BULLEN AND LEAKE'S
PRECEDENTS
OF
PLEADINGS.

FOURTH EDITION.

BULLEN AND LEAKE'S PRECEDENTS OF PLEADINGS

With Notes

AND

RULES RELATING TO PLEADING.

FOURTH EDITION

REVISED AND ADAPTED TO THE PRESENT PRACTICE IN THE QUEEN'S BENCH DIVISION OF THE HIGH COURT OF JUSTICE.

BY

THOMAS J. BULLEN, ESQ.,
OF THE INNER TEMPLE,

AND

CYRIL DODD, ESQ.,
OF THE INNER TEMPLE, BARRISTER-AT-LAW.

"Formulas agendi diversas in unoquoque genere colligito. Nam et practicæ hoc interest; et certè pandunt illæ oracula et occulta legum. Sunt enim non pauca quæ latent in legibus, at in formulis agendi meliùs et fusiùs perspicuntur.'
BACON, *Aph. de Leg.*, lxxxviii.

IN TWO PARTS.

PART I.

LONDON:
STEVENS AND SONS, 119, CHANCERY LANE,
Law Publishers and Booksellers.
1882.

LONDON:
BRADBURY AGNEW, & CO., PRINTERS WHITEFRIARS.

PREFACE

TO THE FOURTH EDITION.

In preparing the present edition it has been the aim of the Editors to preserve so far as practicable the notes to the former editions, adding new matter where necessary, and referring to subsequent statutes and cases. The alteration in the system of pleading, which requires material facts to be stated instead of the legal result of those facts, has rendered necessary a re-drawing of the forms. It is not presumed that the forms given in this edition can be used without alteration to suit each particular case; or that they will be of the same assistance to the pleader under the present system as precedents were under the former system. At the same time, it is hoped that they will be found useful to the practitioner in framing his pleadings.

Owing to the increased bulk of the work, it is deemed advisable to issue the present edition in two parts.

The Editors desire to express their thanks to the many members of the profession who have aided them in the course of their work: especially to Mr. C. W. Clifford, of the Midland Circuit, whose assistance has been invaluable throughout.

The Editors' acknowledgments are also due to Mr. G. B. Allen, of the Inner Temple, for the use of many forms and precedents.

T. J. B.
C. D.

Inner Temple,
December 1881.

PREFACE

TO THE THIRD EDITION.

THE Editor, to whose great experience and reputation as a pleader, may be justly attributed, the favourable acceptance of two former editions of this work, having died whilst a third was passing through the press, it is right that the Profession should be informed to what extent the edition now presented to them in his name may be relied upon as having received the sanction of his authority. At the date of Mr. Bullen's death the work had been printed off to p. 480; the two following sheets, comprising forty-eight pages, were then in type, and a few pages more were ready for delivery to the printer. For the alterations and additions in the remainder of the work, as compared with the last edition, the surviving editor must be held responsible; but they are, to a considerable extent, founded on notes made by the late Mr. Bullen for the preparation of the present edition.

The general plan of the work has not been altered; but the preliminary notes on pleading, with reference to declarations and pleas respectively, have been enlarged and rearranged with the view of forming a more complete introduction to the use of the Precedents. The Forms have been revised and adapted, where necessary, to the changes in the law. The Notes on the various topics of law throughout the work have been revised and extended. The Statutes passed, and the Cases reported since the publication of the last edition will be found noted either in the body of the work or in the list of Additions and Corrections, to which the attention of the reader is particularly requested.

An acknowledgment is due to Mr. Thomas J. Bullen for the diligent care and attention with which he has assisted in the labour of carrying the work through the press.

S. M. L.

MIDDLE TEMPLE,
November, 1868.

PREFACE

TO THE FIRST EDITION.

THIS Work was undertaken in consequence of the want, experienced in actual practice and expressed generally by the profession, of a collection of Precedents settled in conformity with the recent alterations in the System of Pleading. It was begun only when the lapse of time seemed to render it hopeless that the task would be performed by other hands; and it is now presented to the profession with sincere diffidence, but with a hope that it may serve in some degree to supply the existing want.

The system of pleading has recently passed through a period of transition, in which it has undergone most extensive and important amendments. These, for the most part, have been the result of the labours of Her Majesty's Commissioners for inquiring into the Process, Practice, and System of Pleading in the Superior Courts of Common Law, and have been framed upon the recommendations contained in their Reports. They have been effected at intervals, by the Common Law Procedure Acts of 1852 and 1854, and by the subsidiary Rules of Court made by the Judges. The Commissioners have now closed their labours and issued their final Report, in which they appear to consider that very few points affecting Pleading remain in want of amendment. The period of transition may therefore be considered to have passed; and this branch of the law is now left in a state in which it will probably rest for some years to come.

Preface to the First Edition.

The effect of the recent alterations in Pleading has not been to destroy the system or to change its essential principles. The object proposed by the learned Commissioners and effected by the late statutes and rules has been only to prefer substance to form, and to prevent unnecessary technicality from working injustice. Although particular forms of expression are no longer indispensable, it is obviously most important that pleadings should as far as possible be uniform, and that precedents or forms which have acquired an ascertained and understood meaning should be used in preference to new modes of expression, the meaning of which must necessarily contain the elements of uncertainty and doubt. Without the use of precedents it is almost impossible, particularly in pleadings of a complicated nature, for any one but an accurate lawyer and experienced draftsman to avoid overlooking some points of a case absolutely essential to the maintenance of the right or defence. This was never more apparent than it has been in some of the specimens of pleadings which have been met with since the recent changes in the law, drawn by unpractised hands without precedent or guide.*

---

* The very learned editors of Smith's Leading Cases (Mr. Justice Willes and Mr. Justice Keating, the former of whom was a member of the Royal Commission), adverting to the effect produced on the art of pleading by the relaxation of the former rules of criticism, and by the powers of amendment given by the Common Law Procedure Act, 1852, make the following valuable remarks: "It must, however, be remembered that the accurate statement of such of the facts and circumstances of each case as are necessary to enable the plaintiff on the one hand to establish his entire cause of action, and the defendant on the other to set up his entire defence, is still an essential part of the duty of counsel; and that although a final defeat of justice upon merely formal grounds may be averted by the provisions already referred to, no legislative enactment can in all cases prevent the expense and delay which result from the necessity for amending untrue or imperfect narratives of the facts relied upon by the respective parties. Such inconveniences are to be avoided by taking care in the first instance to make the pleadings true and perspicuous, adopting the known and understood formulæ used for the sake of brevity in cases of frequent occurrence, and, where there is no such formula, stating the material facts as they can be proved to exist in intelligible language."—1 Smith's Leading Cases, 4th ed. 103.

A necessary consequence of the extensive changes in the law of Pleading is, that the valuable and elaborate works previously existing have been rendered comparatively useless, except to those persons who possess an intimate acquaintance as well with the former practice as with the recent changes. The object of the Authors of this Work has been to supply a collection of precedents, with instructions for their use, adapted to the law and practice of Pleading in its present state.

In settling the Precedents they have attempted to follow as closely as possible the examples given in the Schedule to the Common Law Procedure Act of 1852. They have endeavoured to render the collection sufficiently complete to meet the cases of most frequent occurrence in practice.

Numerous references have also been given to precedents in reported cases, from which it is hoped the practitioner may derive assistance in drawing pleadings in cases of less common occurrence. Care should, however, be taken in using the forms found in the Reports to settle them as nearly as possible in accordance with the forms contained in the Schedule to the Common Law Procedure Act. It is also hoped that these references to reported forms will be found useful as a guide to the most recent or to the leading cases on the particular points of law to which they relate; and it will be seen that some of the references have been introduced more especially with this view.

The Precedents have been arranged in conformity with the plan adopted by the Common Law Procedure Act of 1852, where the division of causes of actions into the two, so to speak, natural divisions of actions on contracts and actions for wrongs independent of contract (irrespective of the technical distinction between forms of action) received an authoritative recognition. This division has been found very convenient in the compilation of the Work; and it is hoped that it will be found equally convenient in its use.

The Notes contain references to the statutes, rules of court, and principal decisions relating to the pleadings to which they are appended, with such practical observations on the object and effect of the pleadings as appeared necessary for their more convenient use.

The Authors have endeavoured, by a careful selection of the matter, to keep the Work within moderate limits, in order to present it to the profession in a form which, it is hoped, will prove most generally useful.

MIDDLE TEMPLE,
May, 1860.

TABLE OF CONTENTS.

CHAPTER I.

PLEADING IN GENERAL AND STATEMENT OF CLAIM.

CHAPTER II.

STATEMENTS OF CLAIM IN ACTIONS ON CONTRACTS.

CHAPTER III.

STATEMENTS OF CLAIM IN ACTIONS ON WRONGS.

TABLE OF CASES.

PRECEDENTS.

CHAPTER I.

Ordinary Form of Commencement and Conclusion of a Statement of Claim.

18—. B. No. ——

In the High Court of Justice.
Queen's Bench Division.
Writ issued ——, 18—.
Between A.B., Plaintiff,
and
C.D., Defendant.

Statement of Claim.

Delivered on the —— of ——, 18—, by E.F., of No. —, —— street, ——, Solicitor to the above-named Plaintiff.

1. &c., [*here state the cause of action, setting forth concisely in separate paragraphs the material facts relied upon, each paragraph being numbered consecutively and containing, as nearly as may be, a separate allegation.*]

The Plaintiff claims :—

1. £—— [*or* £—— damages, *or as the case may be*].
2. Such further or other relief as the nature of the case may require [*state each distinct claim for relief in a separate paragraph, and number such paragraphs consecutively*].

The Plaintiff proposes that this action should be tried in the county of ——(*a*).

(*a*) *Statement of claim—when necessary.*] The plaintiff must in all cases where the defendant has appeared to the writ, except those hereinafter mentioned, deliver a statement of claim (or a notice in lieu of statement of claim, see *post*, p. 26) to the defendant. (O. XIX. r. 2; O. XXI. r. 1). The cases excepted are as follows :—

1st. Where the defendant at the time of his appearance to the writ states that he does not require the delivery of a statement of claim. (O. XIX. r. 2.)

2nd. Where leave has been given under O. XIV. to a defendant to defend and no order has been made as to delivery of a statement of claim. (O. XXII. r. 3, and note thereto in Wils. Jud. Acts, p. 208.)

In both these last mentioned cases it is optional on the part of the plaintiff to deliver a statement of claim, but if he delivers a statement of claim without being required to do so, and it appears that the delivery of the pleading was unnecessary or improper, he does so at the risk of being ordered to pay the costs occasioned thereby. (O. XXI. r. 1 (c); R. S. C. (Costs), r. 18.) In cases coming within these exceptions where the facts are at all complicated, or, where admissions are likely to be obtained on the pleadings, it is often advisable, notwithstanding the above risk, to deliver a statement of claim, and in such cases the costs of and occasioned by the delivery of a statement of claim would in all probability be allowed.

When the writ is specially indorsed, and the defendant has not dispensed with a statement of claim, the plaintiff may deliver as his statement of claim a notice to the effect that his claim is that which appears by the indorsement upon the writ, unless ordered to deliver a further statement. See *post*, "*Notice in lieu of statement of claim,*" p. 26, and "*Special indorsement upon the writ,*" p. 27.

Description, title and date, &c.] "Every pleading in an action shall be delivered between parties, and shall be marked on the face with the date of the day on which it is delivered, and with the reference to the letter and number of the action, the division to which, and the Judge (if any) to whom the action is assigned, the title of the action, the description of the pleading, and the name and place of business of the solicitor and agent (if any) delivering the same, or the name and address of the party delivering the same if he does not act by a solicitor." (O. XIX. r. 7.) "Non-compliance with any of these rules"—*i.e.*, the rules of the Supreme Court—"shall not render the proceedings in any action void, unless the Court or a judge shall so direct, but such proceedings may be set aside either wholly or in part as irregular, or amended, or otherwise dealt with in such manner and upon such terms as the Court or Judge shall think fit." (O. LIX.) Deviations therefore from the requirements of O. XIX. r. 7, would be irregularities and might afford ground for a summons by the opposite party to have the pleading set aside or amended. The order usually made upon such summons is that the pleading should be so amended as to cure the irregularity. (See, under the former practice, as to delivering a pleading on a day after that on which it bears date, *Newnham* v. *Hanny*, 5 Dowl. 259; *Hodson* v. *Pennell*, 4 M. & W. 373;—as to omissions of date, *Holland* v. *Tealdi*, 8 Dowl. 320;—as to omissions of title, *Ripling* v. *Watts*, 4 Dowl. 290;—and as to omissions of solicitor's name, *White* v. *Feltham*, 3 C. B. 658.) The date of delivery of the pleading is by some pleaders placed at the end instead of the commencement of the pleading, but it is more convenient in practice to have it placed at the commencement.

Parties.] The statement of claim should correspond with the writ, in the names of the parties, in the number of the parties and in the characters in which they sue and are sued. A material variance between the statement of claim and the writ is an irregularity and is ground for an application to set aside or amend the statement of claim. (See, under former practice, *Tory* v. *Stevens*, 6 Dowl. 275; *Kitchen* v. *Brooks*, 5 M. & W. 522.)

Names of the parties.] The Christian names and surnames of the plaintiff and the defendant should be stated in full and correctly in the writ, and in the statement of claim. Titles and names of dignity should be added, as: the Right Honourable ——, Duke of, or Marquis of, or Earl of, or Viscount or Baron ——, or the Right Reverend Father in God —— Lord Bishop of ——, or Sir —— ——, Bart. A person having a title by courtesy is frequently designated by his proper name, with the addition "commonly called Lord ——." In the case of a clergyman it is usual, but not necessary to prefix the term "Reverend" to his name, or to add "Clerk," after it.

In the case of a corporation the full corporate name should be used. "Any two or more persons claiming or being liable as co-partners may sue, or be sued in the name of their respective firms, if any." (O. XVI. r. 10.) In like manner, "any person carrying on business in the name of a firm apparently consisting of more than one person may be sued in the name of such firm." (O. XVI. r. 10*a*.) This use of the name of the firm is merely optional, and the names of the various partners may, if desired, be set out in full in the writ and statement of claim, as in the case of persons who are not in co-partnership, but wherever the name of a firm is used in the writ, it should be likewise used in the statement of claim and subsequent pleadings. (O. XII. rr. 12, 12*a*.) See further, "*Partners*," *post*, p. 290; "*Corporations*," *post*, p. 162.

By 3 & 4 Will. IV. c. 42, s. 12, in actions on bills of exchange or promissory notes or other written instruments, any of the parties to which are designated by the initial letter or letters, or some contraction of the Christian or first name or names, it is sufficient to designate such persons by the same initial letter or letters, or contraction of the Christian or first name or names. A person who executes a deed by a wrong name should be sued by the name in which he executed it. See *Williams* v. *Bryant*, 5 M. & W. 447; *Mayor of Lynne's case*, 10 Rep. 122 *b*.

Misnomer.] A name wrongly spelt, in a manner *idem sonans*, is no material misnomer. (*R.* v. *Shakespeare*, 10 East, 83; *Ahitbol* v. *Benditto*, 2 Taunt. 401; *Williams* v. *Ogle*, 2 Str. 889.) If there be a misnomer in the writ, it seems the defendant, if he appears, can take no advantage of it. (1 Chit. Pr. 13th ed. 158.) But the misnomer should be corrected in the statement of claim, by inserting the right name, with a statement that the party misnamed had sued or been sued by the name in the writ. The defendant can take no advantage of the alteration. (*Hobson* v. *Wadsworth*, 8 Dowl. 601; *Williams* v. *Bryant*, 5 M. & W. 447.)

If there be a material misnomer in the statement of claim, the defendant may take out a summons supported by affidavit to amend it. (See, as to former practice, 3 & 4 Will. IV. c. 42, s. 11.) The costs of such summons would now be regulated by O. LV.

The objection must be taken within the time for pleading. (*Kitchen* v. *Brooks*, 5 M. & W. 522.) A misnomer cannot be objected to after any admission of identity by the defendant. (*Fisher* v. *Magnay*, 1

D. & L. 40.) A person served with a writ issued against another person is not bound to appear, and is not affected by proceedings taken in default of appearance. (*Walley* v. *M'Connell*, 13 Q. B. 903; *Kelly* v. *Lawrence*, 3 H. & C. 1; 33 L. J. Ex. 197; *De Mesnil* v. *Dakin*, L. R. 3 Q. B. 18; 37 L. J. Q. B. 42.)

Number of the parties.] "All persons may be joined as plaintiffs in whom the right to any relief claimed is alleged to exist, whether jointly, severally, or in the alternative. And judgment may be given for such one or more of the plaintiffs as may be found to be entitled to relief, for such relief as he or they may be entitled to, without any amendment. But the defendant, though unsuccessful, shall be entitled to his costs occasioned by so joining any person or persons who shall not be found entitled to relief, unless the Court in disposing of the costs of the action shall otherwise direct." (O. XVI. r. 1.)

"All persons may be joined as defendants against whom the right to any relief is alleged to exist, whether jointly, severally, or in the alternative. And judgment may be given against such one or more of the defendants as may be found to be liable, according to their respective liabilities, without any amendment." (O. XVI. r. 3.)

Persons injured by the same libel may join as plaintiffs, although no joint injury is shown, but the damages would have to be separately assessed. (*Booth* v. *Briscoe*, 2 Q. B. D. 496.)

As to joining two or more defendants in one action where the right to relief exists alternatively against one, or some, of them, see *Honduras Ry. Co.* v. *Lefevre*, 2 Ex. D. 301; 46 L. J. Ex. 391; *Child* v. *Stenning*, 5 Ch. D. 695; 46 L. J. Ch. 523; *Edward* v. *Lowther*, 45 L. J. C. P. 417; 34 L. T. 255.

"Where in any action, whether founded upon contract or otherwise, the plaintiff is in doubt as to the person from whom he is entitled to redress, he may, in such manner as hereinafter mentioned, or as may be prescribed by any special order, join two or more defendants, to the intent that in such action the question as to which, if any, of the defendants is liable, and to what extent, may be determined as between all parties to the action." (O. XVI. r. 6.)

"No action shall be defeated by reason of the misjoinder of parties, and the Court may in every action deal with the matter in controversy so far as regards the rights and interests of the parties actually before it." (O. XVI. r. 13.)

"It shall not be necessary that every defendant to any action shall be interested as to all the relief thereby prayed for, or as to every cause of action included therein; but the Court or a judge may make such order as may appear just to prevent any defendant from being embarrassed or put to expense by being required to attend any proceedings in such action in which he may have no interest." (O. XVI. r. 4.)

A defendant who can show that he would be embarrassed, or put to expense by being required to attend proceedings in the action in which he had no interest, should apply for relief by summons at Judges Chambers, as occasion may arise.

"The plaintiff may, at his option, join as parties to the same action, all or any of the persons severally, or jointly and severally liable on any one contract, including parties to bills of exchange and promissory notes." (O. XVI. r. 5.)

"Trustees, executors, and administrators may sue and be sued on behalf of or as representing the property or estate of which they are trustees or representatives, without joining any of the parties beneficially interested in the trust or estate, and shall be considered as representing such parties in the action; but the Court or a judge may, at any stage of the proceedings, order any of such parties to be made parties to the action, either in addition to or in lieu of the previously existing parties thereto." (O. XVI. r. 7.)

"Where there are numerous parties having the same interest in one action, one or more of such parties may sue, or be sued, or may be authorised by the Court to defend in such action, on behalf or for the benefit of all parties so interested." (O. XVI. r. 9.) For an example of the application of this rule, see *De Hart* v. *Stevenson*, 1 Q. B. D. 313; 45 L. J. Q. B. 575.

"In any case in which the right of an heir-at-law or the next of kin or a class shall depend upon the construction which the Court may put upon an instrument, and it shall not be known or be difficult to ascertain who is or are such heir-at-law or next of kin or class; and the Court shall consider that in order to save expense, or for some other reason, it will be convenient to have the question or questions of construction determined before such heir-at-law, next of kin, or class shall have been ascertained by means of inquiry or otherwise, the Court may appoint some one or more person or persons to represent such heir-at-law, next of kin, or class, and the judgment of the Court in the presence of such person or persons shall be binding upon the party or parties or class so represented." (O. XVI. r. 9*a*.) For an example of the application of this rule, see *In re Peppitt's Estate*, 4 Ch. D. 230; 46 L. J. Ch. 95.

As to using the name of the firm in actions by or against a person or persons trading under a firm, style, or name, see "*Names of the parties*," *ante*, p. 3.

As a general rule all persons jointly entitled or liable to sue or be sued in respect of the cause of complaint, should be joined both in the writ and in the statement of claim, unless they come within the class of cases excepted by O. XVI. rr. 7, 9, 9*a*, 10, or 11; or unless they are incorporated, or authorised by a statute to sue or defend by a name or title, or by a public officer, chairman, secretary, &c. (See forms in such cases, *post*, "*Bankers*," p. 72, "*Company*," p. 145, "*Corporations*," p. 162.) If a party not in the writ be joined in the statement of claim without leave of the Court or a Judge, the statement of claim may be set aside as irregular. (See, under old practice, *Haigh* v. *Conway*, 15 East, 1; *Rogers* v. *Jenkins*, 1 B. & P. 383.) Where several statements of claim are delivered to the several defendants in an action, they should be identical in their contents. A plaintiff may deliver a statement of claim against one or some of several defendants only, without proceeding against the others, for the statement of claim may narrow the operation of the writ. A defendant not proceeded against in the statement of claim, may, however, at the expiration of the time allowed for the delivery of the statement of claim, apply by summons to have the action dismissed as against him with costs for want of prosecution. (O. XXIX. r. 1.) See further, "*Time for delivering statement of claim*," p. 28.

Formerly in actions of or founded upon contract, the non-joinder as defendant of a co-contractor could in general be objected to by plea in abatement only, whilst the non-joinder of a necessary co-plaintiff might be objected to by such plea, or by a notice given under the C. L. P. Act, 1852, s. 35, or by a plea traversing the contract as alleged, and thus showing a *variance* at the trial, or, where the declaration showed the defect, by demurrer. See further Day's C. L. P. Acts, 3rd ed. p. 39, *notes*, and C. L. P. Act, 1852 (15 & 16 Vict. c. 76), ss. 34, 35.

In actions for wrongs independent of contract the non-joinder of a necessary co-plaintiff could in general be objected to by plea in abatement, or by notice as above. In such actions no objection could be taken to the non-joinder of a co-tort-feasor as a defendant, wrongs being in their nature separable.

A plea in abatement could not be pleaded in respect of the non-joinder of a defendant co-contractor not resident within the jurisdiction, or whose place of residence could not be given (see 3 & 4 Will. IV. c. 42, s. 8); or of one against whom the claim had become barred by the Statute of Limitations, 9 Geo. IV. c. 14 (see 9 Geo. IV. c. 14, ss. 1 & 2; 19 & 20 Vict. c. 97, s. 14). A plea in abatement could not be pleaded in actions founded upon contract in respect of the non-joinder of a bankrupt co-contractor (see 3 & 4 Will. IV. c. 42, s. 9, and "The Bankruptcy Act, 1869," 32 & 33 Vict. c. 71, s. 112). Nor was the non-joinder in such actions of one incapable at law of contracting, as a feme covert, &c., ground for such a plea.

By 11 Geo. IV. & 1 Will. IV. c. 68, s. 5, it is enacted that no action for loss or injury to any parcel, package, or person shall abate for want of joining as defendant any co-proprietor in any such coach or other public conveyance by land for hire as therein mentioned.

Now, by O. XIX. r. 13, it is provided that "no plea or defence shall be pleaded in abatement." Consequently that mode of objecting to the non-joinder of parties is abolished, though by O. XVI. r. 13, "The Court or a Judge may, at any stage of the proceedings, either upon or without the application of either party, and on such terms as may appear to the Court or Judge to be just, order that the name or names of any party or parties, whether as plaintiffs or as defendants, improperly joined, be struck out, and that the name or names of any party or parties, whether plaintiffs or defendants, who ought to have been joined, or whose presence before the Court may be necessary in order to enable the Court effectually and completely to adjudicate upon and settle all the questions involved in the action, be added," subject to the proviso that "No person shall be added as a plaintiff suing without a next friend, or as the next friend of a plaintiff under any disability without his own consent thereto." (See *Turquand* v. *Fearon*, 4 Q. B. D. 280; 48 L. J. Q. B. 341; *Sheehan* v. *G. E. Ry. Co.*, 16 Ch. D. 59, 63; 50 L. J. Ch. 68; *Val de Travers Co.* v. *London Tram. Co.*, 48 L. J. C. P. 312).

Where a plea in abatement in respect of non-joinder could have been pleaded, the defendant may, in general, and subject to the above-cited rules as to one or more persons representing all the parties, take out a summons to add the party who ought to have been joined and obtain an order for such party to be joined, the action where necessary being in the meantime stayed (see *Kendall* v. *Hamilton*, 4 App. Cas. 504; 48 L. J. C. P. 705; *Sheehan* v. *G. E. Ry. Co., supra*).

By O. XVI. r. 14, "Any application to add or strike out or substitute a plaintiff or defendant may be made to the Court or a Judge at any time before trial by motion or summons, or at the trial of the action in a summary manner."

In the case of non-joinder of a necessary party in an action founded on contract the defendant should, it would seem, object to the non-joinder by summons at chambers (*Werdermann* v. *The Société Générale d'Electricité*, C. A. Nov. 13th, 1881, and see *Hancocks* v. *Lablache*, 3 C. P. D. 197 ; 47 L. J. C. P. 514 ; *Duckett* v. *Gover*, 6 Ch. D. 82 ; 46 L. J. Ch. 407).

See further "*Amendment of Pleadings*," *post*, p. 24 ; "*Partners*," p. 290, and O. XVI. r. 2, providing for the addition or substituting a plaintiff in the case of a *bonâ fide* mistake, whether of law or fact (*Clowes* v. *Hilliard*, 4 Ch. D. 413 ; 46 L. J. Ch. 271 ; *Duckett* v. *Gover*, *supra*), and "*Husband and Wife*," *post*. As to third parties, see O. XVI. rr. 17—21. As to when contracts are *joint and several*, or *joint* or *several*, see Leake on Contracts, 455 *et seq.*

Character in which parties sue or are sued.] Where parties sue or are sued in a representative character, the indorsement on the writ must show the fact by specifically stating in what capacity it is that the parties sue, or are sued (O. III. r. 4), and the statement of claim should correspond with the writ, and show specifically the capacity in which the parties sue or are sued.

If the writ does not fulfil this requirement, a summons at Chambers may be taken out by the plaintiff to amend it.

Parties under disabilities.] As to these, see *post*, "*Husband and Wife*," "*Infant*," "*Lunatic*," &c.

Pleading in general.] In drawing the statement of claim as well as all subsequent pleadings, it must be constantly borne in mind that it is a first principle of pleading that material facts only are to be stated, and that all material facts are to be stated. (O. XIX. rr. 4, 18 ; *Dawkins* v. *Lord Penrhyn*, 6 Ch. D. 318, 324 ; *Davy* v. *Garrett*, 7 Ch. D. 473, 485 ; 46 L. J. Ch. 218). Matters of law or mere inferences of law should not be pleaded ; for it is for the Court to declare the law arising upon the facts pleaded. (*Hanmer* v. *Flight*, 35 L. T. 127 ; *reversed on appeal*, 36 L. T. 279 ; *Watson* v. *Rodwell*, 3 Ch. D. 380, 383 ; 45 L. J. Ch. 744 ; *Day* v. *Brownrigg*, 10 Ch. D. 294, 302 ; 48 L. J. Ch. 173 ; *Williamson* v. *L. & N. W. Ry. Co.*, 12 Ch. D. 787, 793 ; 48 L. J. Ch. 559.)

It is not in general enough in a pleading to allege that a right exists, but the facts must be set forth which give rise to such right. Similarly, where the act complained of appears on the pleading to afford no cause of action the pleading will be held bad on demurrer in spite of any allegation to the effect that the act was "*unlawful*," or "*wrongful*," or "*improper*," or "*done without any justification therefor or right so to do*" (*Day* v. *Brownrigg*, *supra* ; *Hurdman* v. *N. E. Ry. Co.*, 3 C. P. D. 168 ; 47 L. J. C. P. 368). See further "*Negligence*," *post*, p. 480. Where fraud is intended to be charged, it must be distinctly charged. See "*Fraud*," *post*, p. 427.

Where it is desired to contend that the pleading, or any part of it, setting up a distinct cause of action, ground of defence, set off, counterclaim, reply, or rejoinder is bad in law, such pleading or part should be demurred to. See O. XXVIII. and "*Demurrer*," "Defences." Statements in pleadings which are not demurrers, but allege only matters of law which might be raised by demurrer, are in general embarrassing and liable to be struck out under O. XXVII. r. 1 (*Stokes* v. *Grant*, 4 C. P. D. 25; *Philipps* v. *Philipps*, 4 Q. B. D. 127, *per* Brett, L. J., 132, 136). It is to be noted that by O. LIX. non-compliance with any of the Rules shall not render the proceedings in any action void unless the Court or a Judge shall so direct, but such proceedings may be set aside, either wholly or in part, as irregular, or amended, or otherwise dealt with in such manner, and upon such terms as the Court or Judge shall think fit; and by O. XXVII. r. 1, pleadings which may tend to prejudice, embarrass, or delay the fair trial of an action may be struck out or amended. See "*Amendment of Pleadings*," *post*, p. 24. Consequently, it is not sufficient to entitle a party to have his opponent's pleadings struck out to show that the pleading offends against the rules, unless it is also shown that it tends to prejudice, embarrass, or delay the fair trial of the action. (*Millington* v. *Loring*, 6 Q. B. D. 190; 50 L. J. Q. B. 214.)

Nothing need be stated which the Court takes notice of judicially. Thus the Court takes judicial notice not only of the law of the realm, but also of the general law of nations; the law and custom of parliament, including the privileges and procedure of each branch of the legislature; the prerogatives of the Crown; the maritime, civil, and ecclesiastical laws; the articles of war both in the land and marine service; royal proclamations; the custom of merchants, at least where such custom has been settled by judicial determinations; the special customs of gavelkind and borough English lands; the customs of the City of London which have been certified by the Recorder; the rules and course of procedure of the superior Courts, and the limits of their jurisdiction; the power of the Ecclesiastical Courts, and the limits of their jurisdiction; the division of England into counties, provinces, and dioceses; the commencement and ending of legal terms and sittings; the coincidence of the years of the reign of any sovereign of this country with the years of our Lord; the coincidence of the days of the week with days of the month; the order of the months; the meaning of ordinary English words and terms of art; the names and quantities of legal weights and measures, and the value of the coin of the realm.

But judicial notice is not taken of private Acts of Parliament; nor of particular local customs or usages of trade; nor of the jurisdiction of inferior courts; nor of the laws, usages, or customs of foreign countries or courts of justice, nor of the situation of any particular place. Any of these matters when relied upon must be alleged like other facts; and even in the case of relying on those things of which the Court takes judicial notice it is necessary to allege any facts which are required to apply them to the plaintiff or defendant, or to the facts on which the right of action or defence rests.

A more complete enumeration of the matters of which the Court does or does not take judicial notice, (including those above stated,) may be found in 1 Chit. Pl. 7th ed. p. 236; and in Taylor on Evidence.

The following are the principal rules of the Judicature Acts which relate more especially to pleading in general, and which are substituted by O. XIX. r. 1, for those heretofore used.

"Every pleading shall contain as concisely as may be a statement of the material facts on which the party pleading relies, but not the evidence by which they are to be proved, such statement being divided into paragraphs, numbered consecutively, and each paragraph containing, as nearly as may be, a separate allegation. Dates, sums, and numbers shall be expressed in figures and not in words. Signature of counsel shall not be necessary. Forms similar to those in Appendix (C) hereto may be used." (O. XIX. r. 4.) As to the effect of the forms, see Jud. Act, 1873 (36 & 37 Vict. c. 66), s. 100, which enacts that rules of court shall include forms, and Jud. Act, 1875 (38 & 39 Vict. c. 77), s. 16, which enacts that the rules as to all matters to which they extend shall regulate the proceedings in the High Court of Justice and Court of Appeal, and *Harris* v. *Warre*, 4 C. P. D. 125; 48 L. J. C. P. 310; and *Turquand* v. *Fearon*, 40 L. T. 543, 545.

"Every pleading which shall contain less than [ten] folios of 72 words each (every figure being counted as one word) may be either printed or written, or partly printed and partly written, and every other pleading, not being a petition or summons, shall be printed." (O. XIX. r. 5, *as altered by r.* 9 *of* R. S. C. June, 1876.)

"Every pleading or other document required to be delivered to a party, or between parties, shall be delivered in the manner now in use to the solicitor of every party who appears by a solicitor, or to the party if he does not appear by a solicitor, but if no appearance has been entered for any party, then such pleading or document shall be delivered by being filed with the proper officer." (O. XIX. r. 6.)

"Every pleading in an action shall be delivered between parties, and shall be marked on the face with the date of the day on which it is delivered, and with the reference to the letter and number of the action, the Division to which and the Judge (if any) to whom the action is assigned, the title of the action, the description of the pleading, and the name and place of business of the solicitor and agent, if any, delivering the same, or the name and address of the party delivering the same if he does not act by a solicitor." (O. XIX. r. 7.)

"Every statement of claim shall state specifically the relief which the plaintiff claims, either simply or in the alternative, and may also ask for general relief. And the same rule shall apply to any counter-claim made, or relief claimed by the defendant, in his statement of defence. If the plaintiff's claim be for discovery only the statement of claim shall show it." (O. XIX. r. 8.)

"Where the plaintiff seeks relief in respect of several distinct claims or causes of complaint founded upon separate and distinct facts, they shall be stated, as far as may be, separately and distinctly. And the same rule shall apply where the defendant relies upon several distinct grounds of defence, set-off, or counter-claim founded upon separate and distinct facts." (O. XIX. r. 9.)

"Where any defendant seeks to rely upon any facts as supporting a right of set-off or counter-claim, he shall, in his statement of defence, state specifically that he does so by way of set-off or counter-claim." (O. XIX. r. 10.)

"If either party wishes to deny the right of any other party to claim as executor, or as trustee, whether in bankruptcy or otherwise, or in any representative or other alleged capacity, or the alleged constitution of any partnership firm, he shall deny the same specifically." (O. XIX. r. 11.)

"No plea or defence shall be pleaded in abatement." (O. XXI. r. 13.)

"No new assignment shall hereafter be necessary or used. But everything which has heretofore been alleged by way of new assignment may hereafter be introduced by amendment of the statement of claim." (O. XIX. r. 14.)

"No defendant in an action for the recovery of land who is in possession by himself or his tenant need plead his title, unless his defence depends on an equitable estate or right or he claims relief upon any equitable ground against any right or title asserted by the plaintiff. But, except in the cases hereinbefore mentioned, it shall be sufficient to state by way of defence that he is so in possession. And he may nevertheless rely upon any ground of defence which he can prove, except as hereinbefore mentioned." (O. XIX. r. 15.)

"Nothing in these rules contained shall affect the right of any defendant to plead not guilty by statute. And every defence of not guilty by statute shall have the same effect as a plea of not guilty by statute has heretofore had. But if the defendant so plead he shall not plead any other defence without the leave of the Court or a Judge." (O. XIX. r. 16.)

"Every allegation of fact in any pleading in an action, not being a petition or summons, if not denied specifically or by necessary implication, or stated to be not admitted in the pleading of the opposite party, shall be taken to be admitted, except as against an infant, lunatic, or person of unsound mind not so found by inquisition." (O. XIX. r. 17.)

"Each party in any pleading, not being a petition or summons, must allege all such facts not appearing in the previous pleadings as he means to rely on, and must raise all such grounds of defence or reply, as the case may be, as if not raised on the pleadings would be likely to take the opposite party by surprise, or would raise new issues of fact not arising out of the pleadings, as for instance, fraud, or that any claim has been barred by the Statute of Limitations or has been released." (O. XIX. r. 18.)

"No pleading, not being a petition or summons, shall, except by way of amendment, raise any new ground of claim or contain any allegation of fact inconsistent with the previous pleadings of the party pleading the same." (O. XIX. r. 19.)

"It shall not be sufficient for a defendant in his defence to deny generally the facts alleged by the statement of claim, or for a plaintiff in his reply to deny generally the facts alleged in a defence by way of counter-claim, but each party must deal specifically with each allegation of fact of which he does not admit the truth." (O. XIX. r. 20.)

"Subject to the last preceding rule, the plaintiff by his reply may join issue upon the defence, and each party in his pleading, if any, subsequent to reply, may join issue upon the previous pleading. Such joinder of issue shall operate as a denial of every material allegation of fact in the pleading upon which issue is joined, but it may except any facts which the party may be willing to admit, and shall then operate as a denial of the facts not so admitted." (O. XIX. r. 21.)

"When a party in any pleading denies an allegation of fact in the previous pleading of the opposite party, he must not do so evasively, but answer the point of substance. Thus, if it be alleged that he received a certain sum of money, it shall not be sufficient to deny that he received that particular amount, but he must deny that he received that sum or any part thereof, or else set out how much he received. And so when a matter of fact is alleged with divers circumstances, it shall not be sufficient to deny it as alleged along with those circumstances but a fair and substantial answer must be given." (O. XIX. r. 22.)

"When a contract is alleged in any pleading, a bare denial of the contract by the opposite party shall be construed only as a denial of the making of the contract in fact, and not of its legality or its sufficiency in law, whether with reference to the Statute of Frauds or otherwise." (O. XIX. r. 23.)

"Wherever the contents of any document are material, it shall be sufficient in any pleading to state the effect thereof as briefly as possible, without setting out the whole or any part thereof unless the precise words of the document or any part thereof are material." (O. XIX. r. 24.)

"Wherever it is material to allege malice, fraudulent intention, knowledge, or other condition of the mind of any person, it shall be sufficient to allege the same as a fact without setting out the circumstances from which the same is to be inferred." (O. XIX. r. 25.)

"Wherever it is material to allege notice to any person of any fact, matter, or thing, it shall be sufficient to allege such notice as a fact, unless the form or the precise terms of such notice be material." (O. XIX. r. 26.)

"Wherever any contract or any relation between any persons does not arise from an express agreement, but is to be implied from a series of letters or conversations, or otherwise from a number of circumstances, it shall be sufficient to allege such contract or relation as a fact, and to refer generally to such letters, conversations, or circumstances without setting them out in detail. And if in such case the person so pleading desires to rely in the alternative upon more contracts or relations than one as to be implied from such circumstances, he may state the same in the alternative." (O. XIX. r. 27.)

"Neither party need in any pleading allege any matter of fact which the law presumes in his favour, or as to which the burden of proof lies upon the other side, unless the same has first been specifically denied."

"[*E.g.*—Consideration for a bill of exchange where the plaintiff sues only on the bill, and not for the consideration as a substantive ground of claim.]" (O. XIX. r. 28.)

See "*The Body of the Statement of Claim,*" *infra*, "*Agreements,*" *post*, p. 50.

The body of the statement of claim.] The body of the statement of claim consists of the statement of the material facts on which the plaintiff relies. (O. XIX. r. 4, *ante*, "*Pleading in General;*" *Millington* v. *Loring*, 6 Q. B. D. 190; 50 L. J. Q. B. 214; *Philipps* v. *Philipps*, 4 Q. B. D. 127, 133; 48 L. J. Q. B. 135.) It should contain statements of facts only. (*Dawkins* v. *Lord Penrhyn*, 6 Ch. D.

318, 324.) It is no part of the statement of claim to anticipate the defence, or to state what answer the plaintiff makes to the anticipated defence. (*Hall* v. *Eve*, 4 Ch. D. 341, 345, 348; 46 L. J. Ch. 145; *Dawkins* v. *Lord Penrhyn*, *supra*.) Evidence should not be pleaded, whether consisting of admissions or not. (*Davy* v. *Garrett*, 7 Ch. D. 473, 485; 47 L. J. Ch. 218.) If alternative cases are alleged, the facts ought to be stated so as to show on what facts each alternative to the relief sought is founded. (*Per* Thesiger, L. J. in *Davy* v. *Garrett*, *supra*. See O. XIX. r. 9, *ante*, "*Pleading in General*," p. 7 and *post*, "*Fraud*," p. 428.)

The object of the rules is threefold. Firstly, that the plaintiff may state what his case is for the information of the defendant, and that he may be tied down to it and not spring a new case on the defendant; secondly, that the defendant may be at liberty to say that the statement is not sufficient in law, and to raise the point on demurrer; and thirdly, that the defendant, instead of being driven to deny everything by an ambiguous and uncertain statement involving conclusions of law as well as actual facts, and going down to try an expensive issue, may be at liberty to single out any one statement and to answer it. (*Philipps* v. *Philipps*, *supra*, *per* Bramwell, L. J.). Such facts ought to be stated as a person would have stated in a special case. (*Philipps* v. *Philipps*, *supra*, *per* Brett, L. J., at p. 133; *Turquand* v. *Fearon*, 40 L. T. 543, *per* Bramwell, L. J., at p. 544.) If parties were held strictly to their pleadings under the present system they ought not to be allowed to prove at the trial as a fact on which they would have to rely to prove their case any fact which is not stated in their pleading. (*Philipps* v. *Philipps*, 4 Q. B. D. 143; 48 L. J. Q. B. 138, *per* Brett, L. J.). Facts relevant and material to the question of damages may be stated in the claim. (*Millington* v. *Loring*, 6 Q. B. D. 190; 50 L. J. Q. B. 214; see further *post*, "*Damages*," p. 19. In an action for defamation the defamatory words used are the material facts, and they must be set out. (*Harris* v. *Warre*, 4 C. P. D. 125, 129; 48 L. J. C. P. 310, 312, *per* Coleridge, C. J.). A general statement which prevents the defendant from demurring and at the same time does not allege the facts material to the case is embarrassing because it gives the defendant no knowledge of the case the plaintiff is going to set up. (*Philipps* v. *Philipps*, 4 Q. B. D. 132; 48 L. J. Q. B. 137, *per* Brett, L. J.).

The statement of claim contains, generally speaking, two principal parts, namely, the statement of the right of the plaintiff which has been violated, and the statement of the wrong or violation of that right by the defendant. Following the body of the statement of claim there must be a specific statement of the relief or remedy claimed, and there may also be a claim for general relief. (O. XIX. r. 8, *ante*, "*Pleading in General*," and see *post*, "*Damages*," p. 19, and "*Relief other than Damages*," p. 23.) Causes of action are conveniently divided into those arising on contracts, and those for wrongs independent of contract, and there are important differences in the manner of stating the cause of action in these two divisions. (See *post*, "*Carriers*," p. 120.)

In stating the *contract* when it is contained in a written instrument, whether a deed or a simple contract, it is open to the pleader either to state it according to its legal effect, or to set out the document itself *verbatim*. This was so under the former system and is so still, (O. XIX. r. 24, *Philipps* v. *Philipps*, 4 Q. B. D. 127, 130; 48

L. J. Q. B. 135, 137.) In the former case he takes upon himself to give the true meaning of the instrument, whatever its terms may be, and if it is traversed he runs the risk of a variance when it is produced in evidence; in the latter case, he leaves the construction of it to the Court (except that the meaning is necessarily assumed in alleging the breach); and, although upon a traverse of it the only question of fact is whether an instrument in those very terms was made or not, yet a question of law may arise upon the face of the statement of claim, namely, whether, supposing it to be in those terms, it will support the breach and the cause of action alleged. In the generality of cases, and where the meaning of the instrument is clear and obvious, the best and most usual course is to state the legal effect of the document; but where the meaning is doubtful, and it is wished to raise in the easiest and most direct form the question of its sufficiency to support the action, it is often set out *verbatim*, or (according to the technical expression) *in hæc verba.*

Even when a contract is stated in the statement of claim according to the legal effect attributed to it by the plaintiff, the defendant may raise the question of its sufficiency to support the action by setting out the document *verbatim* in the statement of defence, with an allegation that it is the contract mentioned in the statement of claim. (*Sim* v. *Edmands*, 15 C. B. 240.) Under such circumstances the plaintiff's best course may be to amend his statement of claim by himself setting out the contract *verbatim.*

Where the contract is set out *verbatim*, there should be an allegation identifying the parties; or innuendoes may be introduced parenthetically after their names, "*(meaning the plaintiff)*," and "*(meaning the defendant)*."

Where the legal effect is given it is not necessary to follow the words of the instrument (1 Marsh. 216, 217). Generally, however, the safest and best course, even in pleading an instrument according to its legal effect, is to follow the terms and order of the document itself so far as practicable, instead of attempting to reform it or to use supposed equivalent expressions, but to omit all portions of the document not material to the cause of action.

Where there are several covenants in the same deed, or several promises in the same instrument or forming parts of one verbal contract, it is sufficient to state those covenants or promises only of which breaches are to be afterwards alleged, provided the parts omitted do not materially qualify or alter the nature of the covenants or promises alleged to have been broken. (*Cotterill* v. *Cuff*, 4 Taunt. 285; *Tempest* v. *Rawling*, 13 East, 18; and see *Clarke* v. *Gray*, 6 East, 564; *Howell* v. *Richards*, 11 East, 633; 1 Wms. Saund. 1871 ed. 277 (1).)

Where there are several covenants or promises in the same deed or agreement of which breaches are intended to be alleged, the whole of such promises or covenants should be set out consecutively before alleging any of the breaches.

Where there are two or more distinct deeds or contracts of which breaches are to be alleged, each deed or contract, and the breach or breaches of it, should be separately and distinctly stated. (O. XIX. r. 9, *ante*, p. 9.)

Where an agreement between the parties has been altered or modified by a subsequent agreement, the plaintiff may either state them in their order according to the fact, or he may state the contract as it stands modified or altered, without noticing the original terms which have been dispensed with. (*Boone* v. *Mitchell*, 1 B. & C. 18; *Thresh* v. *Rake*, 1 Esp. 53; *Robinson* v. *Tobin*, 1 Stark. 336; *Carr* v. *Wallachian Petroleum Co.*, L. R. 1 C. P. 636; 35 L. J. C. P. 314.)

Where the contract is by deed this must be stated. It is not necessary in such a case to show that there was any consideration for the defendant's covenants, because a specialty contract requires no consideration to support it.

"Wherever any contract or any relation between any persons does not arise from an express agreement, but is to be implied from a series of letters or conversations, or otherwise from a number of circumstances, it shall be sufficient to allege such contract or relation as a fact, and to refer generally to such letters, conversations, or circumstances without setting them out in detail. And if in such case the person so pleading desires to rely in the alternative upon more contracts or relations than one as to be implied from such circumstances, he may state the same in the alternative." (O. XIX. r. 27.)

For an example of this method of pleading, *see* Form 5, in App. (C.), to Jud. Act, 1875.

Where the statement of claim is upon a simple contract, it is essential that it should show that there was a good and sufficient *consideration* to support the defendant's promise. If no sufficient consideration were alleged, or if the consideration were shown upon the face of it to be illegal, the contract would appear to be void; and in either case the statement of claim would be bad in substance. (*Robertson* v. *Howard*, 3 C. P. D. 280; 47 L. J. C. P. 480.) It is also necessary that the whole consideration on which the promise depends should be stated, for if any part of an entire consideration, or of a consideration consisting of several things, is omitted, the agreement will be incorrectly alleged. (*Symonds* v. *Carr*, 1 Camp. 361; *King* v. *Roxbrough*, 2 C. & J. 418; *King* v. *Sears*, 2 C. M. & R. 48; *Shackell* v. *Rosier*, 2 Bing. N. C. 634; *Guthing* v. *Lynn*, 2 B. & Ad. 232; *Thomas* v. *Thomas*, 2 Q. B. 851.) This important distinction therefore exists between the statement of the promise and of the consideration, namely, that the whole of the latter should be alleged; whereas it is sufficient to state so much only of the promise as the defendant is charged with having broken.

The promise and the consideration together constitute the contract.

Where the consideration was executory at the time of the promise, and formed a condition precedent, the execution of it has to be alleged (see *post*, "*Conditions Precedent*," p. 158.)

The consideration must not be alleged as past or executed, because, generally speaking, a past consideration is insufficient to support a promise; but where a contract is set out *in hæc verba* the past tense may be held to be an apt form of expression for a concurrent act. (*Steele* v. *Hoe*, 14 Q. B. 431, 445; *Payne* v. *Wilson*, 7 B. & C. 423; *Streeter* v. *Horlock*, 1 Bing. 34; *Bainbridge* v. *Wade*, 16 Q. B. 89; *Hoad* v. *Grace*, 7 H. & N. 494; 31 L. J. Ex. 98.)

If the consideration or the promise or covenant is in the alternative, it must be stated according to the fact. So also whenever the covenant or promise is conditional. (*Penny* v. *Porter*, 2 East, 2; *Tate* v. *Wellings*, 3 T. R. 531; *White* v. *Wilson*, 2 B. & P. 116.)

When the promise or covenant itself contains an exception or proviso qualifying the defendant's liability, the exception or proviso should be stated, and it is incorrect to state the contract as an absolute one. As, where the promise by a carrier was to carry and deliver safely, fire and robbery excepted (*Latham* v. *Rutley*, 2 B. & C. 20); where a horse was warranted sound everywhere except a kick in the leg (*Jones* v. *Cowley*, 4 B. & C. 445); where a covenant to repair contained an exception in case of fire and certain other casualties. (*Tempany* v. *Burnand*, 4 Camp. 20; *Browne* v. *Knill*, 2 B. & B. 395; *Howell* v. *Richards*, 11 East, 633; *Dawson* v. *Wrench*, 3 Ex. 359.) But if the covenant or clause in an agreement is absolute in itself, without any exception or proviso or any reference to any, it may be stated as an absolute contract, although in a distinct part of the deed or instrument there is a proviso defeating or qualifying it under certain circumstances; such a proviso is in the nature of a defeasance and must be set up, if the facts permit it, by the other side. Sometimes the covenant or clause, although it does not contain the exception or proviso, refers to it by such words as "except as hereinafter excepted," and in this case the exception or proviso must be stated in the declaration, for *verba relata inesse videntur*. (*Vavasour* v. *Ormrod*, 6 B. & C. 430.)

If the agreement be in writing this fact should, in general, be stated. (See *post*, "*Agreements*," p. 50.)

After the statement of the contract come the *averments*.

In statements of claim on contracts where the statement of the contract shows a promise conditional only, or to be performed at a future time or on the happening of some event, it becomes necessary, in order to show a cause of action, to allege that the event has happened or the time has elapsed or the condition requisite to render the promise absolute has been fulfilled. Such allegations are commonly called *averments*.

Before the C. L. P. Act, 1852, all the averments which the form and effect of the contract as alleged in the declaration showed to be necessary had to be specifically alleged, but by sec. 57 of the above statute it was enacted as follows:—

"It shall be lawful for the plaintiff or defendant in any action to aver performance of conditions precedent generally, and the opposite party shall not deny such averment generally, but shall specify in his pleading the condition or conditions precedent the performance of which he intends to contest."

Advantage was usually taken of this enactment under the former system of pleading to state the performance of conditions precedent generally where such conditions were numerous, or where there was any difficulty in determining what were, or what were not, conditions precedent. (See "*Bullen and Leake's Precedents*," 3rd ed., pp. 8, 61, 147.) In practice it is still usual to aver the performance of conditions precedent generally where it is convenient so to do. (See *post*, "*Conditions Precedent*," *notes*, p. 158.) Whenever the plaintiff pleads the averments specifically, care must be taken to allege whatever is made necessary by the contract according to its intent and legal effect, and according to whether the conditions are positive or negative, or in the conjunctive or disjunctive. (Com. Dig. Pleader, (C.) 58, (C.) 59, (C.) 60; *Burgess* v. *Brazier*, 1 Str. 594); and the things alleged to have been done must be identified as those required to be done by the contract. (*Wallis* v. *Scott*, 1 Str. 88.)

It is still necessary, as it was under the former system of pleading, to aver specifically the facts which afford *excuse* for a non-performance, and the plaintiff must still allege his readiness and willingness to perform the condition or contract on his part, and then go on to show that the defendant prevented him or discharged him from performing it. (See forms *post*, "*Conditions Precedent.*")

All the allegations of a similar kind which are necessary to the cause of action, are included under the term *averments*.

After the averments comes the *breach*. The terms of the breach must obviously depend on the terms of the contract. It should be *assigned* in the words of the covenant or promise, either negatively or affirmatively, according to whether the contract is affirmative or negative, or in words co-extensive with the effect and meaning of it. Generally speaking, it is enough to follow the very words of the contract. It may be dangerous to make the breach unnecessarily narrow or particular. As where the covenant was to use a farm in a husbandlike manner, and the breach assigned was that the defendant had not used the farm in a husbandlike manner, but, on the contrary, had committed *waste*, it was held that no misconduct could be shown which did not amount to waste. (*Harris* v. *Mantle*, 3 T. R. 307.) Care should be taken not to use the words "but on the contrary thereof" or even "but"; their effect, as in that case, is to destroy the generality of the preceding words, and to limit the breach to what follows them (see, *per* Willes, J., *Carpenter* v. *Parker*, 3 C. B. N. S. 206, 243); any expressions of details or of particular acts should be charged cumulatively by using the word "and." No inconvenience can arise from superadding particular breaches, provided they are so alleged as not to exclude or narrow the previous general breach; the plaintiff will then retain the benefit of both, and may recover for any part which he can establish, though he may not succeed in proving the whole. Care, however, must be taken so to allege the particular breach as to make it manifest that it is not intended to limit the general breach previously stated. (See *Byrd* v. *Nunn*, 5 Ch. D. 781; affirmed on appeal, 7 Ch. D. 284; 47 L. J. Ch. 1; *Collette* v. *Goode*, 7 Ch. D. 842; 47 L. J. Ch. 370, as to the effect of particular allegations in narrowing general allegations occurring in the same pleading.) If the covenant or promise is in the alternative or disjunctive, the breach must allege that the defendant did not do either the one act or the other. (*Legh* v. *Lillie*, 6 H. & N. 165; 30 L. J. Ex. 25.)

The assignment of the breach may assume whatever is implied by law; as, the continuance of an existing state of things. By O. XIX. r. 28, "Neither party need in any pleading allege any matter of fact which the law presumes in his favour, or as to which the burden of proof lies on the other side, unless the same has first been specifically denied."

If the covenant or agreement, as alleged in the statement of claim, contains any exception or proviso, it will be necessary to qualify the breach accordingly; as, where there is a covenant to repair premises, except damage by fire, it must appear that the defendant failed to repair other damage than damage by fire. And where the covenant was to repair a fence, except on the west side thereof, a breach should show that the want of repair was in other parts of the fence than on the west side. (Com. Dig. Pleader (C.) 47.) As to contracts of insurance (certain losses or perils excepted), see *post*, "*Insurance*," p. 217.

In actions for wrongs, independent of contract, the right is generally an existing fact, and is so stated, without showing the origin or creation of the right; as in actions for trespasses to land, or goods, where the statement of claim alleges that the land was the plaintiff's and the defendant broke and entered or trespassed upon it; or that the goods were the plaintiff's and the defendant seized and carried them away.

Certain rights are implied in law and are inseparably annexed to the person of the plaintiff, as the right to security of life and limb, liberty and reputation; and these it is unnecessary to allege. In such cases the pleading states only the violation of the right, as, that the defendant assaulted and beat the plaintiff, or that the defendant imprisoned the plaintiff, or that the defendant spoke of the plaintiff certain defamatory words. (See, *per* Patteson, J., *Cotton* v. *Browne*, 3 A. & E. 312, 314.)

In some cases, in stating the act complained of it becomes necessary also to show on the pleading that it was committed in a certain manner, as "negligently", or "maliciously", or "without reasonable or probable cause", or *scienter*, that is to say, with knowledge of a certain fact; for the act in itself may not be actionable, but may have been made so only by the way in which it was done; as in actions for driving negligently, for defamation, for malicious prosecution, for keeping a mischievous animal with knowledge of its mischievous nature; in these cases the mode of doing the act is of the gist of the cause of action, and constitutes a necessary part of the statement of the wrongful act.

"Wherever it is material to allege malice, fraudulent intention, knowledge, or other condition of the mind of any person, it shall be sufficient to allege the same as a fact without setting out the circumstances from which the same is to be inferred." (O. XIX. r. 25.)

Again, in some cases of wrongs the act complained of is not in itself necessarily injurious to the plaintiff, but becomes so only by reason of the special damage caused to him by it, and it then becomes necessary in the statement of claim to allege the special damage as the gist of the action. (See *post*, "*Damages*," p. 19.)

Joinder of causes of action.] "Subject to the following Rules, the plaintiff may unite in the same action and in the same statement of claim several causes of action, but if it appear to the Court or a Judge that any such causes of action cannot be conveniently tried or disposed of together, the Court or Judge may order separate trials of any of such causes of action to be had, or may make such other order as may be necessary or expedient for the separate disposal thereof." (O. XVII. r. 1.) For an instance of the exercise of this discretion see *Smith* v. *Richardson*, 4 C. P. D. 112; 48 L. J. C. P. 140, where a claim in which the vendor of goods and the indorsees of a bill given for the price of the goods jointly sued the purchaser to recover the price and also upon the bill was struck out as embarrassing.

"No cause of action shall unless by leave of the Court or a Judge be joined with an action for the recovery of land, except claims in respect of mesne profits or arrears of rent in respect of the premises claimed, or any part thereof, and damages for breach of any contract under which the same or any part thereof are held." (O. XVII. r. 2.) An application for leave under the above rule must be made before the writ is issued. (*Pilcher* v. *Hinds*, 11 Ch. D. 905; 48 L. J. Ch. 587). An action for the establishment of title to land only, and not for possession of the land, is not an action for recovery of land within the above rule. (*Gledhill* v. *Hunter*, 14 Ch. D. 492; 49 L. J.

Ch. 333); neither is an action for foreclosure. (*Tawell* v. *Slate Co.*, 3 Ch. D. 629.) For instances of cases in which leave has been given under this rule, see *Cook* v. *Enchmarch*, 2 Ch. D. 111; 45 L. J. Ch. 504; and *Kitching* v. *Kitching*, 24 W. R. 901.

"Claims by a trustee in bankruptcy as such shall not, unless by leave of the Court or a Judge, be joined with any claim by him in any other capacity." (O. XVII. r. 3.)

"Claims by or against husband and wife may be joined with claims by or against either of them separately." (O. XVII. r. 4.)

"Claims by or against an executor or administrator as such may be joined with claims by or against him personally, provided the last-mentioned claims are alleged to arise with reference to the estate in respect of which the plaintiff or defendant sues or is sued as executor or administrator." (O. XVII. r. 5.) It has been held that a defendant must not set up by way of counterclaim against the claim of a plaintiff, suing only in a distinct personal character, claims against him personally and also as an executor. (*Macdonald* v. *Carrington*, 4 C. P. D. 28; 48 L. J. C. P. 179.)

"Claims by plaintiffs jointly may be joined with claims by them or any of them separately against the same defendant." (O. XVII. r. 6.)

"The last three preceding Rules shall be subject to Rule 1 of this Order, and to the Rules herein-after contained." (O. XVII. r. 7.)

"Any defendant alleging that the plaintiff has united in the same action several causes of action which cannot be conveniently disposed of in one action, may at any time apply to the Court or a Judge for an order confining the action to such of the causes of action as may be conveniently disposed of in one proceeding." (O. XVII. r. 8.)

"If, on the hearing of such application as in the last preceding Rule mentioned, it shall appear to the Court or a Judge that the causes of action are such as cannot all be conveniently disposed of in one action, the Court or a Judge may order any of such causes of action to be excluded, and may direct the statement of claim, or, if no statement of claim has been delivered, the copy of the writ of summons, and the indorsement of claim on the writ of summons, to be amended accordingly, and may make such order as to costs as may be just." (O. XVII. r. 9.)

The claim of debt or damages.] The claim at the conclusion of the statement of claim should be sufficient to cover the largest amount of debt or damages likely to be recovered; for the jury in the absence of amendment cannot give more than the amount thus claimed. (*Cheveley* v. *Morris*, 2 W. Bl. 1300.)

If the jury assess the damages at a greater amount, an amendment might in some exceptional cases be allowed. (O. XXVII. r. 1. See also *Knowlman* v. *Bluett*, L. R. 9 Ex. 1; 43 L. J. Ex. 29.)

Where the cause of action is one which entitles the plaintiff to interest, the claim should be large enough to include the full amount. (*Watkins* v. *Morgan*, 6 C. & P. 661; *Hudson* v. *Fawcett*, 7 M. & G. 348.) The amount of the claim is not restricted by the indorsement of the debt on the writ.

Where the plantiff's claim can be ascertained exactly, it is better to claim only the precise amount. Otherwise, if the defendant should pay money into court, or plead a defence to the exact sum in dispute, and also plead in denial to the residue, the plaintiff might have to discontinue under O. XXIII., and pay the defendant the costs occasioned by the residue, or might have judgment against him in respect of such residue. Where the plaintiff seeks to recover interest up to the time of judgment, the precise amount cannot be inserted. In order to avoid this difficulty, some pleaders have adopted the following form :—"The plaintiff claims £—— (*the exact amount of the debt, and interest up to the date of the writ of summons*), with interest on £—— (*the exact amount of the debt only*) at £—— per cent. per annum, from the date of the writ of summons herein until payment or judgment."

With the above-mentioned exceptions, the amount claimed in the conclusion of the statement of claim is immaterial. It is treated as meaning any sum which the plaintiff can prove not exceeding the amount named.

Damages.] Damages are distinguished in law as *general* and *special* damages : the former being the necessary and immediate loss occasioned by the injurious act of the defendant ; the latter comprising the loss which actually followed under the special circumstances of the case as its natural and proximate consequence beyond its necessary and immediate effect. This distinction leads to the following rule in pleading : that if special damage is intended to be claimed, it must be stated with particularity : but general damage requires no particular mention, and is covered by the general claim at the conclusion. (See *Boorman* v. *Nash*, 9 B. & C. 145, 152 ; *Rodgers* v. *Nowill*, 5 C. B. 109.)

Where the act of the defendant complained of is in itself a legal injury to the plaintiff, as a breach of contract or a trespass, the law always implies general damage at least to a nominal amount. (*Ashby* v. *White*, 1 Smith's L. C., 8th ed. 264 ; *Marzetti* v. *Williams*, 1 B. & Ad. 415 ; and see *Beaumont* v. *Greathead*, 2 C. B. 494.) Where the act complained of is not in itself necessarily injurious to the plaintiff, but becomes so only by reason of the special damage caused by it, the special damage has then to be stated and proved as the gist of the action and in order to establish the injury, and not merely in the sense of damage. As, for example, in the case of speaking defamatory words, not actionable in themselves but only by reason of their special consequences, and in the case of placing a nuisance upon a highway, which is actionable at the suit of a private person only when it is the cause of special loss or damage to him. (*Leake on Contracts*, 1044 ; *Benjamin* v. *Storr*, L. R. 9 C. P. 400 ; 43 L. J. C. P. 162 ; *Iveson* v. *Moore*, 1 *Ld. Raymond*, 486 ; see *post*, "*Defamation*," "*Nuisance*," "*Negligence*," "*Sheriff*," &c.)

The object of stating special damage in the statement of claim where not alleged as an essential part of the cause of action, is to give notice to the defendant of the nature and extent of the claim made against him, and of the particular facts by which it is to be supported, so as to enable him to come to trial prepared with evidence to meet it. The charge of general damage is sufficiently notified in the statement of the injury, which imports all its necessary and immediate effects, and no further particularity is required in respect of it. (*Smith* v. *Thomas*, 2 Bing. N. C. 372, 380.) The special damage must be charged with sufficient particularity to inform the defendant what the plaintiff intends to prove, and the plaintiff is not allowed to give evidence of any special damage which is not sufficiently stated. (See

1 Wms. Saund., 1871 ed., p. 321, n. (5); *Hartley* v. *Herring*, 8 T. R. 130.) Thus, in an action for an imprisonment, the plaintiff cannot prove as damage that he suffered in health, unless he has charged it in the statement of claim (*Pettit* v. *Addington*, Peake, 62); or that he was stinted of food in prison. (*Lowden* v. *Goodrick*, Peake, 46.)

So, in an action by a tradesman for defamation whereby several customers left him, he cannot prove as damage that any particular customer has left him unless the customer be named in the statement of claim (*Browning* v. *Newman*, 1 Strange, 666; 1 Wms. Saund., 1871 ed., p. 322, n. (5)); and, in an action by a woman for defamation, an allegation that she thereby lost several suitors is insufficient to admit evidence of any particular suitor having deserted her (*Hartley* v. *Herring*, 8 T. R. 130, 132); and, under an allegation of special damage by a loss of the plaintiff's lodgers, he was not allowed to prove the loss of a particular lodger. (*Westwood* v. *Cowne*, 1 Stark. 172.)

But in an action for defamation by the preacher at a chapel, it was held sufficient to allege generally as special damage, that some persons of his congregation had withdrawn their support, without naming them (*Hartley* v. *Herring*, 8 T. R. 130); and a general loss of business or custom may be alleged and proved without having recourse to particular instances. (*Rose* v. *Groves*, 5 M. & G. 613; *Evans* v. *Harries*, 1 H. & N. 251; 26 L. J. Ex. 31; *Riding* v. *Smith*, 1 Ex. D. 91; 45 L. J. Ex. 281.)

The statement of the special damage must sufficiently show its connection with the injurious act as a natural and proximate consequence, otherwise it cannot be recovered even though assessed by the jury. (*Crouch* v. *G. N. Ry. Co.*, 11 Ex. 742; 25 L. J. Ex. 137; *Hoey* v. *Felton*, 11 C. B. N. S. 142; 31 L. J. C. P. 105; *Hobbs* v. *L. & S. W. Ry. Co.*, L. R. 10 Q. B. 111; 44 L. J. Q. B. 49; *and see the observations on this last case in McMahon* v. *Field*, 50 L. J. Ex. 552.) The damages recoverable do not include damages merely connected with the breach of contract or wrong through a series of causes intervening between the immediate consequence of the breach of contract or wrong and the damage or injury complained of. (Per Cockburn, C. J., in *Hobbs* v. *L. & S. W. Ry. Co.*, *ante*; *Glover* v. *L. & S. W. Ry. Co.*, L. R. 3 Q. B. 25; 37 L. J. Q. B. 57; *Sharp* v. *Powell*, L. R. 7 C. P. 253; 41 L. J. C. P. 95; Leake on Contracts, 1046.) Nor do the damages for a breach of contract include damages purely speculative, and not within the contemplation of the contracting parties at the time of the contract. (*The Parana*, 2 P. D. 118.)

The damages in an action for breach of contract include not only such consequences as may be considered as arising naturally, *i.e.* according to the usual course of things, from the breach itself, but such also as may reasonably be supposed to have been in the contemplation of the parties, at the time when they made the contract, as the probable result of the breach of it. See *Horne* v. *Mid. Ry. Co.*, L. R. 8 C. P. 131, 137; 42 L. J. C. P. 59; *Hadley* v. *Baxendale*, 9 Ex. 341; 23 L. J. Ex. 179; *Sanders* v. *Stuart*, 1 C. P. D. 326; 45 L. J. C. P. 682: and *post*, "*Carriers*." In some cases notice to the defendant of the facts out of which the latter damages arose may be essential, and when this is so, the fact of notice, but not the evidence of it, should be alleged in the statement of claim. (O. XIX. r. 23.) Mere notice of the special circumstances will not, generally, render the party breaking the contract liable for the special consequences of the breach of contract, but in order to render him liable for such consequences the contract must have been impliedly made upon the basis of such circumstances, see *British Columbia Saw Mills Co.* v. *Nettleship*, L. R. 3 C. P. 499 : 37 L. J. C. P. 235 ; *per* Willes, J., *Horne* v. *Mid. Ry. Co.*, L. R. 8 C. P. 131 ; 42 L. J. C. P. 59, or the notice so given and received, that an actual contract was thereby made that the defendant should bear the exceptional loss. See *per* Blackburn, J., in *Horne* v. *Mid. Ry. Co.*, *supra;* and see *Simpson* v. *L. & N. W. Ry. Co.*, 1 Q. B. D. 274 ; 45 L. J. Q. B. 182. In pleading in such cases it will be prudent to allege the fact of notice, and that the contract the breach of which is complained of, was made upon the basis of the special circumstances of which notice has been given.

Matter which would constitute a distinct cause of action should be so pleaded. If, however, such matter is also evidence in support of the cause of action stated upon the pleadings it may be proved at the trial, in general, without being pleaded. Thus, in an action for defamation, subsequent libels published by the defendant of the plaintiff are admissible in evidence to prove the malicious motive of the defendant, and cannot be excluded on the ground that they may disclose distinct causes of action. (*Pearson* v. *Lemaitre*, 5 M. & G. 700 ; and see *Hemmings* v. *Gasson*, E. B. & E. 346 ; 27 L J. Q. B. 252.) If the subsequent libels are relied upon merely as evidence to prove the malice charged they should not be set out in the statement of claim. (O. XIX. rr. 4, 25.)

If the plaintiff fails in proving the special damage alleged, he may still resort to and recover his general damages. (*Smith* v. *Thomas*, 2 Bing. N. C. 372, 380.) Thus, in an action for defamation, the plaintiff was held entitled to prove and recover for a general loss of trade, though the declaration also alleged a loss of particular customers which he failed to prove. (*Evans* v. *Harries*, 1 H. & N. 251 ; 26 L. J. Ex. 31 ; *Riding* v. *Smith*, 1 Ex. D. 91 ; 45 L. J. Ex. 281.)

All the circumstances under which an injury was committed may be stated and proved in order to aggravate and enhance the damages (*Millington* v. *Loring*, 6 Q. B. D. 190 ; 50 L. J. Q. B. 214 ; *Newman* v. *Smith*, 1 Salk. 642 ; *Dix* v. *Brookes*, 1 Str. 61) ; thus in an action for breach of a promise to marry the plaintiff may allege that she was seduced under such promise of marriage (*Millington* v. *Loring*, *supra*) ; in an action of trespass for entering the plaintiff's house, that the defendant did it under a false charge that the plaintiff had stolen goods therein (*Bracegirdle* v. *Orford*, 2 M. & S. 77) ; and the jury may take all the circumstances into their consideration in assessing the amount of damages. (*Merest* v. *Harvey*, 5 Taunt. 442 ; and see *Wilson* v. *Hicks*, 26 L. J. Ex. 242 ; *Emblen* v. *Myers*, 6 H. & N. 54 ; 30 L. J. Ex. 71 ; *Bell* v. *Mid. Ry. Co.*, 10 C. B. N. S. 287 ; 30 L. J. C. P. 273.) There is, however, a distinction between actions of tort and of contract in this respect ; in the latter, in general, no damages more than nominal can be recovered that are not capable of being specifically stated and appreciated, except in the case of a breach of a contract to marry, where the injury to the plaintiff's feelings may also be taken into account. (*Hamlin* v. *G. N. Ry. Co.*, 1 H. & N. 408 ; 26 L. J. Ex. 20 ; *Frost* v. *Knight*, L. R. 7 Ex. 111, 116 ; 41 L. J. Ex. 81 ; *Smith* v. *Woodfine*, 1 C. B. N. S. 660 ; *Berry* v. *Da Costa*, L. R. 1 C. P. 331 ; 35 L. J. C. P. 191, and see *Emblen* v. *Myers*, *supra.*)

When the injury, whether a tort or a breach of contract, has (as a natural and proximate consequence) led the plaintiff to incur expense, this should be laid as special damage. It should be alleged that the plaintiff has *paid* the money when that is the case; but a *liability* to pay is sufficient to entitle the plaintiff to recover, and it should then be alleged that the plaintiff has incurred or has become liable to pay the expenses in question. (*Spark* v. *Heslop*, 1 E. & E. 563; 28 L. J. Q. B. 197; *Randall* v. *Raper*, E. B. & E. 84; 27 L. J. Q. B. 266; *Josling* v. *Irvine*, 6 H. & N. 512; 30 L. J. Ex. 78; *Richardson* v. *Chasen*, 10 Q. B. 756.)

Damages may be claimed and assessed for prospective loss which it is reasonably certain will occur by reason of the cause of action (2 Wms. Saund., 1871 ed., p. 496, n. (*g*); *Hodsoll* v. *Stallebrass*, 11 A. & E. 301; *Lamb* v. *Walker*, 3 Q. B. D. 389; 47 L. J. Q. B. 451; *Phillips* v. *L. & S. W. Ry. Co.*, 5 Q. B. D. 78; 49 L. J. Q. B. 233); but not if such future damage constitutes itself a new cause of action; thus in the case of a continuing breach of contract, as a breach of covenant by an apprentice to serve his master, or a breach of covenant to repair premises, damages are recoverable only to the time of action brought, the continuation of the breach forming a new cause for which a fresh action must be brought. (*Ibid.*; *Horn* v. *Chandler*, 1 Mod. 271; *Coward* v. *Gregory*, L. R. 2 C. P. 153; 36 L. J. C. P. 1.)

Damages, whether existing or prospective, resulting from one and the same cause of action can only be assessed and recovered once for all. (*Lamb* v. *Walker*, 3 Q. B. D. 389, 395, 403; *Gibbs* v. *Cruickshank*, L. R. 8 C. P. 454; 42 L. J. C. P. 273; Leake on Contracts, 1050.) It is further laid down that a mode of estimating the damages in some cases is that if the party bound to perform the contract do not perform it, the other contracting party may perform it as nearly as he can, and charge as damage the reasonable expenses of so doing. (Leake on Contracts, 1050; *Hamlin* v. *G. N. Ry. Co.*, 1 H. & N. 408; 26 L. J. Ex. 20; *Leblanche* v. *L. & N. W. Ry. Co.*, 1 C. P. D. 286; 45 L. J. C. P. 521; *Prehn* v. *Royal Bank of Liverpool*, L. R. 5 Ex. 92; 39 L. J. Ex. 41.) Upon this principle, where the vendor has failed to supply goods at the time contracted for, the purchaser may go into the market and buy goods similar, or as nearly similar as possible to those contracted for, and charge the vendor with the loss. (*Hinde* v. *Liddell*, L. R. 10 Q. B. 265; 44 L. J. Q. B. 105; Leake on Contracts, 1051.)

The allegation of special damage, if denied, should be traversed in the statement of defence, otherwise it will be taken to be admitted. (O. XIX. r. 17.)

The defendant may give evidence to rebut the proof of special damage offered by the plaintiff, or in mitigation of the damage proved; as in an action of libel the defendant may give evidence in mitigation of damages, that the plaintiff published libels of him, and was of bad reputation. (*Watts* v. *Fraser*, 7 A. & E. 223; *Richards* v. *Richards*, 2 M. & Rob. 557; *Kelly* v. *Sherlock*, L. R. 1 Q. B. 686.) In an action for injuries caused by the defendant's negligence, a sum received by the plaintiff on an accidental insurance policy cannot be taken into account in reduction of damages. (*Bradburn* v. *G. W. Ry. Co.*, L. R. 10 Ex. 1; 44 L. J. Ex. 9). As to the right of the insurers to withhold or recover the amount of the policy from the insured who has been compensated by the wrongdoer, see *Darrell* v. *Tibbitts*, 5 Q. B. D. 560; 50 L. J. Q. B. 33; *Burnand* v. *Rodocanachi*, 6 Q. B. D. 633; 50 L. J. Q. B. 284. But matter which, if pleaded, would amount to an answer or justification of the cause of action cannot, without being pleaded, be proved in mitigation of damages. (*Linford* v. *Lake*, 3 H. & N. 276; and see *Perkins* v. *Vaughan*, 4 M. & G. 988.)

As to the measure of damages in particular actions, see the separate titles, *post*; and Mayne on the Law of Damages; Sedgwick on the Measure of Damages.

As to damages under Lord Cairns' Act (21 & 22 Vict. c. 27, s. 2), see *post*, "*Injunction*," p. 439.

Relief other than damages or payment of debt.] "The High Court of Justice and the Court of Appeal respectively, in the exercise of the jurisdiction vested in them by this Act in every cause or matter pending before them respectively, shall have power to grant, and shall grant, either absolutely or on such reasonable terms and conditions as to them shall seem just, all such remedies whatsoever as any of the parties thereto may appear to be entitled to in respect of any and every legal or equitable claim properly brought forward by them respectively in such cause or matter; so that, as far as possible, all matters so in controversy between the said parties respectively may be completely and finally determined, and all multiplicity of legal proceedings concerning any of such matters avoided." (Jud. Act, 1873, sec. 24, sub-sec. 7. See also the other sub-sections of section 24 and section 25 of the same Act, and Wils. Jud. Acts, 3rd ed., *notes*, pp. 20—31.)

The remedy or relief which is sought in the action should in general be expressly claimed both on the writ and in the statement of claim whether it be damages, the appointment of a receiver, a mandamus, an injunction, or specific performance of a contract, or whatever else it may be. (O. II. r. 1; O. XIX. r. 2.) If the writ is defective, it can be amended so as to claim the required relief by leave obtained upon summons at Chambers. (O. III. r. 2.)

If the claim for a mandamus, or injunction, or the appointment of a receiver is a substantive part of the relief for the obtaining of which the action is brought, the indorsement upon the writ ought to show such claim, but if the necessity therefor arises incidentally in the course of the action, the required relief will be granted, though not claimed upon the writ. (Wils. Jud. Acts, p. 131. See also Jud. Act, 1873, sec. 25, sub-sec. 8; O. II. r. 1; O. LII. r. 4, and *Colebourne* v. *Colebourne*, 1 Ch. D. 690; 45 L. J. Ch. 749.)

In dealing with claims for specific performance, for rectification of instruments in writing, or for an account, or other claims with which the Chancery Division of the High Court is more competent to deal than the Queen's Bench Division, it must be remembered that there are ample powers of transfer of actions from one division to another. (See Jud. Act, 1873, sec. 34; Jud. Act, 1875, sec. 11; O. V. rr. 4, 4*a*; O. LI. rr. 1—3; Wils. Jud. Acts, pp. 39, 300—303.) If the defendant by way of counter-claim seeks relief which the Chancery Division alone has the requisite machinery to administer (*e.g.*, where specific performance is sought), this may afford good reason for an order to transfer the whole action to the Chancery Division. (*Holloway* v. *York*, 2 Ex. D. 333; *Hillman* v. *Mayhew*, 1 Ex. D. 132; 45 L. J. Ex. 334; Wils. Jud. Acts, p. 303); but a defendant in such case is not entitled as of course to such an order, as otherwise any defendant might put in a counterclaim for the specific performance of some agreement, and then apply for a transfer, and thus everything might, at the will of the defendant, be brought into the Chancery Division. (*Storey* v. *Waddle*, 4 Q. B. D. 289, 290.) As to Injunctions and Mandamus, see further under those titles, *post*.

Venue.] The venue is the statement of the county (or place treated as a county for assize purposes) in which the action is to be tried, as "The County of Devon," &c.

Venues were formerly either *local*, or *transitory*. By O. XXXVI. r. 1, it is provided that "there shall be no local venue for the trial of any action, but, when the plaintiff proposes to have the action tried elsewhere than in Middlesex, he shall in his statement of claim name the county or place in which he proposes that the action shall be tried, and the action shall, unless a Judge otherwise orders, be tried in the county or place so named. Where no place of trial is named in the statement of claim, the place of trial shall, unless a Judge otherwise orders, be the county of Middlesex. Any order of a Judge, as to such place of trial, may be discharged or varied by a Divisional Court of the High Court."

The plaintiff has thus the power of laying the venue where he pleases in the first instance, but either party may at any time before trial apply by summons at Chambers to change the venue to a more suitable or convenient place. This application may be made either where the venue has been selected by the plaintiff, or where it has been fixed by a Judge's order, subject, of course, to the risk of having to pay the costs of the summons if refused, or, indeed, in some cases, even if successful. Upon the hearing of the summons the trial will be directed to be held at whatever place appears upon the facts to be the most proper and convenient place.

By an Order in Council dated the 4th May, 1864 (made in pursuance of the 3 & 4 Will. IV. c. 71), the county of Lancaster is divided for the purposes of the Assizes into "Lancashire, Northern Division," "Lancashire, West Derby Division," and "Lancashire, Salford Division;" and the venue must be so stated in the statement of claim, according to whether the action is intended to be tried at Lancaster, Liverpool, or Manchester. In like manner by an Order in Council dated the 10th June, 1864, appointing assizes to be held at two places in the county of York, the venue is to be laid in "Yorkshire, North and East Riding Division," if the action is to be tried at York, or "Yorkshire, West Riding Division," if it is to be tried at Leeds.

Power is given by the Jud. Act, 1875, sec. 23, to regulate the various circuits by Orders in Council. Orders in Council dated 5th Feb., and 17th May, 1876 (see Wils. Jud. Acts, p. 538), regulate the circuits as at present constituted, and provide for the issue of commissions for the county of Surrey.

As to former practice, see Bullen and Leake, 3rd ed. p. 2.

Amendment of pleadings.] In all cases, except those provided for by O. XXVII. rr. 2 and 3 *infra*, it is necessary to obtain leave before amending pleadings. If this leave is required before trial, it must be applied for by summons at Judges' Chambers; if it is required at the trial, application for it must be made to the presiding Judge. If a demurrer is pending, no order will be made for amendment, except on payment of the costs of the demurrer. (O. XXVIII. r. 7.) As to amendments by striking out or adding parties, see *ante* "*Number of the Parties*," p. 4, and O. XVI. rr. 13 to 16.

As to claims which cannot conveniently be tried together, and which it is desired to have separately tried, see O. XVII. rr. 1, 8, 9, *ante*, "*Joinder of Causes of Action*," p. 17, and O. XXXVI., r. 6. As to counter-claims which ought to be disposed of in a separate action, see O. XXII. r. 9.

The Court of Appeal has power to amend. (O. LVIII. r. 5.) The subject of amendment of pleadings is dealt generally with in O. XXVII., which is as follows:—

"1. The Court or a Judge may, at any stage of the proceedings, allow either party to alter his statement of claim or defence or reply, or may order to be struck out or amended any matter in such statements respectively which may be scandalous, or which may tend to prejudice, embarrass, or delay the fair trial of the action, and all such amendments shall be made as may be necessary for the purpose of determining the real questions or question in controversy between the parties." As to what are embarrassing pleadings, see *ante*, "*Pleading in general*," p. 7; *Cashin* v. *Cradock*, 3 Ch. D. 376; *Golding* v. *Wharton Salt Works Co.*, 1 Q. B. D. 374; *Watson* v. *Rodwell*, 3 Ch. D. 380; 45 L. J. Ch. 744; *Heap* v. *Marris*, 2 Q. B. D. 630; 46 L. J. Q. B. 761; *Pullen* v. *Snelus*, 48 L. J. C. P. 394; 40 L. T. 363; *Davy* v. *Garrett*, 7 Ch. D. 473; 47 L. J. Ch. 218; *Tildesley* v. *Harper*, 10 Ch. D. 393; 48 L. J. Ch. 495; *Newby* v. *Sharpe*, 8 Ch. D. 39; 47 L. J. Ch. 617; *Laird* v. *Briggs*, 16 Ch. D. 440; 50 L. J. Ch. 260; *Williamson* v. *L. & N. W. Ry. Co.*, 12 Ch. D. 787.

"2. The plaintiff may, without any leave, amend his statement of claim once at any time before the expiration of the time limited for reply and before replying, or, where no defence is delivered, at any time before the expiration of four weeks from the appearance of the defendant who shall have last appeared."

[The time for replying is within three weeks after the defence, or the last of the defences has been delivered, unless there is a special order extending the time. (O. XXIV. r. 1.)]

"3. A defendant who has set up in his defence any set-off or counter-claim may, without any leave, amend such set-off or counter-claim at any time before the expiration of the time allowed him for pleading to the reply, and before pleading thereto, or in case there be no reply, then at any time before the expiration of twenty-eight days from the filing of his defence."

"4. Where any party has amended his pleading under either of the last two preceding Rules, the opposite party may, within eight days after the delivery to him of the amended pleading, apply to the Court, or a Judge, to disallow the amendment, or any part thereof, and the Court or Judge may, if satisfied that the justice of the case requires it, disallow the same, or allow it subject to such terms as to costs or otherwise as may seem just."

"5. Where any party has amended his pleading under Rule 2 or 3 of this Order, the other party may apply to the Court or a Judge for leave to plead or amend his former pleading within such time and upon such terms as may seem just."

"6. In all cases not provided for by the preceding Rules of this Order, application for leave to amend any pleading may be made by either party to the Court or a Judge in Chambers, or to the Judge at the trial of the action, and such amendment may be allowed upon such terms as to costs or otherwise as may seem just."

"7. If a party who has obtained an order for leave to amend a pleading delivered by him does not amend the same within the time limited for that purpose by the order, or if no time is thereby limited, then within fourteen days from the date of the order, such order to amend shall, on the expiration of such limited time as aforesaid, or of such fourteen days, as the case may be, become *ipso facto* void, unless the time is extended by the Court or a Judge."

"8. A pleading may be amended by written alterations in the pleading which has been delivered, and by additions on paper to be interleaved therewith if necessary, unless the amendments require the insertion of more than 144 words in any one place, or are so numerous or of such a nature that the making them in writing would render the pleading difficult or inconvenient to read, in either of which cases the amendment must be made by delivering a print of the pleading as amended."

"9. Whenever any pleading is amended, such pleading when amended shall be marked with the date of the order, if any, under which the same is so amended, and of the day on which such amendment is made, in manner following, viz.: 'Amended —— day of ——.'"

"10. Whenever a pleading is amended, such amended pleading shall be delivered to the opposite party within the time allowed for amending the same."

The above rules have been amended with regard to time. By O. LVII. r. 6a, R. S. C. April 1880, r. 42, "the time for delivering or amending any pleading may be enlarged by consent in writing without application to the Court or a Judge." By O. LIX. r. 2, R. S. C. April, 1880, r. 44,) "the Court or a Judge may at any time, and on such terms as to costs or otherwise as to the Court or Judge may seem just, amend any defect or error in any proceedings; and all such amendments may be made as may be necessary for the purpose of determining the real question or issue raised by or depending on the proceedings."

When an application is made by an opponent for leave to amend, care should be taken to have it imposed as a term of the order, if any, giving such leave, that all alterations or amendments of the pleadings necessitated by the amendment of the opponent's pleading may be made, otherwise a summons for leave to make such amendments or alterations may be necessary.

Where a plaintiff has amended his statement of claim after delivery of statement of defence, and, no other pleading having been delivered, moves for judgment on the amended statement of claim, the defendant may either obtain leave to amend his statement of defence, or put in a new defence, or, he may proceed with his original defence, in which case the uncontradicted amendments in the amended statement of claim will be taken to be admitted, and the statement of defence will stand as an answer *pro tanto*. (*Boddy* v. *Wall*, 7 Ch. D. 164; 47 L. J. Ch. 112.) This rule is also applicable to other pleadings.

Notice in lieu of statement of claim.] Where the writ is specially indorsed, and the defendant has not dispensed with a statement of claim, the plaintiff may deliver as his statement of claim a notice to the effect that his claim is that which appears by the indorsement upon the writ, unless the Court or a Judge shall order him to deliver a further statement. Such notice may be either written or printed, or partly written and partly printed, and must be marked on the face in the same manner as an ordinary statement of claim. (O. XXI. r. 4.) A form of such notice is given in App. (B) to the Jud. Act, 1875. See Form 3, the body of which is as follows: "*The particulars of the plaintiff's complaint herein and of the relief and remedy to which he claims to be entitled, appear by the indorsement upon the writ of summons.*" If a further statement is ordered, it must be delivered within six weeks from the date of appearance, or, if any other time for delivery is directed by the order, within the time so directed; unless an extension of time is obtained. (O. XXI. r. 4, O. LVII. r. 6.) The object of delivering a notice in lieu of statement of claim is to avoid the delivery of a formal statement of claim where the nature and items of the plaintiff's claim have been fully shown upon the indorsement upon the writ, and so to lessen the expense of the proceedings. This notice may be used in cases within the rule in which the facts are simple and uncomplicated, or likely to be uncontested, but care should be taken in such cases to see not only that the special indorsement includes all the plaintiff's claims, but also that the claims are so stated as to show a legal cause of action. In the case of *Robertson* v. *Howard*, 3 C. P. D. 280; 47 L. J. C. P. 480, it was held by Lindley, J., that a specially indorsed writ coupled with notice under O. XXI. r. 4, was to be treated as a statement of claim for all purposes, and might be demurred to. In all cases, however, coming within O. XXI. r. 4, where the facts are complicated or likely to be contested, it is advisable to deliver a statement of claim, so as to have a clear narrative of the facts in support of the plaintiff's case upon the pleadings in the first instance. If this is not done it may happen that the defendant in his statement of defence will so state the facts as to necessitate the substitution by the plaintiff of a statement of claim in lieu of his notice, and thus the proceedings would be delayed and at the same time the expense thereof would be increased.

Special indorsement upon the writ.] "In all actions where the plaintiff seeks merely to recover a debt or liquidated demand in money payable by the defendant, with or without interest, arising upon a contract, express or implied, as, for instance, on a bill of exchange, promissory note, cheque, or other simple contract debt, or on a bond or contract under seal for payment of a liquidated amount of money, or on a statute where the sum sought to be recovered is a fixed sum of money or in the nature of a debt, or on a guaranty, whether under seal or not, where the claim against the principal is in respect of such debt or liquidated demand, bill, cheque, or note, or on a trust, the writ of summons may be specially indorsed with the particulars of the amount sought to be recovered, after giving credit for any payment or set-off." (O. III. r. 6.)

The advantage to be derived from a specially indorsed writ, in addition to that above mentioned in O. XXI. r. 4, is that "where the defendant appears to a writ of summons specially indorsed under O. III. r. 6, the plaintiff may, on affidavit made by himself, or by any other person who can swear positively to the debt or cause of action, verifying the cause of action, and stating that in his belief there is no defence to the action, call on the defendant to show cause before the

Court or a Judge why the plaintiff should not be at liberty to sign final judgment for the amount so indorsed, together with interest, if any, and costs. A copy of the affidavit shall accompany the summons or notice of motion. The Court or a Judge may thereupon, unless the defendant, by affidavit or otherwise, satisfy the Court or a Judge that he has a good defence to the action on the merits, or disclose such facts as may be deemed sufficient to entitle him to defend, make an order empowering the plaintiff to sign judgment accordingly." (O. XIV. r. 1 *a.*) See as to proceedings on such summons, O. XIV., and notes in Wils. Jud. Acts, p. 170, and *Girvin* v. *Grepe*, 13 Ch. D. 174; 49 L. J. Ch. 63; *Wallingford* v. *Mutual Society*, 5 App. Cas.; 685; 50 L. J. Q. B. 49; *Crump* v. *Cavendish*, 5 Ex. D. 211; 49 L. J. Ex. 491.

In order to constitute a special indorsement the particulars of the amount sought to be recovered should be clear and intelligible, and should be such as to inform the defendant of the exact nature of the plaintiff's claim, and enable him to see whether it is one to which he has any defence. (*Walker* v. *Hicks*, 3 Q. B. D. 8; 47 L. J. Q. B. 27; *Smith* v. *Wilson*, 4 C. P. D. 392; 5 C. P. D. 25; 49 L. J. C. P. 96; *Parpaite Frères* v. *Dickinson*, 38 L. T. 178; *Aston* v. *Hurwitz*, 41 L. T. 521.) For this purpose it should furnish the requisite dates, and though it need not, where the account is a long one, give a list of items, it should afford sufficient information to enable the defendant to satisfy his mind whether he ought to pay or resist. See cases cited, *supra*.

Interest must not be endorsed, unless payable under a contract to that effect, or upon bills of exchange or promissory notes. See *Rodway* v. *Lucas*, 10 Ex. 66.

Time for delivering statement of claim.] The time for delivering the statement of claim is fixed by O. XXI. In all actions (except Probate actions, and Admiralty actions *in rem*) it may be delivered after the issue of the writ, at any time before appearance, or, if the defendant has appeared before its delivery, at any time within six weeks from the time of the entering of appearance by the defendant. If a longer time is required for delivering the statement of claim, it is necessary to obtain an order to that effect at Judges' Chambers, or a written consent from the opposite party under O. LVII. r. 6 a. If the plaintiff makes default in delivering a statement of claim, where one is requisite, the defendant may at the expiration of the time allowed for the delivery of the statement of claim apply (by summons at Judges' Chambers) to have the action dismissed with costs, for want of prosecution, and upon the hearing of such application the action may be so dismissed, or such other order made upon such terms as shall seem just. (O. XXIX. r. 1.)

It is usual in practice to wait until after appearance by the defendant before delivering the statement of claim. The reason for this is, that in actions for liquidated demands, debts, pecuniary damages, detention of goods, recovery of land, or any of the above matters, no statement of claim is requisite if no appearance has been entered; provision being made by Order XIII. for judgment in such cases upon default of appearance, whilst Order XXI. r. 1 (*c*), directs that "Where a plaintiff delivers a statement of claim without being required to do so, the Court or a Judge may make such order as to the costs occasioned thereby as shall seem just, if it appears that the delivery of a statement of claim was unnecessary or improper."

Rule 18 of "The Rules of the Supreme Court (Costs)" also gives similar power to disallow the costs of unnecessary pleadings, and that, whether any objection is raised as to such costs by the parties or not.

An order for the extension of time for the delivery of a pleading may be made at any time before the action has been actually dismissed, although the application for such extension of time is not made until after the expiration of the time appointed or allowed for the delivery of the pleading. (O. LVII. r. 6.) An order extending the time for delivering the statement of claim will be made upon the defendant's application to dismiss for want of prosecution, where it seems just to make such order. (See *Higginbottom* v. *Aynsley*, 3 Ch. D. 288.)

After an action has been actually dismissed by an order duly made, no extension of time can be given for the delivery of a statement of claim, the action being at an end (*Whistler* v. *Hancock*, 3 Q. B. D. 83; 47 L. J. Q. B. 152; *King* v. *Davenport*, 4 Q. B. D. 402; 48 L. J. Q. B. 606); but before an application is made for an extension of time for delivery of pleadings in such a case, the action must be revived by procuring a rescission or reversal of the order dismissing it. Such an order may be made after the time for appealing against the original order dismissing the action has expired, by virtue of the power given by O. LVII. r. 6, which is as follows: "A Court or a Judge shall have power to enlarge or abridge the time appointed by these rules, or fixed by any order enlarging time, for doing any act or taking any proceeding, upon such terms (if any) as the justice of the case may require, and any such enlargement may be ordered although the application for the same is not made until after the expiration of the time appointed or allowed." (*Burke* v. *Rooney*, 4 C. P. D. 226; 48 L. J. C. P. 601; *Carter* v. *Stubbs*, 6 Q. B. D. 116; 50 L. J. C. P. 4.) Pleadings cannot be amended or delivered in the long vacation without an order for that purpose, nor does the long vacation count in the computation of time for delivering pleadings. (O. LVII. rr. 4 and 5.) The long vacation commences on the 10th August, and terminates on the 24th October in each year. (O. LXI. r. 2.)

Where the plaintiff has been allowed less than six days further time for the delivery of his statement of claim, Sunday, Christmas Day and Good Friday shall not be reckoned in the computation of such time. (O. LVII. r. 2.)

Every pleading in an action must be delivered to the solicitor of every party who appears by a solicitor, or to the party if he does not appear by a solicitor, but if no appearance has been entered for any party, then such pleading is to be delivered by being filed with the proper officer. (O. XIX. r. 6.)

Particulars and their effect on pleading.] When the cause of action is not sufficiently disclosed by the pleading, an order will be made, upon an application by summons at Judges' Chambers, either that the pleading shall be amended or that the party pleading shall deliver particulars giving all such information as may be needful in order to enable his opponent to deal with the case intended to be made against him. So, too, particulars will be ordered to be delivered in respect of individual paragraphs or allegations in pleadings, whether statements of claim, or other pleadings which are too general, or with which an opponent cannot fairly deal, without further or more specific information. (*Saunders* v. *Jones*, 7 Ch. D. 435 ; 47 L. J. Ch. 440 ; *Godden* v. *Corsten*, 5 C. P. D. 17 ; 49 L. J. C. P. 112 ; *Philipps* v. *Philipps*, 4 Q. B. D. 127, 130 ; 48 L. J. Q. B. 135.)

If no particulars are delivered, or ordered, anything may be proved within the scope of the pleadings. If the particulars delivered are not sufficiently explicit, an application for further and better particulars should be made. Particulars of negligence are frequently ordered to be delivered when a statement of claim charging negligence does not specially point out the particular negligence, or acts of negligence, complained of; or where the statement of claim, after alleging specific acts of negligence, also charges negligence in general terms. So, too, particulars will be ordered to be given where the damage claimed is not alleged with such particularity as to render further information as to it needless. (*Brindley* v. *G. N. Ry. Co.*, *Notes of Cases*, 1878, p. 57.)

Again, where fraud is pleaded in general terms, particulars will, where necessary, be ordered of the fraud charged. So also, where a libel, or a slander, is justified in general terms, particulars will be ordered of the justification. Indeed in all cases where further information than that contained in the general allegations in the pleadings ought, under the circumstances of the action, reasonably to be given, an order for particulars will be made, and made as a rule upon the terms that the costs shall be costs in the cause, though of course this is not an inflexible rule. See for forms of orders for particulars Sch. to R. S. C. April, 1880, Forms H. 10, H. 11.

Amendments of pleadings when made must not be inconsistent with, and are controlled by, the particulars delivered in the action, and if any such amendments go beyond the scope of, or are at variance with, the particulars already delivered, such particulars should be amended.

It is optional with the plaintiff to give credits for payments or matters of set-off in his particulars. (*Randall* v. *Ikey*, 4 Dowl. 682 ; *Penprase* v. *Crease*, 1 M. & W. 36 ; *Luck* v. *Handley*, 4 Ex. 486 ; 19 L. J. Ex. 29 ; *Fussell* v. *Gordon*, 13 C. B. 847.)

Where credits are given in the particulars, the plaintiff is considered as suing only for the balance claimed (*Russell* v. *Bell*, 10 M. & W. 352); so that if he proves no balance beyond what is credited, the defendant is entitled to a verdict. (*Smethurst* v. *Taylor*, 12 M. & W. 545.) The defence of payment or set-off when pleaded is taken with reference to the balance claimed in the particulars (*Eastwick* v. *Harman*, 6 M. & W. 13); the proof under it must be of items other than those credited. The items proved would be *primâ facie* applicable to the balance, and it lies upon the plaintiff to show that they are identical with those already credited. (*Townson* v. *Jackson*, 13 M. & W. 374 ; *Lamb* v. *Micklethwait*, 1 Q. B. 400.)

A copy of the particulars is annexed to the record, but they do not form part of the record for all purposes of pleading. (*Jubb* v. *Ellis*, 3 D. & L. 367 ; *Roche* v. *Champain*, 1 Ex. 10.)

It may happen that the particulars whether indorsed on the writ or delivered under an order are afterwards found to be incorrect or insufficient, and it may become necessary to amend them. This can generally be done only by leave. (As to particulars indorsed on writ, see O. III. r. 2.) If, however, particulars are delivered without leave for the purpose of superseding or supplementing the particulars indorsed on a writ, or particulars previously delivered in an action, such particulars are irregular, and may be set aside upon an application for that purpose, but if received by the opposite party, they will, if not set aside, supersede or supplement, as the case may be, the original particulars, the irregularity being one that is waived by the receipt of the fresh particulars and continuation of the action without making application to have such particulars set aside on the ground of irregularity. (*Fromant* v. *Ashley*, 1 E. & B. 723; *Jones* v. *Fowler*, 4 Dowl. P. C. 232.) If fair and proper particulars have been delivered without leave, an application to have them set aside could rarely be attended with any material advantage, as on application under such circumstances, an order would probably be made that the fresh particulars should stand.

There are certain actions with regard to which it has been enacted by various statutes, or directed by various rules, that particulars should be delivered with the declaration, or the pleas, as the case may be; as for example by the Patent Law Amendment Act, 1852, s. 41, it is enacted, that in any action for the infringement of letters-patent, the plaintiff shall deliver with his declaration particulars of the breaches complained of in the said action, and the defendant, on pleading thereto, shall deliver with his pleas, particulars of any objections on which he means to rely at the trial in support of the pleas in the said action; and at the trial of such action no evidence shall be allowed to be given in support of any alleged infringement or of any objection impeaching the validity of such letters-patent which shall not be contained in the particulars delivered as aforesaid: provided always that the place or places at or in which and in what manner the invention is alleged to have been used or published prior to the date of the letters-patent shall be stated in such particulars. So under Lord Campbell's Act, 9 & 10 Vict. c. 93, it is enacted by s. 4, as to actions under that Act, "that in every such action the plaintiff on the record shall be required, together with the declaration, to deliver to the defendant or his attorney a full particular of the person or persons for whom and on whose behalf such action shall be brought, and of the nature of the claim in respect of which damages shall be sought to be recovered." See also r. 19 of H. T. 1853. It is presumed that these and similar enactments and directions are no longer in force, declarations and pleas being abolished, and all enactments inconsistent with the Jud. Acts being by sec. 33 (2) of the Jud. Act, 1875, repealed. (See, however, Jud. Act, 1873, s. 23; Jud. Act, 1875, s. 21.) The present system of pleading requiring all material facts to be stated would seem to render such particulars superfluous. (See O. XIX. rr. 1, 4, 18, &c.) When, however, the pleadings do not afford the information which such particulars would have furnished, doubtless, whether such acts or rules are repealed or not, an order would be made on application at Chambers that such particulars should be delivered. (*Sykes* v. *Howarth*, 12 Ch. D. 826; 48 L. J. Ch. 769; *Flower* v. *Lloyd*, 45 L. J. Ch. 746; 35 L. T. 454.) As to the general principle of the repeal by the Jud. Acts of inconsistent enactments, see *Garnett* v. *Bradley*, 3 App. Cas. 944; 48 L. J. H. L. 186; *Parsons* v. *Tinling*, 2 C. P. D. 119; 46 L. J. C. P. 230; *Dodds* v. *Shepherd*, 1 Ex. D. 75; 45 L. J. Q. B. 457; *Tenant* v. *Ellis*, 6 Q. B. D. 46; 50 L. J. Q. B. 143. As to particulars under the Copyright Act, 5 & 6 Vict. c. 45, s. 16, see "*Defences*," "*Copyright.*" See further "*Patents*," p. 496.

Debts in general.] As to when a formal statement of claim can be dispensed with, see "*Notice in lieu of statement of claim*," *ante*, p. 26. It is convenient to note that under the former system of pleading concise forms of counts were used for suing upon simple contracts resulting in mere debts, in which the cause of action was stated by a general description, the particular circumstances of the debt being reserved to be given in evidence upon the trial, and to be explained by particulars which were as a matter of course required to be delivered with such counts. (See Bullen and Leake, 3rd ed., p. 35 *et seq.*, C. L. P. Act, 1852, and forms in Schedule (B.) to that Act; and as to the particulars, R. 19, H. T., 1853.) These counts were designated *indebitatus counts*, *money counts*, or *common counts*, whilst counts stating the cause of action more particularly and more at length, were termed *special counts*. The common indebitatus counts formerly in use were eight in number, and were as follows :—

1. For money payable by the defendant to the plaintiff for goods sold and delivered by the plaintiff to the defendant.
2. For money payable by the defendant to the plaintiff for goods bargained and sold by the plaintiff to the defendant.
3. For money payable by the defendant to the plaintiff for work done and materials provided by the plaintiff for the defendant at his request.
4. For money payable by the defendant to the plaintiff for money lent by the plaintiff to the defendant.
5. For money payable by the defendant to the plaintiff for money paid by the plaintiff for the defendant at his request.
6. For money payable by the defendant to the plaintiff for money received by the defendant for the use of the plaintiff.
7. For money payable by the defendant to the plaintiff for interest upon money due from the defendant to the plaintiff, and forborne at interest by the plaintiff to the defendant at his request.
8. For money payable by the defendant to the plaintiff for money found to be due from the defendant to the plaintiff on accounts stated between them.

Under the present system it would generally be held that the statement was not sufficiently specific if these counts were exactly followed, and a statement of claim so drawn might be set aside, or ordered to be supplemented by particulars giving the amount of the debt claimed with dates and items. Besides, these counts might perhaps, in some cases, be open to objection as rather stating the legal result of the facts than the contract or facts themselves out of which the debt arose.

CHAPTER II.

Statements of Claim in Actions on Contracts.

Accounts Stated (*a*).

Statement of Claim on accounts stated.

1. Accounts were on the —— of ——, 18—, stated between the plaintiff and the defendant, and £—— was upon such stating of accounts found to be due from and payable by the defendant to the plaintiff.

2. The said £—— has never been paid.

(*a*) An account stated is an admission of a sum of money being due from the defendant to the plaintiff. It affords a distinct cause of action, and may be so stated in the statement of claim. (See *per* Lord Abinger, C.B., *Irving* v. *Veitch*, 3 M. & W. 90, 106.)

Where there has been no express agreement as to the amount due between the parties, or their agents, but the admission relied on as the foundation for the claim upon an account stated, is to be implied from letters, conversations, or circumstances, probably, the correct mode of pleading is to allege that the sum claimed has been found to be due upon an account, or accounts, stated between the parties, and to refer generally to such letters, conversations, or circumstances (see O. XIX. r. 27, and "*Pleading in General*," *ante*, p. 7).

When the account stated, or admission of liability, has been reduced to writing it is correct so to state, the drawing up or giving of the writing being, it is conceived, in general, a fact proper to be pleaded. (See "*Pleading in General*," *ante*, p. 7; "*The Body of the Statement of Claim*," *ante*, p. 11; and "*Agreements*," *post*, p. 50.)

It generally happens that claims for money due upon accounts stated are joined with claims upon the original debt, or debts, in respect of which such accounts were stated. Where this is the case, it is usual to insert the claims upon accounts stated after those upon the original debt or debts.

Where the facts and circumstances amounting to an account stated are set out in detail in the statement of claim, so that it clearly appears therefrom that there has been an account stated between the parties, it is unnecessary to allege that there has been a statement of accounts, that being in such case the legal inference from the facts stated. (See Form No. 1 App. (C) to Jud. Act, 1875; "*Pleading in General*," *ante*, p. 7.)

The claim upon an account stated lies where there is an absolute acknowledgment made by the defendant to the plaintiff of a debt due from him to the plaintiff and payable at the time of action brought. (*Wayman* v. *Hilliard*, 7 Bing. 101; *Knowles* v. *Michel*, 13 East, 249; *Highmore* v. *Primrose*, 5 M. & S. 65; *Porter* v. *Cooper*, 1 C. M. & R. 387; *Wray* v. *Milestone*, 5 M. & W. 21, 24; *Buck* v. *Hurst*, L. R. 1 C. P. 297.)

An account stated alone does not extinguish or supersede or alter the previous debts respecting which it was stated. (*Fidgett* v. *Penny*,

The like, where the accounts are stated of matters in respect of which claims are also made in the Statement of Claim.

In respect of the above debts and causes of action [*Proceed as in preceding form.*]

---

1 C. M. & R. 108; *Smith* v. *Page*, 15 M. & W. 683; *Perry* v. *Attwood*, 6 E. & B. 691; 25 L. J. Q. B. 408.) But an account stated respecting debts on both sides may by agreement between the parties effect an extinction of the cross demands, and so operate as payment *pro tanto*. (*Ashby* v. *James*, 11 M. & W. 542; *Callander* v. *Howard*, 10 C. B. 290.) And where upon an account containing cross demands a balance is struck and agreed upon, the discharge of the other items is a sufficient consideration to support the debt for the balance, though the account might have contained claims for which an action would not lie. (*Laycock* v. *Pickles*, 4 B. & S. 497; 33 L. J. Q. B. 43.)

An account stated alone is not conclusive between the parties, but the debts respecting which it was stated may be examined. Thus, the defendant may show that the account was stated by mistake (see *Trueman* v. *Hurst*, 1 T. R. 40, 42; *Thomas* v. *Hawkes*, 8 M. & W. 140; *Perry* v. *Attwood*, *supra*); that the account was stated respecting a debt not then due, as an I O U given as security for a prospective debt (*Lemere* v. *Elliott*, 6 H. & N. 656; 30 L. J. Ex. 350); that the account was stated respecting debts void for want of consideration, or upon a consideration which has failed (*Jacobs* v. *Fisher*, 1 C. B. 178; *Gough* v. *Findon*, 7 Ex. 48; *Wilson* v. *Wilson*, 14 C. B. 616); that the debts were upon an illegal consideration or for an illegal purpose (*Rose* v. *Savory*, 2 Bing. N. C. 145); that the debt was for an attorney's costs, which could not be recovered for want of a bill delivered (*Scadding* v. *Eyles*, 9 Q. B. 858); that the debt was for the advocacy of a barrister. (*Kennedy* v. *Brown*, 13 C. B. N. S. 677; 32 L. J. C. P. 137.) But it is no defence that the account was stated respecting a debt due for an executed consideration under a contract within the Statute of Frauds, of which there was no memorandum in writing (*Seago* v. *Deane*, 4 Bing. 459; *Knowles* v. *Michel*, 13 East, 249; *Cocking* v. *Ward*, 1 C. B. 858); *aliter*, if the consideration was within the statute, and still executory. (*Lord Falmouth* v. *Thomas*, 1 C. & M. 89.)

The acknowledgment may be proved by writing, as by a bill of exchange or promissory note (*Wheatley v. Williams*, 1 M. & W. 533), if properly stamped (*Green* v. *Davies*, 4 B. & C. 235; *Jones* v. *Ryder*, 4 M. & W. 32); which is evidence of an account stated between immediate parties to the instrument, but not between remote parties (*Burmester* v. *Hogarth*, 11 M. & W. 97); or by an I O U, which is evidence of an account stated with the person to whom it is addressed (*Jacobs* v. *Fisher*, 1 C. B. 178; *Wilson* v. *Wilson*, 14 C. B. 616); and if it bears no address, then with the holder, in the absence of evidence to the contrary (*Curtis* v. *Rickards*, 1 M. & G. 46; *Fesenmayer* v. *Adcock*, 16 M. & W. 449); or the acknowledgment may be by oral statement. (*Newhall* v. *Holt*, 6 M. & W. 662.) An account stated respecting a debt, which has not accrued within six years of action brought, must be in writing, by reason of the 9 Geo. IV. c. 14, s. 8, requiring a written acknowledgment (*Jones* v. *Ryder*, 4 M. & W. 32; and see *Hopkins* v. *Logan*, 5 M. & W. 241, 248); but upon an account

The like, referring to letters by which the accounts were stated.

1. By letters bearing date the —— of ——, 18—, and the —— of ——, 18—, respectively, accounts were stated between the plaintiff and the defendant in respect of the above debts and causes of action, and £—— was upon such stating of accounts found to be due from the defendant to the plaintiff, and payable by the defendant to the plaintiff.

2. The said £—— has never been paid.

For a like form, see "Broker," post, p. 119.

Form No. I. in App. (C.) to Jud. Act, 1875.

1. Between the 1st of January and the 28th of February, 1875, the plaintiff supplied to the defendant various articles

---

stated respecting items on both sides and admitting a balance, it is no objection to the recovery of the balance that some of the earlier items were barred by the Statute of Limitations. (*Ashby* v. *James*, 11 M. & W. 542.)

The acknowledgment must be made before action (*Spencer* v. *Parry*, 3 A. & E. 331, 332; *Allen* v. *Cook*, 2 Dowl. 546); and it must show either expressly or by sufficient reference that an ascertained sum is due. (*Hughes* v. *Thorpe*, 5 M. & W. 656; *Kirton* v. *Wood*, 1 M. & Rob. 253; *Lane* v. *Hill*, 18 Q. B. 252; 21 L. J. Q. B. 318.) The acknowledgment must be made either to the plaintiff himself or to his agent, and is not sufficient if made to a stranger (*Breckon* v. *Smith*, 1 A. & E. 488; *Tucker* v. *Barrow*, 7 B. & C. 623), and it must be made by the defendant or by his agent. An arbitrator is not an agent, and a claim on an account stated will not be supported by his award. (*Bates* v. *Townley*, 2 Ex. 152.)

An acknowledgment of a debt payable at a future time is evidence of an account stated, upon which the right of action does not commence until the time of payment has arrived, as a promissory note payable at some period after date (*Wheatley* v. *Williams*, 1 M. & W. 533; *Fryer* v. *Roe*, 12 C. B. 437); or a note given to secure a debt payable by instalments. (*Irving* v. *Veitch*, 3 M. & W. 90.) As to an acknowledgment of a debt payable upon a contingency, see *Baker* v. *Heard*, 5 Ex. 959.

An acknowledgment under seal will not support a claim upon an account stated. From such an acknowledgment a covenant to pay is implied. (*Middleditch* v. *Ellis*, 2 Ex. 623; *Isaacson* v. *Harwood*, L. R. 3 Ch. Ap. 225; 37 L. J. Ch. 209; *Baber* v. *Harris*, 9 A. & E. 532.)

A subsequent account stated respecting the same matter is not of itself a defence to an action on a previous one. (*Fidgett* v. *Penny*, 1 C. M. & R. 108.)

Under a common count alleging "an account stated" one occasion of accounting only was allowed to be proved. (*Kennedy* v. *Withers*, 3 B. & Ad. 767.) See *ante* "*Debts in General*," p. 32.

of drapery; and accounts and invoices of the goods so supplied, and their prices, were from time to time furnished to the defendant, and payments on account were from time to time made by the defendant.

2. On the 28th of February, 1875, a balance remained due to the plaintiff of £75 9*s.*, and an account was on that day sent by the plaintiff to the defendant showing that balance.

3. On the 1st of March following, the plaintiff's collector saw the defendant at his house, and asked for payment of the said balance, and the defendant then paid him by cheque £25 on account of the same. The residue of the said balance, amounting to £50 9*s.*, has never been paid.

See also for a form, Meyerhoff v. *Froehlich,* 3 C. P. D. 333.

Agent.

Statement of Claim for the Price of Work, &c., done by an Agent (a).

1. The plaintiff was employed by the defendant during the months of April and May, 1879, as his agent to obtain orders for certain jewellery and other goods manufactured or sold by the defendant, at a salary of £—— per month, and a commission of — per cent. upon the amount of sales effected through his, the plaintiff's, agency.

2. The sales of the said jewellery and other goods effected through the plaintiff's agency in pursuance of the said employment amounted to £——.

3. The defendant has paid to the plaintiff £——, and no more, on account of the said salary and commission, and there is now due and payable by the defendant to the plaintiff, as the balance of the said salary and commission, the sum of £——.

(*a*) An action will not lie against an agent for merely omitting to perform a commission, unless he is bound by some contract or duty to undertake it; but if he does undertake it, though gratuitously, he is liable to an action for misfeasance in the performance. (*Elsee* v. *Gatward*, 5 T. R. 143; *Dartnall* v. *Howard*, 4 B. & C. 345; *Whithead* v. *Greetham*, 2 Bing. 464; *Hart* v. *Miles*, 4 C. B. N. S. 371; 27 L. J. C. P. 218; *Balfe* v. *West*, 13 C. B. 466; 22 L. J. C. P. 175.)

As to the law of agency with regard to contracts generally,

The like.

1. The plaintiff was during —— retained and employed by the defendant as his solicitor and agent.

2. The plaintiff as such solicitor and agent did during the said —— certain work and made certain journeys, and paid and expended certain monies, and bestowed certain attendances for the defendant, full particulars whereof have been delivered to the defendant [*or the particulars whereof are as follows*].

3. The sum of £—— is now due, and payable by the defendant to the plaintiff in respect of the matters aforesaid.

By a House Agent for Commission.

1. The plaintiff is a house agent carrying on business at ——, and the defendant is and was the owner of a warehouse at ——.

2. In the month of ——, 18—, the defendant requested the plaintiff as such house agent to endeavour to procure for him a tenant of the said warehouse at a rent of not less than £—— per annum, and the plaintiff then agreed to comply with the said request.

3. The plaintiff complied with the said request, and succeeded in procuring one —— to become tenant to the plaintiff of the said warehouse at a rent of not less than £—— per annum. (*See note, post*, p. 42.)

4. No express agreement was made as to the remuneration to be paid to the plaintiff for so procuring a tenant for the defendant, but the ordinary and reasonable terms are that in such cases an agent shall receive 5 per cent. upon the first year's rent of the premises for which he has procured a tenant [*or as the case may be*].

---

see Story on Agency; Leake on Contracts, 464—536; Notes to *Thompson* v. *Davenport*, 2 Sm. L. C.; *Ireland* v. *Livingston*, L. R. 5 H. L. 395, 407—413; 41 L. J. Q. B. 201, 205; *Sims* v. *Bond*, 5 B. & Ad. 393; and see the notes *post*.

An agent signing a contract in his own name is personally liable upon the contract, unless it appears clearly upon the face of the contract that he signs as the mere agent of some other person, and that the signature was not intended to bind him personally. (*Deslandes* v. *Gregory*, 2 E. & E. 602; 29 L. J. Q. B. 93; *Gadd* v. *Houghton*, 1 Ex. D. 357; 46 L. J. Ex. 71; *Southwell* v. *Bowditch*, 1 C. P. D. 374; 45 L. J. C. P. 630; *Fairlie* v. *Fenton*, L. R. 5 Ex. 169; 39 L. J. Ex. 107; *Hough* v. *Manzanos*, 4 Ex. D. 104; 48 L. J. Ex. 398.)

5. This commission would in the present case amount to £——, and that sum is now due and payable by the defendant to the plaintiff in respect of his said services.

By a Commission Agent to recover a Balance due in respect of Advances on Goods Shipped.

1. The plaintiff is a commission agent carrying on business at ——, and the defendants are merchants carrying on business at ——.

2. In or about Dec., 1878, the defendants applied to the plaintiff for an advance upon certain oils about to be shipped to Sydney, which they proposed to consign for sale to the plaintiff's agents at that place, and the plaintiff agreed to make them an advance thereon of £——, and to ship the said oils to Sydney upon the terms of a letter written and signed by the defendants and sent to him, which was as follows:—

Dec. 20th, 1878.

DEAR SIR,

We beg to hand you invoice of oils consigned for sale to your agents at Sydney, and on which we have to receive from you an advance of £——.

We authorise your agents to sell the above either by private contract or by auction, the commission charged by the broker or auctioneer on such sale to be borne by us, as well as your and your agent's usual commission charges and *del credere*, and we hereby agree to pay you any deficiency between the amount of such advance and the net proceeds of such sales.

Yours, &c.

3. The agreed advance of £—— was made by the plaintiff to the defendants.

4. The said oils were shipped to Sydney and there sold by the plaintiff's said agents as agreed.

5. Upon such sales there was a deficiency of £—— between the amount of such advance and the net proceeds of such sales, whereof the defendants had notice.

6. The defendants have not paid the plaintiff the said deficiency or any part of it, and the said amount thereof is now due to the plaintiff, and payable by the defendants to him.

By an Agent against his Employer for Breach of Agreement to accept a Draft for the Price of Goods bought under the Employment (*b*).

1. The plaintiffs are commission agents at the Mauritius, and the defendant is a merchant at Liverpool.

2. The defendant by letter bearing date the —— day of —— 18—, offered to employ the plaintiffs, as such commission agents, to purchase for him at the Mauritius 500 tons or thereabouts of cane sugar, Nos. 10 and 12, at a maximum price of 26*s.* 9*d.* per cwt., to cover cost, freight, and insurance, and to ship the same for Liverpool, and offered to accept and promised them that he would accept their draft for the price of the said sugar upon presentation.

3. The plaintiffs accordingly accepted the said offer and employment, and bought the said sugar at a price within the said limit, namely, at 26*s.* 7*d.* per cwt., and shipped it for Liverpool, and drew upon the defendant for £——, the amount of the said price thereof, in accordance with the terms of the said offer and employment.

4. The plaintiffs' said draft for £—— was duly presented to the defendant for acceptance, but he refused to accept, and has not accepted it.

Against an Agent Employed to sell Goods, for not accounting or paying over.

1. The plaintiff, who is a wholesale draper carrying on business at Manchester, employed the defendant during the years —— and —— as his agent and traveller to sell certain drapery and other goods for him upon the terms contained in a letter bearing date the —— of —— 18—, and written by the plaintiff to the defendant [*or as the case may be*] which so far as is material were that the defendant should upon request render to the plaintiff a true and full account of the said goods, and of the sale

---

(*b*) A commission agent employed to purchase goods does not in general bind himself absolutely to supply the goods ordered, but merely to use due diligence to fulfil the order, and to get the goods as cheap as he reasonably can for his principal. (*Ireland* v. *Livingston*, L. R. 5 H. L. 407; 41 L. J. Q. B. 201.) The authority of an agent employed to buy in a particular market is in general to be construed with reference to the usages of such market. (*Johnston* v. *Kershaw*, L. R. 2 Ex. 82; 36 L. J. Ex. 44; *Ireland* v. *Livingston*, *supra*.)

thereof, and of the moneys arising from such sale, and pay over to him the net proceeds thereof.

2. The defendant accordingly under and in pursuance of the said employment received from the plaintiff large quantities of drapery and other goods for sale, and sold the same, and received the proceeds thereof.

3. The plaintiff has frequently in and since the month of —— 18— requested the defendant to render to him a true and full account of the said goods, and of the sale thereof, and of the moneys arising from such sale, and to pay over to him the net proceeds thereof.

4. The defendant has had ample time allowed him for complying with such requests, and has made many promises to render such account to the plaintiff, and to pay over to him the said net proceeds.

5. The defendant has never rendered to the plaintiff a true or full account either of the said goods or of the sale thereof, or of the moneys arising from such sale, and has never paid over to the plaintiff the said net proceeds or any portion of them.

6. The only account which the defendant has rendered to the plaintiff was one which was rendered on the —— day of —— 18—, and which was untrue, and was upon the face of it defective. It showed a sum of £50 to be then due and payable by the defendant to the plaintiff, a sum, however, which is much less than the true amount.

Against an Agent for not using due care and diligence in collecting Moneys.

1. The plaintiff is a draper at Leeds.

2. On or about the —— of ——, 18—, it was orally [*or as the case may be,*] agreed between the plaintiff and the defendant that the defendant should become the agent and collector of the plaintiff at a salary of £10 per month, and that the defendant should use due care and diligence in and about collecting outstanding accounts due or which should become due to the plaintiff from his customers.

3. The defendant entered upon the said employment upon the said terms and remained therein for nine months, and from time to time received payments amounting to £60 from the plaintiff on account of his said salary.

4. All conditions were fulfilled, and all things happened, and all times elapsed necessary to entitle the plaintiff to have due care and diligence used by the defendant in and about collecting the said accounts (*c*).

5. The defendant did not use due care or diligence in and about collecting the same.

6. The defendant by reason of such want of due care and diligence failed entirely to collect large numbers of the said accounts, whereby the plaintiff lost the use of the moneys due to him from his said customers for a long time, and is likely altogether to lose the value of many of such accounts, and has paid to no purpose the said sum of £60 to the plaintiff on account of his said salary.

Against an Agent for Selling Goods for a less price than ordered.

1. The plaintiff, who is &c., employed the defendant as his agent to sell clocks and watches for him upon the terms, orally agreed upon between the plaintiff and the defendant, that the defendant should obey the lawful and reasonable orders of the plaintiff in respect of the sale of the said clocks and watches.

2. In ——, 18—, the plaintiff sent to the defendant as such agent 100 clocks and 25 watches for sale by him, and ordered him not to sell the said clocks for a less price than 50*s*. each, and not to sell the said watches at a less price than 40*s*. each.

3. This was a lawful and reasonable order.

4. The defendant received the said clocks and watches as such agent, but he sold them at prices much less than those so ordered as above stated.

Against Commission Agents charging them as del credere Agents for the price of goods sold, or in the alternative for negligence in selling to an insolvent person.

(*Form No. 5 in App.* (C.) *to Jud. Act,* 1875.) (*d.*)

1. The plaintiffs are manufacturers of artificial man-

(*c*) See "*Conditions Precedent*," *post*, p. 158.

(*d*) A *del credere* agent guarantees to his principal the performance of the contracts by the persons to whom he sells, thus affording an additional security to the principal, but not otherwise affecting the

ures, carrying on business at ——, in the county of ——.

2. The defendants are commission agents, carrying on business in London.

3. In the early part of the year ——, the plaintiffs commenced, and down to the ——, 187—, continued to

---

principal's rights or duties in respect of the contract of sale. (*Ex parte White*, L. R. 6 Ch. Ap. 397, 403; 40 L. J. B. 73; *Morris* v. *Cleasby*, 4 M. & S. 574; *Catterall* v. *Hindle*, L. R. 1 C. P. 191; 31 L. J. C. P. 161; Leake on Contracts, 521.)

The agreement of a *del credere* agent is in its immediate object a guarantee of the agent's own conduct and skill in effecting sales to solvent customers. It is not an agreement to answer for the debt of another within the 4th section of the Statute of Frauds, and need not, therefore, be in writing. (*Couturier* v. *Hastie*, 8 Ex. 40; 22 L. J. Ex. 97; Leake on Contracts, 245; *Fleet* v. *Murton*, L. R. 7 Q. B. 126, 132; 41 L. J. Q. B. 49.)

Where an agent's authority is revoked by his principal, he is, as a general rule, in the absence of contract or custom to the contrary, entitled to payment for work done and for services actually rendered. See Leake on Contracts, 66, 485, 488.

House agents, estate agents, and the like, however, have in general no right to any remuneration, unless they succeed in obtaining a tenant or purchaser, as the case may be, on the appointed terms, for the property put into their hands for the purpose of being let or sold. (*Read* v. *Rann*, 10 B. & C. 438; *Green* v. *Wales*, 30 L. J. C. P. 343; *Simpson* v. *Lamb*, 17 C. B. 603; 25 L. J. C. P. 113; *Broad* v. *Thomas*, 7 Bing. 99; 4 C. & P. 338; *Prickett* v. *Badger*, 1 C. B. N. S. 296; 26 L. J. C. P. 33; *Wilkinson* v. *Alston*, 48 L. J. Q. B. 733; *Bayley* v. *Chadwick*, 39 L. T. 429.) The contract in such cases is, by the custom of the trade in general, revocable at the will of the principal at any time before the agent has actually procured a person ready to take, or purchase, as the case may be, on the terms arranged. (*Simpson* v. *Lamb*, *supra*; *Prickett* v. *Badger*, *supra*.) If the relation of buyer and seller, or landlord and tenant, as the case may be, is actually brought about by the agent, he is, in general, entitled to his commission. (*Per* Erle, C. J., *Green* v. *Bartlett*, 14 C. B. N. S. 685; 32 L. J. C. P. 262; see also *Mansell* v. *Clements*, L. R. 9 C. P. 139.)

The general rule in the absence of contract or custom to the contrary would appear to be that commission is not due until the agent has completely performed his task, but if the contract is not fulfilled because of the default of the principal in spite of the agent having done all on his part to be done commission is nevertheless payable. (*Fisher* v. *Drewitt*, 48 L. J. Ex. 32; 39 L. T. 253; *Green* v. *Lucas*, 33 L. T. 584.)

Where, however, the principal by any wrongful conduct prevents such agent from procuring the required purchaser, or tenant, the agent may sue the principal for such conduct, and recover compensation for the labour, or expense, actually bestowed, or incurred, by him in endeavouring to procure a purchaser or tenant. (*Prickett* v. *Badger*, 1 C. B. N. S. 296; 26 L. J. C. P. 33; see also *Inchbald* v. *Western Neilgherry Coffee Co.*, 17 C. B. N. S. 733; 34 L. J. C. P. 15.)

consign to the defendants, as their agents, large quantities of their manures for sale, and the defendants sold the same and received the price thereof and accounted to the plaintiffs therefor.

4. No express agreement has ever been entered into between the plaintiffs and the defendants with respect to the terms of the defendants' employment as agents. The defendants have always charged the plaintiffs a commission at —— per cent. on all sales effected by them, which is at the rate of commission ordinarily charged by *del credere* agents in the said trade. And the defendants, in fact, always accounted to the plaintiffs for the price, whether they received the same from the purchasers or not.

5. The plaintiffs contend that the defendants are liable to them as *del credere* agents, but if not so liable are under the circumstances hereinafter mentioned liable as ordinary agents.

6. On the ——, the plaintiffs consigned to the defendants for sale a large quantity of goods, including —— tons of ——.

7. On or about the ——, the defendants sold —— tons of ——, part of such goods, to one G. H. for £——, at three months' credit, and delivered the same to him.

8. G. H. was not, at that time, in good credit, and was in insolvent circumstances, and the defendants might, by ordinary care and diligence, have ascertained the fact.

9. G. H. did not pay for the said goods, but before the expiration of the said three months for which credit had been given was adjudicated a bankrupt, and the plaintiffs have never received the said sum of £——, or any part thereof.

Against a Broker liable by usage of the trade as though he were a del credere Agent (*e*).

1. The plaintiffs are merchants in London, and the defendants are brokers in the fruit trade in London.

(*e*) By the usage of a trade, a broker in such trade may be liable personally, as though he were a *del credere* agent, upon a written contract which is in such a form as to render it a contract upon which, apart from such usage, the principal alone would be liable. A usage that such liability should arise upon default of giving the name of the principal within a given time, or the like, is reasonable,

2. In October, 1878, the defendants were employed by the plaintiffs as such brokers upon the terms usual in the London fruit market, to sell for them a certain consignment of raisins in the London fruit market.

3. One of the said terms usual in the London fruit market was, that if selling brokers do not name the purchaser in the contract note furnished by them to their principals, they are liable as *del credere* agents for the price of the fruit sold.

4. The defendants accordingly sold in the London fruit market the said consignment of raisins for a sum of £——, and furnished to the plaintiffs a contract note showing such sale; but the purchaser was not named in such contract note.

5. The said purchaser of the said consignment of raisins did not at the proper time pay and has not paid the said price or any part of the said price of the said fruit.

6. The defendants have not paid to the plaintiffs the said price or any part thereof, and the same is still due and payable by the defendants to the plaintiffs.

Against an Agent on the implied warranty that he had authority to contract with the plaintiff (f).

1. The defendant, assuming to be the agent of G. H., invited the plaintiff to enter into a contract with him

---

and may be proved by parol evidence of trade usage. (*Fleet* v. *Murton*, L. R. 7 Q. B. 126; 41 L. J. Q. B. 49; *Hutchinson* v. *Tatham*, L. R. 8 C. P. 482; 42 L. J. C. P. 260; *Humfrey* v. *Dale*, 2 E. & B. 266; 27 L. J. Q. B. 390; *Imperial Bank* v. *London Docks*, 5 Ch. D. 195; 46 L. J. Ch. 335; and see *Southwell* v. *Bowditch*, 1 C. P. D. 374; 45 L. J. C. P. 630; and further as to usages, see *Mollett* v. *Robinson*, L. R. 7 H. L. 802.)

(*f*) A person professing to contract as agent for another, impliedly, if not expressly, warrants, or promises to the person who enters into such contract upon the faith of such profession, that the authority which he professes to have does in fact exist. (*Collen* v. *Wright*, 7 E. & B. 301; 27 L. J. Q. B. 215; *Cherry* v. *The Colonial Bank of Australasia*, L. R. 3 P. C. 24, 31; 38 L. J. P. C. 49; *Richardson* v. *Williamson*, L. R. 6 Q. B. 276; 40 L. J. Q. B. 145; 2 Smith's L. C. 8th ed. 395.)

This principle was applied to directors, as agents of their company, in *Weeks* v. *Propert*, L. R. 8 C. P. 427; 42 L. J. C. P. 129; *Richardson* v. *Williamson*, *supra*, and *Cherry* v. *The Colonial Bank of Australasia*, *supra*. If the person who deals with the agent is fully aware in point of fact what the extent of the authority of the agent is, but makes a mistake as to whether that authority is sufficient in point of

as such agent for the sale by the plaintiff to the said G. H. of certain goods [*or state what the contract was*], and asserted and warranted to the plaintiff that he the defendant was authorised by the said G. H. to make the said contract for him as his agent.

2. The plaintiff upon the faith of such assertion and warranty, duly entered into the said contract with the defendant as and assuming to be the agent of the said G. H., and was always ready and willing to perform the same on his part.

3. The defendant was not authorised by G. H. to make the said contract for him as his agent, and the said G. H. has always repudiated the said contract, and refused to be bound by it.

---

law, or not, to bind the principal with regard to the proposed contract, there is in the absence of an express agreement to that effect, no warranty or promise to the said person on the part of the agent that he has authority to bind his principal with regard to such contract. (*Beattie* v. *Lord Ebury*, L. R. 7 Ch. Ap. 777, 800; L. R. 7 H. L. 102; 41 L. J. Ch. 804; *Eaglesfield* v. *Lord Londonderry*, 4 Ch. D. 693; 38 L. T. (H. L.) 303; see also *Dickson* v. *Reuter's Teleg. Co.*, 3 C. P. D. 1; 47 L. J. C. P. 1.)

In an action against an agent founded on the above principle, the statement of claim must show that the agent had not in fact the authority which by his conduct, or by actual statements, he asserted he had. (*Oxenham* v. *Smythe*, 6 H. & N. 690; 31 L. J. Ex. 110.)

The measure of damages in this action is the loss which the plaintiff has sustained by reason of the supposed contract not being binding: thus, where the contract was for the sale of a ship at a certain price, which the plaintiff afterwards resold at a less price, the measure of damages was the difference in price. (*Simons* v. *Patchett*, 7 E. & B. 568; 26 L. J. Q. B. 195.) And where the contract was for the purchase of goods, the measure of damages was the difference between the contract price and the value of the goods. (*Hughes* v. *Graeme*, 33 L. J. Q. B. 335.)

So where two directors of a joint stock company notified to the company's bankers that the manager had authority to draw cheques on account of the company, which was not the fact (owing to the requirements of the Act of Incorporation of the company), it was held that the two directors were personally liable to the bankers for the amount of the cheques of the manager honoured by the bankers upon the faith of such notification. (*Cherry* v. *The Colonial Bank of Australasia*, *supra*.)

The plaintiff is also, in general, entitled to recover as special damage the costs of an unsuccessful action on the contract against the alleged principal. (*Randell* v. *Trimen*, 18 C. B. 786; 25 L. J. C. P. 307; and see *Richardson* v. *Dunn*, 8 C. B. N. S. 655; 30 L. J. C. P. 44), or of an unsuccessful suit for specific performance (*Collen* v. *Wright*, *supra*; *Spedding* v. *Newell*, L. R. 4 C. P. 212; 38 L. J. C. P. 133), if such action or suit would have been a valid and appropriate remedy, but for the want of authority in the agent, and would, but

4. By reason of the premises the plaintiff was not able to enforce performance of the said contract, and has lost the benefit thereof, and [*state the special damage, if any*].

The like.

1. The defendant in certain letters bearing date the 18th, 24th, and 27th of Dec., 18—, sent by him to the plaintiff, and in a conversation which took place between the plaintiff and the defendant on the 2nd of Jan., 18—, asserted and warranted to the plaintiff that he was authorised by A. B., the owner thereof, to sell a farm at ——, known as the Manor Farm, and to enter into a contract

---

for such want of authority, have been successful. (*Pow* v. *Davis*, E. B. & E. 222 ; 30 L. J. Q. B. 257 ; *Hughes* v. *Graeme*, 33 L. J. Q. B. 335.) But if the plaintiff persists in the action or suit against the alleged principal after the agent has absolutely withdrawn the assertion of authority, or after it is known to the plaintiff that the agent had no authority to bind his alleged principal, he cannot recover costs incurred after such withdrawal or knowledge.

F. and four others were joint owners of an estate, which they had advertised for sale. F., representing to the plaintiff that he had authority from the other joint owners to do so, contracted to sell the estate to him and sent him an abstract of title. The other joint owners repudiated the contract and sold the estate at a higher price to some other person. The plaintiff erroneously conceiving that the advertisement had bound all the joint owners, sued them for breach of contract, and continued his action after they had all sworn (in answer to interrogatories) that F. had no authority to contract, and was nonsuited. He then brought an action against F. for this misrepresentation of authority, in which it was held that the proper measure of damages was,—

(1.) The costs of investigating the title.

(2.) The costs of the former action, both the plaintiff's own and those paid to the defendant, down to the time when the answers to interrogatories were put in and were considered by his legal advisers.

(3.) The difference between the contract price and the market price of the estate.

(*Godwin* v. *Francis*, L. R. 5 C. P. 295 ; 39 L. J. C. P. 121. See also *Spedding* v. *Newell*, L. R. 4 C. P. 212 ; 38 L. J. C. P. 133, and *Richardson* v. *Williamson*, L. R. 6 Q. B. 276 ; 40 L. J. Q. B. 145.)

The *liability* to pay such costs is sufficient to sustain the claim for special damage, see "*Damages*," *ante*, p. 19.

Under the present procedure it is permissible, and in some cases advisable, to join in the same action the agent and his alleged principal, and to state the case in the alternative, claiming to have damages against the agent, if he has not the authority to bind his principal asserted by him, and to have damages against the principal, or, in proper cases, specific performance of contract, if the agent in fact has the authority which he asserted, see "*Number of the parties*," *ante*, p. 4.

on behalf of the said owner, ——, for the sale thereof by the said owner to the plaintiff.

2. The plaintiff, on the faith of such assertion and warranty, entered into a written contract with the defendant on behalf of such owner for the purchase of the farm.

3. The plaintiff was always ready and willing to carry out this contract on his part, but A. B., the said owner of the farm, at all times wholly repudiated the said contract, and denied that the defendant was authorised to sell the farm or to enter into the said contract on his behalf.

4. Thereupon the plaintiff on the faith of such assertion and warranty commenced an action against the said A. B., founded upon the said contract, to recover damages against him for not carrying out the said contract, and for wrongfully repudiating it.

5. This action proceeded to trial and was tried at, &c., and resulted in judgment being given for the said A. B., with costs against the plaintiff.

6. The defendant was not authorised by the said A. B. to sell the farm or to enter into the said contract, and on that account the said judgment was given for A. B. as above stated, with costs against the plaintiff.

7. By reason of the absence of the authority which as above stated the defendant asserted and warranted he possessed, the plaintiff has been unable to enforce the said contract, and has lost the value thereof, and has incurred costs amounting to £—— in prosecuting the said action, and has become liable to pay [and has paid] £—— to the said A. B., the costs payable to him under the said judgment.

Against an Agent to Recover the Amount of a Secret Commission received by him from Vendors to his Principals, upon a Purchase effected by him for his Principals (g).

1. The plaintiffs were and are an incorporated company carrying on business as colliery proprietors and coal

(*g*) No agent is permitted to derive or retain any pecuniary benefit or profit beyond his proper remuneration as agent without the sanction or knowledge of his principal. (*Hay's case*, L. R. 10 Ch. Ap. 601; 44 L. J. Ch. 721; *Fawcett* v. *Whitehouse*, 1 Russ. & My. 132; *Parker* v. *McKenna*, L. R. 10 Ch. Ap. 96, 110, 124; 44 L. J. Ch. 425; *Har-*

miners in Yorkshire and elsewhere, and the defendant was, until very recently, their manager.

2. The defendant, as such manager, agreed on behalf of the plaintiffs with Messrs. —— to purchase from the said Messrs. —— a steam-engine and other machinery for use in the plaintiffs' colliery at ——, at the price of £——, the said engine and other machinery to be made according to certain specifications and conditions, and to the satisfaction of the defendant.

3. The said Messrs. —— accordingly supplied a steam-engine and other machinery, and the defendant expressed his satisfaction therewith, and the plaintiffs paid the said price to the said Messrs. —— for the same.

4. The defendant, without the knowledge or consent of the plaintiffs, secretly and corruptly received from the

---

rington v. *Victoria Graving Dock Co.*, 3 Q. B. D. 549; 47 L. J. Q. B. 594; *Bagnall* v. *Carlton*, 6 Ch. D. 371.) All pecuniary benefit or profit which an agent so receives he receives for the benefit of his principal, and can be compelled to account to his principal for it, and it is immaterial whether it is received by the agent under some secret bargain for it, or whether it is in the shape of a discount, or of a douceur for services rendered. (*McKay's case*, 2 Ch. D. 1, 5; 45 L. J. Ch. 148; *Hay's case*, L. R. 10 Ch. Ap. 601, 603, 604; 44 L. J. Ch. 721; *Morison* v. *Thompson*, L. R. 9 Q. B. 480; 43 L. J. Q. B. 215; *Pearson's case*, 5 Ch. D. 336; 46 L. J. Ch. 339; *De Bussche* v. *Alt*, 8 Ch. D. 286, 316; 47 L. J. Ch. 381; *Metr. Bank* v. *Heiron*, 5 Ex. D. 319; *Phosphate Sewage Co.* v. *Hartmont*, 5 Ch. D. 394, 457.)

The fact that the agent was not influenced by the douceur, or profit, so wrongly obtained in the course of his agency, will not render the transaction legitimate, or entitle the agent to retain such douceur or profit as against his principal. (*De Bussche* v. *Alt*, *supra*; *Harrington* v. *Victoria Graving Dock Co.*, *supra*.)

Any surreptitious dealing between one principal and the agent of the other principal is a fraud on the latter. (*The Panama Telegraph Co.* v. *Indiarubber, &c., Works Co.*, L. R. 10 Ch. Ap. 515; 45 L. J. Ch. 125; Leake on Contracts, 480; *Harrington* v. *Victoria Graving Dock Co.*, *supra*.) As to rescinding a contract upon the ground of such dealings, see *The Panama Telegraph Co.* v. *Indiarubber, &c., Works Co.*, *supra*; *Smith* v. *Sorby*, 3 Q. B. D. 552, *note*, and "Defences," "*Fraud*."

An agent cannot maintain an action to recover such illegal profit or commission from the person who has promised to pay it to him. (*Harrington* v. *Victoria Graving Dock Co.*, *supra*.)

Where, however, the trade practice is for the agent to be remunerated by allowances or discounts made to him by the other contracting party, and that practice is known to, and acquiesced in by the principal, there is nothing illegal in the agent accepting such allowances or discounts. (*G. W. Insurance Co.* v. *Cunliffe*, L. R. 9 Ch. Ap. 525; 43 L. J. Ch. 741; *Baring* v. *Stanton*, 3 Ch. D. 502; and see *Williamson* v. *Barbour*, 9 Ch. D. 529; 37 L. T. 698.)

said Messrs. —— a sum of £—, being 2½ per cent. upon the price of the said engine and other machinery.

5. He received such sum either as a present for procuring for the said Messrs. —— the agreement for supplying the said engine and other machinery to the plaintiffs in accordance with an agreement or understanding made between himself and the said Messrs. —— before the said agreement for supplying the said engine and machinery was finally entered into, or else he received it in payment for his services to the said Messrs. —— in expressing his satisfaction with the said engine and other machinery supplied by them.

For a claim by a Company against a Director to recover a bribe paid him, see The Met. Bank v. *Heiron,* 5 Ex. D. 319.

AGISTMENT (*a*).

Statement of Claim for the Agistment of Horses and Cattle.

1. The plaintiff, in the months of Nov. and Dec., 1878, agisted, fed, and took care of 3 horses, 14 oxen, and 4 cows, for the defendant at his request.

2. There is due from and payable by the defendant to the plaintiff in respect of the matters above mentioned, the sum of £—.

For the Keep of Horses.

1. The plaintiff, from the —— of ——, 18—, to the —— of ——, 18—, kept, fed, groomed, trained, provided with food and stabling, and otherwise cared for and at-

---

(*a*) The common-law duty of an agister of cattle with whom cattle are left to be fed, is to keep and take care of them and feed them, and permit the owner to retake them, but not to redeliver them to him. (*Broadwater* v. *Blot,* Holt, N. P. C. 547; *Corbett* v. *Packington,* 6 B. & C. 268, 271.) An agister is not an insurer of the safety of the cattle intrusted to him; but if they are injured through his negligence or want of care he is liable. (*Smith* v. *Cook,* 1 Q. B. D. 79, 81; 45 L. J. Q. B. 122.) A contract to take in cattle to feed does not give an interest in land within section 4 of the Statute of Frauds. (*Jones* v. *Flint,* 10 A. & E. 753.)

tended to — race-horses of the defendant for the defendant at his request.

2. [*As in paragraph 2 of the preceding claim.*]

For the Use of Pasture.

1. From the —— of ——, 18—, to the —— of ——, 18—, the defendant used, by the permission of the plaintiff, — pasture fields of the plaintiff situate at ——, and the eatage of the grass growing thereon for the depasturing of cattle.

2. [*As in paragraph 2 of claim next but one above.*]

Agreements (*a*).

Statement of Claim upon a Written Agreement.

1. By an agreement in writing bearing date the 15th of March, 1878, it was agreed between the plaintiff and

---

(*a*) Where the agreement alleged to have been broken is an express agreement made by word of mouth, it is generally unnecessary, and even objectionable, to set out in the statement of claim the whole of the conversation or conversations by which the agreement was made. It is sufficient to set out as a fact the actual agreement made, giving, where practicable, such details as to time and place as to render particulars as to these matters unnecessary.

Where an agreement is to be implied from a series of letters or conversations, or from circumstances, it is sufficient to allege the agreement as a fact, and to refer generally to the letters, conversations, or circumstances, without setting them out in detail. (O. XIX. r. 27. See *ante*, "*Pleading in General*," p. 7, and Leake on Contracts, 191.)

Where the agreement relied upon has been reduced to writing it is correct to state or show that it is in writing, and to identify the writing, by stating the date it bears, or in some other way. (*Turquand* v. *Fearon*, 40 L. T. 543.) At common law it was formerly unnecessary to state this; because facts were not required to be stated in pleadings, but only the legal result of facts. (*Young* v. *Austen*, L. R. 4 C. P. 553; 38 L. J. C. P. 233; *Corkling* v. *Massey*, L. R. 8 C. P. 395; 42 L. J. C. P. 153; Leake on Contracts, 169.)

In equity, however, where the pleadings consisted of statements of fact, the practice was otherwise. Wherever, in order to establish ground for relief, it was necessary to prove a written agreement, it was essential that the bill should show a written agreement. (See Leake on Contracts, 169, 170; *Barkworth* v. *Young*, 4 Drew. 1; 26 L. J. Ch. 153.)

It was not, however, in equity necessary where signature was requisite to the validity of the agreement to allege the fact of such signature, for it was said the allegation of a written agreement imported signature. (*Rist* v. *Hobson*, 1 S. & St. 543; Leake on Contracts, 295.)

the defendant (amongst other things) that [*here first state the material parts of the agreement either verbatim or giving the substance and effect of it, care being taken to show the consideration for the defendant's agreement* (*b*). *Then set out the necessary averments. Next allege the breach or breaches of the agreement, and conclude with the statement of the special damage (if any) claimed, each separate allegation being, as nearly as may be, stated in a separate paragraph*].

For Forms see App. (*C.*) *to Jud. Act*, 1875, *Nos.* 8, 10, 16; *Sanguinetti* v. *The Pacific Steam Navigation Co.*, 2 Q. B. D. 238; 46 L. J. Q. B. 105 (*held bad as to part of the claim on demurrer*); *Bennett* v. *Gamgee*, 35 L. T. 764; 46 L. J. Ex. 33; *Swansea Shipping Co.* v. *Duncan, Fox, & Co.*, 1 Q. B. D. 644; *Ashdown* v. *Ingamells*, 5 Ex. D. 280; *Met. Ry. Co.* v. *Defries*, 2 Q. B. D. 189; *Heap* v. *Marris*, 2 Q. B. D. 630; 46 L. J. Q. B. 761.

For Form of Claim upon an Agreement partly verbal and partly contained in Letters: see Cowdy v. *Thomas*, 36 L. T. 22.

Statement of Claim upon a verbal Agreement.

1. It was orally agreed between the plaintiff and the defendant on the —— of ——, 18—, that [*here state the agreement so far as is material, and proceed as directed in the form first above given*].

See further for a form, Davey v. *Shannon*, 4 Ex. D. 81; 48 L. J. Ex. 459.

Upon a Deed (*b*).

1. By an indenture bearing date the —— of ——, 18—, and made between the plaintiff and the defendant, the

---

As to agreements required by the Statute of Frauds to be in writing in order to be valid, see "Defences," "*Frauds, Statute of;*" *Catling* v. *King*, 5 Ch. D. 660; 46 L. J. Ch. 384. See further as to the mode of alleging agreements in pleadings, "*Pleading in General*," *ante*, p. 7, and "*The Body of the Statement of Claim*," *ante*, p. 11.

(*b*) Consideration is necessary to the validity of a simple contract, therefore it must, in general, be shown upon the statement of claim. See "*The Body of the Statement of Claim*," *ante*, p. 11. In the case of bills of exchange, promissory notes, and cheques it is not necessary to state the consideration upon the face of the statement of claim, because it is presumed that consideration is given for them until evidence to the contrary is produced. See *post*, "*Bills of Exchange*,"

defendant covenanted with the plaintiff [*here set out the covenant, the breach of which is complained of, and then proceed to set out the necessary averments, then the breach, and the special damage (if any) claimed, each separate allegation being, so far as may be, stated in a separate paragraph*].

For forms see App. (C.) to Jud. Act, 1875, *Nos.* 14 *and* 18; *Holme* v. *Brunskill,* 38 L. T. 103; 3 Q. B. D. 495; 47 L. J. C. P. 81; *Wooler* v. *Knott,* 1 Ex. D. 124; 45 L. J. Ex. 313 (*held bad on demurrer*); *and "Apprentice," post,* p. 53, "*Bonds," post,* p. 115.

Upon an Agreement to be implied from circumstances.

See for Forms App. (C.) to Jud. Act, 1875, *Form No.* 5, *which is set out ante, "Agent,"* p. 41. *It was referred to with approval by Thesiger, L. J., in Davy* v. *Garrett,* 7 Ch. D. 489. *And see Siddons* v. *Short,* 2 C. P. D. 572; 46 L. J. C. P. 795; 37 L. T. 230.

For other methods of stating causes of action upon agreements, whether in writing or otherwise, see the Forms given of Statements of Claim on Contracts, passim. See further "The Body of the Statement of Claim," ante, p. 11.

---

p. 86, O. XIX. r. 28, *ante,* p. 11.) A gratuitous promise, if it rests in agreement only, is void of legal effect. (*Plowden,* 308; *Kekewich* v. *Manning,* 21 L. J. Ch. 581; 1 De G. M. & G. 176.) A contract by deed is in general valid without consideration. It is therefore not necessary in a statement of claim founded upon a deed to state the consideration.

Under the provisions of certain statutes some deeds without consideration, or voluntary deeds, are made voidable as against certain persons, *e.g., bonâ fide* purchasers for value, &c.; but unless the statement of claim itself shows that the defendant is one of such persons, it would be unnecessary to allege the consideration for the deed in the statement of claim. It is incorrect, in general, to anticipate the defence in the statement of claim. (*Hall* v. *Eve,* 4 Ch. D. 341, 345 *et seq.*; 46 L. J. Ch. 145; see "*The Body of the Statement of Claim," ante,* p. 11.)

In a case such as that above suggested, where a statement of claim discloses a cause of action without any statement of consideration appearing upon the face of the statement of claim, and where the necessity for consideration is first shown by the facts alleged in the defence, it is correct to reply specially the facts showing the consideration. (See "Defences," and O. XIX. rr. 18, 28, *ante,* "*Pleading in General,*" p. 7; *Hall* v. *Eve, supra*; App. (C) to Jud. Act, 1875, Form No. 6.)

ANNUITY. See *post*, "*Bond.*"

APOTHECARY. See *post*, "*Medical Attendance.*"

APPRAISER. See *post*, "*Auctioneer.*"

APPRENTICE (*a*).

By an Apprentice against his Master on the Indenture of Apprenticeship.

1. By an indenture of apprenticeship dated the —— of ——, 18—, the plaintiff put himself apprentice to the

---

(*a*) The covenants in an indenture of apprenticeship are usually independent covenants; and therefore mere disobedience or misconduct is not, in general, a complete defence to an action against the master upon his covenants in the deed (*Winstone* v. *Linn*, 1 B. & C. 460; *Phillips* v. *Clift*, 4 H. & N. 168; 28 L. J. Ex. 153), but such disobedience or misconduct may be relied upon by way of counterclaim or in a cross action. In some cases it is however expressly provided that misconduct shall relieve the master from liability on his covenants, or the covenants of the master to teach, &c., are made conditional upon the good behaviour or conduct of the apprentice; and when this is so, such misconduct affords to the master a complete defence when sued upon his covenants (*Westwick* v. *Theodor*, L. R. 10 Q. B. 224; 44 L. J. Q. B. 110.) But it is a good defence to an action for not teaching and providing for the apprentice, that he quitted the service without leave (*Hughes* v. *Humphreys*, 6 B. & C. 680), or that he refused to be taught. (*Raymond* v. *Minton*, L. R. 1 Ex. 244; 35 L. J. Ex. 153.) And it is a good defence to an action against the father for the desertion of the apprentice, that the master had abandoned one of three trades which he covenanted to teach. (*Ellen* v. *Topp*, 6 Ex. 424.)

As in other contracts for personal services the covenant that the apprentice shall serve is conditional upon his continued capability, and the performance thereof is excused by illness or insanity. (*Boast* v. *Firth*, L. R. 4 C. P. 1; 38 L. J. C. P. 1; *Robinson* v. *Davison*, L. R. 6 Ex. 269; 40 L. J. Ex. 172.) So too, as in other personal contracts, the death of the master or the apprentice puts an end to the contract of apprenticeship. (*Whincup* v. *Hughes*, L. R. 6 C. P. 78; 40 L. J. C. P. 104; *Farrow* v. *Wilson*, L. R. 4 C. P. 744; 38 L. J. C. P. 326.) By an express provision to that effect the contract

defendant to learn the defendant's trade of a boot and shoe maker, and to serve him as an apprentice for the term of five years then next following.

2. The defendant by the said indenture covenanted with the plaintiff to instruct the plaintiff in the said trade by the best means, and to provide for the plaintiff sufficient food, drink, lodging and other necessaries, during the said term.

3. After the making of the said indenture the plaintiff entered into the said service of the defendant as such apprentice, and has always performed all things in the said indenture to be performed on his part.

4. The defendant, however, did not nor would during the said term instruct the plaintiff in the said trade, and

---

may of course be extended to the executors, or surviving partners of the master, or to other persons, carrying on the trade. (*Cooper* v. *Simmons*, 7 H. & N. 707; 31 L. J. M. C. 138.)

The form of covenant usually inserted in indentures of apprenticeship, "for the true performance of all and every the said covenants and agreements, each of the said parties bindeth himself unto the others by these presents," is held to render the father liable for the performance of the articles by the son. (*Whitley* v. *Loftus*, 8 Mod. 190; *Branch* v. *Ewington*, Doug. 518.) An action will not lie against an infant on a covenant in an indenture of apprenticeship. (*Gilbert* v. *Fletcher*, Cro. Car. 179; see Smith's Mast. and Serv. p. 9, n. (*g*), 3rd ed.) An infant apprentice may bind himself by covenant by the custom of London. (*Stanton's case*, Moore, 135; *Eden's case*, 2 M. & S. 226.)

An infant apprentice cannot, during infancy, avoid the apprenticeship on the ground of his infancy, but he may, unless there exists a custom to bind for a longer period, or unless the binding is under the authority of a statute, avoid it upon attaining full age. (*Cuming* v. *Hill*, 3 B. & Ald. 59; Leake on Contracts, 550; *R.* v. *Hindringham*, 6 T. R. 557; *Cooper* v. *Simmons*, 7 H. & N. 707; 31 L. J. M. C. 138.) The father, or person, who has covenanted for him, is not discharged, however, by such avoidance. (*Ex p. Davis*, 5 T. R. 715; *Ex p. Gill*, 7 East, 376; *King* v. *Wigston*, 3 B. & C. 484; *Cuming* v. *Hill*, *ante;* Leake on Contracts, 550.)

There is in general no right to the return of the premium upon the death of the master. (*Whincup* v. *Hughes*, L. R. 6 C. P. 78; 40 L. J. C. P. 104.) In the case however of an articled clerk to a solicitor, the Court may order a return of a portion of the premium in the exercise of their jurisdiction over solicitors as officers of the Court. (*Ex p. Prankerd*, 3 B. & Ald. 257; *Ex p. Bayley*, 9 B. & C. 691; see also *In re Thompson*, 1 Ex. 864.)

In an action against the father for removing the apprentice, the master is not in general, the breach being a continuing one, entitled to prospective damages for the whole term, but only up to time of action brought. (*Lewis* v. *Peachey*, 1 H. & C. 518; 31 L. J. Ex. 496.)

did not nor would during the said term provide sufficient food, drink, lodging and other necessaries, for the plaintiff.

5. By reason of the above-mentioned breaches of covenant [*state the special damage, if any*].

By the Master against the Father of the Apprentice on the Indenture of Apprenticeship.

1. By an indenture of apprenticeship dated the 24th of April, 1878, and made between G. B., therein described as the son of the defendant, of the first part, the defendant of the second part, and the plaintiff of the third part, the said G. B. with the consent of the defendant put himself apprentice to the plaintiff to learn his trade and business of a cabinet-maker, and with him after the manner of an apprentice to serve from the said 24th of April, 1878, for the term of three years then next following.

2. The defendant by the said indenture covenanted with the plaintiff, amongst other things, that the said G. B. should faithfully serve the plaintiff, his lawful commands obey and do, and should not absent himself from the plaintiff's service day or night unlawfully, but in all things as a faithful apprentice should behave himself towards the plaintiff and all his during the said term.

3. After the making of the said indenture the plaintiff received the said G. B. into his said service as such apprentice, and was always ready and willing to perform, and did in fact perform all things in the said indenture on his part to be performed.

4. The said G. B. nevertheless on the 14th and 15th of July, 1878, absented himself from the plaintiff's said service during the whole of such days unlawfully, and on the 18th of July, 1878, absented himself altogether from the plaintiff's said service unlawfully, and has not since returned thereto.

5. In absenting himself on the above 14th and 15th of July, 1878, he disobeyed the lawful commands of the plaintiff who had previously commanded him not to absent himself on those days.

6. By reason of the premises [*state special damage, if any.*]

ARBITRATION AND AWARD (*a*).

Statement of Claim upon an Award, upon a reference, under a Judge's Order made by consent, of a cause and all matters in difference between the Parties.

1. By an order bearing date the 1st of July, 1878, it was, by consent of the now plaintiff and the now defen-

---

(*a*) Where the submission to arbitration cannot be made a rule of court (a very unusual case since the C. L. P. Act, 1854, s. 17) the award can only be enforced by action. An award can, in general, be enforced either by action or, when made a rule of court, by attachment, or, if it be an award to pay money, by execution (1 & 2 Vict. c. 110, s. 18; O. XLII., r. 20). The latter are the more speedy and convenient remedies; but if there be any doubt about the validity of the award, the Court will not interfere to give these summary remedies, and the party will be left to an action. The Court will not order payment of money under an award where a legal set-off might be pleaded to an action upon it. (*Swayne* v. *White*, 31 L. J. Q. B. 260.)

An award, although made a rule of court, may be enforced by an action in the Chancery Division for specific performance in cases where the subject-matter of the award is such as to render a decree for specific performance an apt remedy, as, for instance, where the award is to convey an estate, or the like. (*Blackett* v. *Bates*, L. R. 1 Ch. Ap. 117; 34 L. J. Ch. 515; *Wood* v. *Griffith*, 1 Swanst. 54.) Such award supposes an agreement between the parties, and contains no more than the terms of such agreement ascertained by a third person. (*Per* Lord Eldon in *Wood* v. *Griffith*, 1 Swanst. 54.)

The limitation of an action of debt upon any award where the submission is not by specialty, is six years. (3 & 4 Will. IV. c. 42, s. 3; see "Defences," "*Limitations*.")

Interest cannot be recovered on a motion for an attachment (*Churcher* v. *Stringer*, 2 B. & Ad. 777); nor on an execution under stat. 1 & 2 Vict. c. 110. (*Doe* v. *Squire*, 2 Dowl. N. S. 327.) See further "*Interest*," *post*. Where by an award costs are duly awarded it is not in general a condition precedent to an action on the award that the costs should have been settled by taxation. (*Holdsworth* v. *Wilson*, 4 B. & S. 1; 32 L. J. Q. B. 289; *Met. Dist. Ry. Co.* v. *Sharpe*, 5 App. Cas. 425; 50 L. J. H. L. 14; 4 Q. B. D. 645; 48 L. J. Q. B. 325; *Lewis* v. *Rossiter*, 44 L. J. Ex. 136.)

Specific performance of an agreement to refer existing or future differences to arbitration will not in general be ordered. (*Per* Eldon, L. C., in *Street* v. *Rigby*, 6 Ves. 818; *Gourlay* v. *Duke of Somerset*, 19 Ves. 431; Leake on Contracts, 958.) An action may be brought to recover damages for the breach of an agreement to refer to arbitration, but it is said that in general the damages recoverable, would, in the absence of any express agreement as to damages to be recovered for such breach, be nominal, because there could be no proof of the money loss from the not making of the award. (*Livingston* v. *Ralli*, 5 E. & B. 132; 24 L. J. Q. B. 269; *Street* v. *Rigby*, 6 Ves. 814; but see *Thomas* v. *Fredricks*, 10 Q. B. 775.) An action to recover damages may, however, usefully be brought in those cases where by the terms of the contract, the price or damages have to be ascertained by arbitra-

dant, ordered by the Honourable Mr. Justice ——, one of the Judges of Her Majesty's High Court of Justice,

---

tion as a condition precedent to their recovery by action, and the party liable for such price or damages fails to carry out, or repudiates, his agreement to have such price or damages ascertained by arbitration. (*Goldstone* v. *Osborn*, 2 C. & P. 551; *Scott* v. *Avery*, 8 Ex. 487; 5 H. L. C. 811.)

Agreements by deed, or in writing, to refer existing or future differences to arbitration, are now of much greater value and importance than they were before the C. L. P. Act, 1854, ss. 11, 12, 13. By the first of these sections the Court or a judge may, under the circumstances therein mentioned, stay the proceedings in any action brought in contravention of such an agreement contained in any deed or instrument in writing made after the Act came into operation.

As to the effect given to these sections, see Russell on Arbitration; Leake on Contracts, 957; *Willesford* v. *Watson*, L. R. 8 Ch. Ap. 480; 42 L. J. Ch. 450; *Piercy* v. *Young*, 14 Ch. D. 200; *Dawson* v. *Fitzgerald*, L. R. 9 Ex. 11; 43 L. J. Ex. 22; *Moffat* v. *Cornelius*, 39 L. T. 102; *Randell* v. *Thompson*, 1 Q. B. D. 748; 45 L. J. Q. B. 713.

Where a person has been invited by both parties to an arbitration to act as paid arbitrator, he can, if he so act, maintain an action for his reasonable charges as such arbitrator, and the parties to such arbitration would, it is conceived, be jointly liable to him for such charges, however the liability might ultimately be adjusted as between the parties themselves. An arbitrator generally protects himself by retaining his lien upon the award until his fees are paid. If an excessive charge is paid to him in order to take up the award, the party paying it may recover back the overcharge in an action. (*Barnes* v. *Braithwaite*, 2 H. & N. 569; *Re Coombs*, 4 Ex. 839, 841, 843; *Fernley* v. *Branson*, 20 L. J. Q. B. 178.)

All arbitrators are not paid arbitrators. Whether the arbitrator is entitled to payment for his services depends in each case upon the express or implied terms of the employment. (*Hoggins* v. *Gordon*, 3 Q. B. 466, 474; *Swinford* v. *Burn*, 1 Gow. 7, 8; *Virany* v. *Warne*, 4 Esp. 47; *Burroughes* v. *Clarke*, 1 Dowl. 48; and Russell on Arbitration, 5th ed., p. 474.)

An arbitrator is in a quasi judicial position, and cannot, at any rate if he acts *bonâ fide*, be sued in respect of his decision or conduct as such arbitrator. (*Tharsis Sulphur Co.* v. *Loftus*, L. R. 8 C. P. 1; 42 L. J. C. P. 6; *Pappa* v. *Rose*, L. R. 7 C. P. 32; *ib.* 525; 41 L. J. C. P. 11; *ib.* 187; *Stevenson* v. *Watson*, 4 C. P. D. 148; 48 L. J. C. P. 318.)

A mere valuer, not exercising functions of a judicial, or quasi judicial, character, may be sued for misconduct as such valuer by his employer, or for want of that reasonable skill as a valuer which he is held to warrant himself to possess by holding himself out as a professional valuer. (*Jenkins* v. *Betham*, 15 C. B. 168; 24 L. J. C. P. 94; *Turner* v. *Goulden*, L. R. 9 C. P. 57; 43 L. J. C. P. 60.)

As to references under the Judicature Acts of questions arising before the Court in any cause or matter (other than a criminal proceeding) for inquiry and report, or trial, see Jud. Act, 1873, secs. 56, 57, and Orders; *Longman* v. *East*, *Pontifex* v. *Severn*, *Mellin* v. *Monico*, 3 C. P. D. 142—163; 47 L. J. C. P. 211; *Ward* v. *Pilley*, 5 Q. B. D. 427; 49 L. J. Q. B. 705; *Hoch* v. *Boor*, 49 L. J. C. P. 665.

that a cause then pending in the said Court between the now plaintiff and the now defendant and all matters in difference between them should be referred to the award, arbitrament, final end and determination of X. Y., of &c., so as that he should make and publish his award in writing of and concerning the said matters referred, ready to be delivered to the said parties or such of them as should require the same on or before the 2nd of November, 1878, or on or before such further day as he the said X. Y. should appoint, and signify in writing under his hand to be endorsed on the said order at any time; and it was thereby further ordered with the like consent that the costs of the said cause should abide the event of the said award, and that the costs of the said reference and of the said award should be in the discretion of the said arbitrator.

2. The said X. Y. having taken upon himself the burthen of the said reference, did, in the manner abovementioned, duly enlarge the time for the making and publishing of his award until the 2nd of December, 1878.

3. The said X. Y. on the 20th of November, 1878, duly made and published his award in writing of and concerning the said matters so referred to him, which said award, so far as is material, was as follows :—

"I the said X. Y. award adjudge and direct that the defendant do pay to the plaintiff the sum of £350 in full satisfaction and discharge of all claims and demands made by the plaintiff against the defendant in respect of the matters referred to me; And I further award and direct that the defendant do pay to the plaintiff his costs of this reference, and the costs of this my award, and that the defendant do bear his own costs of the same; And I do further find all the issues in the said cause in favour of the plaintiff, and do find and award that the defendant has no just claim against the plaintiff, and that the plaintiff does owe nothing to the defendant."

4. The costs of the plaintiff of the said cause and of the said reference and of the said award were afterwards taxed, and amounted to £103.

5. The plaintiff has applied to the defendant for payment of the said sums of £350 and £103, but the defendant has not paid the same or any part thereof, and the same are still due from and payable by the defendant to the plaintiff.

Upon an Award made upon a reference to Arbitration under an Agreement referring certain existing differences.

1. The plaintiff and the defendant on the —— of ——, 18—, by an agreement [*in writing*] agreed to refer certain differences then existing between them to the award and arbitrament of X. Y. of [&c.], and to be bound and to abide by his award concerning the same.

2. The said X. Y. having taken upon himself the burthen of the said reference did on the —— of ——, 18—, duly make and publish his award concerning the said matters so referred to him, and the said award was that the defendant should abstain from taking any water from the watercourse running through the lands of the plaintiff and the defendant except for domestic purposes, and that the defendant should pay to the plaintiff the sum of £50.

3. The defendant on the —— of ——, 18— (*after the date of the said award*), contrary to the said award, took water from the said watercourse for purposes other than domestic purposes.

4. The defendant has not paid to the plaintiff the said sum of £50, or any part thereof.

For Form of Claim against an Architect acting as Arbitrator (held bad, no fraud or collusion being alleged), see Stevenson v. *Watson,* 4 C. P. D. 148; 48 L. J. C. P. 318.

For Form of Claim on an Award, see Stone v. *Mayor of Yeovil,* 1 C. P. D. 691; *Melhado* v. *Watson,* 2 C. P. D. 281.

Assignment of Debts and Choses in Action.

Statement of Claim by the Assignee of a Debt under the Companies Act, 1862, *ss.* 95, 157 (*a*).

1. The —— Company, Limited, was, before and at the times of the sale and delivery hereinafter mentioned, a

---

(*a*) By *The Companies Act*, 1862 (25 & 26 Vict. c. 89), s. 95, the official liquidators, in case of the winding up by the Court of a company registered under that Act, may sell and transfer things in action of the company; and by s. 133 the liquidators, in the case of a voluntary winding-up of the company, may exercise all the powers given to official liquidators. Then, by s. 157, it is provided that any person to whom anything in action belonging to the company is assigned in pursuance of the Act may bring or defend any action relating to such thing in action in his own name.

The *Companies Act*, 1862, is amended by *The Companies Act*, 1867 (30 & 31 Vict. c. 131), *The Companies Act*, 1877 (40 & 41

company duly registered under and subject to the provisions of the Companies Act, 1862, and the Acts amending the same.

2. On the —— of ——, 18—, the said company sold and delivered to the defendant — tons of iron at £—— per ton, payable on delivery.

3. The defendant has not paid the said company the said price or any part thereof.

4. After the said sale and delivery, and whilst the said price was a debt due from and payable by the defendant to the said company, the said company was duly wound up voluntarily [*or* by the High Court of Justice, Chancery Division, *or as the case may be*], under and according to the provisions of the said Acts, and under such winding-up liquidators [*or* official liquidators] were duly appointed for the purpose of winding up the affairs of the said company and distributing the property of the same.

5. The liquidators [*or* official liquidators] so appointed sold and assigned the said debt, the same being a thing in action belonging to the said company, to the plaintiff in pursuance of the said Acts, and the said debt is still due and unpaid.

For Statement of Claim by the Assignee of the Book debts of a bankrupt or liquidating debtor under the Bankruptcy Act, 1869 (32 & 33 Vict., c. 71, s. 25, sub-sec. 6, and s. 111) *see "Bankruptcy," post.*

For Statement of Claim under "The Policies of Assurance Act, 1867," 30 & 31 Vict., c. 144 (Life), *by the assignee of a policy, see "Insurance," post.*

Upon an Assignment of a Debt within the provisions of the Judicature Act, 1873, *s.* 25, *sub-sec.* 6 (*b*).

1. At the time of the assignment hereinafter mentioned,

Vict. c. 26), *The Companies Act*, 1879 (42 & 43 Vict. c. 76), and by *The Companies Act*, 1880 (43 Vict. c. 19). The amendments, however, do not affect the sections of *The Companies Act*, 1862, as to the sale of things in action.

(*b*) By the Jud. Act, 1873, sect. 25 (6), "Any absolute assignment, by writing under the hand of the assignor (not purporting to be by way of charge only), of any debt or other legal chose in action, of which express notice in writing shall have been given to the debtor, trustee, or other person from whom the assignor would have been entitled to receive or claim such debt or chose in action, shall be, and be deemed to have been effectual in law (subject to all equities which would have been entitled to priority over the right of the assignee if this Act had not passed), to pass and transfer the legal right to such debt or chose in action from the date of such notice, and all legal or other remedies for the same, and the power to give a good discharge for the same, without the concurrence of the assignor: Provided always, that if the debtor, trustee, or other person liable in respect of such debt or chose in action shall have had notice that such assignment is disputed by the assignor or any one claiming under him, or of any other opposing or conflicting claims to such debt or chose in action, he shall be entitled, if he think fit, to call upon the several persons making claim thereto to interplead concerning the same, or he may, if he think fit, pay the same into the High Court of Justice, under and in conformity with the provisions of the Acts for the relief of trustees."

The *Trustee Relief Acts* are 10 & 11 Vict. c. 96 (*sect.* 3 *is repealed by* 35 *&* 36 *Vict. c.* 44, *s.* 26; *sect.* 1, *from* "*or of the East*" *to* "*sea company*," *and sect.* 6 *are repealed by the Stat. Law Rev. Act*, 1875, *and sect.* 4 *is repealed by* 42 *&* 43 *Vict. c.* 78, *s.* 29); and 12 & 13 Vict. c. 74 (*sect.* 1 *is repealed from* "*the East*" *to* "*sea company*," *and sect.* 2 *is entirely repealed by the Stat. Law Rev. Act*, 1875.)

Before this enactment a debt or chose in action was not, with the exception of contracts assignable by the law merchant, as bills of exchange and the like, and certain contracts assignable by statute (as, for instance, policies of assurance assignable by stat. 30 & 31 Vict. c. 144, and 31 & 32 Vict. c. 86), assignable at law. In the Equity Courts it was otherwise, those Courts regarding such assignments in general as agreements by the assignor to permit the assignee to sue at law in his name, and compelling the assignor, when the assignment was for valuable consideration, thus to allow his name to be used, upon receiving a proper indemnity. Such assignments were regarded in equity as binding the debt or chose in action in the hands of the debtor, or trustee, or other person liable to the assignor in respect thereof from the time when such debtor, trustee, or other person received due notice of such assignment. (Leake on Contracts, 1166—1186, 1189 *et seq.*; *Row* v. *Dawson*, 1 Ves. Sen. 331; 1 White & Tudor, L. C. 726, 729 *et seq.* 5th ed.)

A Court of Equity would not permit the assignee to sue for the debt or chose in action assigned in his own name where he had an adequate remedy at law in the name of the assignor, though he was so allowed to sue when there were special circumstances obstructive of his right to the debt or chose in action which rendered the assistance of a Court of Equity needful to enforce his right (*Hammond* v. *Messenger*, 9 Sim. 327; *Keys* v. *Williams*, 3 Y. & C. Ex. 466; *Rose* v. *Clarke*, 1 Y. & C. Ch. 534; *Hoskins* v. *Holland*, 44 L. J. Ch. 273), or where specific performance, a remedy only obtainable before the Jud. Acts in a Court of Equity, was the appropriate remedy or relief. (*Nelthorpe* v. *Holgate*, 1 Coll. C. 203; Leake on Contracts, 1169; and see *Brice* v. *Bannister*, 3 Q. B. D. 569, 573, 575, *per* Lord Coleridge, C. J.) Where the assignee sued in his own name in a Court of Equity the assignor was, in general, a necessary party to the bill. (*Nelthorpe* v. *Holgate*, *supra*; *Brice* v. *Bannister*, 3 Q. B. D. 575; 47 *L. J. Q. B.* 722.)

The rights of the assignee of a chose in action under the Jud. Act, 1873, s. 25 (6), are thereby expressly made subject to all equities which may be entitled to priority. (See as to equities affecting such assignments, *Mangles* v. *Dixon*, 3 H. L. C. 702, 731; *Brice* v. *Bannister, supra; Young* v. *Kitchin*, 3 Ex. D. 127; 47 L. J. Ex. 579; and White & Tudor's L. C. 5th ed. pp. 779—808.)

In order to create a valid assignment under the Jud. Act, 1873, s. 25 (6), the assignment must among other things be absolute, not purporting to be by way of charge only, and must be in writing. (*Nat. Prov. Bank* v. *Harle*, 6 Q. B. D. 626; 50 L. J. Q. B. 437). It may be of an accruing debt, for an accruing debt may be a "chose in action." (*Brice* v. *Bannister*, 3 Q. B. D. 569; 47 L. J. Q. B. 722; *Buck* v. *Robson*, 3 Q. B. D. 686; 48 L. J. Q. B. 250; *British Waggon Co.* v. *Lea*, 5 Q. B. D. 149, 154; 49 L. J. Q. B. 321.)

Notice in writing of the assignment must be given to the person from whom payment is claimed, in order to bring the case within the Jud. Act. 1873, and to enable the assignee to sue thereon in his own name, although a debt or chose in action may be effectually assigned, as between assignor and assignee, without notice to the party liable to pay. (*Withington* v. *Tate*, L. R. 4 Ch. Ap. 288; 20 L. T. 637; *Pickering* v. *Ilfracombe Ry. Co.*, L. R. 3 C. P. 235, 248; 37 L. J. C. P. 118; *Robinson* v. *Nesbitt*, L. R. 3 C. P. 264; 37 L. J. C. P. 124; and see *Watts* v. *Porter*, 3 E. & B. 743; 23 L. J. Q. B. 345, *a case overruled as to the precise point decided, but not as to the general principle, by Robinson* v. *Nesbitt, supra, and Beavan* v. *Lord Oxford*, 6 De G. Mac. & G. 507; 25 L. J. Ch. 299.)

The fact that the assignment and notice thereof are in writing should be pleaded. (O. XIX. r. 4; see "*Agreements*," *ante*, p. 50.)

The notice required by the above statute is an express notice in writing to the party liable to pay, whereas in equity a formal notice was not requisite; it was and is enough to create an equitable liability that such party had notice in fact. (*Alletson* v. *Chichester*, L. R. 10 C. P. 319; 44 L. J. Ch. 153; *Lloyd* v. *Banks*, L. R. 3 Ch. Ap. 488; 37 L. J. C. P. 881.)

After notice of the assignment, the debt or chose in action, (subject to any equities which may be entitled to priority), is bound in the hands of the party liable, and he cannot pay the assignor, nor can he set off against the assignee any claim against the assignor arising out of matters subsequent to the receipt of such notice and not already existing, or arising out of circumstances which existed, before the date of the receipt of such notice. (*Brice* v. *Bannister*, 3 Q. B. D. 569, 578; 47 L. J. Q. B. 722; *Jeffryes* v. *Agra and Masterman's Bank*, L. R. 2 Eq. 674; 35 L. J. Ch. 686; *Cavendish* v. *Geaves*, 24 Beav. 163, 173; 27 L. J. Ch. 314; *Watson* v. *Mid Wales Ry. Co.*, L. R. 2 C. P. 593; 36 L. J. C. P. 285.)

Claims subsisting against the assignor at the date of the receipt of the notice, but not payable till afterwards, may however be set off against the assignee. (*Jeffryes* v. *Agra and Masterman's Bank, supra; Watson* v. *Mid Wales Ry. Co., supra; Young* v. *Kitchin*, 3 Ex. D. 127; 47 L. J. Ex. 579; *Ex p. Mackenzie*, L. R. 7 Eq. 240; 38 L. J. Ch. 199.)

When it is sought to set up claims against the assignor as a defence to the action by the assignee of a debt or chose in action, this should be done by way of set-off or counter-claim stating the facts, and showing that it is only sought to reduce or answer the claim of the

the defendant was indebted (*c*) to one A. B. in the sum of £——, for money payable by the defendant to the said A. B. [*state the nature of the debt according to the fact, as for instance* for a loan of that amount which was advanced by the said A. B. to the defendant on or about the —— of ——, 18—.]

2. The said A. B., on the —— of ——, 18—, by writing under his hand assigned to the plaintiff absolutely (and not by way of charge only), the said sum of £——, then due and payable by the defendant as aforesaid (*d*).

---

assignee, and not to recover damages from him beyond his claim on the debt, or chose in action, assigned to him. (*Young* v. *Kitchin*, *supra.*)

A mere order or request to a debtor to pay a third party, not communicated to such third party, is not an equitable assignment. (*Scott* v. *Porcher*, 3 Mer. 652, *per* Grant, M. R.)

A cheque is not an equitable assignment of the fund, or any part of the fund drawn on. (*Hopkinson* v. *Forster*, L. R. 19 Eq. 74; *Schroeder* v. *Central Bank of London*, 34 L. T. 735; 24 W. R. 710.)

A document in these terms, "I hereby assign to Messrs. Robson the sum of £40, or any other sum now due, or that may hereafter become due in respect of the steam launch which I am building for you. I will thank you to hold the same at their disposal, and their receipt for the amount will be a full and sufficient discharge," signed by the assignor, and sent to the debtor, was held a valid equitable assignment of £40, accruing to the assignor from the debtor, and not to require a stamp as "an order for the payment of money," under 33 & 34 Vict. c. 97, ss. 48, 53, but capable of being stamped at the trial on payment of the stamp duty and penalty. (*Buck* v. *Robson*, 3 Q. B. D. 686; *Fisher* v. *Calvert*, 27 W. R. 301; *Hamilton* v. *Spottiswoode*, 4 Ex. 200; See *Ex p. Shellard*, L. R. 17 Eq. 109.) See further, Leake on Contracts, 1165, *et seq.*

It is immaterial whether the debtor, trustee, or other person liable in respect of the debt or chose in action accept the notice or agree to pay the assignee, or not (*per* Lord Coleridge, C. J., *Brice* v. *Bannister*, 3 Q. B. D. 574); if, however, he does accept and agree with the assignee to pay him, there is a novation, and he becomes directly bound by contract with the assignee to pay him. (*Tatlock* v. *Harris*, 3 T. R. 180.)

Contracts in which the personal qualifications of the parties form an essential ingredient, are not, from their nature, assignable, either at law or in equity, such as, for example, a contract of service, or a contract between the publisher and author of a book. (*Stevens* v. *Benning*, 1 K. & J. 168; 24 L. J. Ch. 153.)

(*c*) If the defendant is likely to dispute his indebtedness to the assignor at the time of the assignment, the material facts which gave rise to the debt should be stated, so as to compel the defendant to deal specifically in his pleading with such facts.

(*d*) In many cases it may be desirable to set out in full the written assignment and the written notice of the assignment.

3. Express notice in writing of the said assignment was given to the defendant on the —— of ——, 18—.

4. The defendant has not paid the said sum of £——, or any part of it.

Upon an Assignment of a Debt and other choses in action under the provisions of the Judicature Act, 1873, *s.* 25, *sub-sec.* 6.

1. Before the making of the assignment hereinafter mentioned, an agreement in writing bearing date the 25th day of June, 1877, was made and entered into between A. B. and the defendant, whereby it was agreed that the said A. B. should erect for the defendant certain buildings therein mentioned for the price or sum of £500, to be paid by the defendant to the said A. B. as follows, viz., £200 when the outer walls of the said buildings should be erected, £100 when they should be roofed in, and the residue, £200, when the said buildings should be finally completed.

2. At the time of the assignment hereinafter mentioned the said A. B. had completed the erection of the said outer walls, and was duly proceeding with the performance of the said agreement, and the first mentioned sum of £200 had become and was due and payable by the defendant to him under the provisions of the said agreement.

3. The said A. B., on the 15th day of August, 1877, by writing under his hand assigned to the plaintiff absolutely (and not by way of charge only), the said sum of £200 then due and payable by the defendant to the said A. B. as aforesaid, and also all other sums which should thereafter become due to him from the defendant under the said agreement.

4. Express notice in writing of the said assignment was given on or about the 20th day of August, 1877, to the defendant.

5. After the making of the said assignment and before the commencement of this action, the said A. B. duly roofed in and finally completed the said buildings in accordance with the said agreement, and in addition to the said sum of £200 which was due and payable by the defendant as aforesaid at the time of the said assignment, the said further sums of £100 and £200 became and were

due and payable by the defendant under the provisions of the said agreement.

6. The defendant, however, has not paid the said sums, and the amount thereof remains wholly due and unpaid by the defendant to the plaintiff.

For a like Statement of Claim, see Brice v. *Bannister*, 3 Q. B. D. 569; and see *Young* v. *Kitchin*, 3 Ex. D. 127; 47 L. J. Ex. 579.

Assurance. See Insurance, *post*, p. 214.

Auctioneer (*a*).

Statement of Claim by an Auctioneer and Valuer for his Services.

1. The plaintiff is an auctioneer and valuer carrying on business in Ladbroke Grove, Notting Hill.

(*a*) Auctioneers, in general, contract in their own name, and are, in that case, liable to be sued, and capable of suing, whether they disclose the name of their principal or not. (*Franklyn* v. *Lamond*, 4 C. B. 637; *Fisher* v. *Marsh*, 6 B. & S. 411; 34 L. J. Q. B. 177; *Woolfe* v. *Horne*, 2 Q. B. D. 355; 46 L. J. Q. B. 534.) The sale of each lot at an auction is a separate contract. (*Emmerson* v. *Heelis*, 2 Taunt. 38; *Roots* v. *Lord Dormer*, 4 B. & Ad. 77). Property passes at a sale by auction upon the falling of the hammer, unless the conditions of sale otherwise provide. (*Sweeting* v. *Turner*, L. R. 7 Q. B. 310; 41 L. J. Q. B. 58.) Either party may revoke the bid, or the offer to sell, before the fall of the hammer (*Payne* v. *Cave*, 3 T. R. 148), and that, even if the conditions provide that the sale shall be without reserve, or that no person shall retract his bidding. (*Warlow* v. *Harrison*, 1 E. & E. 295; 29 L. J. Q. B. 14; and see *Harris* v. *Nickerson*, L. R. 8 Q. B. 286; 42 L. J. Q. B. 171.) As to the remedies where a sale is falsely advertised "without reserve," see *Warlow* v. *Harrison*, *supra*; Benj. on Sales, 2nd ed. 380-382; *Harris* v. *Nickerson*, *supra*. There is no contract of sale till the fall of the hammer.

An auctioneer, in general, receives the deposit as a stakeholder, and not as the mere agent of the vendor. (*Harington* v. *Hoggart*, 1 B. & Ad. 577; Leake on Contracts, 144, 481.) He cannot usually be sued for the deposit till the result is known. (*Harington* v. *Hoggart*, *supra*.)

An auctioneer is the agent of both parties at a public sale to charge them by signing a memorandum of the sale to satisfy the Statute of

2. In August, 18—, he was retained and employed by the defendant as such auctioneer and valuer to value and sell by auction, and duly catalogue and advertise for the defendant, certain household furniture and effects, upon the terms [then agreed upon in conversation between the plaintiff and the defendant, *or as the case may be*,] that he should be paid therefor at the rate of 5 per cent. upon the amount realised by such sale.

3. The plaintiff duly valued, sold by auction, catalogued, and advertised the said household furniture and effects in accordance with his said retainer and employment.

4. The sum realised by such sale amounted to £800.

5. The sum of £40 thereupon became due and payable by the defendant to the plaintiff under and by virtue of the said terms of his said retainer and employment.

6. The defendant has not paid the said sum or any part thereof.

By an Auctioneer against a Purchaser of Lots at an Auction.

1. The plaintiff is an auctioneer carrying on business at ——.

Frauds. (*Hinde* v. *Whitehouse*, 7 East, 558; *Emmerson* v. *Heelis*, *supra*; *Peirce* v. *Corf*, L. R. 9 Q. B. 214; 43 L. J. Q. B. 52.)

An auctioneer's clerk openly employed at a public auction to take down the buyers' names, is also considered an agent to bind both the seller and the buyer by his signature. (*Peirce* v. *Corf*, *supra*; *Bird* v. *Boulter*, 4 B. & Ad. 443.) It is only at a public sale that the auctioneer, or his clerk, is thus authorised to bind the purchaser. (*Mews* v. *Carr*, 1 H. & N. 484; 26 L. J. Ex. 39; Leake on Contracts, 277; Benj. on Sales, 2nd ed., p. 202.) If the auctioneer sues the purchaser in his, the auctioneer's, own name in a case where a written memorandum is required to satisfy the Statute of Frauds, it is not sufficient that there should be a signature by the auctioneer himself; because a vendor cannot be an agent for the purchaser within that statute. (*Sharman* v. *Brandt*, L. R. 6 Q. B. 720; 40 L. J. Q. B. 312; *Farebrother* v. *Simmons*, 5 B. & Ald. 333.) His clerk's signature would suffice.

An auctioneer has a lien for his charges, and for the auction duty, upon the goods sold. (*Williams* v. *Millington*, 1 H. Bl. 81; *Woolfe* v. *Horne*, 2 Q. B. D. 355; 46 L. J. Q. B. 534; Leake on Contracts, 522.)

The secret employment of "*puffers*," that is to say of persons to run up the price against the public, is deemed a fraud. (*Bexwell* v. *Christie*, 1 Cowp. 395; *Howard* v. *Castle*, 6 T. R. 642; *Thornett* v. *Haines*, 15 M. & W. 367.) See further, "*Sale of Land*," *post*; Leake on Contracts, 368; Benj. on Sales, 2nd ed., 378, 382, 383.

2. The plaintiff sold by auction to the defendant, on the —— of ——, 18—, three lots of wines, at the prices of £——, £——, and £—— respectively upon the terms [contained in the printed conditions of sale] that the defendant should within —— days take away and pay for the said lots.

3. The defendant paid to the plaintiff as deposits, and in part payment of the said prices of the said lots, £—— and no more.

4. The said —— days elapsed before this action, and the plaintiff has always been ready and willing to carry out the said contract on his part, and to deliver the said lots to the defendant upon payment of the said prices therefor.

5. The defendant has not paid any part of the said prices of the said lots except the said sum so paid as above stated as deposits, and the residue of the prices of the said lots amounting to £—— remains due and payable by the defendant to the plaintiff.

By an Auctioneer against the Purchaser of a Lot by Auction for not clearing away the Lot purchased according to the Conditions of Sale or at all, and for not paying the Price.

1. The plaintiff is an auctioneer carrying on business at ——, and the defendant is a furniture broker at ——.

2. The plaintiff sold by auction to the defendant at ——, on the —— of ——, 18—, drawing-room furniture, at prices amounting to £——, upon the terms, amongst others [contained in the conditions of sale], that the defendant should clear away the same within —— days from the said —— of ——, and before clearing away the same should pay the said prices thereof to the plaintiff.

3. [*Same as in par.* 4 *of form next above.*]

4. The defendant did not clear away the said furniture, or any part thereof, within the said time or at all, and did not pay to the plaintiff the said prices thereof, or any part of such prices.

5. By reason of the premises, the plaintiff has been put to £—— expense in warehousing the said furniture.

By a Vendor against a Purchaser who has refused to take a Lot purchased at Auction for loss on a re-sale according to the Conditions of Sale (*b*).

1. The plaintiff, by A. B. his agent and auctioneer, sold by auction to the defendant, on the —— of ——, 18—, a certain farm called the College Farm, at ——, at the price of £3000.

2. The said sale was subject to the following amongst other conditions of sale, namely, that the purchaser should pay to the vendor a deposit of £5 per cent. in part payment of the purchase money immediately after the sale, and the remainder of the purchase money on the —— of ——, 18—, on which day the purchase should be completed, and that the vendor should on or before the said —— of ——, 18—, deduce and make a good title to the premises commencing with (*according to the fact*), and that on payment of the remainder of the said purchase money as aforesaid, the vendor should execute a conveyance of the said premises to the purchaser at the purchaser's expense, and that if the purchaser should fail to comply with the said conditions his

---

(*b*) Goods sold at an auction cannot legally be re-sold in case of default of the purchaser in carrying them away, or paying for them according to the conditions, unless there is a condition enabling them to be so dealt with. (*Woolfe* v. *Horne*, 2 Q. B. D. 355; 46 L. J. Q. B. 534; and see as to general principle, *Valpy* v. *Oakeley*, 16 Q. B. 941; 20 L. J. Q. B. 380; *Griffiths* v. *Perry*, 1 E. & E. 680; 28 L. J. Q. B. 204; *Martindale* v. *Smith*, 1 Q. B. 389.) The same rule applies to land. See as to the power of the Court or a Judge to order a sale of goods upon the application of a party to an action, Jud. Acts, O. LII. r. 2; *Bartholomew* v. *Freeman*, 3 C. P. D. 316. If goods sold are re-sold, where there is no condition as to re-sale on default, the original purchaser can claim the profit on the re-sale, or if there is no profit can recover, at least, nominal damages. (Benj. on Sales, 2nd ed., p. 649; *Valpy* v. *Oakeley*, *supra*; and *Griffiths* v. *Perry*, *supra*.) He would, however, in case of an action for such wrongful re-sale be liable to be met by a counter-claim for his breach of contract, the claim upon which might be sufficient, or even more than sufficient, to afford a defence to such action.

An auctioneer contracting in his own name is liable if he resells, or refuses to deliver, after the time fixed by the conditions of sale for the taking away of the goods by the purchaser has expired, in the absence of conditions to the contrary, the goods being, notwithstanding the default, for which a cross action may be brought, or a counter-claim pleaded, the property of the purchaser. (*Woolfe* v. *Horne*, *supra*; *Saint* v. *Pilley*, L. R. 10 Ex. 137; 44 L. J. Ex. 33.)

As to the general averment of conditions precedent, see "*Conditions Precedent*," *post*, p. 158.

said deposit should thereupon be forfeited, and the vendor should be at liberty to re-sell the said premises by public auction or private contract as he should think fit, and the deficiency if any, in price between the said sum of £3000 and the price realised by such re-sale, and all expenses attending such re-sale, should be paid by the purchaser to the vendor.

3. The defendant paid the vendor the said deposit, and all conditions were fulfilled, and all times elapsed, and all things happened necessary to entitle the plaintiff to maintain this action for the breaches hereinafter mentioned.

4. The defendant did not pay the remainder of the said purchase money, nor complete the said purchase on his part.

5. Thereupon the plaintiff as such vendor as aforesaid, in accordance with the said conditions of sale, re-sold the said premises by public auction on the —— of ——, 18—.

6. The said premises only realised upon such re-sale the price of £2,700, and the expenses attending such re-sale amounted to £—.

7. The plaintiff further by reason of the said breaches by the defendant of his said contract, lost the expenses incurred by him in preparing to complete the said sale and purchase, and endeavouring to procure the completion thereof by the defendant. [These expenses were as follows: *set out expenses, or* Full particulars of these expenses have been delivered.]

8. The sum of £— is due and payable by the defendant to the plaintiff in respect of the matters aforesaid, but the defendant has not paid the same or any part thereof.

AVERAGE. See "*Insurance,*" *post, p.* 219.

AWARD. See "*Arbitration,*" *ante, p.* 56.

Bailments (*a*).

Statement of Claim by a Warehouseman for keeping and taking care of Goods (*b*).

1. The plaintiff is a warehouseman at ——.

2. From the —— of ——, 18—, to the —— of ——, 18—, the plaintiff, as such warehouseman, kept, took care of and warehoused certain goods for the defendant at his request at £—— per month.

3. Before and at the commencement of this action the sum of £—— was due from and payable by the defendant to the plaintiff in respect of the matters aforesaid, full particulars of which have been delivered by the plaintiff to the defendant [*or*, are as follows].

4. The said sum is still due and unpaid.

By a Wharfinger for Wharfage and Warehouseroom.

1. The plaintiff is the proprietor of a wharf and warehouse at ——, and carries on the business there of a wharfinger and warehouseman.

2. On the —— of ——, 18—, the plaintiff, at the request of the defendant, landed at his said wharf, and afterwards stowed and kept in his said warehouse for —— weeks from the said date —— sacks of flour for the defendant.

3. The price agreed [by letters bearing date, &c., *or as the case may be*] to be paid by the defendant to the plaintiff in respect of the matters aforesaid amounts to £——.

4. The said sum of £—— was due from and payable by the defendant to the plaintiff before the commencement of this action, and is still due and unpaid.

(*a*) Bailment is a delivery of goods to another for some purpose upon a contract, express or implied, that after the purpose has been fulfilled they shall be redelivered to the bailor or otherwise dealt with according to his directions, or (as the case may be) kept till he reclaims them. For the law of bailments see the notes to *Coggs* v. *Bernard*, 1 Smith's L. C. (7th ed.) p. 206.

(*b*) When a chattel is detained under a claim of lien against the owner, and charges are incurred in keeping and taking care of it, no claim can be made against the owner in respect of such charges. (*Somes* v. *British Empire Shipping Company*, 8 H. L. C. 338 ; 30 L. J. Q. B. 229.)

Against a Picture Dealer for not taking proper care of a Picture entrusted to him for the purpose of being cleaned.

1. The defendant is a picture cleaner and restorer, carrying on business at ——.

2. On or about the —— of ——, 18—, the plaintiff took a valuable picture belonging to him to the defendant's shop and requested the defendant as such picture-cleaner and restorer as aforesaid to clean and restore the said picture for him upon the usual terms as to payment.

3. The defendant accordingly received the said picture from the plaintiff, and then promised the plaintiff that he would take proper care of the same, and thoroughly clean and restore it, and return it to the plaintiff in a proper condition.

4. The defendant did not take proper care of the said picture, whereby the canvas of the said picture was torn, and the said picture was and is greatly and permanently injured, and is very much lessened in value.

Against a Livery Stable Keeper for not taking care of a Horse.

1. The defendant is a livery stable keeper, carrying on business at ——.

2. In the month of ——, 18—, the plaintiff entrusted the defendant with his horse upon the terms amongst others that the defendant should take proper care of the said horse in a separate stall in his stable for the plaintiff for the sum of £—— per week.

3. The defendant accordingly received the said horse for the purpose and on the terms aforesaid.

4. The defendant did not take proper care of the said horse, and did not keep the said horse in a separate stall, whereby the said horse was kicked and wounded by another horse in the said stable, and was thereby injured and became of no use to the plaintiff.

Against a Railway Company for not safely keeping Goods left in the Cloak Room at one of their Stations (c).

1. The defendants are a railway company carrying on business amongst other places at the —— railway station.

(c) A railway company receiving goods in their cloak room for safe custody are bailees of such goods for reward ; and, in the absence of

2. The defendants have provided at the said station a cloak room for the convenience and accommodation of passengers travelling on their line, and the defendants undertake for the payment of 2*d*. per parcel to take care of any parcels which may be left at the cloak-room in their charge by any passenger, and to redeliver the same to such passenger upon request.

3. On the —— of ——, 18—, the plaintiff, who was a passenger upon the defendants' said railway, left his portmanteau at the said cloak-room in charge of the defendants so to be taken care of and redelivered upon request as aforesaid, and paid the defendants the said fee of 2*d*. in respect thereof.

4. The defendants did not take care of the said portmanteau, and did not redeliver the same to the plaintiff upon his requesting them to do so.

5. In consequence of the defendants' said breaches of contract the said portmanteau and its contents were and are lost to the plaintiff, and he suffered great inconvenience and was put to £—— expense in endeavouring to recover the same.

Bankers (*a*).

Commencement and Conclusion of a Statement of Claim by the Public Officer of a Banking Copartnership suing as Nominal Plaintiff.

1. The plaintiff is one of the registered public officers of a banking copartnership called the —— Banking

---

any contract containing special conditions limiting their liability, they are responsible to the depositors for the full value of the goods so received in case they are unable to return them when demanded. If, however, goods are received by a railway company for safe custody in their cloak room subject to any special condition restricting the liability of the company in certain specified circumstances, the company will not be held liable for the loss of such goods in cases where the specified circumstances existed, provided they can show that they did what was reasonably sufficient to give the depositor notice of the condition, and thereby made it a part of the contract. (*Parker* v. *South Eastern Ry. Co.*, 2 C. P. D. 416; 46 L. J. C. P. 768; *Burke* v. *South Eastern Ry. Co.*, 5 C. P. D. 1; 49 L. J. C. P. 107.) See other forms, *post*, "*Carriers*," "Wrongs," "*Bailments*," "*Innkeeper*."

(*a*) Banking copartnerships governed by the 7 Geo. 4, c. 46, s. 9, and 7 & 8 Vict. c. 113, s. 47, re-enacted by sec. 205 of "The Companies Act, 1862," are bound to sue, and must be sued in the name

Company, and is duly appointed and entitled under and by virtue of the statutes in that behalf to sue in this action as nominal plaintiff for the said copartnership.

[*Proceed to state the cause of action in separate paragraphs, alleging the debt or cause of action to have accrued to, or the agreement, covenant or bond, etc., to have been made with or to the copartnership, not the plaintiff, and conclude in a separate paragraph as follows :*—]

The plaintiff as such public officer as aforesaid, for and on behalf of the said co-partnership, claims £——.

Commencement and Conclusion of a Statement of Claim against the Public Officer of a Banking Copartnership sued as Nominal Defendant.

1. The defendant is one of the registered public officers of a banking copartnership called ——, and is duly appointed and liable under and by virtue of the statutes in that behalf to be sued as nominal defendant for the said copartnership.

[*Proceed to state the cause of action in separate paragraphs, alleging the debt or cause of action to have accrued against the copartnership, not the defendant.*]

---

of their public officer, and not in the names of the trustees, or otherwise. (*Chapman* v. *Milvain*, 5 Ex. 61 ; *Steward* v. *Greaves*, 10 M. &. W. 711 ; see also 27 & 28 Vict. c. 32, s. 1).

Banking Companies incorporated by registration under "The Companies Act, 1862," or to which that Act applies, sue and are sued in the ordinary form by their registered names. See *post*, "*Company*," p. 145.

Where the statement of claim is framed upon a covenant, bond, or other instrument entered into with trustees for the copartnership, the contract with them must be alleged according to the fact, and then a distinct allegation should be added "that the said deed [*or* bond] relates to the concerns of the said copartnership, and was made and entered into by the defendant with the said *G. H.* and *J. K.* for and on behalf of the said copartnership, and not otherwise."

By Bankers on an Overdrawn Account and for Money lent to and paid for a Customer (*b*).

1. The plaintiffs carry on the business of bankers at Lombard Street, in the city of London.

2. Between the —— of ——, 18—, and the —— of ——, 18—, the defendant kept a banking account with the plaintiffs at their said place of business.

3. During the said period the plaintiffs acted as the bankers of the defendant, and on several occasions they as such bankers advanced the defendant money at interest, and allowed the defendant to overdraw his said account, and paid various sums of money for him at his request.

4. At the commencement of this action the sum of £—— was [*or*, After allowing the defendant full credit for all sums which have been paid into his said account with the plaintiffs, a balance of £—— was at the commencement of this action] and still is due from and payable by the defendant to the plaintiffs in respect of the matters aforesaid.

5. Full particulars of the said account and of the said money advanced, overdrawn, and paid, and of the said interest have been delivered by the plaintiffs to the defendant [*or*, are as follows].

Against a Firm of Bankers for not Paying a Customer's Cheque (*b*).

1. The plaintiff is a corn dealer, carrying on business at Clapham, in the county of Surrey, and the defendants

---

(*b*) The relation between a banker and his customer who pays money into the bank is the ordinary relation of debtor and creditor, with a superadded obligation arising out of the custom of bankers to honour the customer's cheques, the money paid in to the banker being, in fact, money lent to the banker on the terms that it should be repaid when called for by cheque. See *Pott* v. *Clegg*, 16 M. & W. 321, 328; *Foley* v. *Hill*, 2 H. L. C. 28; *Ex parte Waring*, 36 L. J. Ch. 151. See also *Hopkinson* v. *Forster*, L. R. 19 Eq. 74.

A banker is bound to honour a customer's cheque if he has sufficient assets of the customer in his hands, and he cannot under ordinary circumstances set up a *jus tertii* against the order of the customer, or refuse to honour his cheque on any other ground than some sufficient one resulting from an act of the customer himself. (*Per* Lord Westbury, *Gray* v. *Johnston*, L. R. 3 H. L. 14. See, however, *per* Lord Cairns, *Ibid.* 11.) If, however, an executor, or trustee, who is indebted to a banker, applies a portion of the trust assets in the banker's hands to the payment of his debt to the banker,

are a firm of bankers, carrying on business at a banking-house in Broad Street, in the city of London.

---

the banker is not justified in accepting such portion, if he is cognisant of the fact that the assets are trust assets, as in so doing he would be participating in the breach of trust for his own personal benefit. (*Per* Lord Westbury, *Gray* v. *Johnston*, *supra*. See also *Bailey* v. *Finch*, L. R. 7 Q. B. 34 ; 41 L. J. Q. B. 83.)

A banker who refuses to pay a customer's cheque, having assets in his hands applicable to that purpose, is liable to pay at least nominal damages (*Marzetti* v. *Williams*, 1 B. & Ad. 415); and the jury may give substantial damages without proof of actual loss. (*Rolin* v. *Steward*, 14 C. B. 595 ; 23 L. J. C. P. 148 ; see also *Larios* v. *Gurety*, L. R. 5 P. C. 346.)

Where the usual dealing of a banker was to credit a customer in his books against bills, etc., paid in, and to honour the cheques of the customer accordingly, he was held liable for refusing to pay a cheque without having given notice that he discontinued such dealing. (*Cumming* v. *Shand*, 5 H. & N. 95 ; 29 L. J. Ex. 129.)

Where money has been paid into a bank upon a joint account it cannot in general be withdrawn without the joint order of all to whose account it was paid in, and the banker is not discharged by a payment to one only. (*Innes* v. *Stephenson*, 1 M. & Rob. 145 ; Leake on Contracts, 905.)

Branch banks are agencies of one principal banking corporation or firm (*Prince* v. *Oriental Bank*, 3 App. Cas. 325 ; 47 L. J. P. C. 42 ; *Garnett* v. *McKewan*, L. R. 8 Ex. 10 ; 42. L. J. Ex. 1). They are, however, distinct for the purpose of estimating the time at which notice of dishonour should be given (*Clode* v. *Bayley*, 12 M. & W. 51) ; and bankers are only bound to pay a customer's cheque at the branch where he keeps his account. (*Woodland* v. *Fear*, 7 E. & B. 519 ; 26 L. J. Q. B. 202.)

A banker paying a forged or altered cheque cannot, in general, charge the customer with the amount. (*Hall* v. *Fuller*, 5 B. & C. 750.) A banker having paid a cheque in ignorance that he then had no assets of the customer, cannot recover back the amount from the payee. (*Chambers* v. *Miller*, 13 C. B. N. S. 125 ; 32 L. J. C. P. 30 ; *Pollard* v. *Bank of England*, L. R. 6 Q. B. 623 ; 40 L. J. Q. B. 233.)

With respect to the liability of bankers in paying cheques drawn payable to order, it is enacted by 16 & 17 Vict. c. 59, s. 19, that any draft or order drawn upon a banker for a sum of money payable to order on demand which shall, when presented for payment, purport to be indorsed by the person to whom the same shall be drawn payable, shall be a sufficient authority to such banker to pay the amount of such draft or order to the bearer thereof; and it shall not be incumbent on such banker to prove that such indorsement or any subsequent indorsement was made by or under the sanction or authority of the person to whom the said draft or order was or is made payable either by the drawer or any indorser thereof. See *Halifax Union* v. *Wheelwright*, L. R. 10 Ex. 183 ; 44 L. J. Ex. 121.

An indorsement of a cheque payable to order, purporting to be by the agent of the person to whose order the cheque is payable, is within 16 & 17 Vict. c. 59, s. 19, a sufficient authority to the banker to pay the amount of such cheque, though the person who indorsed the

2. At the times hereinafter mentioned the plaintiff was a customer of the defendants' said firm and kept a bank-

---

cheque had no authority to indorse. (*Charles* v. *Blackwell*, 2 C. P. D. 151; 46 L. J. C. P. 368.)

"The Crossed Cheques Act, 1878" (39 & 40 Vict. c. 81), contains the following enactments as to bankers' obligations and liabilities in respect of crossed cheques:—

S. 7. "Where a cheque is crossed generally, the banker on whom it is drawn shall not pay it otherwise than to a banker."

"Where a cheque is crossed specially, the banker on whom it is drawn shall not pay it otherwise than to the banker to whom it is crossed, or to his agent for collection."

S. 8. "Where a cheque is crossed specially to more than one banker, except when crossed to an agent for the purpose of collection, the banker on whom it is drawn shall refuse payment thereof."

S. 9. "Where the banker on whom a crossed cheque is drawn has in good faith and without negligence paid such cheque, if crossed generally to a banker, and if crossed specially to the banker to whom it is crossed, or his agent for collection being a banker, the banker paying the cheque and (in case such cheque has come to the hands of the payee) the drawer thereof shall respectively be entitled to the same rights, and be placed in the same position in all respects, as they would respectively have been entitled to and have been placed in if the amount of the cheque had been paid to and received by the true owner thereof."

S. 10. "Any banker paying a cheque crossed generally otherwise than to a banker, or a cheque crossed specially otherwise than to the banker to whom the same shall be crossed, or his agent for collection, being a banker, shall be liable to the true owner of the cheque for any loss he may sustain owing to the cheque having been so paid."

S. 11. "Where a cheque is presented for payment, which does not at the time of presentation appear to be crossed, or to have had a crossing which has been obliterated, or to have been added to or altered otherwise than as authorised by this Act, a banker paying the cheque in good faith and without negligence, shall not be responsible or incur any liability, nor shall the payment be questioned, by reason of the cheque having been crossed, or of the crossing having been obliterated, or having been added to or altered otherwise than as authorised by this Act, and of payment being made otherwise than to a banker or the banker to whom the cheque is or was crossed, or to his agent for collection being a banker (as the case may be)."

S. 12. "A person taking a cheque crossed generally or specially, bearing in either case the words 'not negotiable,' shall not have and shall not be capable of giving a better title to the cheque than that which the person from whom he took it had."

"But a banker who has in good faith and without negligence received payment for a customer of a cheque crossed generally or specially to himself shall not, in case the title to the cheque proves defective, incur any liability to the true owner of the cheque by reason only of having received such payment." (*Mathiessen* v. *Lond. & Coy. Bank*, 5 C. P. D. 7; 48 L. J. C. P. 529.)

See sec. 4 of the Act as to what are 'general' and 'special' crossings, *post*, "*Bills of Exchange*," p. 106.

A person, other than a banker in the course of business, obtaining

ing account with them at their said banking-house upon the agreed terms (amongst others) that the defendants would from time to time, out of any moneys of the plaintiff in their hands applicable to that purpose, pay on presentment any cheque which might be drawn by the plaintiff on the defendants and duly presented at the said banking-house of the defendants for payment by any person lawfully entitled to receive the amount of such cheque, not exceeding the amount of the moneys of the plaintiff in the hands of the defendants applicable to the payment thereof at the time of the presentment thereof.

3. On the —— of ——, 18—, the plaintiff drew upon the defendants a cheque or order directed to them requiring them to pay to H. B., or bearer, the sum of £——.

4. The plaintiff [in the course of his business] delivered the said cheque or order to the said H. B.

5. Whilst the said H. B. was the bearer of the said cheque and lawfully entitled to receive the amount thereof, he duly presented the said cheque at the said banking-house of the defendants for payment.

6. At the time of the said presentment there were moneys of the plaintiff in the hands of the defendants exceeding the amount of the said cheque applicable to the payment thereof.

7. The defendants did not pay the said cheque when so presented as aforesaid.

8. In consequence of the non-payment of the said cheque the plaintiff was greatly injured in his said business, and in his credit and reputation. [*State special damage if any.*]

---

payment of a cheque through a forged indorsement thereof may be proceeded against by the lawful owner of the cheque, as such person is not protected by any statute. (*Ogden* v. *Benas*, L. R. 9 C. P. 513; 43 L. J. C. P. 259; *Arnold* v. *Cheque Bank*, 1 C. P. D. 578; 45 L. J. C. P. 562; *Bobbett* v. *Pinkett*, 1 Ex. D. 368; 45 L. J. Ex. 555.) See further, *post*, "*Bills of Exchange.*" *For form of claim against bankers for conversion of a cheque, and to recover the proceeds, see Matthiessen* v. *Lond. & Coy. Bank, supra.*

Upon the death of one partner in a firm the survivors are in general entitled to draw cheques upon the partnership account. (*Backhouse* v. *Charlton*, 8 Ch. D. 444.)

As to the liability of bankers for loss of securities deposited with them, see "*Bailments*," "Wrongs," *post*, p. 359.

As to the right of lien of bankers, see "Defences," "*Lien*," and *Lond. Chartered Bank of Australia* v. *White*, 4 App. Cas. 413; 48 L. J. C. P. 75; *Misa* v. *Currie*, 1 App. Cas. 554; 45 L. J. Ex. 852.

Bankruptcy (*a*).

Statement of Claim by a Trustee in Bankruptcy upon a cause of action accrued before the Bankruptcy.

1. The plaintiff is the duly appointed trustee of the property of A. B., who was adjudicated bankrupt in the

---

(*a*) The Bankruptcy Act, 1869, provides three different modes of dealing with the property or arranging the affairs of a debtor who is unable to pay his debts in full, viz.: (1) *Bankruptcy;* (2) *Liquidation by Arrangement;* (3) *Composition with Creditors.*

Proceedings for adjudication in Bankruptcy are available wherever one or more creditors to whom the debtor owes, either singly or in the aggregate, not less than £50, petition the Bankruptcy Court to adjudicate the debtor bankrupt in respect of any of the acts of bankruptcy specified in s. 6 of the Act. The petitioner's debt must be a liquidated sum. (*Ex pte. Charles,* 14 East, 197.) As to what is a liquidated debt, see *Ex pte. Broadhurst,* 2 De G. M. & G. 953; *Walter* v. *Broadhurst,* 23 L. J. Ex. 71; *Owen* v. *Routh,* 23 L. J. C. P. 105; *Johnson* v. *Diamond,* 24 L. J. Ex. 217. After the presentation of such petition the Bankruptcy Court may restrain further proceedings in any action against the debtor for any debt provable in bankruptcy, or may allow such proceedings, whether in progress at the commencement of the bankruptcy, or commenced during its continuance, to proceed upon such terms as it may think just (Bk. Act, s. 13).

This last section does not apply to demands in the nature of unliquidated damages arising otherwise than by reason of a contract or promise. (Bk. Act, s. 31. *Ex pte. Harold,* 3 Ch. D. 119; 45 L. J. B. 121; *Ex pte. Baum,* L. R. 9 Ch. Ap. 673; 44 L. J. B. 25.) By s. 49 of the Bk. Act, 1869, it is provided that an order of discharge shall not release a bankrupt "from any debt or liability incurred by means of any fraud or breach of trust." A liquidating debtor is placed in the same position in this respect by s. 125 (10) of the same Act. A creditor who, before the order of discharge is obtained, takes proceedings against the person or property of a debtor, in respect of a debt or liability incurred by means of fraud may be restrained. (*Cobham* v. *Dalton,* 10 Ch. Ap. 655; 44 L. J. Ch. 702; *Ex pte. Hemming,* 13 Ch. D. 163; 49 L. J. B. 17.) But when the order of discharge has been obtained, such creditor is entitled to enforce his remedy. (*Ex pte. Hemming, supra; Cobham* v. *Balfour, supra.*) See further as to debts provable in bankruptcy, Bk. Act, 1869, s. 31; *Ex pte. Neal,* 14 Ch. D. 579, and Williams on Bankruptcy, 2nd ed., p. 160.

After a debtor is adjudicated bankrupt, no creditor has any remedy against his property or person in respect of any debt provable in bankruptcy, except in manner directed by the Bk. Act, 1869. A *secured creditor* may, however, deal with or realise, as in any other case, any security he has upon the property of the bankrupt. (Bk. Act, s. 12.) A secured creditor is any creditor holding any mortgage charge or lien on the bankrupt's estate, or any part thereof as security for a debt due to him. (Bk. Act, s. 16 (5).) See further as to secured creditors, Williams on Bankruptcy, 2nd ed., p. 60.

London Bankruptcy Court [*or,* in the County Court of —— holden at ——] on the 15th of April, 1879.

When a debtor is adjudicated bankrupt, his property, as defined in s. 15 of the Bk. Act, 1869, becomes divisible amongst his creditors, and a trustee of such property is appointed by the creditors. (Bk. Act, ss. 14, 83.) Until a trustee is appointed, the Registrar is the trustee for the purposes of the Bankruptcy Act, and immediately upon the order of adjudication being made the property vests in the Registrar. On the appointment, however, of a trustee, the property forthwith passes to and vests in the trustee (Bk. Act, s. 17), and his title relates back to the time of the act of bankruptcy being completed on which the order of adjudication is made, or to the first act of bankruptcy proved to have been committed within twelve months next preceding such order, provided that at the date of such prior act there existed a debt or debts of not less than £50, and that such debt or debts still is or are due at the date of the adjudication. (Bk. Act, s. 11.)

The property of the bankrupt divisible amongst his creditors does not comprise property held on trust by him for other persons, or the tools of his trade, necessary wearing apparel, and bedding of himself, his wife, and children, to a value altogether not exceeding £20; but it comprises all property belonging to or vested in the bankrupt at the commencement of the bankruptcy, or acquired by or devolving on him during its continuance. (Bk. Act, s. 15.) See s. 4 of the Act as to what is included under the word "property." See also Williams on Bankruptcy, 2nd ed., p. 68, as to what constitutes trust property within s. 15. The divisible property comprises "all goods and chattels being at the commencement of the bankruptcy in the possession, order, or disposition of the bankrupt, being a trader, by the consent and permission of the true owner, of which goods and chattels the bankrupt is reputed owner, or of which he has taken upon himself the sale or disposition as owner; provided that things in action, other than debts due to him in the course of his trade or business, shall not be deemed goods and chattels within the meaning of this clause." (Bk. Act, s. 15 (5).) Shares in a company are not things in action within the meaning of this clause (*Ex pte. Union Bank of Manchester*, L. R. 12 Eq. 354; 40 L. J. B. 57); but a policy of life assurance is. (*Ex pte. Ibbetson*, 8 Ch. D. 519.) So, too, is a debenture of a Joint Stock Company. (*Ex pte. Rensburg*, 4 Ch. D. 685.) If there is no trustee, the Registrar having jurisdiction in the bankruptcy acts as such trustee. (Bk. Act, s. 83(3).). The property of the bankrupt passes from trustee to trustee, including the Registrar when he fills the office of trustee, and vests in the trustee for the time being, without any conveyance, assignment or transfer whatever. (Bk. Act, s. 83 (6).).

The trustee may, by writing under his hand, disclaim any unmarketable shares, or determine any unprofitable contract of the bankrupt, or surrender any lease burdened with onerous covenants. (Bk. Act, s. 23, Bk. Rules, 1871, r. 28; *Smalley* v. *Hardinge*, 50 L. J. Q. B. 367; *Ex pte. Ladbury*, 17 Ch. D. 532; *Ex pte. Walton*, 17 Ch. D. 746; 50 L. J. Ch. 657; *Ex pte. East India Dock Co.*, 17 Ch. D. 759.) The trustee's time for so disclaiming is limited in certain cases specified in s. 24 of the Bankruptcy Act. The disclaimer has been held not to affect the rights *inter se* of lessor and

2. On the 12th of June, 1878, the said A. B. sold and delivered a horse to the defendant for the price of £——.

lessee where the assignee of the lessee is bankrupt. (*Smyth* v. *North*, L. R. 7 Ex. 242 ; 41 L. J. Ex. 103 ; and see *Ex pte. East India Dock Co., supra.*)

A trustee who takes actual possession of leasehold property of a bankrupt, and who does not disclaim, either when called upon by the lessor under the Bk. Act, s. 24, to decide whether he will disclaim or at all, is personally liable for rent accruing due during the time that he is in possession. (*Ex parte Dressler*, 9 Ch. D. 252, 48 L. J. B. 20 ; *Ex parte Carter*, 8 Ch. D. 731 ; *Wilson* v. *Wallani*, 5 Ex. D. 155 ; 49 L. J. Ex. 437 ; *Lowrey* v. *Barker*, 5 Ex. 6, 170 ; 49 L. J. Ex. 433.)

The severance by a trustee in bankruptcy of fixtures which belonged to the lessor unless removed during the existence of the lease is, when made between the time of his appointment as trustee and his disclaimer of a lease, a wrongful act, giving to the landlord a right of action against such trustee personally. (*Ex pte. Brook*, 10 Ch. D. 100 ; 48 L. J. B. 22 ; *Ex pte. Stephens*, 7 Ch. D. 127 ; 47 L. J. B. 22.)

The trustee has power to bring or defend any action relating to the property of the bankrupt. (Bk. Act, s. 25 (3) ; *Leeming* v. *Murray*, 13 Ch. D. 123 ; 48 L. J. Ch. 737.) Any action brought by or against the trustee in his official capacity, must be brought in his official name of "the trustee of the property of ——, a bankrupt." (Bk. Act, ss. 22, 83 (7) ; and see Jud. Act, 1875, O. III. r. 4.) Claims by a trustee in bankruptcy cannot, except by leave obtainable by summons at Chambers, be joined with any claim by him in any other capacity. (Jud. Act, 1875, O. XVII. r. 3.)

A right of action in respect of a wrong or injury to the person, feelings, or reputation of a bankrupt, such as an assault, breach of promise of marriage, bodily injury, defamation of character and the like, does not, whether such wrong or injury was committed before, or during a bankruptcy, pass to the trustee. (*Beckham* v. *Drake*, 8 M. & W. 846 ; 11 M. & W. 315 ; 2 H. L. C. 579 ; *Ex pte. Vine*, 8 Ch. D. 364 ; 47 L. J. B. 116 ; *Rogers* v. *Spence*, 13 M. & W. 571 ; 12 Cl. & F. 700.) Consequently, in respect of such causes of action, the bankrupt alone can sue, or continue an action commenced before bankruptcy. All rights of action which have accrued before bankruptcy in respect of breaches of contract affecting the personal estate or property of the bankrupt pass, in general, to the trustee, and the bankrupt cannot sue, or take any legal proceedings in respect of them. (*Beckham* v. *Drake, ante* ; *Morgan* v. *Steble*, L. R. 7 Q. B. 611 ; 41 L. J. Q. B. 260 ; *Wadling* v. *Oliphant*, 1 Q. B. D. 145 ; 45 L. J. Q. B. 173 ; *Rochfort* v. *Battersby*, 2 H. L. C. 388 ; *Ex pte. Carter*, 2 Ch. D. 806 ; 45 L. J. B. 145.) The trustee is, in general, entitled to sue in respect of such rights of action accruing during the continuance of the bankruptcy, though in the case of a contract made by the bankrupt pending the bankruptcy, if the trustee does not sue, or interpose, an action may be brought in respect thereof by the bankrupt himself. (*Herbert* v. *Sayer*, 5 Q. B. 965; *Jameson* v. *Brick & Stone Co.*, 4 Q. B. D. 208 ; 48 L. J. Q. B. 249.)

The earnings of a bankrupt by his personal labour during the continuance of the bankruptcy, do not, it would seem, so far as they may

3. The price of the said horse was due from and payable by the defendant to the said A. B. before the said A. B. became bankrupt.

4. The defendant has not paid the said price or any part thereof either to the said A. B. or to the plaintiff, and the said sum is due from and payable by the defendant to the plaintiff as trustee as aforesaid.

By a Trustee upon a Contract with him as such Trustee.

1. [*As in paragraph* 1 *of the first form.*]

2. On the 10th May, 1879, the plaintiff as trustee as aforesaid, sold and assigned to the defendant by public auction [*or*, by private contract], for the sum of £——, certain household furniture which belonged to the said A. B. at the commencement of the said bankruptcy [*or*, which was acquired by, or devolved on the said A. B. during the continuance of the said bankruptcy].

3. Full particulars of the said furniture and of the price thereof have been delivered by the plaintiff to the defendant [*or*, are as follows].

---

be necessary for the support of himself and family, vest in the trustee (*Williams* v. *Chambers*, 10 Q. B. 337; *Wadling* v. *Oliphant*, *ante*); therefore a bankrupt may apparently sue for such earnings.

The proceeds derived from the carrying on of a trade, as, for instance, that of a furniture broker (*Crofton* v. *Poole*, 1 B. & Ad. 568), a painter (*Ex pte. Banks*, 4 Ch. D. 689; 46 L. J. B. 74), an architect (*Emden* v. *Carte*, 17 Ch. D. 169 *ib.* 768; 50 L. J. Ch. 492), or an apothecary (*Elliott* v. *Clayton*, 16 Q. B. 581; 20 L. J. Q. B. 217), are not considered personal earnings within the above exception, and such proceeds, though earned during the continuance of the bankruptcy, pass to the trustee.

Executory contracts depending upon the personal qualifications of the bankrupt, such as a contract of partnership, a contract to paint a picture, and the like (Leake on Contracts, 1274; *Gibson* v. *Carruthers*, 8 M. & W. 333, 343), do not pass to the trustee, and afford an exception to the general rule that a trustee is entitled to the benefit of the executory or uncompleted contracts of the bankrupt.

In the case of a plaintiff becoming bankrupt in the course of an action which is of such a nature that the cause of action is divested out of the plaintiff and vested in the trustee, it seems that the action should be continued in the name of the trustee. (*Wright* v. *Swindon, &c., Ry. Co.*, 4 Ch. D. 164; 46 L. J. Ch. 199; *Jackson* v. *N. E. Ry. Co.*, 5 Ch. D. 844; 46 L. J. Ch. 723; *Eldridge* v. *Burgess*, 7 Ch. D. 411; 47 L. J. Ch. 342.) The trustee may be called upon by summons to elect to continue such action, and to give security for costs, but if he thereupon elects not to continue such action, he is not precluded from commencing a fresh action for the same cause. (*Bennett* v. *Gamgee*, 2 Ex. D. 11; 46 L. J. Ex. 204; Leake on Contracts, 1272.) *See* further Jud. Acts O. L.; Wils. 298.

4. The said sum of £—— was at the commencement of this action, and still is, due from and payable by the defendant to the plaintiff as such trustee as aforesaid in respect of the said sale.

By a Trustee where the affairs of the Debtor are being Liquidated by Arrangement under s. 125 of the Bankruptcy Act, 1869 (*b*).

1. The plaintiff is the duly appointed trustee of the property of one A. B., whose affairs are, under and by

---

(*b*) *Liquidation by arrangement.*] A debtor unable to pay his debts may summon a general meeting of his creditors, and they may at such meeting by a special resolution, as defined by the Bk. Act 1869, declare that the affairs of the debtor are to be liquidated by arrangement and not in bankruptcy, and then, or at some subsequent meeting within a week, appoint a trustee. (Bk. Act, s. 125 (1).) All the property of the debtor which would if he were made bankrupt be divisible amongst his creditors vests in the trustee on his appointment, and is divisible amongst the debtor's creditors, and all such settlements, conveyances, transfers, charges, payments, obligations, and proceedings as would be void against the trustee in bankruptcy are void against the trustee in liquidation by arrangement. (Bk. Act, s. 125 (5).) The proceedings are instituted by the filing of a petition by the debtor. (Bk. Act, r. 252, *et seq.*)

The trustee has the same powers, and performs the same duties, and distributes the property in the same manner as a trustee in bankruptcy, and, with the modification referred to in s. 125 (7), all the provisions of the Bk. Act, so far as the same are applicable, apply to liquidation by arrangement. (Bk. Act, s. 125 (7).) His title relates back, as in bankruptcy, to the petition (*Ex pte. Todhunter*, L. R. 10 Eq. 425; 39 L. J. B. 17; *Ex pte. Duignan*, L. R. 6 Ch. Ap. 605; 40 L. J. B. 69), or to any prior act of bankruptcy committed within twelve months of the commencement of the liquidation. (*Ex pte. Eyles*, L. R. 16 Eq. 99; 42 L. J. B. 55; *ex pte. Attwater*, 5 Ch. D. 27.)

The Court may, as in the case of a bankruptcy, at any time after the presentation of a petition by a debtor restrain legal proceedings against him in respect of any provable debt. (Bk. Rules, 1870, r. 260; *ex pte. Isaac*, L. R. 6 Ch. Ap. 58; 40 L. J. B. 19. *See preceding note.*)

Composition with creditors.] The creditors of a debtor unable to pay his debts may without any proceedings in bankruptcy by an extraordinary resolution resolve that a composition shall be accepted in satisfaction of the debts due to them from the debtor. (Bk. Act, s. 126.) See this section as to what is an extraordinary resolution, and how it is passed.

The provisions of a composition so accepted are binding on all creditors whose names, addresses, and debts are shown in the statement of the debtor produced to the meetings at which the resolution has passed, but do not affect or prejudice the rights of any other creditors (Bk. Act, s. 126). A creditor whose name is not inserted

virtue of section 125 of the Bankruptcy Act, 1869, and the rules made in pursuance of the said Act, being liquidated by arrangement, and not in bankruptcy.

2. [*Continue by stating the cause of action*].

By a Trustee for the Non-acceptance of goods agreed to be sold by the Bankrupt to the Defendant.

1. [*As in paragraph* 1 *of first form.*]

2. On the —— of ——, 18—, before the said A. B. became bankrupt, it was agreed in writing by and between the said A. B. and the defendant that the said A. B. should sell to the defendant, and the defendant should buy from the said A. B. —— sacks of flour, at the price of £—— per sack, upon the terms that the

---

in the debtor's statement of debts is not bound by the resolution unless he voluntarily joins in passing it, and obtains his share of the composition. (*Wilson* v. *Breslauer*, 2 C. P. D. 314; *Breslauer* v. *Brown*, 3 App. Cas. 672; 47 L. J. C. P. 729; *ex pte. Lacey*, 16 Ch. D. 131; 50 L. J. Ch. 207; *ex pte. Lang*, 5 Ch. D. 971.)

Before a debtor makes default in payment of a composition, a creditor, bound by the resolution, cannot bring an action for payment of the original debt. (*Slater* v. *Jones*, *Capes* v. *Ball*, L. R. 8 Ex. 186; 42 L. J. Ex. 122.)

A non-assenting creditor may sue for his original debt where the debtor fails to pay or tender the composition within the time agreed on, or within a reasonable time. (*Edwards* v. *Coombe*, L. R. 7 C. P. 519; 41 L. J. C. P. 202; *Goldney* v. *Lording*, L. R. 8 Q. B. 182; 42 L. J. Q. B. 103; *Tea Company* v. *Jones*, 43 L. T. 255.) This applies also to an assenting creditor. (*In re Hatton*, L. R. 7 Ch. Ap. 723; 42 L. J. B. 12.) See also *Edwards* v. *Hancher*, 1 C. P. D. 111; and *Newell* v. *Van Praagh*, L. R. 9 C. P. 96; 43 L. J. C. P. 94.

The right of the creditor to sue under these circumstances upon the original debt is subject to the jurisdiction of the Court of Bankruptcy to restrain him from doing so upon equitable grounds. (*Ex pte. King*, L. R. 17 Eq. 332; 43 L. J. B. 41; *ex pte. Lang*, *supra*.) The creditor may sue the debtor for the balance of the original debt where the debtor has paid some of the instalments of the composition, and has failed to pay or tender the remainder. (*Ex pte. Gilbey*, 8 Ch. D. 248; 47 L. J. B. 49.)

If a trustee appointed for distribution of composition makes default in payment thereof through no fault of the debtor, the latter is not liable, and an action brought against him would be restrained. (*Ex pte. Waterer*, 43 L. J. B. 25.)

Where resolutions accepting a composition have been passed and registered under sec. 126, a creditor will be restrained from vexatiously bringing an action to try the validity of the resolutions. (*Ex pte. Hartel*, L. R. 8 Ch. Ap. 743; 42 L. J. B. 34; *Ex pte. Lopez*, 5 Ch. D. 64; 46 L. J. B. 95; *Ex pte. Watson*, 2 Ch. D. 63; *Ex pte. Paper Staining Co.*, L. R. 8 Ch. Ap. 595.)

said A. B. should deliver the said flour to the defendant, and that the defendant should accept the same from the said A. B., and pay him the said price for the same upon such delivery.

3. The said A. B. was always ready and willing to deliver the said —— sacks of flour to the defendant in accordance with the said agreement, and the said A. B., before he became bankrupt, duly offered and tendered to the defendant, in pursuance of the said agreement, the said —— sacks of flour of such quality and in such manner and at such time as to entitle him to have the same accepted by the defendant.

4. The defendant did not accept the said —— sacks of flour or any of them, and expressly refused so to do, and did not nor would pay the said price for the same.

5. In consequence of such breach of agreement the said A. B. was obliged to sell the said flour to other persons at —— shillings less per sack than the said price agreed to be paid by the defendant.

By the Trustee of a Bankrupt Partner in his own name and that of a Solvent Partner (c).

1. The plaintiff E. F. [*proceed as in paragraph* 1 *of the first form*].

2. The said A. B., previously to being adjudicated a bankrupt as aforesaid, carried on business as a wine merchant, in partnership with the plaintiff G. H., in Oxford Street, London.

3. The said A. B. and the plaintiff G. H., on the 9th of November, 1878, sold and delivered — cases of champagne to the defendant, at £—— per case, to be paid for on delivery.

4. The defendant has not paid for the said champagne,

(c) By s. 105 of the Bk. Act, 1869, the Court of Bankruptcy, with the sanction of a special resolution of the creditors, may authorise the trustee of a bankrupt who at the time of his bankruptcy was a member of a partnership, to commence and prosecute any action in the names of the trustee and of the bankrupt's partner, and may give directions as to indemnifying such partner against costs, and otherwise securing his rights.

By s. 112, where a bankrupt is a contractor in respect of any contract jointly with any other person or persons, such person or persons may sue or be sued in respect of such contract without the joinder of the bankrupt.

or for any part thereof, and the price of the same is due from, and payable by the defendant to the plaintiff E. F., as trustee as aforesaid, and to the plaintiff G. H.

By the Assignee of Book Debts sold to him by the Trustee of a Bankrupt (d).

1. On the —— of ——, 18—, A. B. sold and delivered to the defendant — bales of cloth at the price of £——.

2. On the —— of ——, 18— [*any date after the sale and delivery*], the said A. B. was duly adjudicated a bankrupt in the [London Bankruptcy Court,] and such proceedings thereupon ensued that C. D. was on the —— of —— duly appointed trustee of the property of the said A. B. under the said bankruptcy.

3. On the —— of ——, 18—, the defendant not having paid the said price, or any part thereof, the said C. D., as trustee as aforesaid, sold the said debt of £——, which was a book debt due [*or*, growing due] to the said A. B. within the meaning of the Bankruptcy Act, 1869, to the plaintiff for £—— by public auction [*or*, private contract], and duly assigned the same to the plaintiff before the commencement of this action.

4. The said debt was due from, and payable by the defendant to the plaintiff at the commencement of this action, and is still due and unpaid.

(*d*) By s. 25 (6) of the Bk. Act, 1869, the trustee has power to sell all the property of the bankrupt (including the goodwill of his business, if any, and the book debts due or growing due to him) by public auction or private contract, either altogether to one person, or in separate parcels to different persons. As to what are book debts, see *Shipley* v. *Marshall*, 14 C. B. N. S. 566; 32 L. J. C. P. 258; *Ex pte. Roberts*, 33 L. J. B. 8. In cases where a bankrupt has acquired property during bankruptcy which the trustee cannot claim (*e.g.* proceeds of manual labour), he himself may, out of such property, purchase and acquire property in the book debts. (*Kitson* v. *Hardwick*, L. R. 7 C. P. 473.)

By s. 111, any person to whom a chose in action belonging to the bankrupt has been assigned by the trustee in pursuance of the Act (see s. 25 (6)), may bring or defend an action relating to such chose in action in his own name without joining the bankrupt. (*Seear* v. *Lawson*, 15 Ch. D. 426; 49 L. J. B. 69.)

BARRISTER (*a*).

BILLS OF EXCHANGE, BANKERS' CHEQUES, PROMISSORY NOTES.

I. INLAND BILLS OF EXCHANGE.

Statement of Claim by Drawer against Acceptor on a Bill payable to Drawer.

1. The plaintiff by his bill of exchange, bearing date the —— of ——, 18—, now overdue, directed to the defendant, required the defendant to pay to the plaintiff —— months after date (*aa*) the sum of £——.

2. The defendant accepted the said bill.

3. The defendant has not paid the same.

[*The expenses of noting, &c., may be laid as special damage by adding as follows* (*b*):

4. By reason of the non-payment of the said bill, the plaintiff incurred expenses to the amount of £—— in and about the presenting and noting of the said bill, and incidental to the dishonour thereof.]

(*a*) A barrister cannot bring an action for the recovery of fees for professional services, nor upon a contract the consideration of which is professional services, as, an account stated in respect of professional remuneration. (*Kennedy* v. *Broun*, 13 C. B. N. S. 677; 32 L. J. C. P. 137; *Mostyn* v. *Mostyn*, L. R. 5 Ch. Ap. 457; 39 L. J. Ch. 780; *Robertson* v *McDonogh*, 6 L. R. Ir. 433.) But where a barrister had been employed as returning-officer in an election of guardians for a union, under an express contract for remuneration at so much per day, he was held entitled to recover. (*Egan* v. *Guardians of Kensington Union*, 3 Q. B. 935 n.)

(*aa*) Or "sight." As the fact of the acceptor having had sight of the bill (which means legal sight) is involved in the allegation of acceptance, this form requires no other modification to make it applicable in the case of a bill payable after sight. Legal sight is proved by acceptance or by protest for non-acceptance. (*Campbell* v. *French*, 6 T. R. 212.) A bill or note payable "at sight," or on presentation, is immediately payable, and is equivalent to one payable on demand. (34 & 35 Vict. c. 74, s. 2.)

(*b*) An inland bill is not commonly noted or protested. It is necessary that this should be done in those cases only where any of the parties are to be sued abroad. The expenses are not recoverable, unless charged as special damage. (*Rogers* v. *Hunt*, 10 Ex. 474; *Kendrick* v. *Lomax*, 2 C. & J. 407.)

By Drawer against Acceptor setting forth Consideration (c).

Form No. 7 *in App.* (*C.*) *to Jud. Act,* 1875.

1. The plaintiffs are —— merchants, factors, and commission agents, carrying on business in London.

(c) In actions between immediate parties it is often advisable to add a claim on the consideration for the bill and upon accounts stated, as the bill itself is evidence of an account stated between immediate parties to it. (*Early* v. *Bowman,* 1 B. & Ad. 892; and see *ante,* "*Accounts stated,*" p. 33.)

Interest is claimable on bills of exchange and promissory notes by the custom of merchants from all the parties liable, although not expressed on the face of the bill or note. (*Windle* v. *Andrews,* 2 B. & Ald. 696.) It is recoverable as damages, and need not be charged in the body of the statement of claim. The rate of interest allowed on inland bills and notes is usually £5 per cent., unless another rate is mentioned in the bill or note. (*Keene* v. *Keene,* 3 C. B. N. S. 144; 27 L. J. C. P. 88.) On foreign bills interest is recoverable at the rate of interest at the place where the bill was drawn, accepted or indorsed, as the case may be, according to the liability of the party sued. (*Allen* v. *Kemble,* 6 Moore, P. C. 314; *Gibbs* v. *Fremont,* 9 Ex. 25.)

If persons have become parties to a bill of exchange in the name of a firm, and sue or are sued otherwise than in the name of the firm, it may be alleged that "the plaintiffs" [*or* the defendants, *or* certain persons, *as the case may be*] by the name or style of A. and Co., drew [*or* accepted, *or* indorsed, *as the case may be*], etc." See *Kirk* v. *Blurton,* 9 M. & W. 284; *Ball* v. *Gordon,* 9 M. & W. 345; *Tigar* v. *Gordon,* 9 M. & W. 347; *Smith* v. *Ball,* 9 Q. B. 361. Where any of the parties are designated in the bill by the initial letter, or some contraction of the Christian name, it is sufficient in the statement of claim to follow the designation so used. (See 3 & 4 Will. IV. c. 42, s. 12, *ante,* p. 3.)

It is sometimes doubtful whether a document is a bill of exchange or a promissory note (*Shuttleworth* v. *Stephens,* 1 Camp. 407; *Allan* v. *Mawson,* 4 Camp. 115; *Miller* v. *Thomson,* 3 M. & G. 576; *Fielder* v. *Marshall,* 9 C. B. N. S. 606), in which cases it may be found convenient to set out the document in the statement of claim *verbatim,* with averments of identity of the persons mentioned in it and the parties to the action. See *Price* v. *Taylor,* 5 H. & N. 540; 29 L. J. Ex. 331; see also "*The body of the statement of claim,*" *ante,* p. 11.

Although bills of exchange drawn and accepted by the same parties may be in strictness promissory notes rather than bills, yet where the intention to give and receive such documents as instruments capable of being negotiated in the market as bills of exchange is clear, both the holders and the parties may treat them accordingly. (*Willans* v. *Ayers,* 3 App. Cas. 133; 47 L. J. P. C. 1.) To constitute a valid acceptance it is not necessary that any words indicating an intention on the part of the drawee to be bound by the bill should appear on the face of the bill. The bare signature of the drawee on the bill is sufficient (41 Vict. c. 13, s. 1).

2. The defendants are merchants and commission agents, carrying on business at Hong Kong.

3. For several years prior to the ——, 1875, the plaintiffs had been in the habit of consigning goods to the defendants for sale, as their agents, and the defendants had been in the habit of consigning goods to the plaintiffs for sale, as their agents; and each party always received the price of the goods sold by him for the other; and a balance was from time to time struck between the parties, and paid.

On the —— of ——, the moneys so received by the defendants for the plaintiffs, and remaining in their names, largely exceeded the moneys received by the plaintiffs for the defendants, and a balance of £—— was accordingly due to the plaintiffs from the defendants.

4. On or about the ——, 1875, the plaintiffs sent to the defendants a statement of the accounts between them, showing the said sum as the balance due to the plaintiffs from the defendants, and the defendants agreed to the said statement of accounts as correct, and to the said sum of £—— as the balance due by them to the plaintiffs, and agreed to pay interest on such balance if time were given to them.

5. The defendants requested the plaintiffs to give them three months time for payment of the said sum of £——, and the plaintiffs agreed to do so upon the defendants accepting the bills of exchange hereinafter mentioned.

6. The plaintiffs thereupon on the —— drew two bills of exchange upon the defendants, one for £——, and the other for £——, both payable to the order of the plaintiffs three months after date, and the defendants accepted the bills.

The said bills became due on the ——, 187—, and the defendants have not paid the bills, or either of them, nor the said sum of £——.

The plaintiffs claim:—

£—— and interest to the date of judgment.

By Drawer against Acceptor on a Bill payable to a Third Party.

1. The plaintiff by his bill of exchange, bearing date the —— of ——, 18—, now overdue, directed to the defendant, required the defendant to pay to G. H. or order —— months after date the sum of £——.

2. The plaintiff delivered the said bill to the said G. H.

3. The defendant accepted the said bill, but did not pay the same.

4. The said bill was thereupon returned to the plaintiff.

By Drawer against Acceptor on a Bill accepted payable at a particular place (*d*).

1. [*The same as in the first form.*]

2. The defendant accepted the said bill, payable at Messrs. Goslings & Sharpe, bankers, London, and not otherwise or elsewhere.

(*d*) A bill accepted payable at a banker's or other place was, at common law, a qualified acceptance, and required a presentment according to the tenor of the acceptance. But 1 & 2 Geo. 4, c. 78, after reciting "that according to law, when a bill is accepted, payable at a banker's, the acceptance is not a general, but a qualified acceptance," enacts, "that if any person shall accept a bill, payable at the house of a banker or other place, without further expression in his acceptance, such acceptance shall be deemed and taken to be, to all intents and purposes, a general acceptance of such bill; but if the acceptor shall in his acceptance express that he accepts the bill, payable at a banker's house or other place *only, and not otherwise or elsewhere*, such acceptance shall be deemed and taken to be, to all intents and purposes, a qualified acceptance of such bill; and the acceptor shall not be liable to pay the said bill, except in default of payment when such payment shall have been first duly demanded at such banker's house or other place."

Since the above statute, a bill accepted payable at a banker's or other place, without further restriction in the acceptance, is a general acceptance as against the *acceptor*, and may be declared upon accordingly. (*Blake* v. *Beaumont*, 4 M. & G. 7; *Halstead* v. *Skelton*, 5 Q. B. 86.) A bill so accepted, however, may also be validly presented at the place specified (*ib.*; *Wilmot* v. *Williams*, 7 M. & G. 1017; *Walter* v. *Cubley*, 2 C. & M. 151; *Shelton* v. *Braithwaite*, 8 M. & W. 252); but if not so presented, the assets of the acceptor remain there at his own risk. (*Turner* v. *Hayden*, 4 B. & C. 1.) The effect of the statute is restricted to the acceptor; as against all other parties to the bill, the qualifications of the acceptance remain the same as at common law (*Cranley* v. *Hillary*, 2 M. & S. 120; *Walton* v. *Mascall*, 13 M. & W. 458); and the bill must be duly presented according to the qualifications of the acceptance, in order to charge the drawer (see *Gibb* v. *Mather*, 8 Bing. 214, 220), or the indorser. (*Saul* v. *Jones*, 1 E. & E. 59; 28 L. J. Q. B. 37.) The statute applies equally to bills in which the drawer, in making the bill, has, in the body of it, required payment to be made at a particular place; the acceptance is general as against the acceptor, unless it contains the negative expressions required by the statute. (*Selby* v. *Eden*, 3 Bing. 611; *Fayle* v. *Bird*, 6 B. & C. 531.)

3. The said bill was duly presented for payment at Messrs. Goslings & Sharpe, bankers, London, aforesaid, and was dishonoured.

By Drawer against Acceptor on a Bill accepted payable on a contingency (*e*).

1. [*The same as in the first form.*]

2. The defendant accepted the said bill, payable on the death of G. H.

3. Before the commencement of this action the said G. H. died.

4. The defendant has not paid the said bill.

By Payee against Acceptor.

1. G. H. by his bill of exchange, bearing date the —— of ——, 18—, now overdue, directed to the defendant, required the defendant to pay to the plaintiff, —— months after date, the sum of £ ——.

2. The defendant accepted the said bill.

3. G. H. delivered the said bill to the plaintiff (*f*).

4. The defendant has not paid the said bill.

By Indorsees against Acceptor (*g*).

Form No. 6 *in App.* (*C.*) *to Jud. Act,* 1875.

1. Messrs. M. N. & Co., on the —— day of ——, drew a bill of exchange upon the defendants for £——, pay-

---

(*e*) A conditional acceptance cannot properly be referred to in the statement of claim as an absolute one, although the condition has been fulfilled. (*Langston* v. *Corney*, 4 Camp. 176.)

(*f*) This form mentions the delivery of the bill to the plaintiff. An averment to this effect was held not necessary under the former system of pleading. (*Churchill* v. *Gardner*, 7 T. R. 596.)

(*g*) In order to constitute a valid indorsement of a bill of exchange or note, as against the indorser, there must be a writing of the name of the indorser, and a delivery by him of the bill, with the intention not only to pass the property in it, but to guarantee the payment if the acceptor makes default. (*Denton* v. *Peters*, L. R. 5 Q. B. 475. See also *Foster* v. *Mackinnon*, L. R. 4 C. P. 704; 38 L. J. C. P. 310.) The statement of the indorsement includes the delivery for the purpose of transfer (*Brind* v. *Hampshire*, 1 M. & W. 371), and imports the transfer of the property in, and the right of action on, the bill (*Marston* v. *Allen*, 8 M. & W. 494; *Law* v. *Parnell*, 7 C. B. N. S. 282; 29 L. J. C. P. 17; *Keene* v. *Beard*, 8 C. B. N. S. 372, 381; 29

able to the order of the said Messrs. M. N. & Co. three months after date, and the defendants accepted the same.

2. Messrs. M. N. & Co. indorsed the bill to the plaintiffs.

3. The bill became due on the ——, and the defendants have not paid it.

By Payee against Drawer, for default of Acceptance (*h*).

1. The defendant by his bill of exchange, bearing date the —— of ——, 18—, directed to G. H., required the said G. H. to pay to the plaintiff —— months after date the sum of £——.

2. The said bill was duly presented by the plaintiff

L. J. C. P. 287, 290); but a statement of delivery merely would not include indorsement, and would render the statement of claim bad on demurrer. (*Cunliffe* v. *Whitehead*, 3 Bing. N. C. 828.) The allegation of indorsement is sufficiently proved in an action against the acceptor by proof of a transfer of the property in the bill, although no right of action be given against the indorser by the transfer. (*Smith* v. *Johnson*, 3 H. & N. 222; 27 L. J. Ex. 363.) The delivery of a bill payable to his own order by the drawer to the plaintiff, without indorsement, though with the intention of transferring the property in the bill, was held to give no authority to the plaintiff to indorse the drawer's name, and no right of action against the acceptor. (*Harrop* v. *Fisher*, 10 C. B. N. S. 196; 30 L. J. C. P. 283.) A conditional indorsement transfers the bill subject to the condition. (*Robertson* v. *Kensington*, 4 Taunt. 30.)

When a bill has been indorsed in blank its negotiability cannot afterwards be restricted by a special indorsement, except as against the special indorser himself. (*Smith* v. *Clarke*, 1 Peake, N. P. C. 295; *Walker* v. *Macdonald*, 2 Ex. 527.) Hence the plaintiff may in the pleadings be described as the immediate indorsee of the first or any intermediate indorser. The indorsements not stated must be struck out at the trial, and the remedy against those indorsers is lost. See as to the striking out of indorsements, *Bartlett* v. *Benson*, 14 M. & W. 733; 3 D. & L. 274; Byles on Bills, 12th ed. 154; Chalmers, 96. Indorsements stated, though unnecessarily, must, in the absence of amendment of the pleading, be proved, if denied. (*Waynam* v. *Bend*, 1 Camp. 175.)

(*h*) This cause of action arises immediately on the refusal to accept, and due notice thereof to the defendant, and dates from that time. (*Whitehead* v *Walker*, 9 M. & W. 506.) No new cause of action arises afterwards on non-payment. (*Ib.*) Notice of dishonour by non-acceptance must be given at once, and cannot be reserved until default in payment. (*Bartlett* v. *Benson*, 14 M. &. W. 733.) As to notice of dishonour, and how and when it is to be alleged, or the want of it excused, see *post*, p. 93, n. (*k*).

for acceptance to the said G. H. on the —— of ——, 18—.

3. The said G. H. then refused to accept the said bill, and has not accepted it.

4. The defendant had due notice of the said presentment and dishonour.

5. The defendant has not paid the said bill.

By Indorsee against Drawer, for default of Acceptance.

1. The defendant by his bill of exchange, bearing date the —— of ——, 18—, directed to G. H., required the said G. H. to pay to K. L. or order, —— months after date, the sum of £——.

2. The said K. L. indorsed the said bill to M. N.

3. The said M. N. indorsed the said bill to the plaintiff.

4. [*Continue with paragraphs* 2, 3, 4, *and* 5 *of the last preceding form.*]

By Payee against Drawer, for default of Payment (*i*).

1. The defendant by his bill of exchange, bearing date the —— of ——, 18—, now overdue, directed to G. H., required the said G. H. to pay to the plaintiff, —— months after date, the sum of £——.

2. The defendant delivered the said bill to the plaintiff.

3. The said bill was duly presented for payment.

4. The said bill was dishonoured.

5. The defendant had due notice of the dishonouring of the said bill.

6. The defendant has not paid the said bill.

(*i*) This cause of action arises only when the bill has not been presented for acceptance, or has been accepted, and payment has been refused, and notice given of the dishonour. When acceptance has been refused, no new cause of action can arise on non-payment. (*Whitehead* v. *Walker*, 9 M. & W. 506.)

It is not necessary to state an acceptance, whether general or at a particular place, against any party except the acceptor. (*Parks* v. *Edge*, 1 C. & M. 429.)

By Payee against Drawer, for default of Payment on a Bill drawn payable at a particular place. (*j*).

1. The defendant, by his bill of exchange bearing date the —— of ——, 18—, now overdue, directed to G. H., required the said G. H. to pay to the plaintiff, in London, —— months after date, the sum of £——.

2. [*Continue with paragraphs* 2, 3, 4, 5, *and* 6 *of the last preceding form, but averring presentment for payment in London.*]

By Payee against Drawer for default of Payment, excusing Notice of Dishonour (*k*).

[*Proceed for the first four paragraphs as in the form of Payee against Drawer for default of Payment, and continue as follows.*]

5. The said G. H. had not at any time any effects of the defendant.

(*j*) A general averment that the bill was duly presented for payment would perhaps be sufficient, as in the last form. (*Lyon* v. *Holt*, 5 M. & W. 250; *Parks* v. *Edge*, 1 C. & M. 429; but see *Boydell* v. *Harkness*, 3 C. B. 168.) Where a bill is drawn or accepted, payable at a particular place, the drawer or indorser can only be rendered liable upon presentment and dishonour at that place. (*Gibb* v. *Mather*, 8 Bing. 214; *Saul* v. *Jones*, 1 E. & E. 59; 28 L. J. Q. B. 37.) A general acceptance of a bill drawn payable at a particular place renders the acceptor generally liable by force of the statute 1 & 2 Geo. IV. c. 78; *ante*, p. 89; but does not enlarge or alter the liability of the drawer or indorser. (*Ib.*; *Fayle* v. *Bird*, 6 B. & C. 531.) A qualified acceptance of a bill drawn generally, qualifies the liability of the drawer to the same extent, so that the bill must be presented according to the acceptance in order to charge the drawer (*Shelton* v. *Braithwaite*, 8 M. & W. 252); and so also with the indorser. (*Saul* v. *Jones*, *supra*.) An indorsement payable at a banker's does not constitute the banker agent to receive notice of dishonour. (*Re Leeds Banking Company*, L. R. 1 Eq. 1; 35 L. J. Ch. 33.) A bill must be presented at a banker's within business hours; in other cases at a reasonable hour. (*Wilkins* v. *Jadis*, 2 B. & Ad. 188; *Parker* v. *Gordon*, 7 East, 385; *Barclay* v. *Bailey*, 2 Camp. 527; *Bank of Van Diemen's Land* v. *Bank of Victoria*, L. R. 3 P. C. 526; 40 L. J. P. C. 28.)

(*k*) Notice of dishonour is necessary because it is a matter within the peculiar knowledge of the holder of the bill; and it must be given immediately for two reasons; first, because the person entitled to it may have effects in the hands of the parties dishonouring the bill, which he may wish to withdraw; secondly, because he may have a remedy upon the bill against other parties arising upon the dishonour which he may wish to enforce. (See authorities cited in notes to *Bickerdike* v. *Bollman*, 2 Smith's L. C. 6th ed. 52; where see also

6. The defendant had not at any time any reasonable ground to expect that the said G. H. would have any such effects, or would pay the said bill.

7. There never was any value or consideration for the payment of the said bill by the said G. H.

8. The defendant has not sustained any damage by reason of not having notice of the dishonour of the said bill.

9. The defendant has not paid the said bill.

By Payee against Drawer, for default of Payment, excusing Presentment because the Drawee could not be found.

1. The defendant by his bill of exchange bearing date the —— of ——, 18—, now overdue, directed to G. H., required the said G. H. to pay to the plaintiff, —— months after date, the sum of £——.

2. The defendant delivered the said bill to the plaintiff.

3. When the said bill became due the plaintiff made diligent search and inquiry for the said G. H., in order to present the said bill to him for payment.

---

what excuses for want of notice of dishonour are sufficient, as showing that the defendant has not been damnified by the want of notice in either of the above respects.) In all cases where notice of dishonour is excused or dispensed with, the matter of excuse or dispensation is a material fact and must be averred (O. XIX. rr. 2, 4). See under former practice to same effect, *Burgh* v. *Legge*, 5 M. & W. 418; *Allen* v. *Edmundson*, 2 Ex. 719; and see *Rabey* v. *Gilbert*, 6 H. & N. 536, 538; 30 L. J. Ex. 170, 172.

The facts above pleaded form a good excuse for default in notice of dishonour, or in presentment as against the drawer of the bill, but not as against an indorser who has no notice of the facts. (*Saul* v. *Jones*, 1 E. & E. 59; 28 L. J. Q. B. 37.) A delay in giving notice of dishonour, unavoidable or reasonable under the circumstances of the particular case, need not be excused, but may be averred as due notice of dishonour. (*Firth* v. *Thrush*, 8 B. & C. 387; *Lundie* v. *Robertson*, 7 East, 231.) As to reasonable time within which notice of dishonour can be given, see *Gladwell* v. *Turner*, L. R. 5 Ex. 59. A promise to pay or acknowledgment of liability on the bill is a waiver of notice. (*Woods* v. *Dean*, 3 B. & S. 101; 32 L. J. Q. B. 1; and see *Cordery* v. *Colvin*, 14 C. B. N. S. 374; 32 L. J. C. P. 210.) Such an acknowledgment made by the defendant to a party to the bill other than the plaintiff, may be used by the plaintiff as evidence of notice of dishonour or waiver of such notice (*Potter* v. *Rayworth*, 13 East, 417); as where the defendant suffered judgment by default in a prior action brought against him on the same bill, by a different holder. (*Rabey* v. *Gilbert*, 6 H. & N. 536; 30 L. J. Ex. 170.)

4. The said G. H. could not be found, nor could his place of abode be discovered.
5. The said G. H. did not pay the said bill.
6. The defendant had due notice of the facts stated in the above 3rd, 4th, and 5th paragraphs.
7. The defendant has not paid the said bill.

By Payee against Drawer, for default of Payment, where the Drawee was dead, and no Executor or Administrator was appointed at the time the Bill became due.

1. and 2. [*The same as in paragraphs* 1 *and* 2 *of the last preceding form.*]
3. After the drawing of the said bill, and before the same became due, the said G. H. died.
4. When the said bill became due, no person had become executor of any will of the said G. H., or administrator of his estate or effects.
5. The said bill was duly presented for payment at the last place of abode of the said G. H.
6. The said bill has not been paid.
7. The defendant had due notice of the facts stated the above 3rd, 4th, 5th, and 6th paragraphs.
8. The defendant has not paid the said bill.

By Payee against Drawer, for default of Payment alleging Notice of Dishonour, and also as an alternative case facts excusing Notice of Dishonour.

[*Proceed as in the first five paragraphs of the form above for Payee against Drawer for default of Payment,* p. 92, *and continue as follows :*—]

6. If, however (which the plaintiff does not admit), the defendant had not due notice of the dishonour of the said bill the defendant excused such notice by [*state the facts relied on.*]
7. The defendant has not paid the said bill.

By Payee against Drawer, for default of Payment, where the Defendant dispensed with Presentment.

1. and 2. [*The same as in paragraphs* 1 *and* 2 *of the form above for Payee against Drawer for default of Payment.*]
3. When the said bill became due the defendant re-

quested the plaintiff not to present it to the said G. H. for payment, and discharged the plaintiff from so presenting it.

4. The said G. H. has not paid the said bill.

5. The defendant had notice of the non-payment of the said bill by the said G. H.

6. The defendant has not paid the said bill.

By Indorsee against Drawer, for default of Payment, on a Bill payable to the Drawer or Order.

1. The defendant by his bill of exchange, bearing date the —— of ——, 18—, now overdue, directed to G. H., required the said G. H. to pay to the defendant or order, —— months after date, the sum of £——.

2. The defendant indorsed the said bill to J. K.

3. The said J. K. indorsed the said bill to the plaintiff.

4. The said bill was duly presented for payment.

5. The said bill was dishonoured.

6. The defendant had due notice of the said dishonour of the said bill.

7. The defendant has not paid the said bill.

By Indorsee against Drawer, for default of Payment, on a Bill payable to a third Party or Order.

1. The defendant, by his bill of exchange, bearing date the —— of ——, 18—, now overdue, directed to G. H., required the said G. H. to pay to J. K. or order, —— months after date, the sum of £—.

2. The said J. K. indorsed the said bill to L. M.

3. The said L. M. indorsed the said bill to the plaintiff.

4. [*Continue with paragraphs* 4, 5, 6, *and* 7 *as in last preceding form.*]

By Indorsee against Indorser, for default of Acceptance (*l*).

1. G. H., by his bill of exchange bearing date the —— of ——, 18—, now overdue, directed to J. K.,

---

(*l*) As to striking out intermediate indorsements, see *ante*, p. 91. The indorser of a bill guarantees the acceptance of the bill, and the payment of it by the acceptor at maturity, and so far is in the same position as the drawer. (*Penny* v. *Innes*, 1 C. M. & R. 439; *Matthews* v. *Bloxsome*, 33 L. J. Q. B. 209.)

required the said J. K. to pay to the said G. H., or order, —— months after date, the sum of £——.

2. The said G. H. indorsed the said bill to the defendant.

3. The defendant indorsed the said bill to the plaintiff.

4. The said bill was duly presented for acceptance.

5. The said J. K. did not accept the said bill, and the said bill was dishonoured.

6. The defendant had due notice of the said non-acceptance and dishonour of the said bill.

7. The defendant has not paid the said bill.

By Executor or Administrator of Drawer against Acceptor.

1. The plaintiff is the executor of the last will and testament of C. D., deceased [*or*, the administrator of the personal estate and effects which were of C. D., deceased, who died intestate; *as the case may be*].

2. The said C. D. in his lifetime, by his bill of exchange, bearing date the —— of ——18—, now overdue, directed to the defendant, required the defendant to pay to the said C. D. —— months after date the sum of £——.

3. The defendant then accepted the said bill.

4. The defendant has not paid the same.

By Executor or Administrator of Payee against Acceptor.

1. [*The same as in the last preceding form.*]

2. In the lifetime of the said C. D., J. K., by his bill of exchange, bearing date the —— of ——, 18—, now overdue, directed to the defendant, required the defendant to pay to the said C. D., —— months after date, the sum of £——.

3. The said J. K. delivered the said bill to the said C. D. in his lifetime.

4. The defendant then accepted the said bill.

5. The defendant has not paid the said bill.

By Executor or Administrator of Indorsee against Acceptor.

1. [*The same as in the two preceding forms.*]

2. In the lifetime of the said C. D., J. K., by his bill

of exchange, bearing date the —— of ——, 18—, now overdue, directed to the defendant, required the defendant to pay to the said J. K., or order, —— months after date, the sum of £——.

3. The defendant then accepted the said bill.

4. The said J. K. indorsed the same to the said C. D. in his lifetime.

5. The defendant has not paid the said bill.

By Drawer against Executor or Administrator of Acceptor.

1. The defendant is the executor of the last will and testament of G. H., deceased [*or*, the administrator of the personal estate and effects which were of G. H., deceased, who died intestate ; *as the case may be*].

2. In the lifetime of the said G. H., the plaintiff, by his bill of exchange, bearing date the —— of ——, 18—, now overdue, directed to the said G. H., required the said G. H. to pay to the plaintiff, —— months after date, the sum of £——.

3. The said G. H. then accepted the said bill.

4. The said bill has not been paid.

By Indorsee of Executor of Drawer against Acceptor.

1. G. H., by his bill of exchange, bearing date the —— of ——, 18—, now overdue, directed to the defendant, required the defendant to pay to the said G. H., or order, —— months after date the sum of £——.

2. The defendant accepted the said bill.

3. The said G. H. afterwards died, having first duly made his will and appointed J. K. executor thereof.

4. Afterwards the said J. K., as and being such executor, indorsed the said bill to the plaintiff.

5. The defendant has not paid the said bill.

By Indorsee of Administrator of Drawer against Acceptor.

1 and 2. [*The same as in last preceding form.*]

3. The said G. H. afterwards died intestate, and thereupon administration of the personal estate and effects which were of the said G. H. at the time of his death, was duly granted to J. K.

4. Afterwards the said J. K., as and being such administrator, indorsed the said bill to the plaintiff.

5. The defendant has not paid the said bill.

By Trustee of a Bankrupt Drawer against Acceptor.

1. The plaintiff is the duly appointed trustee of the property of E. F., who was adjudicated bankrupt in the London Bankruptcy Court [*or as the case may be,*] on the —— of ——, 18—.

2. The said E. F., on the —— of ——, 18—, before he became a bankrupt, by his bill of exchange, now overdue, directed to the defendant, required the defendant to pay to the said E. F., —— months after date, the sum of £——.

3. The defendant then accepted the said bill.

4. The defendant has not paid the said bill.

By Husband and Wife on a Bill drawn by her before Marriage against Acceptor (*m*).

1. The plaintiff C. is the wife of the plaintiff A. B.

2. The plaintiff C., whilst she was unmarried, by her bill of exchange, bearing date the —— of ——, 18—, now overdue, directed to the defendant, required the

---

(*m*) When a non-negotiable bill or note is given to a single woman and she marries, the husband and wife must join in the action, but it would seem that a husband may sue alone in his own name on a bill or note made payable to his wife or order before the marriage, although the bill or note is not indorsed by her. (*McNeilage* v. *Holloway*, 1 B. & Ald. 218; and see Byles on Bills, 12th ed. p. 65.) In cases not within the "Married Women's Property Act, 1870," (33 & 34 Vict. c. 93,) which see *post*, "*Husband and Wife*," a husband may sue alone on a promissory note made payable to his wife during the marriage (*Burrough* v. *Moss*, 10 B. & C. 558), or may join with his wife in suing (*Philliskirk* v. *Pluckwell*, 2 M. & S. 393). A bill or note made payable to a wife survives to her on the death of her husband, if he has not previously reduced it into possession. (*Gaters* v. *Madeley*, 6 M. & W. 423; *Howard* v. *Oakes*, 3 Ex. 136); and in case of her dying before her husband without his having reduced it into possession, passes to her administrator, and her husband cannot sue upon the bill except in that character. (*Hart* v. *Stephens*, 6 Q. B. 937.)

As to reduction into possession, see "*Husband and Wife*," *post*, p. 201.

defendant to pay to her, —— months after date, the sum of £——.

3. The defendant then accepted the said bill.
4. The defendant has not paid the said bill.

By Drawer against Husband and Wife on a Bill accepted by her before Marriage (*n*).

1. The defendant G. is the wife of the defendant, E. F.
2. On the 30th April, 1879, whilst the defendant G. was unmarried, the plaintiff, by his bill of exchange, now overdue, directed to the defendant G., required the defendant G. to pay to the plaintiff, —— months after date, the sum of £——.
3. The defendant G. then accepted the said bill.
4. The said bill has not been paid.

By a surviving Drawer against Acceptor.

1. The plaintiff and G. H., since deceased, by their bill of exchange, bearing date the —— of ——, 18—, now overdue, required the defendant to pay to the plaintiff and the said G. H., —— months after date, the sum of £——.
2. The defendant accepted the said bill.
3. The defendant has not paid the same.

II. Foreign Bills of Exchange (*a*).

By Drawer against Acceptor.

1. The plaintiff by his foreign bill of exchange, bearing date the —— of —— 18—, now overdue, drawn

---

(*n*) If a single woman has rendered herself liable on a bill or note, and has afterwards married, the husband and wife must be sued jointly on the bill or note (*Hancocks* v. *Lablache*, 3 C. P. D. 197 ; 47 L. J. C. P. 514), and in cases within the "Married Women's Property Act (1870) Amendment Act (1874)," (37 & 38 Vict. c. 50), the husband is responsible to the extent of the assets specified in s. 5 of that Act.

See "*Husband and Wife*," *post*, p. 196.

(*a*) A foreign bill of exchange, as distinguished from an inland bill, is one which is drawn or payable out of the United Kingdom. As to foreign bills, see Byles on Bills, 13th ed., 397, *et seq.;* and see the Mercantile Law Amendment Act, 1856 (19 & 20 Vict., c. 97), s. 7.

at Paris, in France, directed to the defendant, required the defendant to pay to the plaintiff —— months after date [*if the bill was drawn in a set or parts add* that his first of exchange (second and third not paid)] —— francs, a sum amounting to £—— (*b*).

2. The defendant accepted the said bill.

3. The defendant has not paid the said bill.

By Payer supra protest for honour of Drawer against Acceptor.

1. G. H. by his foreign bill of exchange, bearing date the —— of ——, 18—, now overdue, drawn at Paris, in France, directed to the defendant, required the defendant to pay to J. K. or order —— months after date —— francs, a sum amounting to £——.

2. The defendant accepted the said bill.

3. The said J. K. indorsed the said bill to L. M.

4. The said L. M. indorsed the said bill to N. O.

It is necessary to show in the statement of claim that the bill is a foreign bill, as otherwise the presumption is that it is an inland bill. (*Armani* v. *Castrique*, 13 M. & W. 443.)

The bill may be stated in English, as above, although it is in a foreign language. (*Atty.-Gen.* v. *Valabreque*, 1 Wightw., p. 9.)

The drawer of a dishonoured foreign bill may recover as damages from the acceptor, not only the amount of the bill and interest, but also all such expenses as may have been necessarily caused by the dishonour (*Prehn* v. *The Royal Bank of Liverpool*, L. R. 5 Ex. 92; 39 L. J. Ex. 41), including the expenses of re-exchange, if any. (*In re General South American Co.*, 7 Ch. D. 637; 47 L. J. Ch. 67; *Willans* v. *Ayers*, 3 App. Cas. 133; 47 L. J. P. C. 1.)

Such expenses, if sought to be recovered, must be stated as special damage. See form as to expenses of noting and protesting, *ante*, p. 86. Interest on foreign bills is calculated according to the rate at the place where they are drawn, accepted, or indorsed, as the case may be, according to the liability of the party sued. (*Allen* v. *Kemble*, 6 Moore, P. C. 314; *Gibbs* v. *Fremont*, 9 Ex. 25; and see *ante*, p. 87.)

Foreign bills drawn or negotiated within the United Kingdom must be stamped under 33 & 34 Vict., c. 97, s. 51. By s. 52 of that Act bills and notes purporting to be drawn or made out of the United Kingdom are, for the purposes of the Act, to be deemed to have been so drawn or made, although in fact drawn or made within the United Kingdom. See, further, Chitty on Bills, 11th ed., p. 78.

(*b*) When a bill is drawn in parts all the set constitute but one bill. (Byles on Bills, 13th ed. 394.) The legal holder of the bill is entitled to the possession of all the sets, but he cannot sue a previous indorser for them unless they came to the possession of the latter. (*Pinard* v. *Klockmann*, 3 B. & S. 388; 32 L. J. Q. B. 82.)

5. The said bill was duly presented to the defendant for payment.

6. The said bill was dishonoured.

7. The said bill was duly protested for non-payment.

8. Afterwards the plaintiff, according to the custom of merchants, for the honour of the said drawer, upon protest duly made in that behalf, paid to the last-mentioned indorsee, then being the holder of the said bill, the amount of the said bill, together with certain reasonable and necessary charges of and attending the said presentment and protest, amounting to £——.

9. The defendant had due notice of all the above-mentioned facts.

10. The defendant has not paid the said bill, or the said money so paid by the plaintiff, or any part thereof.

By Payee against Acceptor supra Protest (*c*).

1. G. H. by his foreign bill of exchange, bearing date the —— of ——, 18—, now overdue, drawn at Paris, in France, and directed to J. K., required the said J. K. to pay to the plaintiff —— months after date, —— francs, a sum amounting to £——.

2. G. H. delivered the said bill to the plaintiff.

3. The said bill was duly presented to the said J. K. for acceptance.

4. The said J. K. refused to accept the said bill.

5. The said bill was thereupon duly protested for the non-acceptance thereof.

6. The defendant had due notice of the above-mentioned facts.

7. Afterwards the defendant accepted the said bill under the said protest.

8. When the said bill became due it was duly presented to the said J. K. for payment.

9. The said J. K. did not pay the said bill.

10. The said bill was thereupon duly protested for the non-payment thereof.

11. The defendant had due notice of the facts mentioned in the last three paragraphs.

12. The defendant has not paid the said bill.

(*c*) To support this action, a protest for non-acceptance and also a protest for non-payment are necessary. (*Hoare* v. *Cazenove*, 16 East, 391; *Williams* v. *Germaine*, 7 B. & C. 468.)

By Indorsee against Acceptor on a Foreign Bill payable at Usances (d).

1. G. H. by his foreign bill of exchange, bearing date the —— of ——, 18—, now overdue, drawn at Vienna, in Austria, and directed to the defendant, required the defendant to pay to J. K., or order, at —— usances, that is to say, at —— months after the date of the said bill, —— thalers, a sum amounting to £——.

2. The said J. K. indorsed the said bill to the plaintiff.

3. The defendant accepted the said bill.

4. The defendant has not paid the said bill.

By Payee against Drawer for default of Acceptance (e).

1. The defendant by his foreign bill of exchange, drawn at Paris, in France, on the 19th January, 1879, and directed to G. H., required the said G. H. to pay to the plaintiff —— months after date, —— francs, a sum amounting to £——.

2. The defendant delivered the said bill to the plaintiff.

3. The said bill was duly presented for acceptance.

4. The said bill was dishonoured.

5. Thereupon the said bill was duly protested for the non-acceptance thereof.

6. The defendant had due notice of the facts mentioned in the last three paragraphs.

7. The defendant has not paid the said bill.

8. By reason of the premises, the plaintiff incurred expenses amounting to £——, in and about the presenting, noting, protesting, and re-exchange of the said bill, and incidental to the dishonour thereof.

(d) See a list of usances between different places, (Byles on Bills, 13th ed., 209; Chitty on Bills, 11th ed., 260.) The length of the usance should be alleged in the statement of claim. (Chitty on Bills, 11th ed., 263.)

(e) The transferor for value of a bill warrants to the transferee that the bill shall be accepted by the drawee, and, having been accepted, shall, on being presented at the time it becomes due, be paid. The liability of the transferor is, therefore, to be measured by that of the acceptor, whose surety he is; and as the obligations of the acceptor are determined by the *lex loci* of performance, so also must be those of the surety. (*Rouquette* v. *Overmann*, L. R. 10 Q.B. 525; 44 L. J. Q. B. 221.)

By Indorsee against Drawer, for default of Payment.

1. The defendant by his foreign bill of exchange, bearing date the —— of ——, 18—, now overdue, drawn at Paris, in France, and directed to G. H., required the said G. H. to pay to the defendant, or order, —— months after date —— francs, a sum amounting to £——.

2. The defendant indorsed the said bill to the plaintiff.

3. The said bill was duly presented for payment.

4. The said bill was dishonoured.

5. The said bill was thereupon duly protested for the non-payment thereof (*f*).

6. The defendant had due notice of the above-mentioned presentment and dishonour of the said bill.

7. The defendant has not paid the said bill.

A statement of Claim by Indorsee against Indorser can be framed from the above forms (*g*).

III. Bankers' Cheques (*a*).

By Payee of Cheque against Drawer.

1. The defendant on the 10th of June, 1879, by his cheque, or order for the payment of money, directed to

---

(*f*) Protest seems to be unnecessary in the case of a foreign promissory note. (Chalmers on Bills, p. 138 ; *Bonar* v. *Mitchell*, 5 Ex. 415.)

(*g*) The drawer or indorser of a foreign bill, drawn or indorsed in England, and payable abroad, is liable for the re-exchange, that is the value of the foreign money at the rate of exchange on the day of dishonour, with interest and expenses ; and evidence of a custom of merchants for the holder to have the option of recovering the sum he gave for the bill in England was held inadmissible, as being inconsistent with the bill. (*Suse* v. *Pompe*, 8 C. B. N. S. 538 ; 30 L. J. C. P. 75.)

(*a*) The cheque should be presented within a reasonable time, after which time the bearer holds it at his own risk against the insolvency of the banker. The day after the receipt of the cheque, if received at the town in which it is payable, is held to be the reasonable time given to the bearer for presentment ; but if no loss is occasioned by holding it, the drawer remains liable for any length of time within six years. (*Alexander* v. *Burchfield*, 7 M. & G. 1061 ; *Robinson* v. *Hawksford*, 9 Q. B. 52 ; *Laws* v. *Rand*, 3 C. B. N. S. 442 ; 27 L. J. C. P. 76 ; *Bailey* v. *Bodenham*, 16 C. B. N. S. 288 ; 33 L. J. C. P. 252.) Where the cheque is payable at a distance from the place at which it is received a further time would be in general reasonable. (*Rickford* v. *Ridge*, 2 Camp. 537 ; *Hare* v. *Henty*, 10

Messrs. G. H. & Co., bankers, required them to pay to the plaintiff, or bearer, £——, and delivered the said cheque to the plaintiff.

2. The said cheque was duly presented for payment on the 11th of June, 1879.

3. The said cheque was dishonoured.

4. The defendant had due notice of the said presentment and dishonour.

5. The defendant has not paid the said cheque.

For Statement of Claim on a Cheque excusing notice of dishonour, on the ground that the drawer had no effects in the hands of the drawee, see p. 93, *ante, and under old practice, Kemble* v. *Mills*, 1 M. & G. 757

By Bearer or Indorsee of Cheque against Drawer.

1. The defendant on the 10th of June, 1879, by his cheque, or order for the payment of money, directed to Messrs. G. H. & Co., bankers, required them to pay J. K., or bearer [*or* order] £——, and the plaintiff became the bearer of the said cheque [*or*, and the said J. K. indorsed the said cheque to the plaintiff].

2. [*Continue with paragraphs* 2, 3, 4, *and* 5, *as in the form of payee of cheque against drawer.*]

A like Form, Gattie v. *Fry*, 36 L. T. 182.

By Indorsee of Cheque against Indorser (*b*).

1. G. H. on the 10th of June, 1879, by his cheque, or order for the payment of money, directed to Messrs. J.

C. B. N. S. 65; 30 L. J. C. P. 302; *Prideaux* v. *Criddle*, L. R. 4 Q. B. 455; 38 L. J. Q. B. 232; *Heywood* v. *Pickering*, L. R. 9 Q. B. 428; 43 L. J. Q. B. 145.) A cheque may be presented by sending it to the drawees by post. (*Bailey* v. *Bodenham*, *supra*; *Prideaux* v. *Criddle*, *supra*; *Heywood* v. *Pickering*, *supra*.) See further Roscoe, N. P. Ev. 14th ed. p. 377.

A post-dated cheque payable "to order," on demand is valid, and available even by a person who took it with notice that it was post-dated. (*Bull* v. *O'Sullivan*, L. R. 6 Q. B. 209; 40 L. J. Q. B. 141.) So, too, is a post-dated cheque payable "to bearer" on demand. (*Gatty* v. *Fry*, 2 Ex. D. 265; 46 L. J. Ex. 605.)

(*b*) Cheques are transferable and negotiable instruments, and although a cheque may be drawn payable "to bearer," it may be indorsed so as to make the indorser liable. (*Keene* v. *Beard*, 8 C. B. N. S. 372; 29 L. J. C. P. 287; see also *Currie* v. *Misa*, L. R. 10 Ex. 153; 1 App. Cas. 554; 44 L. J. Ex. 94; 45 L. J. H. L. 852.)

K. & Co., bankers, required them to pay to L. M. [or order] £——.

2. The said L. M. indorsed the said cheque to the defendant.

3. The defendant indorsed the said cheque to the plaintiff.

[*Proceed as in paragraphs* 2, 3, 4, *and* 5, *of form of payee of cheque against drawer.*]

By Bearer of a Crossed Cheque against Drawer (c).

1. The defendant on the 10th of June, 1879, by his

(c) By "The Crossed Cheques Act, 1876" (39 & 40 Vict. c. 81), the 19 & 20 Vict. c. 25, and the 21 & 22 Vict. c. 79, which related to crossed cheques, are repealed, and the law as to crossed cheques is considerably altered and extended. By s. 4 of the Crossed Cheques Act, 1876, "Where a cheque bears across its face an addition of the words '*and company,*' or any abbreviation thereof, between two parallel transverse lines, or of two parallel transverse lines simply, and either with or without the words 'not negotiable,' that addition shall be deemed a crossing, and the cheque shall be deemed to be crossed generally."

"Where a cheque bears across its face an addition of the name of a banker, either with or without the words '*not negotiable,*' that addition shall be deemed a crossing, and the cheque shall be deemed to be crossed specially, and to be crossed to that banker."

By s. 5.—"Where a cheque is uncrossed, a lawful holder may cross it generally or specially."

"Where a cheque is crossed generally, a lawful holder may cross it specially."

"Where a cheque is crossed generally or specially, a lawful holder may add the words, '*not negotiable.*'"

"Where a cheque is crossed specially, the banker to whom it is crossed may again cross it specially to another banker, his agent for collection."

By s. 6.—"A crossing authorized by this Act shall be deemed a material part of the cheque, and it shall not be lawful for any person to obliterate or, except as authorized by this Act, to add to or alter the crossing."

See ss. 7, 8, 9, 10, 11, and 12 of the Act, *ante*, p. 76.

The effect of adding the words "*not negotiable*" on a cheque is that whereas prior to the Crossed Cheques Act, 1876, the law merchant gave to the *bonâ fide* holder of a negotiable instrument a title which previous holders might not possess, now the principle of "*Nemo dat quod non habet,*" applies to the transfer of cheques bearing those words.

Cheques are included under the term, "Bill of Exchange," in the Stamp Act, 1870 (33 & 34 Vict., c. 97, s. 48), and when payable on demand they are, whether post-dated or otherwise, admissible in evidence with only a penny stamp. (*Bull* v. *O'Sullivan*, *supra*; *Gatty* v. *Fry*, *supra.*)

See "*Bankers,*" *ante*, p. 76.

cheque, or order for the payment of money, directed to Messrs. G. H. & Co., bankers, required them to pay to J. K., or bearer, £——.

2. The said cheque before presentment for payment was duly crossed with the name of Messrs. L. M. & Co., bankers [*or*, with the words, "and Company," *or* an abbreviation of the words "and Company," between two parallel transverse lines, *or* with two parallel transverse lines simply], and the plaintiff afterwards became the bearer of the said cheque.

3. The said cheque was duly presented by the said Messrs. L. M. & Co., bankers [*or*, by a banker], for payment.

[*Proceed as in paragraphs* 3, 4, *and* 5, *of form of payee of cheque against drawer.*]

IV. Promissory Notes.

Statement of Claim by Payee against Maker.

Form No. 22 *in App.* (*C.*) *to Jud. Act*, 1875.

1. The defendant, on the —— day of ——, made his promissory note, whereby he promised to pay to the plaintiff or his order £—— three months after date.

2. The note became due on the —— day of —— 1874, and the defendant has not paid it.

The plaintiff claims:—

The amount of the note and interest thereon to judgment.

A like Form.

1. The defendant by his promissory note, bearing date the —— of ——, 18—, now overdue, promised to pay to the plaintiff, —— months after date, the sum of £——.

2. The defendant has not paid the same.

By Payee against Maker on a Note payable on Demand (*a*).

1. The defendant, on the —— of ——, 18—, by his promissory note promised to pay to the plaintiff on demand the sum of £——.

2. The defendant has not paid the same.

(*a*) A note payable on demand is a present debt, and is due and payable at once without demand; and the Statute of Limitations runs from the date of the note. (*Norton* v. *Ellam*, 2 M. & W. 461;

Payee against Maker on a Note payable after Notice (*b*).

1. The defendant, on the 4th of April, 1879, by his promissory note promised to pay to the plaintiff, three months after notice, the sum of £——.

2. On the 20th of May, 1879, the plaintiff gave notice to the defendant to pay the said note three months after the said notice.

3. The time for payment of the said note elapsed before the commencement of this action.

4. The defendant has not paid the said note.

By Payee against Maker on a Note made payable at a particular Place in the body of it (*c*).

1. The defendant by his promissory note, bearing date the —— of ——, 18—, now overdue, promised to pay to the plaintiff, at Messieurs G. H. & Co.'s, Lombard-street, London, —— months after date, the sum of £——.

2. The said note was duly presented at Messieurs G. H. & Co.'s, Lombard-street, London, aforesaid.

3. The said note has not been paid.

Byles on Bills, 12th ed. 345.) But where such a note, accompanied by a written memorandum, was given as security for an account with a banker, it was held that the Statute of Limitations did not begin to run upon it until a balance was struck and a claim made. (*Hartland* v. *Jukes*, 1 H. & C. 667; 32 L. J. Ex. 162: but see *Watkins* v. *Figg*, 11 W. R. 258.) Such a note is not considered as overdue, so as to affect an indorsee with its equities. (*Brooks* v. *Mitchell*, 9 M. & W. 15.)

Promissory notes purporting to be payable *at sight*, or on presentation, are now, by the Bills of Exchange Act, 1871 (34 & 35 Vict. c. 74), s. 2, equivalent in all respects to promissory notes payable on demand.

(*b*) In this case notice must be given; so where a note is payable *after sight*, a presentment for sight is necessary. (*Dixon* v. *Nuttall*, 1 C. M. & R. 307.) So too, where a note is payable *after demand*, a demand is necessary. (*Re Rutherford*, 14 Ch. D. 687; 49 L. J. Ch. 654.)

(*c*) The presentment at the specified place is necessary, and must be averred. (*Spindler* v. *Grellett*, 1 Ex. 384; *Emblin* v. *Dartnell*, 12 M. & W. 830; *Sanderson* v. *Bowes*, 14 East, 500.) A memorandum of the place of payment in the margin or foot of the note has not the same restrictive effect. (*Exon* v. *Russell*, 4 M. & S. 505; *Williams* v. *Waring*, 10 B. & C. 2; *Price* v. *Mitchell*, 4 Camp. 200.) It is not sufficient excuse of presentment that the defendant has absconded and not left any effects at the place specified. (*Sands* v. *Clarke*, 8 C. B. 751.)

Payee against Maker on a Note payable by Instalments (*d*).

1. The defendant by his promissory note, bearing date the 1st of January, 1879, promised to pay to the plaintiff the sum of £100 in manner following; namely, £30 on the 1st Feb., 1879, £30 on the 1st March, and the remainder of the said sum on the 1st April respectively in the year aforesaid.

2. All the periods for payment [*or* the periods for payment of the said first and second instalments *as the case may be*] elapsed before the commencement of this action.

3. The defendant did not pay the said note or any part thereof [*or*, did not pay the said instalments or either of them.]

By Payee against Maker on a Note payable by Instalments in which the whole sum is made payable on any Default.

1. The defendant, on the 9th of Feb., 1879, by his promissory note, promised to pay to the plaintiff the sum of £300 in manner following; namely, £50 on the 1st of May then next ensuing, and £50 on the 1st day of each succeeding month until the whole of the said sum should be fully paid, and further by his said note promised that in case default should be made in payment of any of the said instalments, the whole of the said sum of £300 remaining unpaid at the time of such default should become immediately payable.

2. The defendant made default in payment of the first of the said instalments.

3. The defendant has not paid the whole of the said sum of £300 or any part thereof.

By Bearer against Maker on a Note payable to Bearer (*e*).

1. The defendant by his promissory note, bearing date the —— of ——, 18—, now overdue, promised to pay

---

(*d*) A note payable by instalments is assignable within the statute 3 & 4 Anne, c. 8 (c. 9 Ruff.); and the maker is entitled to the days of grace upon the falling due of each instalment. (*Oridge* v. *Sherborne*, 11 M. & W. 374; *Carlon* v. *Kenealy*, 12 M. & W. 139.)

(*e*) A note drawn by the defendant, payable to his own order, is not a negotiable note within the 3 & 4 Anne, c. 8 (c. 9 Ruff.) until it is indorsed. If it is indorsed in blank it becomes a note payable to bearer, and may be so described in the statement of claim. (*Hooper* v. *Williams*, 2 Ex. 13; *Brown* v. *De Winton*, 6 C. B. 336; *Flight* v. *Maclean*, 16 M. & W. 51.)

If specially indorsed it becomes a note payable to the indorsee or order (*Gay* v. *Lander*, 6 C. B. 336), and should be so described.

to G. H., or bearer, —— months after date, the sum of £——.

2. The plaintiff became the bearer of the said note.

3. The defendant has not paid the said note.

By Bearer against Maker on a Country Bank-Note payable in Town or Country.

1. The defendants are bankers carrying on business at Manchester under the style or firm of A. B. & Co.

2. The defendants by their promissory bank-note, bearing date the —— of ——, 18—, promised to pay the bearer thereof on demand £—— at their bank at Manchester, or at Messieurs G. H. & Co.'s, bankers, London.

3. The plaintiff became the bearer of the said note.

4. The said note was duly presented for payment at the defendant's said bank at Manchester [*or*, at the said Messieurs G. H. & Co.'s, bankers, London aforesaid.]

5. The said note has not been paid.

By Indorsee against Maker.

1. The defendant by his promissory note, bearing date the —— of ——, 18—, now overdue, promised to pay to G. H. or order, —— months after date, the sum of £——.

2. The said G. H. indorsed the said note to the plaintiff.

3. The defendant has not paid the said note.

By Indorsee against Payee.

1. G. H. by his promissory note, bearing date the —— of ——, 18—, now overdue, promised to pay to the defendant, or order, —— months after date, the sum of ——.

2. The defendant indorsed the said note to the plaintiff.

3. The said note was duly presented for payment.

4. The said note was dishonoured.

5. The defendant had due notice of the said presentment and dishonour.

6. The defendant has not paid the said note.

As to excuses for notice of dishonour and the mode of averring them, see ante, p. 93.

By Indorsee against Indorser.

1. G. H. by his promissory note, bearing date the —— of ——, 18—, now overdue, promised to pay to J. K. or order, —— months after date, the sum of £——.

2. The said J. K. indorsed the said note to the defendant.

3. [*Proceed as in paragraphs* 2, 3, 4 *and* 5 *of last preceding form.*]

7. The defendant has not paid the said note, and the same remains unpaid.

V. Miscellaneous Statements of Claims relating to Bills.

For the Breach of a Promise to retire a Bill at Maturity in Consideration of a Renewal.

1. On the 5th of May, 1879, the plaintiff accepted and delivered to the defendant a bill of exchange of that date, drawn by the defendant upon the plaintiff, requiring him to pay to the defendant or order, three months after date, the sum of £50.

2. Subsequently the plaintiff desired a renewal of the said bill, and thereupon it was on the 3rd of August, 1879, agreed between the plaintiff and the defendant that the plaintiff should accept and deliver to the defendant a bill of exchange dated the said 3rd of August, 1879, drawn by the defendant upon the plaintiff, requiring him to pay to the defendant or order three months after date the sum of £55, and that the defendant should upon receiving such last-mentioned bill retire the said first-mentioned bill for £50.

3. The plaintiff accordingly accepted and delivered to the defendant, and the defendant received from the plaintiff, the said bill for £55, upon the said terms.

4. The defendant did not upon receiving the said bill for £55, or within a reasonable time in that behalf retire the said bill for £50. The said bill for £50 has not been retired.

5. In consequence of the defendant not retiring the said last-mentioned bill, the plaintiff was obliged to pay to G. H. as and being the indorsee and holder thereof the sum of £50 and £— for interest thereon.

Against a person entrusted with a Bill to Discount for Negotiating the same for his own Use.

1. On the —— of ——, 18—, the plaintiff delivered to the defendant, and the defendant received from the plaintiff, a bill of exchange dated the —— of ——, 18—, drawn by G. H. upon and accepted by the plaintiff, for £——, payable to the order of the said G. H. —— months after date, and indorsed in blank by him, for the purpose and upon the terms of the defendant discounting the said bill for the plaintiff, and paying over to the plaintiff the proceeds of such discounting.

2. The defendant did not discount the said bill for the plaintiff and pay over to him the proceeds of such discounting, although a reasonable time for him so to do elapsed before this action, and the defendant wrongfully negotiated the said bill for his own benefit, and applied to his own use the proceeds thereof.

3. In consequence of the said breaches of contract upon the part of the defendant the plaintiff was deprived of the said proceeds and was afterwards compelled to pay the said bill and £—— interest thereon [*State special damage, if any.*]

For forms of statement of claim on contracts of indemnity relating to Bills of Exchange, see "Indemnities," post, p. 211.

BILLS OF LADING. *See "Shipping," post, p.* 326.

BOARD AND LODGING. *See "Landlord and Tenant," post, p.* 239.

BONDS (*a*).

(*a*) *Bonds.*]—By the common law, the whole penalty of a bond was recoverable upon a breach of the condition. The Court of Chancery, however, gave relief against the judgment at law, upon payment of the amount really due, or the damages arising from the breach of the condition. A power of granting similar relief in certain cases was afterwards given to the Courts of law by statute.

Thus actions upon *common money bonds* are subject to certain provisions of the statute 4 & 5 Anne, c. 3 (c. 16 Ruff.). By s. 12 of that statute, where an action is brought upon any bond which has a condition to make void the same upon payment of a lesser sum at a day or place certain, if the obligor has, before the action brought, paid to the obligee the principal and interest due by the condition of such bond, though such payment was not made strictly according to the condition, yet it may be pleaded in bar of such action, and shall be as effectual a bar thereof as if the money had been paid at the day and place according to the condition, and had been so pleaded. By s. 13, power is given to the defendant, pending the action, to bring into Court the principal and interest due on the bond, with such costs as have been expended in any suit in law or equity upon such bond, in full satisfaction and discharge of the bond; and the Court may give judgment to discharge the defendant from the same accordingly.

Previously to the Common Law Procedure Act, 1860, payment into Court under this section could not be pleaded, but by s. 25 of the Common Law Procedure Act, 1860, it was expressly enacted that payment into Court might be pleaded in any actions on money bonds by leave of the Court or a Judge. And now payment into Court in satisfaction and discharge of the bond is regulated by the Jud. Acts, Ord. XXX., and may be pleaded without leave in the same manner as any other defence.

Bonds with *special conditions* are subject to certain provisions of the statute 8 & 9 Will. III. c. 11. By s. 8 of this statute it is enacted, that in all actions upon any bond, or on any penal sum for non-performance of any covenants or agreements in any deed or writing contained, the plaintiff may assign as many breaches as he shall think fit, and the jury shall assess not only such damages and costs of suit as were before usually done, but also damages for such of the said breaches as the plaintiff shall prove to have been broken; and that the like judgment shall be entered on the verdict as before had been usually done in such actions; and that if judgment shall be given for the plaintiff on demurrer, or by confession, or *nil dicit*, he may suggest upon the roll as many breaches as he shall think fit, upon which shall issue a writ to the sheriff to summon a jury before the justice or justices of assize (or now by the 3 & 4 Will. IV. c. 42, s. 16, before the sheriff), to inquire of the truth of those breaches, and to assess the damages that the plaintiff shall have sustained thereby. The section then provides, that in case the defendant shall pay into Court the damages assessed for the breaches, a stay of execution shall be entered; or if the plaintiff is satisfied by execution, the defendant shall be thereby discharged; but, notwithstanding, in each case the judgment shall remain as a security against any further breaches, upon which the plaintiff may have a *scire facias*. Accordingly the judgment is entered in the usual form for the whole penalty and costs, with the addition, "that the plaintiff have execution against the defendant of the damages aforesaid to £—— by the jury assessed, according to the statute." (See form, Chit. Forms, 11th ed., p. 354.)

The provisions of the 8 & 9 Will. III. c. 11, respecting the assignment and suggestion of breaches, and the judgment for the penalty as a security for further breaches, are not affected by the Common Law Proced. Act, 1852 (see s. 96) or it would seem by the Jud. Acts. (See Roscoe, N. P. Ev. 14th ed. p. 675; Chitty's Forms, 11th ed., pp. 643, 644.) The distinction between common money bonds within the 4 & 5 Anne, c. 3 (c. 16 Ruff.), and bonds with special conditions, within the 8 & 9 Will. III. c. 11, is discussed in the judgment of the Court in *Smith* v. *Bond*, 10 Bing. 125; and see Leake on Contracts, 143, 1083.

Covenants and agreements in writing containing a penal sum for non-performance are regulated by 8 & 9 Will. III. c. 11 (2 Wms. Saund. 1871 ed. p. 541, n. (1), and see, *per* Bramwell, B., *Betts* v. *Burch*, 4 H. & N. 506, 510 ; 28 L. J. Ex. 267, 269 : *Ex parte Capper*, 4 Ch. D. 724 ; 46 L. J. B. 57). So, too, is a bond conditioned for the payment of a sum by instalments. (*Preston* v. *Dania*, L. R. 8 Ex. 19 ; 42 L. J. Ex. 33.)

As to *replevin bonds*, see 19 & 20 Vict. c. 108, ss. 63—70 ; 23 & 24 Vict. c. 126 (C. L. P. Act, 1860), s. 22 ; and 11 Geo. II. c. 19, s. 23.

In suing upon a *common money bond* it was, and would appear still to be sufficient to frame the statement of claim for the penalty without assigning any breach of the condition.

In suing upon a *bond within* the 8 & 9 Will. III. c. 11, there were, before the coming into operation of the Judicature Acts, two courses open to the plaintiff. (2 Wms. Saund. 1871 ed. 541 (1), 544 (*e*) ; *Webb* v. *James*, 8 M. & W. 645.) The count might have been framed for the penalty only, without mentioning the condition or assigning any breach of it ; or the condition might have been set out and breaches of it assigned in the declaration. In the latter case, the statute was complied with at once, and the defendant was able to plead either by denying, or by confessing and avoiding the bond and condition, or the breaches, or both. In the former case, where the count was framed for the penalty only, the defendant might have set out the condition in his plea and averred performance thereof, or any matter in excuse of performance. If he pleaded performance, the performance might, in some cases, have been pleaded generally ; and then it was necessary for the plaintiff, in obedience to the statute, to have assigned in his replication the breaches on which he relied (2 Wms. Saund. 1871 ed. p. 541 (1), 544 (*e*) ; 1 Wms. Saund. 1871 ed. p. 133), or the performance might have been pleaded with particularity according to the terms of the condition ; and then it was sufficient for the plaintiff in his replication to take issue on the performance, or such portion of it as he disputed. (See *Bush* v. *Leake*, 3 Doug. 255 ; *Darbishire* v. *Butler*, 5 Moo. 198; *Turner* v. *McNamara*, 2 Chit. R. 697 ; *Roakes* v. *Manser*, 1 C. B. 531.) If, instead of pleading performance in either form, the defendant pleaded *non est factum*, or some plea in excuse or otherwise, on which the plaintiff took issue, then the plaintiff was obliged, in pursuance of the statute, to *suggest* upon the record, after the joinder of issue, all the breaches upon which he intended to rely. This same course of *suggesting* the breaches was also adopted in the event of his obtaining judgment upon demurrer, or by default, whenever the breaches had not been assigned in the declaration or replication by any of the above means. (*Ethersey* v. *Jackson*, 8 T. R. 255 ; *Homfray* v. *Rigby*, 5 M. & S. 60 ; *Lawes* v. *Shaw*, 5 Q. B. 322 ; *Webb* v. *James*, 8 M. & W. 645.) And the statute in this respect was compulsory, *i. e.*, the plaintiff must either have assigned or suggested breaches, as the case might be, and could only recover damages for the breaches assigned or suggested. (*Roles* v. *Rosewell*, 5 T. R. 538 ; *Hardy* v. *Bern*, 5 T. R. 636 ; *Walcot* v. *Goulding*, 8 T. R. 126 ; *Welch* v. *Ireland*, 6 East, 613.) If the defendant pleaded performance as to part of the condition, and matter of excuse to other part, the plaintiff's proper course was to assign breaches in his replication to the former, and to take issue and to enter a suggestion of breaches as to the latter. (*Webb* v. *James*, 8 M. & W. 645.)

It is now considered the best course in all cases to assign the

On a Bond, without assigning a Breach (*b*).

1. The defendant, by his bond, bearing date the 15th of June, 1879, became bound to the plaintiff in the sum of £100 to be paid by the defendant to the plaintiff.

---

breaches in the statement of claim, because, if not denied specifically, or by necessary implication, or stated not to be admitted by the defendant, they are in general taken to be admitted (O. XIX. r. 17); whereas the breaches, if suggested, must be proved. It is further somewhat open to doubt whether the practice of suggesting breaches is not so inconsistent with the new rules of pleading, as to be no longer admissible. (See Jud. Act, 1873, s. 23; Jud. Act, 1875, ss. 21, 33 (2); and O. XIX. r. 1.)

Before the Common Law Procedure Act, 1852, enabled the defendant to plead several matters by way of rejoinder, there was an advantage in reserving the assignment of breaches to the replication, as the defendant was thereby restricted to a single answer to each breach. At common law the plaintiff could only assign a single breach, whether in the declaration or in the replication, otherwise his pleading was open to the objection of duplicity; because he claimed the same thing, viz., the penalty, in respect of each breach. (*Monser's case*, 2 Co. Rep. 4a; *Cornwallis* v. *Savery*, 2 Burr. 773.) But the above statute, 8 & 9 Will. III. c. 11, enabled him to assign as many breaches as he should think fit.

He cannot assign or suggest any breaches which occurred after action brought, but for these he must proceed by *scire facias* upon the judgment when obtained. (See *Willoughby* v. *Swinton*, 6 East, 550.) And it is important to remark that the plaintiff cannot, on a *scire facias*, suggest any breach which he might have originally assigned or suggested. (2 Wms. Saund. 1871 ed. 546, n. (*f.*)) As to the proceedings by *scire facias* on the judgment to recover damages for further breaches see 2 Chit. Pr. 13th ed. 824; see form, Chit. Forms, 11th ed. p. 651; *Tabor* v. *Edwards*, 4 C. B. N. S. 1; 27 L. J. C. P. 183.

On an inquiry to assess damages upon the suggestion of breaches, the defendant cannot set up any matters in excuse or justification of the breaches; all such matters must be pleaded. (*Abp. Canterbury* v. *Robinson*, 1 C. & M. 690.)

In an action on a bond within this statute conditioned for the payment of an annuity, or the performance of other things, the Court will not stay the proceedings on the payment of the money in arrear and costs, unless the defendant also gives a judgment to secure future breaches. (*Van Sandau* v. ——, 1 B. & Ald. 214; 2 Chit. Pr. 13th ed. 1102.)

The liability of the obligor on the whole is limited to the amount of the penalty. (*Wilde* v. *Clarkson*, 6 T. R. 303; *Branscombe* v. *Scarbrough*, 6 Q. B. 13.)

(*b*) It is not necessary in drawing a statement of claim upon a bond to aver a breach by the non-payment of the money. It is sufficient if the statement of claim states the debt under the bond; and it lies upon the defendant to discharge himself. (*Ashbee* v. *Pidduck*, 1 M. & W. 564.)

The claim at the end of a statement of claim on a bond is the amount of the penalty.

For Claim against an Heir on the Bond of his Ancestor: see " Heir and Devisees," post, p. **196.**

On an Annuity Bond stating the condition and assigning a Breach (*c*).

1. The defendant, by his bond bearing date the 21st of November, 1878, became bound to the plaintiff in the sum of £3,000, to be paid by the defendant to the plaintiff subject to a condition thereunder written, that if the defendant should pay to the plaintiff £25 half-yearly, on the 1st of January and the 1st of July in every year during the life of the plaintiff, the said bond should be void.

2. Afterwards the defendant failed to pay to the plaintiff, and has not paid the half-yearly payment under the said bond which became due on the 1st of July, 1879.

On a Bond with a special Condition, setting out the Condition and assigning Breaches.

1. The defendant by his bond, bearing date the —— of ——, 18—, became bound to the plaintiff in the sum of £——, to be paid by the defendant to the plaintiff, subject to a condition thereunder written, whereby, after reciting that [*here state the material recitals, if any, in the condition,*] the condition of the said bond was declared to be that if [*here state the condition,*] then the said bond should be void.

2. [*Here assign the breach in respect of which the plaintiff seeks to recover damages. If there are several breaches each breach should be stated in a separate paragraph.*]

For like Forms of Statements of Claim, see Croydon Gas Co. v. *Dickinson*, 1 C. P. D. 787 ; *Holme* v. *Brunskill*, 38 L. T. 103 ; 3 Q. P. D. 495.

See for Form of Claim upon a Replevin Bond, Dix v. *Groom*, 5 Ex. D. 91.

(*c*) Annuity bonds are within 8 & 9 Will. III. c. 11. (*Walcot* v. *Goulding*, 8 T. R. 126.

Broker (*a*).

Statement of Claim by a Broker for Commission on a purchase of Shares, and for Repayment of Money paid by him for his Principal in the Purchase of such Shares.

1. The plaintiff is a stock and share broker carrying on business at &c.

2. On or about the —— of ——, 18—, it was agreed [*state how agreed*] between the plaintiff and the defendant·

(*a*) A broker is an agent making it a trade to find purchasers for those who wish to sell goods or shares, and vendors for those who wish to buy, and to negotiate and superintend the making of the bargain between them. (Blackburn, Contract of Sale, adopted by Hannen, J., in *Mollett* v. *Robinson*, L. R. 7 C. P. 97 ; 41 L. J. C. P. 74 ; and see in L. R. 7 H. L. 802 ; 44 L. J. H. L. 362 ; *Baring* v. *Corrie*, 2 B. & Ald. 137 ; Leake on Contracts, 516.)

The employment of a person carrying on business as a broker in a particular trade or market, authorises him, in general, to contract, as to the form and terms of the contract, according to the usages of the trade or market, so far as they are not inconsistent with his employment and position as broker. (*Mollett* v. *Robinson*, L. R. 7 H. L. 802, 836 ; 44 L. J. H. L. 362, 379 ; *Sutton* v. *Tatham*, 10 A. & E. 27 ; *Ireland* v. *Livingston*, L. R. 5 H. L. 407 ; 41 L. J. Q. B. 201 ; and see *Baring* v. *Stanton*, 3 Ch. D. 506, *per* Mellish, L. J. ; and *Grissell* v. *Bristowe*, L. R. 4 C. P. 36 ; 38 L. J. C. P. 10.)

A person employing a broker on the London Stock Exchange authorises him to act according to the rules and usages of the Exchange, and is bound to indemnify against payments made by him under and in compliance with such rules and usages (*Taylor* v. *Stray*, 2 C. B. N. S. 175 ; 26 L. J. C. P. 185 ; *Stray* v. *Russell*, 1 E. & E. 888 ; 29 L. J. Q. B. 118 ; *Smith* v. *Lindo*, 4 C. B. N. S. 395 ; 5 C. B. N. S. 567 ; *Thacker* v. *Hardy*, 4 Q. B. D. 685 ; 48 L. J. Q. B. 289 ; Leake on Contracts, 56, 763, and see *Lacey* v. *Hill*, 43 L. J. Ch. 551 ; L. R. 18 Eq. 182) ; unless the liability to such payments is occasioned by his own misconduct, or default. (*Duncan* v. *Hill*, L. R. 8 Ex. 242 ; 42 L. J. Ex. 179.)

A London broker if not licensed (pursuant to 6 Anne, c. 68 (c. 16, Ruff.), and 33 & 34 Vict. c. 60) cannot recover any commission for work done as a broker, but he may recover for money paid for his employer, at his request, or which he was compelled to pay for him according to the usage of the market. (*Pidgeon* v. *Burslem*, 3 Ex. 465 ; *Jessop* v. *Lutwyche*, 10 Ex. 614 ; *Smith* v. *Lindo*, 4 C. B. N. S. 395 ; 5 *ib.* 587 ; 27 L. J. C. P. 196 ; *ib.* 335 ; *Chapman* v. *Shepherd*, L. R. 2 C. P. 228 ; 36 L. J. C. P. 113.)

It is a usage of the Stock Exchange that a member or jobber buying upon such Exchange may discharge his contract by passing the name of a consenting person as a substituted party to whom the right or liability in respect of such contract attaches, and to whom, if of legal capacity to contract, objection can only be taken within a certain limited time, and if not then taken, the person whose name is so passed is deemed to have been accepted as the

that the plaintiff should purchase for the defendant and pay the price of fifteen shares in the —— Company, and that the defendant should repay to the plaintiff the money expended by him in purchasing the same, and also pay to him commission and reward for such purchase at the rate of [*state rate where practicable*].

3. The plaintiff accordingly purchased the said shares for the defendant, and expended for the defendant in so purchasing the same £——.

4. The said shares were accordingly transferred to the

---

contracting party in lieu of the member. (*Grissell* v. *Bristowe*, L. R. 4 C. P. 36; 38 L. J. C. P. 10; *Coles* v. *Bristowe*, L. R. 4 Ch. Ap. 3; 38 L. J. Ch. 81; *Torrington* v. *Lowe*, L. R. 4 C. P. 26; 38 L. J. C. P. 121; *Maxted* v. *Paine*, L. R. 6 Ex. 132; 40 L. J. Ex. 57; *Bowring* v. *Shepherd*, L. R. 6 Q. B. 309; 40 L. J. Q. B. 129; *Hawkins* v. *Maltby*, L. R. 3 Ch. Ap. 188; 37 L. J. Ch. 58; *Hodgkinson* v. *Kelly*, L. R. 6 Eq. 496; 37 L. J. Ch. 837; *Davis* v. *Haycock*, L. R. 4 Ex. 373; 38 L. J. Ex. 155; and as to persons not of capacity to contract, see *Nickalls* v. *Merry*, L. R. 7 H. L. 530; 45 L. J. Ch. 575; *Heritage* v. *Paine*, 2 Ch. D. 594; 45 L. J. Ch. 285. See further, Roscoe's N. P. Evid., 14th ed. p. 519 *et seq.*)

It is a usage upon the London and Liverpool Stock Exchanges that all members of these Exchanges are regarded *inter se* as principals, and deal with each other upon that footing. (*Taylor* v. *Stray*, 2 C. B. N. S. 175; 26 L. J. C. P. 185; *Bayliffe* v. *Butterworth*, 1 Ex. 425; Roscoe's N. P. Ev., 14th ed. p. 519; and see cases cited, *ante*.)

In some trades and markets there is a usage that a broker who, as broker, buys for a principal without disclosing the name of his principal, is liable to the vendor as though a *del credere* agent, for the price of the goods, in case the buyer does not pay. (*Imperial Bank* v. *London and St. Catherine Docks Co.*, 5 Ch. D. 195, 200; 46 L. J. Ch. 335; *Humfrey* v. *Dale*, 7 E. & B. 266; E. B. & E. 1004; 26 L. J. Q. B. 137; 27 L. J. Q. B. 390; *Fleet* v. *Murton*, L. R. 7 Q. B. 126; 41 L. J. Q. B. 49; *Hutchinson* v. *Tatham*, L. R. 8 C. P. 482; 42 L. J. C. P. 260: and *see* "*Agent*," *ante*, p. 43.)

Wagers as to the present or future price of shares or stocks are not illegal, but are simply void (8 & 9 Vict. c. 109, s. 18); consequently a broker who has at the request of his principal made payments for him upon time bargains, or speculative bargains, as to stocks or shares can recover such payments by action against his principal. (*Jessop* v. *Lutwyche*, 10 Ex. 614; 24 L. J. Ex. 65; *Knight* v. *Cambers*, 15 C. B. 562; 24 L. J. C. P. 121; *Rosewarne* v. *Billing*, 15 C. B. N. S. 316; 33 L. J. C. P. 55; Leake on Contracts, 763.) Such request need not be an express request, it may arise from the employment of the broker to enter into such bargains in such a way that by the usages or rules of the Exchange or market upon which the bargains are made the broker is bound generally to make such payments. (*Thacker* v. *Hardy*, 4 Q. B. D. 685; 48 L. J. Q. B. 289; *Cooper* v. *Neil*, 27 W. R. 159; *Ex pte. Rogers*, 15 Ch. D. 207. See also *Sutton* v. *Tatham*, 10 A. & E. 27.)

See further, notes to "*Agent*," *ante*, p. 36, and Leake on Contracts, 56, 516, 517, 495, 496.

defendant, who accepted the transfer thereof, and became the owner of the said shares.

5. The said sum of £——, and also the sum of £—— as such commission and reward as aforesaid, became due and payable by the defendant to the plaintiff in respect of the matters aforesaid, but the defendant has not paid the above-mentioned sums, or any part of them.

By a Broker to be indemnified by his Principal for Payments made in the course of Dealings upon the London Stock Exchange for his Principal, and for his Commission and Reward.

1. The plaintiff is a broker upon the London Stock Exchange.

2. The defendant employed the plaintiff as such broker to purchase and sell for him upon the London Stock Exchange, in accordance with the rules and usages of the said Stock Exchange for commission and reward, certain stock and shares as follows: [*set forth particulars with dates and items where practicable.*]

3. The plaintiff did accordingly, as directed by the defendant, purchase and sell the said stock and shares for the defendant upon the said Stock Exchange in accordance with the rules and usages thereof.

4. In accordance with such rules and usages the plaintiff was compelled to pay and did in so purchasing as above mentioned pay for the defendant the sum of £—— made up as follows: [*set forth particulars where practicable.*]

5. The commission and reward due to the plaintiff as such broker from the defendant in respect of such purchases and sales amounted to £——, [*where practicable add, made up as follows, and set forth particulars.*]

6. The said sums of £—— and £——became due and payable by the defendant to the plaintiff, but the defendant has not paid the same, or any part thereof.

7. [*Where there has been an account stated, add,* Accounts have been sent in on the —— of ——, 18—, and the —— of —— 18—, by the plaintiff to the defendant showing the above amount of £—— to be due from the defendant to the plaintiff, and the defendant has admitted [*state how admitted*] to the plaintiff his liability to pay that amount to the plaintiff, *or as the case may be*].

Against a Sharebroker for not purchasing according to Order.

1. [*As in form next above*].

2. It was [by letters bearing date the 23rd, the 25th, and 28th of Feb., 1879,] agreed between the plaintiff and the defendant, that the defendant, as and being such broker, should purchase for the plaintiff twenty-five shares in the —— Company, at the then market price of such shares, for commission to the defendant [*state the rate of commission where practicable*].

3. The defendant could then have purchased such shares at the then market price thereof, and a reasonable time for such purchase elapsed.

4. The defendant did not then purchase and has not purchased for the plaintiff the said shares, or any of them.

5. [*State the damage.*]

Carriers (*a*), (*b*), (*c*).

(*a*) An action against a common carrier for not safely carrying is an action for a breach of the common law duty, independent of contract. The entrusting of the goods to the carrier in the way of his business to be carried, or, similarly, the becoming a passenger to be carried, casts a duty on the carrier. (*Pozzi* v. *Shipton*, E. B. & E. 963 ; *Marshall* v. *York, Newcastle, and Berwick Ry. Co.*, 11 C. B. 655 ; *Austin* v. *Great West. Ry. Co.*, L. R. 2 Q. B. 442, 446 ; *Foulkes* v. *Met. Dist. Ry. Co.*, 5 C. P. D. 157 ; 49 L. J. C. P. 361 ; see also *Keys* v. *Belfast, &c., Ry. Co.*, 9 H. L. C. 556 ; 8 Jur. (N. S.) 367.) The law also, from the same fact of employment, implies a contract identical in its terms with the duties so imposed by law. (See *Morgan* v. *Ravey*, 6 H. & N. 265 ; 30 L. J. Ex. 131, 134.) In whichever point of view the transaction is regarded, the duties and liabilities arising from the mere fact of employment may be varied or qualified by lawful terms or stipulations introduced by express agreement. (See *per* Erle, J. *M'Manus* v. *Lancashire and Yorkshire Ry. Co.*, 4 H. & N. 327, 336 ; 28 L. J. Ex. 353.)

(*b*) *Form of Claim.*]—Under the former system of pleading, the declaration in an action against a carrier might in general be framed either upon the contract, charging the injury as a breach of contract, or upon the duty imposed by law, charging the injury as a breach of duty, or wrong.

Statements of claim now consist simply of narrations of facts, consequently in actions against carriers, and the like, it is by no means always easy to say whether the claim is to be regarded as one upon a contract, or in *tort*. (See *Pontifex* v. *Midland Ry. Co.*, 3 Q. B. D. 23, 26 ; 47 L. J. Ex. 2.) The facts in many such cases disclose a cause of action which may be regarded either as arising out of contract, or, in *tort*. See, also, "*Carriers*," *post*, p. 361.

Except for the convenience of classification, and for the purposes of the County Courts Acts as to costs, and the remitting of actions to those Courts, it is unimportant whether an action is to be regarded as in *tort*, or founded on *tort*, or in *contract*, or founded on *contract*. By 30 & 31 Vict. c. 142, s. 5 (which, by Jud. Act, 1873, s. 67, is applied to all actions in the High Court of Justice in which any relief is sought which can be given in a County Court), it is enacted that ". . . . if the plaintiff shall recover a sum not exceeding twenty pounds, if the action is founded on *contract*, or ten pounds, if founded on *tort*, whether by verdict, judgment by default, or on demurrer, or otherwise, he shall not be entitled to any costs of suit unless the Judge certify on the record that there was sufficient reason for bringing such action in such superior Court, or unless the Court or a Judge at Chambers shall by rule or order allow such costs."

In the construing of this enactment as to costs the substance of the matter is to be looked at, not merely the form of pleading. (*Bryant* v. *Herbert*, 3 C. P. D. 389; 47 L. J. C. P. 354; *Fleming* v. *Manchester, Sheffield, and Lincolnshire Ry. Co.*, 4 Q. B. D. 81; *Baylis* v. *Lintott*, L. R. 8 C. P. 345; 42 L. J. C. P. 119; *Pontifex* v. *Midland Ry. Co.*, 3 Q. B. D. 23; 47 L. J. Q. B. 28.) If there is an express contract, and the act complained of is a breach of it, the action is founded on contract, and should in general be regarded as an action of contract; whilst if there is no contract at all, but an unauthorised intermeddling with property, the action is founded on *tort*, and should be regarded as in *tort*. (*Pontifex* v. *Midland Ry. Co., supra.*)

A statement of claim charging the defendant as a common carrier upon the delivery of the goods to him in that capacity imports that he is liable to the duties imposed by the common law as incident to the position of a common carrier.

It is therefore generally advisable not to describe the defendant as a *common* carrier, but to describe him as a carrier merely.

Where a breach of duty is charged, the facts from which the duty arises must be stated. It is not enough merely to allege a duty, without showing facts to support that duty. An allegation of a duty is a mere inference of law, and is of no avail if the facts do not support it. (*Benett* v. *Peninsular and Oriental Steamboat Co.*, 6 C. B. 785; *Gautret* v. *Egerton*, L. R. 2 C. P. 371, 374; *Collis* v. *Selden*, L. R. 3 C. P. 495. And see *per* Maule, J., *Brown* v. *Mallett*, 5 C. B. 599; *Dutton* v. *Powles*, 2 B. & S. 174; 30 L. J. Q. B. 169.)

The terms of the undertaking, employment, or promise, should be stated correctly, with all the exceptions, and qualifications of liability, to which it may be subject; as a promise to carry safely, fire and robbery excepted. (*Latham* v. *Rutley*, 2 B. & C. 20; *White* v. *Great Western Ry. Co.*, 2 C. B. N. S. 7; 26 L. J. C. P. 158. See "*The Body of the Statement of Claim*," *ante*, p. 11.) Conditions which are void under the Railway and Canal Traffic Act cannot be set up in variance of the carriers' duties. (*Rooth* v. *North Eastern Ry. Co.*, L. R. 2 Ex. 173, 181.) As to these see "*Carriers*," "Defences."

As to stating special damage, see "*Damages*," *ante*, p. 19, and "*Particulars and their Effect upon Pleading*," *ante*, p. 29.

(*c*) *Parties to the Action.*]—An action against a carrier for the loss of goods or for any breach of duty, or of contract, whether express or implied, is, as a general rule, to be brought in the name of the person who, by himself or his agent, employed the defendant, or delivered the goods to him. He may be either the absolute or special owner of the goods. (*Freeman* v. *Birch*, 3 Q. B. 492.)

In some instances, particularly in cases of the sale of goods which are forwarded by the vendor to the purchaser through a carrier, it becomes a matter of considerable nicety to determine whether the action should be in the name of the consignor or in that of the consignee. The action is to be brought in the name of the consignor when there is an express agreement between him and the carrier as to the employment of the carrier on his account (*Davis* v. *James*, 5 Burr. 2680; *Moore* v. *Wilson*, 1 T. R. 659; *Sergent* v. *Morris*, 3 B. & Ald. 277; *Dunlop* v. *Lambert*, 6 Cl. & F. 600); and where the consignor, by necessary implication, employs the carrier on his account, which is usually the case where property has not passed to the consignee, and where the goods remain during the carriage at the risk of the consignor, as where goods are forwarded for sale on approval (*Swain* v. *Shepherd*, 1 M. & Rob. 223; *Sergent* v. *Morris*, *supra*; *Freeman* v. *Birch*, *supra*); and where the contract of sale is within the Statute of Frauds, and there is not sufficient evidence to charge the consignee (*Coats* v. *Chaplin*, 3 Q. B. 483). Delivery to, and acceptance by the carrier is not a sufficient acceptance to charge the purchaser under the Statute of Frauds, even where the carrier has been selected and paid by the purchaser (*Norman* v. *Phillips*, 14 M. & W. 277; *Meredith* v. *Meigh*, 2 E. & B. 364); and in such case the consignor must sue the carrier (*Coombs* v. *The Bristol and Exeter Ry. Co.*, 3 H. & N. 510; 27 L. J. Ex. 401). But if the buyer, knowing the goods to be in the possession of the carrier or warehouseman, and to be lying at his disposal, does not notify to the seller within a reasonable time his refusal of them, he may be taken to have accepted and received them (*Bushell* v. *Wheeler*, 15 Q. B. 443; see *Norman* v. *Phillips*, *supra*).

But, generally speaking, the action must be in the name of the consignee, for, except in such cases as those referred to, the delivery to the carrier is a delivery to the consignee; it is for him that the goods are carried, and the consignor in employing the carrier is considered as the agent of the consignee for that purpose, as where goods are delivered to a carrier under a contract of sale by order of the consignee (*Dawes* v. *Peck*, 8 T. R. 330; and see *Dutton* v. *Solomonson*, 3 B. & P. 582; *per* Parke, B., *Wait* v. *Baker*, 2 Ex. 1, 7); and where goods are shipped under a bill of lading by order and on account of the consignee. (*Brown* v. *Hodgson*, 2 Camp. 36.) In such cases it is immaterial that the consignor paid the carriage. (*King* v. *Meredith*, 2 Camp. 639.)

The principle of law is to refer all transactions of agents to the principal on whose account they were entered into. (See *Dawes* v. *Peck*, *supra*, *per* Parke, B.)

In cases where the consignee receives the goods and promises either expressly, or by implication, to pay the carriage, he may in general be sued by the carrier for the carriage of the goods, as the waiving by the carrier of his lien on the goods affords sufficient consideration to support the contract to pay such carriage. (See *Jesson* v. *Solly*, 4 Taunt. 52; *Moller* v. *Young*, 4 E. & B. 755; 25 L. J. Q. B. 94.)

In an action for the loss of a passenger's luggage it was held that the owner might sue in his own name, though he travelled as the servant of another person who paid his fare for him and took his ticket. (*Marshall* v. *York and Berwick Ry. Co.*, 11 C. B. 655.) Where,

CARRIERS I. OF GOODS BY LAND (*d*).

Statement of Claim by a Carrier for the Carriage of Goods.

1. The plaintiff is a carrier.
2. On the 1st of Feb., 1879, it was agreed between the

---

a box containing property of two persons was addressed to one only and sent on behalf of both, it was held they might join in suing for the loss of the goods. (*Metcalf* v. *London and Brighton Ry. Co.*, 4 C. B. N. S. 317.)

Where a servant had taken with him as part of his luggage as a passenger upon a railway a portmanteau belonging to his master, it was held that the master could not maintain an action against the railway company for its loss upon the journey. (*Becher* v. *Great Eastern Ry. Co.*, L. R. 5 Q. B. 241; 39 L. J. Q. B. 122; see, too, *Alton* v. *Midland Ry. Co.* 14 C. B. N. S. 213; 34 L. J. C. P. 292; and *Martin* v. *Great Indian Peninsular Ry. Co.*, L. R. 3 Ex. 9.)

In case of doubt as to the proper parties to sue or be sued it may be advisable, though at the risk of having to pay costs occasioned by the joinder of unnecessary parties, to join all who may be supposed proper to sue or be sued, see O. XVI. and *ante*, p. 4, "*Number of the Parties.*"

As to parties to be made defendants where several carriers are concerned, see the next note. As to the rights and liabilities of the consignee of goods named in a bill of lading, and of the indorsee of a bill of lading, see *post*, "*Shipping*," p. 326.

(*d*) *Carriers of Goods by Land.*]—The duties of a common carrier of goods imposed by law in the absence of special agreement are:—To receive for carriage all goods offered, provided he has convenience to carry them, and the goods are of a proper kind, and the employer is ready and willing to pay the proper and reasonable hire (*Pickford* v. *Grand Junction Ry. Co.*, 8 M. & W. 372; *Johnson* v. *Midland Ry. Co.*, 4 Ex. 367; *Jackson* v. *Rogers*, 2 Show. 330); to carry for a reasonable reward, and to deliver the goods within a reasonable time (*Hales* v. *London and North Western Ry. Co.*, 4 B. & S. 66; 32 L. J. Q. B. 292); to insure their safety during the carriage and until delivery, the act of God and the Queen's enemies excepted. (*Forward* v. *Pittard*, 1 T. R. 27; *Pozzi* v. *Shipton*, 8 A. & E. 963; *Riley* v. *Horne*, 5 Bing. 217; *Bourne* v. *Gatliffe*, 3 M. & G. 643; *Richards* v. *London, Brighton, and South Coast Ry. Co.*, 7 C. B. 839; *Wyld* v. *Pickford*, 8 M. & W. 443; *Nugent* v. *Smith*, 1 C. P. D. 423; 45 L. J. C. P. 697.)

The events excepted as acts of God seem to include all disturbances of nature so sudden or violent as to be practically irresistible. (*Nichols* v. *Marsland*, L. R. 10 Ex. 258; 44 L. J. Ex. 134; 2 Ex. D. 1; 46 L. J. Ex. 174; *Nugent* v. *Smith*, 1 C. P. D. 34, 423; 45 L. J. C. P. 28, 697.) A frost of extraordinary severity that could not be foreseen has been held to constitute *vis major*, or, in this sense, an act of God (*Blyth* v. *Birmingham Waterworks Co.*, 11 Ex. 781); so, too, has a great and unexpected fall of snow (*Briddon* v. *Great Northern Ry. Co.*, 28 L. J. Ex. 51); as, also, a violent tempest (*Nugent* v. *Smith*, *ante*; *River Wear Commissioners* v. *Adamson*, 2 App. Cas. 743, 749; 47 L. J. Q. B. 193). See further "*Nuisance*," *post*, p. 490.

A common carrier is not responsible for damage accruing to the thing carried, from its inherent vice, or natural defects, or deteriora-

plaintiff and the defendant that the plaintiff should carry for the defendant for the sum of £—— certain household

---

tion, or, as it has been termed, happening from the "*vice propre de chose*," or from improper packing by the sender; at all events, where there has been nothing to indicate to the carrier the defective nature of the packing. Thus, he is not liable for the loss of, or injury to an animal, caused by its own violence or want of temper, if he has secured it in a proper manner. (*Blower* v. *Great Western Ry. Co.*, L. R. 7 C. P. 655, 663, 664, and cases there cited; 41 L. J. C. P. 268; *Kendall* v. *London and South Western Ry. Co.*, L. R. 7 Ex. 373, 377; 41 L. J. Ex. 184; *Barbour* v. *S. E. Ry. Co.*, 34 L. T. 67; *Brass* v. *Maitland*, 6 E. & B. 470; 26 L. J. Q. B. 49; *Nugent* v. *Smith, ante;* see, also, *Richardson* v. *North Eastern Ry. Co.*, L. R. 7 C. P. 78.)

Where, however, the deterioration is caused by the default of the carrier, or the vice, in the case of an animal, is brought out by the negligence or default of the carrier, the liability of the carrier attaches. (*Wilson* v. *Lanc. Ry. Co.*, 9 C. B. N. S. 632; 30 L. J. C. P. 232; *Gill* v. *M. S. and L. Ry. Co.*, L. R. 8 Q. B. 186; 42 L. J. Q. B. 89; see *Blower* v. *G. W. Ry. Co.*, L. R. 7 C. P. 655, *per* Willes, J., p. 663.)

As to who are common carriers, see *Morse* v. *Slue*, Vent. 190, 238; *Gisbourn* v. *Hurst*, 1 Salk. 249; *Brind* v. *Dale*, 8 C. & P. 207; 2 M. & Rob. 80; *Nugent* v. *Smith, supra; Liver Alkali Co.* v. *Johnson*, L. R. 7 Ex. 267; L. R. 9 Ex. 338; 43 L. J. Ex. 216, and *Scaife* v. *Farrant*, L. R. 10 Ex. 358; 44 L. J. Ex. 36; *Bergheim* v. *Great Eastern Ry. Co.*, 3 C. P. D. 221, 222; 47 L. J. C. P. 318.

A common carrier is justified in refusing to carry, if his conveyance is already full, and he has not convenience to carry that which otherwise he would be bound to carry according to his profession (*Lovett* v. *Hobbs*, 2 Show. 428; *Riley* v. *Horne*, 5 Bing. 217); or if from any cause the goods offered, either by reason of the mode in which they are packed, or otherwise, are unusually dangerous, or unusually hazardous to carry (*Edwards* v. *Sherratt*, 1 East, 604); or if the goods are brought at an unreasonable time (*Lane* v. *Cotton*, 1 Ld. Raym. 652; *Pickford* v. *Grand Junction Ry. Co.*, 12 M. & W. 766).

Though common carriers are by common law obliged to carry for all persons as above stated for reasonable reward, they are not obliged to charge all persons alike or equally. In the case of railway companies there is, in general, statutory provision requiring them to charge equally to all persons (*Evershed* v. *London and North Western Ry. Co.*, 2 Q. B. D. 254; 3 Q. B. D. 135; 3 App. Cas. 1029; 46 L. J. Q. B. 289; 48 L. J. Q. B. 22; *Great Western Ry. Co.* v. *Sutton*, L. R. 4 H. L. 226; 38 L. J. Ex. 177; *Gidlow* v. *L. & Y. Ry. Co.*, L. R. 7 H. L. 517; 45 L. J. H. L. 625; *Parker* v. *Great Western Ry. Co.*, 7 M. & G. 253; *Baxendale* v. *Eastern Counties Ry. Co.*, 4 C. B. N. S. 63; *Piddington* v. *South Eastern Ry. Co.*, 5 C. B. N. S. 111; *Bramley* v. *South Eastern Ry. Co.*, 12 C. B. N. S. 63; 31 L. J. C. P. 286); and see *post*, p. 133, "The Railway Clauses Act, 1845," sec. 90, and "The Railway and Canal Traffic Act, 1854."

The power of railway companies by special contracts to vary their liabilities in respect of loss of, or injury done to, animals, goods, or things, in the receiving, forwarding, or delivering thereof, by neglect or default of their servants, is limited to such conditions, signed by the party, as may be adjudged by the Court or Judge before whom any

furniture and effects of the defendant from York to Birmingham, and deliver the same to the defendant at Number 9, New-street, Birmingham.

---

question relating thereto shall be tried to be just and reasonable, "The Railway and Canal Traffic Act, 1854," (17 & 18 Vict. c. 31,) s. 7; (*Peek* v. *North Staffordshire Ry. Co.*, 10 H. L. C. 473; 32 L. J. Q. B. 241; *M'Manus* v. *L. and Y. Ry. Co.*, 4 H. & N. 327; 28 L. J. Ex. 353; *Lewis* v. *Great Western Ry. Co.*, 3 Q.B.D. 195; 47 L. J. Q. B. 131; *Ashenden* v. *L. B. & S. C. Ry. Co.* 5 Ex. D. 190); and this enactment is extended to the traffic carried by railway companies on steam vessels by "The Regulation of Railways Act, 1868," (31 & 32 Vict. c. 119,) s. 16; and 34 & 35 Vict. c. 78, s. 12 (*Cohen* v. *South Eastern Ry. Co.*, 2 Ex. D. 253; 46 L. J. Ex. 417; *Doolan* v. *The Directors, &c., of Midland Ry. Co.*, 2 App. Cas. 792).

As to what conditions have been held just and reasonable, see "Defences," "*Carriers*."

The above provisions of 17 & 18 Vict. c. 31, s. 7, do not extend to conditions relating to the carriage of goods or animals by one railway company over the line of another. (*Zunz* v. *South Eastern Ry. Co.*, L. R. 4 Q. B. 539; 38 L. J. Q. B. 209.)

The liability of a carrier extends throughout the entire distance over which he professes to carry. Thus the liability of a railway company professing to carry over the lines of other companies, extends over the whole distance. (*Muschamp* v. *Lancaster and Preston Ry. Co.*, 8 M. & W. 421; *Welby* v. *West Cornwall Ry. Co.*, 2 H. & N., 703; 27 L. J. Ex. 181; *Blake* v. *Great Western Ry. Co.*, 7 H. & N. 987; 31 L. J. Ex. 346; *Collins* v. *Bristol and Exeter Ry. Co.*, 29 L. J. Ex. 41; *Thomas* v. *Rhymney Ry. Co.*, L. R. 6 Q. B. 266; 39 L. J. Q. B. 141.)

The contracting company can alone be sued for any breach of the contract to carry over its own line and that of other railway companies unless the circumstances are such as to constitute the several companies carrying the goods, or passengers, partners in the transaction. (*Coxon* v. *Great Western Ry. Co.*, 5 H. & N. 274; 29 L. J. Ex. 165; *Collins* v. *Bristol and Exeter Ry. Co.*, *ante*; *Gill* v. *M. S. & L. Ry. Co.*, L. R. 8 Q. B. 186; *Foulkes* v. *Met. Dist. Ry. Co.*, 5 C. P. D. 157; 49 L. J. C. P. 361.) But, as the law imposes upon all a duty to do no act to injure another, such other companies may be liable for acts of misfeasance causing injury to passengers or goods entrusted to them (*Foulkes* v. *Met. Dist. Ry. Co.*, *supra*, *per* Bramwell, L. J.; *Self* v. *L. B. & S. C. Ry. Co.*, 42 L. T. 173); or for breaches of the duty cast upon them by the receipt of such passengers or goods to be carried by them (*Foulkes* v. *Met. Dist. Ry. Co.*, *supra*; *Marshall* v. *York & Berwick Ry. Co.*, 11 C. B. 655; *Hooper* v. *L. & N. W. Ry. Co.*, 43 L. T. 570; 50 L. J. C. P. 103).

A common carrier receiving goods within the realm to carry to a place without the realm is subject to the duties of a common carrier for the whole distance. (*Crouch* v. *London and North Western Ry. Co.*, 14 C. B. 255; *Nugent* v. *Smith*, 1 C. P. D. 423; 45 L. J. C. P. 697.) As to goods received without the realm, see *Bramley* v. *South Eastern Ry. Co.*, 12 C. B. N. S. 63; 31 L. J. C. P. 286; *Le Conteur* v. *London and South Western Ry. Co.*, L. R. 1 Q. B. 54; 35 L. J. Q. B. 40.

Where goods are accepted by a railway company to be carried to a

3. The plaintiff did accordingly carry the said household furniture and effects for the defendant from York to Birmingham, and deliver the same to the defendant at Number 9, New-street, Birmingham.

4. The defendant has not paid to the plaintiff the said sum of £——, or any part thereof.

The like, there being several Consignments.

1. The plaintiffs are carriers between York and London, and the defendant is a corn and hay dealer at York.

2. The defendant delivered to the plaintiffs as such carriers as aforesaid, 8 quarters of corn on the 1st of May, 1879; 5 quarters of oats on the 3rd of May, 1879, and 11 tons of hay and 5 quarters of corn on the 19th of June, 1879, to be by them carried at the ordinary and reasonable rate of charges for such carriage from York to London, and there delivered to the defendant or his agent.

3. The plaintiffs received from the defendant the said goods upon the terms and for the purposes aforesaid.

4. The plaintiffs thereupon duly carried the said goods from York to London, and there delivered the same to the defendant [or his agent].

5. The charges for the carriage of such goods at the ordinary and reasonable rate of charge therefor amounts to £——.

6. The defendant has not paid for the said carriage of the said goods, and the sum of £—— is due from and payable by the defendant to the plaintiffs in respect thereof.

---

place beyond their line, subject to special conditions, the conditions apply throughout the whole distance. (*Collins* v. *Bristol and Exeter Ry. Co.*, 29 L. J. Ex. 41; 7 H. L. C. 194; *Hall* v. *North Eastern Ry. Co.*, L. R. 10 Q. B. 437; 44 L. J. Q. B. 164.) As to passengers' luggage see *post*, p. 143.

The carrier, in the absence of special agreement as to time for delivery, is bound, as above stated, to deliver within a reasonable time; what this may be, depends upon his available means of forwarding the goods entrusted to him, and upon the whole of the circumstances, and is, in each case, a question of fact. (*Hales* v. *London and North Western Ry. Co.*, 4 B. & S. 61; 32 L. J. Q. B. 292; *Taylor* v. *Great Northern Ry. Co.*, L. R. 1 C. P. 385; 35 L. J. C. P. 210; *Ellis* v. *Thompson*, 3 M. & W. 445, *per* Alderson, B., and see "*Shipping*," *post*, p. 332.)

Against a Common Carrier for injury to Goods.

1. The defendants are common carriers of goods from Hull to London.

2. The plaintiff delivered ——bales of wool to be by the defendants as such carriers safely carried for hire from Hull to London, and there delivered to the order of the plaintiff.

3. The defendants received the said —— bales of wool from the plaintiff in good condition, and upon the terms and for the purposes aforesaid.

4. The defendants carried the said —— bales of wool from Hull to London, but did not safely carry the same. The said wool was damaged in the course of the said journey, and was delivered in London in a damaged condition by the defendants to the order of the plaintiff.

5. [*Give the details of the damage where practicable* (*e*).]

Against a Carrier for injury to Goods, charging him as a Carrier of Goods for Hire, and in the alternative as a Common Carrier.

1, 2, 3 & 4. [*As in last preceding form.*]

5. If the defendants are not common carriers, or if they did not receive the said —— bales of wool as common carriers, then they received them as carriers of goods for hire upon the terms that they should carefully carry them from Hull to London, and there deliver them as above stated.

6. The damage above complained of was caused by want of care on the part of the defendants in the conveying of the said wool from Hull to London.

7. [*As in paragraph 5 of last preceding form* (*e*).]

Against a Carrier for loss of Goods.

1. The plaintiff by his agent A. B. on the —— of ——, 18—, delivered at Bradford to the defendants, who are carriers of goods for hire, two boxes containing the following articles [*set out the articles*] to be by them safely and carefully carried for hire, for the plaintiff from Bradford to No. 30, Barker-street, Shrewsbury, and there delivered to the plaintiff within a reasonable time in that behalf.

2. The defendants then received the said boxes with their said contents on the terms and for the purposes aforesaid.

3. A reasonable time for the said carriage and delivery to the plaintiff of the said boxes and their said contents has elapsed.

4. The defendants have not delivered either of the said boxes or their said contents, or any part of their said contents, to the plaintiff at No. 30 Barker-street, Shrewsbury, or at all.

5. The plaintiff has by reason of the premises been deprived of and has lost the said two boxes and their said contents.

For a like claim, see Fleming v. *M. S. & L. Ry. Co.*, 4 Q. B. D. 81.

Against a Carrier for not carrying in time for a particular Market (*e*).

1. The plaintiff, on the —— of ——, 18—, delivered at Sheffield to the defendants, who are carriers of goods for

---

(*e*) *Damages.*]—Whenever the object of the sender is specially brought to the notice of the carrier, or circumstances are known to the carrier from which the object ought in reason to be inferred, so that the object may be taken to have been within the contemplation of both parties, damages may be recovered for the natural consequences of the failure of that object by the carrier's default. (*The Parana*, 2 P. D. 118, 120; *Horne* v. *Midland Ry. Co.*, L. R. 8 C. P. 131; 42 L. J. C. P. 59; *Simpson* v. *London and North Western Ry. Co.*, 1 Q. B. D. 274; 45 L. J. Q. B. 182.)

A miller, in an action against a carrier for delay in delivering a shaft of his mill, was held not entitled to recover as damages, the loss of profits by the stoppage of the mill (*Hadley* v. *Baxendale*, 9 Ex. 341); so the owner of a cotton mill, in an action against a carrier for delay in delivering cotton to be used in his mill, was held not entitled to recover damages for the wages paid to workmen, and the loss of profits while the mill was stopped for want of cotton (*Gee* v. *L. & Y. Ry. Co.*, 6 H. & N. 211; 30 L. J. Ex. 11). In the same way where a box containing part of the machinery of a saw mill was lost by a carrier, it was held that the carrier was not liable for the loss incurred by the stoppage of the works, though the absence of the lost portion made the rest of the machinery useless, and the carrier when he received the box knew that it contained machinery. (*British Columbia Saw Mill Co.* v. *Nettleship*, L. R. 3 C. P. 499; 37 L. J. C. P. 235.) Where a commercial traveller was kept waiting in idleness at a hotel the arrival of a case of samples which ought to have been, but was not, within a reasonable time, delivered to him by a carrier to whom it had been entrusted for carriage, it was held that the carrier was not liable for hotel expenses

hire, a box containing cutlery, to be by them carried from Sheffield to Nottingham, and there delivered by the ——

---

so incurred, the contents of the case not having been stated, nor the object with which they were sent brought to the notice of the carrier. (*Woodger* v. *Great Western Ry. Co.*, L. R. 2 C. P. 318; 36 L. J. C. P. 177; see also *Candy* v. *Midland Ry. Co.* 38 L. T. 226; *Anderson* v. *North Eastern Ry. Co.*, 4 L. T. 216; 9 W. R. 519.)

If goods are sent by a carrier by land to be sold at a particular market, and by reason of delay on the part of the carrier, they have not arrived in time for the market, damages for loss of market, may, in the absence of conditions to the contrary, be recovered. (*The Parana, suprâ.*)

In estimating damages, circumstances peculiar to the plaintiff, and of which the carrier had no notice, or with reference to which he did not contract, cannot be used in aggravation, as for instance, that when the goods did at length arrive at their destination, the plaintiff's traveller who would have sold them had left, or that a special bargain was lost. (*Great Western Ry. Co.* v. *Redmayne*, L. R. 1 C. P. 329; *Horne* v. *Midland Ry. Co.*, L. R. 7 C. P. 583; L. R. 8 C. P. 131; 42 L. J. C. P. 59.)

If goods are sent for the purpose of being sold in a particular season when they are at a higher price than at other times, and if by reason of breach of contract they do not arrive in time, damages for loss of market, may, as against a carrier by land, in general, be recovered. (*The Parana, supra; Wilson* v. *L. & Y. Ry. Co.*, 30 L. J. C. P. 232; 9 C. B. N. S. 632. See also *Collard* v. *South Eastern Ry. Co.*, 30 L. J. Ex. 393; 7 H. & N. 79.)

Mere knowledge or notice of the purpose of a sender of goods will not suffice to render a common carrier, who by his breach of contract defeats that purpose, liable for the loss consequent upon the purpose being so defeated. The knowledge must be acquired, or the notice given, under such circumstances as to make the fulfilling of the sender's purpose a common object of both parties, or to make it a term of the contract that the carrier will be liable for such damages if the contract is broken. (*British Columbia Saw Mill Co.* v. *Nettleship, supra*; and *Horne* v. *Midland Ry. Co., supra.*)

Thus in an action against a railway company for delay in delivering goods, a notice given to the company at the time of consigning the goods that the senders are under contract to deliver the goods by a certain day, was held insufficient to charge the company with the loss of the contract price. (*Horne* v. *Midland Ry. Co., supra.*)

As to what circumstances are sufficient to constitute notice of the special purpose for which the goods are sent, and to create a contract to carry so as to fulfil the special purpose, see *Simpson* v. *London and North Western Ry. Co.*, 1 Q. B. D. 274; 45 L. J. Q. B. 182; and *Candy* v. *Midland Ry. Co.*, 38 L. T. 226. See further "*Damages*," *ante*, p. 19, and *post*, "*Carriers of Passengers*," p. 137.

In an action against a carrier for the loss of goods, the plaintiff is, in general, entitled to recover the market value of the goods at the place to which they are consigned. (*Rice* v. *Baxendale*, 7 H. & N. 96; 30 L. J. Ex. 371; *British Columbia, &c.* v. *Nettleship, ante.*) If there is no market for such goods at the place of delivery, the cost price, together with the cost of carriage and a reasonable allowance for

of ——, 18—, in time for the Nottingham Fair, held on that and the following days, to the plaintiff for the purpose of being sold at such fair.

2. The defendants then received the said box containing cutlery on the terms and for the purposes aforesaid, and promised the plaintiff to deliver the same by the said —— of ——, 18—, in time for the said fair, for the purpose of being sold at such fair.

3. The defendants did not, however, carry the said box containing the said cutlery to Nottingham, and there deliver the same to the plaintiff by the said —— of —, or in time for the said fair, or in time to be sold at such fair.

4. By reason of the premises the plaintiff lost the profits which he would otherwise have made by the sale of the said cutlery at such fair, and also lost the benefit of the expenses incurred by him in travelling to such fair and in preparing for the sale of the said cutlery thereat.

5. The loss of such profits amounts to £——. The said expenses, the benefit of which the plaintiff has lost, were as follows: [*set out the same*].

Against a Carrier for Breach of a Contract to supply Horse boxes to carry Horses to a particular Fair (e).

1. The defendants were possessed of a railway from York to London, and of horse boxes for the conveyance of horses upon the said railway for hire.

2. It was by certain letters, bearing date the 10th, 11th, 14th, and 16th of Feb., 1879, agreed between the plaintiff and the defendants, that the plaintiff should deliver to the defendants at their station at York on the 20th of Feb., 1879, twelve horses to be conveyed in horse boxes of the defendants upon the said railway of the defendants from York to London, for reward to the defendants, and delivered in London on the 21st of Feb., 1879, in time for a certain fair to be held at ——, near London, for the

---

importer's profit would appear to be a proper measure of damages. (*O'Hanlan* v. *Great Western Ry. Co.*, 6 B. & S. 484; 34 L. J. Q. B. 154.) Loss of hire of goods sent for hire cannot be recovered where the carrier has no notice that they are sent for that purpose. (*Hales* v. *London and North Western Ry. Co.*, 4 B. & S. 66; 32 L. J. Q. B. 292.) As to the effect of conditions relieving carriers from liability see "Defences," "*Carriers*," and see, *ante*, p. 124.

sale of horses on the 22nd of Feb., 1879, and that the defendants should convey the said horses in their said horse boxes from York to London, and deliver them in London on the said 21st of Feb. in time for the said fair, for the purpose of being sold thereat.

3. The plaintiff sent the said horses to the said station of the defendants at York on the said 20th of Feb., and there tendered them to the defendants for the purpose of so being conveyed as aforesaid.

4. The plaintiff was always ready and willing to pay the defendants for the conveyance of the said horses as aforesaid.

5. The defendants did not, however, provide horse boxes for the conveyance of the said horses, or convey the said horses, but refused and failed so to do.

6. By reason of the premises the plaintiff was unable to send the said horses to or to sell them at the said fair, and lost the profits, amounting to £——, which he would have made by so selling them, and lost the expense of £—— to which he was put in so delivering and tendering the said horses to the defendants at York as aforesaid.

By a Carrier for Expenses occasioned by the non-removal of a Horse within a reasonable time after arrival at Destination (*f*).

1. The plaintiffs are carriers of horses for hire.

2. It was on the —— of ——, 18—, agreed between the plaintiffs and the defendant that the plaintiffs should carry a certain horse for the defendant from Doncaster to York, and there have the horse ready within a reasonable time at their station to be taken away by the defendant,

(*f*) Carriers, after a refusal by the consignee of the goods carried, or when delivery at the place, or to the person named cannot be effected, become "involuntary bailees" of the goods thus left upon their hands, and are only bound to act with reasonable care and caution with respect to such goods. (*Heugh* v. *London and North Western Ry. Co.*, L. R. 5 Ex. 51; 39 L. J. Ex. 48.)

If under such circumstances it becomes reasonable to incur expenses in taking care of the goods, the carrier can, in general, recover such expenses from the person with whom the contract of carriage was made. (*Cargo ex Argos*, L. R. 5 P. C. 134; *Great Northern Ry. Co.* v. *Swaffield*, L. R. 9 Ex. 132; 43 L. J. Ex. 89.) In the latter case, the railway company recovered the livery charges paid by them in respect of a horse not fetched away by the consignee at the proper time.

and that the defendant should upon the arrival of the horse at the said station at York, or within a reasonable time thereafter, take away the said horse and pay the reasonable charges of the plaintiffs for its carriage from Doncaster to York.

3. The plaintiffs accordingly received the said horse and carried it from Doncaster to York, and there had the horse ready within a reasonable time at their station to be taken away by the defendant.

4. The plaintiffs further gave to the defendant upon arrival of the said horse at their station at York a notice in writing [*or* print] stating that it had arrived, and that unless fetched away at once it would be put at livery at the expense of the defendant.

5. The defendant, however, did not upon arrival of the said horse at the said station at York, or within a reasonable time in that behalf, take away the said horse, or pay the reasonable charges of the plaintiffs for its carriage from Doncaster to York.

6. The plaintiffs accordingly, upon the default of the defendant to take away the said horse as agreed and as above stated, put the said horse at livery, and have paid therefor £——.

7. The said reasonable charges of the plaintiffs for the carriage of the said horse from Doncaster to York amounted to £——.

8. The said sums of £—— and £—— were not paid, and are now due and payable by the defendant to the plaintiffs.

Against a Railway Company to recover back Charges made in excess of those charged to other persons for Packed Parcels (g).

1. The defendants are the —— Railway Company incorporated under and by virtue of [*set out the statute, or statutes, incorporating the company*].

(*g*) A railway company, which is liable by statute to carry for all persons upon equal terms (*ante*, p. 124), cannot charge more for a parcel consigned to one person containing several packed parcels belonging to different persons, than for a parcel containing similar goods belonging all to one person; and if any overcharge is made and exacted it may be recovered back. (*Pickford* v. *Grand Junction Ry. Co.*, 10 M. & W. 399; *Crouch* v. *Great Western Ry. Co.*, 11 Ex. 742; *Parker* v. *Great Western Ry. Co.*, 11 C. B. 545; *Garton* v. *Bristol and*

2. The plaintiff, in the course of his business, has during the period between the —— of ——, 18—,

---

Exeter Ry. Co., 4 H. & N. 33; 28 L. J. Ex. 169; *Piddington* v. *South Eastern Ry. Co.*, 5 C. B. N. S. 111; 27 L. J. C. P. 295; *Great Western Ry. Co.*, v. *Sutton*, L. R. 4 H. L. 226; 38 L. J. Ex. 177.) It is immaterial that the several parcels are addressed to different persons if they are consigned collectively. (*Baxendale* v. *London and South Western Ry. Co.*, L. R. 1 Ex. 137; 35 L. J. Ex. 108.) But where the several parcels belonging to different persons are not enclosed in one package, although they are all consigned at one time by and to the same persons, the company is justified in charging an increased rate in respect of the increased trouble in weighing, entering, and taking care of the different parcels. (*Baxendale* v. *Eastern Counties Ry. Co.*, 4 C. B. N. S. 63; 27 L. J. C. P. 137.)

The company may charge different rates to different persons where the services rendered are different. (*Strick* v. *The Swansea Canal Co.*, 16 C. B. N. S. 245; 33 L. J. C. P. 240.)

The 90th section of "The Railway Clauses Consolidation Act, 1845," (8 & 9 Vict. c. 20,) provides that "all such tolls" "shall be at all times charged equally to all persons, and after the same rate, whether per ton, per mile, or otherwise, in respect of all passengers, and of all goods, or carriages of the same description, and conveyed or propelled by a like carriage or engine passing only over the same portion of the line of railway under the same circumstances."

The word "*tolls*," by the definition given in that Act, includes, in the above section, "any rate or charge or other payment payable under the special Act for any passenger, animal, carriage, goods, merchandize, articles, matters, or things conveyed on the railway." (See *London and North Western Ry. Co.* v. *Evershed*, 2 Q. B. D. 254; 3 Q. B. D. 134; 3 App. Cas. 1029; 46 L. J. Q. B. 289; 47 L. J. Q. B. 284; 48 L. J. Q. B. 22.)

By "The Railway and Canal Traffic Act, 1854," (17 & 18 Vict. c. 31,) s. 2:—"Every railway company, canal company, and railway and canal company shall, according to their respective powers, afford all reasonable facilities for the receiving, and forwarding, and delivering of traffic upon and from the several railways and canals belonging to or worked by such companies respectively, and for the return of carriages, trucks, boats, and other vehicles, and no such company shall make or give any undue or unreasonable preference or advantage to or in favour of any particular person or company, or any particular description of traffic, in any respect whatsoever, nor shall any such company subject any particular person or company, or any particular description of traffic to any undue or unreasonable prejudice or disadvantage in any respect whatsoever." (See *Evershed* v. *London and North Western Ry. Co., supra.*)

As to railway companies carrying goods by sea, see "*Shipping*," *post*, p. 338.

Charges exacted by a railway company from one person in excess of those paid by other persons may be recovered back as money paid under compulsion. (*Great Western Ry. Co.* v. *Sutton*, L. R. 4 H. L. 226; 38 L. J. Ex. 177; *L. & Y. Ry. Co.* v. *Gidlow*, L. R. 7 H. L. 517; 45 L. J. H. L. 625; *L. & N. W. Ry. Co.* v. *Evershed*, *supra*, and cases *supra*. See further "*Money Received*," *post*, p. 280.) The proper mode of

and the —— of ——, 18—, delivered from time to time to the defendants, for conveyance by them along their railways and other railways in connection therewith, divers large consignments of goods, consisting of parcels collected by the plaintiff or his agents destined for the same town, and sent in one consignment to the plaintiff's agents or to the plaintiff at such town.

3. The invariable practice of the defendants during the said period has been not to require or receive from the plaintiff or his agents any declaration, or description of the contents of the parcels so consigned as aforesaid, and to charge him by weight for all such consignments, without regard to the contents of the parcels and without knowledge of the same, at a certain uniform rate of charge known as the fifth-class rate.

4. The plaintiff, in order to induce the defendants to carry his said goods, has been compelled to pay and has paid daily to the defendants in all cases the said uniform rate of charge upon all the goods delivered by him each day to them for the purpose of being carried during the said period.

5. During the said period divers large wholesale houses in the city of London and elsewhere dealing in goods of various descriptions and of various classes according to the defendants' tariff of charges for the carriage of goods by weight, have been in the habit of delivering to the defendants for conveyance by them along their railways and other railways in connection therewith divers large consignments of goods of like description and conveyed in the same way and under the same circumstances in every respect with those of the plaintiff above named. Such consignments consisted partly of various descriptions and classes of goods belonging to such consignors, and partly of parcels of goods belonging to various other persons, and houses deal-

---

stating the claim is as above; since if the claim is merely for money payable for money received for the use of the plaintiff, or paid under compulsion, stringent particulars of the circumstances with dates and items will be ordered if applied for. (*Sutton* v. *Great Northern Ry. Co.*, Court of Appeal, December, 1878.)

A railway company acting as common carriers, and carrying beyond and off their line, may charge a through rate, lower than the rates on their line, in proportion to the distance. (*Baxendale* v. *London and North Western Ry. Co.*, L. R. 1 Ex. 137; 35 L. J. Ex. 108.)

ing in goods of various descriptions and classes other than those in which the consignors dealt, which were received by such consignors for the purpose of being forwarded together with their own goods in one consignment by the defendants' railway and other railways in connection therewith to the town or place of destination.

6. The defendants, during the said period, have been well aware of the said practice, and with knowledge of the same it has been the practice of the defendants, during the whole of the said period, not to require or receive from the said houses any declaration or description of the contents of the parcels so consigned by them as aforesaid, and to charge them by weight for all such consignments without regard to the contents of the parcels, and without knowledge of the same, at a certain uniform rate of charge known as the fourth-class rate, such rate being a lower rate of charge than the rate charged by the defendants to the plaintiff.

7. [*Give such details as to amounts of overcharges as may be practicable.*]

Against a Railway Co. to recover Charges made in excess of those charged to other Persons for like Services (g).

1. The plaintiffs are, and were during the entire period hereinafter mentioned brewers at Burton. The defendants are and were during the said period a railway company incorporated under and by virtue of [*set out the statute or statutes incorporating the company*], and subject to the provisions of those statutes and of "The Railways Clauses Consolidation Act, 1845" (8 & 9 Vict. c. 20), and "The Railway and Canal Traffic Act, 1854" (17 & 18 Vict. c. 31), conveying goods for hire by their railway from and to Burton.

2. The plaintiffs, during the period between —— and —— have from time to time employed the defendants as such carriers as aforesaid to carry goods for them from and to Burton, and during that period the defendants have as such carriers carried for the plaintiffs from and to Burton goods, the total weight of which amounted to —— tons.

3. The plaintiffs, in order to induce the defendants to carry for the plaintiffs the said goods, have been compelled to pay, and have paid, to the defendants all rates, tolls, and charges which they demanded and claimed

against them in and about the carriage of the said goods.

4. The defendants, in breach of their duty, did not carry, and refused to carry the said goods of the plaintiffs for tolls and charges charged to them equally and at the same rate with those charged to other persons, namely, to A. B., P. Q., and R. S. for goods of the same description conveyed and carried by the defendants over the same portion of their said line of railway, in like manner and under the same circumstances, and the defendants made rebates and deductions from the said tolls to and in favour of the above-mentioned persons, which they did not make in favour of the plaintiffs, and the defendants made and gave unreasonable preferences and advantages to and in favour of the above-mentioned persons, and rendered gratuitous services to them, which they did not render and refused to render to or in favour of the plaintiffs, whereby the defendants, in breach of their duty in that behalf as such carriers of goods by railway as aforesaid, and also contrary to the provisions of the said statutes, subjected the plaintiffs to undue and unreasonable prejudice and disadvantage.

5. As regards the said A. B., P. Q., and R. S., the defendants have during the entire period hereinbefore mentioned made and allowed to them respectively a rebate or deduction of —— per ton on all the goods which the defendants during the period aforesaid carried for them, although the defendants did not make or allow a like rebate or deduction to the plaintiffs in respect of their said goods, which were carried by the defendants under precisely similar circumstances.

6. Had the like rebate or deduction been made to the plaintiffs, their payments to the defendants would have been £—— less than they actually were during the said period.

7. The defendants have also during the whole of the said period in regard to the said goods which they have as hereinbefore mentioned carried for the said A. B., P. Q., and R. S. upon the defendants' line of rail to or from Burton aforesaid, gratuitously carted the said goods to and from the defendants' railway station at Burton from and to the respective breweries in Burton of the said persons, whereas in regard to the plaintiffs' said goods the defendants have in the instances in which they carted the said goods to or from their said station

at Burton from or to the plaintiffs' brewery in Burton, charged the plaintiffs the sum of —— per ton on their said goods so carted by the defendants as aforesaid.

8. The sum so paid by the plaintiffs to the defendants for cartage during the said period amounted to £——.

9. The said several preferences and advantages which the defendants granted to the said A. B., P. Q., and R. S. were secretly made and given, and the plaintiffs were not aware thereof when they paid the rates, tolls, and charges hereinbefore in the third paragraph mentioned.

10. By reason of the said preferences and advantages so made and granted by the defendants as aforesaid, the plaintiffs have been put to unfair and undue competition in their said business, and have made less profit from their said business than they would otherwise have made.

11. The said amounts of £——, and £——, so paid by the plaintiffs to the defendants as above stated are now due from and payable by the defendants to plaintiffs as and being money received by the defendants for the use of the plaintiffs.

CARRIERS II. OF PASSENGERS (*a*).

Claim by a Passenger against a Railway Company in respect of Personal Injuries sustained in a Collision.

1. On the —— of ——, 18—, it was agreed between the plaintiff and the defendants that the plaintiff should

(*a*) *Carriers of Passengers.*]—Carriers of passengers are not bound to receive as passengers persons who offer themselves in an unfit state to be carried, or who are not willing to conform to reasonable regulations as to carriage, or who are not ready and willing to pay the proper and reasonable fare, or for whom the carrier has not sufficient room in his carriage. (*Lovett* v. *Hobbs*, 2 Show. 428.) Carriers of passengers do not insure the safety of passengers during the journey, but they undertake, in the absence of any special contract to the contrary, that due care shall be used in the conveyance of the passenger. (*Readhead* v. *Midland Ry. Co.*, L. R. 2 Q. B. 412; *ib.*, 4 Q. B. 379, 393; 36 L. J. Q. B. 181; 38 L. J. Q. B. 169; *Daniel* v. *Metropolitan Ry. Co.*, L. R. 5 H. L. 45, 55; 40 L. J. C. P. 121.) In the case of a railway company contracting to carry a passenger to a place beyond their own line, the company undertake that due care shall be used in conveying him so far as regards railway management throughout the entire journey, and are, in general, liable upon the contract for

become a passenger to be carefully carried by the defendants upon their railway from A. to B. for reward then paid to the defendants.

---

the negligence with regard to his conveyance of the servants of the companies employed by them to carry him beyond their own line, as though such servants had been their own (*Great Western Ry. Co.* v. *Blake*, 7 H. & N. 991 ; 31 L. J. Ex. 346 ; *Buxton* v. *North Eastern Ry. Co.*, L. R. 3 Q. B. 549 ; 37 L. J. Q. B. 258 ; *Thomas* v. *Rhymney Ry. Co.*, L. R. 5 Q. B. 226 ; *ib.*, 6 Q. B. 266 ; 39 L. J. Q. B. 141 ; 40 L. J. Q. B. 89 ; see also *John* v. *Bacon*, L. R. 5 C. P. 437, 441, 442, 443 ; 39 L. J. C. P. 365) ; they are also liable for the defective construction of stations and carriages used (*Foulkes* v. *Met. Dist. Ry. Co.*, 5 C. P. D. 157, 168 ; 49 L. J. C. P. 361) ; but they are not liable for the wrongful acts of third parties over whom they have no control. (*Wright* v. *Midland Ry. Co.*, L. R. 8 Ex. 137 ; 42 L. J. Ex. 89 ; *Daniel* v. *Metropolitan Ry. Co.*, L. R. 5 H. L. 45, 55 ; 40 L. J. C. P. 121.) A passenger may make a special contract relieving a railway company from any liability for negligence in his conveyance, and free passes usually contain a condition to that effect. (*McCawley* v. *Furness Ry. Co.*, L. R. 8 Q. B. 57; 42 L. J. Q. B. 4 ; *Gallin* v. *London and North Western Ry. Co.*, L. R. 10 Q. B. 212 ; 44 L. J. Q. B. 89.)

As in the case of valid special conditions with regard to the conveyance of goods, a special condition with regard to the conveyance of a passenger is, in general, operative throughout the entire journey, even though it is in part to be performed on the line of another company employed by the contracting company. (*Hall* v. *North Eastern Ry. Co.*, L. R. 10 Q. B. 437 ; 44 L. J. Q. B. 164.)

A passenger taking a ticket from one company for a journey extending over the lines of other companies contracts with that company which issued the ticket, and cannot sue the others upon the contract, unless he can show a partnership between the company issuing the ticket and the other companies. (*Gill* v. *Manchester, Sheffield, and Lincolnshire Ry. Co.*, L. R. 8 Q. B. 186 ; 42 L. J. Q. B. 89.) But, as to the liability of such other companies for acts of misfeasance, or breaches of duty, see *ante*. p. 125.

Carriers by land do not warrant that the carriages are "roadworthy," and they are not liable to a passenger injured in consequence of a latent defect in the carriage, which it was impossible to detect either during construction or afterwards. (*Readhead* v. *Midland Ry. Co.*, L. R. 4 Q. B. 379 ; 38 L. J. Q. B. 169.)

They are, however, liable if the defect is one that could, by the exercise of care and skill, be discovered during construction, or is a defect in construction which could have been, by the exercise of care and skill, avoided, even though the carriage be made for them by an independent contractor. (*Francis* v. *Cockrell*, L. R. 5 Q. B. 184, 194 ; *ib.* 5 Q. B. 501, 508, 513 ; 39 L. J. Q. B. 113 ; *ib.* 291 ; and see *Sharp* v. *Grey*, 9 Bing. 457, 459.)

Railway companies are bound to provide reasonable accommodation for their passengers, including reasonable facilities for entering or leaving their trains. (*Praeger* v. *Bristol and Exeter Ry. Co.*, 24 L. T. 107, cited L. R. 7 C. P. 323 ; *Bridges* v. *North London Ry. Co.*, L. R. 7 H. L. 213 ; 43 L. J. Q. B. 151 ; as explained in *Jackson* v. *Metropolitan Ry. Co.*, 3 App. Cas. 193 ; 47 L. J. C. P. 303 ; *Robson*

2. The plaintiff accordingly became such passenger for the said purpose, and upon the said terms.

3. The plaintiff was not, however, carefully carried from

---

v. *North Eastern Ry. Co.*, 2 Q. B. D. 85, 88; 46 L. J. Q. B. 50; *Rose* v. *North Eastern Ry. Co.*, 2 Ex. D. 248; 46 L. J. Ex. 374; *Nicholson* v. *L. and Y. Ry. Co.*, 3 H. & C. 534; 34 L. J. Ex. 84; *Longmore* v. *Great Western Ry. Co.*, 19 C. B. N. S. 183.)

The action for a breach of duty in carrying a passenger or his luggage, is so far independent of contract that the passenger may maintain an action in his own name, though another person took and paid for the ticket for him. (*Marshall* v. *York, Newcastle and Berwick Ry. Co.*, 11 C. B. 655; 21 L. J. C. P. 34; *Martin* v. *Great Indian Peninsula Ry. Co.*, L. R. 3 Ex. 9.) But where a servant took and paid for a ticket, and took with him, as though his own luggage, a portmanteau belonging to his master, it was held that the master who had authorised the servant so to take it, could not sue for its loss. (*Becher* v. *Great Eastern Ry. Co.*, L. R. 5 Q. B. 241; 39 L. J. Q. B. 122.)

A person having taken, and had delivered to him by the railway company tickets for his servants which he kept in his own possession, was held entitled to sue the company for not conveying his servants, whom the company had refused to carry because they could not produce their tickets. (*Jennings* v. *Great Northern Ry. Co.*, L. R. 1 Q. B. 7; 35 L. J. Q. B. 15.)

A carrier, in the absence of any special contract as to time, contracts with regard to passengers, as with regard to goods, to carry within a time which is, under all the circumstances, reasonable. (*Hurst* v. *Great Western Ry. Co.*, 19 C. B. N. S. 310; 34 L. J. C. P. 264; *Fitzgerald* v. *Midland Ry. Co.*, 34 L. T. 771; and see notes to "*Carriers of Goods*," *ante*, p. 123.)

Damages for not carrying a Passenger, or for Delay.]—Loss occasioned to a passenger prevented from attending business appointments or engagements by unreasonable delay in carrying him to his destination, cannot, in the absence of a special contract to that effect, be recovered against a carrier, as such damage is too remote (*Hamlin* v. *Great Northern Ry. Co.*, 1 H. & N. 408; 26 L. J. Ex. 20; *Hobbs* v. *London & South-Western Ry. Co.*, L. R. 10 Q. B. 111, 117, 118; 44 L. J. Q. B. 49).

In *Hobbs* v. *London & South-Western Ry. Co.*, *supra*, the plaintiffs took tickets to travel by a midnight train from W. to H. The train did not go to H., and the plaintiffs were taken to E., which was a station farther from the plaintiff's house than H. was. The plaintiffs walked home in the wet from E., there being no conveyance to be had. It was there held, that damages might be given for the personal inconvenience and discomfort of having so to walk, but not for illness brought on by the dampness of the night. But where an innkeeper contracted to provide stabling for twelve horses for the plaintiff during a particular fair, and failed to do so, it was held that the plaintiff could recover damages for injury caused to the horses by exposure to the weather while he was engaged in finding other stables for them (*McMahon* v. *Field*, 50 L. J. Ex. 552).

If a carrier engages to put a person down at a given place, and

A. to B. but was, whilst such passenger upon the said journey, injured by the train in which he was being carried coming into collision with certain goods waggons standing or being upon the said railway.

4. This collision was caused by the negligence of the servants of the defendants [in not stopping the said train before it came into collision with the said goods waggons, or in not removing the said goods waggons before the said train came into collision with them, *or as the case may be. Specify the nature of the negligence complained of, where practicable*].

---

does not put him down there, but puts him down somewhere else, such person may, in the absence of any special agreement to the contrary, adopt reasonable means of getting to the place at which he ought to have been put down, and recover the costs thereof as damages against the carrier for his breach of contract (*Hobbs* v. *London and South-Western Ry. Co., supra; Le Blanche* v. *London & North-Western Ry. Co.*, 1 C. P. D. 286, 313 ; 45 L. J. C. P. 521).

In general, railway companies impose special conditions upon passengers carried by them with regard to the times of starting and arrival of trains, and with regard to delay. Such conditions bind passengers, to whose knowledge they are brought, and also, it would seem, passengers who have not become aware of them, if the company has done all that reasonably should be done to make such passengers aware of them, and has dealt as if, and in the belief that they had become aware of them (*Le Blanche* v. *London & North Western Ry. Co., supra* ; *Fitzgerald* v. *Midland Ry. Co.*, 34 L. T. 771 ; *Thompson* v. *Midland Ry. Co.*, 34 L. T. 34; *Parker* v. *South-Eastern Ry. Co.*, 2 C. P. D. 416, 422, 423 ; 46 L. J. C. P. 768 ; *Burke* v. *South Eastern Ry. Co.*, 5 C. P. D. 1 ; 49 L. J. C. P. 107 ; see also *Johnson* v. *Great Southern & Western Ry. Co.*, 9 (Ir.) L. R. Com. Law, 108). See further, "*Damages*," *ante*, p. 19, and notes to "*Carriers of Goods*," *ante*, p. 123, and see *Denton* v. *Great Northern Ry. Co.*, 5 E. & B. 860 ; 25 L. J. Q. B. 129, and observations on that case in Pollock on Contracts, 2nd ed. pp. 177—184.

Damages for personal injuries.]—In an action by a passenger against a carrier for personal injury, the jury in assessing damages are warranted in taking into consideration the pain and personal suffering of the injured passenger, the expense incurred by him for medical and other necessary treatment and attendance, and the business loss he has sustained, and is likely to sustain, through inability to continue, as he otherwise would have done, to attend to his business (*Phillips* v. *L. & S. W. Ry. Co.*, 5 C. P. D. 280 ; 49 L. J. C. P. 233 ; *Fair* v. *L. & N. W. Ry. Co.*, 21 L. T. 326). But where the passenger has, under a policy of insurance against accidents, received a sum of money in respect of the accident in question, they are not entitled to deduct such sum from the compensation to be awarded to such passenger. (*Bradburn* v. *Great Western Ry. Co.*, L. R. 10 Ex. 1 ; 44 L. J. Ex. 9.) As to death caused by negligence see "*Executors*," *post*, p. 416.

5. The plaintiff was by reason of the premises thrown forwards with violence and injured. [*Give details as far as practicable.*]

6. The plaintiff has in consequence been put to expense [*or,* has incurred liability] for medical attendance and for nursing [and has been compelled to incur hotel and lodging expenses in endeavouring to cure himself of his said injuries, and has been prevented from attending to his business of a tailor, and has lost profits which he otherwise would have earned in his said business of a tailor, *or, as the case may be, giving amounts and dates as far as practicable*].

The like, where the Collision took place owing to negligence of Servants of a Company over whose line the defendants contracted to carry the Passenger.

1. It was on the ——of ——, 18—, agreed between the plaintiff and the defendants that the plaintiff should become a passenger to be carefully carried by railway by the defendants and their agents the X. Y. Co. from A. to B. for reward then paid to the defendants.

2 and 3. [*As in form next above.*]

4. This collision took place on the line of the X. Y. Co., and was caused by the negligence of the servants of that company then having the control and management of the said line [*or,* having the control and management of the said train], in not stopping the said train in which the plaintiff was before it came into collision with the said goods waggons [*or as the case may be, stating the nature of the negligence complained of as far as practicable*].

5 and 6. [*As in form next above.*]

Claim by a Passenger against a Railway Company in respect of Personal Injuries caused by being carried in a Defective Carriage.

1 and 2. [*As in form next but one above.*]

3. The plaintiff was not, however, carried from A. to B., but was whilst upon the said journey negligently placed by the servants of the defendants, for the purpose of being carried upon the said journey, in a carriage which, by reason of defects was unfit to perform, or to be used upon, the said journey. [*State the defects charged, if practicable.*]

4. This carriage, by reason of the said defects, broke down, whilst the plaintiff was being carried in it upon the said journey, and thereby caused the train of which it formed part to run off the line of rails [*or, as the case may be*].

5. By reason of the premises the plaintiff was thrown out and injured. [*Give details as far as practicable.*]

6. [*As in paragraph* 6 *of form next but one above. State special damage, if any.*]

A like Form, Foulkes v. Met. Dist. Ry. Co., 4 *C. P. D.* 267.

Claim by a Husband and Wife against a Railway Company in respect of injuries to the wife as a Passenger, and consequent loss of her services by the Husband.

1. The plaintiff A. B. is a farmer residing and carrying on his business at X., and the plaintiff Sarah is his wife, and before and at the times of the grievances hereinafter alleged, assisted him in his said business and otherwise.

2. The defendants on the —— of ——, 18—, at X. received the plaintiff Sarah, then being the wife of the plaintiff A. B., to be carefully carried as a passenger on their railway from X. to Y. for reward to the defendants.

3. The defendants did not carefully carry the said plaintiff Sarah on her said journey, but so negligently conducted themselves in that behalf and in the management of an engine and of the train and carriage in which the said plaintiff Sarah was received as aforesaid, that the said engine was driven violently against the said train and carriage, and the plaintiff Sarah was thereby thrown down and wounded and injured.

4. By reason of the premises the plaintiff Sarah suffered, and is suffering, and will suffer great pain, and was, and is permanently injured and incapacitated from attending to her household and other duties.

5. By reason of the premises the plaintiff A. B. has lost and will lose the comfort, society, assistance, and services of his said wife, and has incurred and will incur expense for nursing and medical and other attendance in endeavouring to cure his said wife of her said injuries. [*Where practicable give details.*]

Claim against a Railway Company for injuries to a Passenger caused by negligently bringing a Train to a standstill where there was no proper facility for alighting.

1. The plaintiff on the —— of ——, 18—, became a passenger to be carried by railway by the defendants from A. to B. for reward to the defendants.

2. Upon the arrival at B. of the train in which the plaintiff was being carried by the defendants as such passenger, the said train was by the negligence of the defendants drawn up and brought to a standstill at a place beyond the platform of the defendants at their station at B., at a spot where there was no platform or proper accommodation for alighting.

3. Upon the said train being so drawn up and brought to a standstill, the servants of the defendants called out the name of the said station, and invited the plaintiff to alight without giving him sufficient, or any warning of the absence of any platform or proper accommodation for alighting.

4. Thereupon it being dark, and the plaintiff being unaware of the said absence of any platform or accommodation for alighting, endeavoured carefully to alight.

5. In consequence of the said absence of any platform or proper accommodation for alighting, the plaintiff fell upon the ground in so endeavouring to alight, and put his knee out of joint, and was much shaken, and bruised.

6. The plaintiff was by reason of the premises put to great pain and [compelled to expend £—— upon medical attendance, and was prevented for six weeks from attending to his business of a ——, and lost £—— profits which he would otherwise have made from his said business, *or, as the case may be*].

See other Forms by Railway Passengers against Railway Companies for Injuries and Negligence, post, pp. 481—488.

By a Passenger against a Railway Company for loss of his Luggage (*b*).

1. The plaintiff on the —— of ——, 18—, was received by the defendants as a passenger for the purpose

(*b*) Carriers are liable for loss of, or injuries caused to, passengers' luggage, by negligence of themselves or their servants, whilst in their charge (*Cohen* v. *South Eastern Ry. Co.*, 2 Ex. D. 253; 46 L. J. Ex.

of being carried with his luggage by rail in a certain train by the defendants from London to Exeter for reward to the defendants.

2. The defendants thereupon received and took charge of the said luggage, which consisted of two trunks, containing the plaintiff's wearing apparel, and placed it [*or*, promised the plaintiff that they would place it] in their luggage van in London in the said train in which the plaintiff was about to be carried by them as aforesaid, for the purpose of so carrying the said luggage from London to Exeter.

417; *Bergheim* v. *Great Eastern Ry. Co.*, 3 C. P. D. 221, 226; 47 L. J. C. P. 318), and it would seem in the case of luggage taken by them out of the care and control of the passenger, that they are liable as insurers, as in the case of other goods, in the absence of any special contract to the contrary. (*Cohen* v. *South Eastern Ry. Co.*, 2 Ex. D. 253, 259; 46 L. J. Ex. 417; *Bergheim* v. *Great Eastern Ry. Co.*, *supra; Robinson* v. *Dunmore*, 2 B. & P. 416; *Le Conteur* v. *London and South Western Ry. Co.*, L. R. 1 Q. B. 54; 35 L. J. Q. B. 40; *Butcher* v. *London and South Western Ry. Co.*, 16 C. B. 13; 24 L. J. C. P. 137; *Richards* v. *London, Brighton, and South Coast Ry. Co.*, 7 C. B. 839; 18 L. J. C. P. 251.)

With regard to luggage placed by a railway company in the same carriage with the passenger, at the request, or with the consent of the passenger, the company are not liable as insurers, but are liable merely for loss or injury occasioned by negligence of their servants. (*Bergheim* v. *Great Eastern Ry. Co.*, *supra; Talley* v. *Great Western Ry. Co.*, L. R. 6 C. P. 44; 40 L. J. C. P. 9.)

A passenger by railway who takes merchandise as his personal luggage cannot claim in respect of it against the company, unless the company have voluntarily and knowingly accepted it as personal luggage, and waived their right to charge for it as merchandise, as, for example, by raising no objection when informed of its nature either by the passenger or by its appearance. (*Cahill* v. *London and North Western Ry. Co.*, 13 C. B. N. S. 818; 31 L. J. C. P. 271; *Great Northern Ry. Co.* v. *Shepherd*, 8 Ex. 30; 21 L. J. Ex. 114, 296; *Belfast, &c., Ry. Co.* v. *Keys*, 9 H. L. C. 556.)

"Personal or ordinary luggage" means articles of the kind which passengers usually carry as their luggage. (See as to this *Hudston* v. *Midland Railway Co.*, L. R. 4 Q. B. 366; 38 L. J. Q. B. 213; *Macrow* v. *Great Western Ry. Co.*, L. R. 6 Q. B. 612; 40 L. J. Q. B. 300; *Mytton* v. *Midland Ry. Co.*, 4 H. & N. 615; 28 L. J. Ex. 385.)

The carrier is bound to be ready to deliver luggage of which he takes charge to the passenger at the end of the journey. As to what is a sufficient delivery see *Patscheider* v. *Great Western Ry. Co.*, 3 Ex. D. 153; *Richards* v. *London, Brighton, and South Coast Ry. Co.*, 7 C. B. 839, 860; 18 L. J. C. P. 251; and see Redfield on "*Carriers*," at p. 61. As to what is a taking in charge by the carrier see *Lovell* v. *London, Chatham, and Dover Ry. Co.*, 45 L. J. Q. B. 476; 34 L. T. 127; *Leach* v. *South Eastern Ry. Co.*, 34 L. T. 134. As to damages see "*Carriers of Goods*," *ante*, p. 128.

3. The defendants did not carry the said luggage to Exeter by the said train, and did not there deliver the said luggage to the plaintiff on the arrival of the said train, or within a reasonable time thereafter, although the plaintiff was then ready and willing to take delivery of the said luggage.

4. The defendants have either lost or retained the said luggage, whereby the plaintiff has been and still is deprived of the said trunks and wearing apparel, and has suffered great inconvenience, and has incurred expense amounting to —— in endeavouring to recover possession thereof.

Company (*a*).

(*a*) Public companies and other corporations aggregate, whether incorporated by charter, or by Act of Parliament, or by statutory registration, sue and are sued by their corporate name. When corporations have been once mentioned by their corporate name in the title of the pleadings, they may be styled "the plaintiffs" or "the defendants" throughout the body thereof.

An action cannot be brought by or against an indeterminate body of persons, unless they are incorporated or are made capable of suing or being sued by statute. (*Russell* v. *Men of Devon,* 2 T. R. 667; *Sloman* v. *New Zealand Government,* 1 C. P. D. 563; 46 L. J. C. P. 185.)

Railway and canal companies, and many other companies which are formed for carrying out undertakings requiring the aid of statutory powers, are incorporated by special Acts of Parliament, and all such companies sue and are sued by the name by which they are incorporated.

Ordinary joint stock companies are now regulated by The Companies Acts, 1862, 1867, 1877, 1879 and 1880, which may be referred to as "The Companies Acts, 1862 to 1880." The Companies Act, 1862 (25 & 26 Vict. c. 89), is now the principal Act upon the subject, although its provisions have been to some extent amended and modified by the Companies Acts, 1867, 1877, 1879, and 1880 (30 & 31 Vict. c. 131, 40 & 41 Vict. c. 26, 42 & 43 Vict. c. 76, and 43 Vict. c. 19).

The Act of 1862, by s. 176, applies to companies formed and registered under the Acts of 1856 and 1857, in the same manner as if they were formed and registered under the Companies Act, 1862, subject to certain modifications in that section.

Companies incorporated by registration under the Companies Act, 1862, or to which that Act applies, such as those formed or registered under the previous Acts of 1856 and 1857 (see ss. 175, 176, 177 of the Act of 1862), sue and are sued by their registered name. (See s. 18 of the Act of 1862, *Wolf* v. *The City Steamboat Co.*, 7 C. B. 103.) Where a company is formed on the principle of limited liability, the word "Limited" must be added as the last word in its name.

Statement of Claim for a Call by a Company formed by special Act of Parliament incorporating the provisions of the Companies Clauses Consolidation Act, 1845 (8 *&* 9 *Vict. c.* 16) (*b*).

1. The plaintiffs are a company incorporated by and under the provisions of [*state the company's special Act*

(Companies Act, 1862, ss. 8 and 9.) Where there is a change in the name of the company, the change of name is not complete until the certificate of incorporation in the new name has been issued. (*Shackleford, Ford & Co.* v. *Dangerfield*, L. R. 3 C. P. 407 ; 37 L. J. C. P. 151.)

By s. 9 of the Companies Act, 1867, power is given to a *limited* company to reduce its capital, and by s. 10 the company, after exercising this power, must, during such period as shall be fixed by the Court therein mentioned, add to its name the words "and reduced" as the last words in its name, and those words shall during that period be deemed to be part of the name of the company within the meaning of the Companies Act, 1862. And by the Companies Act, 1877, sec. 3, it is enacted that such power of reduction shall extend and apply to the paid-up capital of a company as well as to capital not paid-up, and s. 4 of that Act gives the Court in certain cases a discretionary power to dispense with the addition of the words "and reduced" to the name of a company reducing its capital. As to re-registration of an unlimited company as a limited one, see 42 & 43 Vict. c. 76, s. 4.

During the winding-up of a company under the Companies Act, 1862, actions are still brought by or against the company in its own name, whether in respect of calls or other matters. On a compulsory winding-up the official liquidator, by s. 95, has power, with the sanction of the Court in which the winding-up is proceeding, to bring or defend any action in the name and on behalf of the company. By s. 133 (7) the liquidator appointed to conduct a voluntary winding-up may exercise the same power without the necessity for obtaining any such sanction ; and by s. 151, the liquidator appointed to conduct a voluntary winding-up, subject to the supervision of the Court, may (subject to any restriction imposed by the Court) exercise the same powers as the liquidators in an ordinary voluntary winding-up.

After a winding-up order has been made for the winding-up of any company under the Companies Acts, 1862 and 1869, the Judge, in whose Court such winding-up is pending, has power to order the transfer to himself of any action pending in any other Division brought or continued by or against such company. (R. S. C. 1876, r. 18.)

As to obtaining a stay of proceedings after the commencement of a winding-up, see "Defences," "*Company.*"

See further "*Bankers,*" *ante*, p. 72, and "*Corporations,*" *post*, p. 162.

(*b*) Several of the Acts of Parliament relating to companies contain provisions for simplifying the pleadings and proofs in actions against shareholders for calls. As to how far these enactments are now in force, see *infra*.

The Companies Clauses Consolidation Act, 1845 (8 & 9 Vict. c. 16

or Acts], incorporating the provisions of the Companies Clauses Consolidation Act, 1845.

2. The defendant is [*or* was] the holder of —— shares in the said company.

---

contains the following provisions relating to actions for calls by companies to which that Act applies:—By s. 25, "if at the time appointed by the company for the payment of any call any shareholder fail to pay the amount of such call, it shall be lawful for the company to sue such shareholder for the amount thereof, in any Court of law or equity having competent jurisdiction, and to recover the same, with lawful interest, from the day on which such call was payable." By s. 26, "in any action or suit to be brought by the company against any shareholder to recover any money due for any call, it shall not be necessary to set forth the special matter, but it shall be sufficient for the company to declare that the defendant is the holder of one share or more in the company (stating the number of shares), and is indebted to the company in the sum of money to which the calls in arrear shall amount in respect of one call or more upon one share or more (stating the number and amount of each of such calls), whereby an action hath accrued to the company by virtue of this and the special Act." By s. 27, "on the trial or hearing of such action or suit, it shall be sufficient to prove that the defendant at the time of making such call was a holder of one share or more in the undertaking, and that such call was in fact made, and such notice thereof given as is directed by this or the special Act; and it shall not be necessary to prove the appointment of the directors who made such call, nor any other matter whatsoever; and thereupon the company shall be entitled to recover what shall be due upon such call, with interest thereon, unless it shall appear either that any such call exceeds the prescribed amount, or that due notice of such call was not given, or that the prescribed interval between two successive calls had not elapsed, or that calls amounting to more than the sum prescribed for the total amount of calls in one year had been made within that period." By s. 28, "the production of the register of shareholders shall be *primâ facie* evidence of such defendant being a shareholder, and of the number and amount of his shares."

Before the Judicature Acts it was held that the statutory form given by the above Act must, if adopted, be strictly followed (*Moore* v. *Metropolitan Sewage Co.*, 3 Ex. 333), and that it ought to be adopted in all cases to which it was applicable (*Wolverhampton Waterworks Co.* v. *Hawkesford*, 6 C. B. N. S. 336; 7 Ib., 795; 11 Ib., 456; *Wilson* v. *Birkenhead Ry. Co.* 6 Ex. 624). As the action in this form charged the defendant only upon his liability as a shareholder, it was held that it was necessary to insert the express averment that he is a shareholder. (*Wolverhampton Waterworks Co.* v. *Hawkesford*, *supra*.) That averment meant that he *was* a shareholder at the time the call was made (*Belfast, &c., Ry. Co.* v. *Strange*, 1 Ex. 739); and therefore the form was not applicable to the executor of a deceased shareholder who had died after the calls were made (*Birkenhead, Lancashire, and Cheshire Ry. Co.* v. *Cotesworth*, 5 Ex. 226); and in such case it was necessary that the averments should be framed according to the facts.

A person may be a shareholder within s. 27, although there is not

3. Before the commencement of this action, and while the defendant was such shareholder as aforesaid a call of £——, payable on the 5th of April, 1879, was made upon each of the said shares, and due notice thereof was given to the defendant.

---

a duly sealed register of shareholders under s. 9. (*Wolverhampton Waterworks Co.* v. *Hawkesford*, 11 C. B. N. S. 456; 31 L. J. C. P. 184; and see *Burke* v. *Lechmere*, L. R. 6 Q. B. 297; 40 L. J. Q. B. 98.)

Under the Companies Clauses Consolidation Act a call may be made payable by instalments (*North Western Ry. Co.* v. *M'Michael*, 6 Ex. 273; *Birkenhead, Lancashire, and Cheshire Junction Ry. Co.* v. *Webster*, 6 Ex. 277); but it would seem that before the Judicature Acts the instalments could not be sued for in the statutory form until all the instalments were due and payable (Ib.; *Ambergate Ry. Co.* v. *Coulthard*, 5 Ex. 459; and see *Rudder* v. *Price*, 1 H. Bl. 547). That view, however, as it was occasioned only by the form of action, the statutory form being framed in *debt* and not in *assumpsit*, would appear to be no longer of any importance.

With respect to companies registered under the Companies Act, 1862, that Act, by s. 70, enacts that "In any action or suit brought by the company against any member to recover any call or other moneys due from such member in his character of member, it shall not be necessary to set forth the special matter, but it shall be sufficient to allege that the defendant is a member of the company, and is indebted to the company in respect of a call made or other moneys due, whereby an action or suit hath accrued to the company."

To establish a *primâ facie* case in actions for calls by such last mentioned companies it is, generally speaking, only necessary to prove that the calls sued for were in fact made, that the defendant was then a shareholder in the company, that he had due notice of the making of the calls, and that the time appointed for their payment elapsed before action. (See Lindley on Partnership, 4th ed., p. 1033.)

The fact that the defendant is or was a shareholder may be *primâ facie* proved by the production of the company's register of shareholders (see Companies Act, 1862, ss. 26 and 37); and the minutes in the company's books of the resolutions making the calls (if duly signed) will, in the absence of proof to the contrary, be sufficient evidence that the calls were duly made. (See Companies Act, 1862, s. 67.)

By the provisions of s. 70 above cited, the statutory mode of pleading in actions by companies registered under the Act of 1862 was rendered applicable to actions by such companies to recover moneys other than calls due from a shareholder in his character of member of the company, as, for instance, to recover money payable on allotment of shares where the applicant had become a shareholder in respect of the shares allotted, and had become liable to pay the allotment-money by the provisions of the company's articles of association.

With respect to unincorporated Cost-book Mining Companies within the Stannaries Act, 1869, (32 & 33 Vict. c. 19,) it is enacted by s. 13 of that Act that it shall be lawful for the company to sue its shareholders for calls in any court of law having competent jurisdiction in the name of the purser for the time being of the company (as

4. The defendant has not paid the said call, or any part of it, whereby an action has accrued to the plaintiff company by virtue of the said Act [*or* Acts], and of the Companies Clauses Consolidation Act, 1845, to demand and have

---

nominal plaintiff for the company) to recover the amount of the call due, together with interest and the costs of suit, and a short statutory form of "declaration or other proceeding" in such action (analogous to the form given by the first mentioned Acts) is also given by the same section. Before this enactment it was held that a cost-book mining company could not empower the purser of the mine to sue one of the members of the company for calls. (*Hybart* v. *Parker*, 4 C. B. N. S. 209; 27 L. J. C. P. 120.)

It is at least doubtful whether the forms of pleadings given by the above cited enactments would now be held sufficient, inasmuch as they do not state all the material facts required to be proved by the plaintiffs at the trial. (See Jud. Act, O. XIX. rr. 1 and 4, and ss. 21 and 33 (2) of the Jud. Act, 1875), and it would therefore appear that a statement of claim in such actions should be somewhat more specific. But it is not necessary to state any facts except those which are required to be proved. It is not necessary to state facts which would be presumed in favour of the plaintiffs, or as to which the onus of proof would lie upon the defendant. (See O. XIX. r. 28). With respect to the proof which is ordinarily requisite to support an action for calls, see ss. 27 and 28 of the Companies Clauses Consolidation Act, 1845, *supra*, and the foregoing observations on the Companies Act, 1862. Under ordinary circumstances, and in the absence of some special provision to the contrary in the Act of Parliament or Articles of Association constituting or regulating the company, the person liable to pay a call on shares is the person who was the holder of the shares at the time the call was made, and, in the case of a transfer of the shares after the making of the call but before it has become payable, the transferor, and not the transferee, is the person ordinarily liable for its payment. (See the Companies Clauses Consolidation Act, 1845, s. 27, *supra*; *Belfast, &c. Ry. Co.* v. *Strange*, 1 Ex. 739; *Aylesbury Ry. Co.* v. *Mount*, 4 M. & G. 651; 7 *ib.* 898; *Aylesbury Ry. Co.* v. *Thompson*, 2 Ry. Cas. 668; and as to companies under the Companies Act, 1862, see s. 70 of that Act, *supra*; and Table A, art. 4 (though see also art. 6), and *Dawes' case*, 38 L. J. Ch. 512. See also *North American Colonial Association* v. *Bentley*, 19 L. J. Q. B. 427; and *Welland Ry. Co.* v. *Blake*, 6 H. & N. 410; 30 L. J. Ex. 161.)

For forms of declaration under the old practice in actions for calls by a company incorporated by acts of a colonial legislature, see *Welland Ry. Co.* v. *Blake*, *supra*; and *Welland Ry. Co.* v. *Berrie*, 6 H. & N. 416; 30 L. J. Ex. 163.

Unincorporated companies, in the absence of special statutory authority, have no power to sue one of the shareholders for calls in the name of an officer of the company, and must sue and be sued like ordinary partners. (See *Hybart* v. *Parker*, *supra*; and see *Gray* v. *Pearson*, L. R. 5 C. P. 568; *Evans* v. *Hooper*, 1 Q. B. D. 45; 45 L. J. Q. B. 206; but see Lindley on Partnership, 4th ed. pp. 469, 501.)

from the defendant the said sum of £——, together with interest thereon at the rate of —— per cent. per annum, from the said 5th day of April, 1879.

Statement of Claim by a Company incorporated and registered under the Companies Act, 1862, *for a Call and Interest thereon against a Shareholder of the Company.*

1. The plaintiffs are a company incorporated and registered under "the Companies Act, 1862" [*or* "under the Companies Acts of 1862 and 1867," *or as the fact may be, according to the date of the company's incorporation and registration, but it is unnecessary to mention the later Acts of* 1867, 1877, 1879, *or* 1880, *except in cases where the provisions of those Acts are material to the cause of action*].

2. The defendant is [*or* was] a member of the plaintiff company, and a holder of —— shares therein.

3. Before the commencement of this action, and while the defendant was such shareholder as aforesaid, a call of £—— per share was duly made upon the said shares, in pursuance of the registered articles of association of the said company, under the provisions of the said Act [*or* Acts].

4. Due notice of the said call was given to the defendant, and the said call became due and payable by the defendant on the 15th day of June, 1879.

5. The defendant, as such member and shareholder as aforesaid, thereupon became, and still is indebted to the plaintiff company in the sum of £—— in respect of the said call, and is also indebted, as such member and shareholder, to the plaintiff company for money payable by him to the plaintiff company for interest at the rate of —— per cent. per annum from the said 15th day of June, 1879 [*state the rate of interest specified by the articles*] on the said call so due from the defendant to the plaintiff company as aforesaid, and forborne at interest by the plaintiff company to the defendant at his request, whereby an action has accrued to the plaintiff company.

A like Form by a Company registered under the Companies Act, 1862, *against a Shareholder, for Money payable by him as such Shareholder upon an Allotment of Shares* (*c*).

1. [*Same as paragraph* 1 *of the last precedent.*]

2. The plaintiff company, on the —— of ——, 18—, allotted to the defendant, on his application, —— of the shares of £—— each into which the capital of the said company was divided.

3. The plaintiff company thereupon gave the defendant notice of such allotment, and the defendant accepted the said shares, so allotted to him, and became, and is [*or* was] a member and shareholder of the said company in respect thereof.

4. Under and by virtue of the provisions of the articles of association of the said company, which were registered under the said Act [*or* Acts], the sum of £—— per share upon each of the said shares so allotted became due and payable by the defendant to the plaintiff company immediately upon the giving of the said notice.

5. The defendant, as such member and shareholder as aforesaid, is indebted to the plaintiff company in the sum of £—— in respect of the moneys so due and payable by him as aforesaid, whereby an action has accrued to the plaintiff company.

Statement of Claim by a Company upon an Agreement with the Company to pay Money on Allotment of Shares (*c*).

1. The plaintiffs are a company incorporated &c. [*State the mode of incorporation of the Company.*]

(*c*) Money payable on allotment of shares is not, properly speaking, a call (See *Crosskey* v. *Bank of Wales*, 4 Giff. 314); and therefore a statement of claim in an action to recover money payable on allotment should ordinarily state a contract for the payment thereof, or otherwise show how the liability to such payment has arisen. (As to cases within s. 70 of the Companies Act, 1862, see note (*b*), *ante*, p. 146.)

The applicant for shares is bound by his offer to accept the shares and pay the allotment-money on them, if an allotment is duly made in accordance with such offer, and due notice of allotment is sent to him, even though such notice is not actually received by him. (*Wall's case*, L. R. 15 Eq. 18; *Harris's case*, L. R. 7 Ch. Ap. 587; *Beck's case*, L. R. 9 Ch. Ap. 392; *Household Fire Company* v. *Grant*, 4 Ex. D. 216; 48 L. J. Ex. 577.) For an example of a count under the old system in an action by a company on an agreement to pay

2. On the —— of ——, 18—, the defendant [by a letter of that date] promised the plaintiffs that, if they would allot to him —— of the shares of £—— each into which the capital of the said Company was divided, he the defendant in consideration thereof would thereupon pay to the plaintiffs £—— upon each of the shares so to be allotted.

3. The plaintiffs accordingly within a reasonable time duly allotted —— of the said shares to the defendant, and duly gave him notice of the said allotment, [and requested him to pay the said sum of £—— on each of the said shares so allotted, in accordance with his said promise.]

4. The said notice was received and accepted by the defendant [*see note* (c), p. 151, *as to this averment*], and the said sum of £—— on each of the said shares became due and payable by the defendant to the plaintiffs.

5. The defendant did not pay to the plaintiffs the said sum of £—— on each of the said shares so allotted, and the said sums, amounting in the whole to £——, remain due from and payable by the defendant to the plaintiffs.

Statement of Claim against a Company under s. 65 *of the Companies Clauses Consolidation Act,* 1845, *for Costs and Expenses incurred in obtaining the Company's special Act* (*d*).

1. The defendants are a company incorporated by and under the provisions of the —— Act. [*State the Company's special Act or Acts.*]

---

money on allotment, see *Ramsgate Hotel Co.* v. *Montefiore*, 4 H. & C. 164; 35 L. J. Ex. 90; and for like counts by a committee of management, see *Woolmer* v. *Toby*, 10 Q. B. 691; *Duke* v. *Dive*, 1 Ex. 36; *Duke* v. *Forbes*, *ib.* 356.

(*d*) By the Companies Clauses Consolidation Act, 1845 (8 Vict. c. 16), s. 65, it is enacted, "That all the money raised by the company —whether by subscription of the shareholders, or by loan, or otherwise—shall be applied, firstly, in paying the costs and expenses incurred in obtaining the special Act, and all expenses incident thereto; and secondly, in carrying the purposes of the company into execution." A sum of money agreed to be paid by the promoters of a railway company to a landowner for his countenance and support to their bill is not within this section; and a covenant to pay it is not binding on the company. (*Earl of Shrewsbury* v. *North Staffordshire Ry. Co.*, 35 L. J. Ch. 156; L. R. 1 Eq. 593.)

For a declaration in the old form under this section, see *Hitchins*

2. Before the passing of the said Act the plaintiff in February and March, 18—, expended moneys of the plaintiff to the amount of £—— in obtaining the said Act and in other matters incident thereto.

---

v. *Kilkenny Ry. Co.*, 9 C. B. 536; and for like counts under special Acts, *Tilson* v. *Warwick Gas Light Co.*, 4 B. & C. 962; *Carden* v. *General Cemetery Co.*, 5 Bing. N. C. 253; *Wyatt* v. *Metropolitan Board of Works*, 11 C. B. N. S. 744; 31 L. J. C. P. 217; *Savin* v *Hoylake Ry. Co.*, L. R. 1 Ex. 9; 35 L. J. Ex. 52.

Where the promoters of an Act had employed a parliamentary agent to obtain the Act, which contained a similar clause, it was held that the agent must sue his immediate employers, and that the promoters only, and not the agent, could recover under the clause. (*Wyatt* v. *Metropolitan Board of Works*, 11 C. B. N. S. 744; 31 L. J. C. P. 217; and see *Scott* v. *Lord Ebury*, L. R. 2 C. P. 255; *In re Kent Tramway Co.*, 12 Ch. D. 312, and the cases cited below.) It seems, therefore, that the above section cannot be relied upon as giving a right of action against the company in respect of work done or moneys expended in obtaining the Company's Act, by a person who has been employed by the promoters and has done the work or expended the moneys under a contract entitling him to claim remuneration or reimbursement from the promoters personally. Except in cases falling within the last-cited section or other similar enactments, the preliminary expenses incurred in the formation of a company were not recoverable against the company in an action at law under the former practice, a contract made by promoters on behalf of the intended company for the repayment of such expenses, being legally incapable of ratification by the company when subsequently formed. (See *Kelner* v. *Baxter*, L. R. 2 C. P. 174; 36 L. J. C. P. 94; *In re Empress Engineering Co.*, 16 Ch. D. 125; *Scott* v. *Lord Ebury*, *supra*.) This was so even where the articles of association of the company, which was formed under the Companies Act, 1862, expressly provided that such preliminary expenses should be paid by the company. (*Melhado* v. *Porto Allegre Ry. Co.*, L. R. 9 C. P. 503; 43 L. J. C. P. 253.) In equity, however, where the company can be properly considered to have adopted and derived benefit from the services of promoters rendered prior to the registration of the company payment for such services would appear to be enforceable. (*In re Hereford, &c. Co.*, 2 Ch. D. 621; 45 L. J. Ch. 461; *Touche* v. *Met. Ry. Warehousing Co.*, L. R. 6 Ch. Ap. 671; 40 L. J. Ch. 496; *In re Empress Engineering Co.*, *supra*.)

As to the provisions of s. 38 of the Companies Act, 1867, with reference to the disclosure of contracts entered into by promoters, directors, or trustees of a company, see "*Fraud*," *post*, p. 432.

For a former declaration in an action against a company on a Lloyd's bond, see *Chambers* v. *Manchester and Milford Ry. Co.*, 5 B. & S. 588; 33 L. J. Q. B. 268; and as to the validity of such bonds, see *ib.*, and *Blackmore* v. *Yates*, L. R. 2 Ex. 225; *White* v. *Carmarthen Ry. Co.*, 33 L. J. Ch. 93; *Re Cork and Youghal Ry.* L. R. 4 Ch. Ap. 748; 39 L. J. Ch. 277.

For a statement of claim by an assignee of a debt under ss. 95 and 157 of the Companies Act, 1862, see "*Assignment*," *ante*, p. 59.

As to foreign companies, see "*Corporations*," *post*, p. 165.

3. Particulars of the moneys so expended are contained in an account furnished by the plaintiff to the defendants before action [*or*, are as follows; *state such particulars where practicable, if not contained in accounts previously rendered.*]

4. The moneys so expended by the plaintiff were costs and expenses necessarily and properly incurred in obtaining the said Act and in matters incident thereto.

5. After the passing of the said Act moneys to an amount exceeding the said sum of £——, and applicable to the payment thereof, were raised by the defendants by subscriptions of the shareholders of the Company, and by loans and otherwise [*where practicable, specify in what mode the moneys were raised*], and at the time of the request hereinafter mentioned were in the hands of the defendants, and were moneys which in accordance with the provisions of the said Act and of the Lands Clauses Consolidation Act, might have been applied and ought to have been applied by the defendants in paying the said sum of £—— to the plaintiff for the moneys so expended by him as aforesaid.

6. The plaintiff requested the defendants to pay him the said sum of £—— out of the moneys so raised by the defendants as aforesaid, and a reasonable time for such payment elapsed before the commencement of this action.

7. The defendants did not apply any part of the moneys so raised in or towards paying the said sum of £—— to the plaintiff, and the said sum of £—— has not been paid and remains wholly due from and payable by the defendants to the plaintiff.

For Forms of Statements of Claim by and against Banking Companies, see ante, "Bankers," p. 72.

Statement of Claim against a Company for a Mandamus, requiring them to issue their warrant to the Sheriff to summon a jury to assess the value of Land in respect of which Notice to Treat has been given under the Lands Clauses Consolidation Act, 1845, *and for Damages* (*e*).

1. The defendants are a company incorporated [*state the mode of incorporation of the company showing that*

(*e*) A notice to treat for the sale of lands under the provisions of the Lands Clauses Consolidation Act, 1845, creates what for most purposes amounts to a relation of vendor and purchaser between the

the Lands Clauses Consolidation Act, 1845, *applies thereto.*]

2. The defendants, on the —— of ——, 18—, gave notice to the plaintiff that for the purposes of their under-

---

landowner and the company giving the notice, even where the land has not been actually taken by the company. The company, after giving such notice, may be compelled to have the value of the land assessed in the statutory manner, and if they neglect or refuse to issue their warrant to the sheriff for that purpose, and after the proper steps have been taken by the landowner, an action may be brought against them for a mandamus to compel them to perform that duty. (See *post*, "*Mandamus*," and *Fotherby* v. *Metropolitan Ry. Co.*, L. R. 2 C. P. 188; 36 L. J. C. P. 88; *Morgan* v. *Metropolitan Ry. Co.*, L. R. 3 C. P. 553; 4 Ib. 97; 37 L. J. C. P. 265; 38 L. J. C. P. 87; see also *Guest* v. *Poole and Bournemouth Ry. Co.*, L. R. 5 C. P. 553; 39 L. J. C. P. 329.) As soon as the value of the land is thus fixed, the relation of vendor and purchaser becomes complete. (See *Harding* v. *Metropolitan Ry. Co.*, 41 L. J. Ch. 371; L. R. 7 Ch. Ap. 154; and the cases there cited.)

Whenever land has been actually taken by the company or injuriously affected by the execution of their works, and the compensation claimed exceeds the amount of £50, it is in effect enacted by s. 68 of the last-mentioned Act that, where due notice has been given by the party entitled to compensation of his desire to have the amount of such compensation settled by the verdict of a jury, and the company have not paid or entered into a written agreement to pay the amount of compensation claimed, and have neglected to issue within due time their warrant to the sheriff to summon a jury to settle the amount of such compensation, the company thereby become liable to pay to the party entitled to compensation the whole amount claimed by him. (See forms of action in such cases under the old system, *Railstone* v. *York, Newcastle, and Berwick Ry. Co.*, 15 Q. B. 404; *Burkinshaw* v. *Birmingham and Oxford Junction Ry. Co.*, 5 Ex. 475; *Eastham* v. *Blackburn Ry. Co.*, 9 Ex. 758; *Glyn* v. *Aberdare Ry. Co.*, 6 C. B. N. S. 359; 28 L. J. C. P. 271; *Wale* v. *Westminster Palace Hotel Co.*, 8 C. B. N. S. 276; *Knapp* v. *London, Chatham, and Dover Ry. Co.*, 2 H. & C. 212; 32 L. J. Ex. 236.)

But so far as regards railway companies, the provisions of the last-mentioned section have been modified by the Regulation of Railways Act, 1868 (31 & 32 Vict. c. 119), which in substance enacts, by s. 41, that in every case of lands purchased or taken otherwise than by agreement, and in every case of lands injuriously affected as therein mentioned, either the company or the landowner may, at any time before the issue of the company's warrant to the sheriff, apply for a Judge's order for the trial of the question of compensation, to be stated in an issue which is to be tried in the same manner as any issue joined in an ordinary action. The jurisdiction given by this section is now vested in the High Court of Justice and the Judges thereof; and the same Act by s. 42 enacts that whenever the company, under the provisions of the Lands Clauses, &c., Act, are bound to issue their warrant to the sheriff to summon a compensation jury, the obtaining by the company of such Judge's order as above mentioned, shall be a satisfaction of such duty on the part of the company.

taking they required to purchase and take certain lands and premises therein mentioned, situated at —— in the county of ——, belonging to the plaintiff.

3. The plaintiff had a greater interest in the said lands

But it seems doubtful whether the provisions of the two last-cited sections apply to the case of lands in respect of which a railway company has merely given notice to treat without having actually taken or had possession of them.

In an action for the amount of compensation assessed by a jury, under the provisions of the Lands Clauses Consolidation Act, 1845, the verdict of the jury is, generally speaking, conclusive as to the amount of compensation, but not as to the right, which may be disputed in an action for the amount. (*R.* v. *London & North-Western Ry. Co.*, 3 E. & B. 443; *Read* v. *Victoria Station and Pimlico Ry. Co.*, 1 H. & C. 826; 32 L. J. Ex. 167; and see *Barber* v. *Nottingham & Grantham Ry. Co.*, 15 C. B. N. S. 726; 33 L. J. C. P. 193; *Mortimer* v. *South Wales Ry. Co.*, 1 E. & E. 375; 28 L. J. Q. B. 129.) So it is also with the award of an arbitrator as to the amount, unless it appears that he has included non-compensable items of claim in his award. (*Beckett* v. *Midland Ry. Co.*, L. R. 1 C. P. 241; 35 L. J. C. P. 163; *Rhodes* v. *Airedale Commissioners*, 1 C. P. D. 380, 402; 45 L. J. C. P. 861; *Duke of Buccleuch* v. *Metropolitan Board of Works*, L. R. 3 Ex. 306; L. R. 5 H. L. 418; 37 L. J. Ex. 177; 39 L. J. Ex. 136; 41 L. J. H. L. 137.)

Compensation under the statute includes all damage for injuries which could be reasonably anticipated and ascertained at the time of assessing it. (*Croft* v. *London & North-Western Ry. Co.*, 3 B. & S. 436; 32 L. J. Q. B. 113; and see *Stone* v. *Mayor of Yeovil*, 1 C. P. D. 691; 2 *ib.* 99; 45 L. J. C. P. 657; 46 *ib.* 137.)

As to the meaning of "injuriously affected," see *Chamberlain* v. *West-End, &c. Ry. Co.*, 2 B. & S. 605, 617; 31 L. J. Q. B. 201 *Rickett* v. *Metropolitan Ry. Co.*, L. R. 2 H. L. 175; 36 L. J. H. L. 205; *Beckett* v. *Midland Ry. Co.*, L. R. 3 C. P. 82; *Hammersmith Ry. Co.* v. *Brand*, L. R. 4 H. L. 171; 38 L. J. H. L. 265; *Duke of Buccleuch* v. *Met. Board of Works*, and other cases cited *supra*, and *M'Carthy* v. *Met. Board of Works*, L. R. 7 H. L. 243; 43 L. J. C. P. 385.

To entitle a party, none of whose land has been taken, to compensation under the Lands Clauses Consolidation Act, or the Railway Clauses Consolidation Act, for injurious affection of land or buildings, the injury or damages sustained must be such as, but for the statute authorising the acts done by the company or undertakers, would have supported an action against them, and there must be permanent injury and damage affecting the land or buildings, as distinguished from a mere personal inconvenience or damage to any particular trade which may be carried on there. (See *M'Carthy* v. *Metropolitan Board of Works*, L. R. 7 H. L. 243; 43 L. J. C. P. 385, and cases cited above.)

For declarations under the old system to recover compensation under the Lands Clauses Consolidation Act, 1845, assessed by the sheriff's jury, and for the costs of the inquiry, see *South-Eastern Ry. Co.* v. *Richardson*, 15 C. B. 810; *Chapman* v. *Monmouthshire Ry. Co.*,

and premises than as tenant for a year, or from year to year, and the compensation claimed by him exceeded £50.

4. No agreement was come to between the plaintiff and the defendants as to the amount of compensation to be paid to the plaintiff by the defendants for his said interest in the said lands and premises, and for the damage sustained by him by reason of the execution of the works authorised by the said Act and the Acts incorporated therewith.

5. The plaintiff desired to have the amount of such compensation settled by the verdict of a jury and not by arbitration, and gave notice of such desire to the defendants, stating in his said notice the nature of his interest in the lands and premises in respect of which he claimed compensation, and the amount of compensation so claimed by him, and duly required the defendants to issue a warrant to the sheriff of the said county to summon a jury to assess and settle the amount of such compensation as aforesaid in manner required by law and by the several statutes in that behalf.

6. All conditions were fulfilled and all times elapsed necessary to entitle the plaintiff to have the defendants issue their warrant to such sheriff to summon a jury to assess and settle the amount of the said compensation.

---

2 H. & N. 267 ; 27 L. J. Ex. 97 ; *Mortimer* v. *South Wales Ry. Co.*, 1 El. & El. 375 ; 28 L. J. Q. B. 129 ; *Fletcher* v. *Great Western Ry. Co.*, 4 H. & N. 242 ; 28 L. J. Ex. 147 ; *Read* v. *Victoria Station & Pimlico Ry. Co.*, 1 H. & C. 826 ; 32 L. J. Ex. 167.

For like declarations for compensation awarded by arbitration under ss. 23, 68, see *Evans* v. *Lancashire & Y. Ry. Co.*, 1 E. & B. 754 ; *Chamberlain* v. *West-End & Crystal Palace Ry. Co.*, 2 B. & S. 605, 617 ; 3 *ib.* 768 ; 31 L. J. Q. B. 201 ; 32 *ib.* 173 ; *Beckett* v. *Midland Ry. Co.*, L. R. 1 C. P. 241 ; 35 L. J. C. P. 163 ; *Eagle* v. *Charing Cross Ry. Co.*, L. R. 2 C. P. 638 ; *Duke of Buccleuch* v. *Metropolitan Board of Works*, L. R. 3 Ex. 306. See further, "*Arbitration*," *ante*, p. 56.

For a former count against a railway company for compensation for minerals, the working of which was prevented by the company, as likely to damage the works of the railway, under s. 78, see *Fletcher* v. *Great Western Ry. Co.*, 4 H. & N. 242 ; 5 *ib.* 689 ; 28 L. J. Ex. 147 ; and see, for an instance of a former declaration against a canal company for compensation for mines under the canal, the working of which the company prevented, under a local Act, *Swindell* v. *Birmingham Canal Co.*, 9 C. B. N. S. 241 ; 29 L. J. C. P. 364 ; and see *R.* v. *Aire and Calder Navigation*, 30 L. J. Q. B. 337, and *Dunn* v. *Birmingham Canal Co.*, 7 L. R. Q. B. 244 ; 8 *ib.* 42 ; and see *Smith* v. *Great Western Ry. Co.*, 3 App. Cas. 165 47 L. J. Ch. 97, as to the right to compensation in such cases.

7. The plaintiff was and is personally interested in the performance of that duty by the defendants, and such performance thereof was demanded by the plaintiff of the defendants.

8. The defendants wholly neglected and refused, and still neglect and refuse to perform the said duty, and to issue such warrant as aforesaid to the sheriff.

9. By reason of the matters hereinbefore complained of the amount of the said compensation has never been assessed or settled, and the payment thereof has been and will be delayed. [*State any special damage sustained.*]

The plaintiff claims—

1. £—— damages.

2. A peremptory writ of mandamus directed to the defendants, requiring them to issue their warrant to the said sheriff to summon a jury to assess and settle the amount of the said compensation.

3. Such further or other relief as the nature of the case may require.

For a Statement of Claim for Compensation awarded by arbitration under the Lands Clauses Consolidation Act, 1845, *see Stone* v. *Mayor of Yeovil,* 1 C. P. D. 691; 2 *ib.* 99; 45 L. J. C. P. 657.

Conditions Precedent (*a*).

General averment of the Performance of Conditions precedent.

All conditions were performed, and all things happened, and all times elapsed necessary to entitle the plaintiff to

---

(*a*) *Conditions precedent.*] As to the averment of the performance of conditions precedent, and as to the necessity of alleging conditions precedent in the statement of the contract, and the performance of them, see *ante*, p. 15, and *Grafton* v. *Eastern Counties Ry. Co.*, 8 Ex. 699; *Mason* v. *Harvey*, 8 Ex. 819; *Scott* v. *Avery*, 8 Ex. 487; 5 H. & C. 811; *Milner* v. *Field*, 5 Ex. 829; *Worsley* v. *Wood*, 6 T. R. 710.

As to what are conditions precedent in a contract, see the notes to *Pordage* v. *Cole*, 1 Wms. Saund. 548 (ed. 1871), and to *Peeters* v. *Opie*, 2 Wms. Saund. 742, and to *Cutter* v. *Powell*, 2 Sm. L. C., 8th ed., p. 1; and see Leake on Contracts, 633—669.

By the C. L. P. Act, 1852, s. 57, "It shall be lawful for the plaintiff or defendant in any action to aver performance of conditions precedent generally, and the opposite party shall not deny such averment generally, but shall specify in his pleading the condition or conditions precedent, the performance of which he intends to contest."

[have the said agreed cargo loaded on board the said ship, *or as the case may be, or*] have a performance of the said promise [*or* agreement *or* covenant] of the defendant, and to maintain this action for the breach thereof hereinafter

---

It would seem doubtful whether this provision, which is a most salutary one, is still in force unaffected by the Judicature Acts.

By sec. 33 (2) of the Judicature Act, 1875, all enactments inconsistent with the Judicature Acts are repealed, whilst by sec. 21 of the same Act all forms and methods of procedure, save as otherwise provided by the Judicature Acts and Rules, which were in force in any of the Courts whose jurisdiction is transferred to the High Court of Justice, and which are not inconsistent with the Judicature Acts and Rules, may continue to be used and practised. (See as to power to make rules, Judicature Act, 1875, ss. 16, 17, 24.)

The question, therefore, is whether the above provisions are so inconsistent as to be repealed. Now O. XIX. r. 1 enacts that the rules thereinafter given shall be substituted for former rules of pleading. Whilst O. XIX. r. 4 requires a statement of material facts, and no express provision is made for such a general averment of performance of conditions precedent in the rules. See further, "*Pleading in General*," *ante*, p. 7.

But, on the other hand, O. XIX. r. 4 enacts that the material facts are to be stated concisely, and that forms similar to those in App. (C) to Judicature Act, 1875, may be used, and Form (6) in App. (C) (which see *post*, p. 160), gives a general averment of conditions precedent.

Further, the practice has, since the Judicature Acts, been to allege performance of conditions precedent generally, where convenient. It will be found that the view that conditions precedent may still be alleged generally, is taken in Leake on Contracts, 669; see also for an example of the use of such a general averment, *Macdonald* v. *Carington*, 4 C. P. D. 28.

It is to be noted, that by O. LIX. non-compliance with any of the Rules shall not render the proceedings in any action void, unless the Court or a Judge shall so direct, but such proceedings may be set aside, either wholly or in part, as irregular, or amended, or otherwise dealt with in such manner and upon such terms as the Court or Judge shall think fit, and by O. XXVII. r. 1, pleadings which may tend to prejudice, embarrass or delay the fair trial of an action may be struck out or amended. Consequently, it may perhaps be, that it is not strictly regular to allege such performance generally, but that such allegations would not be struck out in cases where they did not prejudice, embarrass, or delay the fair trial of the action (see *Millington* v. *Loring*, 6 Q. B. D. 190; 50 L. J. Q. B. 214; "*Pleading in general*," *ante*, p. 7).

If it is no longer permissible to aver generally the performance of conditions precedent, the pleader must, as before the passing of the C. L. P. Act, 1852, anxiously determine what are conditions precedent to the right of action, &c., and aver their performance with certainty and particularity.

The general averment of the performance of conditions precedent prevents all danger of a demurrer upon the ground that performance of some condition precedent has not been alleged. The

alleged; [*where there are negative conditions also, add:* and nothing happened to disentitle the plaintiff from maintaining this action for the same, *or* for the breach hereinafter alleged.]

The like. (*This is given in Form No. 6 of App.* (*C*) *to Jud. Act*, 1875, *Stat. of Defence.*)

The [defendants] did all things which were necessary to entitle them to delivery by the said Messrs. M. N. & Co. of the said 1200 tons of coal under their said contract, and the time for delivery has long since elapsed.

General Averment, excusing some, and stating the Performance of all other Conditions precedent.

Before and at the time for [payment of the said £—— by the plaintiff, the defendant excused the plaintiff from

---

opposite pleader is not tempted to raise unnecessary questions, and is compelled to state specifically the conditions precedent, the fulfilment or performance of which he contests. (C. L. P. Act, 1852, sec. 57, *supra*; O. XIX. r. 20.)

Where a condition has not been performed, the above general averment would be untrue, and might be met by a denial of the performance of the particular condition. The ground which the party may have for excusing the non-performance could not be set up in answer to this denial, and in support of his original averment of the performance of all conditions; for this would be a departure in pleading. In the case therefore of any necessary condition remaining unperformed, the party should state the matter of excuse in the first instance. This was the rule before the C. L. P. Act, 1852, and it is not altered. (Co. Lit. 304, *a*; O. XIX. r. 19; *Manby* v. *Cremonini*, 6 Ex. 808; *Cort* v. *Ambergate Ry. Co.*, 17 Q. B. 127; 20 L. J. Q. B. 460; 24 L. J. Q. B. 460.) The conditions excused, and the excuses of performance should be averred with particularity, and not in a general form. (*London Dock Co.* v. *Sinnott*, 8 E. & B. 347.)

The general averment of the performance and happening of all things necessary to the plaintiff's right of action, imports a sufficient statement of his being ready and willing to do all things necessary to be done on his part in future. (*Bentley* v. *Dawes*, 9 Ex. 666.) But the general averment of readiness and willingness is not sufficient in the case of a condition precedent which requires either performance or an excuse for non-performance. (*Roberts* v. *Brett*, 6 C. B. N. S. 611, 633); and a general averment of all conditions precedent having been performed and fulfilled will not supply the omission of specific averments of other facts essential to the cause of action or defence. (See *Bloomer* v. *Darke*, 2 C. B. N. S. 165; *Irving* v. *Gray*, 3 H. & N. 34; *Tabor* v. *Edwards*, 4 C. B. N. S. 1; *Hollis* v. *Marshall*, 2 H. & N. 755.)

paying or tendering the same *state the conditions excused, and the mode by which they were excused*], and except as aforesaid, all conditions were performed, and all things happened, and all times elapsed, necessary to entitle the plaintiff to maintain this action for the breach of the said promise [*or* agreement *or* covenant] hereinafter alleged.

General Averment where the Performance of some of the Conditions precedent has been prevented by the Defendant's breach of the Contract.

The plaintiff has always been ready and willing to perform the said agreement [*or* covenant] on his part, and has performed the same except so far as he was prevented from so doing by the defendant's breach of the said agreement [*or* covenant] hereinafter mentioned; and, except as aforesaid, all conditions were fulfilled, and all things happened, and all times elapsed, necessary to entitle the plaintiff to maintain this action for the breach of the said agreement [*or* covenant] by the defendant hereinafter alleged.

Averment of Waiver of Conditions precedent by the Promiser absolutely disabling himself from performing the Promise or Contract on his part (*b*).

1. Afterwards the defendant by [*state the mode*] absolutely disabled himself from performing the said contract on his part, and waived and excused the performance by the plaintiff of all conditions precedent on his part to be performed.

2. The plaintiff had until the time when the defendant so disabled himself as aforesaid been always ready and willing to perform all conditions precedent to be performed on his part, and to carry out the said contract, and all conditions up to such time to be performed by the plaintiff had in fact been performed.

(*b*) If the promiser disables himself from performing the contract on his part, he thereby waives or excuses the performance of future conditions precedent to his liability. (Leake on Contracts, 668, 869; *Ford* v. *Tiley*, 6 B. & C. 325; *Short* v. *Stone*, 8 Q. B. 358; *Caines* v. *Smith*, 15 M. & W. 189; *Lovelock* v. *Franklyn*, 8 Q. B. 371.) The mode by which the promiser has disabled himself should be stated where practicable.

Averment of Waiver of Conditions precedent by the Promiser by an absolute Refusal to perform and Repudiation of the Agreement on his part (c).

1. Afterwards (and before the time for the performance of the said agreement) the defendant absolutely repudiated his said agreement and refused to be any longer bound thereby, and gave express notice to the plaintiff that he would not perform the same (by letter dated the —— of ——, 18—, *or as the case may be*).

2. Until the time when the defendant so absolutely repudiated his said agreement and refused to be any longer bound thereby and gave the said notice, the plaintiff was always ready and willing to perform all conditions precedent to be performed on his part, and to carry out the said agreement, and all conditions up to such time to be performed by the plaintiff had in fact been performed.

Corporations (*a*).

Commencements and Conclusions of Statements of Claim by and against Corporations.

(*c*) An absolute refusal to perform an agreement and a repudiation of it by the promiser, communicated by him to the opposite party, is a waiver and excuse of the performance by such party of future conditions precedent, and, if accepted as a termination of the agreement, gives to the opposite party, in general, an immediate right of action, even though the time for performance by the promiser has not arrived. Thus, where the defendant agreed to marry the plaintiff whenever his father should die, and afterwards repudiated his agreement, and expressly stated that he never would marry the plaintiff, and refused to consider himself any longer engaged, it was held that he could be sued immediately upon such repudiation, though his father was still alive. (*Frost* v. *Knight*, L. R. 7 Ex. 111; 41 L. J. Ex. 79; see also to same effect, *Cherry* v. *Thompson*, L. R. 7 Q. B. 574; 41 L. J. Q. B. 243; *Hochster* v. *Delatour*, 2 E. & B. 678; 22 L. J. Q. B. 455; *Roper* v. *Johnson*, L. R. 8 C. P. 167; 42 L. J. C. P. 65; *Brown* v. *Muller*, L. R. 7 Ex. 319; 41 L. J. Ex. 214; *Danube and Black Sea Ry.* v. *Xenos*, 13 C. B. N. S. 825; 31 L. J. C. P. 284; *Ex parte Chalmers*, L. R. 8 Ch. Ap. 289; 42 L. J. Bk. 37; *Re Phœnix Bessemer Steel*, 4 Ch. D. 108; 46 L. J. Ch. 115.) See also Leake on Contracts, 871—875.

(*a*) For the mode generally in which corporations sue and are sued, see *ante*, "*Company*," p. 145. In actions brought by or against corporations, the fact of their incorporation should usually be shown in the statement of claim. In the case of an English corporation duly constituted and bearing a name which is conferred or recognised by

Form of Statement of Claim by a Municipal Corporation (*b*).

In the High Court of Justice. 18— M. No.—.

Queen's Bench Division.

Writ issued ——, 18—.

Between the Mayor, Aldermen, and Burgesses of the Borough of M. . *Plaintiffs.*

and

John Smith . . . . . *Defendant.*

Statement of Claim.

1. The plaintiffs are the Municipal Corporation of the borough of M. in the county of ——.

2. The defendant is &c. [*State the defendant's address and description, where material.*]

3, &c. [*State the cause of action.*]

The plaintiffs claim &c. [*State the debt, damages, or relief claimed as in the ordinary forms.*]

Statement of Claim against a Board of Guardians (*c*).

[*Formal heading as above.*]

Between John Jones . . . . *Plaintiff.*

and

The Guardians of the Poor of the —— Union in the county of —— , *Defendants.*

Statement of Claim.

---

statute, it is not however requisite that there should be an express statement of the fact of incorporation. As to the rule requiring the contracts of corporations to be under seal and the numerous exceptions which have been established to that rule, see *South of Ireland Col. Co.* v. *Waddle*, L. R. 4 C. P. 617; 38 L. J. C. P. 338; Leake on Contracts, 588, *et seq.*, and the cases there cited. Where, as in the case of an Urban Sanitary Authority under the Public Health Act, 1875 (38 & 39 Vict. c. 55, s. 174), a corporation is by statute required to contract under seal in respect of certain matters, such corporation cannot contract otherwise in regard to such matters than under seal. (*Hunt* v. *Wimbledon Local Board*, 3 C. P. D. 208; 4 *ib.* 48; 47 L. J. C. P. 540; 48 *ib.* 207.)

(*b*) The proper style of the municipal corporation of a borough (by 5 & 6 Will. IV. c. 76, s. 6,) is "The Mayor, Aldermen, and Burgesses of the Borough of ——," and the proper style of the municipal corporation of a city is "The Mayor, Aldermen, and Citizens of the City of ——" (*Attorney-General* v. *City of Worcester*, 2 Phill. 3; 15 L. J. Ch. 398; *Rochester* v. *Lee*, 15 Sim. 376).

(*c*) By 5 & 6 Will. IV. c. 69, s. 7, the guardians of the poor of every union and of every parish placed under the control of a board of guardians shall be for all the purposes of that Act a corporation by the name of "the guardians of the poor of the —— union (or of the parish of ——), in the county of ——"; and they are

1. The plaintiff is &c. [*State the plaintiff's address and description, where material.*]

2. The defendants are a body corporate [*or* are the guardians of the poor of the above-mentioned Union] under the statutes relating to the execution of the poor laws.

3, &c. [*State the cause of action.*]

The plaintiff claims &c. [*State the debt, damages, or relief claimed.*]

As to Statements of Claim by or against Sanitary Authorities under "The Public Health Act, 1875," *see below, note* (*d*).

---

thereby empowered to take and hold buildings, lands, or hereditaments, goods, effects, or other property, and may use a common seal, and are further empowered by that name to bring actions and to sue and be sued, and to take or resist all other proceedings in relation to any such property, or any bonds, contracts, securities, or instruments given to them in virtue of their office; and it is enacted that in every such action relating to any such property it shall be sufficient to state the property to be that of the guardians of the —— union or of the parish of ——. And by the 5 & 6 Vict. c. 57, s. 16, it is enacted that every such board of guardians may in all cases sue and be sued in their corporate name.

(*d*) By the Public Health Act, 1875 (38 & 39 Vict. c. 55), s. 5, England (with the exception of the metropolis, as defined by s. 4), is divided for the purposes of the Act into districts called respectively "urban sanitary districts" and "rural sanitary districts," and subject respectively to the jurisdiction of authorities called "urban sanitary authorities" and "rural sanitary authorities." By s. 6 it is in effect enacted (subject to certain provisoes therein mentioned) that the boroughs, Improvement Act districts, and local government districts therein described shall be urban sanitary districts, and that the municipal corporations, improvement commissioners, and local boards respectively therein specified shall be urban sanitary authorities for those districts respectively. By s. 7 it is enacted that every local board, and any improvement commissioners being an urban authority and not otherwise incorporated, shall continue to be or be a body corporate, designated (in the case of local boards and commissioners being urban authorities at the time of the passing of the Act) by such name as they then bore, and (in the case of local boards constituted after the passing of the Act) by such name as they may with the sanction of the local government board adopt, with a perpetual succession and a common seal, and with power to sue and be sued in such name.

By s. 9 it is enacted that the area of any union not coincident with an urban district nor wholly included in it, with the exception of those portions (if any) of that area which are included in any urban district shall be a rural district, and that (subject to the provisoe therein mentioned) the guardians of the union shall form the rural

As to Actions by or against School Boards, see below, note (e).

Statement of Claim by a Foreign Corporation (f).

[Formal heading as above.]

---

authority of such district, and that (subject to the provisions of that Act) all statutes, orders, and legal provisions applicable to any board of guardians shall apply to them in their capacity of rural authority under that Act for the purposes of that Act. And by s. 4 the word "union" "means a union of parishes incorporated or united for the relief or maintenance of the poor under any public or local Act of Parliament, and includes any parish subject to the jurisdiction of a separate board of guardians." Where the municipal corporation of a borough sue or are sued in their capacity of urban sanitary authority, they may be styled "The mayor, aldermen, and burgesses of the borough of ——, acting as [*or* being] the urban sanitary authority for [the urban sanitary district of] that borough" (see *Baker* v. *Mayor, &c., of Portsmouth*, 3 Ex. D. 4; Ib. 157; 47 L. J. Ex. 223; Ib. 289); but in such a case the municipal corporation and the sanitary authority are not two distinct and separate corporations, and it was held, before the passing of the Public Health Act, 1875, that such corporations might sue or be sued in their ordinary corporate names as municipal corporations on contracts entered into in their character of a local board or sanitary authority. (See *Nowell* v. *The Mayor, &c., of Worcester*, 9 Ex. 457; *Southampton, &c., Bridge Co.* v. *Local Board of Health of Southampton*, 8 E. & B. 801, 805; 28 L. J. Q. 41; *Andrews* v. *Mayor, &c., of Ryde*, L. R. 9 Ex. 302; 43 L. J. Ex. 174.) So where the guardians of a union sue or are sued in the capacity of a rural sanitary authority, they may be styled "The guardians of the poor of the —— union in the county of ——, acting as [*or* being] the rural sanitary authority for [the rural sanitary district of] that union." The Local Boards and Improvement Commissioners mentioned in s. 7 above cited, must sue and be sued by their proper corporate names as therein mentioned.

For examples of actions against Local Boards of Health, see *Davies* v. *Mayor, &c., of Swansea*, 8 Ex. 808; *Burland* v. *Local Board of Kingston-upon-Hull*, 3 B. & S. 271; 32 L. J. Q. B. 17; *Foreman* v. *Mayor, &c., of Canterbury*, L. R. 6 Q. B. 215; 40 L. J. Q. B. 138; *Smith* v. *The West Derby Local Board*, 3 C. P. D. 423; 47 L. J. C. P. 607; *Hunt* v. *Wimbledon Local Board*, 3 C. P. D. 108; 4 *ib.* 48; 47 L. J. C. P. 540; 48 *ib.* 207.

The provisions of s. 174 of the Public Health Act, 1875, prescribed the mode in which urban authorities must contract with reference to the matters therein specified. The provisions of s. 264 with respect to the venue of actions against sanitary authorities, &c., are no longer obligatory. See *ante*, "*Venue*," p. 24.

(*e*) By s. 30 of the Elementary Education Act, 1870 (33 & 34 Vict. c. 75), it is enacted that every school board under the Act "shall be a body corporate by the name of the school board of the district to which they belong," and shall have a perpetual succession and a common seal.

(*f*) A foreign corporation duly created according to the laws of a foreign state recognised by her Majesty, may sue and be sued by its

Between the Rio de Janeiro Railway Company . . . . . . *Plaintiffs.*
and
John Jones . . . . . . *Defendant.*

Statement of Claim.

1. The plaintiffs are a body of persons duly constituted and incorporated without the dominions and jurisdiction

---

corporate name in the English Courts; but the fact of its incorporation according to the law of the foreign state must be proved, unless admitted. (*National Bank of St. Charles* v. *De Bernales*, 1 C. & P. 569; *General Steam Navigation Co.* v. *Guillou*, 11 M. & W. 877; *Bank of Scotland* v. *Ker*, 8 Sim. 246; *Lewis* v. *Baldwin*, 11 Beav. 153; *Buenos Ayres Ry. Co.* v. *Northern Ry. Co. of Buenos Ayres*, 2 Q. B. D. 210; and see Lindley on Partnership, 4th ed., p. 1483, *seq.*, and the cases below cited.)

A colonial corporation is regarded as a foreign one, and a liability which, by a foreign or colonial statute, is declared to be a specialty debt, is regarded in this country as a debt by simple contract only. (*Welland Ry. Co.* v. *Blake*, 6 H. & N. 410; 30 L. J. Ex. 161; *Welland Ry. Co.* v. *Berrie*, 6 H. & N. 416; 30 L. J. Ex. 165; where see forms of declaration in actions by a colonial company for calls.)

A foreign trading corporation may sue in this country in a name only acquired by reputation. (*Dutch West India Co.* v. *Van Moses*, 1 Stra. 612; *Henriquez* v. *Dutch West India Co.*, 2 Ld. Ray. 1532.)

It was held that a foreign corporation was not liable to be served with a writ out of the jurisdiction under ss. 16, 18, and 19 of the C. L. P. Act, 1852 (*Ingate* v. *Austrian Lloyd's Co.*, 4 C. B. N. S. 704; 27 L. J. C. P. 323, and see *Royal Mail Steam Co.* v. *Braham*, 2 App. Cas. 381; 46 L. J. P. C. 67); but an order may now be made under the provisions of the Jud. Acts, O. XI. r. 1, for service of a notice of a writ out of the jurisdiction upon such foreign corporation. (*Westman* v. *Aktiebolaget, &c., Fabrik*, 1 Ex. D. 237; 45 L. J. Ex. D. 327; *Scott* v. *Royal Wax Candle Co.*, 1 Q. B. D. 404; 45 L. J. Q. B. D. 585.)

As to actions by or against foreign sovereigns or states, see *Emperor of Brazil* v. *Robinson*, 5 Dowl. 522; *King of Greece* v. *Wright*, 6 Dowl. 12; *United States of America* v. *Wagner*, L. R. 2 Ch. Ap. 582; 36 L. J. Ch. 624; *Prioleau* v. *United States of America*, L. R. 2 Eq. 659; 36 L. J. Ch. 36; *Republic of Peru* v. *Weguelin*, L. R. 20 Eq. 140; 44 L. J. Ch. 583; *Vavasseur* v. *Krupp*, 9 Ch. D. 351; *Republic of Costa Rica* v. *Erlanger*, 1 Ch. D. 171; *Twycross* v. *Dreyfus*, 5 Ch. D. 605; 46 L. J. Ch. 510; *Strousberg* v. *Republic of Costa Rica*, 44 L. T. 199; 29 W. R. 125.

Corporations are frequently empowered by statute to sue or be sued in the name of some member or officer of the corporation as nominal plaintiff or defendant. See *ante*, "*Bankers*," p. 72, and "*Company*," p. 145. This is the case with friendly societies (see 38 & 39 Vict. c. 60, ss. 21 and 16 (5), and "*Friendly Societies*," *post*, p. 182, where see forms); with trade unions (see 34 & 35 Vict. c. 31, s. 9, and "*Friendly Societies*," *post*, p. 185); with some insurance companies and the like under their special Acts; and with many public bodies.

of the Queen, that is to say, in the empire of Brazil, and are entitled and empowered by the law and customs of the said empire [to make and enter into the contract hereinafter mentioned and] to sue and be sued in and by their name and style above mentioned.

2. The defendant is, &c. [*State the defendant's address and description, where material.*]

3, &c. [*State the cause of action.*]

The plaintiffs claim &c. [*State the debt, damages, or relief claimed.*]

COVENANT. See "*Agreements*," *ante*, p. 50.

CROPS.

Statement of Claim for Crops Sold.

1. On the —— of ——, 18—, the plaintiff bargained and sold to the defendant —— acres of growing wheat at the price of £—— per acre.

Building societies under "The Building Societies Acts, 1874, 1875, 1877" (37 & 38 Vict. c. 42; 38 Vict. c. 9; 40 & 41 Vict. c. 63), and industrial and provident societies under "The Industrial and Provident Societies Act, 1876" (39 & 40 Vict. c. 45), are bodies corporate, and must sue and be sued accordingly in their corporate name. (See *post*, "*Friendly Societies.*")

For a form of declaration under the old practice in an action by churchwardens and overseers under 59 Geo. III. c. 12, s. 17, see *Ward* v. *Clarke*, 12 M. & W. 747.

The action against the inhabitants of a hundred, or district in the nature of a hundred is given by statute. (See *Jackson* v. *The Inhabitants of Colesworth*, 1 T. R. 71; *Russell* v. *Men of Devon*, 2 T. R. 667.) The proceedings in the action are now regulated by the 7 & 8 Geo. IV. c. 31, as modified by the provisions of the Judicature Acts. The hundredors are sued in the ordinary form by the name of "the men inhabiting within the hundred of ——, in the county of ——." The action must be brought against the inhabitants of the hundred collectively, and cannot be brought against some individual inhabitants. (*Jackson* v. *Pearson*, 1 B. & C. 304.) The venue in such action was formerly local, but now see *ante*, "*Venue*," p. 24.

Corporations Sole.]—Where a corporation sole has a name of dignity, he should sue and be sued in that name, his own Christian name being prefixed to his name of office, as for instance, "John Lord Bishop of ——." (See *ante*, p. 3.) In other cases, even in actions brought by or against him in his corporate capacity, he sues and is sued in his individual name (see *ante*, p. 3, and 2 Inst. 666); but where he sues in his corporate capacity, his name of office should be added after his own Christian and surname.

2. The said price was due from and payable by the defendant to the plantiff before the commencement of this action.

3. The defendant has not paid the said price or any part thereof.

By an Outgoing Tenant against the Landlord for Tillages, &c., according to the custom of the Country (*a*).

1. The plaintiff became tenant to the defendant of the Glebe Farm, in the parish of ——, in the county of ——, for a term of three years from the —— of ——, 18—, upon the terms amongst others that the plaintiff should during the said tenancy till and cultivate the lands belonging to the said farm in a husbandlike manner, according to the custom of the country in the said county, and that the defendant should at the expiration of the said tenancy pay to the plaintiff all such reasonable allowances as the plaintiff as off-going tenant should, according to the said custom, be entitled to receive from the defendant in respect of any benefit which the plaintiff should then give up to the defendant of any tillages, sowing, or cultivation by the plaintiff of the said lands, according to the said custom.

2. During the said tenancy the plaintiff tilled and cultivated the said lands in a husbandlike manner, according to the said custom, and at the expiration of the said tenancy gave up to the defendant the benefit of certain

---

(*a*) Where a tenant is entitled by the terms of his tenancy to be paid for the seeds, tillages, &c., surrendered by him at the expiration of the tenancy, the landlord is the person *primâ facie* liable to pay for the same, and, in the absence of a contract between the outgoing and incoming tenant, the latter is not in any way liable. (*Bradburn* v. *Foley*, 3 C. P. D. 129; 47 L. J. C. P. 331; see also *per* Willes, J., in *Stafford* v. *Gardner*, L. R. 7 C. P. 242, 249; and *Sucksmith* v. *Wilson*, 4 F. & F. 1083.)

Such a contract between an incoming and an outgoing tenant may be either express, or implied from circumstances; but the mere fact of an incoming tenant entering upon a holding in which by custom the outgoing tenant is entitled to payment for seeds, manure, tillages, or the like, and obtaining the benefit thereof, is not sufficient to give rise to such an implied contract. (*Codd* v. *Brown*, 15 L. T. 536; *Sucksmith* v. *Wilson*, *ante*; *Bradburn* v. *Foley*, *ante*.)

Where by the agreement or custom, a valuation is a condition precedent to payment, this condition, and its performance, should be stated, or else its non-performance excused.

tillages, sowing, and cultivation by the plaintiff of the said lands according to the said custom.

3. The plaintiff thereupon as off-going tenant became entitled, according to the said custom, to receive from the defendant the sum of £—— by way of reasonable allowances in respect of the said benefit so given up by him to the defendant as aforesaid.

4. The defendant had notice of the premises, and a reasonable time thereafter for the payment by him of the said sum elapsed before the commencement of this action.

5. The defendant has not paid the said sum or any part thereof.

By an Outgoing Tenant against an Incoming Tenant upon an Agreement for Tillages &c., according to the Custom of the Country.

1. [*Proceed as in Paragraph* 1 *of last form, substituting throughout the name of the lessor for the word "defendant."*]

2. During the said tenancy the plaintiff tilled and cultivated the said lands in a husbandlike manner, according to the said custom, and at the expiration of the said tenancy was prepared to give up, and offered to give up, to the said A. B. [*Insert the name of the lessor*] the benefit of certain tillages, sowing, and cultivation by the plaintiff of the said lands according to the said custom, and it was thereupon agreed between the plaintiff and the said A. B. and the defendant, who was the incoming tenant of the said farm, that, instead of the plaintiff giving up the said benefit to the said A. B., and receiving from him the said allowances in respect thereof, the plaintiff should give up the said benefit to the defendant, and the defendant should receive the same from the plaintiff and should pay to the plaintiff in respect thereof all such reasonable allowances as the plaintiff would otherwise have been entitled to receive, according to the said custom, from the said A. B.

3. The plaintiff in accordance with the said agreement gave up to the defendant the benefit of the said tillages, sowing, and cultivation by the plaintiff of the said land according to the said custom.

4. Had the plaintiff given up the said benefit to the said A. B. he would have been entitled, according to the

said custom, to receive from the said A. B. the sum of £—— by way of reasonable allowances in respect of the such benefit.

[*Repeat paragraphs 4 and 5 of last form.*]

DAMAGES. See *ante*, p. 19, and see "*Liquidated Damages*," *post*, p. 262.

DEMURRAGE (*a*).

Claim for Demurrage of Wagons at an agreed rate.

1. The plaintiffs let on hire to the defendants —— wagons for the conveyance of coal from —— colliery to London upon the terms [*state, where practicable, how the terms were agreed on, and if in writing, in what writing*], amongst others, that the defendants should load the said wagons with coal at the said colliery within 3 days after their arrival at the said colliery, and then forward them filled to London, or if they should take a longer time to load the said wagons at the said colliery, that they should pay to the plaintiffs a further sum of £—— per day for each day

---

(*a*) The word "demurrage," strictly speaking, signifies the agreed additional payment (generally per day) for an allowed detention beyond the period specified in the contract; but it is popularly used also to signify compensation for undue detention. (Leake on Contracts, 1081; *per cur.* in *Lockhart* v. *Falk*, L. R. 10 Ex. 135; 44 L. J. Ex. 108; see also *per* Brett, J., in *Sanguinetti* v. *Pacific Steam Navig. Co.*, 2 Q. B. D. 238, 251; 46 L. J. Q. B. 105.)

Where the contract is silent as to the time within which a ship, or a truck, or the like, is to be unloaded by the hirer, it is, in general, an implied term of the contract that the hirer will use reasonable diligence in unloading. (*Ford* v. *Cotesworth*, L. R. 4 Q. B. 127; L. R. 5 Q. B. 544; 39 L. J. Q. B. 188; Leake on Contracts, 695.)

But where a certain number of days are allowed by the contract for the loading or unloading by the hirer, a contract is, in the absence of anything to indicate the contrary, implied by the hirer that he will load or unload within the allowed days, and he takes upon himself the risk of any ordinary vicissitudes which may occur to prevent him doing so. (*Thiis* v. *Byers*, 1 Q. B. D. 244, 249; 45 L. J. Q. B. 511; *Randall* v. *Lynch*, 2 Camp. 352, 355, 356; 12 East, 179.)

The dates of the hiring and of the delays complained of should be inserted where practicable in the statement of claim. (See further, *post*, "*Shipping*.")

beyond the said 3 days for the demurrage of the said wagons.

2. The defendants accordingly received the said wagons upon the terms aforesaid, but they did not load them with coal at the said colliery within 3 days after their arrival at the said colliery or then forward them to London, but took 14 days to load them at the said colliery beyond the said 3 days after their arrival at the said colliery, whereby the sum of £—— became, and still is, due and payable by the defendants to the plaintiffs for the demurrage of the said wagons beyond the said three days.

Claim for Detention of Wagons beyond a reasonable time in Loading and Unloading.

1. The plaintiffs let on hire to the defendants —— wagons for the conveyance of coal from —— colliery to London upon the terms [*state, where practicable, how the terms were agreed on, and if in writing, in what writing*], amongst others, that the defendants should use reasonable despatch in loading the said wagons with coal at the said colliery, and in unloading the same upon their arrival in London.

2. The defendants accordingly received the said wagons upon the terms aforesaid, but they did not use reasonable despatch in loading them, or any of them, with coal at the said colliery, nor did they use reasonable despatch in unloading them, or any of them, upon their arrival.

3. The defendants detained the said wagons —— days in loading them at the said colliery, which was —— days beyond what was reasonable in that behalf.

4. The defendants further detained the said wagons —— days in unloading them upon their said arrival in London, which was further —— days beyond what was reasonable in that behalf.

5. The plaintiffs thereby lost the use and hire of the said wagons for —— days, and the value of such use and hire for the said —— days, which amounted to £——.

DIVIDENDS. See "*Company,*" *ante*, p. 145, and *post*, p. 369.

EXCHANGE.

Statement of Claim upon a Contract of Exchange.

1. On or about the —— of ——, 18—, it was agreed by and between the plaintiff and the defendant [in writing bearing date &c.], that the plaintiff should deliver a horse of his called —— to the defendant in exchange for a bay mare of the defendant.

2. The plaintiff thereupon, in performance of the said agreement on his part, delivered his said horse to the defendant, and the defendant then received the same upon the terms aforesaid.

3. The plaintiff has always been ready and willing to receive the said bay mare from the defendant, and a sufficient time elapsed before the commencement of this action to entitle the plaintiff to have the said bay mare delivered to him by the defendant.

4. The defendant has not delivered the said bay mare to the plaintiff.

EXECUTORS AND ADMINISTRATORS.

Statement of Claim by an Executor on Causes of Action accrued to the Deceased (*a*).

1. The plaintiff is the executor of the last will and testament of C. D., deceased, who carried on the business

---

(*a*) *Actions by executors and administrators.*]—An executor or administrator may sue upon all *personal* contracts made with the testator, in respect of the damages accrued to the personal estate from the breach of them (*Chamberlain* v. *Williamson*, 2 M. & S. 408; *Bradshaw* v. *Lancashire and Yorkshire Ry. Co.*, L. R. 10 C. P. 189; 44 L. J. C. P. 148; *Twycross* v. *Grant*, 4 C. P. D. 40, 46; 48 L. J. Q. B. 1, 3), and whether the breach occurred before or after the testator's death; but for breaches of contract which affect the person of the testator only, and not his transmissible personal estate, as a breach of promise to marry where there is no special damage to the estate, an executor or administrator cannot sue. (*Chamberlain* v. *Williamson*, 2 M. & S. 408; 1 Wms. Exs. 8th ed., 792, 807.)

Contracts with a testator affecting his *real* estate, and which run with the land, as covenants for title, covenants to repair, etc., pass with the estate to the heir or devisee if it be freehold, and to the executor where it is a chattel interest in the land. And in the former case, if the testator has not sued for breaches of such covenants in his life time, the executor cannot sue afterwards, unless in respect of some distinct loss or injury to the testator's personal estate. But, except

of a piano manufacturer at Bristol in the county of Gloucester.

2. On the —— of ——, 18—, the said C. D. sold and delivered to the defendant in Bristol aforesaid a cottage piano at the price of £——.

---

as above, where the reversion descends to an heir or devisee such heir or devisee alone can sue after the testator's death in respect of such covenants. (*Kingdon* v. *Nottle*, 1 M. & S. 355; *Jones* v. *King*, 4 M. & S. 186; 5 Taunt. 417; and see 1 Wms. Exs. 8th ed. 810 *et seq.* See further, Leake on Contracts, 1250 *et seq.*)

O. III., r. 4, of the Judicature Act, 1875, provides that if the plaintiff sues, or the defendant, or any of the defendants is sued in a representative capacity, the indorsement of claim upon the writ shall show in what capacity the plaintiff or defendant sues or is sued. (See forms, Judicature Act, App. (A), part ii. sect. viii.) O. XVI. r. 7, provides that "trustees, executors, and administrators may sue and be sued on behalf of, or as representing the property or estate of which they are trustees or representatives, without joining any of the parties beneficially interested in the trust or estate, and shall be considered as representing such parties in the action; but the Court or a judge may, at any stage of the proceedings, order any of such parties to be made parties to the action, either in addition to or in lieu of the previously existing parties thereto." (See further, r. 11 of this Order, which, subject to the Jud. Act, 1875, and the rules thereunder, incorporates the Chancery Procedure Act, 15 & 16 Vict. c. 86, s. 42.)

Before the coming into operation of the Judicature Act, 1875, a plaintiff could not join in the same declaration a claim as executor or administrator with a claim in his own right. Now, however, by O. XVII. r. 5, "claims by or against an executor or administrator, as such, may be joined with claims by or against him personally; provided the last-mentioned claims are alleged to arise with reference to the estate in respect of which the plaintiff or defendant sues, or is sued, as executor or administrator."

Where the cause of action arose in the lifetime of the deceased, the executor or administrator must sue in his representative character. (2 Wms. Exs. 8th ed. 1879.) Where the cause of action arose wholly after the death, the executor or administrator may sue either in his own name personally (as being the party contracted with), or in his representative character, if the money to be recovered would be assets of the estate. (*Ib.* 1880; *Aspinall* v. *Wake*, 10 Bing. 51; *Moseley* v. *Rendell*, L. R. 6 Q. B. 338; 40 L. J. Q. B. 111; *Abbott* v. *Parfitt*, L. R. 6 Q. B. 346; 40 L. J. Q. B. 115.) But if he continues to carry on the business of the deceased solely for his own benefit, and enters into contracts in the course of doing so, he must sue on such contracts in his own right, and cannot sue in his representative capacity. (*Bolingbroke* v. *Kerr*, L. R. 1 Ex. 222, explained in *Abbott* v. *Parfitt*, *supra*.) If the executor sues in his personal character, he would be exposed to a set-off or counterclaim of any debt due from, or liability incurred by himself to the defendant; but before the Judicature Acts came into operation, so long as he sued in his personal character no set-off could be pleaded in such action against him in his representative capacity, and it

3. The said price was due from and payable by the defendant to the said C. D. during the lifetime of the said C. D. and is still due and unpaid.

The plaintiff as executor as aforesaid claims £——.

Commencement of Statement of Claim by an Executor of an Executor.

1. The plaintiff is the executor of the last will and testament of E. F. deceased, who in his lifetime and at the time of his death was executor of the last will and testament of C. D. deceased.

Statement of Claim by an Administrator on Causes of Action accrued to the Deceased.

1. The plaintiff is the administrator of the personal estate and effects which were of C. D., deceased, who died intestate.

2. The said C. D. on the —— of——, 18—, lent to the defendant £—— for three months.

3. The said three months expired and the said loan became repayable during the lifetime of the said C. D. and is still unpaid.

The plaintiff as administrator as aforesaid claims £——.

---

would seem that if he now sues in his personal character only, no counterclaim or set-off will be allowed to be pleaded against him as executor. (*Macdonald* v. *Carington*, 4 C. P. D. 28; 48 L. J. C. P. 179; O. XIX. r. 3; O. XXII. r. 9.)

An executor may commence an action before probate, and it is sufficient if he obtains probate in time to prove his title in case it should be disputed. But the letters of administration must issue before the administrator can commence an action, for without them he has no right of action. (1 Wms. Exs. 8th ed. 311, 411.) As to the title of an executor or administrator relating back to the death, see 1 Wms. Exs. 8th ed. 636; *Foster* v. *Bates*, 12 M. & W. 226; *Bodger* v. *Arch*, 10 Ex. 333; *Welchman* v. *Sturgis*, 13 Q. B. 552.

All the executors appointed in the will, except such as have renounced probate, should join as coplaintiffs in an action on a contract made by the deceased. Those who have renounced probate need not be joined. (See 20 & 21 Vict. c. 77, s. 79.)

Where the contract was made since the death of the testator, and with some of the executors only, those only should join who were parties to the contract. By O. XVI. r. 1, however, all persons may be joined as plaintiffs in whom the right to any relief claimed is alleged to exist, whether jointly, severally, or in the alternative; and by O. XVI. r. 13, no action shall be defeated by reason of the misjoinder of parties; and see further, "*Number of the parties*," *ante*, p. 4.

Commencement of Statement of Claim by an Administrator with the Will annexed.

1. The plaintiff is the administrator of the personal estate and effects which were of C. D., deceased, with the last will and testament of the said C. D. annexed.

The like by an Administrator de bonis non *with the Will annexed.*

1. The plaintiff is administrator, with the last will and testament of C. D., deceased, annexed, of the personal estate and effects which were of the said C. D. left unadministered by E. F. and G. H. in their lifetime, now respectively deceased, who were the executors of the last will and testament of the said C. D.

The like by an Administrator de bonis non *after the Death of the first Administrator.*

1. The plaintiff is the administrator of the personal estate and effects which were of C. D., deceased, left unadministered by E. F. in his lifetime, now deceased, who was the administrator of the personal estate and effects of the said C. D.

The like by an Administrator during the Minority of an Executor (*b*).

1. The plaintiff is the administrator of the personal estate and effects which were of C. D., deceased, during the minority of E. F., an infant under the age of twenty-one years, who is executor of the last will and testament of the said C. D.

The like by an Administrator during the Absence of the Executor (*c*).

1. The plaintiff is the administrator of the personal estate and effects which were of C. D., deceased, during

---

(*b*) An administrator during the minority of an executor has, for the time, all the powers of an ordinary administrator. (*In re Cope*, 16 Ch. D. 49 ; 50 L. J. Ch. 13.)

(*c*) As to the title of an administrator *durante absentiâ*, see 1 Wms. Exs. 8th ed. p. 509 ; *Clare* v. *Hedges*, 1 Lutw. 342 ; 2 P. Wms. 579 ; *Slater* v. *May*, 2 Ld. Raym. 1071 ; *Webb* v. *Kirkby*, 7 De Gex, M. & G. ; 25 L. J. Ch. 872 ; 26 *Ib.* 145 ; *Suwerkrop* v. *Day*, 8 A. & E. 624.

the absence of E. F., who is the executor of the last will and testament of the said C. D. and who is now beyond the seas.

Statement of Claim by an Executor or Administrator on Causes of Action accrued since the Death of the Deceased.

1. The plaintiff is the executor of the last will and testament of C. D., deceased [*or* the administrator of the personal estate and effects which were of C. D., deceased, who died intestate and] who carried on the business of a bookseller at No. —— Oxford-street in the county of Middlesex.

2. The defendant also carries on the business of a bookseller in Oxford-street aforesaid.

3. On the —— of ——, 18—, after the death of the said C. D., the plaintiff, as executor [*or* administrator], as aforesaid, for the purpose of realizing the assets belonging to the estate of the said C. D., sold and delivered to the defendant the whole of the books and stock-in-trade of the said C. D. for the price of £——.

4. The said price was at the commencement of this action, and still is, due from, and payable by the defendant to the plaintiff, as executor [*or* administrator] as aforesaid, as assets of the said estate of the said C. D.

Statement of Claim against an Executor or Administrator on Causes of Action accrued against the Deceased in his Lifetime (*d*).

1. The plaintiff is a builder and house decorator, carrying on business at Croydon in the county of Surrey.

2. The defendant is the executor of the last will and testament of G. H., deceased [*or* the administrator of

---

(*d*) *Actions against executors and administrators.*]—The executor is in general liable upon all contracts made by the testator for breaches before or after death, to the extent of the assets which have come to his hands to be administered. (*Wilson* v. *Wigg*, 10 East, 313; 2 Wms. Exs. 8th ed. 1728. See further, Leake on Contracts, 1250, *et seq.*)

Contracts of agency, or for personal acts or services, are in general revoked by death, and the executor or administrator cannot be sued upon them except for breaches which occurred in the lifetime of the testator or intestate. (*Farrow* v. *Wilson*, L. R. 4 C. P. 744; *Stubbs* v. *Holywell Ry. Co.*, L. R. 2 Ex. 311, 313; *Werner* v. *Humphreys*, 2 M. & G. 853; *Campanari* v. *Woodburn*, 15 C. B. 400; *per* Parke, B., *Siboni* v. *Kirkman*, 1 M. & W. 418, 423; 2 Wms. Exs.

the personal estate and effects which were of G. H., deceased, who died intestate].

3. In the years 18— and 18—, during the lifetime of the said G. H., and at his request, the plaintiff did

---

8th ed. 796, n. (*o*), 1731; and see *Tasker* v. *Shepherd*, 6 H. & N. 575; 30 L. J. Ex. 207.)

Where a contract which is not rescinded by death is made with a person who dies before it is completed, and it is completed after his death, the statement of claim in an action upon the contract against the executor or administrator of the deceased party must state the contract specially as made with the deceased, and aver the completion after his death, and the breach by the defendant. (See, for form of declaration, *Campanari* v. *Woodburn*, 15 C. B. 400; and see also *Corner* v. *Shew*, 3 M. & W. 350.)

An executor cannot be liable, as executor, for goods sold to him, or work done at his request, or for money received by him for the use of the plaintiff, or for money lent to him. Claims against him as executor on these causes of action are construed as claims against him personally. (*Ashby* v. *Ashby*, 7 B. & C. 444; *Farhall* v. *Farhall*, L. R. 7 Ch. Ap. 123; 41 L. J. Ch. 146; *Corner* v. *Shew*, 3 M. & W. 350.) Nor is an executor liable, as such, in an action for interest on a debt due from him as executor, and forborne at his request; though he would be liable for interest due on a contract with the testator. (*Bignell* v. *Harpur*, 4 Ex. 773.) An executor may be liable in his representative capacity on accounts stated, and also for money paid for him as executor at his request. (*Ashby* v. *Ashby*, 7 B. & C. 444; see also *Farhall* v. *Farhall*, *supra*; and 2 Wms. Exs. 8th ed. 1778 *et seq.*) As to the liability of an executor for his testator's funeral, see "*Funeral Expenses*," *post*, p. 189.

A court of equity considers an executor trustee for the legatees in respect to their legacies, and will compel him to perform his trusts. (2 Wms. Exs. 8th ed. 298.)

After assent by an executor to a specific legacy, though not before, he is liable at law to an action by the legatee, because the property vests in the legatee upon the assent. (*Williams* v. *Lee*, 3 Atk. 223; 2 Wms. Exs. 8th ed. 1943.) For cases where the assent may be retracted, see 2 Wms. Exs. 8th ed. 1385.

So in the case of a general pecuniary legacy, after the executor has admitted to the legatee that he has received the money, and holds it to the use of the legatee, it becomes a debt to the latter, who may recover it in an action. (*Topham* v. *Morecraft*, 8 E. & B. 972; and see 2 Wms. Exs. 8th ed. 1945; *Whitehouse* v. *Abberly*, 1 C. & K. 642.)

By the Statute of Frauds (29 Car. II. c. 3, s. 4), it is enacted that no action shall be brought whereby to charge any executor or administrator, upon any special promise to answer damages out of his own estate, unless the agreement upon which such action shall be brought, or some memorandum or note thereof, shall be in writing, and signed by the party to be charged therewith, or some other person thereunto by him lawfully authorized. And a promise by an executor or administrator to answer personally is not binding unless supported by a new and sufficient consideration. (2 Wms. Exs. 8th ed. 1781.)

various work, and provided various materials for the said G. H., in and about making various alterations, additions, and improvements to the house of the said G. H., at Croydon aforesaid. [*State the particulars where practicable.*]

4. The price agreed to be paid by the said G. H. to the plaintiff for the said work and materials amounted to the sum of £——, and became due and payable from the said G. H. to the plaintiff during the lifetime of the said G. H., and before the commencement of this action.

5. The said sum is still due and unpaid.

For a Form of Claim by an Executrix of a Creditor against a Residuary Legatee of the Debtor, see Hunter v. *Young,* 4 Ex. D. 256; 48 L. J. Ex. 689 (*e*).

All the executors who have proved the will should be joined as co-defendants, though the non-joinder of any defendants would not be fatal, but might afford ground for a summons to show cause why they should not be made parties to the action. (See "*Number of the parties,*" *ante,* p. 4.)

Where any of the parties to an action die after the commencement thereof, and the cause of action survives or continues, the action does not become abated (O. L. r. 1), and an order may be obtained *exparte,* on application to the Court or a judge, that the proceedings in the action shall be carried on between the continuing parties to the action and such new party or parties. (O. L. r. 4; *Ashley* v. *Taylor,* 10 Ch. D. 768.) See further, as to the service and effect of such order, O. L. r. 5.

The injury to the personal estate should be shown at the time when application is made to add the executor or administrator as a party to the action. It is not necessary that it should appear in express terms upon the pleadings; it is sufficient if the fact appears by necessary implication. (*Per* Brett, L. J., *Twycross* v. *Grant,* 4 C. P. D. 40, 46; 48 L. J. Q. B. 1, 3.)

Executor de son tort.]—An executor de son tort is a person who, without having been appointed executor, or without having taken out letters of administration, intermeddles with the goods of the deceased, or does any other act characteristic of the office of executor or administrator. (1 Wms. Exs. 8th ed. 261; where see also what acts constitute an executor de son tort.) Where a person has acted in such manner as to have become an executor de son tort, he has all the liabilities, though none of the privileges that belong to an executor. (*Carmichael* v. *Carmichael,* 1 Phill. C. C. 103, *per* Lord Cottenham; *Rayner* v. *Koehler,* L. R. 14 Eq. 262; *Coote* v. *Whittington,* L. R. 16 Eq. 534; *Ambler* v. *Lindsay,* 3 Ch. D. 198; 1 Wms. Exs. 8th ed. 269.) It is not necessary to describe him as *executor de son tort* in the pleadings, but he should be sued and described as in the case of an ordinary executor. (1 Wms. *Ib.* 269, 270.)

(*e*) When an executor has administered assets and paid over the

FACTOR (*a*).

See "*Agent,*" *ante, p.* 36, and "*Broker,*" *ante, p.* 117.

---

residue of an estate, a creditor of the testator is entitled to follow the residue to the extent of his debt, and residuary legatees who have received their legacies, may be compelled to refund so much of the amounts paid to them as may be requisite to satisfy his claim. (*Hall* v. *Palmer*, 3 Hare, 532; *Fordham* v. *Wallis*, 10 Hare, 217; *Hunter* v. *Young*, 4 Ex. D. 256; 48 L. J. Ex. 689.) See further 22 & 23 Vict. c. 35, s. 29, which enacts that "where an executor or administrator shall have given such or the like notices as in the opinion of the Court in which such executor or administrator is sought to be charged would have been given by the Court of Chancery in an administration suit, for creditors and others to send in to the executor or administrator their claims against the estate of the testator or intestate, such executor or administrator shall, at the expiration of the time named in the said notices or the last of the said notices for sending in such claims, be at liberty to distribute the assets of the testator or intestate, or any part thereof, amongst the parties entitled thereto, having regard to the claims of which such executor or administrator has then notice, and shall not be liable for the assets or any part thereof so distributed to any person of whose claim such executor or administrator shall not have had notice at the time of distribution of the said assets or a part thereof, as the case may be; but nothing in the present Act contained shall prejudice the right of any creditor or claimant to follow the assets or any part thereof into the hands of the person or persons who may have received the same respectively." (*Newton* v. *Sherry*, 1 C. P. D. 246; 45 L. J. C. P. 257.)

As to married women, see O. XVI. r. 8; and "*Husband and Wife,*" *post*, 202.

See further, notes to "Defences," "*Executors and Administrators.*" See also other forms of Statements of Claim by and against Executors, "*Landlord and Tenant,*" *post*, pp. 248, 252.

(*a*) A factor is a person to whom goods are consigned for sale by a merchant residing abroad or at a distance, in general, from the place of sale; and he usually sells in his own name, without disclosing that of his principal; the latter, therefore, with full knowledge of these circumstances, trusts him with the actual possession of the goods, and gives him authority to sell in his own name. (*Per* Abbott, C. J., in *Baring* v. *Corrie*, 2 B. & Ald. 143; Leake on Contracts, 514, *et seq.*)

A factor in general acquires a lien upon the goods entrusted to him for sale for advances made to his principal, and for the general balance of account arising out of his employment as factor. (*Houghton* v. *Matthews*, 3 B. & P. 485.)

As to sales and pledges by factors, see the Factors' Acts, 1823 to 1877 (4 Geo. IV. c. 83; 6 Geo. IV. c. 94; 5 & 6 Vict. c. 39; 40 & 41 Vict. c. 39); and see Roscoe's N. P. Ev., 14th ed., 885 and Leake on Contracts, 514, *et seq.*

Farrier.

Against a Farrier [or Veterinary Surgeon] for not using due care, &c., in his treatment of the Plaintiff's Horse, which was lame.

1. The defendant is a farrier carrying on business at ——.

2. The plaintiff in the months of —— and ——, 18—, employed the defendant as a farrier for reward to treat and endeavour to cure a certain horse of the plaintiff, which was lame, upon the terms amongst others that the defendant should use and exercise due care and skill in treating the said horse and endeavouring to cure it.

3. The defendant entered upon the said employment upon the said terms.

4. The defendant treated the said horse but did not use or exercise due care or skill in treating or endeavouring to cure it.

5. The said horse in consequence became more lame and wholly incurable, and of no use or value to the plaintiff.

Fixtures (*a*).

Claim for the price of Fixtures.

1. The plaintiff sold and gave up to the defendant certain fixtures [particulars whereof are as follows, *give details where practicable*], in a house No. ——, —— Street, ——, formerly occupied by the plaintiff, upon the terms [contained in certain letters bearing date &c., *or as the case may be*] that the defendant should upon such giving up pay the plaintiff therefor the sum of £——.

2. The defendant has not paid the plaintiff the said sum of £—— or any part thereof.

The like where the Defendant was to pay a reasonable Price therefor (b).

1. The plaintiff at the request of the defendant sold and gave up to the defendant certain fixtures [particulars

---

(*a*) The sale and giving up possession of fixtures by a tenant who has a right to remove them to his landlord or to an incoming tenant, is not a sale of an interest in land within the Statute of Frauds. (*Hallen* v. *Runder*, 1 C. M. & R. 266; *Lee* v. *Gaskell*, 1 Q. B. D. 700; 45 L. J. Q. B. 540.)

(*b*) See as to "reasonable price," "*Sale of Goods*," *post*, p. 302.

whereof are as follows, *give details where practicable*], in a house formerly occupied by the plaintiff, being No. ——, —— Street, ——, upon the terms [contained in certain letters &c., *or as the case may be*] that the defendant should upon such giving up pay to the plaintiff a reasonable price for the same.

2. A reasonable price for the same is £——.

3. The defendant has not paid the plaintiff the said price or any price whatever.

FORBEARANCE (*a*).

Claim on a Promise in consideration of abstaining from further Prosecution of an Action.

1. The plaintiff on the 18th of August, 1879, sold to the defendant certain yarn at the price of £——, and

---

(*a*) Forbearance of an action commenced for a *bonâ fide* claim is a sufficient consideration for a promise, as the forbearing an action instituted or proposed to try a question which is, or which is fairly and honestly believed by the party seeking to enforce the promise, to be a doubtful question. (*Longridge* v. *Dorville*, 5 B. & Ald. 117; *Cook* v. *Wright*, 1 B. & S. 559; 30 L. J. Q. B. 321; *Callisher* v. *Bischoffsheim*, L. R. 5 Q. B. 451; 39 L. J. Q. B. 181; *Wilby* v. *Elgee*, L. R. 10 C. P. 497; 44 L. J. C. P. 254.) But forbearing an action in which the plaintiff had no cause of action, and knew it, will not support a promise. (*Wade* v. *Simeon*, 2 C. B. 548; *Ex pte. Banner*, 17 Ch. D. 480; and see *Smith* v. *Monteath*, 13 M. & W. 427; and *Callisher* v. *Bischoffsheim*, *supra*.)

Where a claim is *bonâ fide* made, respecting which doubt honestly exists, forbearing to sue is a good consideration. (*Cook* v. *Wright*, *supra*.) So, forbearing to sue for an alleged balance of unsettled accounts as to which there was a *bonâ fide* dispute between the plaintiff and defendant is a good consideration for a promise (*Llewellyn* v. *Llewellyn*, 3 D. & L. 318); but where there is no foundation for the dispute, and it is not a *bonâ fide* dispute on the part of the plaintiff, the plaintiff cannot enforce a promise, the consideration of which is his forbearing to take legal proceedings to enforce his unfounded claim. (*Edwards* v. *Baugh*, 11 M. & W. 641; *Lloyd* v. *Lee*, 1 Str. 94; and see *Cook* v. *Wright*, *and cases cited*, *supra*.) So, generally, any giving up or forbearing by agreement to enforce a legal right may afford a valid consideration for a promise. (*Lamb* v. *Brewster*, 4 Q. B. D. 220; 48 L. J. Q. B. 277.) It would seem that now an order can be made in the original action itself, and that the institution of a separate action is not necessary to enforce a compromise *bonâ fide* made in an action, where at any rate, such compromise involves only the questions in the action. (*Eden* v. *Naish*, 7 Ch. D. 781; 47 L. J. Ch. 325; *Scully* v. *Lord Dundonald*, 8 Ch. D. 658; Jud. Act, 1873, s. 24, sub.-s. 7.)

agreed to deliver the said yarn to the defendant at Manchester within a reasonable time in that behalf.

2. The plaintiff afterwards offered to deliver the said yarn to the defendant at Manchester on the 12th of September, 1879, and the defendant then absolutely refused to accept the same, and repudiated his said contract, and refused to be any longer bound thereby.

3. The plaintiff alleged and believed and still alleges and believes that he offered to deliver the said yarn within a reasonable time in that behalf, and that the defendant wrongfully refused to accept the same, and wrongfully repudiated his said contract, and wrongfully refused to be any longer bound thereby.

4. The plaintiff on the 1st of November, 1879, commenced an action in the High Court of Justice, Queen's Bench Division, to recover damages against the defendant in respect of his said refusal to accept the said yarn and repudiation of and refusal to be bound by his said contract.

5. Thereupon the defendant promised the plaintiff that if he would abstain from further prosecuting his said action he would pay to him the sum of £——.

6. The plaintiff accordingly agreed to abstain and did abstain from further prosecuting his said action.

7. The defendant has not paid to the plaintiff the said sum of £——, so promised, or any part thereof, although a reasonable time for such payment has elapsed.

Friendly Societies, Building Societies, &c. (*a*).

Commencement of Statement of Claim by a Friendly Society.

Between A. B. and C. D., Trustees
of the [*state the title of the society*]. *Plaintiffs.*
and
X. Y. . . . . *Defendant.*

(*a*) The principal enactments now in force relating to Friendly Societies are 38 & 39 Vict. c. 60, and 39 & 40 Vict. c. 32, which may be cited together with 42 & 43 Vict. c. 9, as "The Friendly Societies Acts." This last-mentioned statute is declaratory merely of the true meaning of s. 30 of "The Friendly Societies Act, 1875."

Section 8 of 38 & 39 Vict. c. 60, "The Friendly Societies Act, 1875," gives a list of societies which may be registered under that Act. (*As to earlier societies, see sect. 6.*)

Statement of Claim.

1. The above-named plaintiffs are the trustees of the [*state the title of the society*], which is a friendly society

---

By sect. 16 (3): "All property belonging to a society, whether acquired before or after the same is registered, shall vest in the trustees for the time being of the society, for the use and benefit of the society and the members thereof, and of all persons claiming through the members according to the rules of the society; and the property of any branch of a society shall vest in the trustees of such branch, or in the trustees of the society if the rules of the society so provide, for the use and benefit either of the members of such branch, and persons claiming through such members, or of the members of the society generally, and persons claiming through them, according to the rules of the society."

By sect. 16 (4): "Upon the death, resignation, or removal of a trustee, whether of a society or branch, the property vested in such trustee vests in the succeeding trustees of such society or branch either solely or together with any surviving or continuing trustees, and until the appointment of succeeding trustees, in such surviving or continuing trustees only, or in the executors or administrators of the last surviving or continuing trustee, as personal estate (whether the same be real or personal), subject to the same trusts, without conveyance or assignment, except that stocks and securities in the public funds of Great Britain and Ireland shall be transferred into the names of the succeeding trustees, either solely or jointly with any surviving or continuing trustees."

By sect. 16 (5): "In all legal proceedings whatsoever concerning any such property the same shall be stated to be the property of the trustees for the time being in their proper names as trustees for the society or branch (as the case may be) without further description."

By sect. 21: "With respect to legal proceedings against registered societies the following provisions shall have effect:

"(1). The trustees of any society or branch, or any other officers authorised by the rules thereof, may bring or defend, or cause to be brought or defended, any action, suit, or other legal proceeding in any court whatsoever, touching or concerning any property, right, or claim of the society or branch, as the case may be, and shall sue and be sued, implead and be impleaded, in their proper names, without other description than the title of their office.

"(2). In legal proceedings which may be brought under this Act by a member or person claiming through a member, the society may also be sued in the name, as defendant, of any officer or person who receives contributions or issues policies on behalf of the society within the jurisdiction of the court in which the legal proceeding is brought, with the addition of the words 'on behalf of the society' (naming the same).

"(3). No legal proceeding shall abate or be discontinued by the death, resignation, or removal from office of any officer, or by any act of such officer after the commencement of the proceedings." (See also Jud. Act, 1875, O. L.)

By 38 & 39 Vict. c. 60, s. 31 (1). "The rules bind the society and the members thereof, and all persons claiming through them respec-

established and registered under and in pursuance of the Statutes relating to Friendly Societies.

2, &c. [*State the cause of action as in ordinary cases, showing the right of the society, and the matter in respect of which damages or other relief is sought.*]

Commencement of Statement of Claim against a Friendly Society.

1. The above-named defendants are the trustees of the [*state the title of the society*], which is a friendly society established and registered under and in pursuance of the Statutes relating to Friendly Societies.

Commencement of Statement of Claim by a Friendly Society where the Trustees have died since the Writ was issued, and new ones have been appointed.

Between P. Q. and X. Y., Trustees
of the Z. Friendly Society . . *Plaintiffs.*
and
L. M. . . . . . . *Defendant.*

Statement of Claim.

1. This action was commenced by A. B. and C. D., since deceased, who at the time of the commencement of

---

tively, to the same extent as if each member had subscribed his name and affixed his seal thereto, and there were in such rules contained a covenant on the part of himself, his heirs, executors, and administrators, to conform to such rules subject to the provisions of this Act."

The statutes relating to friendly societies contain special provision for the settlement of disputes between members of the society or persons claiming through members, or under the rules of a registered society, and the society or its officers, in the manner directed by the rules of the society (38 & 39 Vict. c. 60, ss. 22, 30 (10) &c.) Such disputes, therefore, are not in general within the cognizance of the High Court of Justice.

Where however the dispute is not one between the member, *quà* member, and the society or its officers, but is independent of his membership, the jurisdiction of the High Court of Justice is, in general, not ousted by the above special provisions as to the settlement of disputes. (*Morrison* v. *Glover*, 19 L. J. Ex. 20 ; 4 Ex. 430 ; *Mulkern* v. *Lord*, 4 App. Cas. 182 ; 47 L. J. Ch. 228 ; *Kelsall* v. *Tyler*, 25 L. J. Ex. 153 ; 11 Ex. 513 ; *Sinden* v. *Bankes*, 30 L. J. Q. B. 102 ; 7 Jur. N. S. 910 ; *Davie* v. *Friendly Society of Colington*, 9 Macph. 96. See *post*, note (*c*)).

this action were the trustees of the Z. Friendly Society, which was and is a friendly society established and registered under and in pursuance of the Statutes relating to Friendly Societies.

2. After the death of the said A. B. and C. D., the above-named plaintiffs P. Q. and X. Y. were duly appointed and now are trustees of the said Z. Friendly Society.

3. By an order made in this action and dated the —— day of —— 18—, the above-named P. Q. and X. Y. were made plaintiffs in this action.

4, &c. [*State the cause of action, &c.*]

Commencement of Statement of Claim by a Trade Union (b).

1. The above-named plaintiffs are the trustees of the [*state the title of the union*], which is a trade union regis-

(*b*) As in friendly societies, so in TRADES' UNIONS, all real and personal estate belonging to a union registered under the Acts 34 & 35 Vict. c. 31, and 39 & 40 Vict. c. 22, is vested in trustees, and in all actions, or indictments, or summary proceedings, the same must be stated to be the property of the trustees, in their proper names as trustees of such trade union. (34 & 35 Vict. c. 31, s. 8; 39 & 40 Vict. c. 22, s. 3.) The above Acts may be cited together as the "Trade Union Acts, 1871 and 1876."

The trustees of any trade union so registered, or any other officer of such trade union who may be authorized so to do by the rules thereof, are empowered to bring or defend, or cause to be brought or defended, any action, prosecution, or complaint touching or concerning the property, right, or claim to property of the trade union; and may in all cases concerning the real or personal property of such trade union, sue and be sued in their proper names, without other description than the title of their office; and no such action, suit, prosecution, or complaint, will be discontinued or will abate by the death or removal from office of such persons, or any of them, but the same may be proceeded in by their successors. (34 & 35 Vict. c. 31, s. 9.)

The Act of 1871 (34 & 35 Vict. c. 31, s. 4), enacts that nothing therein contained shall enable any Court to entertain any legal proceedings instituted with the object of directing, enforcing, or recovering damages for any breach of any agreement for the application of the union funds to provide benefits to the members, or for any breach of any agreement between members of a trade union as such, concerning the conditions on which any members of such union shall or shall not sell their goods, transact business, employ, or be employed.

Consequently, as before the Act, the members, as such, as between themselves and the unions have no legal status, and depend entirely on mutual good faith. The reason being that, apart from this Act, such

tered under and in pursuance of the "Trade Union Acts, 1871 and 1876."

2. &c. [*State the cause of action as in ordinary cases, showing the right of the union, and the matter in respect of which damages or other relief is sought.*]

Commencement of Statement of Claim by a Building Society (c).

1. The above-named plaintiffs are a building society incorporated under and in pursuance of "The Building Societies Acts."

---

unions were regarded as established in restraint of trade and not entitled to the assistance of the Courts. (*Hornby* v. *Close*, L. R. 2 Q. B. 153; 36 L. J. M. C. 43; *Farrer* v. *Close*, L. R. 4 Q. B. 602; 38 L. J. Q. B. 263; *Rigby* v. *Connol*, 14 Ch. D. 482; 49 L. J. Ch. 328; *Duke* v. *Littleboy*, 49 L. J. Ch. 802; 43 L. T. 216.) The term trade union is defined by 39 & 40 Vict. c. 22, s. 16, in conjunction with 34 & 35 Vict. c. 31, s. 23 (which is in part repealed by 39 & 40 Vict. c. 22).

(c) With regard to BUILDING SOCIETIES the principal enactments now in force are 37 & 38 Vict. c. 42; 38 & 39 Vict. c. 9; and 40 & 41 Vict. c. 63 (which may be cited together as "The Building Societies Acts").

Upon obtaining a certificate of incorporation under "The Building Societies Acts," the society becomes a body corporate by its registered name. (37 & 38 Vict. c. 42, s. 9.)

The society, therefore, sues and is sued by its corporate name. By section 27 of 37 & 38 Vict. c. 42, as amended by 40 & 41 Vict. c. 63, s. 3, all rights of action and other rights, and all estates and interests in real and personal estate whatsoever, belonging to or held in trust for any society certified under the repealed Act 6 & 7 Wm. 4, c. 32, on the incorporation of the society under the Act 37 & 38 Vict. c. 42, vest in the society without any conveyance or assignment whatsoever, except in the case of stocks and securities in the public funds of Great Britain and Ireland, and estates in copyhold or customary hereditaments, the title to which cannot be transferred without admittance.

By section 4 of 40 & 41 Vict. c. 63, s. 4, all rights of action and other rights and interests in real and personal estate whatsoever held in trust for any society theretofore incorporated under 37 & 38 Vict. c. 42, on the passing of 40 & 41 Vict. c. 63, vested in the society without any conveyance or assignment whatsoever, except in the case of stocks and securities in the public funds of Great Britain and Ireland, and estates in copyhold or customary hereditaments, the title to which cannot be transferred without admittance.

By 37 & 38 Vict. c. 42, s. 16, it is enacted that the rules of every society thereafter established shall, amongst other things, set forth the mode of settling disputes between the society and any of its members, or any person claiming by or through any member, or under the rules.

By 37 & 38 Vict. c. 42, s. 21, the rules are binding on the members

2, &c. [*State the cause of action as in ordinary cases, showing the right of the Society, and the matter in respect of which damages or other relief is sought.*]

---

and officers of the society, and on all persons claiming on account of a member or under the rules.

The provisions as to the settlement of disputes contained in "The Building Societies Acts" do not apply where the dispute is independent of membership. (*Morrison* v. *Glover*, 19 L. J. Ex. 20; 4 Ex. 430; *Mulkern* v. *Lord*, 4 App. Cas. 182; 47 L. J. Ch. 228; *Farmer* v. *Giles*, 30 L. J. Ex. 65; 5 H. & N. 753; *Cutbill* v. *Kingdom*, 17 L. J. Ex. 177; 1 Ex. 494; *Bottomley* v. *Fisher*, 31 L. J. Ex. 417; 1 H. & C. 211; *Fleming* v. *Self*, 3 De G. M. & G. 997; 24 L. J. Ch. 29; *Prentice* v. *London*, L. R. 10 C. P. 679; 44 L. J. C. P. 353.)

Thus where the society has lent money to members on the security of mortgages, or where members have entered into express covenants with the society, disputes relating to such mortgages or covenants are cognisable by the High Court of Justice, and may be enforced as in ordinary cases. (*Doe* v. *Glover*, 15 Q. B. 103; and cases cited *supra*.) So, too, in actions against sureties for members, the sureties cannot take advantage of the rules unless they are expressly incorporated in their contracts. (*Brown* v. *Langley*, 4 M. & G. 466; *Brown* v. *Williamson*, 13 M. & W. 14; *Price* v. *Kirkham*, 3 H. & C. 437; 34 L. J. Ex. 35.)

An incorporated building society is not legally entitled to act as a freehold land society. A freehold land society buys land with the funds subscribed by members, and divides that land among them; but a building society advances to members, out of the subscriptions of the members, money to be laid out in the purchase of land or buildings, which are then mortgaged to the society. (*Grimes* v. *Harrison*, 28 L. J. Ch. 823; 26 Beav. 435.) It is *ultrà vires* of an incorporated building society to purchase land for sale or division amongst members. (*In re Kent Benefit Building Society*, 30 L. J. Ch. 787; 4 L. T. 610; 37 & 38 Vict. c. 42, s. 37.)

Industrial and Provident Societies are regulated by 39 & 40 Vict. c. 45 (which may be cited as "The Industrial and Provident Societies Act, 1876"). By sect. 6 the societies which may be registered under this Act are societies for carrying on any labour, trade or handicraft, whether wholesale or retail, including the buying and selling of land, of which societies no member, other than a society registered under this Act, shall have or claim an interest in the funds exceeding £200.

As to the business of banking, this Act contains certain special provisions (see ss. 6, 10 (2)).

By sect. 11: (1) "The registration of a society shall render it a body corporate by the name described in the acknowledgment of registry by which it may sue and be sued, with perpetual succession and a common seal."

(2) "The rules of the society shall bind the society and all members thereof, and all persons claiming through them respectively, to the same extent as if each member had subscribed his name and affixed his seal thereto, and there were contained in such rules a covenant on the part of himself, his heirs, executors, and administrators to conform thereto, subject to the provisions of this Act."

By a Building Society whose Rules were certified under 6 & 7 W. IV., c. 32, and which was subsequently incorporated under "The Building Societies Act, 1874," upon a Covenant in a Mortgage Deed made with Trustees before such Incorporation.

1. The plaintiff society, on and previous to the 16th of November, 1870, was a benefit building society, the rules of which had been and were certified under "An Act for the Regulation of Benefit Building Societies," 6 & 7 W. 4, c. 32.

2. The plaintiff society continued to exist and was afterwards and before this action incorporated under "The Building Societies Act, 1874," 37 & 38 Vict. c. 42, and under "The Building Societies Act, 1877," 40 & 41 Vict. c. 63.

3. By an indenture bearing date the 16th of November, 1870, and made between the defendant and certain persons as trustees of the plaintiff society, it was witnessed that in consideration of £200 advanced by the said persons as trustees of the plaintiff society out of the funds of the said society to the defendant, the defendant covenanted with the said persons, as trustees of the plaintiff society, that he would pay to the trustees or trustee for the time being of the plaintiff society the several weekly contributions or sums of money which by virtue of the said indenture and the rules for the time being of the said society should become due and payable in respect of the said advance.

4. The said several weekly contributions or sums of money which by virtue of the said indenture and the rules

---

As to notes, bills of exchange, and contracts of any such society, see s. 11 (10), (12).

Sect. 14 contains provisions for the settlement of disputes between a member or person claiming through a member or under the rules of a registered society, and the society or an officer thereof ousting the jurisdiction in general of the High Court of Justice. As to what are such disputes, see notes on Friendly and Building Societies, *ante*, pp. 184, 187.

LOAN SOCIETIES are regulated by 3 & 4 Vict. c. 110 [repealed in part by Stat. Law Rev. Act, 1874 (No. 2)], and by 38 & 39 Vict. c. 60, s. 10 (4), "The Friendly Societies Act, 1875."

These societies cannot sue or be sued in their own name. The trustees in whom their property is vested must sue or be sued for them (sect. 8 of 3 & 4 Vict. c. 110). The rules when certified are, by sect. 4, binding on the several members and officers of the society, and the borrowers and sureties and all other persons having interest therein.

for the time being of the said society became due and payable in respect of the said advance amounted to ten shillings and tenpence per week.

5. The defendant did not pay the said several weekly contributions or sums of money, and the following of the said weekly contributions or sums of money, amounting in the whole to £——, are now due and payable by the defendant to the plaintiff society in respect of the said advance [*set out the particulars*].

FUNERAL EXPENSES (*a*).

Statement of Claim by an Undertaker for Funeral Expenses.

1. The plaintiff is an undertaker carrying on business at ——.

2. The defendant requested the plaintiff, as such undertaker [*if by letters add:* by letters bearing date the —— of —— and the —— of ——, &c.], to provide a hearse, coaches, horses, goods, and necessary things for a funeral upon the —— day of ——, 18—, and to conduct and manage the same.

(*a*) An executor, having assets, is liable personally, *de bonis propriis*, upon an implied contract, to pay for the funeral expenses of his testator; and he may be sued by the undertaker without any express order given by him, unless the undertaker has given exclusive credit to a third party. The executor may defeat an action founded on the implied contract only, by proving that he has no assets. (*Tugwell* v. *Heyman*, 3 Camp. 298; *Rogers* v. *Price*, 3 Y. & J. 28; *Corner* v. *Shew*, 3 M. & W. 350, 356; and see *Green* v. *Salmon*, 8. A. & E. 348; 2 Wms. Exs., 8th ed. 1796.) But the executor is only liable upon this implied contract for the expenses of a funeral suitable to the degree of the testator. (*Brice* v. *Wilson*, 8 A. & E. 349; *Lucy* v. *Waldrond*, 3 Bing. N. C. 841.) In order to charge the executor with any greater expense it must be shown that he sanctioned, or ordered it. (See cases *suprà*.)

A husband is liable for the expenses of his wife's funeral, and where a person in his absence necessarily employs an undertaker, and pays the expense of the funeral of the wife, such person may recover the amount as money paid for and on behalf of the husband, under an agency, or authority to act in the matter on the husband's behalf, implied by the law. (*Jenkins* v. *Tucker*, 1 H. Bl. 90; *Ambrose* v. *Kerrison*, 10 C. B. 776; *Bradshaw* v. *Beard*, 12 C. B. N. S. 344; 31 L. J. C. P. 273.) An infant widow may render herself liable for the funeral of her husband as for necessaries. (*Chapple* v. *Cooper*, 13 M. & W. 252.)

Where the liability is implied as above from circumstances, and there is no express contract, the circumstances giving rise to the liability should be referred to in the claim, and the contract stated as a fact. (O. XIX. r. 27; *see ante*, "*Pleading in General*," p. 7, and "*Agreements*," *ante*, p. 50.)

3. The plaintiff did, in accordance with the above request, provide a hearse, coaches, horses, goods, and necessary things for the said funeral, and conduct and manage the same.

4. The plaintiff has delivered to the defendant an account giving the details of his charges therefor, which amount to £—— [*or* The particulars of the plaintiff's charges therefor are as follows:], which said charges are fair and reasonable.

5. The defendant has not paid the plaintiff the said sum of £——, or any part thereof.

6. [*If there has been an account stated, add:* The defendant admitted to the plaintiff that the account delivered as above stated was correct, *or as the case may be. See ante, "Accounts Stated,"* p. 33.]

GAMING (*a*).

GOODS. See "*Sale of Goods,*" *post*, p. 301.

GOODWILL. See "*Trade,*" *post*, p. 341.

GUARANTEES (*aa*).

Statement of Claim on a Guarantee for the Price of Goods supplied to a Third Person.

1. The plaintiff is a woollen cloth manufacturer at Huddersfield, in the county of York.

(*a*) See 5 & 6 Will. IV. c. 41, ss. 1, 2, as revised by "The Stat. Law Rev. Act, 1874," and see also Leake on Contracts, 748 *et seq.* As to recovering deposits on bets from keepers of betting houses, see 16 & 17 Vict. c. 119, s. 5, and *Doggett* v. *Catterms*, 19 C. B. N. S. 765; 34 L. J. C. P. 159. As to the recovery of money deposited in the hands of a stakeholder upon a wager, see "*Money Received,*" *post*, p. 280. And see further, "*Money Paid,*" *post*, p. 278.

(*aa*) The Statute of Frauds, 29 Car. II. c. 3, s. 4, provides that no action shall be brought whereby to charge the defendant upon any special promise to answer for the debt, default, or miscarriage of another person, unless the agreement upon which such action shall be brought, or some memorandum or note thereof, shall be in writing and signed by the party to be charged therewith, or some other person thereunto by him lawfully authorised.

In order to constitute a guarantee within the statute the person whose debt is answered for by the guarantee must be some person other than the promisor or promisee, and he must be liable for such

2. The defendant is a retired tradesman, and resides at Brighton, in the county of Sussex.

3. On the 15th of June, 1879, the defendant wrote and sent a letter to the plaintiff, guaranteeing and pro-

---

debt and continue liable for the same whilst the guarantee is in force, and the promisee must be himself the creditor. (*Simpson* v. *Penton*, 2 C. & M. 430; *Eastwood* v. *Kenyon*, 11 A. & E. 438; *Hargreaves* v. *Parsons*, 13 M. & W. 561; *Mountstephen* v. *Lakeman*, L. R. 7 H. L. 17, 24; 39 L. J. Q. B. 275.) A mere promise of indemnity, or a promise to answer for a debt of the promisee, is not within the statute. (*Thomas* v. *Cook*, 8 B. & C. 728; *Wildes* v. *Dudlow*, L. R. 19 Eq. 198; 44 L. J. Ch. 341.) Nor is a promise to pay for goods, where the goods are supplied to another upon the sole credit of the promisor. (*Simpson* v. *Penton*, 2 C. & M. 430; *Birkmyr* v. *Darnell*, Salk. 27; 1 Smith's L. C. 8th ed. p. 326.)

A guarantee must be construed according to the intention of the parties as expressed in the writing, and evidence of the position and circumstances of the parties may be given at the trial for the purpose of ascertaining such intention. (*Wood* v. *Priestner*, L. R. 2 Ex. 282; 36 L. J. Ex. 127; *Coles* v. *Pack*, L. R. 5 C. P. 65; 39 L. J. C. P. 63; *Heffield* v. *Meadows*, L. R. 4 C. P. 595; *Laurie* v. *Scholefield*, L. R. 4 C. P. 622; 38 L. J. C. P. 290; *Morrell* v. *Cowan*, 7 Ch. D. 151; 47 L. J. Ch. 73.)

As to when the death of the guarantor brought to the knowledge of the promisee operates as a determination of a continuing guarantee, see *Lloyd's* v. *Harper*, 16 Ch. D. 290; 50 L. J. Ch. 140; *Coulthart* v. *Clementson*, 5 Q. B. D. 42; 49 L. J. Q. B. 204.

By the Mercantile Law Amendment Act, 1856 (19 & 20 Vict. c. 97), s. 3, "no special promise to be made by any person after the passing of this Act to answer for the debt, default, or miscarriage of another person, being in writing and signed by the party to be charged therewith or some other person by him thereunto lawfully authorised, shall be deemed invalid to support an action, suit, or other proceeding to charge the person by whom such promise shall have been made, by reason only that the consideration for such promise does not appear in writing, or by necessary inference from a written document."

Under this section the consideration for the promise may be proved by parol evidence, but the promise must still be complete in the writing under the Statute of Frauds, and the parol evidence admissible to prove the consideration cannot be used to explain the written promise. (*Holmes* v. *Mitchell*, 7 C. B. N. S. 361; 28 L. J. C. P. 301.) A written guarantee (where the subject-matter of the contract makes it liable to an agreement stamp) is not exempt from the stamp merely by reason of the consideration not being contained in the writing, but proved by parol evidence. (*Glover* v. *Halkett*, 2 H. & N. 487; 26 L. J. Ex. 416.)

As to whether the guarantee should be set out verbatim in the statement of claim, or the effect thereof merely stated, see "*The Body of the Statement of Claim*," *ante*, p. 11.

A surety is not entitled to a demand for payment upon the default of the debtor, or to notice of the default, unless he has expressly stipulated for it (*Sicklemore* v. *Thistleton*, 6 M. & S. 9; *Hitchcock* v.

mising the plaintiff that he would be responsible to him for the due payment [to the extent of £200] of the price of any cloths and woollen stuffs which he might sell and deliver on credit to one G. H., who was a clothier tailor and outfitter in Brighton aforesaid.

4. The plaintiff accepted the said guarantee and promise, and accordingly afterwards sold and delivered on credit to the said G. H., in the said month of June, various cloths and woollen stuffs at various prices, amounting to £150.

5. Full particulars of the said goods and prices have been delivered by the plaintiff to the defendant [*or* particulars of the said goods and prices are as follows: *setting out the particulars*].

6. No particular time was agreed upon for the duration of the said credit, but a reasonable time [*or* —— months, which is the customary time allowed in the plaintiff's said trade] for such credit elapsed before the commencement of this action.

7. The said G. H. has not, nor has the defendant paid to the plaintiff the said £150, or any part thereof.

Humfrey, 5 M. & G. 559; and see *Price* v. *Kirkham*, 3 H. & C. 437; 34 L. J. Ex. 35); and in order to charge a surety upon a contract of guarantee it is not necessary to make a demand upon the principal debtor, unless such demand is necessary to charge the debtor (*Rede* v. *Farr*, 6 M. & S. 121; *Lilley* v. *Hewitt*, 11 Price, 494; *Warrington* v. *Furbor*, 8 East, 242; *Walton* v. *Mascall*, 13 M. & W. 452); or unless the surety has expressly stipulated that such demand shall be made. See also Leake on Contracts, 646.

By the Mercantile Law Amendment Act, 1856, s. 4, "no promise to answer for the debt, default, or miscarriage of another made to a firm consisting of two or more persons, or to a single person trading under the name of a firm, and no promise to answer for the debt, default, or miscarriage of a firm consisting of two or more persons, or of a single person trading under the name of a firm, shall be binding on the person making such promise in respect of anything done or omitted to be done after a change shall have taken place in any one or more of the persons constituting the firm, or in the person trading under the name of a firm, unless the intention of the parties that such promise shall continue to be binding notwithstanding such change, shall appear either by express stipulation or by necessary implication from the nature of the firm or otherwise." (See *Barclay* v. *Lucas*, 1 T. R. 291 n.; 3 Doug. 321; *Metcalf* v. *Bruin*, 12 East, 400; *Backhouse* v. *Hall*, 6 B. & S. 507; 34 L. J. Q. B. 141.)

As to actions on representations respecting the credit of third persons, see 9 Geo. IV. c. 14, s. 6; and see "*Fraud*," *post*, p. 432.

See further, "*Money Paid*," *post*, p. 276.

On a Guarantee of the due Payment of a Bill taken for the Price of Goods supplied to a Third Party.

1. The plaintiff is a tea merchant, carrying on business at Liverpool.

2. In the month of ——, —18, G. H., who was starting in business as a grocer at Liverpool aforesaid, requested the plaintiff to sell and deliver to him —— chests of tea at £—— per chest, and to take from the said G. H., for and on account of the price of the said tea, his acceptance of a bill of Exchange, to be drawn by the plaintiff upon the said G. H., for the said price, payable six months after date to the plaintiff's order.

3. The plaintiff agreed to sell and deliver the said tea to the said G. H. upon the said terms, subject to the condition of the defendant guaranteeing the plaintiff the due payment of the said bill.

4. The defendant thereupon, by a writing bearing date the —— day of ——, 18—, guaranteed and promised the plaintiff that the said bill should be duly paid at maturity [*or*, gave the plaintiff the following guarantee in writing: *setting forth the guarantee verbatim*].

5. The plaintiff, upon receiving such guarantee and promise, accordingly sold and delivered to the said G. H. the said —— chests of tea, at the said price, amounting to £——, and took from the said G. H. his acceptance of such bill as aforesaid, for and on account of the price of the said —— chests of tea.

6. The said bill was not paid at maturity, and is still wholly unpaid.

7. In consequence of the non-payment of the said bill, the plaintiff lost the price of the said tea.

Form No. (16) *in App.* (*C.*) *to Jud. Act*, 1875.

1. The plaintiffs are brewers, carrying on their business at ——, under the firm of X. Y. & Co.

2. In the month of March, 1872, M. N. was desirous of entering into the employment of the plaintiffs as a traveller and collector, and it was agreed between the plaintiffs and defendants and M. N., that the plaintiffs should employ M. N. upon the defendants entering into the guarantee hereinafter mentioned.

3. An agreement in writing was accordingly made and entered into, on or about the 30th March, 1872, between

the plaintiffs and the defendants, whereby in consideration that the plaintiffs would employ M. N. as their collector the defendants agreed that they would be answerable for the due accounting by M. N. to the plaintiffs for and the due payment over by him to the plaintiffs of all moneys which he should receive on their behalf as their collector.

4. The plaintiffs employed M. N. as their collector accordingly, and he entered upon the duties of such employment, and continued therein down to the 31st of December, 1873.

5. At various times between the 29th of September and the 25th of December, 1873, M. N. received on behalf of the plaintiffs and as their collector sums of money from debtors of the plaintiffs amounting in the whole to the sum of £950; and of this amount M. N. neglected to account for or pay over to the plaintiffs sums amounting in the whole to £227, and appropriated the last-mentioned sums to his own use.

6. The defendants have not paid the last-mentioned sums, or any part thereof to the plaintiffs.

Heirs and Devisees (*a*).

Against the Heir and Devisee jointly on a Covenant of the Testator.

1. The defendant A. B. is [and was at the time of the death of E. F., deceased, the eldest son and (*a*)] heir of

(*a*) Under the former system of pleading it was not necessary for the plaintiff in pleading to state how the defendant was heir. (*Denham* v. *Stephenson*, Salk. 355.) Now, however, it would seem, in general, correct to allege the facts which show the defendant to be the heir, thus obtaining specific admissions or denials of the facts alleged. (See *Philipps* v. *Philipps*, 4 Q. B. D. 127, 129, 130; 48 L. J. Q. B. 135, in which case the question was as to how a plaintiff should plead his own title.) But it cannot be always necessary to state the facts showing the heirship; because in some cases those facts are not necessary to be proved, as for example, where the plaintiff proposes to rely upon an admission of heirship made by the defendant. Perhaps in such cases it may be correct to plead the fact of the admission. (See *per* Brett, L. J., *Philipps* v. *Philipps*, 4 Q. B. D. 135, 136; and see Jud. Act, 1875, O. XIX. r. 4.)

It is not necessary, as against an heir, though it may often be convenient, to allege that the ancestor died possessed of any real assets which descended to the heir, as it lies on the heir to show by way of defence that nothing in respect of which he can be rendered liable descended to him. (See "Defences," "*Heirs and Devisees.*")

E. F., deceased, and the defendant C. D. is the devisee of the said E. F. of divers lands and hereditaments [*what these are should, where practicable, be stated*] which were of the said E. F., deceased, by his last will and testament [*it may in some cases be convenient to give details identifying the will relied on*].

2. The said E. F., in his lifetime, by a deed bearing date the —— day of ——, 18—, covenanted for himself and his heirs with the plaintiff that he, the said E. F., would pay to the plaintiff £——, with interest for the same at the rate of £—— per centum per annum, on the —— day of ——, 18—, now elapsed.

3. The said £—— and interest thereon are still unpaid.

At common law an important distinction was made between specialty debts in which the obligor bound himself only, and those in which he also bound his heir by name. The former did not charge the lands of the ancestor which passed by descent to the heir; the latter did, and the obligee could recover upon them against the heir, to the extent of the lands which the latter acquired by descent from the obligor. In neither case could the obligee recover against the devisee of the lands. See further Leake on Contracts, 149-152, 1266.

The statute 11 Geo. IV. and 1 Will. IV. c. 47 (which repealed the 3 W. & M. c. 14) now gives a like remedy against the devisee upon specialty debts of the latter kind to the extent of the lands devised. But debts of the former kind (equally with simple contract debts) are now charged in equity upon the land of the obligor after his decease, by the statute 3 & 4 Will. IV. c. 104, where he has not charged them by his will. See 32 & 33 Vict. c. 46, s. 1.

The action against the heir and devisee of a testator, upon specialties in which the heir is bound, is founded on the 11 Geo. IV. and 1 Will. IV. c. 47. By s. 2, testamentary dispositions of real estate whereof the testator was seised in fee, in possession, reversion, or remainder, are to be deemed void as against any person with whom the testator had entered into any bond, covenant, or other specialty binding his heirs. By s. 3, every such creditor shall have an action upon such specialties against the heir and devisee, or the devisee of such devisee jointly. By s. 4, in case there shall not be any heir, the creditor may maintain an action against the devisee or devisees solely.

The distinction between obligations under seal in which the obligor bound himself only, and those in which he also expressly bound his heir is further much diminished by the "Conveyancing and Law of Property Act, 1881" (44 & 45 Vict. c. 41), s. 59, as to obligations made after the 31st of Dec., 1881, which enacts that the heirs and real estate shall be bound in law by such obligations as well as the executors and administrators of the obligor, as if heirs were expressed, except so far as a contrary intention is expressed by the obligation.

Commencement of Statement of Claim against an Heir on the Bond of his Ancestor.

1. The defendant C. D. is [and was at the time of the death of E. F., deceased, the eldest son and] heir of E. F., deceased.

Husband and Wife.

By Husband and Wife for the Price of Goods sold and delivered by the Wife before Marriage (a).

Between A. B. and C. (*Christian name of the wife*) his wife . .	Plaintiffs.
and	
D. E.	Defendant.

(a) *Husband and Wife.*] Upon contracts made with the wife before marriage, the husband and wife ought in general to sue jointly, but if the husband dies before action, the widow can in general sue. Upon such contracts in general (and subject particularly to the exceptions created by the Married Women's Property Acts, cited p. 205), the husband and wife ought to be sued jointly. If either the husband or the wife sues or is sued alone in cases where both should sue or be sued jointly, and if the facts showing that there is a husband or a wife who ought to have been joined appear on the statement of claim, the objection to the non-joinder may be taken by demurrer. (*Hancocks* v. *Lablache*, 3 C. P. D. 197; 47 L. J. C. P. 514.) But, except in cases where the facts appear on the statement of claim, the usual mode of taking the objection to such non-joinder in the Queen's Bench Division is by a summons at Chambers, and this seems to be the course contemplated by the Judicature Act. (See O. XVI. r. 13.) Pleas in abatement are abolished by O. XIX., r. 13.

A married woman is in general incapable of contracting except as agent for her husband or some other person, though this must be taken as subject to certain exceptions, as for instance, when the contract is one which binds her separate property, or is one valid by reason of the Married Women's Property Acts, cited *post*, p. 205.

It follows, therefore, that in general the husband is the proper party to sue or be sued upon contracts made by the wife during coverture, and that his right and liability depend on the question whether the wife was his agent to contract. The authority of the wife to contract as agent for her husband is a question of fact in each case; but there is, during cohabitation, a *primâ facie* presumption in favour of such authority to contract for such domestic matters as are usually entrusted to the management of the wife, as for the reasonable supply of goods for the use of her husband, herself, or the household, according to the condition in which they live. (*Phillipson* v. *Hayter*, L. R. 6 C. P. 38; 40 L. J. C. P. 14; *Etherington* v. *Parrott*, Ld. Raym. 1006; *Montague* v. *Benedict*, 2 Smith's L. C., 8th ed. p. 483; *Seaton* v. *Benedict*, *ib.* p. 491; *Debenham* v. *Mellon*, 5 Q. B. D. 394;

1. The plaintiff C. [*the Christian name of the wife*] is the wife of the above-named plaintiff, A. B.

2. The plaintiff C., on the —— day of ——, 18—, before her marriage with the above-named plaintiff, A. B.,

---

6 App. Cas. 24; 49 L. J. Q. B. 497; 50 L. J. Q. B. 155; *Lane* v. *Ironmonger*, 13 M. & W. 368; *Reid* v. *Teakle*, 13 C. B. 627; *Reneaux* v. *Teakle*, 8 Ex. 680; *Jewsbury* v. *Newbold*, 26 L. J. Ex. 247; and see *Ryan* v. *Sams*, 12 Q. B. 460; *per* Willes, J., *Cooper* v. *Lloyd*, 6 C. B. N. S. 519, 521.) Such presumption of authority of the wife arising merely from cohabitation may be rebutted by proving the express revocation of the husband without notice of the revocation to the parties dealing with her. (*Jolly* v. *Rees*, 15 C. B. N. S. 628; 33 L. J. C. P. 177; *Debenham* v. *Mellon*, *supra*.)

But if there have been previous dealings of the same kind through the wife with the same person, which have been acknowledged by the husband, thus giving a foundation of special consent to the agency, it seems that revocation of authority would not be effectual without notice to the person dealing upon the faith of, and in the belief in, the continuance of the agency. (Leake on Contracts, 486, 570; *Debenham* v. *Mellon*, *supra*; *Trueman* v. *Loader*, 11 A. & E. 589; *Ryan* v. *Sams*, *supra*.)

There is no such presumption of authority during separation; but a married woman living apart from her husband with his consent, or compelled to separate herself from him by his misconduct, and without an adequate maintenance, has an implied authority, which he cannot rebut, to bind her husband by contracts for necessaries (*Manby* v. *Scott*, 2 Smith's L. C. 8th ed. 445; *Debenham* v. *Mellon*, *supra*; *Hindley* v. *Marquis of Westmeath*, 6 B. & C. 200; *Boulton* v. *Prentice*, 2 Strange, 1214; S. C. Selwyn's N. P. 12th ed. p. 334; *Hodgkinson* v. *Fletcher*, 4 Camp. 70; *Mizen* v. *Pick*, 3 M. & W. 481; *Johnson* v. *Sumner*, 3 H. & N. 261; 27 L. J. Ex. 341; *Bazeley* v. *Forder*, L. R. 3 Q. B. 559; *Wilson* v. *Ford*, L. R. 3 Ex. 63; *Biffin* v. *Bignell*, 7 H. & N. 877; 31 L. J. Ex. 189; *Forristall* v. *Lawson*, 34 L. T. 903); unless she has been guilty of adultery (*Govier* v. *Hancock*, 6 T. R. 603; *Atkyns* v. *Pearce*, 2 C. B. N. S. 763; 26 L. J. C. P. 252; *Cooper* v. *Lloyd*, 6 C. B. N. S. 519); or, unless she is living apart from her husband under an agreement with him by which he is to pay to her, and pays, a certain maintenance, and by which she is not to have recourse to him for anything further. (*Eastland* v. *Burchell*, 3 Q. B. D. 432; 47 L. J. Q. B. 500.)

In the case of a wife living apart from her husband the *onus* of proving that the circumstances are such as to render the husband liable to be charged lies on the party seeking to charge the husband. (*Per* Abbott, C. J., in *Mainwaring* v. *Leslie*, M. & M. 18; *Johnson* v. *Sumner*, 3 H. & N. 261; 27 L. J. Ex. 341.)

As in the case of any other agent, a husband may, by ratification, become liable on contracts made by his wife in excess of the authority given to her to contract as his agent. (*Montague* v. *Bendict*, *antè*; *Seaton* v. *Bendict*, *antè*; *Millard* v. *Harvey*, 34 Beav. 237.)

In cases where a husband would be liable for necessaries, he may be liable for money lent to his wife and applied in procuring necessaries, or paying for necessaries procured. (*Harris* v. *Lee*, 1 P. Wms. 482; *Jenner* v. *Morris*, 3 D. F. & J. 45; 30 L. J. Ch. 361; *Davidson*

sold and delivered to the defendant 20 tons of hay [*or as the case may be*] at the agreed price of £——.

3. The defendant has not paid the said price, or any part thereof.

---

v. *Wood*, 1 D. J. & S. 465; 32 L. J. Ch. 400; *Deare* v. *Soutten*, L. R. 9 Eq. 151.)

As to marriage pending action, see O. L.

It is a general rule that where a husband seeks to recover property of the wife not belonging to her for her separate use, the action should be brought in the names of the husband and wife jointly, as where the action is brought to recover a chose in action of the wife not being her separate property, or to recover real estate of the wife not belonging to her for her separate use, or personal property in respect of which she has a subsisting equity to a settlement. (Dan. Ch. Prac., p. 85 *et seq.*) Where an action is brought to recover separate property of the wife (not being property in respect of which she is entitled to sue alone in her own name under the provisions of the Married Women's Property Act, 1870), the general rule is that the wife should bring the action by her next friend. (See *post*, p. 202.) But subject to the above rules, and to the exceptions created by the last-mentioned Act, the old practice still appears to prevail that where a promise is made *to* a married woman on a consideration proceeding from her solely, as a contract with her to pay for her services rendered, (wherever, as it is said, the wife is the meritorious cause of action,) the husband may, at his election, sue alone in his own name, or jointly in the name of himself and wife. (*Bidgood* v. *Way*, 2 W. Bl. 1236; *Dalton* v. *Midland Ry. Co.*, 13 C. B. 474; *Jones* v. *Cuthbertson*, L. R. 7 Q. B. 218; L. R. 8 Q. B. 504; 41 L. J. Q. B. 145; 42 L. J. Q. B. 221.)

Thus, on a bond given to the wife during coverture, husband and wife may have a joint action during their lives; or the husband may sue during coverture in his own name. (*Day* v. *Padrone*, 2 M. & S. 396 n. (*b*); *Ankerstein* v. *Clarke*, 4 T. R. 616.) On a note made *to* a wife during coverture, the husband may sue alone, or husband and wife may sue jointly. (*Philliskirk* v. *Pluckwell*, 2 M. & S. 393; *Howard* v. *Oakes*, 3 Ex. 136; *Burrough* v. *Moss*, 10 B. & C. 558.) A statement of claim by husband and wife jointly upon such contracts as these made since the marriage (if simple contracts, other than bills or notes), must state the interest of the wife or the consideration as proceeding from the wife: thus, a claim upon accounts stated with them must show that the accounting was in respect of debts for which she had a right to sue. (*Bidgood* v. *Way*, 2 W. Bl. 1236; *Johnson* v. *Lucas*, 1 E. & B. 659.)

On a bond or covenant or promissory note made *to husband and wife*, the husband may sue alone (*Ankerstein* v. *Clarke*, 4 T. R. 616), or may join the wife. (*Philliskirk* v. *Pluckwell*, 2 M. & S. 393.) If the husband dies before suit, the right of action survives to the wife, and does not pass to the husband's representative. If he survives, it belongs to him.

Where a husband becomes bankrupt, his trustee must join the wife in suing on causes of action accrued in right of the wife, which if vested in the husband would pass to the trustee. (*Richbell* v. *Alexander*, 10 C. B. N. S. 324; 30 L. J. C. P. 268.) The trustee of

By Husband and Wife upon an Agreement in Writing made with the Wife before Marriage (a).

1. [*As in form next above.*]

2. By an agreement in writing, made between the defendant and the above-named plaintiff C. [*the Christian name of the wife*], before her marriage with the above-named plaintiff, A. B., which said agreement bears date the —— day of ——, 18—, it was agreed [*set out the agreement as in ordinary cases, as to which see "Agreements," ante, p.* 50.]

3, &c. [*As in ordinary cases.*]

Commencement of Claim by a Married Woman suing by her Next Friend (b).

Between A. B., a married woman, who sues by C. D., her next friend } Plaintiff.

and

E. F. . . . . Defendant.

---

a bankrupt husband cannot sue alone on a bill or note made payable to the wife. (*Sherrington* v. *Yates*, 12 M. & W. 855.)

Where a *chose in action* has been conferred upon the wife, and has not during coverture been reduced into possession by the husband, it passes on the death of the wife to her administrator. (*Fleet* v. *Perrins*, L. R. 3 Q. B. 536; L. R. 4 Q. B. 500; 37 L. J. Q. B. 233; 38 L. J. Q. B. 257; *Jones* v. *Cuthbertson*, L. R. 8 Q. B. 504; 42 L. J. Q. B. 221.)

Thus the right of action on a bond or note made *to* a wife, or on any other contract on which she has a right to sue, remains in the wife on the death of the husband before action (*Howard* v. *Oakes*, 3 Ex. 136; *Gaters* v. *Madeley*, 6 M. & W. 423; *Richards* v. *Richards*, 2 B. & Ad. 447); and if the wife dies before action the right of action passes to her administrator (*Day* v. *Padrone*, 2 M. & S. 396, n. (*b*); *Hart* v. *Stephens*, 6 Q. B. 937); and the husband cannot sue except in that capacity.

(*b*) *Married Woman.*] A married woman cannot in general commence or maintain an action by herself in her own name. In cases where a married woman sues without her husband, as plaintiff, *e.g.*, cases relating to her separate estate, she must sue by her next friend unless an order is granted enabling her to sue alone, O. XVI. r. 8, and see *notes*, "*Next Friend*," *post*, p. 202, and "*Separate Estate*," *post*, p. 203. She may however sue or be sued alone, where she has obtained a judicial separation and the separation continues (20 & 21 Vict. c. 85, ss. 25, 26, which see *infra*), or where the marriage has been dissolved, or where, upon her husband being convicted of an aggravated assault upon her, the Court or magistrate before whom he is so convicted makes an order under 41 & 42 Vict. c. 19, that she shall be no longer bound to cohabit with her husband, or where her husband is *civiliter mortuus*, or where she is deserted by her husband and has obtained a protection order under 20 & 21 Vict. c. 85, s. 21, or 21 & 22 Vict. c. 108, ss. 6, 7, 8, *infra*, and see *Kingsman* v. *Kingsman*, 6 Q. B. D. 122; 50 L. J. Q. B. 81. A married woman may sue alone to recover any wages, earnings, money, or property by the Married Women's Property Act, 1870, declared to be her separate property, or to enforce any remedies for the protection of such wages, earnings, money, or property, or of any chattels or other property purchased or obtained by means thereof for her own use under the provisions of s. 11 of that Act (which see, *post*, *note*, p. 206).

By 20 & 21 Vict. c. 85, s. 25, (Divorce and Matrimonial Causes Act,) "in every case of a judicial separation the wife shall, from the date of the sentence and whilst the separation shall continue, be considered as a *feme sole* with respect to property of every description which she may acquire, or which may come to or devolve upon her; and such property may be disposed of by her in all respects as a *feme sole*, and on her decease the same shall, in case she shall die intestate, go as the same would have gone if her husband had been then dead; provided, that if any such wife should again cohabit with her husband, all such property as she may be entitled to when such cohabitation shall take place shall be held to her separate use, subject, however, to any agreement in writing made between herself and her husband whilst separate."

By s. 26, "in every case of a judicial separation the wife shall, while so separated, be considered as a *feme sole* for the purposes of contract, and wrongs and injuries, and suing and being sued in any civil proceeding; and her husband shall not be liable in respect of any engagement or contract she may have entered into, or for any wrongful act or omission by her, or for any costs she may incur as plaintiff or defendant; provided, that where upon any such judicial separation alimony has been decreed or ordered to be paid to the wife, and the same shall not be duly paid by the husband, he shall be liable for necessaries supplied for her use."

By s. 21, a wife deserted by her husband may obtain an order of a magistrate or of the Court protecting her earnings and property, acquired since the commencement of such desertion, from her husband and all creditors and persons claiming under him, and such earnings and property shall belong to the wife as if she were a *feme sole*; and the wife shall, during the continuance of such order of protection, be and be deemed to have been, during such desertion of her, in the like position in all respects, with regard to property and contracts, and suing and being sued, as she would be under this Act if she obtained a decree of judicial separation. This section applies only to lawful earnings. (*Mason* v. *Mitchell*, 3 H. & C. 528; 34 L. J. Ex. 68.)

Whilst the protection order is in force the wife is by virtue of the above enactments in the same position as if she were a *feme sole* with respect to property of every description which she may acquire, or which may come to, or devolve upon her, after the date of such order. (*In re Coward and Adams Purchase*, L. R. 20 Eq. 179; 44 L. J. Ch. 384; *Nicholson* v. *Drury Buildings Estate Company*, 7 Ch. D. 48; 47 L. J. Ch. 192.) By 21 & 22 Vict. c. 108, s. 6, the application for a protection order may be made to the Judge Ordinary. The effect of decrees for judicial separations and of protection orders, is by 21 & 22 Vict. c. 108, s. 7, extended to property to which the wife has become or shall become entitled as executrix, administratrix, or trustee since the sentence of separation or the commencement of the desertion (as the case may be), and the death of the testator or intestate is to be deemed to be the time when the wife became entitled as executrix or administratrix..

By 21 & 22 Vict. c. 108, s. 8, "Property of or to which the wife is possessed or entitled for an estate in remainder or reversion at the date of the desertion or decree (as the case may be), shall be deemed to be included in the protection given by the order or decree." Sects. 8 and 10 of the above statute (*In re Insole*, L. R. 1 Eq. 470; 35 L. J. Ch. 177), protect dealings with the wife under orders or decrees which are afterwards discharged, reversed, or varied.

An order of protection obtained by a married woman deserted by her husband, under s. 21 of 20 & 21 Vict. c. 85, *supra*, though it protects her property acquired since the commencement of the desertion, does not entitle her to maintain an action commenced before the date of the order. (*Midland Ry. Co.* v. *Pye*, 10 C. B. N. S. 179; 30 L. J. C. P. 314.)

Choses in action of the wife not reduced into possession by the husband at the date of the protection order, or decree for judicial separation, become, under 20 & 21 Vict. c. 85, s. 25, upon such order or decree being made, the wife's property, as though she were a *feme sole*. (*Johnson* v. *Lander*, L. R. 7 Eq. 228; 38 L. J. Ch. 229. *In Re Coward and Adams Purchase*, L. R. 20 Eq. 179; 40 L. J. Ch. 384; *Nicholson* v. *Drury Buildings Estate Company*, 7 Ch. D. 48, 55; 47 L. J. Ch. 192.) "Reduction into possession as regards *choses in action* means actual payment to the husband in his character as husband, not as trustee, or what is equivalent to it; if the property has been paid to *his* agent, or so dealt with that the property is under the exclusive control of the husband, or has been, in the exercise of his exclusive control, placed by him in the hands of, or transferred to, other persons upon some trust inconsistent with the existence of the wife's possible title by survivorship, that will be considered as a reduction into possession." (2 Spence, Eq. Jur., p. 478; cited in *Nicholson* v. *Drury Buildings Estate Company*, 7 Ch. D. 55). Nothing has ever been held to amount to reduction into possession of a wife's *chose in action* which does not give the husband for some moment of time absolute dominion over the property without any concurrence of the wife. (*Per* Fry, J., *in Nicholson* v. *Drury Buildings Estate Co.*, 7 Ch. D. 48, 55; 47 L. J. Ch. 192; *Aitchison* v. *Dixon*, L. R. 10 Eq. 589; 39 L. J. Ch. 705; *Scrutton* v. *Pattillo*, L. R. 19 Eq. 369; 44 L. J. Ch. 249.) A wife who has been deserted by her husband and has a protection order under 20 & 21 Vict. c. 85, s. 21, is by that section placed in the like position with regard to all actions, as if she had obtained a decree of judicial separation. (See *Ramsden* v. *Brearley*, L. R. 10 Q. B. 147; 44 L. J. Q. B. 46, *an action for libel.*)

The status of a married woman is not affected by the pronouncing of a decree *nisi* for the dissolution of the marriage. She continues subject to all the disabilities of coverture until the decree is made absolute. (*Norman* v. *Villars*, 2 Ex. D. 359; 46 L. J. Ex. 579.)

A wife, after being divorced, cannot bring an action against her husband in respect of any personal tort committed during coverture by him, as for example an assault; for, during coverture, husband and wife are in law one person. (*Phillips* v. *Barnet*, 1 Q. B. D. 436; 45 L. J. Q. B. 277.)

1. The plaintiff A. B. is a married woman, and she sues by C. D., her next friend duly appointed (*c*).

2, &c. [*As in ordinary cases.*]

Commencement of Claim by Husband and Wife, coupled with a Claim by Husband alone (*d*).

Between A. B. and C. [*Christian name of wife*] his wife . . } Plaintiffs.

and

D. E. . . . . Defendant.

1. The plaintiff C. [*Christian name of the wife*] is the wife of the above-mentioned plaintiff, A. B.

Commencement of Claim by Wife Executrix, joining her Husband as Co-plaintiff (*e*).

Between A. B. and C. [*Christian name of the wife*], his wife, executrix of the last will and testament of D. E., deceased } Plaintiffs.

and

F. G. . . . . Defendant.

1. The plaintiff C. [*Christian name of the wife*] is the wife of the above-named plaintiff A. B., and the

---

A woman after divorce is solely entitled to such of her property as was not reduced into possession by her husband during the coverture. (*Wells* v. *Malbon*, 31 Beav. 48 ; 31 L. J. C. 344.)

(*c*) *Next friend*]. Where a married woman sues as plaintiff by her next friend, she does so in the manner practised in the Court of Chancery before the passing of the Jud. Act, 1875, see O. XVI. r. 8. By s. 11 of 15 & 16 Vict. c. 86, which was an act to amend the Practice and Course of Proceeding in the High Court of Chancery, it was enacted that " before the name of any person shall be used in any suit to be instituted in the said Court as next friend of any infant, married woman or other party, or as relator in any information, such person shall sign a written authority to the solicitor for that purpose, and such authority shall be filed with the bill, information, or claim." It would seem now under the new procedure that the authority must be filed when the writ of summons is issued, as the obtaining of the written authority is a necessary preliminary to the commencement of the action. See Dan. Ch. Forms, 3rd ed., p. 31, n. (*c*).

(*d*) By O. XVII. r. 4, claims by or against husband and wife may be joined with claims by or against either of them separately.

(*e*) *Wife executrix or administratrix.*] Where a married woman is executrix or administratrix her husband must be joined with her in actions by her or against her in that capacity.

executrix of the last will and testament of D. E., deceased.

Commencement of Claim against a Married Woman Administratrix joining her Husband as Co-defendant (e).

Between A. B. . . . . . . Plaintiff.

and

C. D. and E. [*Christian name of the wife*], the wife of C. D., administratrix of the estate and effects which were of F. G., deceased. . . . . . } Defendants.

1. The above-named defendant E. [*Christian name of the wife*] is the wife of the above-named defendant C. D., and the administratrix of the estate and effects of F. G., deceased.

Statement of Claim against a Married Woman, in which it is sought to charge her Separate Estate (f).

1. The defendant C. D. is and was at the time of making the contract hereinafter alleged, a married woman

---

(*f*) *Separate estate.*] A married woman may have property settled to her separate use exclusively of her husband, either with or without restraint being placed upon her power of dealing with such property. If no restraint is placed upon her power of dealing with her separate property she may charge it specifically, or may contract generally with the effect of subjecting it to her debts or contracts. She does not, however, in such cases, in general, become absolutely personally liable, and cannot be made bankrupt in respect of such debts (*ex parte Jones, In re Grissell*, 12 Ch. D. 484 ; 48 L. J. Bk. 109), but a relation of debtor and creditor is created with a right to go against a particular fund (*Robinson* v. *Pickering*, 29 W. R. 385 ; 44 L. T. 165) ; and where her trustees are not made parties to the action, and no particular fund is sought to be charged, but only a personal remedy against her is sought, the action cannot in general be sustained. (*Aylett* v. *Ashton*, 1 M. & Cr. 105 ; *Johnson* v. *Gallagher*, 3 D. F. & J. 494 ; *Picard* v. *Hine*, L. R. 5 Ch. Ap. 274, and see *Pike* v. *Fitzgibbon*, 17 Ch. D. 454 ; 50 L. J. Ch. 394.)

Unless an intention appear to the contrary, the separate estate which she has at the time of contracting is available in equity, as being the fund intended to be bound by a married woman in entering as a principal into contracts. (*Pike* v. *Fitzgibbon*, 17 Ch. D. 454 ; 50 L. J. Ch. 394 ; *Barber* v. *Gregson*, 49 L. J. Ex. 731 ; *Picard* v. *Hine*, L. R. 5 Ch. Ap. 274 ; *London Chartered Bank of Australia* v. *Lemprière*, L. R. 4 P. C. 572 ; 42 L. J. P. C. 49 ; *Johnson* v.

possessed of, or entitled to the benefit of considerable separate property. [She is and was the wife of the defendant G. D.]

2. The said defendant C. D. on the —— day of ——, 18—, purchased of, and received from the plaintiff a brougham, at the price of £160, upon her own credit and upon the credit of her said separate property.

3. The said defendant C. D. has not paid the said price of the said brougham nor any part of the said price.

4. [*State, where practicable, the circumstances of the*

Gallagher, 3 D. F. & J. 494; 30 L. J. Ch. 306; *McHenry* v. *Davies*, L. R. 10 Eq. 88; 39 L. J. Ch. 866; *Murray* v. *Barlee*, 3 M. & K. 210.)

If, however, the trust for the separate use of a married woman is attended with a restraint upon anticipation, or alienation, the power of disposition is taken away, except as to dividends or interest accrued and retained for her separate use. (*Arnold* v. *Woodhams*, L. R. 16 Eq. 29; 42 L. J. Ch. 578; *Waldrond* v. *Waldrond*, Joh. 18; 28 L. J. Ch. 99; *Stanley* v. *Stanley*, 7 Ch. D. 589; 47 L. J. Ch. 256; *Pike* v. *Fitzgibbon*, *supra*.) See further, Leake on Contracts, 554, *et seq*.

Where an action is brought against a married woman in respect of her separate estate, it is in general necessary to make her husband a co-defendant. (*Holmes* v. *Penney*, 3 K. & J. 90; *Hancocks* v. *Lablache*, 3 C. P. D. 197; 47 L. J. C. P. 514.)

If the trustees have not been made parties to proceedings against the separate estate of the married woman, the judgment will not be permitted to prejudice them. (*Collett* v. *Dickenson*, 11 Ch. D. 687; 4 Ex. D. 285; and see *Atwood* v. *Chichester*, 3 Q. B. D. 722; 47 L. J. Q. B. 300.) It is in general necessary to make the trustees parties to such proceedings. (*Atwood* v. *Chichester*, 3 Q. B. D. 722, 725; 47 L. J. Q. B. 300; *Robinson* v. *Pickering*, *supra*; see, however, *Davies* v. *Jenkins*, 6 Ch. D. 728; 46 L. J. Ch. 761; *Collett* v. *Dickenson*, *suprà*.)

Where an action is brought to recover separate property of the wife (not being property in respect of which she is entitled to sue alone in her own name under the provisions of the "Married Women's Property Act, 1870," as to which see *post*), the general rule is that the wife should bring the action by her next friend (O. XVI. r. 8; Dan. Ch. Prac. p. 102), making her husband a defendant. (*Roberts* v. *Evans*, 7 Ch. D. 830; 47 L. J. Ch. 469; Dan. Ch. Prac., p. 103; *Wake* v. *Parker*, 2 Kee. 59.) The next friend is named as such on the writ and in the statement of claim.

O. XVI. r. 8, gives, it will be observed, power, where requisite, to permit a wife to sue alone, and that either with or without imposing terms as to her giving security for costs. A wife cannot thus sue alone without an order enabling her to do so. (See Archibald's Forms, pp. 49, 50; Dan. Ch. Forms, 3rd ed. p. 74, *et seq.*) As to the claim for relief, see a form given in *Hancocks* v. *Lablache*, 38 L. T. 753; and conf. decree set out in *Picard* v. *Hine*, 5 Ch. Ap 274; and see observations thereon in *Pike* v. *Fitzgibbon*. *supra*.

purchase, as for instance. The said defendant C. D. at the time when she so purchased the said brougham was living at Dover apart from her husband, and maintaining an establishment separate from her husband.]

5. The said separate property of the defendant C. D., is and was vested in the defendant E. F., as trustee thereof for her sole and separate use and benefit.

The plaintiff claims as follows:

(1). To have the separate property of the said C. D. which was at the time of making the contract hereinbefore alleged, and which remains at this present date, vested in her or in the defendant E. F. or any other person in trust for her, charged with the payment of the sum of £160.

(2). To have an inquiry directed of what the said separate property of the said defendant C. D. consists at the present date, and in whom it is vested.

(3) To have such further inquiries directed and accounts taken as may be necessary.

(4). To have such further and other relief as may be necessary.

Statement of Claim by a Wife to Recover Wages gained by her after the passing of the "Married Women's Property Act, 1870" *(9th August,* 1870), *in an employment in which she was engaged separately from her Husband* (*g*).

1. Between the —— day of ——, 18—, and the —— day of ——, 18— (*dates after the passing of the "Married Women's Property Act,* 1870"), the plaintiff, being

(*g*) *Married Women's Property Acts.*] By the "Married Women's Property Act, 1870" (33 & 34 Vict. c. 93, passed 9th August, 1870), sect. 1, "The wages and earnings of any married woman acquired or gained by her after the passing of this Act in any employment, occupation, or trade in which she is engaged or which she carries on separately from her husband, and also any money or property so acquired by her through the exercise of any literary, artistic, or scientific skill, and all investments of such wages, earnings, money, or property, shall be deemed and taken to be property held and settled to her separate use, independent of any husband to whom she may be married, and her receipts alone shall be a good discharge for such wages, earnings, money, and property."

By sect. 2, deposits in savings banks by a married woman, or by a woman who afterwards marries, and annuities granted to such

then, as she still is, a married woman, was employed by the defendant as a ——, at the wages of £—— per month [*or as the case may be*].

---

women by the Commissioners for the Reduction of the National Debt are to be deemed to be the separate property of such women, and the same are to be accounted for and paid to them as if they were unmarried women; provided that if any such deposit is made by or such annuity granted to a married woman by means of moneys of her husband, without his consent, the Court may upon application under section 9 of the Act, order such deposit or annuity, or any part thereof, to be paid to the husband.

Sect. 3 deals with investments by a married woman in public stocks and funds; see further 34 & 35 Vict. c. 47, s. 14, which deals with her investments in the Metropolitan Board of Works.

Sect. 4 deals with her investments in companies.

Sect. 5 with those in industrial and provident societies, friendly societies, benefit building, or loan societies.

Sect. 9 provides for the decision in a summary way of questions between husband and wife as to property declared by the Act to be separate property of the wife.

By sect 11, "A married woman may maintain an action in her own name for the recovery of any wages, earnings, money, and property by this Act declared to be her separate property, or of any property belonging to her before her marriage, and which her husband shall, by writing under his hand, have agreed with her shall belong to her after her marriage as her separate property, and she shall have in her own name the same remedies, both civil and criminal, against all persons whomsoever for the protection and security of such wages, earnings, money, and property, and of any chattels or other property purchased or obtained by means thereof for her own use, as if such wages, earnings, money, chattels, and property belonged to her as an unmarried woman; and in any indictment or other proceeding it shall be sufficient to allege such wages, earnings, money, chattels, and property to be her property." The effect as to such property &c., is, that she can sue as though a *feme sole*, but cannot be sued without her husband being made a party as defendant. (*Hancocks* v. *Lablache*, 3 C. P. D. 197; 47 L. J. C. P. 514.)

The business carried on by a married woman may be a separate business, although her husband lives with her. (*Ashworth* v. *Outram*, 5 Ch. D. 923; 40 L. J. Ch. 687; *Lovell* v. *Newton*, 4 C. P. D. 7.) A banking account kept by a married woman who carries on a separate business is so incidental to such separate business, that the married woman may in her own name sue the banker for improperly dishonouring her cheques drawn on that account (*Summers* v. *City Bank*, L. R. 9 C. P. 581), or for any breach of the contract which as such banker he has entered into with her. So a married woman living apart from her husband may recover damages for being wrongfully expelled from a beer-house, the goodwill and stock-in-trade of which had been purchased by her with her separate earnings. (*Moore* v. *Robinson*, 48 L. J. 156; 40 L. T. 99.)

By sect. 12 of the above Act, "A husband shall not by reason of any marriage which shall take place after this Act has come into operation, be liable for the debts of his wife contracted before mar-

2. The said employment of the plaintiff was an employment in which she was engaged, and which she carried on, separately from her husband.

---

riage, but the wife shall be liable to be sued for, and any property belonging to her for her separate use shall be liable to satisfy such debts, as if she had continued unmarried."

By the common law a husband became on marriage responsible for the debts of his wife contracted before marriage. The above section in some cases, as for instance where a husband took the whole property of the wife on marriage, thus leaving no separate estate out of which debts contracted by her before marriage were payable, worked an injustice to creditors of the wife in respect of debts contracted before marriage. Consequently it was by the "Married Women's Property Act (1870) Amendment Act, 1874," 37 & 38 Vict. c. 50, passed 30th July, 1874, enacted as follows:—

Sect. 1. "So much of the Married Women's Property Act, 1870, as enacts that a husband shall not be liable for the debts of his wife contracted before marriage is repealed so far as respects marriages which shall take place after the passing of this Act, and a husband and wife married after the passing of this Act may be jointly sued for any such debt."

Sect. 2. "The husband shall, in such action, and in any action brought for damages sustained by reason of any tort committed by the wife before marriage, or by reason of the breach of any contract made by the wife before marriage, be liable for the debt or damages respectively to the extent only of the assets hereinafter specified; and in addition to any other plea or pleas may plead that he is not liable to pay the debt or damages in respect of any such assets as hereinafter specified; or, confessing his liability to some amount, that he is not liable beyond what he so confesses; and if no such plea is pleaded the husband shall be deemed to have confessed his liability so far as assets are concerned."

Sect. 3. "If it is not found in such action that the husband is liable in respect of any such assets, he shall have judgment for his costs of defence, whatever the result of the action may be against the wife."

Sect. 4. "When a husband and wife are sued jointly, if by confession or otherwise it appears that the husband is liable for the debt or damages recovered, or any part thereof, the judgment to the extent of the amount for which the husband is liable shall be a joint judgment against the husband and wife, and as to the residue, if any, of such debt or damages, the judgment shall be a separate judgment against the wife."

Sect. 5. "The assets in respect of and to the extent of which the husband shall in any such action be liable are as follows:—

(1.) The value of the personal estate in possession of the wife, which shall have vested in the husband:

(2.) The value of the choses in action of the wife which the husband shall have reduced into possession, or which with reasonable diligence he might have reduced into possession:

(3.) The value of the chattels real of the wife which shall have vested in the husband and wife:

(4.) The value of the rents and profits of the real estate of the wife

3. The defendant has not paid to the plaintiff the said wages, or any portion of them, and there is now due and payable from the defendant to the plaintiff in respect thereof £——.

---

which the husband shall have received, or with reasonable diligence might have received :

(5.) The value of the husband's estate or interest in any property, real or personal, which the wife in contemplation of her marriage with him shall have transferred to him or to any other person :

(6.) The value of any property, real or personal, which the wife in contemplation of her marriage with the husband shall with his consent have transferred to any person with the view of defeating or delaying her existing creditors :

"Provided that when the husband after marriage pays any debts of his wife, or has a judgment *boná fide* recovered against him in any such action as is in this Act mentioned, then to the extent of such payment or judgment the husband shall not in any subsequent action be liable."

In actions to recover debts contracted by a married woman before her marriage, if the marriage took place after the passing of the "Married Women's Property Act (1870) Amendment Act, 1874," the husband is made a co-defendant with the wife, but if he proves that he is exempt from liability in accordance with the provisions of the "Married Women's Property Act (1870) Amendment Act, 1874," (which see *supra*) he will as against the plaintiff be entitled to his costs of defence, though the plaintiff will in general be entitled to add these costs to the amount recoverable against the separate property of the wife. (*London and Provincial Bank* v. *Boyle*, 7 Ch. D. 773 ; 47 L. J. Ch. 301.)

In suing a husband and wife jointly under the last-mentioned Act, it is not necessary to set out in the statement of claim that the husband has assets of the kind specified in that Act, or to specify the assets in respect of which it is sought to make him liable ; but it is for the defence to deny assets if the possession of them is not admitted. (*Matthews* v. *Whittle*, 13 Ch. D. 811 ; 49 L. J. Ch. 359.) In practice, however, it may sometimes be convenient to give details in the statement of claim of the assets in respect of which it is alleged that the husband is liable, so as to compel the pleader in drawing the defence to deal specifically with the allegations as to such assets in the statement of claim. (O. XIX., r. 20.)

Where a married woman sues in respect of matters in respect of which she is entitled to sue alone by virtue of sects. 1 and 11 of the Married Women's Property Act, 1870 (which see *ante*), the statement of claim should show that the matters in respect of which she sues are within those sections, if it discloses the fact of her coverture.

Where the marriage took place after the passing of the "Married Women's Property Act (1870) Amendment Act, 1874" (which see *ante*), and a judgment is obtained against the wife in respect of a debt contracted by her before the marriage, such judgment may be satisfied out of her separate property, and there should be a declaration that such property stands charged. (See *London and Provincial Bank* v. *Boyle*, 7 Ch. D. 773 ; 47 L. J. Ch. 301.)

As to separate estate, see *note (f), ante*, p. 203.

Statement of Claim against Husband and Wife jointly to recover a Debt for Money Lent, contracted by the Wife before the Marriage [the date of the Marriage being subsequent to the passing of the "Married Women's Property Act (1870) *Amendment Act,* 1874"] (*g*).

1. The defendant C. [*the Christian name of the wife*], is the wife of the defendant A. B. She became his wife on the —— day of ——, 18— [*shewing the date to be after the passing of the said Act, 30th July,* 1874; *or state* She became his wife after the passing of the "Married Women's Property Act (1870) Amendment Act, 1874"].

2. The said defendant C. on the —— day of ——, 18—, before she became the wife of the defendant A. B., and while unmarried, borrowed from the plaintiff the sum of £—— upon the terms that she should repay the same with interest at the rate of —— per centum per annum to the plaintiff within two years from the —— day of ——, 18—.

3. The said period of two years has elapsed, but the said sum of £—— has not been repaid, nor has any part of it, nor has any interest been paid thereon.

4. [Personal estate in possession of the said defendant C., more than sufficient in value to satisfy the claim of the plaintiff in this action, vested in the defendant A. B., upon his said marriage with the said defendant C., *or state when it so vested.*]

5. The said defendant C. has property belonging to her for her separate use.

The plaintiff claims as follows :—

(1). To have judgment against the said defendants A. B. and C. jointly for the said sum of £——, and his costs of action.

(2). If it shall be found that the defendant A. B. is not liable, then to have judgment against the defendant C. for the said sum of £——, and costs of action, including any costs he may have to pay the defendant A. B.

(3). To have it declared that the separate property of the defendant C. at present vested in her, or in any other person in trust for her, is chargeable with the said sum of £——, and £—— for interest thereon, and with the costs of this action, including any costs payable by the plaintiff to the defendant A. B., and to have the same charged accordingly.

(4). To have an inquiry what property C. at present has belonging to her for her separate use, and in whom it is vested.

(5). To have such further or other relief as may be necessary.

Statement of Claim against Husband and Wife for the Price of Goods supplied to the Wife during coverture, to recover Payment out of Property made her Separate Property by the "Married Women's Property Act, 1870," *the Goods not having been supplied on the Credit of the Husband* (*g*).

1. The defendant C. [*Christian name of the wife*] is the wife of the defendant A. B. and carries on the trade of a dressmaker at ——.

2. The defendant C. has for many years since the passing of the "Married Women's Property Act, 1870," carried on the said trade at —— separately from the defendant A. B. who was and is her husband, and she acquired or gained thereby considerable money or property.

3. Whilst carrying on such trade, on the —— day of ——, 18—, the defendant C. bought of the plaintiff a parcel of old lace [*or as the case may be*] upon the credit of her said money or property so acquired or gained as aforesaid, at the price of £——, and the said defendant C. then promised the plaintiff that she would pay the said price by two equal instalments at three and six months from the said —— day of ——, 18—, intending thereby to charge her separate property, being the money or property so acquired as aforesaid.

4. The said defendant C. has not paid the said price, or any part of it, although the time for the payment of both of the said instalments has elapsed.

The plaintiff claims as follows :—

(1). To have it declared that the separate property of the defendant C. vested in her, or in any other person in trust for her, is chargeable with the said sum of £——, and with the costs of this action, and to have the same charged accordingly.

(2). To have an inquiry of what the separate property of C. consists at the present time, and in whom it is vested.

(3). To have such further or other relief as may be necessary.

[*For a like Form* see *Hancocks* v. *Lablache*, 38 L. T. 753.]

INDEMNITIES (*a*).

By the Acceptor of an Accommodation Bill on the Contract to indemnify him (*b*).

1. The defendant, on the —— of ——, 18—, requested

(*a*) A promise to answer for a debt or liability incurred by the promisee himself, is not within s. 4 of the Statute of Frauds, and therefore need not be in writing. (*Thomas* v. *Cook*, 8 B. & C. 728; *Eastwood* v. *Kenyon*, 11 A. & E. 438; *Hargreaves* v. *Parsons*, 13 M. & W. 561; *Reader* v. *Kingham*, 13 C. B. N. S. 344; 32 L. J. C. P. 108; *Batson* v. *King*, 4 H. & N. 739; 28 L. J. Ex. 327; *Wildes* v. *Dudlow*, L. R. 19 Eq. 198; 44 L. J. Ch. 341.) See also "*Guarantees*," *ante*, p. 190; Leake on Contracts, 246; and Addison, 7th ed., 151. Notice of the damnification is not a condition precedent in the contract, unless such notice was expressly stipulated for (*Cutler* v. *Southern*, 1 Wms. Saund., 1871 ed., p. 133; *Duffield* v. *Scott*, 3 T. R. 374); but the effect of notice of a claim or action may be to give the indemnifying party the opportunity of resisting it, and of estopping him from afterwards saying that it was not payable. (*Duffield* v. *Scott, supra; Smith* v. *Compton*, 3 B. & Ad. 407; *Jones* v. *Williams*, 7 M. & W. 493; and see Mellish, L. J., in *Parker* v. *Lewis*, L. R. 8 Ch. Ap. 1058.)

Apart from any express promise, a contract of indemnity may in general be implied where one who is only secondarily liable performs under compulsion of law an obligation for which another person is primarily liable. (*Per* Willes, J., *Roberts* v. *Crowe*, L. R. 7 C. P. 636, 637; 41 L. J. C. P. 200, 201.)

Such contract may also be implied "where two persons are equally liable for a debt, and the person who is not in the enjoyment of the property in respect of which the debt arises, and therefore only secondarily liable, is called upon to pay." (*Per* Willes, J., *Roberts* v. *Crowe, supra*, p. 636; see also *Nevill's case*, L. R. 6 Ch. Ap. 43; 40 L. J. Ch. 1.) Thus there is an implied agreement between the original lessee and each successive assignee of a term that the latter shall whilst in possession indemnify the former from liability on breaches of the covenants of the lease. (*Moule* v. *Garrett*, L. R. 5 Ex. 132; *ib.* 7 Ex. 101; 39 L. J. Ex. 69; 41 L. J. Ex. 62, and see *Crouch* v. *Tregoning*, L. R. 7 Ex. 88.) So an agent is in general entitled to indemnity from his principal against any liabilities incurred in executing the orders of his principal, unless those orders are illegal, or unless the liabilities are incurred by reason of the default or misconduct of such agent. (*Thacker* v. *Hardy*, 4 Q. B. D. 685, 687; 48 L. J. Q. B. 289; *Adamson* v. *Jarvis*, 4 Bing. 66; *Dugdale* v. *Lovering*, L. R. 10 C. P. 196; 44 L. J. C. P. 197.) As to pleading an agreement to indemnify implied from circumstances, see O. XIX., r. 27, and *ante*, "*Agreements.*"

(*b*) The drawer or acceptor of an accommodation bill is entitled to

the plaintiff to accept, for the defendant's accommodation, a bill of exchange, bearing date the —— of ——, 18—, drawn by the defendant on the plaintiff, requiring him to pay to the defendant, or order, £——, —— months after date, and promised the plaintiff that if the plaintiff would accept the said bill and deliver the same to the defendant, in order that the defendant might negotiate it for his own use, the defendant would indemnify and save harmless the plaintiff from any loss or damage by reason of his so accepting and delivering the same to the defendant.

2. The plaintiff accordingly accepted the said bill for the defendant's accommodation, and delivered the same to him for the purpose and on the terms aforesaid.

3. The defendant did not indemnify or save harmless the plaintiff from loss or damage by reason of his so accepting and delivering the said bill to the defendant, and the plaintiff, as acceptor of the said bill, was obliged to pay to G. H., the holder thereof, the amount of the said bill, with £—— interest thereon.

On a Promise to Indemnify the Plaintiff against Defending an Action (c).

1. In the month of ——, 18—, G. H. brought an action against the plaintiff in the Queen's Bench Division of the High Court of Justice to recover £—— then

---

recover against the party accommodated, not only the amount of the bill, but also the costs, which he has been compelled to pay (*Jones* v. *Brooke*, 4 Taunt. 464; *Stratton* v. *Mathews*, 3 Ex. 48); but not the costs of an action against him upon the bill which he ought to have paid without action. (*Beech* v. *Jones*, 5 C. B. 696, and see *Bleaden* v. *Charles*, 7 Bing. 246.) Where the costs have been incurred at the defendant's request, and actually paid before the action, they may be recovered as being money paid at the defendant's request. (*Garrard* v. *Cottrell*, 10 Q. B. 679.)

Upon a contract to indemnify an accommodation acceptor the cause of action accrues when the plaintiff is damnified by payment, and the Statute of Limitations begins to run from that date (*Reynolds* v. *Doyle*, 1 M. & G. 753); so on a contract to indemnify against the costs of maintaining an action. (*Collinge* v. *Heywood*, 9 A. & E. 633.)

(c) Upon a contract of indemnity against bringing or defending an action, full costs taxed between solicitor and client are recoverable as damages. (*Smith* v. *Compton*, 3 B. & Ad. 407, 408; *Lloyd* v. *Mostyn*, 2 Dowl. N. S. 476.) The like costs may in some cases be recovered as damages where an action has been brought against the

in the hands of the plaintiff, which was claimed by the defendant.

2. It was thereupon orally agreed between the plaintiff and the defendant that the plaintiff should defend the said action, and that the defendant should indemnify and save harmless the plaintiff from all loss and damage by reason of his defending the same.

3. The plaintiff accordingly defended the said action, and such proceedings were had therein that the said G. H. recovered judgment therein against the plaintiff for the said £——, and for £—— for costs of action.

4. A sufficient time elapsed before the commencement of this action to entitle the plaintiff to have the said agreement performed upon the part of the defendant.

5. The defendant has not indemnified and saved harmless the plaintiff from all loss and damage by reason of his defending the said action, whereby the plaintiff has been obliged to pay and has paid the said £—— for costs of the said action, and a further sum of £—— incurred by the plaintiff for his own costs and expenses in and about defending the said action.

For Statement of Claim by a Broker to be indemnified by his principal for payments made in the course of dealings upon the London Stock Exchange for his principal, see ante, p. 119.

For Further Forms on Contracts of Indemnity, see Webster v. *Petre,* 4 Ex. D. 127; *Bowyear* v. *Pawson,* 6 Q. B. D. 540.

INFANT (*a*).

Commencement of Statement of Claim by an Infant.

Between A. B., an infant, by C. D., his next friend, } Plaintiff.

and

E. F. . . . . Defendant.

1. The plaintiff, A. B., is an infant who sues by C. D., his next friend duly appointed.

---

plaintiff by a third party, where there has been a breach of an agreement to indemnify. (*Howard* v. *Lovegrove*, L. R. 6 Ex. 43; 40 L. J. Ex. 13.)

(*a*) As to actions against Infants, see "Defences," "*Infants.*" By O. XVI., r. 8, infants may sue as plaintiffs by their next friends

Insurance.—I. Marine Policies (*a*).

On a Policy of Insurance on a Ship for a Total Loss.

1. The plaintiff was at the time hereinafter mentioned the owner of a ship called the ——.

2. By a policy of insurance, bearing date the —— day of ——, 18—, the plaintiff caused himself to be insured

---

in the manner practised in the Court of Chancery before the passing of the Jud. Act, 1875, and may in like manner defend any action by their guardians appointed for that purpose. See as to the manner practised formerly in the Court of Chancery, 15 & 16 Vict. c. 86, s. 11, and "*Husband and Wife*," *ante*, p. 202.

(*a*) By sect. 7 of 30 Vict. c. 23, "No contract or agreement for sea-insurance (other than such insurance as is referred to in the 55th section of 'The Merchant Shipping Act Amendment Act, 1862") shall be valid unless the same is expressed in a policy; and every policy shall specify the particular risk or adventure, the names of the subscribers or underwriters, and the sum or sums insured; and in case any of the above-mentioned particulars shall be omitted in any policy, such policy shall be null and void to all intents and purposes."

As to the meaning of "sea-insurance" and "policy," as used in the above statute, see sects. 4 and 12 of the statute.

By sect. 9 of the above statute, "No policy shall be pleaded or given in evidence in any Court, or admitted in any Court to be good or available in Law or in Equity, unless duly stamped." The "slip" or memorandum of insurance, which is initialed by the underwriters before executing the formal policy itself, is void under the statute, and cannot be sued upon. (*Fisher* v. *Liverpool Maritime Insurance Co.*, L. R. 9 Q. B. 418; 43 L. J. Q. B. 114.) The insurance relates back to the time when the real agreement is made between the parties, that is to the date of the "slip," consequently the obligation which attaches to the relation of insurer and insured, viz., that up to the time of insurance all material facts which would affect the judgment of an underwriter must be communicated, attaches up to the time of the making of the "slip" only, and not to that of the executing the formal policy. (*Lishman* v. *Northern Maritime Insurance Co.*, L. R. 8 C. P. 216; L. R. 10 C. P. 179; 42 L. J. C. P. 108; 44 L. J. C. P. 185; *Cory* v. *Patton*, L. R. 7 Q. B. 304; L. R. 9 Q. B. 577; 41 L. J. Q. B. 195 (*n*); 43 L. J. Q. B. 181; *Ionides* v. *Pacific Insurance Co.*, L. R. 6 Q. B. 674; L. R. 7 Q. B. 517; 41 L. J. Q. B. 190; *Rivaz* v. *Gerussi*, 6 Q. B. D. 222; 50 L. J. Q. B. 176.) The "slip," though not itself enforceable, may be given in evidence wherever its contents are material, as for instance to show the intention of the parties as to the nature of the risk. (*Ionides* v. *Pacific Insurance Co.*, *supra*; *Cory* v. *Patton*, *supra*; *Lishman* v. *Northern Maritime Insurance Co.*, *supra*.)

As to what is a sufficient description in a policy of the particular risk or adventure, see *Edwards* v. *Aberayron Mutual Ship Insurance Society*, 1 Q. B. D. 563, 573; 44 L. J. Q. B. 67.

Where a partnership subscribes a policy it is sufficient if the name

at and from the port of —— to the port of ——, upon the body, tackle, apparel, ordnance, munition, artillery, boat, and other furniture of and in the said ship ——, beginning the adventure at the said port of ——, and

---

of the firm is expressed in the policy; and the individual partners are liable upon it, though not individually named. (See *Reid* v. *Allan*, 4 Ex. 326, and *Hallett* v. *Dowdall*, 18 Q. B. 2.)

The action on a policy of marine insurance may be brought in the name of the party nominally effecting the insurance, being the agent or insurance broker, or in the name of the principal or party interested; and where the insurance has been effected by an agent in his own name on behalf of his principal, the principal may sue on the policy, although it contained nothing to show the agency. (*Provincial Insurance Co. of Canada* v. *Leduc*, L. R. 6 P. C. 224; *De Vignier* v. *Swanson*, 1 B. & P. 346, n.; *Browning* v. *Provincial Insurance Co. of Canada*, L. R. 5 P. C. 263; *Watson* v. *Swan*, 11 C. B. N. S. 756; 31 L. J. C. P. 210; Leake on Contracts, 524.)

By 28 Geo. III. c. 56, s. 1, it is not lawful for any person to effect any policy of insurance upon any ship, goods, or other property, without first inserting in such policy the name or names, or usual style and firm of one or more of the persons interested in such insurance, or of the consignors and consignees of the property insured, or of the persons residing in Great Britain who shall receive the order for and effect such policy, or of the persons who shall give the order to the agent immediately employed to effect such policy; and by sect. 2 it is declared that every policy made contrary to the meaning of this Act shall be void.

By 30 Vict. c. 23, s. 8, "No policy shall be made for any time exceeding twelve months."

As to what stamp is required upon a policy of sea-insurance and as to time of stamping see 30 Vict. c. 23; 33 & 34 Vict. c. 97, and 39 Vict. c. 6.

By 39 Vict. c. 6, s. 2, such a policy may now be stamped upon its production as evidence in any court of civil judicature in the United Kingdom on payment of the amount of the unpaid duty and a penalty of one hundred pounds.

In the case of a "time policy" upon a ship there is no implied warranty that the ship is sea-worthy at the commencement of the risk, as there is in the case of voyage policies. (*Gibson* v. *Small*, 4 H. L. C. 353; *Dudgeon* v. *Pembroke*, 2 App. Cas. 284; 46 L. J. Q. B. 409.)

As to the interest of parties insuring, it is enacted by the 19 Geo. II. c. 37, s. 1, "that no assurance or assurances shall be made by any person or persons, bodies corporate or politic, on any ship or ships belonging to his Majesty or any of his subjects, or any goods, merchandises, or effects, laden or to be laden on board of any such ship or ships, interest or no interest, or without further proof of interest than the policy, or by way of gaming or wagering, or without benefit of salvage to the assurer: and that every such assurance shall be null and void to all intents and purposes."

This section does not apply to foreign ships, and it is therefore unnecessary in the case of a policy on a foreign ship to allege that the plaintiff was interested in the ship. (*Thellusson* v. *Fletcher*, 1 Doug.

continuing during her abode there, and until the said ship and premises should be arrived at the said port of ——, and until she should have moored at anchor 24 hours in safety, against perils of the sea [*etc., accord-*

315; *Craufurd* v. *Hunter*, 8 T. R. 13; *Nantes* v. *Thompson*, 2 East, 385. See further as to this section, *Allkins* v. *Jupe*, 2 C. P. D. 375; 45 L. J. C. P. 824.)

As to what constitutes an insurable interest see *Seagrave* v. *Union Marine*, L. R. 1 C. P. 305; 35 L. J. C. P. 172; *Ebsworth* v. *Alliance Marine*, L. R. 8 C. P. 596; 42 L. J. C. P. 305; 43 L. J. C. P. 394, n.; *Anderson* v. *Morice*, L. R. 10 C. P. 609; 1 App. Cas. 713; 46 L. J. H. L. 11.

By the "Policies of Marine Assurance Act, 1868" (31 & 32 Vict. c. 86), s. 1, "Whenever a policy of insurance on any ship, or on any goods in any ship, or on any freight, has been assigned, so as to pass the beneficial interest in such policy to any person entitled to the property thereby insured, the assignee of such policy shall be entitled to sue thereon in his own name; and the defendant in any action shall be entitled to make any defence which he would have been entitled to make if the said action had been brought in the name of the person by whom or for whose account the policy sued upon was effected," and by s. 2, the assignment of a policy may be made by indorsement in the form given in the schedule (and see Judicature Act, 1873, s. 25 (6)).

As to the mode of pleading an assignment, see "*Assignment*," *ante*, p. 59. The statement of claim should show that the assignee suing in his own name is entitled to the property insured by the policy.

The policy may be assigned after loss. (*Lloyd* v. *Fleming*, L. R. 7 Q. B. 299; 41 L. J. Q. B. 93); but it cannot be assigned after the interest of the assignor in the subject matter has ceased. (*North of England Oil Cake Co.* v. *Archangel Maritime Insurance Co.*, L. R. 10 Q. B. 249; 44 L. J. Q. B. 121.)

Before the passing of the "Policies of Marine Assurance Act, 1868," the assignee of a sea-policy of insurance was obliged to sue in the name of the insured. In an action by the assignee of a policy under the above statute the insurers are not entitled to set off a debt incurred with them by the assured for premiums on policies effected with them by the assured after the date of the assignment. (*Pellas* v. *Neptune Marine Insurance Co.*, 5 C. P. D. 34; 49 L. J. C. P. 153.)

In statements of claim on marine policies, the interest in the subject of the policy is averred as being in the plaintiff, if the insured, or in the person or persons on behalf of whom he is suing. (*Cohen* v. *Hannam*, 5 Taunt. 101.) An averment of interest at the time of or before effecting the policy is immaterial; it is sufficient if the plaintiff be interested at the commencement of the risk. (*Rhind* v. *Wilkinson*, 2 Taunt. 237.) If the insured assigns away his interest after effecting the policy and before the loss, he cannot recover upon the policy, except as trustee for the assignee where the policy has been assigned with the interest. (*Powles* v. *Innes*, 11 M. & W. 10; *North of England Oil Cake Co.* v. *Archangel Maritime Insurance Co.*, L. R. 10 Q. B. 249; 44 L. J. Q. B. 121.) If the assignment was

ing to the policy, stating those perils from which the loss arose], the said ship and premises being warranted free from average under £3 per cent., unless general or the ship should be stranded; and the defendant, for a certain

---

only by way of mortgage, he may recover. (*Ward* v. *Beck*, 13 C. B. N. S. 668; 32 L. J. C. P. 113.) In an action on a policy (lost or not lost) it is immaterial that the plaintiff acquired his interest and made the insurance after the loss, provided he had no notice of such loss at the time of making the insurance. (*Sutherland* v. *Pratt*, 11 M. & W. 296.) The interest may be valued in the policy at a fixed sum independently of its real value, and the insured is entitled to recover such fixed sum for a total loss (*Irving* v. *Manning*, 6 C. B. 391; *Barker* v. *Janson*, L. R. 3 C. P. 303; 37 L. J. C. P. 105; *Lidgett* v. *Secretan*, L. R. 6 C. P. 616; 40 L. J. C. P. 257); or a proportionate part for a partial loss. (*Lewis* v. *Rucker*, 2 Burr. 1167; and see *Denoon* v. *Home and Colonial Assurance Co.*, L. R. 7. C. P. 341; 41 L. J. C. P. 162.)

In framing statements of claim on marine policies, when the nature of the claim makes it necessary to refer to the whole contents of the policy, memoranda, etc., it will frequently be found convenient to set out the document verbatim, as the commercial form of these instruments and the blanks left in them make it sometimes difficult to recite them in a satisfactory manner. In other cases, the shortest form, of course, is to give the legal effect of the material parts of the contract as in other statements of claim. Care must be taken to state the contract accurately, with all the exceptions and qualifications of the defendant's liability (*Dawson* v. *Wrench*, 3 Ex. 359), and the statement of claim must negative that the defendant comes within the exceptions. (*Ib.*; but see *Wheeler* v. *Bavidge*, 9 Ex. 668; *Crow* v. *Falk*, 8 Q. B. 467, 471.)

A "constructive total loss" is when the damage is of such a character that the insured is entitled, if he thinks fit, to treat the loss as total, although the subject-matter of the insurance still exists *in specie*.

Under a policy against "total loss only," a constructive total loss may be recovered. (*Adams* v. *M'Kenzie*, 13 C. B. N. S. 442; 32 L. J. C. P. 92.) Notice of abandonment is a condition precedent to the right of the assured to claim for a "constructive total loss." (*Knight* v. *Faith*, 15 Q. B., 649; *Kaltenbach* v. *Mackenzie*, 3 C. P. D. 467; 48 L. J. C. P. 9.) Where, however, there is substantially nothing to abandon, and the insurer would gain nothing by the notice of abandonment, the giving of such notice is held excused or waived. (*Rankin* v. *Potter*, L. R. 6 H. L. 83; 42 L. J. C. P. 169; *Kaltenbach* v. *Mackenzie*, *suprà*.) It has been held that a sale authorized by necessity during the voyage may amount to a total loss, for which the assured may recover without notice of abandonment. (*Roux* v. *Salvador*, 3 Bing. N. C. 266; *Farnworth* v. *Hyde*, 18 C. B. N. S. 835; 34 L. J. C. P. 107; 36 *Ib.* 33; *Rankin* v. *Potter*, *suprà*; and see *Moss* v. *Smith*, 9 C. B. 94.)

Where a shipowner has been compelled to pay damages in consequence of a collision, such damages are not recoverable as loss by perils of the sea under a policy which contains no "collision clause." (*De Vaux* v. *Salvador*, 4 A. & E. 420.) The "collision clause" usually

premium paid to him by the plaintiff, subscribed the said policy for £——, and became an insurer thereon to the plaintiff for that amount on the said ship and premises.

2. The plaintiff, at the time of the said insuring, and thence until and at the time of the loss hereafter mentioned, was interested in the said ship and premises to the amount of all the moneys by him insured thereon.

3. The said ship, with the said other premises on board thereof, departed on her said voyage, and afterwards whilst she was proceeding on the said voyage, and during the continuance of the said risk the said ship and premises were wholly lost by [*here state cause of total loss, showing that it was by perils insured against*].

4. Notice of the said loss was duly given by the plaintiff to the defendant.

5. A sufficient time has elapsed since such loss to entitle the plaintiff to be paid the said £—— by the defendant.

6. The defendant has not paid the same.

On a Policy of Insurance upon Cargo for a Total Loss.

1. The plaintiff is a general merchant, carrying on business at ——.

2. By a policy of insurance, bearing date the ——

---

inserted to insure damage payable for collisions does not include costs incurred by shipowners in successfully defending an action for collision (*Xenos* v. *Fox*, L. R. 3 C. P. 630; 4 *Ib.* 665; 37 L. J. C. P. 294; 38 *Ib.* 351), nor does it include damages payable for personal injury caused by the collision. (*Taylor* v. *Dewar*, 5 B. & S. 58; 33 L. J. Q. B. 141.) An insurer who has paid the loss is entitled to bring an action, in the name of the insured against a wrongdoer who caused such loss, for compensation for the injury. (*Mason* v. *Sainsbury*, 3 Doug. 64; *Randal* v. *Cockran*, 1 Ves. Sen. 97; *Midland Ins. Co.* v. *Smith*, 6 Q. B. D. 561; 50 L. J. Q. B. 329.) But he can only recover such damages as the insured has a right to (*Simpson* v. *Thomson*, 3 App. Cas. 279; *Midland Ins. Co.* v. *Smith*, *supra*).

By the 3 & 4 Will. IV. c. 42, s. 29, the jury may give damages in the nature of interest in actions on policies of insurance.

Where the members of a mutual insurance association agreed that the manager of the association should sue in his own name for all sums payable by members for premiums and contribution, it was held that the manager was not thereby enabled to sue. (*Gray* v. *Pearson*, L. R. 5 C. P. 568; *Evans* v. *Hooper*, 1 Q. B. D. 45; 45 L. J. Q. B. 206.)

See further as to pleadings on policies of marine insurance, Arnold on Marine Insurance 5th ed., p. 1090.

of ——, 18—, the plaintiff caused himself to be insured at and from —— to a port of discharge in the United Kingdom, upon the goods and merchandise in the ship ——, beginning the adventure from the loading of the said goods and merchandise on board the said ship as above, and continuing until they should be safely discharged and landed, against perils of the seas [*etc., according to the policy, stating those perils from which the loss arose*]; corn, fish, salt, fruit, flour, and seed being warranted free from average, unless general, or the ship should be stranded; sugar, tobacco, hemp, flax, hides, and skins being warranted free from average under £5 per cent., and all other goods being warranted free from average under £3 per cent., unless general or the ship should be stranded.

3. The defendant, for the premium of £—— paid to him by the plaintiff, subscribed the said policy for £——, and became an insurer thereon to the plaintiff for that amount on the said goods and merchandise.

4. The said goods and merchandise were shipped on board the said ship at —— aforesaid, to be carried therein on the said voyage.

5. The plaintiff was then and thence, until and at the time of the loss hereinafter mentioned, interested in the said goods and merchandise to the amount of all the moneys by him insured thereon.

6. The said ship, with the said goods and merchandise on board thereof, sailed on the said voyage, and afterwards, whilst the said ship with the said goods and merchandise on board thereof was proceeding on the said voyage, and during the continuance of the said risk, the said goods and merchandise were wholly lost by [*here state cause of loss, showing that it was by perils insured against*].

7. [*Continue as in paragraphs* 4, 5, *and* 6 *of the last form.*]

On a Policy of Insurance upon Goods to recover for a General Average Loss (*b*).

1. The plaintiff, by a policy of insurance, bearing date the —— day of ——, 18—, caused himself to be insured

---

(*b*) "*General average*" is the damage or loss incurred by any particular part of the ship or cargo for the preservation of the rest. Such

at and from —— to a port of discharge in the United Kingdom, upon the goods and merchandise in the ship ——, beginning the adventure from the loading thereof on board the said ship as above, and continuing until they should be safely discharged and landed against perils of the sea [*etc., according to the policy, stating those perils from which the loss arose*]; the said goods and merchandise being warranted free from average, unless general, or the ship should be stranded [*or as the case may be*].

2, 3, and 4. [*Continue as in paragraphs* 3, 4, *and* 5 *of the last form.*]

5. The said ship, with the said goods and merchandise on board thereof, sailed on the said voyage, and whilst she was proceeding on the said voyage and during the continuance of the said risk, the said ship and the said goods and merchandise were by [*here state cause of danger, showing that it was by perils insured against*] brought into great danger of being lost, wherefore the master of the said ship, for the general safety and preservation of the said ship and of the said goods and merchandise, was necessarily obliged to cut away and cast overboard, and did cut away and cast overboard the masts, yards, sails, ropes, anchors, and rigging of the said ship, whereby the same were wholly lost.

6. By reason of the matters aforesaid, the plaintiff, in respect of his interest in the said goods and merchandise, became liable to bear and pay, and bore and paid a proportionable part of the value of the said masts, yards, sails, ropes, anchors, and rigging, and thereby sustained a general average loss amounting to £——, being £—— per cent. for each and every £100 so by him insured as aforesaid.

7, 8, and 9. [*Continue as in paragraphs* 4, 5, *and* 6 *of the last form but one.*]

---

damage or loss having been incurred for the benefit of all concerned in the adventure, all persons interested in the ship freight and cargo are called upon to contribute to indemnify the owner of the particular part which has sustained the damage or loss.

As to the meaning of "*particular average*," see *The Great Indian Peninsular Ry. Co.* v. *Saunders*, 1 B. & S. 41; 2 *Ib.* 266; 30 L. J. Q. B. 218; 31 *Ib.* 206; *Oppenheim* v. *Fry*, 5 B. & S. 348; 33 L. J. Q. B. 267; *Kidstone* v. *The Empire Marine Insurance Co., Lim.*, L. R. 1 C. P. 535; 2 *Ib.* 357; 35 L. J. C. P. 250; 36 *Ib.* 156; 2 Arnould on Marine Insurance, 5th ed., p. 888.

For a Form of Claim for the Return of the Premium paid on a Policy upon Goods which were never in fact placed on Board, See "Money Received," post, p. 286 (*c*).

For a Form of Claim upon a Policy on Freight, see Griffiths v. *Bramley-Moore,* 4 Q. B. D. 70.

Insurance.—II. Life Policies (*a*).

Statement of Claim on a Policy of Insurance on the Life of a Third Person.

1. The defendants are a life insurance company carrying on business at ——.

(*c*) *Return of premium.*] See "*Money received,*" *post,* p. 280. If the risk has once commenced; or if the policy be void for illegality or avoided on the ground of fraud of the insured, the premium is not recoverable, but if the risk has never commenced, as for instance if the ship never sailed, it is recoverable. (3 Kent, Com. 341; *Allkins* v. *Jupe,* 2 C. P. D. 375; 46 L. J. C. P. 824.)

So if the policy is avoided by a material concealment or misrepresentation (without fraud, the premium may be recovered, the risk never having attached. (*Anderson* v. *Thornton,* 8 Ex. 425.) See further, Leake on Contracts, 101, *et seq.*

(*a*) Policies of insurance on lives are subject to the statate 14 Geo. 3, c. 48, which enacts, by s. 1, "That from and after the passing of this act no insurance shall be made by any person or persons, bodies politic or corporate, on the life or lives of any person or persons, or on any other event or events whatsoever, wherein the person or persons for whose use, benefit, or on whose account such policy or policies shall be made shall have no interest, or by gaming or wagering, and that every assurance made contrary to the true intent and meaning hereof shall be null and void to all intents and purposes whatsoever."

By s. 2, "That it shall not be lawful to make any policy or policies on the life or lives of any person or persons, or other event or events, without inserting in such policy or policies the person's or persons' name or names interested therein, or for whose use, benefit, or on whose account such policy is so made or underwrote." It is not sufficient for the name of the party interested merely to appear in the policy, but it must be inserted therein as the name of the party interested. (*Hodson* v. *Observer Life Ass. Soc.,* 8 E. & B. 40; 26 L. J. Q. B. 303; *Evans* v. *Bignold,* L. R. 4 Q. B. 622).

By s. 3, "That in all cases where the insured hath interest in such life or lives, event or events, no greater sum shall be recovered or

2. By a policy of insurance bearing date the —— of ——, 18—, made by the defendants, after reciting that the plaintiff had proposed to effect an insurance with the defendants on the life of G. H. and

---

received from the insurer or insurers, than the amount or value of the interest of the insured in such life or lives, or other event or events."

The interest in this statute means, in general, pecuniary interest The interest of a father in the life of a child is not sufficient alone to support an insurance on the child's life. (*Halford* v. *Kymer*, 10 B. & C. 724; *Worthington* v. *Curtis*, 1 Ch. D. 419; 45 L. J. Ch. 259.) But a wife may insure her husband's life, and the husband his wife's. (*Reed* v. *Key*, Peake's Add. Cases, 70; *Huckman* v. *Fernie*, 3 M. & W. 505.)

A creditor has an insurable interest in the life of his debtor (*Anderson* v. *Edie*, Park Ins., 8th ed., 914–15), provided the debt is not an illegal one (*Dwyer* v. *Edie*, Park Ins., 8th ed., 914); and a *cestui que trust* may insure the life of his trustee (*Collett* v. *Morrison*, 9 Hare, 162.)

Where one person causes another in whose life he has no pecuniary interest to insure such life in his own name, but at the expense and for the benefit of such first person, the policy is void under the statute. (*Wainwright* v. *Bland*, 1 M. & W. 32; 1 M. & Rob. 481; *Shilling* v. *The Accidental Death Ins. Co.*, 2 H. & N. 42; 26 L. J. Ex. 266.) A promise made by a creditor to his debtor not to enforce a debt during his life, made without consideration, is not an insurable interest of the debtor in the life of the creditor. (*Hebden* v. *West*, 3 B. & S. 579; 32 L. J. Q. B. 85.) A contract of employment at a salary for a certain number of years creates an insurable interest in the life of the employer. (*Ib.*) It is sufficient that there is an interest in the life of the person insured at the time of effecting the insurance; and it is immaterial that it ceases afterwards. The value of the interest at the date of the policy may be recovered on death, but no more. (*Dalby* v. *India and Lond. Ins. Co.*, 15 C. B. 365; 24 L. J. C. P. 2; overruling *Godsall* v. *Boldero*, 9 East, 72; 2 Smith's L. C., 8th ed., 271; as to the interest at the date of the policy, see *Law* v. *London Indisputable Life Policy Co.*, 24 L. J. Ch. 196.) If the same interest is insured with several insurers, no more than the value of the interest insured can be recovered. (*Hebden* v. *West*, *supra*.)

By the "Married Women's Property Act, 1870" (33 & 34 Vict. c. 93), s. 10, "A married woman may effect a policy of insurance upon her own life or the life of her husband for her separate use, and the same and all benefit thereof, if expressed on the face of it to be so effected, shall enure accordingly, and the contract in such policy shall be as valid as if made with an unmarried woman. A policy of insurance effected by any married man on his own life, and expressed upon the face of it to be for the benefit of his wife, or of his wife and children or any of them, shall enure and be deemed a trust for the benefit of his wife for her separate use, and of his children, or any of them, according to the interest so expressed, and shall not, so long as any object of the trust remains, be subject to the control of the husband, or to his creditors, or form part of his

had delivered to them a declaration setting forth the age and state of health of the said G. H. and other things, and that it had been agreed that the said declaration should be the basis of the said insurance, and that the plaintiff had paid to the defendants £——, as a consideration for the insurance of the sum of £—— on the life of the said G. H. for a year from the —— of ——, 18—, and had agreed to pay a like sum on the —— of —— in each succeeding year during the continuance of the said policy, it was declared, subject to certain conditions and provisoes set forth in the said policy [*state the conditions and provisoes if material*], that if the said G. H. should depart this life within the said year, or in any succeeding year for which such payment as aforesaid should have been made, the plaintiff should be paid out of the capital stock and funds of the defendants' company within —— calendar months after the decease of the said G. H. should have been duly notified to the directors of the said company in the manner mentioned in the said policy of insurance the said sum of £——.

3. At the time of the making of the said policy of insurance the plaintiff was interested in the life of the said G. H. to the amount so insured thereon as aforesaid.

4. Afterwards on the —— of ——, 18—, whilst the said policy was still in force, the said G. H. died.

5. More than —— calendar months before the commencement of this action, the decease of the said G. H. was duly notified to the directors of the said company in the manner mentioned in the said policy, and [*here state performance of such conditions as are conditions precedent of the right of action or show the waiver thereof* (b)].

6. The plaintiff has not been paid the said £—— out of the capital stock and funds of the said company, and the same is wholly due and unpaid.

---

estate." (See *Holt* v. *Everall*, 2 Ch. D. 266; 45 L. J. Ch. 433; *In re Mellor's Trusts*, 6 Ch. D. 127; 7 Ch. D. 200); "but if it shall be proved that the policy was effected and the premiums paid by the husband with intent to defraud his creditors, they shall be entitled to receive out of the sum secured an amount equal to the premiums so paid."

As to stamping life policies, see 33 & 34 Vict. c. 97. Some life insurance companies are entitled by their special Acts to sue or be sued in the name of their public officer or manager. See Bunyon on Life Assurance, Index to Private Statutes.

(b) See "*Conditions Precedent*," note (a), *ante*, p. 158.

On a Covenant to keep up a Policy of Insurance assigned as Security for a Debt.

1. The defendant by a deed bearing date the —— day of ——, 18—, assigned to the plaintiff a policy of insurance on the life of the defendant, granted by the —— company, dated the —— day of ——, 18—, and numbered ——, for the sum of £——, and subject to the annual premium of £——, together with all moneys insured or to become payable by or under the said policy, for securing to the plaintiff the payment of the sum of £——, with interest thereon.

2. The defendant by the said deed covenanted with the plaintiff that the defendant would from time to time, so long as any money should remain due under the said security, pay the said premium of £——, and any other premiums or sums for the time being necessary for keeping up the said policy, on the first day on which the same respectively ought to be paid, and would forthwith deliver the receipt for the same to the plaintiff, and that in case the defendant should neglect to pay any of such premiums and sums of money as aforesaid, the plaintiff should be at liberty to pay all premiums and other sums of money necessary for keeping up the said policy, and that the defendant would on demand repay to the plaintiff all such sums of money so paid by him as aforesaid, with interest thereon at £—— per centum per annum from the time of the same respectively having been paid.

3. On the —— of ——, 18—, while £—— remained due under the said security, one of the said annual premiums, amounting to the sum of £——, became due under the said policy and was necessary to be paid for keeping up the same.

4. The defendant did not pay the said last-mentioned premium but neglected so to do, and the plaintiff thereupon duly paid the said premium and afterwards duly demanded repayment thereof, with interest thereon as aforesaid, from the defendant.

5. The defendant has not repaid the plaintiff the said sum of £—— or any part thereof, or the said interest thereon.

By the Assignee of a Policy of Insurance on the Life of a Third Person under 30 & 31 *Vict. c.* 144 (*c*).

1, 2, and 3. [*Proceed as in paragraphs* 1, 2, *and* 3 *of the last form but one, substituting the name of the assignor for the word "plaintiff."*]

(*c*) By "The Policies of Assurance Act, 1867," 30 & 31 Vict. c. 144, s. 1, "Any person or corporation now being, or hereafter becoming entitled by assignment, or other derivative title, to a policy of life assurance, and possessing at the time of action brought the right in equity to receive and the right to give an effectual discharge to the assurance company liable under such policy for monies thereby assured or secured, shall be at liberty to sue at law in the name of such person or corporation to recoversuch monies."

By s. 3, "No assignment made after the passing of this Act of a policy of life assurance shall confer on the assignee therein named, his executors, administrators, or assigns, any right to sue for the amount of such policy, or the monies assured or secured thereby, until a written notice of the date and purport of such assignment shall have been given to the assurance company liable under such policy at their principal place of business for the time being, or in case they have two or more principal places of business, then at some one of such principal places of business, either in England, or Scotland, or Ireland, and the date on which such notice shall be received shall regulate the priority of all claims under any assignment; and a payment *boná fide* made in respect of any policy by any assurance company before the date on which such notice shall have been received shall be as valid against the assignee giving such notice as if this Act had not been passed."

By s. 5, "Any such assignment may be made either by indorsement on the policy, or by a separate instrument in the words and to the effect set forth in the schedule hereto, such indorsement or separate instrument being duly stamped."

By s. 6, "Every assurance company to whom notice shall have been duly given of the assignment of any policy under which they are liable, shall, upon the request in writing of any person by whom any such notice was given or signed, or of his executors or administrators, and upon payment in each case of a fee not exceeding five shillings, deliver an acknowledgment in writing under the hand of the manager, secretary, treasurer, or other principal officer of the assurance company of their receipt of such notice; and every such written acknowledgment, if signed by a person being *de jure* or *de facto* the manager, secretary, treasurer, or other principal officer of the assurance company, whose acknowledgment the same purports to be, shall be conclusive evidence against such assurance company of their having duly received the notice to which such acknowledgment relates."

An agreement in writing to execute on request an effectual mortgage of a policy of assurance, deposited at the time of the agreement as security for a loan, is not an assignment of such policy within the meaning of the above Act. (*Spencer* v. *Clarke*, 9 Ch. D. 137; 47 L. J. Ch. 692; *Crossley* v. *Glasgow Life Ass.* 4 Ch. D. 421; 46 L. J. Ch. 65.)

4. On the —— of ——, 18—, the said —— —— duly assigned the said policy by indorsement thereon [*or* by a separate instrument, *as the case may be*] to the plaintiff.

5. Afterwards, on the —— of ——, 18—, a written notice of the date and purport of such assignment was given to the defendant company at ——, their principal place of business for the time being [*or*, at ——, one of their principal places of business in England].

6. On the —— of ——, 18—, whilst the said policy was still in force, the said G. H. died.

7. More than —— calendar months before the commencement of this action the decease of the said G. H. was duly notified to the directors of the said company in the manner mentioned in the said policy.

8. The plaintiff was at the time of the bringing of this action [and still is] the absolute owner of the said policy [*or state facts showing that the plaintiff possessed, at the time of action brought, the right in equity to receive and the right to give an effectual discharge to the company for monies assured or secured by the policy*], and [*here state performance of all conditions which are conditions precedent to the right of action, or show the waiver thereof* (*b*)].

9. The plaintiff has not been paid the said £—— out of the capital stock and funds of the said company, and the same is wholly due and unpaid.

Insurance.—III. Fire Policies (*a*).

Statement of Claim on a Policy of Insurance against Fire.

1. The defendants are a fire insurance company carrying on business at ——.

(*a*) A policy of fire insurance is void and illegal unless the person in whose favour it is made has an insurable interest in the goods insured and his name is inserted in the policy. (See 14 Geo. III. c. 48, ss. 1 and 2, cited *ante*, p. 221.) Such interest must exist at the time of the insuring and of the fire (*Lynch* v. *Dalzell*, 4 Bro. P. C. 431; *Sadlers' Co.* v. *Badcock*, 2 Atk. 554), and should be alleged in the statement of claim. A warehouseman, wharfinger, or common carrier, has a sufficient insurable interest in the goods which are deposited with him. (*Waters* v. *Monarch Ins. Co.*, 5 E. & B. 870; 25 L. J. Q. B. 102; *London and North Western Railway Co.* v. *Glyn*, 1 E. & E. 652; 28 L. J. Q. B. 193.) See, also, as to what is an insurable interest, *Marks* v. *Hamilton*, 7 Ex. 323; 21 L. J. Ex. 109;

2. By a policy of insurance bearing date the —— of ——, 18—, made by the defendants, after reciting that the plaintiff had paid the defendants £—— for insuring against loss or damage by fire as follows namely, £——, on a dwelling-house, No. ——, High Street, Plymouth, in the county of Devon, and £—— on the furniture and goods in the said dwelling-house, for a year from the —— of ——, 18—, and had agreed to pay the defendants on the —— of —— in every succeeding year during the continuance of the said policy the like sum of £——, it was declared that (subject to the conditions indorsed on the said policy, and which constituted the basis of the said insurance) the plaintiff should be paid out of the capital stock and funds of the said company the amount of all such damage and loss as he should suffer by fire on the property in the said policy mentioned, not exceeding the said sums so insured thereon respectively as aforesaid, during the said year from the said —— of ——, 18—, or at any time afterwards so long as the plaintiff should pay the said sum of £—— yearly as aforesaid and the defendants should accept the same.

3. The said conditions indorsed on the said policy are as follows [*here set out verbatim or by way of recital, such of the conditions as are material to the cause of action.*]

4. The plaintiff was at the time of the making of the said policy, and thence until and at the time of the damage and loss hereinafter mentioned, interested in the said several premises so insured as aforesaid to the amounts so insured thereon respectively.

Ebsworth v. *Alliance Marine Ass. Co.*, L. R. 8 C. P. 596; *Collingridge* v. *Royal Exchange Ass. Co.*, 3 Q. B. D. 173; 47 L. J. Q. B. 32; and Leake on Contracts, 756. A policy of fire insurance is a contract of indemnity, and upon payment of the amount of loss the insurer is entitled to be put in the place of the assured (*Darrell* v. *Tibbitts*, 5 Q. B. D. 560; 50 L. J. Q. B. 33; *Midland Ins. Co.* v. *Smith*, 6 Q. B. D. 561; 50 L. J. Q. B. 329); and if at a subsequent time the assured receives compensation from other sources for the loss sustained by him, the insurer is entitled to recover from the assured any sum which he may have received in excess of the loss actually sustained by him. (*Darrell* v. *Tibbitts, supra.*)

By "The Metropolitan Fire Brigade Act, 1865," (28 & 29 Vict. c. 90) s. 12, any damage occasioned by the Metropolitan Fire Brigade "in the due execution of their duties shall be deemed to be damage by fire within the meaning of any policy of insurance against fire." Some Fire Insurance Companies are entitled by their special Acts to sue or be sued in the name of their public officer or manager. See note to "*Marine Policies*," *ante*, p. 218.

5. The plaintiff, until the time of the happening of the said damage and loss hereinafter mentioned, duly paid the defendants the said sum of £—— yearly, in accordance with the terms of the said policy, in every year succeeding the date of the said policy, and the defendants accepted the said payments.

6. On the —— of ——, 18—, whilst the said policy was in full force and effect, the said several premises so insured as aforesaid were burnt down and destroyed [*or* burnt and damaged] by fire.

7. By reason of the said fire the plaintiff suffered damage and loss on the said dwelling-house and on the said furniture and goods respectively, to the several amounts so insured thereon respectively as aforesaid [*or*, on the said dwelling-house to the extent of £——, and on the said furniture and goods to the extent of £——, *as the case may be*].

8. [*Here state performance of all conditions precedent to the right of action, or show the waiver thereof* (*b*)].

9. The defendants have not paid to the plaintiff out of the capital stock and funds of the said company, or otherwise, the said sums of £—— and £——, and the same are wholly due and unpaid.

INSURANCE.—IV. AGAINST ACCIDENTS, ETC. (*a*).

(*b*) See "*Conditions Precedent*," note (*a*), *ante*, p. 158. Where a policy of insurance is made subject to conditions that notice of loss and particulars of damage must be given by the insurer within a certain time, the giving of such notice and particulars within the time mentioned is usually a condition precedent to the right to recover for the loss. (*Roper* v. *Lendon*, 1 E. & E. 825; 28 L. J. Q. B. 260; *Worsley* v. *Wood*, 6 T. R. 710; Leake on Contracts, 647; Addison on Contracts, 7th ed., 931.)

(*a*) As to the meaning of "accident," see *Sinclair* v. *Maritime Passengers Ass. Co.*, 3 E. & E. 478; 30 L. J. Q. B. 77; *Hooper* v. *Accidental Death Ins. Co.*, 5 H. & N. 546; *Hiorns* v. *Railway Passengers Ass. Co.*, 5 H. & N. 211; *Trew* v. *Railway Passengers Ass. Co.*, 6 H. & N. 839; 30 L. J. Ex. 317; *Fitton* v. *Accidental Death Ins. Co.*, 17 C. B. N. S. 122; 34 L. J. C. P. 28; *Smith* v. *The Accident Ins. Co.*, L. R. 5 Ex. 302; 39 L. J. Ex. 211; *Winspear* v. *The Accident Ins. Co.*, 6 Q. B. D. 42; 50 L. J. Ex. 292; *Lawrence* v. *The Accidental Ins. Co.*, 7 Q. B. D. 216; 50 L. J. Q. B. 522; as to the meaning of "railway accident," see *Theobald* v. *Railwa Passengers Ass. Co.*, 10 Ex. 45.

Interest (*a*).

Statement of Claim for Interest upon Money Lent.

1. On the —— of ——, 18—, the plaintiff lent to the defendant £—— upon the terms set forth in two letters

---

(*a*) Interest, when payable, may be payable as a debt according to the terms of the contract, express or implied; or it may be recoverable as damages for the wrongful detention of money which ought to have been paid (*Webster* v. *British Empire Life Ass. Co.* 15 Ch. D. 169, 178; 49 L. J. Ch. 769; *Cameron* v. *Smith*, 2 B. & Ald. 305; *Hudson* v. *Fawcett*, 7 M. & G. 348).

By the Common Law, where the contract is silent as to interest, it is generally presumed not to be within the contemplation of the parties, and so cannot be claimed. (*Frith* v. *Leroux*, 2 T. R. 57; *De Havilland* v. *Bowerbank*, 1 Camp. 50; *Fruhling* v. *Schroeder*, 2 Bing. N. C. 77; *Rhodes* v. *Rhodes*, Johns., 653; 29 L. J. Ch. 418; see also cases cited in Leake on Contracts, 1101.) It is allowable, however, upon mercantile securities by the custom of merchants; also by particular usages of trade, and by the particular course of dealing between the parties, which would be evidence of an implied agreement. (*Higgins* v. *Sargent*, 2 B. & C. 348; *Fruhling* v. *Schroeder*, 2 Bing. N. C. 77.)

Thus, interest is allowed upon bills of exchange, promissory notes, and other written mercantile securities, as in the nature of damages. (*Ib.*; *Calton* v. *Bragg*, 15 East, 223.) So, it has been allowed on the price of goods agreed to be paid for by a bill, although the bill was never given (*Farr* v. *Ward*, 3 M. & W. 25); so, on a guarantee for the payment of a bill (*Hare* v. *Rickards*, 7 Bing. 254); on a promise to pay by a note (*Davis* v. *Smyth*, 8 M. & W. 399); on a loan of money secured by a bill (*Denton* v. *Rodie*, 3 Camp. 493, 496.) As to the rate of interest on foreign bills, see "*Bills of Exchange*," *ante*, p. 101. By the course of dealing between the parties, even compound interest may be claimed. (*Eaton* v. *Bell*, 5 B. & Ald. 34; and see *Mosse* v. *Salt*, 32 Beav. 269; 32 L. J. Ch. 756; *Fergusson* v. *Fyffe*, 8 Cl. & F. 121.) An agent who has improperly retained money of his principal is chargeable with interest for the same, and the amount of such interest depends upon the profits which the agent may be presumed to have made by the employment of the money. (*Burdick* v. *Garrick*, L. R. 5 Ch. Ap. 233; 39 L. J. Ch. 369.) If the agent uses the money in a commercial business, compound interest may be in general recovered. (*Burdick* v. *Garrick*, *supra*.)

By 3 & 4 Will. IV. c. 42, s. 28, it is enacted "that upon all debts or sums certain, payable at a certain time or otherwise, the jury on the trial of any issue, or on any inquisition of damages, may, if they shall think fit, allow interest to the creditor, at a rate not exceeding the current rate of interest, from the time when such debts or sums certain were payable, if such debts or sums be payable by virtue of some written instrument at a certain time; or, if payable otherwise, then from the time when demand of payment shall have been made in writing, so as such demand shall give notice to the debtor that interest will be claimed from the date of such demand until the term of payment; provided that interest shall be payable in all cases in which it is now payable by law." (See on the construction of this

dated respectively the —— of ——, and the —— of —— [*or as the case may be*], namely, that the defendant should, so long as the said sum or any part thereof remained unpaid, pay to the plaintiff interest at the rate of £—— per cent. per annum for the said sum, or for so much thereof as should for the time being remain unpaid, by equal half-yearly instalments, on the —— of —— and the —— of —— in every year.

2. The said sum of £—— [*or* £——, part of the said sum of £——] remained unpaid till the —— of ——, 18— [*or* is still unpaid].

3. The defendant has not paid to the plaintiff the half-yearly instalments of the said interest, which became due to the plaintiff in respect of the said sum of £—— on the —— of ——, 18—, and the —— of ——, 18—, and which amount together to the sum of £——.

---

section, *Duncombe* v. *Brighton Club, &c. Co.*, L. R. 10 Q. B. 371 ; 45 L. J. Q. B. 216 ; *Hill* v. *South Staffordshire Railway Co.*, L. R. 18 Eq. 154 ; 43 L. J. Ch. 556 ; *Ward* v. *Eyre*, 15 Ch. D. 130 ; 49 L. J. Ch. 657 ; *Geake* v. *Ross*, 44 L. J. C. P. 315.) And by s. 29, the jury may give damages in the nature of interest over and above the value of the goods at the time of the conversion or seizure, in all actions of *trover* or *trespass de bonis asportatis*, and over and above the money recoverable in all actions on policies of insurance. But where the delay in payment of monies due under a policy of insurance is caused by the neglect of the plaintiff to clothe himself with a legal title to the money, interest ought not to be given for the period covered by such delay. (*Webster* v. *British Empire Life Ass. Co.*, 15 Ch. D. 169 ; 49 L. J. Ch. 769.) The claim under the statute is in the nature of damages, and must be assessed by the jury (*Berrington* v. *Phillips*, 1 M. & W. 48), who may refuse to allow it (*Attwood* v. *Taylor*, 1 M. & G. 279). The practice of the Court of Chancery as to allowing interest would appear to have been similar in principle to that of the common law courts (*Caledonian Ry. Co.* v. *Carmichael*, L. R. 2 H. L. Sc. 56, 66 ; *Webster* v. *British Empire Life Ass. Co.*, *supra*). Where interest is claimable as damages, no express mention of it is necessary in the body of the statement of claim, as the claim for it at the end of the statement is sufficient. Where, however, interest is claimed under a contract, the contract should be stated in the ordinary manner in the body of the statement of claim.

When a person borrows money for a certain period, with interest at a certain rate down to the day named, a contract for payment of interest at that rate after the day named is not to be implied. The principal and interest, if not then paid, become a debt, and any allowance for its detention or non-payment made by any tribunal before which the payment may be sought, is in the nature of damages, not of interest. (*Cook* v. *Fowler*, 7 L. R. H. L. 27 ; 43 L. J. Ch. 855 ; *In re Roberts*, 14 Ch. D. 49.)

Since the repeal of the usury laws by the 17 & 18 Vict. c. 90, any rate of interest agreed upon between the parties is lawful.

See for a Form of Statement of Claim by Mortgagee against Mortgagor on a Covenant to pay Interest on the Mortgage Debt, "Mortgage," post, p. 290.

JUDGMENTS (*a*).

Statement of Claim on a Judgment of one of the Superior Courts.

1. The plaintiff, on the —— of ——, 18—, commenced an action against the defendant in the Queen's Bench

---

(*a*) By 43 Geo. III. c. 46, s. 4, in actions on any judgments recovered in any court in England or Ireland by plaintiffs, the plaintiff was prevented from recovering any costs of suit, unless the Court or a Judge thereof otherwise ordered. And such an order was not in general made where the plaintiff might have realised his judgment by execution or otherwise. (See 1 Chit. Prac., 12th ed., 404.) Now, it would seem, the costs, as in other actions, are governed by O. LV., see *Garnett* v. *Bradley*, 3 App. Cas. 944; 48 L. J. Ex. 186.

An action will lie on the judgment of an inferior court, whether a court of record or not (*Read* v. *Pope*, 1 C. M. & R. 302; *Williams* v. *Jones*, 13 M. & W. 628; *Herbert* v. *Cook*, Willes, 37 n.), but not on a judgment of a County Court established by 9 & 10 Vict. c. 95 (*Berkeley* v. *Elderkin*, 1 E. & B. 805; 22 L. J. Q. B. 281; *Austin* v. *Mills*, 9 Ex. 288; 32 L. J. Ex. 40). And the statute 19 & 20 Vict. c. 108, s. 27, enacts that "no action shall be brought in a County Court on any judgment of a superior court."

An action will not lie on a Judge's order, or an order of Court, made in interlocutory or collateral proceedings, as an order for costs. (*Emerson* v. *Lashley*, 2 H. Bl. 248; *Sheehy* v. *Professional Life Ass.*, 2 C. B. N. S. 211; 26 L. J. C. P. 301; *Dent* v. *Baskam*, 9 Ex. 469; 23 L. J. Ex. 161; *Hookpayton* v. *Bussell*, 10 Ex. 24; 23 L. J. Ex. 267; *Patrick* v. *Shedden*, 2 E. & B. 14; 22 L. J. Q. B. 283.) An action has been held to lie upon an order for costs which formed part of a final judgment of the House of Lords. (*Marbella Iron Ore Co.* v. *Allen*, 47 L. J. C. P. 601; 38 L. T. 815.)

But if the order is founded on an independent and distinct agreement, an action may lie upon the agreement though the order is superadded. (*Wentworth* v. *Bullen*, 9 B. & C. 840, 850; *Smith* v. *Whalley*, 2 B. & P. 842; *Lievesley* v. *Gilmore*, L. R. 1 C. P. 571; 35 L. J. C. P. 351.) And an action will lie on an award made under a submission by Judge's order. (*Still* v. *Halford*, 4 Camp. 19), or under a rule of *nisi prius* (*Bonner* v. *Charlton*, 5 East, 139.) A Judge's order to repay money, made without consent, is not ground for an action for money received. (*Phillips* v. *Broadley*, 9 Q. B. 744.)

Where an order of a Judge, or of the Court, prescribes the particular remedy to be followed, that remedy alone can, in general, be followed. (*Hookpayton* v. *Bussell*, 10 Ex. 24; 23 L. J. Ex. 267.)

Division of the High Court of Justice, which said action was distinguished in the Cause Book of the said Court as N. No. ——.

2. Afterwards, on the —— of ——, 18—, the plaintiff,

In an action on a judgment of an inferior Court, the statement of claim must show that the original cause of action was within the jurisdiction of such Court. (*See under former practice*, *Read* v. *Pope*, 1 C. M. & R. 302; *Williams* v *Jones*, 13 M. & W. 628.)

A foreign or colonial judgment for a liquidated demand in money establishes a debt between the parties, but does not merge or extinguish the original cause of action. The plaintiff may sue in this country upon the original cause of action, if actionable here, or upon the judgment of the foreign Court, or upon both. (*Walker* v. *Witter*, 1 Doug. 1, 5; *Sadler* v. *Robins*, 1 Camp. 253; *Hall* v. *Odber*, 11 East, 118; per Tindal, C. J., *Smith* v. *Nicholls*, 5 Bing. N. C. 208, 221.)

The judgments and decreets of Irish and Scotch Courts are considered as foreign judgments in English Courts. (*Harris* v. *Saunders*, 4 B. & C. 411; and see *Collins* v. *Mathew*, 5 East, 473). But by "the Judgments Extension Act, 1868," (31 & 32 Vict. c. 54), s. 1, a certificate of a judgment obtained or entered up after the passing of the Act in any of the Courts of Queen's Bench, Common Pleas, or Exchequer at Dublin, for any debt, damages, or costs, may be registered in the High Court of Justice, Queen's Bench Division, within twelve months of the date of such judgment, or within such extended time as may be permitted by the said Division, and "shall from the date of such registration be of the same force and effect, and all proceedings shall and may be had and taken on such certificate, as if the judgment of which it is a certificate had been a judgment originally obtained or entered up on the date of such registration as aforesaid, in the Court in which it is so registered, and all the reasonable costs and charges attendant upon the obtaining and registering such certificate shall be recovered in like manner as if the same were part of the original judgment." This section applies to judgments of the Supreme Court of Judicature in Ireland as constituted by 40 & 41 Vict. c. 57 (see s. 71 of that Act).

And by s. 3, a certificate of a decreet of the Court of Session in Scotland obtained after the passing of the Act for the payment of any debt, damages, or expenses may be registered in a similar manner, and "shall from the date of such registration be of the same force and effect as a judgment obtained or entered up in the Court in which it is so registered, and all proceedings shall and may be had and taken on such certificate as if the decreet of which it is a certificate had been a judgment originally obtained or entered up on the date of such registration as aforesaid in the Court in which it is so registered, and all the reasonable costs, charges, and expenses attendant upon the obtaining and registering such certificate shall be recovered in like manner as if the same were part of the decreet of which it is a certificate."

It need not be expressly alleged in a statement of claim upon the judgment of a Foreign Court that the Court had jurisdiction over the parties or the cause, such jurisdiction being presumed until the contrary is made to appear. (*Robertson* v. *Struth*, 5 Q. B. 941;

by the judgment of the said Court, recovered against the defendant in the said action £——, together with £—— for his costs of action.

3. The said judgment is still in force and unsatisfied.

Statement of Claim upon a Final Order of the House of Lords directing an unsuccessful Appellant to pay the Respondents' Costs, Marbella Iron Ore Co. v. *Allen,* 38 L. T. 815; 47 L. J. C. P. 601.

On a Judgment of a French Court.

1. Previously to the time hereinafter mentioned, the plaintiff commenced an action against the defendant in the Court of ——, in the Republic of France.

2. The said Court was duly constituted and held in accordance with the laws of the said Republic, and had jurisdiction in respect of the said action.

3. On the —— of ——, 18—, the plaintiff, by the judgment of the said Court, and according to the laws of the said Republic, recovered against the defendant in the said action the sum of —— francs, which is equivalent in English money to £——, and which the defendant was by the said Court adjudged and ordered to pay to the plaintiff.

4. The said judgment is still in force and unsatisfied.

Henderson v. *Henderson*, 6 Q. B. 288.) The distinction in this respect between the judgment of a Foreign Court and that of an English Inferior Court is to be noted.

An action will lie on a decree of a colonial Court of Equity for the payment of money. (*Sadler* v. *Robins*, 1 Camp. 253; *Henley* v. *Soper*, 8 B. & C. 16; *Henderson* v. *Henderson*, 6 Q. B. 288.)

It seems now to be settled that when an action is brought on the judgment of a foreign or colonial Court, having jurisdiction over the parties and the subject-matter of the suit, it is conclusive between the parties upon the merits, and that any defences upon the merits, which might have been pleaded in the original action, cannot be pleaded in an action on the judgment. (*Bank of Australasia* v. *Nias*, 16 Q. B. 717; 20 L. J. Q. B. 284; *Henderson* v. *Henderson*, 6 Q. B. 288; *De Cosse Brissac* v. *Rathbone*, 6 H. & N. 301; 30 L. J. Ex. 238; *Munroe* v. *Pilkington*, 2 B. & S. 11; 31 L. J. Q. B. 81, 89; *Ellis* v. *McHenry*, L. R. 6 C. P. 228; 40 L. J. C. P. 109; *Godard* v. *Gray*, L. R. 6 Q. B. 139, 150; 40 L. J. Q. B. 62; and see notes to *Mostyn* v. *Fabrigas*, 1 Smith's L. C., 8th ed. 652.)

As to when a foreign judgment can be impeached, see "Defences," "*Judgment.*"

On a Scotch Decreet.

1. In or about the month of ——, 18—, the plaintiff brought an action against the defendant in the Sheriff's Court of the county of —— in Scotland [for the recovery of £—— for a debt due from the defendant to the plaintiff, for goods sold and delivered by the plaintiff to the defendant].

2. On the —— of ——, 18—, the plaintiff, by the judgment of the said Court in the said action, recovered against the defendant £——, with interest thereon at £—— per cent. per annum, from the date of the said judgment until payment, and the sum of £—— for costs of action, which sums of money and interest the defendant was by the said Court adjudged and ordered to pay to the plaintiff.

3. The said Court had lawful jurisdiction and authority to try the said action and to deliver the said judgment and to make the said order.

4. The said judgment is still in force and unsatisfied.

For a Claim to recover Costs Awarded by the Judgment of a Foreign Court, see Gardner v. *Irvin,* 4 Ex. D. 49.

LAND—RECOVERY OF.

See post, "Recovery of Land," p. 502, and Landlord and Tenant," infra.

LANDLORD AND TENANT.

Statement of Claim for the use of a House and Land by the permission of the Plaintiff (a).

1. The defendant has, by the permission of the plaintiff, used and occupied a house and land of the plaintiff,

---

(*a*) A contract to pay a fair compensation for use and occupation is implied by law from the fact that lands, etc., belonging to the plaintiff have been occupied by the defendant by the plaintiff's permission; the amount of compensation in such case depends on the value of the premises and on the duration of the occupation. As soon as the

situate at ——, from the —— day of ——, 18—, to the —— of ——, 18—.

2. There was no express contract between the plaintiff

---

occupation ceases the implied contract ceases; and as no express time is limited for payment, the compensation accrues due from day to day (*Gibson* v. *Kirk*, 1 Q. B. 850; *Churchward* v. *Ford*, 2 H. & N. 446; 26 L. J. Ex. 354; *Sloper* v. *Saunders*, 26 L. J. Ex. 275.) An implied contract is, of course, negatived by an express agreement on the same matter; and the amount of rent and time of payment would then be determined by the agreement.

The mere fact of the plaintiff's ownership of the land, etc., and of the occupation by the defendant, is sufficient *primâ facie* evidence of a contract to support this action. (*Hellier* v. *Silcox*, 19 L. J. Q. B. 295; *Churchward* v. *Ford*, 2 H. & N. 446; 26 L. J. Ex. 354.) But the presumption from such evidence may be rebutted by showing that the occupation was adverse to the consent of the plaintiff, or that it was under a contract with a third party, a stranger to the plaintiff, or by proof of any circumstances which are inconsistent with a contract between the plaintiff and the defendant. (*Churchward* v. *Ford*, *supra*; *Cox* v. *Knight*, 18 C. B. 645; 25 L. J. C. P. 314; *Turner* v. *Cameron Coal Co.*, 5 Exch. 932; *Sloper* v. *Saunders*, 29 L. J. Ex. 275; *Levy* v. *Lewis*, 6 C. B. N. S. 766; 30 L. J. C. P. 141.) A tenant or party claiming under him cannot dispute the title of the landlord from whom he received possession, but he may show that the title has determined. (See *London and North Western Ry. Co.* v. *West*, L. R. 2 C. P. 553.)

The assignee of the reversion may maintain this action (*Rennie* v. *Robinson*, 1 Bing. 147; *Standen* v. *Chrismas*, 10 Q. B. 135), but can only recover in respect of the use and occupation subsequent to the assignment. (*Mortimer* v. *Preedy*, 3 M. & W. 602.) So also the assignee of a mortgagor who has let a tenant into possession after the mortgage. (*Hickman* v. *Machin*, 4 H. & N. 716; 28 L. J. Ex. 310.) The action will also lie against the assignee of a tenancy created by simple contract who has occupied the premises (*How* v. *Kennett*, 3 A. & E. 659.)

A tenant who has agreed to take premises, but who has never entered, is not liable for use and occupation (*Edge* v. *Strafford*, 1 C. & J. 391; *Lowe* v. *Ross*, 5 Ex. 553; *Towne* v. *D'Heinrich*, 13 C. B. 892; 22 L. J. C. P. 219), but must be sued for breach of his agreement.

One who, having permission to occupy premises of the plaintiff, permits another to occupy them, is liable to the plaintiff for use and occupation, unless and until such other becomes the plaintiff's tenant, or occupies under the plaintiff's permission. The possession of the tenant of a tenant is the possession of the tenant himself as against the superior landlord. (*Bull* v. *Sibbs*, 8 T. R. 327; *Conolly* v. *Baxter*, 2 Stark. 525; *Shine* v. *Dillon*, Ir. 1 C. L. 277.)

The liability for use and occupation extends to any hereditament, corporeal, or incorporeal, as a right of fishery (*Holford* v. *Pritchard*, 3 Ex. 793); a pew (*Israel* v. *Simmons*, 2 Stark. 356); a watercourse (*Davis* v. *Morgan*, 4 B. & C. 8), &c.

An executor or administrator should in respect of occupation by him since the decease be charged as occupying in his own right, and not in his representative capacity. (*Wigley* v. *Ashton*, 3 B. & Ald. 101; *Atkins* v. *Humphrey*, 2 C. B. 654.)

and the defendant as to the amount to be paid by the defendant to the plaintiff in respect of the said use and occupation of the said house and land, and no payment has been made by the defendant to the plaintiff in respect thereof.

3. The fair and reasonable value of such use and occupation thereof by the defendant as aforesaid is £——.

The like at an Agreed Rate (*a*).

1. [*As in last form*].

2. It was on the —— of ——, 18— [*or* by an agreement in writing, &c.], agreed between the plaintiff and the defendant that the defendant should pay the plaintiff for such use and occupation of the said house and land at the rate of £—— per week [*or as the case may be*].

3. The defendant has not paid the plaintiff for such use and occupation in accordance with the said agreement, or at all.

Statement of Claim for the use of Warehouses and Premises pending the completion of the Purchase, Met. Ry. Co. v. *Defries*, 2 Q. B. D. 189 (*affirmed ib.* 387).

A like Form for the use of a Railway Station and Lines, &c., Buenos Ayres and Ensanada Port Ry. Co. v. *Northern Ry. of Buenos Ayres*, 36 L. T. 148.

For Rent due under a Yearly Tenancy (*b*).

1. The plaintiff let to the defendant as tenant thereof to the plaintiff from year to year, a house and garden

---

(*b*) Rent accrued under a demise, whether by deed or simple contract, is recoverable, whether there has been an actual occupation or not.

By the Common Law it was not required that a demise of land, or of any corporeal hereditament, should be by deed, or in writing. But by the Statute of Frauds, 29 Car. II. c. 3, ss. 1, 2, all leases, estates, interests of freehold, or any uncertain interest in any lands or hereditaments, not put in writing, and signed by the parties so making the same, or their agents lawfully authorized by writing,

known as No. ——, —— street, ——, at the yearly rent of £——, payable quarterly upon the usual quarter-days [*or as the case may be*].

2. The defendant took possession of the said house

---

shall have the effect of leases or estates at will only, except leases not exceeding the term of three years from the making thereof, whereupon the rent reserved to the landlord during such term shall amount unto two-third parts at least of the full improved value of the thing demised.

And by Statute 8 & 9 Vict. c. 106, s. 3, a lease required by law to be in writing of any tenements or hereditaments made after the 1st October, 1845, shall be void at law unless made by deed.

An instrument void as a lease under the statute may be good as an agreement for a lease. (*Bond* v. *Rosling*, 1 B. & S. 371 ; 30 L. J. Q. B. 227 ; *Rollason* v. *Leon*, 7 H. & N. 73 ; 31 L. J. Ex. 96 ; *Tidey* v. *Mollett*, 16 C. B. N. S. 298 ; 33 L. J. C. P. 235.)

If a tenant enter into possession under a lease void under the statute, or an agreement for a lease, and pays rent at so much a year under it, the jury may conclude that he entered under a parol demise on such terms contained in the void lease or agreement as are not inconsistent with a yearly tenancy. (See notes to *Doe* d. *Rigge* v. *Bell*, and *Clayton* v. *Blakey*, 1 Smith's L. C.) So if being in possession he admits such rent to be due. (*Cox* v. *Bent*, 5 Bing. 185.) As to what terms are consistent with a yearly tenancy, see *Richardson* v. *Gifford*, 1 A. & E. 52 ; *Martin* v. *Smith*, L. R. 9 Ex. 50 ; 43 L. J. Ex. 43 ; *Sanders* v. *Karnell*, 1 F. & F. 356 ; *Thomas* v. *Packer*, 1 H. & N. 669 ; and see *Tooker* v *Smith*, 1 H. & N. 732 ; *Bowes* v. *Croll*, 6 E. & B. 264 ; and Woodfall's Landlord and Tenant, 11th ed. p. 203.

By the Statute of Frauds, 29 Car. II. c. 3, s. 4, No action shall be brought whereby to charge any person upon any contract or sale of lands, tenements or hereditaments, or any interest in or concerning them, or upon any agreement that is not to be performed within the space of one year from the making thereof, unless the agreement upon which such action shall be brought, or some memorandum or note thereof, shall be in writing, and signed by the party to be charged therewith, or some other person by him thereunto lawfully authorized.

An agreement for a lease is a contract for an interest in lands within this section (*Edge* v. *Strafford*, 1 Tyr. 295 ; 1 Cr. & J. 391) ; so is a contract to procure a lease or assignment of a lease. (*Horsey* v. *Graham*, L. R. 5 C. P. 9 ; 39 L. J. C. P. 58.)

An action for specific performance can be maintained if there have been acts of part performance referable to, and done with a view to perform, the oral agreement for a lease. (*Tomkinson* v. *Straight*, 17 C. B. 697 ; 25 L. J. C. P. 85 ; *Nunn* v. *Fabian*, L. R. 1 Ch. Ap. 35, 40 ; 35 L. J. Ch. 140 ; *Gunter* v. *Halsey*, Amb. 586 ; *Shillibeer* v. *Jarvis*, 8 De G. M. & G. 79.) See further as to sec. 4 of the Statute of Frauds, Leake on Contracts, 249 ; and O. XIX., r. 23, which requires the Statute of Frauds to be pleaded if relied on as a defence.

A lease of incorporeal hereditaments was always required to be by deed, as a lease of a right of shooting (*Bird* v. *Higginson*, 6 A. & E. 824), or a lease of tithes (*Gardiner* v. *Williamson*, 2 B. & Ad. 336.) But if an incorporeal hereditament has been used under a parol

and garden under the said letting and continued as such tenant thereof to the plaintiff for three-quarters of a year, from the 1st of January, 1880, to the 29th of September, 1880.

3. The defendant has not paid to the plaintiff the said rent, or any part of it, in respect of such period of three-quarters of a year.

For Rent due on a Covenant in a Lease by Deed (*b*), (*c*).

1. By a deed bearing date the —— of ——, 18—, and made between the plaintiff and the defendant, the plaintiff let to the defendant certain messuages and land situate at ——, in the county of —— [*give a description of the property*], for a term of —— years, commencing on the —— of ——, 18—.

2. The defendant by the said deed covenanted with the plaintiff that he would yearly and every year during the said term pay to the plaintiff the yearly rent of £—— by equal half-yearly payments, on the 25th of March and the 29th of September [*set out covenant as in deed, or the material part of it*].

3. The defendant during the said term did not on the 29th of September, 18—, pay to the plaintiff the said half-yearly payment of the said rent then due and payable, nor has he paid the same or any part thereof.

A similar Claim (*b*), (*c*).

1. The plaintiff by deed let to the defendant a house and land, situate at ——, to hold for —— years, from the —— day of ——, 18—, at the yearly rent of £—— payable quarterly, on the usual quarter-days, and the defendant by the said deed covenanted with the plaintiff to pay him the said rent as aforesaid.

2. —— quarters of the said rent are due and unpaid.

---

licence for which the defendant agreed to pay, he may be sued for the money due upon such executed consideration. (*Thomas* v. *Fredricks*, 10 Q. B. 775, and see *Bird* v. *Higginson*, *supra*, and see *ante*, note (*a*), p. 234.)

(*c*) An action lies on the express covenant for rent, notwithstanding an assignment of the lease and acceptance by the landlord of the assignee as tenant (1 Wms. Saund. 299; 2 Wms. Saund. 697, n. (3)). Under those circumstances the lessee would not remain liable on the mere reservation of rent in the lease. (*Wadham* v. *Marlowe*, 8 East, 314; 1 H. Bl. 437; 1 Wms. Saund. 305.)

For the Rent of a Furnished House due under an Agreement in Writing (*b*).

1. By an agreement in writing made between the plaintiff and the defendant, and bearing date the —— of ——, 18—, it was agreed between the plaintiff and the defendant that the plaintiff should let to the defendant the house No. ——, —— Street, ——, with the furniture and effects which then were in the said house [*or as the case may be*], at the rent of £—— per month, payable monthly, for a period of —— months.

2. The defendant entered into possession of the said house with the said furniture and effects in accordance with the said agreement, and has continued in possession thereof for —— months under the said agreement.

3. The defendant has not paid the rent due for such —— months, or any part of such rent.

Claim for Board and Lodging (*d*).

1. The plaintiff keeps a lodging-house at ——.

2. The defendant has at his request been boarded and lodged by the plaintiff at the said lodging-house from the —— of ——, 18— to the —— of ——, 18—.

3. £—— is a fair and reasonable charge for the said board and lodging of the defendant for the said period [*or if there was any express agreement as to terms, state it*].

4. The defendant has made no payment to the plaintiff in respect of such board and lodging, and the sum of £—— is due and payable from the defendant to the plaintiff in respect thereof.

Landlord against Tenant for not keeping the Premises in Tenantable Repair (*e*).

1. The defendant became and was tenant to the plaintiff of a messuage and premises of the plaintiff situate at

---

(*d*) A contract for board and lodging, where no specific rooms are demised to the lodger, is not a contract for an interest in land within the Statute of Frauds, 29 Car. II. c. 3, s. 4, and need not be in writing. (*Wright* v. *Stavert*, 2 E. & E. 721 ; 29 L. J. Q. B. 161.)

(*e*) A contract to use premises in a tenant-like and proper manner is implied by law from the mere fact of the tenancy, in the absence of any express agreement on the subject ; but the liability of a tenant from year to year, in the absence of express agreement, for repairs, is limited to keeping the premises demised "wind and water tight,"

——, in the county of ——, upon the terms that the defendant should, during the said tenancy, keep the said messuage and premises in tenantable repair, order, and condition.

2. The defendant, during the said tenancy, did not keep the said messuage or the said premises in tenantable repair, order, and condition. [*Give such details as are practicable.*]

For not using the Premises in a Tenant-like manner (*e*).

1. The defendant became and was tenant to the plaintiff of a messuage and premises of the plaintiff situate at ——, in the county of —— [and of furniture and goods of the plaintiff therein], upon the terms that the defendant should during the said tenancy use the said messuage and premises [and furniture and goods] in a tenant-like and proper manner.

2. The defendant, during the said tenancy, used the said messuage and premises [and furniture and goods] in an untenant-like and improper manner. [*Give such details as are practicable.*]

For not delivering up Fixtures upon the Premises in good Repair.

1. The defendant became and was tenant to the plaintiff of a messuage and premises of the plaintiff, situate at ——, in the county of ——, for a term of —— years from the —— of ——, 18—, upon the terms, amongst others, that the defendant should, at the expiration of the said term, deliver up to the plaintiff the said messuage and premises, with all fixtures thereon, in the same state and condition as they were in at the time of the defendant becoming such tenant as aforesaid, reasonable wear and tear only excepted.

---

and to using them in a "tenant-like" and proper, or "husband-like" manner. (*Leach* v. *Thomas*, 7 C. & P. 337; *Horsfall* v. *Mather*, Holt, N P. 7.)

A tenant at will, or from year to year, is only liable for commissive waste (*Herne* v. *Bembow*, 4 Taunt. 764; *Ferguson* v. ———, 2 Esp. 590), but a tenant for life, or lives, or for years, is liable for permissive waste (6 Ed. I., c. 5; *Harnett* v. *Maitland*, 16 M. & W. 257, 262; *Yellowly* v. *Gower*, 11 Ex. 294), and see further Woodfall's Landlord and Tenant, 11th ed. pp. 558, 559; Roscoe's N. P. Ev., 14th ed. p. 327; and "*Waste*," *post*, p. 539. See further as to obtaining particulars *ante* p. 29.

2. The said term expired by effluxion of time on the —— of ——, 18—, and the defendant then delivered up to the plaintiff the said messuage and premises.

3. The defendant did not then deliver up to the plaintiff, and has not delivered up to the plaintiff, the fixtures, which at the time when he became tenant to the plaintiff of the said messuage and premises were thereon, in the same state and condition as they were in at the time of the defendant becoming such tenant as aforesaid, reasonable wear and tear only excepted.

Lessor against Lessee upon a Covenant to Repair (f).

1. The plaintiff by deed let to the defendant a house, No. 401, Piccadilly, to hold for seven years from the —— of ——, 18—.

2. The defendant by the said deed covenanted with the plaintiff well and substantially to repair the said house during the said term [*according to the covenant*].

3. The defendant did not well and substantially repair the said house during the said term [*follow the wording of the covenant, and give details so far as practicable*].

4. [The said term of the defendant expired by effluxion of time on the —— day of ——, 18—, and the said house then and previously thereto was out of good and substantial repair.]

Lessor against Lessee upon a Covenant to Repair subject to certain exceptions (f).

1. The plaintiff by deed let to the defendant a house, No. ——, —— Street, ——, to hold for —— years from the —— day of ——, 18—.

(*f*) In an action by a landlord against a tenant for breach of promise or covenant to keep the demised premises in repair, the measure of damages during the continuance of the lease is the diminution in value of the reversion (*Turner* v. *Lamb*, 14 M. & W. 412; *Doe* v. *Rowlands*, 9 C. & P. 734; *Smith* v. *Peat*, 9 Ex. 161; *Mills* v. *East London Union*, L. R. 8 C. P. 79; 42 L. J. C. P. 46); but where the plaintiff is a sublessor, whose lease is determined by a forfeiture not shown to have been wholly caused by the breach of the sub-contract by the defendant, the sublessee, to repair, the measure of damages is not the value of the lease or term of the plaintiff, the lessee, but may be the sum it would cost to do the repairs as contracted for. (*Clow* v. *Brogden*, 1 M. & G. 39; *Davies* v. *Underwood*, 2 H. & N. 570; 27 L. J. Ex. 113; and see *Williams* v. *Williams*, L. R. 9 C. P. 659; 43 L. J. C. P. 382). The amount of the damages also depends upon the

2. The defendant by the said deed covenanted with the plaintiff to keep the said house in good and substantial repair during the said term, casualties by fire or tempest [*&c., according to the covenant*] excepted.

3. During the said term the said house was not kept in good and substantial repair, although no casualty by fire or tempest [*&c., according to the covenant*] happened thereto.

The like, where the want of Repair exists at time of action and the Term has not expired.

1 and 2. [*As in form next above.*]

3. The said house is not in good and substantial repair, although no casualty by fire or tempest [*&c., according to the covenant*] has happened thereto, and the said term has not as yet expired.

Landlord against Tenant for not Farming according to the Custom of the Country (g).

1. The defendant became and was tenant to the plaintiff of a farm and land situate at ——, in the county of ——

---

class and condition of the premises at the time of the demise, the extent of the tenant's liability being construed with regard thereto. (*Stanley* v. *Towgood*, 3 Bing. N. C. 4; *Burdett* v. *Withers*, 7 A. & E. 136; *Payne* v. *Haine*, 16 M. & W. 541; *Saner* v. *Bilton*, 7 Ch. D. 815; 48 L. J. Ch. 545.) Where the reversioner after the expiration of the lease granted a new lease, on the terms of pulling down the house and building a new one, it was held that the jury were not obliged to give merely nominal damages for breaches of the covenant to repair contained in the old lease and which breaches had been committed during the term granted by the old lease. (*Rawlings* v. *Morgan*, 18 C. B. N. S. 776; 34 L. J. C. P. 185.) A lessor who covenants with his lessee to repair demised premises is entitled to notice of the want of repair before being sued for non-performance of his covenant. (*Makin* v. *Watkinson*, L. R. 6 Ex. 25; 40 L. J. Ex. 33; *L. & S. W. Ry. Co.* v. *Flower*, 1 C. P. D. 77; 45 L. J. C. P. 54; *Manchester Bonded Warehouse Co.* v. *Carr*, 5 C. P. D. 507; 49 L. J. C. P. 809.) See further "*Waste*," *post*, p. 539.

The covenants in leases to repair absolutely, and to repair after notice, are usually distinct and independent covenants. (*Baylis* v. *Le Gros*, 4 C. B. N. S. 537; *Roe* v. *Paine*, 2 Camp. 520.)

(*g*) From the mere fact of a tenancy of a farm, whether under a written or parol agreement, or under a lease by deed, the law implies a promise on the part of the tenant to cultivate it in a husbandlike manner and according to the custom of the country where it is situate; unless the express contract is inconsistent with such implication. (*Wigglesworth* v. *Dallison*, 1 Doug. 201; *Powley* v. *Walker*, 5 T. R. 373; *Legh* v. *Hewitt*, 4 East, 154; *Williams* v. *Woods*, 17 L. J. Q. B. 319.)

[*give a description of the property*], upon the terms that the defendant should use and cultivate the said farm and land during the said tenancy according to the course of good husbandry and the custom of the country wherein the same were situate.

2. During the said tenancy the defendant did not use and cultivate the said farm and land according to the course of good husbandry and the said custom [in this that he sowed —— acres of the arable land of the said farm with two successive crops of wheat, and that he carried away from the said farm many cart-loads of straw and dung, which had arisen and been made upon the said farm during the said tenancy, and used and consumed the same elsewhere than on the said farm and land [*or as the case may be, giving details where practicable*].

Lessee against Lessor for Breach of Covenant for Quiet Enjoyment and for Title (*h*).

1. The defendant by deed bearing date the —— of ——, 18—, demised to the plaintiff a house, No. 46, Pall

---

(*h*) Under a lease by deed the word "*demise*" or "*let*," or any equivalent words sufficient to constitute a lease, import a covenant for title, and for quiet enjoyment; unless there be an express covenant on either point, in which case no implication can be raised from such words. (*Line* v. *Stephenson*, 4 Bing. N. C. 678; 5 Bing. N. C. 183; *Adams* v. *Gibney*, 6 Bing. 656, 666; *Mostyn* v. *W. Mostyn Coal and Iron Co.*, 1 C. P. D. 145; 45 L. J. C. P. 401.) Such implied covenants are limited to the duration of the lessor's estate, and cease upon its determination. (*Adams* v. *Gibney*, *supra*; see *Penfold* v. *Abbott*, 32 L. J. Q. B. 67.) A warranty of the demise by the lessor is an express covenant, and extends to the whole term granted. (*Williams* v. *Burrell*, 1 C. B. 402.)

Under a parol demise the law will imply a promise for quiet enjoyment during the term, but not for title. (*Bandy* v. *Cartwright*, 8 Ex. 913; 22 L. J. Ex. 285 and xl. *note*; *Hall* v. *City of London Brewery Co.*, 2 B. & S. 737; 31 L. J. Q. B. 257.)

A similar promise is not implied in a mere agreement to demise (*Brashier* v. *Jackson*, 6 M. & W. 549); although in such an agreement there is an implied undertaking by the lessor that he has title to enter into the agreement, and has a good title to let for the agreed term. (*Stranks* v. *St. John*, L. R. 2 C. P. 376; 36 L. J. C. P. 118.) There is no implied warranty in a lease of a warehouse or of an unfurnished house, or of land, that it is reasonably fit for use, habitation, or cultivation (*Sutton* v. *Temple*, 12 M. & W. 52; *Hart* v. *Windsor*, *ib.* 68; *Erskine* v. *Adeane*, 42 L. J. Ch. 835; L. R. 8 Ch. Ap. 756; *Manchester Bonded Warehouse Co.* v. *Carr*, 5 C. P. D. 507; 49 L. J. C. P. 809); but in letting apartments or a furnished house

Mall, to hold for —— years from the —— of ——, 18—, at the rent of £—— a year, and subject to the covenants and conditions therein contained.

2. The defendant by the said deed covenanted with the plaintiff that at the time of the making of the said demise the defendant had full and lawful power and authority to demise the said house to the plaintiff for the said term as aforesaid.

3. The defendant by the said deed further covenanted with the plaintiff that he, the plaintiff, his executors, administrators, and assigns, paying the said yearly rent thereby reserved, and performing and observing the covenants therein contained, by him and them to be performed and observed, should and might lawfully, peaceably, and quietly hold, use, and occupy the said house for the said term, without any lawful denial, let, hindrance, molestation, or interruption whatsoever of or by the defendant, his heirs or assigns, or any person or persons claiming through, under, or in trust for him.

4. The defendant at the time of the making of the said demise had not full or lawful power or authority to demise the said house to the plaintiff for the said term as aforesaid.

5. After the making of the said demise, and during the said term, G. H., then lawfully claiming the said house through and under the defendant [*add, when*

---

a lessor impliedly undertakes or promises, in the absence of express stipulation, that it is reasonably fit for occupation (*Smith* v. *Marrable*, 11 M. & W. 5; *Wilson* v. *Finch-Hatton*, 2 Ex. D. 336; 46 L. J. Ex. 489; *Campbell* v. *Lord Wenlock*, 4 F. & F. 710); and if it is not so, the tenant may quit at once, and is not liable for rent after so quitting. (See cases cited, *supra*.)

The measure of damages is the loss directly sustained through the invalidity of the demise; thus, where a defendant had granted a lease which he had not title to grant, and the plaintiff obtained from the person having title a fresh lease, he was held entitled to recover from the defendant in an action on the covenant for quiet enjoyment the expenses of the void lease and the difference in value of the void and valid lease. (*Lock* v. *Furze*, 19 C. B. N. S. 96; 34 L. J. C. P. 201; 35 *ib.* 141; L. R. 1 C. P. 441; see also *Williams* v. *Burrell*, 1 C. B. 402; *Rolph* v. *Crouch*, L. R. 3 Ex. 44; 37 L. J. Ex. 8; *Godwin* v. *Francis*, L. R. 5 C. P. 295; 39 L. J. C. P. 121; *Collen* v. *Wright*, 8 E. & B. 647; 27 L. J. Q. B. 215; *Spedding* v. *Nevell*, L. R. 4 C. P. 212.)

Where the lease contains the usual clause for re-entry it is unnecessary to allege payment of rent and performance by the plaintiff of his covenants, as in paragraph 6 of this form. It is for the defendant to justify his entry if he can as a re-entry under the power contained in the lease. (*Dawson* v. *Dyer*, 5 B. & Ad. 584).

practicable, the ground of the claim of G. H.], and having a good title to the same and to the possession thereof, through and under the defendant, entered into the said house and evicted the plaintiff therefrom.

[6. The plaintiff did duly pay the said yearly rent in accordance with the above-mentioned covenant, and did, until the time hereinafter mentioned, perform and observe all the said covenants by him to be performed and observed in the said deed contained, and all the covenants in the said deed contained, made, and entered into by the defendant, were duly performed and observed, until the time when the said G. H. entered into possession of the said house as aforesaid.]

Landlord against Tenant for not giving up Possession at the End of the Term.

1. The defendant became and was tenant to the plaintiff of a messuage called ——, situate at ——, in the county of ——, at a rent of £—— a year, payable half-yearly, [*or as the fact is*] upon the terms, amongst others, that the defendant should at the expiration of the said tenancy give up possession of the said messuage to the plaintiff.

2. The said tenancy expired on the —— of——, 18—.

3. The defendant did not on the said —— of ——, 18—, give up possession of the said messuage to the plaintiff, but wrongfully remained in possession thereof from the said —— of ——, 18—, to the —— of ——, 18—; whereby the plaintiff lost the use and possession of the said messuage, and incurred expense in recovering possession of the same [*give details of expense where practicable*].

For a Form of Statement of Claim upon a Covenant to pay Taxes or Rates, see Rawlins v. *Briggs*, 3 C. P. D. 368; 47 L. J. C. P. 487; *in which case, however, it is to be noted that the covenant did not impose the duty to pay the claim sued for* (*i*).

(*i*) As to construction of covenants with regard to rates, taxes, or outgoings imposed on property, or the owners, or the occupiers thereof, see cases collected in Roscoe's N. P. Ev., 14th ed., pp. 668, 669, and cited in *Rawlins* v. *Briggs*, 3 C. P. D. 368; 47 L. J. C. P. 487; and *Hartley* v. *Hudson*, 4 C. P. D. 367; *Budd* v. *Marshall*, 5 C. P. D. 481; 50 L. J. C. P. 24; and see Woodfall's Landlord and Tenant, 11th ed. pp. 518, *et seq.*

Assignee of Lessor against Lessee (*k*).

1. G. H., being seised in fee [*or* possessed for the residue of a term of —— years, commencing the —— of ——,

---

(*k*) *Assignees of Lessor and Lessee.*]—By the common law certain covenants run with the land, so as to attach the benefit or the burden of them to the assignee of the term, but not with the reversion; and by the common law covenants are not assignable. (1 Wms. Saund. 299, n. (*b*).) Consequently the assignee of the reversion could neither sue nor be sued upon a covenant in a lease. To remedy this inconvenience the statute 32 Hen. VIII. c. 34, gave an action to and against the assignee of the reversion. By s. 1 it was enacted that all persons, being grantees or assignees of any reversion, should have like advantage against the lessees and their assigns by action for not performing conditions, covenants, or agreements, expressed in the indentures of lease, as the lessors and grantors, their heirs or successors, might have had; and by s. 2, that all lessees of lands or their assigns should have like action and remedy against all persons having any gift or grant of the reversion of the lands so let, for any condition or covenant expressed in the indentures of their leases, as the same lessees might have had against the lessors.

The statute only applies to leases by deed. (*Brydges* v. *Lewis*, 3 Q. B. 603; *Standen* v. *Chrismas*, 10 Q. B. 135; *Smith* v. *Eggington*, L. R. 9 C. P. 145; 43 L. J. C. P. 140; *Phillips* v. *Miller*, L. R. 10 C. P. 420; 44 L. J. C. P. 265; *Elliott* v. *Johnson*, L. R. 2 Q. B. 120; 36 L. J. Q. B. 41; 8 B. & S. 38.) If the demise be not by deed, the lessor, notwithstanding the assignment, can sue. (*Bickford* v. *Parson*, 5 C. B. 920.) The statute applies to leases by deed of incorporeal hereditaments. (*Martyn* v. *Williams*, 1 H. & N. 817; 26 L. J. Ex. 117; *Hooper* v. *Clark*, L. R. 2 Q. B. 200; 36 L. J. Q. B. 19; *Norval* v. *Pascoe*, 34 L. J. Ch. 82.) The statute applies only to covenants which run with the land, as to which see *Spencer's case*, 5 Co. 18 a; 1 Sm. L. C., 8th ed., 68; *Vyvyan* v. *Arthur*, 1 B. & C. 410; and see Leake on Contracts, 1210. See further, the "Conveyancing and Law of Property Act, 1881" (44 & 45 Vict. c. 41).

In the case of tenancies not under lease by deed, the payment of rent and holding as before the assignment affords evidence of a new tenancy under the terms of the original letting, and thus a conventional law is made equivalent to that of Hen. VIII. in the case of leases under seal, the new contract being that everything shall go on as before the assignment. (*Cornish* v. *Stubbs*, L. R. 5 C. P. 339; 39 L. J. C. P. 205; *Buckworth* v. *Simpson*, 1 C. M. & R. 834; *Brydges* v. *Lewis*, 3 Q. B. 603; *Williams* v. *Heales*, L. R. 9 C. P. 177; 43 L. J. C. P. 80.)

In actions where the plaintiff's claim is upon a demise by himself, the title of the plaintiff to the land demised need not be set out, he may rely on the deed alone; but in an action by an assignee of the reversion, the statement of claim must show that the lessor was seised or possessed of some estate which would pass by assignment. (1 Wms. Saund., 6th ed., p. 233 a.)

In equity the assignment of the benefit and burden of covenants is not thus restricted; by the general principles of equity the benefit of a contract is assignable; and if the covenant concerns specific property it may pass by assignment with the property if the parties so

18—] of a messuage and land situate at ——, let the same, by deed bearing date the —— of ——, 18—, to the defendant to hold for —— years from the —— of ——, 18—.

---

contract. (*Keates* v. *Lyon*, L. R. 4 Ch. Ap. 218; 38 L. J. Ch. 357; *Renals* v. *Cowlishaw*, 9 Ch. D. 125; 11 Ch. D. 866; 48 L. J. Ch. 33; 48 L. J. Ch. 830; *Western* v. *Macdermott*, L. R. 2 Ch. Ap. 72; 36 L. J.Ch. 76; Leake on Contracts, 1233, *et seq.*) So, too, in equity, notice of a covenant may affect an assignee of property with regard to which it has been entered into, so as to render such property liable to the burden of such covenant in his hands. (*Western* v. *Macdermott, supra; Tulk* v. *Moxhay*, 2 Phill. 778; *Whatman* v. *Gibson*, 9 Sim. 196; *Wilson* v. *Hart*, L. R. 1 Ch. Ap. 463; 35 L. J. Ch. 569; *Catt* v. *Tourle*, L. R. 4 Ch. Ap. 654; 38 L. J. Ch. 665; Leake on Contracts, 1234, *et seq.*)

The doctrine of constructive notice applies only in favour of third parties who are entitled to the covenants and equities affecting the property, and not as between vendors and purchasers as to matters which it was the duty of the vendor to communicate. (*Caballero* v. *Henty*, L. R. 9 Ch. Ap. 447; 43 L. J. Ch. 635; Leake on Contracts, 1237.)

Upon the execution of a lease by the lessee he is estopped from denying the lessor's title, as recited in the lease. If the lessor's title is not shown in the lease, the lessee is estopped from setting up any defence founded upon the fact that the lessor *nil habuit in tenementis*; and thus there arises, as between the lessor and lessee, a reversion in the lessor by estoppel. This reversion by estoppel is *primâ facie* a reversion in fee simple, and assignable and capable of passing by devise or descent (*Cuthbertson* v. *Irving*, 4 H. & N. 742; 6 H. & N. 135; 28 L. J. Ex. 306; 29 L. J. Ex. 485; *Gouldsworth* v. *Knights*, 11 M. & W. 337); but the lessee may rebut the *primâ facie* presumption of the reversion being in fee simple by evidence consistent with the estoppel, as by showing that the reversion is an estate for years or for life, &c., but not by showing that the lessor had no estate, for this would be inconsistent with the estoppel. (*Weld* v. *Baxter*, 11 Ex. 816; 1 H. & N. 568; 25 L. J. Ex. 214; 26 *Ib.* 112.) The heir, or assignee, or devisee of a reversion by estoppel may sue upon the covenants in the lease. (*Gouldsworth* v. *Knights*, 11 M. & W. 337; *Sturgeon* v. *Wingfield*, 15 M. & W. 224; *Doe* v. *Ongley*, 10 C. B. 25; *Cuthbertson* v. *Irving, supra.*) See the "Conveyancing and Law of Property Act, 1881" (44 & 45 Vict. c. 41) s. 18, as to the powers of leasing conferred thereby upon mortgagors and mortgagees in possession. An estoppel which binds a party binds those claiming through or under such party. (*Taylor* v. *Needham*, 2 Taunt. 278; *Doe* d. *Bullen* v. *Mills*, 2 A. & E. 17; *London and North Western Ry. Co.* v. *West L. R.*, 2 C. P. 553; 36 L. J. C. P. 245.) All persons taking the estate, term, or reversion, to which the covenants are annexed, under the same title, become bound by, and entitled to the benefit of the covenants, and that whether they take by operation of law as trustees in bankruptcy or heirs, or as administrators, or by act of the party as executors or assignees. (*Spencer's case*, 5 Co., 17 b; *Tremeere* v. *Morison*, 1 Bing. N. C. 89; *Goodwin* v. *Noble*, 8 E. & B. 587; 27 L. J. Q. B. 204; *Williams* v. *Heales*, L. R. 9 C. P. 177; 43 L. J. C. P. 80; *White* v. *Hunt*,

2. The defendant by the said deed covenanted with the said G. H. and his assigns [*state the covenant*].

3. Afterwards and during the said term, the said G. H., by a deed bearing date the —— of ——, 18—, granted and assigned all his reversion of and in the said message and land to the plaintiff.

4. Afterwards and during the said term the defendant [*state breach, giving such particulars as to date, &c., as are practicable*].

Executor of Lessor against Lessee (l).

1. The plaintiff is the executor of the last will and testament of G. H., deceased. [The said G. H. died on

---

L. R. 6 Ex. 32; 40 L. J. Ex. 23; *Ex parte Carter, in re Ware*, 8 Ch. D. 731, 734; *Ex parte Dressler, in re Solomon*, 9 Ch. D. 252; 48 L. J. Bk. 20.) A term passes by assignment so as to carry covenants without possession or actual entry. (*Williams* v. *Bosanquet*, 1 B. & B. 238.) An assignee of the rent reserved in a lease may, without attornment, sue for such rent (4 Anne, c. 16, s. 9; *Allen* v. *Bryan*, 5 B. & C. 512; *Williams* v. *Hayward*, 28 L. J. Q. B. 374); where a termor underleases for a longer period than his term, reserving a rent, the rent so created is assignable, and the assignee can sue for it. (*Williams* v. *Hayward*, *supra*.)

By 8 & 9 Vict. c. 106, s. 9, when the reversion expectant on a lease of any tenements or hereditaments of any tenure, shall be surrendered or merge, the estate which shall for the time being confer as against the tenant under the same lease the next vested right to the same tenements or hereditaments, shall to the extent and for the purpose of preserving such incidents to and obligations on the same reversion as but for the surrender or merger thereof would have subsisted, be deemed the reversion expectant on the same lease.

Where a party is pleading his own title derived by assignment, he must deduce it step by step through the various mesne assignments, it being matter within his own knowledge, and which he is bound to state for the information of his opponent (*Philipps* v. *Philipps*, 4 Q. B. D. 127; 48 L. J. Q. B. 135; *R.* v. *Bishop of Llandaff*, 2 Stra. 1012); but a party alleging title by assignment in his opponent might formerly, and it is conceived may still, plead it by a *que estate*, that is, by a general averment that the estate precedently laid in some other person vested in him by assignments. (*Harries* v. *Beavan*, 4 Bing. 646; *Derisley* v. *Custance*, 4 T. R. 75.)

(*l*) Covenants which run with the land, as covenants to repair, etc., pass with the reversion to the heir or devisee, and not to the executor, unless the reversion passes to the executor as being for a term only. The executor therefore cannot, in general, sue upon covenants running with the land. But in respect to damages caused to the personal estate of the testator exclusively by breaches of such covenants in his lifetime, and apart from the damages to the real estate, the executor may sue. (*Kingdon* v. *Nottle*, 1 M. & S. 355; *Jones* v. *King*, 4 M. & S. 188; 5 Taunt. 418; *Raymond* v. *Fitch*, 2 C. M. & R. 588; *Ric-*

the —— of ——, 18—, and his will was proved by the plaintiff in the High Court of Justice, Probate Division, on or about the —— of ——, 18—.]

2. The said G. H., being possessed of a messuage situate at ——, in the county of ——, for the residue of a term of years, commencing the —— of ——, 18 — [*or*, for a term of years more than sufficient to enable him to make the lease hereinafter mentioned], let the same by deed [*or*, by a deed bearing date the —— of ——, 18 —] to the defendant, to hold for —— years from the —— of ——, 18—.

3. The defendant by the said deed covenanted with the said G. H. [*state the covenant.*]

4. Afterwards, during the last-mentioned term, and in the lifetime of the said G. H., the defendant [*state the breaches which occurred in the lifetime of G. H., as in other cases*].

---

ketts v. *Weaver*, 12 M. & W. 718.) An executor can sue for rent accrued to the testator, seised in fee or for life, in his lifetime, by virtue of 32 Hen. VIII. c 37.

At common law rent was not apportionable in respect of time, but now by 33 & 34 Vict. c. 35, "The Apportionment Act, 1870," which extends the remedies given by former Apportionment Acts (11 Geo. II. c 19; 4 & 5 Wm. IV. c. 22; 6 & 7 Wm. IV. c. 71; 14 & 15 Vict. c. 25; 23 & 24 Vict. c. 154), if a tenancy determines by death, the proportionate part of the rent up to the time of the determination is recoverable, but not until the time arrives when the next payment would but for such determination have fallen due. If the death which determines the tenancy is that of the landlord, his executors or administrators can then sue for such proportionate part.

If the tenancy continues notwithstanding the death of the landlord, and the reversion is one that does not upon his death pass to his executors or administrators, the person to whom the reversion passes must recover the rent from the tenant when the next period for payment of rent after the death arrives, and is liable to the executors or administrators for the proportionate part of the rent up to the time of the death as money received to their use.

By the above statute, s. 2 (subject to the other provisions of the Act), it is enacted that "all rents, annuities, dividends, and other periodical payments in the nature of income (whether reserved or made payable under an instrument in writing or otherwise) shall, like interest on money lent, be considered as accruing from day to day, and shall be apportionable in respect of time accordingly."

By s. 7, the Act is not to apply where the parties have expressly stipulated that there is to be no apportionment. (See further, Woodfall's Landlord and Tenant, 11th ed., pp. 366, *et seq.*) Executors and administrators may join claims in their representative capacity with those in their own right arising with reference to the estate of the deceased. (See O. XVII. r. 5, *ante*, "*Executors.*")

5. And afterwards during the said last-mentioned term, and after the death of G. H. [*similarly state the breaches which occurred after the death*].

Heir of Lessor against Lessee.

1. G. H., being seised in fee of a messuage situate at ——, let the same by a deed bearing date the —— of ——, 18—, to the defendant, to hold for —— years from the —— of ——, 18—.

2. The defendant by the said deed covenanted with G. H. and his heirs [*state the covenant*].

3. Afterwards, during the said term [on the —— of ——, 18—], the said G. H. died.

4. Upon the death of the said G. H. the reversion n fee of, and in, the said messuage descended to the plaintiff, as and being the eldest son and heir of the said G. H.

5. After the death of the said G. H. during the said term, and whilst the plaintiff was seised of the said reversion, the defendant [*state the breach*].

Devisee of Lessor against Lessee.

1. G. H., being seised in fee of a messuage situate at ——, let the same by a deed bearing date the —— of ——, 18—, to the defendant to hold for —— years from the —— of ——, 18—.

2. The defendant by the said deed covenanted with the said G. H. and his assigns [*state the covenant*].

3. Afterwards, during the said term [on the —— of ——, 18—], the said G. H. died.

4. By his last will and testament [which was duly proved, *state when and where, if practicable*] the said G. H. devised all his reversion in the said messuage to the plaintiff.

5. [*As in paragraph 5 of Statement of Claim next above.*]

Lessee against Assignee of Lease (*m*).

1. A. B., by a deed bearing date the —— of ——, 18—, let to the plaintiff a house, No. 11, New Bond Street,

(*m*) An assignee of a lease, whether it is assigned to him by the lessee, or whether there have been other mesne assignments, is under an obligation implied by law to indemnify the original lessee against

London, for a term of 14 years, commencing on the —— of ——, 18—, at a rental of £—— a year, payable by equal half-yearly payments [*or as the case is*].

2. By the said deed the plaintiff covenanted with the said A. B., that he, his executors, administrators, or assigns, would yearly, and every year during the continuance of the said term, pay to the said A. B. the said rent by equal half-yearly payments as in the said deed specified.

3. Afterwards, and during the continuance of the said term, the plaintiff, by a deed bearing date the —— of ——, 18—, assigned the said term to C. D.

4. Afterwards, and during the continuance of the said term, the said term became vested in the defendant by assignment.

5. Whilst the said term was so vested in the defendant, and during the continuance thereof, —— of the said half-yearly payments of the said rent became due and payable [on the —— of ——, 18—, and the —— of ——, 18—, *as the case may be*].

6. The said —— half-yearly payments were not, nor was any part of them, paid by the defendant.

7. The plaintiff was thereupon compellable to pay, and did pay to the said A. B. the said —— half-yearly payments.

8. The defendant has not repaid the same or any portion thereof to the plaintiff.

Lessor against Assignee of Lessee upon a Covenant in the Lease.

1. The plaintiff, by a deed bearing date the —— of ——, 18—, let to G. H. a messuage, situate at ——, to hold for —— years from the —— of ——, 18—.

2. The said G. H., by the said deed, for himself and

---

breaches of covenant running with the land in the lease committed during his own tenancy (*Moule* v. *Garrett*, L. R. 5 Ex. 132; L. R. 7 Ex. 101; 41 L. J. Ex. 62); the lessee is in the position of surety to the lessor for the assignee (*Wolveridge* v. *Steward*, 1 Cr. & M. 644, 659); but this implied obligation of the assignee only extends to breaches committed during his own tenancy. (*Crouch* v. *Tregoning*, L. R. 7 Ex. 88; 41 L. J. Ex. 97; *Wolveridge* v. *Steward*, *supra*.)

Implied promises only exist in the absence of express stipulation between the parties. (*Toussaint* v. *Martinnant*, *per* Buller, J., 2 T. R. 105.) See further, Leake on Contracts, 1231–1233, 79.

his assigns, covenanted with the plaintiff [*state the covenant*].

3. By a deed bearing date the —— of ——, 18—, the said G. H., being then possessed of the said term for the portion thereof then unexpired, assigned to the defendant all the estate of him the said G. H. in the said term.

4. Afterwards, during the said term, the defendant [*state the breach*].

A like Form, Macdonald v. *Carington*, 4 C. P. D. 28.

Lessor against Executor of Lessee (*n*).

1. The plaintiff, by a deed bearing date the ——

(*n*) In actions by the landlord against the executor of the deceased tenant for rent accrued due during the life of the tenant the executor is liable *de bonis testatoris*, and the action must be brought against him in his representative character. For rent accrued due after the death of the tenant, the executor may be charged *de bonis testatoris*, and sued in his representative character; he may also be sued in his own right as assignee of the term generally, and proof that he is executor is sufficient to support the allegation that the term vested in him by assignment (*Wollaston* v. *Hakewill*, 3 M. & G. 297); but when he is thus charged in his own right as assignee generally, he may plead that he is executor only, and has never entered, if such is the fact (*Ib.* 320, 321; *Kearsley* v. *Oxley*, 2 H. & C. 896); or, if he has entered, he may plead that he is assignee only as executor, and that the premises are of no value, or are of less value than the rent, admitting his liability *pro tanto*, and that he has no other assets. (See Wms Exs. 8th ed. p. 1763; *Jevens* v. *Harridge*, 1 Wms. Saund. 1, n. (*i*); *Rubery* v. *Stevens*, 4 B. & Ad. 241; *Hornidge* v. *Wilson*, 11 A. & E. 645; *Hopwood* v. *Whaley*, 6 C. B. 744.)

As to breaches of covenant, the executor of the tenant is, in general, liable *de bonis testatoris*, for breaches of covenant in the lifetime or after the death of the testator. (Wms. Exs. 8th ed. p. 1757; *Wollaston* v. *Hakewill*, 3 M. & G. 297, 320.) And it seems that with respect to breaches of covenant after the death of the testator, the executor is liable *de bonis propriis* as assignee of the term (*Sleap* v. *Newman*, 12 C. B. N. S. 116), except that with respect to covenants to pay rent his liability does not exceed what the property yields. (*Tremeere* v. *Morison*, 1 Bing. N. C. 89.)

By the statute 22 & 23 Vict. c. 35, s. 27, it is provided, that where an executor, after satisfying all present liabilities under a lease of the testator, and setting apart a sufficient sum to answer any future claim in respect of any fixed and ascertained sum under the lease, has assigned the lease to a purchaser, and distributed the residuary estate, he shall no longer be personally liable in respect of any subsequent claim under the lease; but the lessor may follow the assets distributed. (See *Dodson* v. *Samwell*, 30 L. J. Ch. 799.) See further "*Executors*," *ante*, p. 172.

of ——, 18—, let to G. H. a messuage, situate at ——, to hold for —— years from the —— of ——, 18—.

2. The said G. H., by the said deed, covenanted with the plaintiff [*state covenant*].

3. Afterwards, during the said term [on the —— of ——, 18—], the said G. H. died, having made his last will and testament [which was proved, *state when and where, if practicable*], whereby he appointed the defendant his executor.

4. During the said term, and before the death of the said G. H.; the said G. H. [*state such breach as occurred in the lifetime of the said G. H.*].

5. During the said term, and after the death of the said G. H., the defendant [*state such breach as occurred after the death of the said G. H.*].

For a Form of Assignee of Lessor against Assignee of Lessee upon Covenant to repair, &c., see Hudson v. *Williams*, 39 L. T. 632; *but compare note* (*k*), *p.* 246, *ante.*

For Double Value under 4 *Geo.* 2, *c.* 28, *s.* 1 (*o*).

1. The defendant was tenant to the plaintiff of a messuage and land of the plaintiff, situate at —— [*give a*

(*o*) By the statute 4 Geo. II. c. 28, s. 1, it is enacted, "that in case any tenant or tenants for any term of life, lives or years, or other person or persons, who are or shall come into possession of any lands, tenements, or hereditaments, by, from, or under, or by collusion with such tenant or tenants, shall wilfully hold over any lands, tenements, or hereditaments, after the determination of such term or terms, and after demand made, and notice in writing given, for delivering the possession thereof, by his or their landlords or lessors, or the person or persons to whom the remainder or reversion of such lands, tenements or hereditaments shall belong, his or their agent or agents thereunto lawfully authorized, then and in such case such person or persons so holding over shall, for and during the time he, she, and they shall so hold over, or keep the person or persons entitled out of possession of the said lands, tenements, and hereditaments as aforesaid, pay to the person or persons so kept out of possession, their executors, administrators, or assigns, at the rate of double the yearly value of the lands, tenements, and hereditaments so detained, for so long time as the same are detained, to be recovered in any of his Majesty's Courts of Record, by action of debt, whereunto the defendant or defendants shall be obliged to give special bail, against the recovering of which said penalty there shall be no relief in equity."

The double value given by this statute is in the nature of a penalty

description of the property], for a term of years which determined on the ——of ——, 18—.

2. After the said —— of ——, 18— [namely on the —— of ——, 18—], the plaintiff, as and being the defendant's landlord as aforesaid, and the person to whom the reversion of the said messuage and land then belonged [by his agent thereunto lawfully authorised], made a demand upon, and gave notice in writing to, the defendant, for delivery to the plaintiff of the possession of the said messuage and land.

3. The defendant did not in accordance with such demand and notice deliver possession of the said messuage and land to the plaintiff, but wilfully held over the said messuage and land, and kept the plaintiff, then being entitled to the possession thereof, out of the possession of the said land and messuage until the —— of ——, 18—, a period of —— months after the determination of the said term, and after such demand made and notice given as aforesaid.

4. The double of the yearly value of such messuage and land during the above-mentioned period amounts to the sum of £——, which said sum is still wholly due and unpaid.

For Double Rent under 11 *Geo.* 2, *c.* 19, *s.* 18 (*p*).

1. The defendant was tenant to the plaintiff of a messuage and land, as tenant from year to year, at the yearly rent of £——, payable quarterly.

---

given to the party grieved, and therefore must be sued for within two years. (See "Defences," "*Limitation.*") The holding over must be wilful and contumacious, and not either by mistake or under a *bonâ fide* claim of right. (*Soulsby* v. *Neving*, 9 East, 310; *Swinfen* v. *Bacon*, 6 H. & N. 184, 846, 30 L. J. Ex. 33, 368.) A person to whom the landlord has granted a fresh lease, to commence at the expiration of the defendant's term, is not a person entitled to the possession within the meaning of the Act, and cannot maintain this action. (*Blatchford* v. *Cole*, 5 C. B. N. S. 514, 28 L. J. C. P. 140.)

A landlord may also sue his tenant for the special damage occasioned by the tenant holding over after the expiration of the tenancy, as for the damages which he is rendered liable to pay to a third party to whom he has let the premises, and to whom he is unable to give possession in consequence of the tenant holding over. (*Bramley* v. *Chesterton*, 2 C. B. N. S. 592, 27 L. J. C. P. 23.)

(*p*) By 11 Geo. II. c. 19, s. 18, it is enacted, "in case any tenant

2. The defendant [on the —— of ——, 18— duly gave the plaintiff notice of his, the defendant's, intention to quit the said premises at a time mentioned in such notice [namely, on the —— of ——, 18—].

3. The defendant did not at the said time mentioned in such notice deliver up possession of the said messuage and land to the plaintiff, but continued in possession thereof until the —— of ——, 18—.

4. The double rent of the said messuage and land during the said period after the said time for quitting mentioned in such notice amounts to the sum of £——, which said sum is still wholly due and unpaid.

Landlord against Tenant to recover Possession where the Tenancy has been determined by Notice to Quit, with a Claim for Mesne *Profits* (*q*) (*r*) (*s*).

[*Form No.* 24, *App.* (*C*) *to Jud. Act,* 1875.]

1. On the —— day of ——, the plaintiff let to the defendant a house, No. 52, —— Street, in the city of London,

---

or tenants shall give notice of his, her, or their intention to quit the premises by him or them holden at a time mentioned in such notice, and shall not accordingly deliver up the possession thereof at the time in such notice contained, that then the said tenant or tenants, his, her, or their executors or administrators, shall from thenceforward pay to the landlord or landlords, lessor or lessors, double the rent or sum which he, she, or they should otherwise have paid, to be levied, sued for, and recovered at the same time, and in the same manner, as the single rent or sum before the giving such notice could be levied, sued for, or recovered; and such double rent or sum shall continue to be paid during all the time such tenant or tenants shall continue in possession as aforesaid." The double rent given by this statute is not in the nature of a penalty, like the double value under the statute 4 Geo. II. c. 28, but may be levied, sued for, and recovered in the same manner as the single rent. The statute applies only where the tenant had the power of determining his tenancy by a notice, and has given a valid notice sufficient to determine it. (*Johnstone* v. *Huddlestone*, 4 B. & C. 922.)

(*q*) *Title to Recover Possession.*]—Where a landlord seeks to recover the possession of the demised premises, the statement of claim should show the creation of the relation of landlord and tenant between himself and the defendants, and its determination before action, either by lapse of time (as in a lease for years), or by notice to quit (as in a yearly tenancy), or by a determination of the will of the landlord (as in a tenancy at will), or by surrender or forfeiture, and the defendant's continued possession of the premises by himself or his tenant. From these allegations the wrongful nature of the defendant's holding, and the plaintiff's title to immediate possession, are left to be inferred as conclusions of law. It is not necessary for a landlord in such action to deduce a good title as against all the world to the premises, a tenant being estopped from disputing the landlord's title to premises let to him at the time of such letting, though not estopped from showing its subsequent determination. (*Cooke* v. *Loxley*, 5 T. R. 4; *Cuthbertson* v. *Irving*, 4 H. & N. 742, 6 *Ib.* 135, 28 L. J. Ex. 306, 29 *Ib.* 485; *Delany* v. *Fox*, 2 C. B. N. S. 768, Woodfall's Landlord and Tenant, 11th ed., pp. 196–199.) As to estoppels by leases see *ante*, n. (k), p. 247. As to when other claims may be joined with a claim for the recovery of land, see O. XVII. r. 2, "*Joinder of Causes of Action*," *ante*, p. 17. See, generally, notes to "*Recovery of Land*," *post*, p. 502. As to the right after the 31st of December, 1881, of re-entry or forfeiture under any proviso in a lease for breach of any covenant or condition therein, see *post*, p. 260.

(*r*) *Mesne Profits.*]—In actions brought to recover possession of premises by a landlord, a claim is frequently made for mesne profits, which it will be convenient to consider here, though the action for mesne profits is properly an action for a wrong. As soon as a tenant's interest is legally determined his holding becomes wrongful, and is in law a trespass for which damages in the form of mesne profits may be recovered. The action of trespass for mesne profits being an action of trespass, and consequently a possessory action, could formerly only be brought after entry, or judgment in ejectment (*Barnett* v. *Guildford*, 11 Ex. 19, 24 L. J. Ex. 281); but by the C. L. P. Act, 1852 (15 & 16 Vict. c. 76), s. 214, "Whenever it shall appear on the trial of any ejectment at the suit of a landlord against a tenant, that such tenant or his attorney hath been served with due notice of trial, the judge before whom such cause shall come on to be tried shall, whether the defendant shall appear upon such trial or not, permit the claimant on the trial, after proof of his right to recover possession of the whole or of any part of the premises mentioned in the writ in ejectment, to go into evidence of the mesne profits thereof which shall or might have accrued from the day of the expiration or determination of the tenant's interest in the same, down to the time of the verdict given in the cause, or to some preceding day to be specially mentioned therein; and the jury on the trial, finding for the claimant, shall in such case give their verdict upon the whole matter, both as to the recovery of the whole or any part of the premises, and also as to the amount of the damages to be paid for such mesne profits, and in such case the landlord shall have judgment within the time hereinbefore provided, not only for the recovery of possession and costs, but also for the mesne profits found by the jury: provided always that nothing hereinbefore contained shall be construed to bar any such landlord from bringing any action for the mesne profits which shall accrue from the verdict, or the day so specified therein, down to the day of the delivery of possession of the premises recovered in the ejectment."

By O. XXXVI. r. 18, "If, when an action is called on for trial, the plaintiff appears, and the defendant does not appear, then the plaintiff may prove his claim so far as the burden of proof lies upon him."

Consequently in an undefended action the plaintiff must, to recover mesne profits, prove his right to possession, and his title to and the amount of mesne profits; unless, and except so far as, admitted on the pleadings.

By O. XXXVI. r. 22, *a*, "Upon the trial of an action the judge may, at or after the trial, direct that judgment be entered for any or either party, or adjourn the case for further consideration, or leave any party to move for judgment. No judgment shall be entered after a trial without the order of a court or judge."

If the tenant appears at the trial it is not necessary, in order to rely on the above section, to give evidence that he received due notice of trial, his appearance is sufficient. (*Doe* d. *Thompson* v. *Hodgson*, L. M. & R. 283, 12 A. & E. 135, Cole, Eject., pp. 292, 388.)

It would seem that where mesne profits are sought, the statement of claim should contain a specific claim to that effect. (O. XIX. r. 8; and see forms, Nos. 18 and 24, App. (C), to Jud. Act, 1875, set out in the text.) It was not formerly necessary for the issue, there being no pleadings, to show this. (*Smith* v. *Tett*, 9 Ex. 307.) A claim for mesne profits may be joined with one for the recovery of the land or premises in respect of which the claim is made. (O. XVII. r. 2.) Mesne profits may be claimed from the date when the tenant's interest is determined. Where the interest is determined by a forfeiture, it would seem that a proportionate part of the current rent up to the date of the forfeiture may be recovered as rent, and that after that date and up to the time of the recovery of the premises, mesne profits are recoverable. ("*The Apportionment Act*, 1870," 33 & 34 Vict. c. 35; *Swansea Bank* v. *Thomas*, 4 Ex. D. 94; 48 L. J. Ex. 344.)

It is the duty of a tenant at the expiration of his term, not merely to go out himself, but to deliver up complete possession of the demised premises to his landlord; it is therefore no defence that the premises are occupied by his under-tenant, who refuses to give them up (*Harding* v. *Crethorn*, 1 Esp. 57, *per* Lord Kenyon; *Chitty* v. *Tancred*, 7 M. & W. 127, 130, *per* Parke, B.); and the tenant is liable in mesne profits both for the value of the premises whilst his under-tenant holds over, and for the costs of ejecting him. (*Henderson* v. *Squire*, L. R. 4 Q. B. 170, 174; 38 L. J. Q. B. 73, *per* Blackburn, J.) It is the correct course, in such a case, to claim such costs expressly upon the statement of claim.

The damages claimed as mesne profits are usually measured by the rent; but further damages, as *e.g.*, the unsatisfied costs of an ejectment, may be recovered (*Pearse* v. *Coaker*, L. R. 4 Ex. 92, 99; *Goodtitle* v. *Tombs*, 3 Wils. 121; *Doe* d. *Levi* v. *Roe*, 6 C. B. 275, *per* Cresswell, J.; *Henderson* v. *Squire*, *supra*), if claimed upon the statement of claim.

Under the former system of pleading it was held that the allegation in a declaration that the plaintiff "incurred great expense in recovering possession of the said land and messuage," was sufficient to allow the costs of a previous action of ejectment to be recovered. (*Pearse* v. *Coaker*, *supra*.) See further, Mayne on Damages, pp. 392–394. As to the effect of a judgment to recover possession, and generally, see "*Recovery of Land*," *post*, p. 502.

(*s*) *Notice to Quit.*]—A tenancy from year to year can in general be determined by a notice to quit. The notice may be given by either party. When once given it can only be withdrawn by the assent of both parties. (*Blyth* v. *Dennett*, 13 C. B. 178.)

In the absence of express stipulation between the parties, the common law requires the notice to be a half-year's notice to quit at the end of the first or some other year of the tenancy.

as tenant from year to year, at the yearly rent of £120, payable quarterly, the tenancy to commence on the —— day of ——.

A notice to quit, when given on behalf of the landlord by a person not authorised by him, at the time when the notice begins to run, to give it, cannot be made valid by a subsequent ratification. (*Doe* d. *Mann* v. *Walters*, 10 B. & C. 626; *Doe* d. *Lister* v. *Goldwin*, 2 Q. B. 143, 146; *Right* d. *Fisher* v. *Cuthell*, 5 East, 491, 498.)

As to claiming double rent when a tenant, after giving notice to quit, holds over, see a form of claim, and note, *ante*, p. 254.

When the tenancy is other than yearly, a reasonable notice, in the absence of express stipulation, must be given; what is customary is probably the reasonable notice. (*Jones* v. *Mills*, 10 C. B. N. S. 788, 31 L. J. C. P. 66.)

A notice to quit is not rendered unnecessary by the assignment of the term, or of the reversion, whether such assignment is by act of one of the parties, or otherwise. (*Maddon* d. *Baker* v. *White*, 2 T. R. 159; *Doe* d. *Shore* v. *Porter*, 3 T. R. 13; *Doe* d. *Castleton* v. *Samuel*, 5 Esp. 173; *Birch* v. *Wright*, 1 T. R. 378.) See further, Woodfall's Landlord and Tenant, 11th ed., pp. 300 *et seq.*

The Agricultural Holdings Act, 1875 (38 & 39 Vict. c. 92), has in some cases altered the law as to the length of notice requisite to be given. By sec. 51, " Where a half-year's notice, expiring with a year of tenancy, is by law necessary and sufficient for determination of a tenancy from year to year, a year's notice so expiring shall, by virtue of this Act, be necessary and sufficient for the same; but nothing in this section shall extend to a case where the tenant is adjudged bankrupt, or has filed a petition for a composition or arrangement with his creditors."

By sec. 54, " Nothing in this Act shall prevent a landlord and tenant, or intending landlord and tenant, from entering into and carrying into effect any such agreement as they think fit, or shall interfere with the operation thereof."

By sec. 56, the application of the Act may be excluded by an agreement in writing between the landlord and tenant to that effect.

By sec. 57, power is given to exclude the application of the Act from tenancies from year to year existing at the commencement of the Act (14th Feb., 1876) by a notice given within two months after the commencement of the Act.

By sec. 58, " Nothing in this Act shall apply to a holding that is not either wholly agricultural or wholly pastoral, or in part agricultural and as to the residue pastoral, or that is of less extent than two acres."

A yearly tenancy which by express agreement of the parties is determinable on *six months'* notice to quit is not within the above Act. (*Wilkinson* v. *Calvert*, 3 C. P. D. 360, 47 L. J. C. P. 679.)

A notice to quit is only necessary where the tenancy is admitted, and where the tenant disclaims and denies his landlord's title he thereby renders a notice to quit unnecessary, and waives his right to such notice. (*Doe* d. *Calvert* v. *Frowd*, 4 Bing. 560; *Doe* d. *Bennett* v. *Long*, 9 C. & P. 773; *Doe* d. *Grubb* v. *Grubb*, 10 B. & C. 816; *Vivian* v. *Moat*, 16 Ch. D. 730; 50 L. J. Ch. 331.)

2. The defendant took possession of the house, and continued tenant thereof until the —— day of —— last, when the tenancy determined by a notice duly given.

3. The defendant has disregarded the notice, and still retains possession of the house.

The plaintiff claims :—

(1) Possession of the house.

(2) £—— for mesne profits from the —— day of ——.

For a like Form, see Wilkinson v. *Calvert,* 3 C. P. D. 360 ; 47 L. J. C. P. 679.

The like where the Tenancy has determined by effluxion of Time (q), (r), (s).

1. The plaintiff, by deed bearing date the —— day of ——, 18—, let to the defendant certain premises known as ——, situate in ——, for a term of —— years, to commence on the —— day of ——, 18—, at the yearly rent of £——.

2. The defendant continued tenant of the said premises until the —— day of ——, 18—, when the said term expired.

3. The defendant afterwards continued to retain, and still retains, possession of the said premises, and refuses to deliver up possession thereof to the plaintiff.

[*Claim as in form next preceding.*]

Landlord against Tenant to recover Possession of the demised Premises upon a Forfeiture for Breach of Covenant to keep the Premises in repair, &c., joining Claims for Damages for the Breach of Covenant, for Arrears of Rent, and for Mesne *Profits (r) (t).*

[*Form, No.* 18, *App.* (*C*), *to Jud. Act,* 1875.]

1. On the —— day of ——, the plaintiff, by deed, let to the defendant a house and premises, No. 52, —— Street, in the city of London, for a term of 21 years, from

---

(*t*) *Forfeiture.*]—Leases containing conditions of forfeiture upon default of the tenant, as, for not repairing, non-payment of rent, or other breach of covenant, are voidable at the option of the lessor, who must by some unequivocal act, indicating to the lessee his intention to insist upon the forfeiture, exercise his option, in order to avoid them. (*Rede* v. *Farr,* 6 M. & S. 121 ; *Roberts* v. *Davey,* 4 B. & Ad. 664 ;

the —— day of ——, at the yearly rent of £120, payable quarterly.

2. By the said deed the defendant covenanted to keep the said house and premises in good and tenantable repair.

3. The said deed also contained a clause of re-entry, entitling the plaintiff to re-enter upon the said house and premises, in case the rent thereby reserved, whether de-

---

Baylis v. *Le Gros*, 4 C. B. N. S. 537) ; *Jones* v. *Carter*, 15 M. & W. 718, and see *Toleman* v. *Portbury*, L. R. 6 Q. B. 245, *Ib.* 7. Q. B. 344, 40 L. J. Q. B. 125, 41 *Ib.* 98.)

A right of re-entry or forfeiture (other than one arising on non-payment of rent, assigning, underletting or parting with possession of the land leased, bankruptcy or liquidation of lessee, taking in execution of the lessee's interest, or on breaches of certain provisions in mining leases) cannot, after the 31st of Dec., 1881, be enforced "unless and until the lessor serves on the lessee a notice specifying the particular breach complained of, and, if the breach is capable of remedy, requiring the lessee to remedy the breach, and, in any case, requiring the lessee to make compensation in money for the breach, and the lessee fails, within a reasonable time thereafter, to remedy the breach, if it is capable of remedy, and to make reasonable compensation in money, to the satisfaction of the lessor, for the breach." The "Conveyancing and Law of Property Act, 1881" (44 & 45 Vict. c. 41).

As to the right of the Court to afford relief against such forfeiture or re-entry, see s. 14 (2), of the above Statute. See further "Defences," "*Landlord and Tenant.*"

A lease conditioned to be *void* for the benefit of one party is *voidable* only at the option of that party. (*Rede* v. *Farr*, *Roberts* v. *Davey*, *supra*; *Davenport* v. *Reg.* 3 App. Cas. 115 ; 47 L. J. P. C. 8.)

A proviso in a lease for re-entry on a condition broken can operate only during the term (*Johns* v. *Whitley*, 3 Wils. 127), but it will extend to a new implied tenancy from year to year upon the terms of the lease. (*Thomas* v. *Packer*, 1 H. & N. 669 ; see, also, *Martin* v. *Smith*, L. R. 9 Ex. 50, 43 L. J. Ex. 43.)

There are certain conditions annexed by law to particular estates, by which, on the happening of certain things, the landlord is entitled to re-enter. Thus, if a tenant renounces his character as tenant by either setting up title in a third person, or in himself, to the premises against his landlord, his conduct amounts to a disclaimer, and his term is thereby forfeited. (*Doe* v. *Cooper*, 1 M. & G. 135, 139, *per* Tindal, C. J. ; *Doe* d. *Ellerbrock* v. *Flynn*, 1 C. M. & R. 137.) But mere words will not operate as a disclaimer of a lease for a term certain, there must be some act done by the tenant, the effect of which, if acquiesced in, would be to impair the landlord's title. (*Doe* v. *Wells*, 10 A. & E. 427.) See further, Woodfall's Landlord and Tenant, 11th ed., pp. 283, *et seq.*; 324, *et seq.*

Where a lessor re-enters on a forfeiture, the rights of under-lessees are gone, but where a lessor accepts a surrender from a lessee, the rights of the under-lessees remain, although the lease was at the time liable to forfeiture. (*G. W. Ry. Co.* v. *Smith*, 2 Ch. D. 235, 45 L. J. Ch. 235, 241, 244.)

manded or not, should be in arrear for 21 days, or in case the defendant should make default in the performance of any covenant upon his part to be performed.

4. On the 24th June, 18—, a quarter's rent became due, and on the 29th September, 18—, another quarter's rent became due; on the 21st October, 18—, both had been in arrear for 21 days; and both are still due.

5. [On the same 21st October, 18—, the house and premises were not, and are not now, in good or tenantable repair, and it would require the expenditure of a large sum of money to reinstate the same in good and tenantable repair, and the plaintiff's reversion is much depreciated in value. *In actions commenced after the* 31*st of December*, 1881, *it will be necessary to state performance of the requirements of the statute*, 44 & 45 *Vict.* c. 41, s. 14.]

The plaintiff claims :—

(1) Possession of the said house and premises.

(2) £—— for arrears of rent.

(3) £—— damages for the defendant's breach of his covenant to repair.

(4) £—— for the occupation of the house and premises from the 29th September, 18—, to the day of recovering possession.

A like Form by Lessor against Assignee of Lessee, Hanmer v. *Flight*, 35 L. T. 127 (*the actual decision was reversed in C. A., see* 36 L. T. 279).

Statement of Claim to recover Possession on a Forfeiture for Non-payment of Rent (*under the C. L. P. Act*, 1852, s. 210) (*u*).

1. The plaintiff, by deed bearing date the —— of ——, 18—, let to the defendant a messuage and premises

---

(*u*) *Forfeiture for non-payment of rent.*]—If a lease contains a proviso for re-entry for non-payment of rent, a demand by the landlord or his agent duly authorised, of the precise rent due and payable, to save the forfeiture, on the exact day, at the proper place of payment, at a convenient hour between sunrise and sunset, is, at common law, requisite, before the landlord can claim to re-enter for non-payment of rent, unless the demand is expressly dispensed with by the terms of the lease. If no place is named for payment the proper place is at the most notoricus place on the land; therefore if there be a principal dwelling-house it must be there, at the front door. (1 Wms. Saund. 287 *et seq.*; *Acocks* v. *Phillips*, 5 H. & N. 183.)

By 15 & 16 Vict. c. 76 (C. L. P. Act, 1852), s. 210 the necessity of

situate at ——, for a term of —— years, commencing on the —— day of ——, 18—, at a yearly rent of £—— payable quarterly [*or as the case may be*].

2. The said deed contained a clause of re-entry, entitling the plaintiff to re-enter upon the said messuage and premises in case the said rent thereby reserved should be in arrear for 21 days.

3. On the 24th of June, 18—, a quarter's rent became due, and on the 29th of Sept., 18—, another quarter's rent became due; on the 21st of Oct., 18—, both had been in arrear for 21 days, and both are still due.

4. Before this action was commenced, and before the writ was served, half a year's rent was due, and no sufficient distress was to be found on the said messuage and premises, or on any part thereof, countervailing the said arrears of rent then and still due.

For a Form where demand is dispensed with by the Lease, see No. 18 *in App.* (C) *to Jud. Act.*, 1875, *set out ante*, p. 259.

LIQUIDATED DAMAGES (*a*).

Statement of Claim on a Covenant in a Deed of Sale of a Business, to pay Liquidated Damages in the Event of the Defendant carrying on the Business.

1. By a deed bearing date the —— of ——, 18—, made between the plaintiff and the defendant, the de-

---

a legal demand by the landford of the rent is done away with, if it be proved that half a year's rent was due, and that no sufficient distress was to be found on the demised premises countervailing the arrears then due, and that the lessor had power to re-enter. (See the section, and *Cotesworth* v. *Spokes*, 10 C. B. N. S. 103, 30 L. J. C. P. 220; *Doe* d. *Dixon* v. *Roe*, 7 C. B. 134; *Cross* v. *Jordan*, 8 Ex. 149, from which it would appear that a half-year's rent at least must be actually due when the writ is issued.)

The assignee of the reversion cannot eject for non-payment of rent unless the tenant has had notice of the assignment before the forfeiture accrued. (*Mallory's case*, 5 Rep. 1136; *Fraunces' case*, 8 Rep. 92 a, *sub nom. Miller* v. *Francis*, 1 Godb. 272, Co. Litt. 215 b); though where the forfeiture is for causes other than non-payment of rent such notice is not necessary (*Scaltock* v. *Harston*, 1 C. P. D. 106, 45 L. J. C. P. 125.) See further Roscoe's N. P. Ev. 14th ed., pp. 951–953; Woodfall's Landlord and Tenant, 11th ed., pp. 291–295.

(*a*) *Liquidated damages* are a sum agreed upon in a contract by the parties themselves as the damages for a breach of it.

A *penalty* is a sum named in a contract to be forfeited on a breach,

fendant assigned to the plaintiff all the interest, benefit, or profit to be thenceforth made from the profession and practice of a surgeon and apothecary, as theretofore

---

not as an agreed valuation of the damages, but as a security for the due performance of the contract. (*Per* Lord Mansfield, *Lowe* v. *Peers*, 4 Burr. 2225, 2220; *Kemble* v. *Farren*, 6 Bing. 141, 148.)

Wherever there is a sum mentioned at the end of a contract as damages for non-performance of any of a great number of stipulations of various importance, such sum is a penalty, but where it is agreed that if a party do, or omit to do, a particular thing, such a sum shall be paid by him, there the sum may be regarded as liquidated damages (*Kemble* v. *Farren*, *supra; Astley* v. *Weldon*, *per* Heath, J., L. B. & P. 346, 353; *Magee* v. *Lavell*, L. R. 9 C. P. 107; 43 L. J. C. P. 134; *Betts* v. *Burch*, 4 H. & N. 506, 28 L. J. Ex. 267; *Ex parte Capper*, 4 Ch. D. 725, 731; 46 L. J. B. 57.)

Where the sum named is in reality a penalty, only the actual damage sustained can be recovered, even though the parties by the contract term the sum liquidated damages. (*Thompson* v. *Hudson*, L. R. 4 H. L. 1, 30, 38 L. J. Ch. 431; *Magee* v. *Lavell*, *supra; Ex parte Capper*, *supra;* and see *Lea* v. *Whitaker*, L. R. 8 C. P. 70.) See further Leake on Contracts, 1096 *et seq.*

Upon the breach of a contract secured by a penalty the plaintiff may either sue for the penalty assigning the breach—in which case he can recover the amount of damage sustained, not exceeding the penalty; or he may sue for unliquidated damages for the breach, to be assessed by the jury irrespectively of the penalty. In the former case the recovery of the full penalty will be a satisfaction for all breaches of the contract, but in the latter the plaintiff may sue *toties quoties* there are breaches and recover a full indemnity. (See 8 & 9 Wm. 3, c. 11, s. 8, *per* Lord Mansfield in *Lowe* v. *Peers*, *supra; Winter* v. *Trimmer*, 1 W. Bl. 395; *Harrison* v. *Wright*, 13 East, 343; *Astley* v. *Weldon*, *supra*, *per* Bramwell, B., in *Betts* v. *Burch*, *supra.*)

Where the plaintiff sues for liquidated damages the non-payment of the damages must be assigned as a breach of the contract. (*Hurst* v. *Hurst*, 4 Ex. 571.) Where the contract is alternative, either to do a thing or to pay a liquidated sum, both alternatives must be negatived in the statement of claim. (*Legh* v. *Lillie*, 6 H. & N. 165, 30 L. J. Ex. 25.)

In a mortgage bond given to secure the due payment by instalments of a sum due, a provision making the total sum due enforceable on any default is not a penalty. (*Wallingford* v. *Mutual Society*, 5 App. Cas. 685; 50 L. J. Q. B. 49; *Protector Endowment Co.* v. *Grice*, 5 Q.B.D. 592, 596; 49 L. J. Q. B. 812.)

On a bond conditioned not to carry on business within certain limits or to pay liquidated damages, an injunction may be granted to enforce the condition. (*Howard* v. *Woodward*, 34 L. J. Ch. 47.) In such cases the amount payable is usually regarded as liquidated damages, for it cannot be ascertained what damages may be actually sustained from a breach of such a contract. (*Galsworthy* v. *Strutt*, 1 Ex. 663; Leake on Contracts, 1095.) A plaintiff may sue for unliquidated damages for a breach and also claim an injunction. (*Carnes* v. *Nesbitt*, 7 H. & N. 158; *Ib.* 778; 30 L. J. Ex. 348; 31 *Ib.* 273.)

carried on by the defendant at ——, or from any of the patients belonging thereto.

2. The said deed contained a covenant by the defendant with the plaintiff, that the defendant would not at any time afterwards, directly or indirectly, by himself or in co-partnership with any other person or persons, carry on or exercise the practice or profession of a surgeon and apothecary, or either of them, within the distance of three miles from the then place of business of the defendant at —— aforesaid, and that in case of any breach of the above-mentioned covenant, the defendant would pay to the plaintiff the sum of £——, to be recovered against him as and for liquidated damages, and not as a penalty.

3. The defendant afterwards from the —— of ——, 18—, to the —— of ——, 18— [*or as the case may be*], carried on and exercised the practice or profession of a surgeon and apothecary within three miles of —— aforesaid, by visiting, within the said distance from that place, G. H., L. M. [*&c. give details where practicable*], as patients of the defendant in his character, practice, and profession of a surgeon and apothecary.

4. The defendant has not paid to the plaintiff the said sum of £——.

Lunatic (*a*).

Commencement of Statement of Claim by a Person of unsound mind so found by inquisition.

Between A. B., committee of the estate of C. D., a person of unsound mind so found by inquisition and the said C. D. by the said A. B. as his Committee . . . . *Plaintiffs.*

and

E. F. . . . . . . *Defendant.*

The Court will not interfere by injunction where a certain sum has been agreed on as the price of the breach, and the defendant has in effect purchased the right to do the act complained of as a breach. (*Woodward* v. *Gyles*, 2 Vern. 119; *Forbes* v. *Carney*, cited in Joyce on Injunctions, 80; *Sainter* v. *Ferguson*, 1 Mac. & G. 286.)

Thus, where an increased rent was reserved by way of liquidated damages an injunction was refused to restrain the lessee from committing the breach of covenant in respect of which the increased rent became payable. (*Woodward* v. *Gyles*, *supra*.)

(*a*) A person of unsound mind, who has been so found by inqui-

1. The above-named A. B. is committee of the estate of the above named C. D., a person of unsound mind so found by inquisition.

The like against a Person of Unsound Mind not so found by Inquisition, or against a Person of Unsound Mind so found by Inquisition who defends by Guardian.

Between A. B. . . . . . *Plaintiff.*
and
C. D., a person of unsound mind [not] so found by inquisition, who defends by E. F. his guardian . . . . *Defendant.*

1. C. D., the above-named defendant, is a person of unsound mind [not] so found by inquisition, who defends this action by E. F., who has been duly appointed guardian of the said C. D. for the purpose of defending this action.

The like by a Person of Unsound Mind not so found by Inquisition.

Between A. B., a person of unsound mind not so found by inquisition, by C. D., his next friend . . . *Plaintiff.*
and
E. F. . . . . . . *Defendant.*

1. A. B., the above-named plaintiff, is a person of unsound mind not so found by inquisition, who sues by C. D., his next friend.

---

sition, sues, and is sued, by his committee, who must be a co-plaintiff, or co-defendant, as the case may be. If however the interest of the committee is adverse to the lunatic, a guardian *ad litem* may be assigned. (*Worth* v. *Mackenzie*, 3 M. & G. 363 ; see Chitty's Forms, 11th ed., pp. 523—527.)

By O. XVIII., "In all cases in which lunatics, and persons of unsound mind not so found by inquisition might respectively before the passing of the Act," (*i. e.* Jud. Act, 1875,) "have sued as plaintiffs or would have been liable to be sued as defendants in any action or suit, they may respectively sue as plaintiffs in any action by their committee or next friend in manner practised in the Court of Chancery before the passing of the said Act, and may in like manner defend any action by their committees or guardians appointed for that purpose." See as to the Chancery practice, 15 & 16 Vict. c. 86, s. 11, "*Husband and Wife*," *ante*, *note* (*c*), p. 202.

The like against a Person of Unsound Mind so found by Inquisition.

Between A. B. . . . . . *Plaintiff.*

and

C. D., a person of unsound mind so found by inquisition, who defends by E. F., committee of the estate of the said C. D. and the said E. F. *Defendants.*

1. C. D., the above-named defendant, is a person of unsound mind so found by inquisition, who defends by E. F., committee of the estate of the said C. D.

MARRIAGE (*a*). See "*Husband and Wife*," *ante.*

Statement of Claim upon a Breach of Promise to Marry within a reasonable time.

1. In June, 18—, the plaintiff and the defendant agreed to marry one another.

(*a*) Mutual promises to marry are not agreements made upon consideration of marriage within the Statute of Frauds, 29 Car. II. c. 3, s. 4, and need not be proved by writing (*Harrison* v. *Cage*, 1 Ld. Raym. 386); but promises to pay money in consideration of marriage are, and must be proved by writing. (See *Shadwell* v. *Shadwell*, 9 C. B. N. S. 159; 30 L. J. C. P. 145.) A general promise to marry, without any express stipulation as to time, is a promise to marry within a reasonable time. (*Harrison* v. *Cage*, 1 Ld. Raym. 386; and see *Short* v. *Stone*, 8 Q. B. 358.) A promise to marry made by a person who was already married at the time of making the promise, but of which the promisee had no notice, is binding, and an action may be maintained upon it. (*Wild* v. *Harris*, 7 C. B. 999; *Millward* v. *Littlewood*, 5 Ex. 775.)

The marriage of one of the promising parties to a third party after the promise, though before the time for performance has elapsed, is a breach of the contract, and entitles the other party at once to bring an action. (*Short* v. *Stone*, 8 Q. B. 358; *Caines* v. *Smith*, 15 M. & W. 189.)

An absolute unconditional renunciation of a contract or engagement to marry before the time of performance, is, at the election of the promisee, a breach of the contract upon which an action may be immediately maintained. (*Frost* v. *Knight*, L. R. 7 Ex. 111; 41 L. J. Ex. 78.)

An executor or administrator cannot sue for a breach of promise of marriage made to the testator or intestate, except perhaps in respect of special damage caused to the estate by the breach of contract. (*Chamberlain* v. *Williamson*, 2 M. & S. 408.)

2. A reasonable time for such marriage has elapsed.

3. The plaintiff has been always ready and willing to marry the defendant.

4. The defendant has neglected and refused to marry the plaintiff.

For Breach of a Promise contained in Letters to Marry on a particular day.

1. The plaintiff is the daughter of a farmer living at ——; the defendant is a manufacturer carrying on business at ——.

2. By letters bearing date the —— of ——, 18—, the —— of ——, 18—, and the —— of ——, 18, the plaintiff and the defendant agreed to marry one another, and that their said marriage should take place on the —— of ——, 18—.

3. The plaintiff was ready and willing to marry the defendant on the said —— of ——, 18—.

4. The defendant neglected and refused to marry the plaintiff on the said —— of ——, 18—.

In this action the jury may give damages for the injury to the feelings of the plaintiff, as well as for the loss of the marriage (*per* Willes, J., *Smith* v. *Woodfine*, 1 C. B. N. S. 660, 668, *where see further as to the measure of damages, and what may be given in evidence in aggravation and mitigation, as also see Berry* v. *Da Costa*, L. R. 1 C. P. 331 ; 35 L. J. C. P. 191 ; *Millington* v. *Loring*, 6 Q. B. D. 190 ; 50 L. J. Q. B. 214 ; *and Frost* v. *Knight, supra*).

Until the statute 32 & 33 Vict. c. 68, the parties to the action for breach of promise of marriage were not competent witnesses, but now by sect. 2 of that statute "the parties to any action for breach of promise of marriage shall be competent to give evidence in such action ; provided always that no plaintiff in any action for breach of promise of marriage shall recover a verdict unless his or her testimony shall be corroborated by some other material evidence in support of such promise." As to what is such evidence, see *Bessela* v. *Stern*, 2 C. P. D. 265 ; 46 L. J. C. P. 467.

An infant may, by his or her next friend, maintain an action for a breach of a promise to marry (*Holt* v. *Ward*, 2 Str. 937 ; *per* Lord Ellenborough, in *Warwick* v. *Bruce*, 2 M. & S. 209) ; but infancy affords a defence to an action in respect of a breach of such promise, if pleaded. (See "*Marriage*," "Defences.")

The fact that the plaintiff has been seduced under the promise of marriage may be alleged in the statement of claim in aggravation of damages. (*Millington* v. *Loring, supra;* see further. "*The body of the statement of claim,*" *ante*, p. 11.)

For Breach of a promise to Marry the Defendant, by marrying another Person, with a claim for special damage.

1. The plaintiff was formerly a governess at ——, and the defendant was and is a gentleman possessed of considerable property, living at ——.

2. Between the —— of ——, 18—, and the —— of ——, 18—, the defendant frequently promised to marry the plaintiff, who on her part then promised to marry the defendant.

3. The engagement between the plaintiff and the defendant to marry one another continued from the date of such promises to the —— of —— 18—, when the defendant married another woman.

4. The plaintiff until the defendant so married another woman was always ready and willing to marry the defendant.

5. The plaintiff, in view of the then intended marriage between herself and the defendant, and at the defendant's request, on the —— of ——, 18—, gave up her said situation as governess, and incurred an expense of £—— in preparing her clothing and other matters for the said then intended marriage.

6. In consequence of the above conduct of the defendant the plaintiff lost the said marriage and the benefit of the expense incurred as aforesaid, and was injured in her health and feelings.

Upon an Absolute Repudiation of an Engagement to Marry upon the happening of an event, made before the happening of the said event.

1. The plaintiff and the defendant in June 1880, agreed to marry one another upon the death of the defendant's father.

2. On the —— of ——, 18—, before the death of the defendant's father, the defendant absolutely refused ever to marry the plaintiff, and wrongfully repudiated, renounced and determined the said agreement on his part.

3. The plaintiff until such refusal and wrongful repudiation, renunciation, and determination was always ready and willing to marry the defendant upon the death of his father.

Statement of Claim upon an Agreement to Marry on or before a certain day, or in default to pay an Annuity to the Plaintiff, Heap v. *Marris*, 2 Q. B. D. 630; 46 L. J. Q. B. 761.

For a Form alleging in aggravation of Damages a Seduction under the Promise of Marriage, see Millington v. *Loring*, 6 Q. B. D. 190; 50 L. J. Q. B. 214.

MASTER AND SERVANT (*a*).

Statement of Claim by a Servant against his Master for Wages.

1. The plaintiff was employed as a [warehouseman] by the defendant from the —— of ——, 18—, to the

---

(*a*) Where the cause of action is a wrongful discharge or dismissal, whereby the servant has been prevented from earning wages, the statement of claim must be framed accordingly. Where by the contract of service the wages are payable at fixed periods, as yearly, quarterly, or monthly, and the master wrongfully dismisses the servant during the currency of one of those periods, the servant is entitled to recover as part of his damages in an action for the wrongful dismissal, a compensation for the service actually done during the broken period up to the time of the dismissal, or, at his option (instead of suing for damages for the wrongful dismissal), he may treat the contract as rescinded, and sue the master as on a new implied contract for a proportion of wages in respect of the work actually done during the broken period (*Goodman* v. *Pocock*, 15 Q. B. 576; Leake on Contracts, 67); and in either case he is also entitled to claim and recover, as a debt, any amount due to him for wages in respect of any completed periods which have elapsed prior to such dismissal. (See *Hartley* v. *Harman*, 11 A. & E. 798.)

Where the contract has been rescinded (*Lamburn* v. *Cruden*, 2 M. & G. 253), or where a servant has wrongfully left the service (*Taylor* v. *Laird*, 1 H. & N. 266; 25 L. J. Ex. 329), or has been dismissed for misconduct (*Turner* v. *Robinson*, 5 B. & Ad. 789), after a certain period of service, but before any wages have accrued due under the contract, the plaintiff cannot recover for the services rendered, unless a new agreement to pay for such services can be established. (*De Bernardy* v. *Harding*, 8 Ex. 822.)

Where there is a contract for a service to commence on a future day, and the intended employer before the time for the commencement of the service absolutely renounces and refuses to perform the contract on his part, and communicates his renunciation and refusal to the servant, the latter may, if he pleases, treat this conduct on the part of the employer as an immediate breach of the contract, and at once bring an action to recover damages for such breach, instead of

—— of ——, 18—, inclusive, at the wages of £—— a week, payable weekly.

2. Before the commencement of this action, —— weeks' wages, amounting at the rate aforesaid to the sum

---

waiting till the time fixed for the commencement of the service. (*Hochster* v. *De la Tour*, 2 E. & B. 678; 22 L. J. Q. B. 455; *Frost* v. *Knight*, L. R. 7 Ex. 111; 41 L. J. Ex. 78; *Roper* v. *Johnson*, L. R. 8 C. P. 167; 42 L. J. C. P. 65; and see *ante*, "*Marriage*," p. 266.)

A contract of service for an indefinite time is generally presumed, as a matter of fact, to be a contract for a year; but there is no inflexible rule of law to that effect, and each particular case must depend upon its own circumstances. (*Beeston* v. *Collyer*, 4 Bing. 309; *Fawcett* v. *Cash*, 5 B. & Ad. 904; *Baxter* v. *Nurse*, 6 M. & G. 935; *Fairman* v. *Oakford*, 5 H. & N. 635; 29 L. J. Ex. 459; *Creen* v. *Wright*, 1 C. P. D. 591, 594.)

In engagements of service in particular trades and businesses, the custom in the trade or business to determine the contract by notice is incorporated into the contract, unless the terms of the contract expressly or impliedly exclude the custom. (*Metzner* v. *Bolton*, 9 Ex. 518; *Parker* v. *Ibbetson*, 4 C. B. N. S. 346; 27 L. J. C. P. 236.)

In the hiring of menial or domestic servants there is a custom, presumptively forming part of the contract, that the servant may be dismissed with a month's warning or a month's wages. (*Nowlan* v. *Ablett*, 2 C. M. & R. 54.) This custom applies to a servant engaged as head gardener (*Ib.*), to a person hired to assist in garden and stables (*Johnson* v. *Blenkensopp*, 5 Jur. 870), to a huntsman (*Nicoll* v. *Greaves*, 17 C. B. N. S. 27; 33 L. J. C. P. 259); but not to a governess. (*Todd* v. *Kerrich*, 8 Ex. 151; 22 L. J. Ex. 1.)

In cases where the custom applies, the month's wages to be paid upon dismissal without notice are payable as a compensation for the dismissal, and not, properly speaking, as wages (*Fewings* v. *Tisdal*, 1 Ex. 295); but they may perhaps be regarded as a debt due under the contract upon the dismissal. (See *East Anglian Ry. Co.* v. *Lythgoe*, 2 L. M. & P. 221, 226.) For a form of declaration under the old practice by a domestic servant on a contract of service subject to this custom, see *Turner* v. *Mason*, 14 M. & W. 112.

Where there is a contract of hiring for a year, the continuation of the service at the expiration of the year, without further agreement expressly made, is evidence of a new contract for a year on the same terms. (*Beeston* v. *Collyer*, 4 Bing. 309.) Under such circumstances it seems that a new contract arises each year, which is determined at the expiration of the year without notice. Where the parties contracted "for one whole year, and so from year to year, so long as the parties should respectively please," it was held that the contract could not be determined by notice not ending with the current year. (*Williams* v. *Byrne*, 7 A. & E. 177.) And in such case it would seem that reasonable notice is necessary to determine it at the end of the current year. (*Per* Littledale, J., *Ib.*, 182.) A schoolmaster was engaged at an annual salary so long as, by mutual consent, he should retain the office, the appointment to be subject to termination by three months' notice by either party; it was held that the notice might be given at any time. (*Ryan* v. *Jenkinson*, 25 L. J. Q. B. 11.)

A contract of service, "to be binding for twelve months certain,

of £——, became due from and payable by the defendant to the plaintiff for the work and services done and rendered by the plaintiff in the said employment during the period between the above-mentioned dates for the defendant at his request.

3. The defendant has not paid the said sum of £——, and the same remains due and payable to the plaintiff.

---

and continue from time to time, until three months' notice be given by either party to determine the same," was held determinable at the expiration of the first year by three months' previous notice. (*Brown* v. *Symons*, 8 C. B. N. S. 208; 29 L. J. C. P. 251.) And where the contract of service was "for twelve months certain, after which time either party should be at liberty to terminate the agreement by giving the other a three months' notice," it was held (Kelly, C. B., diss.) that at the close of the first twelve months the agreement could be determined by either party without any notice. (*Langton* v. *Carleton*, L. R. 9 Ex. 57.)

A contract of service for a term of more than a year is within s. 4 of the Statute of Frauds. (*Giraud* v. *Richmond*, 2 C. B. 835; *Dobson* v. *Collis*, 1 H. & N. 81; 25 L. J. Ex. 267.) So also is a contract for a year's service to commence at a future day. (*Bracegirdle* v. *Heald*, 1 B. & Ald. 722; *Snelling* v. *Lord Huntingfield*, 1 C. M. & R. 20, *Banks* v. *Crossland*, L. R. 10 Q. B. 97; 44 L. J. M. C. 8; Leake on Contracts, 255; Addison on Contracts, 7th ed., p. 155.) And it was held that such a contract made orally in France was not enforceable in this country, though valid by French law. (*Leroux* v. *Brown*, 12 C. B. 801.) A part performance of a contract of service does not operate to take the case out of the provisions of s. 4 of the Statute of Frauds, 29 Car. II. c. 3. (*Britain* v. *Rossiter*, 48 L. J. Ex. 362; 40 L. T. 240).

A person who enters into a service where the exercise of skilled labour is required impliedly warrants that he is possessed of the requisite skill for such service, and an action may be maintained against him for any breach of such warranty. (*Harmer* v. *Cornelius*, 5 C. B. N. S. 236; 28 L. J. C. P. 85.)

For instances of actions by an employer against his servant for breaches of contract, as for leaving the service before the term of service had expired, or for leaving it without notice, or for doing work under the contract negligently, see *Lees* v. *Whitcomb*, 5 Bing. 34; *Messiter* v. *Rose*, 13 C. B. 162; *Holmes* v. *Onion*, 2 C. B. N. S. 790; 26 L. J. C. P. 261.

Where a servant during the service, and in the course thereof, or in connection therewith, earns and receives money from third persons for work done by him for them, the master may maintain an action against the servant to recover the amount as money received to his use. (*Morison* v. *Thompson*, L. R. 9 Q. B. 480; and see *ante*, "*Agent*," p. 47.)

See the Employers and Workmen Act, 1875 (38 & 39 Vict. c. 90), enlarging the powers of county courts in respect of disputes between employers and workmen, and giving a limited civil jurisdiction in respect of such disputes to courts of summary jurisdiction.

The like for a Wrongful Dismissal.

1. In March, 1878, it was agreed [by letters] between the plaintiff and the defendant that the plaintiff should enter into the defendant's service on the 25th of March, 1878, and serve him for a year from that day [*or* until the service should be determined as hereinafter mentioned] in the capacity of a [foreman] at the wages of £2 per week, and that the defendant should receive and retain the plaintiff in the said service in the capacity and on the terms aforesaid during the said year [*or* until the expiration of a reasonable notice, to be given by the plaintiff or the defendant to the other of them to determine the said service].

2. The plaintiff on the said 25th of March, 1878, entered into the said service in the capacity and on the terms aforesaid, and so continued therein until the dismissal hereinafter mentioned, and was always ready and willing to continue in the said service during the remainder of the said year [*or* until the said service should be determined as aforesaid], whereof the defendant always had notice.

3. The defendant on the 5th of August, 1878, and before the expiration of the said year [*or* without any such notice having been given by either the plaintiff or the defendant to the other of them to determine the said service as aforesaid], dismissed the plaintiff from the said service, and refused to retain him therein for the remainder of the said year [*or* until the said service should be so determined as aforesaid].

4. By reason of the premises the plaintiff has lost the wages and advantages which he would have derived from the said service, and has remained unemployed for a long time, viz. —— months.

For a Form of Statement of Claim by Employer against Servant for Breach of Contract by Servant carrying on Business within a certain distance, see Davey v. *Shannon*, 4 Ex. D. 81; 48 L. J. Ex. 459.

MEDICAL ATTENDANCE (*a*).

Statement of Claim by a Surgeon and Apothecary for Medical Attendance and Medicines.

1. The plaintiff, between the —— of ——, 18—, and the —— of ——, 18—, rendered to the defendant at his

---

(*a*) The Medical Act, 21 & 22 Vict. c. 90 (amended by 22 Vict. c. 21; 23 & 24 Vict. c. 7, and 38 & 39 Vict. c. 66), enacts by s. 31 that every person registered under this Act shall be entitled, according to his qualification, to practise medicine or surgery, and to demand and recover in any court of law, with full costs of suit, reasonable charges for professionalaid, advice, and visits, and the cost of any medicines or other medical or surgical appliances rendered or supplied by him to his patients; provided always, that it shall be lawful for any college of physicians to pass a bye-law to the effect that no one of their fellows or members shall be entitled to sue in manner aforesaid in any court of law, and thereupon such bye-law may be pleaded in bar to any action for the purposes aforesaid commenced by any fellow or member of such college.

By s. 32 it is enacted that "no person shall be entitled to recover any charge in any court of law for any medical or surgical advice, attendance, or for the performance of any operation, or for any medicine, which he shall have both prescribed and supplied, unless he shall prove upon the trial that he is registered under this Act." By s. 27, a copy of the Register is made evidence.

The above section (32) applies not only in actions against the patients who have received the attendance, but also in actions against persons who are sued for the attendance received by others. (*De la Rosa* v. *Prieto*, 33 L. J. C. P. 262; 16 C. B. N. S. 578.) It applies to attendance given on board a foreign man-of-war in an English port. (*De la Rosa* v. *Prieto, supra.*) A medical practitioner engaged by another to attend his patients in his absence, cannot recover the price of his services without proof of registration. (*De la Rosa* v. *Prieto, supra.*) The plaintiff must be qualified and registered at the time he supplied the medicines he prescribed, and rendered the services sued for, in order to recover in the action. (*Leman* v. *Houseley*, L. R. 10 Q. B. 66; 44 L. J. Q. B. 22.)

It seems that if one partner of a firm can prove registration, the partners jointly may recover. (*Per* Erle, C. J., and Byles, J., in *Turner* v. *Reynall*, 14 C. B. N. S. 328; 32 L. J. C. P. 164, as to which case, see *Leman* v. *Houseley, supra.*)

Sec. 31, above, only entitles medical men to recover for services rendered or medicine prescribed and supplied according to their qualification; therefore, a practitioner whose qualification is to practise surgery *only*, cannot recover for attendance in a medical case (*Allison* v. *Haydon*, 4 Bing. 619; *Leman* v. *Fletcher*, L. R. 8 Q. B. 319; 42 L. J. Q. B. 214; see further, *Ellis* v. *Kelly*, 30 L. J. M. C. 35, 37), though for medicine administered as ancillary to a surgical case, such a practitioner might recover. (Roscoe's N. P. Ev. 14th ed., p. 463, and cases cited *supra.*)

Before the Act a physician by custom could not recover his fees in an action, without a special contract for payment. (*Chorley* v. *Bolcot*,

request [*or* to C. D. for and at the request of the defendant] professional aid, advice, and visits, as a surgeon and apothecary, and supplied to the defendant at his request [*or* to the said C. D. for and at the request of the defendant] medicines [and medical and surgical appliances].

2. The reasonable charges due and payable by the defendant to the plaintiff in respect thereof amount to the sum of £——.

3. The said charges have not been paid.

MONEY LENT (*a*).

Statement of Claim arising out of a simple Contract for the repayment of a Loan six months from the date of the making thereof.

1. On the —— of ——, 18—, the plaintiff lent to the

---

4 T. R. 317; *Veitch* v. *Russell*, 3 Q. B. 928; and see *Attorney-General* v. *College of Physicians*, 1 J. & H. 561; 30 L. J. Ch. 757.) Under the statute a physician duly registered may sue and recover without a special contract unless restrained by a bye-law. (*Gibbon* v. *Budd*, 2 H. & C. 92; 32 L. J. Ex. 182.) The Royal College of Physicians has passed a bye-law that "no Fellow of the College shall be entitled to sue for professional aid rendered by him." This bye-law does not extend to members. See 32 L. J. Ex. 182 n. (2).

By the Act for regulating the practice of apothecaries, 55 Geo. III. c. 194, s. 21, it is enacted that no apothecary shall be allowed to recover any charges claimed by him in any court of law, unless such apothecary shall prove on the trial that he has obtained a certificate to practise as an apothecary from the Master Wardens and Society of Apothecaries.

By s. 20, practising as an apothecary without having obtained a certificate (as above) is prohibited under a penalty of £20. See *Leman* v. *Fletcher*, *supra*, and *Leman* v. *Houseley*, *supra*.

Under the above statutes proof of registration, or certificate, as the case may be, is a condition precedent to recovery; but before the Judicature Acts it was not necessary that the fact of registration or of having obtained a certificate should be shown in the declaration, since the statutes merely required proof of the qualification as evidence at the trial, and this would appear still to be the case as to the statement of claim.

By the Dentists' Act, 1878 (41 & 42 Vict. c. 33), s. 5, after the 1st of August, 1879, "a person shall not be entitled to recover any fee or charge, in any court, for the performance of any dental operation, or for any dental attendance or advice, unless he is registered under this Act, or is a legally qualified medical practitioner."

(*a*) A debt arising out of a loan of money on a simple contract may be sued for in a form of the nature above set out, stating the facts according to the circumstances of the case.

defendant the sum of £——, upon the terms that the defendant should repay the said sum to the plaintiff within six months from the said —— of ——, 18—.

2. The said six months elapsed before the commencement of this action.

3. The defendant has not paid the said sum of £—— or any part thereof to the plaintiff.

The like on a Loan repayable at once (b).

1. On the —— of ——, 18—, the plaintiff lent to the defendant the sum of £——.

An I. O. U. alone will not support a claim for money lent, for though it is proof of money owing, it is no more proof of money lent than of goods sold or any other source of a debt. (*Fesenmayer* v. *Adcock*, 16 M. & W. 449.) Nor will a cheque of itself support this claim. (*Pearce* v. *Davis*, 1 M. & Rob. 365.) A loan may be recovered as a simple contract debt, though it has been secured by a mortgage, where the deed contains no covenant to repay. (*Yates* v. *Aston*, 4 Q. B. 182.) But where there is such a covenant, though a limited one, no other contract can be implied, and the action must be brought on the covenant. (*Mathew* v. *Blackmore*, 1 H. & N. 762; 26 L. J. Ex. 150; *Browne* v. *Price*, 4 C. B. N. S. 598; 27 L. J. C. P. 290). A covenant may be sometimes implied from a mere acknowledgment of the debt in the deed, so as to have the effect of merging the simple contract in the specialty; but if the deed has another object, then a covenant will not be implied from that acknowledgment. (*Courtney* v. *Taylor*, 6 M. & G. 851; *Marryat* v. *Marryat*, 28 Beav. 224; 29 L. J. Ch. 665; *Jackson* v. *N. E. Ry. Co.*, 7 Ch. D. 573; *Isaacson* v. *Harwood*, L. R. 3 Ch. Ap. 225; 37 L. J. Ch. 209.) See also Leake on Contracts, 235, 937. Money lent for an illegal purpose, or for an immoral purpose, cannot be recovered. (*Cannan* v. *Bryce*, 3 B. & Ald. 179; *McKinnell* v. *Robinson*, 3 M. &. W. 434; *Pearce* v. *Brooks*, L. R. 1 Ex. 213; 35 L. J. Ex. 134; 4 H. & C. 358.) A bet being merely a void and not an illegal contract, money lent for the purpose of paying bets lost by the defendant to others than the plaintiff may be recovered. (*Hill* v. *Fox*, 4 H. & N. 359.)

(*b*) Where money is lent without any stipulation as to the time of repayment a present debt is created, which is in general repayable at once without any demand (*Birks* v. *Trippet*, 1 Wms. Saund. 1871 ed. p. 38; see also *Norton* v. *Ellam*, 2 M. & W. 464; and *per* Parke, B. in *Walton* v. *Mascall*, 13 M. & W. 458; see also *Kington* v. *Kington*, 11 M. & W. 235; *Waters* v. *Thanet*, 2 Q. B. 757); but if at the time of the making of the loan there was an express stipulation that the repayment should be conditional upon the making of a request, then a request must be made before action, and should be alleged in the statement of claim.

2. The said sum was due from and payable by the defendant to the plaintiff at the commencement of this action.

3. The defendant has not paid the same or any part thereof.

For a Form of Statement of Claim for Money lent on Mortgage, see "Mortgage," post, p. 290.

For a Form for Money lent and Accounts stated, see Meyerhoff v. *Froehlich,* 3 C. P. D. 333.

Money Paid (*a*).

(*a*) An action to recover money paid is maintainable where there has been a payment of money by the plaintiff to a third party at the request or by the authority of the defendant, express or implied, with an undertaking, express or implied, to repay it. (*Brittain* v. *Lloyd,* 14 M. & W. 762; *Lewis* v. *Campbell,* 8 C. B. 541; *Hutchinson* v. *Sydney,* 10 Ex. 438.)

There must be actual payment, or what is equivalent to it (*Power* v. *Butcher,* 10 B. & C. 329, 346), of money of the plaintiff which he is entitled to be repaid. (*Goepel* v. *Swinden,* 1 D. & L. 888.) Giving a note, which is accepted as payment, is equivalent to money paid. (*Barclay* v. *Gooch,* 2 Esp. 571.) Executing a covenant to pay is not equivalent to payment of money (*Power* v. *Butcher,* 10 B. & C. 329); nor is the extinguishment of a debt by giving a new security. (*Taylor* v. *Higgins,* 3 East, 169; *Maxwell* v. *Jameson,* 2 B. & Ald. 51.) It has been held that the proceeds of goods sold as a distress for rent cannot be treated as money paid by the party distrained upon (*Moore* v. *Pyrke,* 11 East, 52). As to money levied by sale of goods under a *fi. fa.*, see *Rodgers* v. *Maw,* 15 M. & W. 444.

The payment must be at the request or by the authority of the defendant; a voluntary payment without request or authority is not sufficient. (*Stokes* v. *Lewis,* 1 T. R. 20; *per* Lord Kenyon, C.J., *Exall* v. *Partridge,* 8 T. R. 308, 310; and see *Pownal* v. *Ferrand,* 6 B. & C. 439.) A request or authority may be implied by the general course of dealing, or by the nature of the particular transaction; thus a person who employs a broker on the Stock Exchange, impliedly authorizes the latter to pay money for him according to the rules of the Stock Exchange (*Sutton* v. *Tatham,* 10 A. & E. 27; *Pawle* v. *Gunn,* 4 Bing. N. C. 445; *Westropp* v. *Solomon,* 8 C. B. 345; *Taylor* v. *Stray,* 2 C. B. N. S. 175; 26 L. J. C. P. 185, 287; *Smith* v. *Lindo,* 5 C. B. N. S. 587; 27 L. J. C. P. 335; *Whitehead* v. *Izod,* L. R. 2 C. P. 228; 36 L. J. C. P. 113; *Mollett* v. *Robinson,* L. R. 7 H. L. 836); but not to pay money in respect of a liability which has been incurred by the broker's own default. (*Duncan* v. *Hill*, L. R. 8 Ex. 242; 42 L. J. Ex. 179.) A request will generally be implied where the defendant has notice of the payment being made for him, and does not dissent. (*Paynter* v. *Williams*, 1 C. & M. 810; *Alexander* v. *Vane*, 1 M. & W. 511.) So where a payment has been compelled through the wrongful act of the defendant, of which he gets the benefit; as where an acceptance of the plaintiff was wrongfully indorsed by the defendant. (*Bleaden* v. *Charles*, 7 Bing. 246.) Where an insolvent, having made a composition with his creditors, gave acceptances to the defendant, being one of his creditors, for a larger amount than his composition, in fraud of the other creditors, and was afterwards compelled to pay the acceptances in the hands of third parties, he was held entitled to recover the amount from the defendant as money paid to his use. (*Bradshaw* v. *Bradshaw*, 9 M. & W. 29; and see *Smith* v. *Cuff*, 6 M. & S. 160; *Horton* v. *Riley*, 11 M. & W. 492.)

A request or authority will be implied where the plaintiff has been legally compelled to pay, or, being legally compellable to pay, has paid, a debt or claim for which the defendant is liable (*per* Tindal, C.J., *Grissell* v. *Robinson*, 3 Bing. N. C. 10, 15; *Jefferys* v. *Gurr*, 2 B. & Ad. 833; *per* Cockburn, C.J., in *Moule* v. *Garrett*, L. R. 7 Ex. 104; 41 L. J. Ex. 64; Leake on Contracts, 77); as where an executor has paid the legacy duty for which the legatee was liable (*Foster* v. *Ley*, 2 Bing. N. C. 269; *Bate* v. *Payne*, 13 Q. B. 900); where the indorser of a bill was made to pay the defendant's acceptance (*Pownal* v. *Ferrand*, 6 B. & C. 439; and see *Sleigh* v. *Sleigh*, 5 Ex. 514); and where the plaintiff, an auctioneer, was compelled to pay the auction duty upon the sale of an estate which he sold for the defendant. (*Brittain* v. *Lloyd*, 14 M. & W. 762.)

Where a surety pays the debt of the principal debtor he may recover it as money paid for the use of such debtor; so where one of several co-contractors (not being partners) pays the whole debt for which the other co-contractors are jointly liable with him, he may sue each co-contractor or the representatives of such as are deceased for contribution in this form. (*Edger* v. *Knapp*, 5 M. & G. 753; *Kemp* v. *Finden*, 12 M. & W. 421; *Batard* v. *Hawes*, 2 E. & B. 287; *Dering* v. *Earl of Winchelsea*, 1 Cox, 318; 1 White & Tudor, L. C. 5th ed., p. 106; and see *Ellis* v. *Emmanuel*, 1 Ex. D. 157; 46 L. J. Ex. 25.) A surety has no claim against his co-sureties until he has paid more than his share of the debt due to the creditor, whilst such co-sureties remain liable to the creditor for the unpaid portion of the debt. (*Ex parte Snowdon*, 17 Ch. D. 44; 50 L. J. Ch. 540.) Where the plaintiff drew and the defendant indorsed a bill as co-sureties for the acceptor, the plaintiff, having paid it, was held entitled to recover contribution. (*Reynolds* v. *Wheeler*, 30 L. J. C. P. 350; 10 C. B. N. S. 561.) But one of two joint wrong-doers having been compelled to pay the whole damage cannot recover a moiety against the other. (*Merryweather* v. *Nixan*, 8 T. R. 186; and see *Shackell* v. *Rosier*, 2 Bing. N. C. 634, 648; and see as to where one wrong-doer can recover against the other upon a promise of indemnity given or implied, *Adamson* v. *Jarvis*, 4 Bing. 66; *Betts* v. *Gibbins*, 2 A. & E. 57; *Toplis* v. *Grane*, 5 Bing. N. C. 650; *Dugdale* v. *Lovering*, L. R. 10 C. P. 196; 44 L. J. C. P. 197.)

Where the plaintiff has been compelled, under a distress or threat of a distress to which he was liable, to pay the rent of the defendant's premises, he may recover the amount from the defendant (*Exall* v. *Partridge*, 8 T. R. 308; and see *Moore* v. *Pyrke*, 11 East, 52; *Rodgers* v. *Maw*, 15 M. & W. 444, 448; *Graham* v. *Allsopp*, 3 Ex. 186; *Johnson* v. *Skafte*, L. R. 4 Q. B., *per* Lush, J., p. 705; 38 L. J. Q. B. 318); but where the plaintiff voluntarily, and without any request from the defendant, placed his goods on the defendant's premises, and he was obliged to pay the defendant's rent to redeem them from a distress, it was held that he could not recover the amount, because the payment was caused by his own voluntary act. (*England* v. *Marsden*, L. R. 1 C. P. 529; 35 L. J. C. P. 259; but see *Ex pte. Bishop*, 15 Ch. D. 400, 417; 50 L. J. Ch. 18.) Where the plaintiff's goods standing on the defendant's land were seized for tithe rent-charge, the plaintiff could not recover, because the rent was charged on the land only, and was not a personal liability of the defendant. (*Griffinhoofe* v. *Daubuz*, 5 E. & B. 746; 25 L. J. Q. B. 237.) So where the plaintiff and the defendant were under-lessees at separate rents of separate portions of premises, the whole of which were held at an entire rent under one lease, the plaintiff having been compelled to pay the whole rent under threat of distress, was held not entitled to recover a portion from the defendant as money paid to his use. (*Hunter* v. *Hunt*, 1 C. B. 300.) Where the defendant is not liable to any one but the plaintiff himself, so that the payment by the plaintiff does not exonerate the defendant from any liability, the plaintiff, having been compelled to pay, can sue the defendant only on the original agreement between them which created the liability, as there is no contract implied in law independently of such agreement. As where a tenant had agreed with his landlord to pay certain taxes for which the landlord only was liable, but having failed to pay them, the landlord was compelled to do so, the landlord could not sue for money paid. (*Spencer* v. *Parry*, 3 A. & E. 331; and see *Lubbock* v. *Tribe*, 3 M. & W. 607.)

Money paid by the plaintiff against the payment of which the defendant had agreed to indemnify him is, in general, equivalent to a payment made at the request of the defendant (*Lewis* v. *Campbell*, 8 C. B. 541; *Hawley* v. *Beverley*, 6 M. & G. 221; *Moule* v. *Garrett*, L. R. 5 Ex. 132; 7 *Ib.* 101; 39 L. J. Ex. 69; 41 *Ib.* 62); as where an accommodation acceptor, drawer, or indorser is obliged to pay the amount of the bill to the holder, this is money paid for the use of the person accommodated (see "*Indemnities*," *ante*, p. 211); and where the plaintiff defended an action upon an accommodation acceptance at the request of the defendant, for whose accommodation he had given the acceptance, he was allowed to recover the costs of the action as money paid to the defendant's use. (*Garrard* v. *Cottrell*, 10 Q. B. 679; and see *Sleigh* v. *Sleigh*, 5 Ex. 514.)

The defendant cannot avoid the effect of his request by showing that the payment was requested and made in execution of a void contract, as on account of a wager lost by him (*Jessop* v. *Lutwyche*, 10 Ex. 614; 24 L. J. Ex. 65; *Knight* v. *Cambers*, 15 C. B. 562; 24 L. J. C. P. 121; *Rosewarne* v. *Billing*, 15 C. B. N. S. 316; 33 L. J. C. P. 55; *Thacker* v. *Hardy*, 4 Q. B. D. 685; 48 L. J. Q. B. 289); but he may avoid it by showing that the payment was requested and made for an illegal purpose; or in execution of an illegal contract. (*Ib. Mortimer* v. *Gell*, 4 C. B. 543.) See further "*Indemnities*," *ante*, p. 211, *note* (*a*).

Statement of Claim for Money Paid by the Plaintiff at the express request of the Defendant (*b*).

1. On the —— of ——, 18—, the plaintiff paid for the defendant, and at his request the sum of £—— to C. D.

2. The defendant has not repaid the said sum to the plaintiff, and the same is now due from and payable by the defendant to the plaintiff.

The like upon an implied request for Money Paid by a Contractor by deed for a co-Contractor.

1. The plaintiff and the defendant were at the time of the making of the indenture hereinafter mentioned possessed for a term of 99 years, commencing the 25th of March, 1864, of a house and premises known as No. ——, Russell Square, in the County of Middlesex.

2. By an indenture, dated the 1st of January, 1879, and made between the plaintiff and the defendant of the one part, and E. F. of the other part, the said house and premises were assigned to the said E. F. by way of mortgage to secure the repayment of the sum of £500 advanced to the plaintiff and the defendant by the said E. F. with interest thereon at the rate of £5 per cent. per annum, and the plaintiff and the defendant and each of them did by the said indenture for themselves, and as separate covenants each of them did thereby for himself, covenant with the said E. F. to repay to the said E. F. the said sum of £500 on or before the 1st of January, 1880, together with interest thereon in the meantime at the rate aforesaid.

3. On the 5th January, 1880, the said sum of £500 and the said interest thereon being still unpaid to the said E. F. the said E. F. gave notice to the plaintiff and the defendant to pay the same to him forthwith (*c*).

(*b*) Wherever a payment of money has been made for the defendant at his express request, it is sufficient to state the fact of such payment having been made, and the date and amount of such payment, and the person to whom it was made, as in the form first given above. If, however, there was no request in fact, and a request is to be implied merely from the circumstances of the case, then the plaintiff should state all the material facts which give rise to the implication of law, as in the form secondly given above. (O. XIX. rr. 4, 27.)

(*c*) Though a notice requiring payment may be alleged to have been given where such is the fact, such notice is, in general, unnecessary, as it is enough if the plaintiff was under a legal obligation to pay.

4. The defendant did not pay the same or any part thereof, and thereupon the plaintiff, before the commencement of this action, paid the said E. F. the said sum of £500 and £25, which was the amount of interest then due thereon to the said E. F. under and by virtue of the said indenture.

5. The defendant has not paid any part of either of the said last mentioned sums to the plaintiff.

Money Received (*a*).

Statement of Claim for Money Received for the Use of the Plaintiff.

1. The defendant received for the use of the plaintiff the sum of £——.

(*a*) Whenever a person has received money which in justice and equity belongs to another, under circumstances which render the receipt of it a receipt by such person to the use of such other, a debt is created which is recoverable by action. (*Per* Lord Mansfield, C. J., *Moses* v. *Macferlan*, 2 Burr. 1005; and see *Marriott* v. *Hampton*, 2 Smith's L. C. 8th ed. 421.)

See as to the former and present systems of pleading, "*Debts in General*," *ante*, p. 32.

If a cheque (*Spratt* v. *Hobhouse*, 4 Bing. 173), foreign money (*Ehrensperger* v. *Anderson*, 3 Ex. 148), a country bank note (*Pickard* v. *Bankes*, 13 East, 20), or the like, has been received by the defendant as money it may be treated as money.

The following cases afford examples of circumstances under which such debt is implied.

Where a sheriff in execution of and under a writ of *fi. fa.* has received money, the execution creditor is entitled to recover it from the sheriff (*Dale* v. *Birch*, 3 Camp. 347; *Longdill* v. *Jones*, 1 Stark. 345; and see *Jefferies* v. *Sheppard*, 3 B. & Ald. 696); so also he may recover the proceeds of the goods seized and sold. (*Swain* v. *Morland*, 1 B. & B. 370). Where the defendant has received *fees* pertaining to an office, asserting his right to the fees or to the office, the plaintiff being the person really entitled to the office and the fees, may recover the amount actually received. (*King* v. *Alston*, 12 Q. B. 971; *Spry* v. *Emperor*, 6 M. & W. 639; *Roberts* v. *Aulton*, 2 H. & N. 432; 26 L. J. Ex. 380; *Pinder* v. *Barr*, 4 E. & B. 105.) So where an agent has received money from his principal under a revocable authority to dispose of it in a particular manner, the principal, if he revokes the authority before it has been acted upon, may recover the money. (*Taylor* v. *Lendey*, 9 East, 49; *Parry* v. *Roberts*, 3 A. & E. 118; *Fletcher* v. *Marshall*, 15 M. & W. 755.) But so long as the authority remains unrevoked, the form of action for any non-compliance with instructions must be for a breach of such instructions (*Ehrensperger* v. *Anderson*, 3 Ex. 148; and see *Duncan* v. *Skip-*

2. The circumstances under which the defendant so received the same were as follows : [*set forth same, as for*

---

with, 2 Camp. 68 ; *Miller* v. *Atlee*, 3 Ex. 799, 801 ; *Hardman* v. *Bellhouse*, 9 M. & W. 596) ; unless such breach amounts to a repudiation of the agency, or a total refusal by the agent to dispose of the money according to his instructions, in which cases the principal may also recover back the money. (*Scott* v. *Surman*, Willes, 400, 404 ; *Thorpe* v. *Thorpe*, 3 B. & Ad. 580 ; *Buchanan* v. *Findlay*, 9 B. & C. 738 ; *Ehrensperger* v. *Anderson*, 3 Ex. 148, 158.)

Where money has been paid by the plaintiff to get rid of *duress* to the person of the plaintiff, or to his goods, the money may be recovered back (*Astley* v. *Reynolds*, 2 Str. 915 ; *Shaw* v. *Woodcock*, 7 B. & C. 73 ; *Skeate* v. *Beale*, 11 A. & E. 983 ; *Atlee* v. *Backhouse*, 3 M. & W. 633 ; *Tamvaco* v. *Simpson*, 19 C. B. N. S. 453 ; 34 L. J. C. P. 268 ; *Wakefield* v. *Newbon*, 6 Q. B. 276 ; *Pratt* v. *Vizard*, 5 B. & Ad. 808 ; *Oates* v. *Hudson*, 6 Ex. 346) ; so also where a mortgagor has paid money to a mortgagee beyond what is justly due to prevent a threatened sale (*Close* v. *Phipps*, 7 M. & G. 586) ; or to obtain a transfer or assignment of the mortgage (*Fraser* v. *Pendlebury*, 31 L. J. C. P. 1) ; so also money may be recovered which has been exacted by other kinds of oppression or extortion (*Smith* v. *Cuff*, 6 M. & S. 160 ; *Valpy* v. *Manley*, 1 C. B. 594 ; *Scarfe* v. *Hallifax*, 7 M. & W. 288 ; *Smith* v. *Sleap*, 12 M. & W. 585 ; *Smith* v. *Bromley*, 2 Doug. 696 *n.* ; *Williams* v. *Hedley*, 8 East, 378) ; or by abuse of legal process (*Duke de Cadaval* v. *Collins*, 4 A. & E. 858). But money paid under the compulsion of legal process cannot in general be recovered in an action so long as the process remains ; the remedy is by application to the Court to set aside the process. (*De Medina* v. *Grove*, 10 Q. B. 152 ; *Pitt* v. *Coomes*, 2 A. & E. 459 ; *Payne* v. *Chapman*, 4 A. & E. 364 ; *Huffer* v. *Allen*, L. R. 2 Ex. 15 ; 36 L. J. Ex. 17.) So, money paid under a distress cannot be recovered back as a debt, but the plaintiff must replevy, or bring an action for the wrongful distress. (*Lindon* v. *Hooper*, 1 Cowp. 414 ; *Gulliver* v. *Cosens*, 1 C. B. 788 ; *Glynn* v. *Thomas*, 11 Ex. 870 ; 25 L. J. Ex. 125 ; *Loring* v. *Warburton*, E. B. & E. 507 ; 28 L. J. Q. B. 31.)

Money paid by the plaintiff in discharge of a demand illegally made under colour of an office may be recovered back as a debt (*Morgan* v. *Palmer*, 2 B. & C. 729 ; *Steele* v. *Williams*, 8 Ex. 625) ; as excessive fees paid to the steward of a manor for admission to copyholds (*Traherne* v. *Gardner*, 5 E. & B. 913 ; 25 L. J. Q. B. 201) ; excessive fees paid to a broker under a distress (*Hills* v. *Street*, 5 Bing. 37) ; overcharges paid to a carrier to induce him to carry goods (*Ashmole* v. *Wainwright*, 2 Q. B. 837) ; payments extorted by a railway company in contravention of their statutory obligations (*Gt. W. Ry. Co.* v. *Sutton*, L. R. 4 H. L. 226 ; 38 L. J. Ex. 177 ; and *per* Lord Chelmsford in *L. & Y. Ry.* v. *Gidlow*, L. R. 7 H. L. 527 ; *Evershed* v. *L. & N. W. Ry.* 2 Q. B. D. 254 ; 46 L. J. Q. B. 289 ; 3 Q. B. D. 134 ; 47 L. J. Q. B. 284 ; 3 App. Cas. 1029 ; 48 L. J. H. L. 22 ; and see *ante* "*Carriers*," p. 132) ; an excessive charge paid to an arbitrator to take up his award (*Re Coombs*, 4 Ex. 839 ; *Barnes* v. *Braithwaite*, 2 H. & N. 569) ; money improperly exacted as a toll at a turnpike. (*Waterhouse* v. *Keen*, 4 B. & C. 200 ; and see *Lewis* v. *Hammond*, 2 B. & Ald. 206.)

instance] The defendant was the collector and agent of the plaintiff, and received the said sum on the ——

Money recovered in an action which the defendant might have successfully defended cannot be recovered back (*Marriott* v. *Hampton*, 7 T. R. 269; 2 Smith's L. C. 8th ed. 421; *Hamlet* v. *Richardson*, 9 Bing. 644; *Duke de Cadaval* v. *Collins*, 4 A. & E. 858; *De Medina* v. *Grove*, 10 Q. B. 152); nor can money paid voluntarily, and with a full knowledge of all the facts, to satisfy a claim which the plaintiff could have successfully resisted. (*Spragg* v. *Hammond*, 2 B. & B. 59; *Bilbie* v. *Lumley*, 2 East, 469; *Denby* v. *Moore*, 1 B. & Ald. 123; *Wilson* v. *Ray*, 10 A. & E. 82; *Barber* v. *Pott*, 4 H. & N. 759; 28 L. J. Ex. 381; *Rogers* v. *Ingham*, L. R. 3 Ch. D. 351; *Freeman* v. *Jeffries*, L. R. 4 Ex. 189; 38 L. J. Ex. 116.)

Money paid by reason of ignorance or mistake of fact, or by reason of an excusable forgetfulness of fact, may be recovered back (*Bize* v. *Dickason*, 1 T. R. 285; *Milnes* v. *Duncan*, 6 B. & C. 671; *Kelly* v. *Solari*, 9 M. & W. 54; *Mills* v. *Alderbury Union*, 3 Ex. 590; *Aiken* v. *Short*, 1 H. & N. 210; 25 L. J. Ex. 321; *Durrant* v. *The Ecc. Com.*, 6 Q. B. D. 234; 50 L. J. Ex. 30); as where a tenant under a landlord who held *pur autre vie* paid rent in ignorance that the life had dropped (*Barber* v. *Brown*, 1 C. B. N. S. 121; 26 L. J. C. P. 41); where an excess of price was paid for a bar of silver sold by weight, upon an erroneous calculation of the weight (*Cox* v. *Prentice*, 3 M. & S. 344); where a like excess was paid upon a wrong calculation of price (*Nevall* v. *Tomlinson*, L. R. 6 C. P. 405); and where one partner purchased another's share in the partnership, for a price dependent upon the amount of the profits, and paid the other more than he was entitled to under a mistake in the calculation of them. (*Townsend* v. *Crowdy*, 8 C. B. N. S. 477; 29 L. J. C. P. 300.) A sheriff who seized goods in excution and paid over the proceeds to the judgment creditor in ignorance of the fact of a previous act of bankruptcy of the judgment debtor, and who was subsequently compelled to pay the amount to the assignees of the bankrupt, was held entitled to recover the proceeds paid to the judgment creditor. (*Standish* v. *Ross*, 3 Ex. 527.)

Where money is paid under a supposed obligation to pay it, and in forgetfulness of a fact which put an end to the obligation, it may be recovered back, as when an insurance office paid the amount of a life policy in forgetfulness of a default which had previously caused the policy to lapse (*Kelly* v. *Solari*, 9 M. & W. 54); but if the money is paid intentionally, without reference to the truth or falsehood of the fact, the plaintiff meaning to waive all inquiry into it, it is a voluntary payment, and cannot be recovered. (*Per* Parke, B., in *Kelly* v. *Solari*, *supra*.) The right to recover money paid under a mistake of fact must have reference to a belief in the existence of a fact which, if true, would have given the person receiving a right against the person paying the money (*per* Bramwell, B., in *Aiken* v. *Short*, 1 H. & N. 210; 25 L. J. Ex. 321.) Upon this principle a banker who pays to a third party the amount of the cheque of his customer, in the mistaken belief that such customer has assets in the bank sufficient to meet such cheque, cannot recover the money so paid from such third party. (*Chambers* v. *Miller*, 13 C. B. N. S. 125; 32 L. J. C. P. 30; and see *Pollard* v. *Bank of England*, L.

of ——, 18—, from one A. B., a debtor of the plaintiff, in payment of a debt of the said A. B. to the plaintiff, as and being such collector and agent as aforesaid.

R. 6 Q. B. 623; 40 L. J. Q. B. 233.) A voluntary gift made under a mistake cannot be recovered back. (*Aiken* v. *Short*, *supra*; *Wilson* v. *Thornbury*, L. R. 10 Ch. Ap. 239.) If the defendant had no notice of the mistake, such notice should in general be given him, and a demand of the money made before action. (*Freeman* v. *Jeffries*, L. R. 4 Ex. 189; 38 L. J. Ex. 116; *per* Parke, B., in *Kelly* v. *Solari*, *supra*.)

Where money is paid voluntarily with a knowledge of the facts, it is not ground for recovering it back that it was paid under a mistake as to, or in ignorance, of the law. (*Bilbie* v. *Lumley*, 2 East, 469; *Stevens* v. *Lynch*, 12 East, 38; *Rogers* v. *Ingham*, 3 Ch. D. 351; *Denby* v. *Moore*, 1 B. & Ald. 123; and see *Ex parte James*, L. R. 9 Ch. Ap. 609; 43 L. J. B. 107.)

Money that has been paid for a consideration that has failed may be recovered. (See *post*, note, (*c*), p. 286.)

Money that has been obtained wrongfully or by fraud may be in general recovered.

Thus, where money was obtained by false pretences from the plaintiff (*Holt* v. *Ely*, 1 E. & B. 795; *Edmeads* v. *Newman*, 1 B. & C. 418; *Martin* v. *Morgan*, 1 B. & B. 289); so where a plaintiff has been induced by fraudulent misrepresentations contained in a prospectus of a company to take and pay for shares in the company he may, before the rights of other persons intervene, avoid his contract as a shareholder upon the discovery of the fraud, and recover back the money paid (*Oakes* v. *Turquand*, L. R. 2 H. L. 325; 36 L. J. Ch. 949); unless the company is then being wound up, in which case he is too late to avoid the contract. (*Stone* v. *City and County Bank*, 3 C. P. D. 282; 47 L. J. C. P. 681; *Collins* v. *City and County Bank* (*ib.*); *Tennent* v. *City of Glasgow Bank*, 4 App. Cas. 615.)

In general where a party is entitled to rescind a contract on the ground of fraud, he may recover back the money he has paid under the contract. (See Leake on Contracts, 90.)

So, money stolen may be treated as a debt, it would seem, and be recovered back. (*Chowne* v. *Baylis*, 8 Jur. N. S. 1028; 31 L. J. Ch. 757; *Wells* v. *Abrahams*, L. R. 7 Q. B. 554; 41 L. J. Q. B. 306.)

Where the plaintiff's goods have been wrongfully obtained and converted into money by the defendant, the plaintiff may waive the wrong and recover the proceeds. (See *post*, note (*b*), p. 285.)

Where the plaintiff has paid money to the defendant upon an *illegal executory contract*, or for a future *illegal object*, there is a *locus pœnitentiæ*, and the plaintiff may, before the contract is executed, or the object accomplished, recover back the money, (*Per* Buller, J., *Lowry* v. *Bourdieu*, 2 Doug. 468; *Jaques* v. *Withy*, 1 H. Bl. 65; *Taylor* v. *Lendey*, 9 East, 49; *Tappenden* v. *Randall*, 2 B. & P. 467; *Bone* v. *Ekless*, 5 H. & N. 925; 29 L. J. Ex. 438.) He must give notice that he demands the money before action. (*Palyart* v. *Leckie*, 6 M. & S. 290; *Savage* v. *Madder*, 36 L. J. Ex. 178; *Busk* v. *Walsh*, 4 Taunt. 290.) Money in the hands of a stakeholder deposited upon a void or illegal wager may be recovered back before it has been paid over. (*Busk* v. *Walsh*, *supra*; *Cotton* v. *Thurland*, 5 T. R. 405;

3. The defendant did not pay the said sum to the plaintiff, and the same is now due and payable by the defendant to the plaintiff.

Gatty v. *Field*, 9 Q. B. 431 ; *Martin* v. *Hewson*, 10 Ex. 737 ; 24 L. J. Ex. 174 ; *Varney* v. *Hickman*, 5 C. B. 271 ; 17 L. J. C. P. 102 ; *Hastelow* v. *Jackson*, 8 B. & C. 221 ; *Hodson* v. *Terrill*, 1 C. & M. 797 ; *Savage* v. *Madder*, *supra* ; *Batson* v. *Newman*, 1 C. P. D. 573 ; *Hampden* v. *Walsh*. 1 Q. B. D. 189 ; 45 L. J. Q. B. 238 ; *Diggle* v. *Higgs*, 2 Ex. D. 422 ; 46 L. J. Ex. 721 ; *Trimble* v. *Hill*, 5 App. Cas. 342 ; 49 L. J. C. P. 49.) After the illegal or void contract or purpose has been executed, the money paid cannot, in general, be recovered. (*Lowry* v. *Bourdieu*, 2 Doug. 468 ; *Andree* v. *Fletcher*, 3 T. R. 266 ; *Thistlewood* v. *Cracroft*, 1 M. & S. 500 : *Wilson* v. *Ray*, 10 A. & E. 82 ; *Howson* v. *Hancock*, 8 T. R. 575 ; *Begbie* v. *Phosphate Sewage Co.*, 1 Q. B. D. 679 ; 44 L. J. Q. B. 233 ; *Re Mapleback*, 4 Ch. D. 150 ; 46 L. J. B. 14.) There are, however, some cases where money paid in execution of, or as the consideration for, an illegal agreement, or purpose, may be recovered back, though the agreement or purpose has been executed, where the party paying is not *in pari delicto* with the party receiving, but is in such a position as to have been subject, or liable, to oppression, or imposition, at the hands of the other party to the transaction, as, for instance, money paid by a bankrupt to obtain his certificate (*Smith* v. *Bromley*, 2 Doug. 696 n.), money paid to compromise a penal action in defiance of the statute (*Williams* v. *Hedley*, 8 East, 378 ; *Unwin* v. *Leaper*, 1 M. & G. 747), money paid by a debtor compounding with his creditors to a creditor in excess of the composition to obtain his consent to the composition (*Atkinson* v. *Denby*, 6 H. & N. 778 ; 7 H. & N. 934 ; 30 L. J. Ex. 361 ; 31 L. J. Ex. 362 ; *Smith* v. *Cuff*, 6 M. & S. 160.)

Although the plaintiff cannot enforce an illegal or void contract, yet if money has been paid to his agent in execution of such contract he may recover it. (*Tenant* v. *Elliott*, 1 B. & P. 3 ; *Farmer* v. *Russell*, 1 B. & P. 296 ; *Bousfield* v. *Wilson*, 16 M. & W. 185 ; *Nicholson* v. *Gooch*, 5 E. & B. 999 ; 25 L. J. Q. B. 137 ; *Johnson* v. *Lansley*, 12 C. B. 468 ; *Sharp* v. *Taylor*, 2 Phill. 801 ; and see *Beeston* v. *Beeston*, 1 Ex. D. 13 ; 45 L. J. Ex. 230.)

Money paid under a compromise of a *bonâ fide*, though possibly mistaken, claim cannot be recovered back. (*Atlee* v. *Backhouse*, 3 M. & W. 633 ; *Callisher* v. *Bischoffsheim*, L. R. 5 Q. B. 449 ; 39 L. J. Q. B. 181, and see *Ex parte* Banner, 17 Ch. D. 480.)

Where the defendant has received the plaintiff's money from a third party, *bonâ fide*, and under a binding contract, he is not in general accountable to the plaintiff. (*Calland* v. *Lloyd*, 6 M. & W. 26 ; *Foster* v. *Green*, 7 H. & N. 881 ; 31 L. J. Ex. 159 ; *Atlee* v. *Backhouse*, *supra*.)

As to money received by an agent, see *post*, *note* (*d*) p. 288 ; and see "*Agent*," *ante*, pp. 39, 47.

As to the recovery by the assignee of debts assigned to him, see "*Assignment*," *ante*, p. 59.

Against a Servant who has wrongfully sold his Master's Goods and has kept the proceeds of the Sale, the Master waiving the Tort and claiming the Proceeds as Money Received for his Use (*b*).

1. The defendant was at the time hereinafter mentioned the bailiff of the plaintiff, and in that capacity had the care and management of certain property of the plaintiff, including a horse called ——.

2. On the —— of ——, 18—, the defendant without the knowledge or consent of the plaintiff, wrongfully sold the said horse.

3. The defendant received £—— as the proceeds of the sale of the said horse.

4. The defendant has not accounted for, or paid over the said £—— to the plaintiff.

The plaintiff claims the said £—— as money received by the defendant for the plaintiff's use.

(*b*) Where the plaintiff's goods have been wrongfully obtained by the defendant and converted into money the plaintiff may waive the wrong and follow the proceeds as money received for his use. (*Lamine* v. *Dorrell*, 2 Ld. Raym. 1216; *Oughton* v. *Seppings*, 1 B. & Ad. 241; *Neate* v. *Harding*, 6 Ex. 349; *Marsh* v. *Keating*, 1 Bing. N. C. 215; *Rodgers* v. *Maw*, 15 M. & W. 448.) So, where the plaintiff's stock was sold by a member of the defendant's firm under a forged power of attorney and the price paid to the firm, the price was thus recovered (*Marsh* v. *Keating*, *supra*); so, if the defendant wrongfully, having no title thereto, converts to his own use a cheque, bill, or other security of the plaintiff. (*Down* v. *Halling*, 4 B. & C. 330; *Symonds* v. *Atkinson*, 1 H. & N. 146; 25 L. J. Ex. 313; *Bobbett* v. *Pinkett*, 1 Ex. D. 368; 45 L. J. Ex. 555.)

So where coal has been wrongfully got by an adjoining owner the true owner may recover the proceeds. (*Powell* v. *Rees*, 7 A. & E. 426; *Jegon* v. *Vivian*, L. R. 6 Ch. Ap. 742; 40 L. J. Ch. 389.)

In cases where the plaintiff waives the wrong in order to claim his money or the proceeds of his goods which have been wrongfully obtained, he thereby precludes himself from claiming any damages for the wrong done. Thus, he cannot claim the proceeds of goods wrongfully sold by the defendant as a debt, and also claim damages in respect of the injurious nature of the act. (*Brewer* v. *Sparrow*, 7 B. & C. 310; and see *Valpy* v. *Sanders*, 5 C. B. 886; *Smith* v. *Baker*, L. R. 8 C. P. 350; 42 L. J. C. P. 155; *per* Bovill, C.J.) Nor can he waive the wrong in part only; so that, having accepted from the defendant part of the price of goods which had been wrongfully sold by the latter, he is bound to treat the balance also as a debt. (*Lythgoe* v. *Vernon*, 5 H. & N. 180; 29 L. J. Ex. 164.)

For a Form of Claim for Wrongful Conversion of a Cheque of the Plaintiff with an Alternative Claim for the Proceeds, see Matthiessen v. *The London and County Bank,* 5 C. P. D. 748, L. J. C. P. 529.

For the return of a Premium paid on a Policy upon Goods which were never in fact placed on Board (*c*).

1. The defendant is an underwriter, carrying on business at ——.

(*c*) Money paid by the plaintiff for a consideration that has failed may be thus recovered (see *Straton* v. *Rastall*, 2 T. R. 366, 369, 370); as, money given for forged railway scrip (*Westropp* v. *Solomon*, 8 C. B. 345); for a forged bank-note or worthless cheque (*Turner* v. Q. B. 202); for a forged bill or bank-note (*Jones* v. *Ryde*, 5 Taunt. *Stone*, 1 D. & L. 122; *Woodland* v. *Fear*, 7 E. & B. 519; 26 L. J. 488; *Gurney* v. *Womersley*, 4 E. & B. 133; as to money paid in discharge of a forged bill see *Wilkinson* v. *Johnston*, 3 B. & C. 428); money given for a bill of exchange that has been avoided by a material alteration (*Burchfield* v. *Moore*, 3 E. & B. 683); money given for bonds sold as valid bonds, but which proved defective and worthless (*Young* v. *Cole*, 3 Bing. N. C. 724); money paid as deposit on a contract of sale which has been rescinded (*Blackburn* v. *Smith*, 2 Ex. 783; *Ashworth* v. *Mounsey*, 9 Ex. 175; *Simmons* v. *Heseltine*, 5 C. B. N. S. 554; 28 L. J. C. P. 129); or which the vendor could not complete (*Gosbell* v. *Archer*, 2 A. & E. 500); or which has been defeated by a condition not fulfilled (*Giles* v. *Edwards*, 7 T. R. 181; *Wright* v. *Newton*, 2 C. M. & R. 124; and see *Beavan* v. *M'Donnell*, 9 Ex. 309, where by the terms of the contract the deposit became forfeited); money paid as deposits on scrip for shares in a railway scheme which turned out abortive (*Moore* v. *Garwood*, 4 Ex. 681; *Watson* v. *Earl Charlemont*, 12 Q. B. 856; *Ward* v. *Londesborough*, 12 C. B. 252; *Mowatt* v. *Londesborough*, 4 E. & B. 1; *Walstab* v. *Spottiswoode*, 15 M. & W. 501); or deposits on shares in an abortive cost-book mine (*Johnson* v. *Goslett*, 25 L. J. C. P. 274; 3 C. B. N. S. 569; 27 L. J. C. P. 122); or a deposit on application for shares in a company to be returned if no allotment made, where no allotment was made, see *Moseley* v. *Cressey's Co.*, L. R. 1 Eq. 405; 35 L. J. Ch. 360; the price of an annuity, the securities for which have been set aside (*Huggins* v. *Coates*, 5 Q. B. 432); or of an annuity which had ceased to exist before the sale (*Strickland* v. *Turner*, 7 Ex. 208); the conduct money paid with a subpœna to a witness whose attendance was countermanded, and who incurred no expense (*Martin* v. *Andrews*, 7 E. & B. 1; 26 L. J. Q. B. 39); so, money paid for a purpose which afterwards became impossible, see *Brown* v. *Overbury*, 25 L. J. Ex. 169; 11 Ex. 715.

The plaintiff cannot recover as upon a failure of consideration where he has obtained that which he bargained for, although it turns out to be not genuine, but valueless (*Begbie* v. *Phosphate, &c., Co.*, 1 Q. B. D. 679; 44 L. J. Q. B. 233; *Lambert* v. *Heath*, 15 M. &

2. By a policy of insurance, bearing date the —— day of ——, 18—, the plaintiff caused himself to be insured against certain perils of the sea upon a voyage from —— to ——, upon certain goods to be carried upon the said voyage in the ship ——, beginning the adventure upon the said goods from the loading thereof aboard the said ship, and continuing until the said goods should be safely discharged and landed, and the defendant, for the premium of £—— then paid to him by the plaintiff, subscribed the said policy for £——, and became an insurer thereon to the plaintiff for that amount on the said goods.

3. The said goods so insured as aforesaid were never loaded aboard the said ship for the said voyage, and the

---

W. 486; *Clare* v. *Lamb*, L. R. 10 C. P. 334; 44 L. J. C. P. 177); as money paid for the use of a patent, which is after being used for some years discovered to be invalid (*Taylor* v. *Hare*, 1 B. & P. N. R. 260; and see *Lawes* v. *Purser*, 6 E. & B. 930; 26 L. J. Q. B. 25); or where the consideration fails partly through his own default (*Straton* v. *Rastall*, 2 T. R. 366; *Stray* v. *Russell*, 28 L. J. Q. B. 279; 29 *ib.* 115; 1 E. & E. 888, 916); as where the plaintiff purchased shares in a bank, but did not get them registered, and the bank afterwards failed (*ib.*); so where the plaintiff paid money to the defendant under a contract which he could not enforce by reason of the Statute of Frauds, it was held that he could not, merely on that account, recover it back. (*Sweet* v. *Lee*, 3 M. & G. 452; *Thomas* v. *Brown*, 1 Q. B. D. 714; 45 L. J. Q. B. 811; but see *Gosbell* v. *Archer*, 2 A. & E. 500.) Where after payment of a deposit a contract for purchase of land fell through from the refusal of the purchaser to accept completion, it was held that he could not recover the deposit (*ex parte Barrell*, L. R. 10 Ch. Ap. 512; 44 L. J. B. 138; *Thomas* v. *Brown*, *supra*).

The failure of consideration must be complete in order to entitle the plaintiff to recover the money paid for it (*Hunt* v. *Silk*, 5 East, 449; *Blackburn* v. *Smith*, 2 Ex. 783; *Anglo-Egyptian Nav. Co.* v. *Rennie*, L. R. 10 C. P. 271; 44 L. J. C. P. 130; *Nicholson* v. *Ricketts*, 29 L. J. Q. B. 55; 6 Jur. N. S. 422); so, where a premium was paid for an apprenticeship for a term of six years and the master died at the end of the first year, and an action was brought to recover the premium, it was held that there was only a partial failure of consideration, and that such action was not maintainable (*Whincup* v. *Hughes*, L. R. 6 C. P. 78; 40 L. J. C. P. 104, dissenting from *Hirst* v. *Tolson*, 2 Mac. & G. 134). But where the consideration is severable, complete failure of part may form a ground for recovering a proportionate part of the money paid for it, see *Astle* v. *Wright*, 25 L. J. Ch. 864; 23 Beav. 77; as where a quantity of goods were ordered at a certain rate of payment, and only a portion was delivered (*Devaux* v. *Conolly*, 8 C. B. 640).

Freight paid in advance is not in general recoverable, although the goods are lost on the voyage (*per* Brett, L. J. in *Allison* v. *Bristol Mar. Ins. Co.*, 1 App. Cas. 225). See further, Leake on Contracts, 105—113.

said ship made the said voyage, and no risk ever commenced upon the said adventure.

4. The plaintiff on the —— of ——, 18—, wrote to the defendant informing him of the matters mentioned in the last preceding paragraph, and requesting the repayment of the said premium.

5. The defendant had before this action ample time to repay the said premium to the plaintiff, but has not repaid the same.

For Money admitted to have been received for the use of the Plaintiff (d).

1. On the —— of ——, 18—, the defendant received from G. H. £—— for the purpose of paying the same over to the plaintiff.

(*d*) Where money has been received by an agent from his principal with instructions to pay it over to the plaintiff, the agent is not accountable to the latter until he has acknowledged to him that he has accepted the charge, and holds the money for his use (*Williams* v. *Everett*, 14 East, 582 ; *Yates* v. *Bell*, 3 B. & Ald. 643 ; *Lilly* v. *Hays*, 5 A. & E. 548 ; *Brind* v. *Hampshire*, 1 M. & W. 365 ; *Baron* v. *Husband*, 4 B. & Ad. 611 ; *Moore* v. *Bushell*, 27 L. J. Ex. 3 ; *Hill* v. *Royds*, L. R. 8 Eq. 290 ; 38 L. J. Ch. 538). Where such acknowledgment is given conditionally, the action will not lie until after fulfilment of the condition (*Malcolm* v. *Scott*, 5 Ex. 601 ; *Hudson* v. *Bilton*, 6 E. & B. 565 ; 26 L. J. Q. B. 27.)

If a trustee admits to the *cestui que trust* that he holds the money the subject of the trust as the money of the *cestui que trust* to be accounted for to the latter, it may in general be recovered by the latter in an action in the Queen's Bench Division, the trustee being by such acknowledgment debarred from relying on his character as trustee, see under former practice *Remon* v. *Hayward*, 2 A. & E. 666 ; *Roper* v. *Holland*, 3 A. & E. 99 ; *Edwards* v. *Lowndes*, 1 E. & B. 81, 89; *Pardoe* v. *Price*, 16 M. & W. 451, 458 ; *Howard* v. *Brownhill*, 23 L. J. Q. B. 23, per Erle, J. ; *L. & N. W. Ry. Co.* v. *Glyn*, 1 E. & E. 652 ; 28 L. J. Q. B. 188, 192. In general, however, and in the absence of such acknowledgment and of any contract between the trustee and the *cestui que trust*, the remedy of the latter is in the Chancery Division.

An agent receiving money rightfully on behalf of his principal is accountable to his principal, and is not, after payment over of the money to his principal without notice of any claim, subject to claims of third parties with regard to such money (*Pond* v. *Underwood*, 2 Ld. Raym. 1210; *Bamford* v. *Shuttleworth*, 11 A. & E. 926; *Holland* v. *Russell*, 4 B. & S. 14 ; 32 L. J. Q. B. 297 ; *Shand* v. *Grant*, 15 C. B. N. S. 324 ; *Stephens* v. *Badcock*, 3 B. & Ad. 354). A mere agent who receives money rightfully on behalf of his principal is, in general, accountable only to his principal (*Holland* v. *Russell; Shand* v. *Grant*, *supra* ; *Sadler* v. *Evans*, 4 Burr. 1985 ; and see Addison on

2. Subsequently, on the —— of ——, 18—, the defendant acknowledged to the plaintiff that he had received the said £—— for the said purpose, and that he held the same to the plaintiff's use.

3. The defendant has not paid the said £—— to the plaintiff.

For the recovery of a Legacy admitted to have been received by the Defendant for the use of the Plaintiff (*e*).

1. The defendant is the executor of the last will of one G. H., deceased, which said will was duly proved by the defendant in the Probate Division of Her Majesty's High Court of Justice on the —— of ——, 18—.

2. By the said will the said G. H. bequeathed to the plaintiff the sum of £——, free of legacy duty.

3. On the —— of ——, 18—, the defendant informed the plaintiff [by letter] that he had realised the estate of the said G. H., and held the amount of the said legacy for the plaintiff's use.

4. The defendant has not paid the plaintiff the said legacy.

Against an Agent employed to sell Goods, for not accounting or paying over, see form, ante, p. 39.

Contracts, 7th ed., p. 67); but where the payment is void, *ab initio*, so that the money never was received for his principal, it may be recovered back from the agent before he has paid it over to his principal or settled with his principal for it, as for example if the payment has been made by mistake (*Buller* v. *Harrison*, 2 Cowp. 565; *Cox* v. *Prentice*, 3 M. & S. 344; *Newall* v. *Tomlinson*, L. R. 6 C. P. 405; Addison on Contracts, 7th ed., p. 67). A principal cannot charge a sub-agent upon a merely unauthorised delegation of agency, there being neither primarily, nor by ratification, any privity of contract between them. (*Stephens* v. *Badcock*, 3 B. & Ad. 354; *Prince* v. *Oriental Bank Corp.*, 3 App. Cas. 325, 334; as to ratification see *Brook* v. *Hook*, L. R. 6 Ex. 89; 40 L. J. Ex. 50.)

(*e*) An executor or administrator is in the position of a trustee, see *note* (*d*) *supra*, and the legacies or distributive shares payable out of the estate of the deceased, cannot be recovered as debts (*Deeks* v. *Strutt*, 5 T. R. 690; *Jones* v. *Tanner*, 7 B. & C. 542; and see 2 Wms. on Executors, 7th ed., 1931). But after an executor or administrator has admitted to the legatee that he holds the money to his use, the legatee may recover it as a debt. (*Topham* v. *Morecraft*, 8 E. & B. 972; and see *Barlow* v. *Browne*, 16 M. & W. 126.) See "*Executors and Administrators*," *ante*, p. 172.

Against a Railway Company for Excessive Charges in Contravention of Equality, see ante, p. 132.

Against an Agent to Recover the Amount of a Secret Commission received in Fraud of his Principal, see ante, p. 47.

MORTGAGE.

Statement of Claim upon a Mortgage Deed on the Covenant for repayment of the Mortgage Money (*a*).

1. The defendant, by a deed bearing date the —— day of ——, 18—, covenanted with the plaintiff to pay to the plaintiff £—— on the —— day of ——, 18—, with interest on the same in the meantime at the rate of £—— per cent. per annum.

2. The defendant did not pay the said sum of £—— on the said —— day of ——, 18—, or at all, or the said interest, or any interest.

3. The said interest at the date of the commencement of this action amounted to £——.

PARTNERS (*aa*).

Commencement of Statement of Claim by and against a Firm in the Firm's name.

Between Brown & Co. . . . . . Plaintiffs.

and

Jones & Robinson . . . . . . Defendants.

(*a*) If the mortgage deed contains no covenant for the repayment of the debt, such debt may be recovered as money lent (*Yates* v. *Aston*, 4 Q. B. 182; *Mathew* v. *Blackmore*, 1 H. & N., 762; 26 L. J. Ex. 150). As to when a covenant may be implied, see "*Money Lent*," *ante*, p. 275.

The Court has a summary jurisdiction under the statute 7 Geo. II., c. 20, to stay proceedings in actions for mortgage debts. As to ejectment by mortgagee, see "*Recovery of Land*," *post*, p. 503. Actions for the redemption or foreclosure of mortgages are, by sec. 34 of the Jud. Act, 1873, assigned to the Chancery Division.

(*aa*) By O. XVI. r. 10, "Any two or more persons claiming, or being liable as co-partners, may sue or be sued in the name of their

Statement of Claim.

Delivered the —— of ——, 18—, by &c.

1. The plaintiffs carry on business at ——, as ——, and the defendants carry on business at ——, as ——.

---

respective firms, if any; and any party to an action may in such case apply by summons to a judge for a statement of the names of the persons who are co-partners in any such firm."

By O. XVI. r. 10 a, "Any person carrying on business in the name of a firm apparently consisting of more than one person may be sued in the name of such firm."

By O. VII. r. 2, "When a writ is sued out by partners in the name of their firm, the plaintiffs or their solicitors shall, on demand in writing by or on behalf of any defendant, declare forthwith the names and places of residence of all the persons constituting the firm. And if the plaintiffs or their solicitor shall fail to comply with such demand, all proceedings in the action may, upon an application for that purpose, be stayed upon such terms as the Court or a judge may direct. And when the names of the partners are so declared, the action shall proceed in the same manner, and the same consequences in all respects shall follow as if they had been named as plaintiffs in the writ. But all proceedings shall, nevertheless, continue in the name of the firm." See further, "*Names of the Parties,*" *ante*, p. 3.

As to service of a writ against a firm see O. IX. rr. 6, 6a. Partners when sued in the name of their firm appear individually in their own names, O. XII. rr. 12, 12a. As to execution see O. XLII. r. 8. See further, Leake on Contracts, 533, and *Ex pte. Blain,* 12 Ch. D. at p. 533.

Formerly the non-joinder of a partner who ought to have been made a co-defendant was ground for a plea in abatement, but now by O. XIX. r. 13, "No plea or defence shall be pleaded in abatement;" so that it would seem that in general the objection should be taken by summons to add the defendant not joined, and to stay the action until he is joined. (*Kendall* v. *Hamilton*, 4 App. Cas. 504, 516, 534, 544; 48 L. J. H. L. 705.)

Where a contract is made in a partnership name, and there are partners who did not appear in the transaction and were unknown to the other contracting party, the secret partners are in the condition of undisclosed principals; and although they may join in suing upon the contract, the other contracting party cannot be compelled to sue them, though he may, if he pleases, sue them jointly with the ostensible partners. (*De Mautort* v. *Saunders*, 1 B. & Ad. 398; *Kendall* v. *Hamilton*, *supra*.)

Where a contract is made *with* one partner in his own name only, without mention of his firm, on account of the partnership business, the other partners may join with him in suing on it (*Skinner* v. *Stocks*, 4 B. & Ald. 437; *Garrett* v. *Handley*, 4 B. & C. 664; *Cothay* v. *Fennell*, 10 B. & C. 671; *Robson* v. *Drummond*, 2 B. & Ad. 303; *Alexander* v. *Barker*, 2 C. & J. 133), or he may sue on it alone, upon the same principle that where an agent contracts for an undisclosed principal either the former or the latter may sue upon it. (*Sims* v. *Bond*, 5 B. & Ad. 389, 393; and see 2 Smith's L. C. 8th ed. 121, 412.) The right of the undisclosed partner to the benefit of the contract is, like that of the undisclosed principal, subject to the equities and defences which the defendant may have against the partner who actually contracted. (*Robson* v. *Drummond*, 2 B. & Ad. 303; *George* v. *Clagett*, 7 T. R. 359.)

Where the contract is made *by* one partner in his own name, on account of the partnership business, he may be sued alone upon it, or the other partners may be sued with him as co-defendants. Thus, where the two ostensible partners in a business signed a written agreement for the services of the plaintiff in their business, the plaintiff was held entitled to sue them jointly with another partner who had not signed the agreement, and who was unknown to him at the time of making it. (*Beckham* v. *Drake*, 9 M. & W. 79; 11 M. & W. 315.)

If, however, judgment is recovered against the ostensible partners, it is a bar, even without satisfaction, to an action against the secret partners for the same cause; the rule being that judgment against a contractor is a bar to a new action for the same cause against his co-contractors. (*Priestley* v. *Fernie*; 3 H. & C. 977; 34 L. J. Ex. 172; *Kendall* v. *Hamilton*, 4 App. Cas. 504, 514 48 L. J. H. L. 705; *King* v. *Hoare*, 13 M. & W. 494.)

The question of liability as a partner, of one who is not ostensibly a partner, depends on whether the trade is carried on on his behalf, and the participation in the profits of the trade is a most important element in determining that question, without being in itself decisive; the test being whether it is such a participation of profits as to constitute the relation of principal and agent between the person taking the profits and those actually carrying on the business. (*per* Blackburn, J. in *Bullen* v. *Sharp*, L. R. 1 C. P. 86, 112; 34 L. J. C. P. 184; and *per* Cotton, L. J. in *ex parte Tennant*, 6 Ch. D. 303, 315; *Cox* v. *Hickman*, 8 H. L. C. 268, 306, *per* Lord Cranworth; 9 C. B. N. S. 47; 30 L. J. C. P. 125.)

Participation in profits, as such, is very cogent evidence of partnership in the business from which the profits are derived, though that evidence is capable of being controlled by the surrounding circumstances (*per* James, L. J. *ex parte Tennant*, 6 Ch. D. 303, 309; Lindley on Partnership, 4th ed. p. 38 *et seq.*).

Each partner is to be regarded as agent for the firm to carry out the objects of the partnership. (*Pooley* v. *Driver*, 5 Ch. D. 458, 476; 46 L. J. Ch. 466.)

There is a distinction between sharing profits, as such, and receiving payment for services rendered, or money lent, in proportion to a given quantum of profits. (*Mollwo, March, & Co.* v. *Court of Wards*, L. R. 4 P. C. 419, 434, 437; *Pooley* v. *Driver*, 5 Ch. D. 458, 478; 46 L. J. Ch. 466; *Re English and Irish Univ. Ins. Soc.*, 1 H. & M. 85; *ex parte Tennant*, *supra.*) An agent or traveller who is paid by a commission on the profits does not thereby become liable or entitled as a partner. (*Cheap* v. *Cramond*, 4 B. & A. 670; *Harrington* v. *Churchward*, 29 L. J. Ch. 521; *Lyon* v. *Knowles*, 3 B. & S. 556; 5 B. & S. 756; 32 L. J. Q. B. 71; *Pott* v. *Eyton*, 3 C. B. 32.)

By Bovill's Act (28 & 29 Vict. c. 86), s. 1, the advance of money by way of loan upon a contract in writing that the lender shall receive interest upon the loan, varying with the profits, or a share of the profits, is not of itself to constitute the lender a partner or responsible as such. By sec. 2, a contract for remuneration of a servant or agent by a share in the profits is not of itself to render the servant or agent responsible as a partner or to give him the rights of a partner. By sec. 3, the widow or child of a deceased partner receiving as an annuity a portion of the profits of a business is not by reason only of such receipt to be deemed a partner. By sec. 4, a person selling the goodwill of a business, and receiving in return, by way of annuity or otherwise, a portion of the profits of the business, is not by reason only of such receipt to be deemed a partner.

The advance under sec. 1 of the Act, must be "by way of loan," the person advancing must be a genuine lender, so that the position is that of debtor and creditor (*Pooley* v. *Driver*, 5 Ch. D. 458, 485; 46 L. J. Ch. 466; Lindley on Partnership, 4th ed. p. 45, 47, *ex parte Delhasse*, 7 Ch. D. 511; 47 L. J. B. 65; *Syers* v. *Syers*, 1 App. Cas. 174). It has been held that the contract required by sec. 1 of the Act, must be signed. (*Pooley* v. *Driver*, *supra.*) The Act applies only to a loan upon the personal responsibility of the trader. (*Ex parte Delhasse, supra;* see further *ex parte Mills*, L. R. 8 Ch. Ap. 569; and *Holme* v. *Hammond*, L. R. 7 Ex. 218, 227; 41 L. J. Ex. 157.)

By sec. 34 of the Jud. Act, 1873, the dissolution of partnerships, and the taking of partnership or other accounts, is assigned to the Chancery Division. One partner could not formerly sue another at law upon any matter involving the partnership accounts. Partners could, and can, sue each other in the Queen's Bench Division in respect of matters independent of the partnership, or on express covenants or agreements. (*Brown* v. *Tapscott*, 6 M. & W. 119; *Blech* v. *Balleras*, 29 L. J. Q. B. 261.) So if one partner advance for the other a sum of money as the share of the other of the partnership capital, he can recover it by action in one of the Queen's Bench Division. (*Venning* v. *Leckie*, 13 East, 7; *French* v. *Styring*, 2 C. B. N. S. 357; 26 L. J. C. P. 181.) So also one partner may sue another for his share of the produce of the partnership transaction, after a final account stated and a balance acknowledged to be due. (*Foster* v. *Allanson*, 2 T. R. 479; *Jackson* v. *Stopherd*, 4 Tyr. 330; *Bovill* v. *Hammond*, 6 B. & C. 149; *Coffee* v. *Brian*, 3 Bing. 54; *Wray* v. *Milestone*, 5 M. & W. 21; *Henley* v. *Soper*, 8 B. & C. 16, 20.) The executors of a deceased partner carrying on the business for the benefit of the estate are liable as partners for debts incurred by them in carrying on the business, and are partners in such business. (*Wightman* v. *Townroe*, 1 M. & S. 412.)

A contract made with a partnership respecting matters connected with the partnership business is generally construed as applicable to the existing partnership and business, and is terminated by a dissolution or change of the partnership or alteration in its business, unless the contrary intention expressly appears. (*Lord Arlington* v. *Meyrricke*, 2 Saund. 414, n. (5); *Robson* v. *Drummond*, 2 B. & Ad. 303; *Dry* v. *Davy*, 10 A. & E. 30; *Chapman* v. *Beckington*, 3 Q. B. 703; *Tasker* v. *Shepherd*, 6 H. & N. 575; 30 L. J. Ex. 207; *Backhouse* v. *Hall*, 6 B. & S. 507; 34 L. J. Q. B. 141.) With respect to contracts of guarantee, see The Mercantile Law Amendment Act, 1856 (19 & 20 Vict. c. 97) s. 4, "*Guarantees*," *ante*, p. 192.

Statement of Claim by a Surviving Partner for the price of goods sold and delivered by himself and his Deceased Partner jointly during the lifetime of the latter (*b*).

1. During the months of March and April, 18—, the plaintiff carried on business in partnership with E. F., since deceased, as grocers at ——.

2. During the said months the plaintiff and the said E. F. sold and delivered to the defendant goods as follows: [*set out the particulars as far as practicable, or* to the value of £——, full particulars whereof have been delivered to the defendant.]

3. The defendant has not paid the price of the said goods or any portion of it, and there is now due and payable from the defendant to the plaintiff in respect thereof £——.

Claim against a New Firm for Money Lent to a Former Firm whose Liabilities the New Firm have by agreement taken upon themselves (*c*).

1. The defendants C. D., E. F., and Co., carry on the business as silk mercers in Stafford which was formerly carried on there by C. D. and G. H.

(*b*) Where the action has been commenced in the name of the firm, and there has been no change in such name, it would seem unnecessary to state in the claim the fact of the death of any member of the firm which may have occurred between the date of the contract and the action or pleading; but where one of the partners having died since the date of the contract, the action has been commenced in the names of the surviving partners as individuals, the death should be stated, so as to shew why upon a contract made with certain partners, only a portion of them (viz., the survivors) are suing. In actions against partners it is not necessary to show upon the claim the fact of the death of any partner who may have died since the cause of action arose; for the non-joinder of a joint contractor as defendant can now only be objected to by summons to add the joint contractor, which is impossible after his death. (O. XIX. r. 13; O. XVI. r. 14.) The former mode of objecting was by plea in abatement, which was also impossible after the death.

(*c*) *Change of firm.*] A person by becoming a partner does not thereby become liable upon the contracts or for the debts of the firm existing at the time of his so becoming a partner (*Beale* v. *Mouls*, 10 Q. B. 976; *Vere* v. *Ashby*, 10 B. & C. 288); nor does a person by leaving a partnership, or by a dissolution of it, become relieved from liability upon the contracts or for the debts of the firm existing at the time of his so leaving it, or of such dissolution.

2. In the year 18— the plaintiff lent £1000 to the said C. D. and G. H. for use in their said business upon the terms that it should be repaid upon a month's notice to repay it being given by the plaintiff and that until such repayment the said C. D. and G. H., their executors or administrators, should pay interest thereon to the plaintiff at the rate of 5 per cent. per annum by equal half-yearly payments, on the 1st of January and the 24th of June in each year, commencing on the 24th of June, 18—.

3. The said C. D. and G. H. continued to pay to the plaintiff the agreed interest on the said loan up to the 1st of January, 18—, inclusive.

4. On the 3rd of February, 18—, the said partnership, which up to that time existed between C. D. and G. H. in the said business, was dissolved by mutual consent [*or as the case may be*].

5. The said business was thenceforth carried on by the defendants C. D., E. F., and Co., the said G. H. thenceforth ceasing to have any interest in the said business, [and being indemnified by a deed bearing date the —— of ——, 18—, made by the defendants, against all claims which might be made upon him for the debts of or arising from the said business, including the said £1000 above mentioned and the interest thereon].

6. It was thereupon afterwards [*state when*] by word of mouth [*or* in writing dated, &c., *or, if by implied contract state the agreement as a fact, and refer generally to the circumstances without setting them out in detail,* O. XIX. r. 27] agreed between the plaintiff and the defendants and the said G. H. that the defendants should become liable to the plaintiff for the repayment of the said loan of £1000 and the said interest thereon to the plaintiff

---

Upon a change of firm a *novation* is often effected by the express or implied agreement of the parties, whereby the creditor of the original firm accepts the liability of the new firm in lieu of that of the original firm.

If a creditor, knowing of the change in the firm, takes security for his debt from the new firm, or takes interest from the new firm upon his debt, or in any other way treats them as his debtors, this affords evidence of such novation. (*Rolfe* v. *Flower*, L. R. 1 P. C. 27; *Bilborough* v. *Holmes*, 5 Ch. D. 255; 46 L. J. Ch. 446; *Kirwan* v. *Kirwan*, 2 Cr. & M. 617; *ex parte Gibson*, L. R. 4 Ch. Ap. 662; 38 L. J. Ch. 673; *Hart* v. *Alexander*, 2 M. & W. 484; 7 C. & P. 746.)

upon the terms aforesaid, and that G. H. should be discharged from all liability in respect thereof.

7. [The defendants paid to the plaintiff the agreed interest on the said loan from the said 1st of January, 18—, up to the 24th of June, 18—, inclusive.]

8. Afterwards [*state when and how*] the plaintiff gave a month's notice to the defendants to repay the said loan of £1000.

9. The defendants have not, though the period of such notice elapsed before this action was commenced, repaid to the plaintiff the said loan of £1000 or any part of it.

Patents (*a*).

See "*Patents*," *post*, p. 494, *and note* (*a*) *below*.

Penal Statutes (*aa*).

Commencement and Conclusion of a Statement of Claim by an Informer in a Qui Tam Action.

1. The plaintiff sues in this action as well for the Queen [*or* for the poor of the parish of ——, in the county of ——,] as for himself.

(*a*) An action will lie to recover money agreed to be paid by the defendant for a licence to use a patent invention belonging to the plaintiff, although the licence under which the defendant has used the invention was not under seal. (*Chanter* v. *Dewhurst*, 12 M. & W. 823; 13 L. J. Ex. 198; *Chanter* v. *Johnson*, 14 M. & W. 408; 14 L. J. Ex. 289; *Lawes* v. *Purser*, 6 E. & B. 930; 26 L. J. Q. B. 25.) On the grant of a licence to use a patent, and on an assignment of a patent, there is no implied warranty that the patent is valid. (*Hall* v. *Conder*, 2 C. B. N. S. 22; 26 L. J. C. P. 138, 288; *Smith* v. *Scott*, 6 C. B. N. S. 771; 28 L. J. C. P. 325; *Clark* v. *Adie*, 3 Ch. D. 134; 2 App. Cas. 423.) But the assignor can take no advantage of the invalidity of the patent as against the assignee. (*Walton* v. *Lavater*, 8 C. B. N. S. 162; 29 L. J. C. P. 275; and see *Oxley* v. *Holden*, 30 L. J. C. P. 68, 72, 75.) Nor can the assignee, in general, dispute the validity of the patent as against the assignor. (*Hills* v. *Laming*, 9 Ex. 256; *Smith* v. *Neale*, 2 C. B. N. S. 67; 26 L. J. C. P. 143; *Lawes* v. *Purser*, 6 E. & B. 930; 26 L. J. Q. B. 25; *Crossley* v. *Dixon*, 10 H. L. C. 293; 32 L. J. Ch. 617.)

(*aa*) The statement of claim in an action for a penalty under a statute should state or show that the act was done against the form of the statute, otherwise it will be bad in arrest of judgment.

2, 3, &c. [*State the facts which constitute the cause of action for recovery of the penalty*].

The plaintiff, as well for the Queen [*or* for the poor of the above-mentioned parish] as for himself, claims £—— [*the amount of the penalty sued for*].

(*Fife* v. *Bousfield*, 6 Q. B. 100.) In *qui tam* actions for a penalty, where the action is given to the party grieved, the statement of claim must state as a fact or show that the plaintiff is a party grieved; and if the consent of the Attorney-General is made necessary, the fact that it has been obtained must also be stated, otherwise the statement of claim would be bad on demurrer. (*Hollis* v. *Marshall*, 2 H. & N. 755; 27 L. J. Ex. 235.) The absence of the Attorney-General's consent, where such consent is necessary, would also be a ground for staying proceedings. (*Hollis* v. *Marshall*, *supra*; *Rochfort* v. *Atherley*, 1 Ex. D. 511; *Fletcher* v. *Hudson*, 5 Ex. D. 287; 49 L. J. Ex. 793.) It is not in general necessary to aver an authority to sue from the crown or from the party entitled to the penalties. (*Cole* v. *Coulton*, 2 E. & E. 695; 29 L. J. M. C. 125, 127). In *qui tam* actions the indorsement of claim on the writ must show the capacity in which the plaintiff sues. (See Jud. Act, 1875, O. III. r. 4, and Appendix A., Part II., s. VIII.)

As to when a person is entitled to sue for a penalty as "a party aggrieved," see *Hollis* v. *Marshall* and cases cited *supra*, and *Robinson* v. *Currey*, *infra*.

In penal actions no damages are recoverable for the detention of the debt, because no debt is due until judgment. (*Frederick* v. *Lookup*, 4 Burr. 2018; *Cuming* v. *Sibly*, 4 *ib.* 2489.)

A corporation cannot sue for penalties as a common informer, unless expressly empowered by statute to do so. (*Guardians of St. Leonard's, Shoreditch* v. *Franklin*, 3 C. P. D. 377; 47 L. J. C. P. 727.)

As to when distinct penalties are incurred by the repetition or continuance of prohibited acts, see *Milnes* v. *Bale*, L. R. 10 C. P. 591; 44 L. J. C. P. 336; *Garrett* v. *Messenger*, L. R. 2 C. P. 583; *Crepps* v. *Durden*, 2 Cowp. 640.

As to the limitation of penal actions, see "*Defences*," "*Limitation*," and see *Dyer* v. *Best*, L. R. 1 Ex. 152; 35 L. J. Ex. 105; *Robinson* v. *Currey*, 6 Q. B. D. 21; 50 L. J. Q. B. 9, *reversed on appeal*, 7 Q. B. D. 465; 50 L. J. Q. B. 561.

Where a statute prohibits an act under a penalty, it does not necessarily follow, even where the penalty is not given to the party grieved, that an action will lie for special damage sustained by the plaintiff from the doing of the prohibited act. Whether in such a case the breach of the statutory prohibition does or does not give a right of action for damages to a party suffering damage from the breach, must depend upon the object and language of the particular statute. (*Atkinson* v. *Newcastle and Gateshead Waterworks Co.* 2 Ex. D. 441; 46 L. J. Ex. 775; *where the dicta* in *Couch* v. *Steel*, 3 E. & B. 402; 33 L. J. Q. B. 121, *are disapproved.*)

Where a statute creating a liability to a penalty contains special provisions for the mode of enforcing it (as, for instance, by proceedings before magistrates), the particular remedy prescribed by the statute must in general be followed, and no action can be maintained for the penalty where the special statutory provisions for its enforce-

See a Form of Statement of Claim in a Qui tam Action for a Penalty under a Local Act relating to the Sale of Coals, Guardians of St. Leonard's, Shoreditch v. *Franklin*, 3 C. P. D. 377; 47 L. J. C. P. 727; *and for Forms of Declarations in Qui tam Actions, under the Old Practice, see Hollis* v. *Marshall*, 2 H. & N. 755 (*where the Informer sued as well for certain Improvement Commissioners as for Himself*); *and Hunt* v. *Hills*, 5 H. & N. 123 (*where the Action was brought by the Treasurer of a Borough, suing as well for the Borough as for Himself*).

For Form of Claim for Voting in the House of Commons without having taken the Oath, see Clarke v. *Bradlaugh*, 44 L. T. 667; 7 Q. B. D. 38.

Statement of Claim for the Penalty for Bribery at an Election, under the Corrupt Practices Prevention Act, 1854 (17 *&* 18 *Vict. c.* 102, *s.* 2), *amended by* 21 *&* 22 *Vict. c.* 87, *and* 26 *Vict. c.* 29, *and continued by those and subsequent Statutes, see* 42 & 43 *Vict. c.* 75 (*b*).

1. On the —— day of ——, 18—, an election was holden in and for the borough of ——, of a member to

---

ment are inconsistent with there being a jurisdiction in the ordinary courts to entertain such action. (*London and Brighton Railway Co.* v. *Watson*, 3 C. P. D. 429; 4 C. P. D. 118; 47 L. J. C. P. 634; 48 L. J. C. P. 361; *Cates* v. *Knight*, 3 T. R. 442; *Fleming* v. *Bailey*, 5 East, 313; and see *Stevens* v. *Evans*, 2 Burr. 1157; *Underhill* v. *Ellicombe*, M'Clell. & Y. 450, 455; *St. Pancras Vestry* v. *Batterbury*, 2 C. B. N. S. 477.)

(*b*) The 26 Vict. c. 29, which amended and continued the "Corrupt Practices Prevention Act," 1854, by s. 6, enacted (*inter alia*) that in any action for any penalty for bribery, treating, or undue influence, it should be sufficient to allege that the defendant was at the election at or in connection with which the offence is intended to be alleged to have been committed guilty of bribery, treating, or undue influence (as the case might require). But it is conceived that this enactment is now superseded by the operation of the Judicature Acts, and that it is necessary in this, as in other cases, that the material facts should be specifically stated in the statement of claim.

It was held in *Milnes* v. *Bale*, 10 L. R. C. P. 591; 44 L. J. C. P. 336, that where a person has been guilty of several acts of bribery at a municipal election, he is liable, under s. 3 of the Corrupt Practices (Municipal Elections) Act, 1872 (35 & 36 Vict. c. 60), to a penalty in

serve in parliament for the said borough, at which said election G. H. was a candidate within the meaning of the Corrupt Practices Prevention Acts.

2. At the said election the defendant by himself [*or* by J. K. on his behalf] gave [*or* agreed to give] money to L. M. [*or* to N. O. on behalf of L. M.], then being a voter at the said election for the said borough, in order to induce the said L. M. to vote at the said election for the said G. H. [*or* to refrain from voting at the said election], contrary to the Corrupt Practices Prevention Act, 1854.

3. The defendant thereby became liable to forfeit and forfeited the sum of £100 to the plaintiff, who sues the defendant for the same in this action under the last-mentioned statute.

For Instances of Declarations under the Old Practice in Actions brought for Penalties under the above Enactment, see Cooper v. *Slade*, 6 E. & B. 447; 25 L. J. Q. B. 324; *Reed* v. *Lamb*, 6 H. & N. 75; 29 L. J. Ex. 452; *and see also Milnes* v. *Bale*, L. R. 10 C. P. 591; 44 L. J. C. P. 336, *where the Action was brought for a Penalty under s.* 3 *of "The Corrupt Practices (Municipal Elections) Act*, 1872 (35 & 36 Vict. c. 60).

---

respect of each of such acts of bribery. That decision clearly applies to s. 2 of the Corrupt Practices Prevention Act, 1854.

Any action under the last-mentioned Act must, by s. 14, be brought within one year from the committing of the offence, and the writ of summons must, under ordinary circumstances, be served within the same period.

It may be useful for purposes of reference to mention the following instances of declarations under the old practice in actions for penalties:—declaration for a penalty under the Commissioners' Clauses Act, 1845 (10 & 11 Vict. c. 16), for acting as a commissioner after having become disqualified:—*Nicholson* v. *Field*, 7 H. & N. 810; 31 L. J. Ex. 233; for acting as commissioner after being concerned in a contract with the commissioners; *Dyer* v. *Best*, L. R. 1 Ex. 152; 35 L. J. Ex. 105. Against an officer of a county court for acting as attorney for a party in a proceeding in the court, 9 & 10 Vict. c. 95, s. 30; *Ackroyd* v. *Gill*, 5 E. & B. 808; *Warden* v. *Stone*, 7 *ib.* 603. Against a magistrate's clerk for taking excessive fees under 26 Geo. II., c. 14, s. 2; *Bowman* v. *Blyth*, 7 E. & B. 26; *Lewis* v. *Davis*, L. R. 10 Ex. 86; 44 L. J. Ex. 86. For penalties for the unauthorised use of the name of a patent under 5 & 6 Will. IV., c. 83, s. 7; *Myers* v. *Baker*, 3 H. & N. 802; 28 L. J. Ex. 90. For penalties for infringing the copyright in a dramatic performance under 3 & 4 Will. IV., c. 15; *Fitzball* v. *Brooke*, 6 Q. B. 873; *Shepherd* v. *Conquest*, 17 C. B. 427; *Chatterton* v. *Cave*, L. R. 10 C. P. 572; 2 C. P. D. 42; 3 App. Cas. 483.

See for Statement of Claim for a Penalty under 21 Geo. III. c. 49, *for Keeping Open an Aquarium as a Place of Public Entertainment and Amusement on Sunday, Girdlestone* v. *The Brighton Aquarium Co.*, 3 Ex. D. 137; 38 L. T. 358; 4 Ex. D. 107; 48 L. J. Ex. 373; *and see also Terry* v. *The Brighton Aquarium Co.*, L. R. 10 Q. B. 306; *and Warner* v. *The Brighton Aquarium Co.*, L. R. 10 Ex. 291.

Action for a Penalty under The Metropolis Management Act, 1855 (18 & 19 Vict. c. 120, s. 6); *for Acting as a Vestryman without being duly qualified as required by the Act, Goodhew* v. *Williams*, 3 C. P. D. 382; 47 L. J. C. P. 313.

See for Form of Claim in an Action by an Officer of the Company of Goldsmiths in London for Penalties under s. 3 of 7 & 8 Vict. c. 22, *Robinson* v. *Currey*, 6 Q. B. D. 21; 50 L. J. Q. B. 9 (*see note*, p. 297).

PENALTY. See "*Liquidated Damages*," *ante*, p. 262.

PRINCIPAL and AGENT. See "*Agent*," *ante*, p. 36.

PRINCIPAL and SURETY. See "*Guarantees*," *ante*, p. 190.

PROMISSORY NOTES. See *ante*, p. 107.

PROVIDENT SOCIETIES. See "*Friendly Societies*," *ante*, p. 182.

RAILWAY. See "*Company*," *ante*, p. 145.

REPLEVIN.

See for Form of Claim upon a Replevin Bond, Dix v. *Groom*, 5 Ex. D. 91.

SALE ; I. OF GOODS (*a*).

Statement of Claim for the Price of Goods Sold and Delivered.

1. The plaintiff is a butter merchant at ——, and the defendant is also a butter merchant at ——.

(*a*) By the Statute of Frauds, 29 Car. II. c. 3, s. 17, it is enacted "that no contract for the sale of any goods, wares, and merchandises for the price of £10 sterling, or upwards, shall be allowed to be good, except the buyer shall accept part of the goods so sold, and actually receive the same ; or give something in earnest to bind the bargain or in part of payment ; or that some note or memorandum in writing of the said bargain be made and signed by the parties to be charged by such contract, or their agents thereunto lawfully authorised."

By Lord Tenterden's Act, 9 Geo. IV. c. 14, s. 7, it is enacted, with respect to the above section, that the said enactments shall extend to all contracts for the sale of goods, of the *value* of £10 sterling and upwards, notwithstanding the goods may be intended to be delivered at some future time, or may not at the time of such contract be actually made, procured, or provided, or fit or ready for delivery, or some act may be requisite for the making or completing thereof, or rendering the same fit for delivery. As to the decisions on these statutes see Leake on Contracts, 293–309 ; Benjamin on Sales, 2nd ed. 72–226; Roscoe's N. P. Ev. 14th ed. *et seq.*

By O. XIX. r. 23, a denial of the contract alleged in the statement of claim is to be construed as a denial of the making of the contract in fact, not of its sufficiency in law, whether with reference to the Statute of Frauds or otherwise ; consequently the defence must distinctly raise the non-fulfilment of the requirements of the above enactments if it is intended to rely upon the non-fulfilment of them. (*Clarke* v. *Callow*, 46 L. J. Q. B. 53 ; *Catling* v. *King*, 5 Ch. D. 660 ; 46 L. J. Ch. 384 ; *Pullen* v. *Snelus*, 48 L. J. C. P. 394.) Where the contract has been reduced to writing this fact should however appear. (See "*Agreements*," *ante.*)

It would, subject to the above observation as to writing, seem unnecessary to show upon the statement of claim that the requirements of the above enactments have been fulfilled in the first instance, though it may sometimes be convenient to do so. When by the defence the absence of fulfilment of the requirements of the above enactments has been raised, the plaintiff may amend the statement of claim by setting forth how the said requirements have been fulfilled, though in general it will be found unnecessary to do more than join issue. See further "Defences," "*Frauds, Statute of.*"

In suing for the price of goods it must appear upon the statement of claim that the price is due and payable, either by necessary implication from the facts stated, or by express averment to that effect. As to the suspension of the right to sue for a simple contract debt caused by the taking of a negotiable security for and on account of the debt, see *Kearslake* v. *Morgan* 5 T. R. 513 ; and "Defences," "*Bills of Exchange.*"

2. Between the —— of ——, 18—, and the —— of ——, 18—, the plaintiff sold and delivered to the defendant certain quantities of butter as follows: [*set out particulars of the same with dates and prices, or say* particulars whereof have been delivered].

Where goods are sold upon a contract to pay for them by a bill and no bill is given, the only cause of action until the proposed period of the bill has elapsed is for the failure to give the bill. It is not until the proposed period has elapsed that the price of the goods can be sued for. (*See under the former system of pleading*, *Mussen* v. *Price*, 4 East, 147; *Dutton* v. *Solomonson*, 3 B. & P. 582; *Paul* v. *Dod*, 2 C. B. 800.)

Where a contract for the sale of goods is silent as to the time for delivery of the goods, the delivery must be within "a reasonable time," and to determine this all the circumstances may be considered (*Ellis* v. *Thompson*, 3 M. & W. 445, *see per* Alderson, B.); so where no price is fixed, a "reasonable price" is to be paid. (*Acebal* v. *Levy*, 10 Bing. 376.) Payment means *primâ facie* payment in cash; but it is in general open to prove that there is a usage for a certain credit. (*Brown* v. *Bryne*, 3 E. & B. 703; 23 L. J. Q. B. 313; *Hoadly* v. *McLaine*, 10 Bing. 482; Leake on Contracts, 200.)

Primâ facie in sales of goods, the delivery of the goods, and the payment of the price are concurrent acts, and each party should in such case at the proper time be ready and willing to perform the act to be done on his part (*Callonel* v. *Briggs*, 1 Salk. 112; *Morton* v. *Lamb*, 7 T. R. 125) or show an absolute refusal on the part of the other party to perform the concurrent act to be done by him, or conduct on the part of such other party equivalent to such a refusal, or a waiver by such other party of the act not done by the former party. "The party must show he was ready; but if the other party stops him, on the ground of an intention not to perform his part, it is not necessary for the first to go further and do a nugatory act." (*Jones* v. *Barkley*, 2 Doug. 684, *per* Lord Mansfield, C. J.) The same rule applies to conditions precedent, see "*Conditions Precedent*," *ante*, p. 158. So a request not to deliver, or to postpone delivery, operates as an excuse for non-delivery, and extends the time for delivery. (*Plevins* v. *Downing*, 1 C. P. D. 220; 45 L. J. C. P. 695.) If the seller forbears delivery at the agreed time, or sends by a new route at the buyer's request, it is said that this is not to be regarded as a new contract, and that the arrangement has only reference to the mode of performance of the original contract. (*Plevins* v. *Downing*, *supra*; *Cuff* v. *Penn*, 1 M. & S. 21; *Tyers* v. *Rosedale Iron Co.*, L. R., 10 Ex. 195; 44 L. J. Ex. 130; *Ogle* v. *Earl Vane*, L. R. 3 Q. B. 272; 37 L. J. Q. B. 77; *Leather Cloth Co.* v. *Hieronimus*, L. R. 10 Q. B. 140; 44 L. J. Q. B. 54, *per* Blackburn, J.) This distinction between a new contract, and a mere agreement that a new mode of performing a contract shall be taken as a satisfaction for, or in lieu of the agreed mode is of importance with regard to the Statute of Frauds, the assent to such substituted performance not requiring writing. (See *per* Blackburn, J. in *Leather Cloth Co.* v. *Hieronimus*, *supra*, and cases cited *supra*.)

If the buyer forbear delivery at the request of the seller, though without binding himself to do so, the damages will be regulated by

3. The plaintiff, from time to time as the said butter was delivered to the defendant, sent to the defendant invoices showing the prices thereof, which were fair and reasonable prices for the same, amounting in the whole to £——.

4. The defendant has not paid the plaintiff for the said butter, and the said sum of £—— is now due from, and payable by the defendant to the plaintiff in respect thereof.

A like Form, Elphick v. *Barnes*, 5 C. P. D. 321.

For the price of Goods Bargained and Sold but not Delivered (*a*) (*b*).

1. The plaintiff, on the —— of ——, 18—, bargained and sold to the defendant 50 tons of steel rails, at £——

---

the state of the market, when he withdraws the forbearance, and he can claim in such case the benefit of a rise (*Ogle* v. *Earl Vane*, *supra*); so also if the seller forbear delivery at the request of the buyer. (*Hickman* v. *Haynes*, L. R. 10 C. P. 598; 44 L. J. C. P. 358; Leake on Contracts, 1059).

Where goods are to be delivered and paid for by instalments, non-payment for an instalment is not, in general, a condition precedent to the delivery of subsequent instalments, but is only ground for damages at any rate where the contract has been partially performed. (See *Simpson* v. *Crippin*, L. R. 8 Q. B. 14; *Honck* v. *Muller*, *infra*; *Roper* v. *Johnson*, L. R. 8 C. P. 167; 42 L. J. C. P. 167; *Johnassohn* v. *Young*, 4 B. & S. 296; 32 L. J. Q. B. 385; *Freeth* v. *Burr*, L. R. 9 C. P. 208: 43 L. J. C. P. 91).

If, however, the default be made with the manifest intention of repudiating the contract, or made under circumstances showing an absolute incapacity to perform it, so that the party in default cannot be regarded as ready in future to perform his part, the seller is discharged from future deliveries. (*Bloomer* v. *Bernstein*, L. R. 9 C. P. 588; 43 L. J. C. P. 588; *Morgan* v. *Bain*, L. R. 10 C. P. 15; 44 L. J. C. P. 47; *ex parte Chalmers*, L. R. 8 Ch. Ap. 289; 42 L. J. Bk. 37; *Honck* v. *Muller*, 7 Q. B. D. 92; 50 L. J. Q. B. 529).

The insolvency or bankruptcy of a buyer, where there is no election by the trustee to carry out the contract, may upon this principle, entitle an unpaid seller to withhold future deliveries (*ex parte Chalmers*, *supra*; *Morgan* v. *Bain*, *supra*: *ex parte Stapleton*, 10 Ch. D. 586, 590; and see *re Phœnix Bessemer Steel Co.*, 4 Ch. D. 108; 46 L. J. Ch. 115).

As to pleading conditions, precedent or concurrent, see "*Conditions Precedent*," *ante*, p. 158.

(*b*) The above form applies to a case where there has been a sale of goods and the property has passed to the purchaser, and the contract has been completed in all respects except delivery, and the

per ton, to be paid for within a month, but not to be removed from the plaintiff's works before payment.

2. The said month elapsed before this action was commenced, but the defendant has not paid the plaintiff for the said rails, and the sum of £—— is due and payable by the defendant to the plaintiff as the price of the said rails.

To recover a Balance of the Price of Goods sold and delivered, and Damages for Repudiation of the Contract and refusal to take delivery of the rest of the Goods contracted for (*c*).

1. The plaintiff is a fruit and potato merchant carrying on business at Kingston-upon-Hull, and the defendants are fruit and potato merchants carrying on business in partnership at Derby.

---

delivery was not a part of the consideration for the price or a condition precedent to its payment. If anything remains to be done under the contract to which the concurrence of the seller is necessary, as to ascertain the price of the goods by weighing, the property in general does not pass until the act is performed. (*Simmons* v. *Swift*, 5 B. & C. 857; *Jenner* v. *Smith*, L. R. 4 C. P. 270.)

An act to be done by the buyer, as the weighing of the goods by him, does not prevent property passing. (*Furley* or *Turley* v. *Bates*, 2 H. & C. 200; 33 L. J. Ex. 33.)

By a contract for the sale of specific ascertained goods, the property immediately vests in the buyer and a right to the price in the seller, unless it appears that such is not the intention of the parties. (*Gilmour* v. *Supple*, 11 Moo. P. C. 551; *Calcutta, &c., Steam Navigation Co.* v. *De Mattos*, 32 L. J. Q. B. 322, 329.)

The question of when property passes is one of intention to be gathered from the circumstances, and a clear intention expressed to pass the property is sufficient to do so, notwithstanding some act remains to be done by either party (*Furley* or *Turley* v. *Bates*, *supra*), or the price has not been definitely agreed on. (*Joyce* v. *Swann*, 17 C. B. N. S. 84.)

A contract for the sale of goods within the 17th section of the Statute of Frauds is not effectual to pass any property in the goods, unless and until the requirements of that section are satisfied. (*Stockdale* v. *Dunlop*, 6 M. & W. 224; *Coats* v. *Chaplin*, 3 Q. B. 483.) See further, Benjamin on Sales, 2nd ed. pp. 228, 232 *et seq.*; Leake on Contracts, 284, 308; Roscoe's N. P. Ev., 14th ed. pp. 470, 491. As to pleading the non-fulfilment of the requirements of the Statute of Frauds, see preceding note, and "Defences," "*Frauds, Statute of.*"

(*c*) The measure of damages in an action for not accepting goods under a contract of sale, is, in general, the difference between the contract price and the market price of similar goods at the time when they ought to have been accepted (*Boorman* v. *Nash*, 9 B. & C. 145;

2. On the —— of ——, 18—, the defendant, A. B., at Hull, acting for the said partnership, ordered of the plaintiff 600 bags of potatoes, to be supplied in two lots of 300 bags each, at the price of £4 7*s*. 6*d*. per score bags.

3. The plaintiff then accepted the said order, and agreed to supply the said potatoes so ordered to the defendants.

4. The plaintiff in accordance with the said order supplied 300 bags of the said potatoes to the defendants.

5. The defendants took delivery of and accepted the said 300 bags of potatoes, but absolutely refused to take the remaining 300 bags of the said potatoes ordered, or to take any more of the said potatoes, and wrongfully repudiated their contract to take 600 bags of the said potatoes at the said price.

6. The plaintiff was always ready and willing to supply the remaining 300 bags of the said potatoes to the defendants as ordered, as above stated [and indeed offered to do so].

7. The defendants would not take, and have not, though the time for so doing has long elapsed, taken delivery of the remaining 300 bags of potatoes or any of them, but, as above stated, they have wrongfully repudiated their contract with regard to them.

8. The defendants have not paid the price of the 300 bags of potatoes which they took delivery of and accepted, but only a part of it, namely, £10. 5*s*. 8*d*., and a balance of £55. 6*s*. 10*d*. is now due from and payable by them to the plaintiff in respect thereof.

Philpotts v. *Evans*, 5 M. & W. 475), and if they are deliverable by instalments the same rule applies to each instalment. (*Brown* v. *Muller*, L. R. 7 Ex. 319; 41 L. J. Ex. 214; *Roper* v. *Johnson*, L. R. 8 C. P. 167; 42 L. J. C. P. 65.) If there is no evidence of any such loss, the damages are, in general, nominal only. (*Valpy* v. *Oakeley*, 16 Q. B. 941; 20 L. J. Q. B. 380.) See as to forbearance at the request of the opposite party, *note* (*a*), *ante*, p. 302.

The purchaser cannot anticipate the claim for damages by giving previous notice of his intention not to accept, unless the vendor assents to, or acts upon, such notice, and terminates the contract. (*Philpotts* v. *Evans*, *supra*; *Ripley* v. *M'Clare*, 4 Ex. 345; *Xenos* v *Danube, &c., Railway Co.*, 11 C. B. N. S. 152; 13 C. B. N. S. 825; 21 L. J. C. P. 84, 284; *Frost* v. *Knight*, L. R. 7 Ex. 111; 41 L. J. Ex. 78.) Where there is no market price for the goods, as, for instance, where they are useless to any one but the purchaser, it would seem that the whole price could be recovered.

9. When the defendants absolutely refused to take delivery of the remaining 300 bags of potatoes, and wrongfully repudiated their said contract with regard to them as above stated, the plaintiff resold the said remaining 300 bags of potatoes, but the market had then fallen, and they only realised at the rate of £3 17*s*. 6*d*. per score bags, and the plaintiff lost upon such re-sale a sum of £7. 10*s*.

Against a Purchaser for not accepting Goods sold to him by Sample (*d*).

1. The plaintiff is a soap manufacturer carrying on business in London, and the defendant is a hairdresser and perfumer carrying on business in High-street, Oxford.

2. On the 15th of June, 1879, it was agreed between the plaintiff (through his traveller) and the defendant that the plaintiff should sell to the defendant and that the defendant should buy of the plaintiff the following quantities of soaps and perfumery [*set out particulars*], and deliver the same to the defendant in the first week of the next July, the same to be equal to the samples then shown to the defendant, for the sum of £—— payable upon the said delivery.

3. The plaintiff delivered the said soaps and perfumery in the said first week of July to the defendant.

4. The said soaps and perfumery so delivered were equal to the said samples.

5. The defendant rejected, and refused to accept, the said soaps and perfumery, and returned the same to the plaintiff without paying the said price thereof or any portion of it.

6. [The plaintiff thereupon sold the said soaps and

(*d*) Goods sold by sample must agree with the sample, and the purchaser is entitled to a reasonable time to ascertain if they so agree, and may then, in general, reject them if they do not so agree. (*Heilbutt* v. *Hickson*, L. R. 7 C. P. 438 ; 41 L. J. C. P. 228 ; *Grimoldby* v. *Wells*, L. R. 10 C. P. 391 ; 44 L. J. C. P. 203.) A sale by sample excludes any implied warranty of matters that can be judged of by the sample. (*Mody* v. *Gregson*, L. R. 4 Ex. 49 ; 38 L. J. Ex. 12.)

The purchaser, having a right to reject goods, is not bound to go to the expense or trouble of returning them to the seller, but may reject them by clearly notifying his rejection to the seller. (*Grimoldby* v. *Wells*, *supra*.)

perfumery for the best price obtainable, which was £——, being £—— less than the said agreed price.]

7. [The plaintiff further in consequence of the defendant's rejection of the said soaps and perfumery, lost £—— which he paid for the carriage thereof to and from the defendant at Oxford.]

The like, where the Terms of the Agreement have been reduced into writing and signed so as to satisfy the Statute of Frauds (*e*).

1. & 2. [*As in form next above.*]

3. The terms of the above agreement were on the same day reduced into writing and signed by the defendant.

4, &c. [*As in paragraphs* 3, *&c., of form next above.*]

The like, where the Contract was made by Letters (*e*).

1. [*As in form next but one above.*]

2. By letters bearing date the 3rd, 4th, 7th, 9th, and 15th of June, 1879, it was agreed between the plaintiff and the defendant that the plaintiff should sell to the defendant, &c. [*as in form next but one above.*]

3, &c. [*As in form next but one above.*]

For a Statement of Claim by an Assignee of a Debt for Goods Sold and Delivered under the Companies Act, 1862, ss. 95, 157, *see "Assignment of Debts," ante,* p. 59.

For a Statement of Claim by Husband and Wife for the Price of Goods Sold and Delivered by the Wife before Marriage, see "Husband and Wife," ante, p. 196.

(*e*) See *ante, note* (*a*), p. 301, and "Defences," "*Frauds, Statute of,*" and "*Agreements,*" *ante,* p. 50.

For a Statement of Claim against a Married Woman Charging her Separate Estate, see "Husband and Wife," ante, p. 203.

For a Statement of Claim against Husband and Wife for the Price of Goods supplied to the Wife during Coverture, to Recover Payment out of Property made her Separate Estate by the "Married Women's Property Act, 1870," *the Goods not being supplied on the Credit of the Husband, see "Husband and Wife," ante, p.* 210.

For a Statement of Claim by a Surviving Partner for Goods Sold and Delivered by Himself and his Deceased Partner jointly, see "Partners," ante p. 294.

For Statements of Claim for Goods Sold and Delivered in other Cases, see "Accounts Stated," "Agent," "Auctioneer," "Bankruptcy," "Crops," &c.

For Damages for failure to deliver Goods contracted for (*f*).

1. On the —— of ——, 18—, the defendant [by an agreement in writing] agreed to sell and deliver to the

---

(*f*) In an action for not delivering goods under a contract of sale the measure of damages is, in general, the difference between the contract price and the market price at the time appointed for delivery (*Gainsford* v. *Carroll*, 2 B. & C. 625; *Startup* v. *Cortazzi*, 2 C. M. & R. 165; *Burrow* v. *Arnaud*, 8 Q. B. 595, 609; *Josling* v. *Irvine*, 6 H. & N. 512; 30 L. J. Ex. 78), and if they are deliverable by instalments the same rule applies to each instalment. (*Brown* v. *Muller*, L. R. 7 Ex. 319; 41 L. J. Ex. 214.) And the damages are calculated upon a similar principle when the action is brought upon a complete breach before the times for delivery are all elapsed, as for instance, upon an absolute repudiation of and refusal to perform the contract. (*Roper* v. *Johnson*, L. R. 8 C. P. 167; 42 L. J. C. P. 65; and see *Frost* v. *Knight*, L. R. 7 Ex. 111; 41 L. J. Ex. 78.) The vendor cannot diminish the claim for damages by giving previous notice of intention not to deliver, unless the purchaser consents to rescind the contract upon such notice. (*Leigh* v. *Paterson*, 8 Taunt. 540; and see *Philpotts* v. *Evans*, 5 M. & W. 475; *Roper* v. *Johnson*, *supra*.)

plaintiff 50 tons of cotton seed pitch at the price of £2. 5*s.* per ton, and the plaintiff agreed to accept and pay for the same.

2. The plaintiff has always been ready and willing to accept and pay for the same.

3. A reasonable time for the delivery of the said pitch has elapsed.

4. The defendant has not delivered the said pitch or any of it.

Where there is no difference between the contract price and the market price the damages are only nominal. (*Valpy* v. *Oakeley*, 16 Q. B. 941.) Where there is no market for goods similar to those contracted for, the purchaser may buy goods as nearly like those contracted for as he is able, and recover the difference in price as damages. (*Hinde* v. *Liddell*, L. R. 10 Q. B. 265; 44 L. J. Q. B. 105.) It was held that where goods of similar quality were not procurable, the price at which the buyer had resold might be taken as the value. (*France* v. *Gaudet*, L. R. 6 Q. B. 199; 40 L. J. Q. B. 121. See further *Elbinger, &c.*, v. *Armstrong*, L. R. 9 Q. B. 476; 43 L. J. Q. B. 211.)

Where a contract was made with a manufacturer for the supply of an article which was not to be procured in the market, and which he knew was intended for shipment and sale abroad, it was held upon a failure to deliver the whole at the time contracted for, and the delivery, after delay, of a part only, that damages were recoverable in respect of a sale to a foreign buyer, and of the extra freight and insurance upon the part delivered caused by the loss of season through the delay. (*Borne* v. *Hutchinson*, 18 C. B. N. S. 445; 34 L. J. C. P. 169.)

Loss of profit on a resale cannot be recovered in general, unless it is at the time of the contract brought to the notice of the seller that such resale is intended, so that such damages are fairly within the contemplation of the seller at the time of the contract, and there is no market in which it is reasonably practicable for the purchaser to buy goods to perform his contract for resale. (*Williams* v. *Reynolds*, 6 B. & S. 495; 34 L. J. Q. B. 221; *Randall* v. *Raper*, E. B. & E. 84; *Cory* v. *Thames Iron Works Co.*, L. R. 3 Q. B. 181; 37 L. J. Q. B. 68; *Hydraulic Eng. Co.* v. *McHaffie*, 4 Q. B. D. 670; "*Damages*," *ante*, p. 19.)

If the price has been paid, the buyer is entitled to recover the whole market value of the goods at the time of delivery; but where the price had been paid by a bill, and after a breach of contract by the vendor in not delivering the goods the bill was dishonoured, the purchaser was held entitled to recover only the difference between the contract price and the market price, as in the case where the price remains unpaid. (*Valpy* v. *Oakeley*, *supra*; *Griffiths* v. *Perry*, 1 E. & E. 680; 28 L. J. Q. B. 204.)

Where the property in the goods has passed under the contract, but the price has not been paid, and the vendor has wrongfully converted and disposed of the goods so as to preclude himself from

5. The market price of such pitch at the time when the defendant should have delivered the same was £5 per ton [and the plaintiff was compelled to and did purchase pitch of like kind, quantity, and quality in the market at the said price of £5 per ton].

For Damages for delivery of Goods not as contracted for (f).

1. The plaintiff on or about the —— of ——, 18—, agreed with the defendants to buy from the defendants, and the defendants agreed with the plaintiff to sell to the plaintiff about 300 tons of rapeseed, *ex* Edgar Gregson, then in warehouse at Leith, at the price of 28*s*. 6*d*. per 424lbs, to be weighed and sound delivered *ex* ship at Hull.

2. The plaintiff duly paid to the defendants the said price of the said rapeseed, amounting to £2,284. 3*s*.

3. The defendants delivered the said rapeseed *ex* ship at Hull, but 920 quarters thereof were not sound delivered, but were delivered *ex* ship at Hull in an unsound condition.

4. On account of the unsound condition of the said 920 quarters the said 920 quarters were of no use to the plaintiff, and the plaintiff sold them by auction in order to dispose of them.

5. Such auction was conducted in a proper manner, and was a reasonable mode of disposing of such rapeseed.

6. The said 920 quarters realised, after deducting the expenses of and incidental to such auction, £811 19*s*. 9*d*. less than the price paid therefor by the plaintiff as above stated to the defendants.

7. The said 920 quarters were in fact worth at Hull £811 19*s*. 9*d*. less than if they had been sound delivered *ex* ship at Hull.

---

delivering them and recovering the price, the vendee can only recover the difference between the value of the goods and the contract price, and cannot recover the full value by suing for the conversion of the goods instead of for the breach of contract (*Chinery* v. *Viall*, 5 H. & N. 288; 29 L. J. Ex. 180); but if the vendor wrongfully retakes the goods after delivery, the vendee may recover the full value in an action of trespass or trover, the vendor having his remedy for the price. (*Gillard* v. *Brittan*, 8 M. & W. 575; *Stephens* v. *Wilkinson*, 2 B. & Ad. 320.)

See further Leake on Contracts, 1058, *et seq.*, and "*Warranty*," *post*.

SALE; II. OF LAND (*a*).

Claim by Vendor against Purchaser on a sale by Private Contract for refusing to complete the Purchase.

1. On the —— day of ——, 18—, it was agreed by and between the plaintiff and the defendant [by an agreement

---

(*a*) By the Statute of Frauds, 29 Car. II. c. 3, s. 4, it is enacted, that no action shall be brought whereby to charge any person upon any contract or sale of lands, tenements, or hereditaments, or any interest in or concerning them, unless the agreement upon which such action shall be brought, or some memorandum or note thereof shall be in writing, and signed by the party to be charged therewith, or some other person thereunto by him lawfully authorized. See the decisions on this section, Roscoe on Evidence, 14th ed., p. 296; Chitty on Contracts, 10th ed., p. 272; Leake on Contracts, 249; "Defences," "*Frauds, Statute of.*"

As to the authority of an auctioneer or his clerk to sign a memorandum of the contract in sales by public auction, see "*Auctioneer,*" *ante*, p. 65.

As to pleading the fact of the contract being in writing see "*Agreements,*" *ante*, p. 50; "*Sale of Goods,*" *ante*, p. 301.

Actions for specific performance are assigned to the Chancery Division; as to them see "*Relief other than damages or payment of debt,*" *ante, note*, p. 23.

In an action against the purchaser, where the estate remains the property of the vendor (though possession may have been given to the purchaser) the vendor is not, in the absence of an agreement to that effect, entitled to claim the amount of the unpaid purchase-money as a debt, and the measure of damages in actions against a purchaser for not completing is, in general, the loss sustained by the vendor from the breach of contract, as the difference between the amount of the agreed purchase-money and the estimated saleable value of the land, together with the amount of the loss of interest on the purchase-money and the costs incurred. See *Laird* v. *Pim*, 7 M. & W. 474; and Dart, V. & P. 5th ed., p. 985.

But ordinarily the amount of the deposit, if any, must be allowed for in the computation of damages, and this even where there is a condition that the purchaser shall make good any loss on a resale, and the vendor sues for the amount of the loss on such resale. (*Ockenden* v. *Henly*, E. B. & E. 485; 27 L. J. Q. B. 361; *Essex* v. *Daniell*, L. R. 10 C. P. 538; 32 L. T. 476.)

A condition that a purchaser's deposit shall be forfeited in the event of his failure to comply with any of the conditions of sale, does not amount to a stipulation that the amount of such deposit shall be taken as liquidated damages for a breach of the contract by the purchaser, and does not prevent the vendor from recovering general damages for such breach, subject to such deduction of the amount of the deposit as above mentioned. (*Icely* v. *Grew*, 6 N. & M. 467; *Essex* v. *Daniell*, *supra*.)

But it is otherwise where there is a stipulation to the effect that in the case of failure to complete the purchase, the deposit shall be

in writing signed by them on that date] that the plaintiff should sell to the defendant and the defendant should purchase from the plaintiff a messuage and land situate and being No. 21, —— Street, in the parish of ——, in

---

forfeited, and the amount of it taken as liquidated damages. In such a case the vendor was held entitled to recover the amount of an I. O. U., which had been given for the deposit money. See *Hinton* v. *Sparkes*, L. R. 3 C. P. 161 ; 37 L. J. C. P. 81.

On a contract for the sale of land, in the absence of any contrary stipulation, the vendor must make out a good title to the estate which he contracts to sell. (*Hall* v. *Betty*, 4 M. & G. 410 ; *Jeakes* v. *White*, 6 Ex. 873 ; 21 L. J. Ex. 265 ; *Stranks* v. *St. John*, L. R. 2 C. P. 376 ; 36 L. J. C. P. 118 ; *Clarke* v. *Willott*, L. R. 7 Ex. 313 ; 41 L. J. Ex. 197 ; *Noble* v. *Edwardes*, 5 Ch. D. 378 ; 37 L. T. 7), and the rule formerly was that he was bound to show such title for a period of at least sixty years, see *Frend* v. *Buckley*, L. R. 5 Q. B. 213 ; 39 L. J. Q. B. 90, but by s. 1 of the Vendor and Purchaser Act, 1874 (37 & 38 Vict. c 78), in the case of any contract of sale of land made after 1874, and subject to any stipulation to the contrary in the contract, forty years is substituted for sixty years as the period of commencement of title which a purchaser may require in ordinary cases.

In the absence of any stipulation to the contrary, the vendor is bound to show a good title to the property sold, both as to the legal estate, and as to the entire equitable estate and interest (*Maberley* v. *Robins*, 5 Taunt. 625 ; *Jeakes* v. *White*, *supra* ; *Stevens* v. *Austen*, 3 E. & E. 685 ; 30 L. J. Q. B. 212 ; *Clarke* v. *Willott*, *supra* ; *Noble* v. *Edwardes*, *supra* ; Leake on Contracts, 828) ; and it is not sufficient to show a title depending on a doubtful question of fact. (*Simmons* v. *Heseltine*, 5 C. B. N. S. 554 ; 28 L. J. C. P. 129 ; and see *Jeakes* v. *White*, and *Clarke* v. *Willott*, above cited.)

But the vendor's obligations as to showing title may be, and usually are, restricted by special stipulations in the contract or conditions of sale, and with respect to sales made after the 31st of December, 1881, certain stipulations diminishing the vendor's obligations as to showing title are, in the absence of agreement to the contrary, to be implied (44 & 45 Vict. c. 41, s. 3).

Upon a contract to grant a lease there is (subject to the provisions of 37 & 38 Vict. c. 78, s. 2, and 44 & 45 Vict. c. 41, s. 13), an implied undertaking by the lessor that he has title to grant such lease (*Stranks* v. *St. John*, L. R. 2 C. P. 376 ; 36 L. J. C. P. 118 ; and see *Roper* v. *Coombes*, 6 B. & C. 534), and it was held that every contract for the sale of a lease, in the absence of a stipulation to the contrary, implied an undertaking to make out the lessor's title to demise, as well as that of the vendor to the lease itself. (*Souter* v. *Drake*, 5 B. & Ad. 992 ; *Hall* v. *Betty*, 4 M. & G. 410 ; *White* v. *Foljambe*, 11 Ves. 337 ; *Ogilvie* v. *Foljambe*, 3 Mer. 53 ; and see *Tweed* v. *Mills*, L. R. 1 C. P. 39.)

But the law on this subject has been materially modified, in the case of contracts made after 1874, by the provisions of s. 2 of 37 & 38 Vict. c. 78, which enacts that (subject to any stipulation to the contrary in the contract) "under a contract to grant or assign a term of years, whether derived or to be derived out of a freehold

the county of ——, with the appurtenances [for an estate of fee simple in possession] at the price of £1000 and upon the terms and conditions hereinafter mentioned.

2. The said terms and conditions (so far as material

---

or leasehold estate, the intended lessee or assign shall not be entitled to call for the title to the freehold," and with regard to contracts made after 1881 by those of s. 13 of 44 & 45 Vict. c. 41, which enacts that (subject to any stipulation to the contrary) "on a contract to grant a lease for a term of years to be derived out of a leasehold interest, with a leasehold reversion, the intended lessee shall not have the right to call for the title to that reversion."

In a contract for the sale of an agreement for a lease, there is no implied undertaking that the lessor has a good title to grant the lease (*Kintrea* v. *Preston*, 1 H. & N. 357; 25 L. J. Ex. 287.)

Under an agreement for the sale of land, the vendor, in the absence of any stipulation to the contrary, is bound to deliver at his own expense to the purchaser or the purchaser's solicitor a proper abstract of his title, and also to verify it, if required, by the production of the title deeds (*Samson* v. *Rhodes*, 6 Bing. N. C. 261; 8 Sc. 544; *Sharland* v. *Liefchild*, 4 C. B. 529; *Steer* v. *Crowley*, 14 C. B. N. S. 337; 32 L. J. C. P. 191; *Oakden* v. *Pike*, 34 L. J. Ch. 620; *Gray* v. *Fowler*, L. R. 8 Ex. 249; 42 L. J. Ex. 161; *Bryant* v. *Busk*, 4 Russ. 1; *Frend* v. *Buckley*, *sup.*; and see Leake on Contracts, 831); this is, however, subject in the case of sales made after 1881 to the provisions of s. 3 of 44 & 45 Vict. c. 41.

An averment of the vendor's readiness and willingness to convey implies the ability to do so, and is a sufficient averment of the vendor's title to the estate (*De Medina* v. *Norman*, 9 M. & W. 820.)

It is not under ordinary circumstances a condition precedent to the vendor's right to sue on the contract that he should have tendered a conveyance, as it is the purchaser's duty, unless there is a stipulation to the contrary, to prepare and tender the conveyance for execution, and it is therefore sufficient if the vendor was ready and willing to execute it. (*Poole* v. *Hill*, 6 M. & W. 835; and see *Stephens* v. *De Medina*, 4 Q. B. 422; *Marsden* v. *Moore*, 4 H. & N. 500.)

By s. 25 (7) of the Judicature Act, 1873, as amended by s. 10 of the Jud. Act, 1875, stipulations in contracts, as to time or otherwise, which would not, before the Act, have been deemed to be or to have become of the essence of such contracts in a court of equity, shall receive in all courts the same construction and effect as they would have theretofore received in Equity. See *Patrick* v. *Milner*, 2 C. P. D. 342; 46 L. J. C. P. 537; *Noble* v. *Edwardes*, *supra;* Leake on Contracts, 846, 847; Dart, V. & P. 5th ed., p. 974. In sales of land, except where the property sold is of a diminishing or fluctuating nature, time is not of the essence of the contract, unless made so by express stipulation or necessary implication; yet, though time may not be of the essence of the contract, where there is great and improper delay on one side, the other party has a right to fix a reasonable time within which the contract is to be completed, and a distinct written notice by that other that he shall consider the contract at an end if not completed within a reasonable time named

to this action) were as follows, viz. [*here state the conditions material to the cause of action, as for instance*], that the defendant should pay to the plaintiff a deposit of £100, in part of the said purchase-money, on the signing

---

is treated as binding on the party to whom it is given (*Patrick* v. *Milner*, *supra;* Sugden, V. & P. 14th ed., p. 268; *King* v. *Wilson*, 6 Beav. 124, 126; *Pegg* v. *Wisden*, 16 Beav. 239, 244; *Wells* v. *Maxwell*, 33 L. J. Ch. 44, 50; *Green* v. *Sevin*, 13 Ch. D. 589; 41 L. T. 724; *Crawford* v. *Toogood*, 13 Ch. D. 153; 49 L. J. Ch. 108.)

By the "Sale of Land by Auction Act, 1867," (30 & 31 Vict. c. 48,) s. 4, it is enacted "that from and after the passing of this Act, whenever a sale by auction of land would be invalid at law by reason of the employment of a puffer, the same shall be deemed invalid in equity as well as at law."

By s. 5, "that the particulars or conditions of sale by auction of any land shall state whether such land will be sold without reserve, or subject to a reserved price, or whether a right to bid is reserved; if it is stated that such land will be sold without reserve, or to that effect, then it shall not be lawful for the seller to employ any person to bid at such sale, or for the auctioneer to take knowingly any bidding from any such person." See *Gilliat* v. *Gilliat*, L. R. 9. Eq. 60; 39 L. J. C. 142.

By s. 6, "where any sale by auction of land is declared either in the particulars or conditions of such sale to be subject to a right for the seller to bid, it shall be lawful for the seller, or any one person on his behalf, to bid at such auction in such manner as he may think proper."

Before the above Act, if an estate was advertised or declared to be sold *without reserve*, and a puffer was, without notice, employed at the sale, the sale was held both at law and in equity to be voidable by the purchaser on the ground of fraud. (*Thornett* v. *Haines*, 15 M. & W. 367; *Meadows* v. *Banner*, 5 Madd. 34; *Robinson* v. *Wall*, 2 Phill. 375.) See further, "*Auctioneer*," *ante*, p. 65.

Where the contract is rescinded for want of title or for default on the part of the vendor, and there is a complete failure of consideration, the purchaser is entitled to recover the deposit as money received to his use; see *ante*, "*Money Received*," p. 286; *Simmons* v. *Heseltine*, 5 C. B. N. S. 554; 28 L. J. C. P. 129; *Gosbell* v. *Archer*, 2 A. & E. 500; and see *Blackburn* v. *Smith*, 2 Ex. 783; *Patrick* v. *Milner*, 2 C. P. D. 342; but interest on the amount of the deposit is recoverable only as damages (*Maberley* v. *Robins*, 5 Taunt. 625; *Bradshaw* v. *Bennett*, 5 C. & P. 48). So also the purchaser is entitled to a return of the deposit where the contract is rescinded on the ground of fraud or mistake (*Aberaman Ironworks Co.* v. *Wickens*, L. R. 4 Ch. Ap. 101; 20 L. T. 89; *Torrance* v. *Bolton*, L. R. 14 Eq. 124; 41 L. J. Ch. 643), or where it is defeated by a condition. (*Giles* v. *Edwards*, 7 T. R. 181; *Wright* v. *Newton*, 2 C. M. & R. 124.) But after conveyance of the land bargained for, the purchaser cannot claim the deposit as money received to his use, on the ground that the vendor had no title to the land. (*Clare* v. *Lamb*, L. R. 10 C. P. 334; 44 L. J. C. P. 177.)

If the purchaser makes default, and by the terms of the contract the deposit is forfeited, he cannot recover it. (*Beavan* v. *M'Donnell*,

of the said agreement, and the remainder thereof on the —— day of ——, 18—, on which day the said purchase should be completed, and that the plaintiff should deduce and make a good title to the said messuage and premises

---

9 Ex. 309; and see *Palmer* v. *Temple*, 9 A. & E. 508; *Casson* v. *Roberts*, 31 Beav. 613; 32 L. J. Ch. 105; *Depree* v. *Bedborough*, 4 Giff. 479; 33 L. J. Ch. 134.) And even where there is no such condition, the purchaser, generally speaking, is not entitled to recover the deposit, if the sale goes off from his default, as, for instance, from his refusal to accept completion or his repudiation of the contract. (*Ex p. Barrell*, L. R. 10 Ch. 512; 44 L. J. B. 138; *Thomas* v. *Brown*, 1 Q. B. D. 714; 45 L. J. Q. B. 811.)

Where, after a sale by auction, the purchaser is entitled to rescind the contract, he may maintain an action for the deposit against the auctioneer if he has received it as a stakeholder on behalf of both parties, or against the vendor if it has been paid to him (*Harington* v. *Hoggart*, 1 B. & Ad. 577); but not against a person to whom the money was paid merely as agent for the vendor. (*Bamford* v. *Shuttleworth*, 11 A. & E. 926; and see *Edgell* v. *Day*, L. R. 1 C. P. 80; 35 L. J. C. P. 7.) He cannot recover interest from the auctioneer although the latter has invested the money at interest. (*Harington* v. *Hoggart, supra.*)

See further "*Auctioneer*," *ante*, p. 65.

In an action by the purchaser against the vendor for not completing the purchase, the purchaser can claim as damages the costs of preparing and entering into the agreement, and the costs of investigating the title, and of endeavouring to procure a good title (*Hodges* v. *Earl of Litchfield*, 1 Bing. N. C. 492; *Hanslip* v. *Padwick*, 5 Ex. 615); and it is sufficient if these costs have been incurred, though not paid before action (*Richardson* v. *Chasen*, 10 Q. B. 756; and see *Pritchet* v. *Boevey*, 1 C. & M. 775; and *ante*, p. 22.) He may also claim interest on the deposit money as special damage (*De Bernales* v. *Wood*, 3 Camp. 258; *Farquhar* v. *Farley*, 7 Taunt. 592; *Hodges* v. *Earl of Litchfield*, *supra*); though not as a debt. (*Maberley* v. *Robins*, 5 Taunt. 625; *Bradshaw* v. *Bennett*, 5 C. & P. 48.) He cannot claim the costs of raising the purchase money in readiness for payment, nor the interest on it while lying idle, where it has been raised prematurely and before ascertaining whether the vendor has a good title (*Hanslip* v. *Padwick*, *sup.*); but where the purchaser has acted reasonably and properly in raising and setting apart the purchase money, and was justified by the circumstances in so doing, it seems that such interest would be recoverable as special damage. See *Sherry* v. *Oke*, 3 Dowl. 349; *Howland* v. *Norris*, 1 Cox, 59.

He cannot claim the costs of a Chancery suit brought by him against the defendant for specific performance, and dismissed for defect of the defendant's title (*Malden* v. *Fyson*, 11 Q. B. 292); nor the extra costs of a Chancery suit brought against him by the defendant and dismissed with costs. (*Hodges* v. *Earl of Litchfield*, *sup.*; and see *Gray* v. *Fowler*, L. R. 8 Ex. 249.) Expenses unnecessarily incurred before entering into the contract cannot be claimed. (*Hodges* v. *Earl of Litchfield*, *sup.*)

The purchaser cannot claim damages for the loss of his bargain, or for loss of profit on a resale, where the vendor fails to complete by

on or before the —— day of —— 18—, and on payment of the said remainder of the said purchase-money as aforesaid should execute to the defendant a proper conveyance of the said messuage and premises to be prepared by and at the expense of the defendant.

---

reason of a defect in his title, provided the vendor acted *boná fide*, and had reasonable grounds for supposing that he had, or could in due time acquire, a good title. (*Flureau* v. *Thornhill*, 2 Bl. 1070; *Walker* v. *Moore*, 10 B. & C. 416; *Pounsett* v. *Fuller*, 17 C. B. 660; 25 L. J. C. P. 145; *Sikes* v. *Wild*, 1 B. & S. 587; 4 *ib.* 421; 30 L. J. Q. B. 325; 32 *ib.* 375; *Bain* v. *Fothergill*, L. R. 7 H. L. 158; 43 L. J. Ex. 423.)

It was laid down in the case of *Hopkins* v. *Grazebrook*, 6 B. & C. 31 (which was followed in *Robinson* v. *Harman*, 1 Ex. 850), that where the vendor contracts to sell an estate, knowing at the time that he has no title, he is liable in an action for the breach of the contract to have damages assessed against him for the loss of the bargain. But in *Bain* v. *Fothergill*, *supra*, the case of *Hopkins* v. *Grazebrook* was overruled, and it was also said (though not expressly decided) that the rule laid down in *Flureau* v. *Thornhill* as to the limits within which damages may be recovered upon the breach of a contract for the sale of a real estate must be taken to be without exception, and that "if a person enters into a contract for the sale of a real estate knowing that he has no title to it nor any means of acquiring it, the purchaser cannot recover damages beyond the expenses he has incurred, by an action for the breach of the contract; he can only obtain other damages by an action for deceit." See *per* Lord Chelmsford, L. R. 7 H. L., at p. 207.

But the rule above-mentioned does not apply where the vendor fails to complete from any other cause than inability from defect of title—*e.g.*, where the sale goes off from his refusing to complete (see *Simons* v. *Patchett*, 7 E. & B. at p. 572), or from his declining, or purposely omitting, to take the necessary steps for giving possession to the purchaser. (*Engell* v. *Fitch*, L. R. 3 Q. B. 314; 4 *ib.* 659; 37 L. J. Q. B. 145; 38 L. J. Q. B. 304; *Simons* v. *Patchett*, 7 E. & B. at p. 572; and see *Bain* v. *Fothergill*, *supra*.) Under such circumstances the purchaser is entitled to recover damages for the loss of his bargain, and the measure of such damages is the difference between the contract price and the value of the land at the time of the breach of contract, and the fact that the purchaser has resold the land at an enhanced price is *primâ facie* evidence of its actual market value. (*Engell* v. *Fitch*, *supra*; *Walker* v. *Moore*, 10 B. & C. 416.) So where, on an agreement to grant a lease, the intended lessor wilfully refused to give possession according to the contract, he was held liable for damages in respect of the loss of profits by delay of a trade, for the purpose of which, as he knew, the premises had been engaged by the intended lessee. (*Jaques* v. *Millar*, 6 Ch. D. 153; 47 L. J. Ch. 544.)

The rule in *Flureau* v. *Thornhill*, *supra*, does not apply where there has been an actual conveyance to the purchaser of the estate bargained for; in such a case the purchaser's remedy under ordinary circumstances is upon the covenants for title (if any) contained expressly or by implication in the conveyance (*Clare* v. *Lamb*, L. R. 10 C. P.

3. [*Here state the fulfilment or waiver of any conditions precedent to the cause of action, as for instance.*] The plaintiff accordingly deduced and made a good title to the said messuage and premises within the time prescribed, as aforesaid, by the said agreement [*or* within due time in that behalf], and was always [*or* at all times material to this action] ready and willing to complete the said sale and purchase, and to execute to the defendant a proper conveyance of the said messuage and premises, and the defendant always had notice of the facts above-mentioned.

4. The defendant did not nor would on the said —— day of ——, 18—, or at any time complete the said purchase on his part or pay the plaintiff the said remainder of the said purchase-money amounting to £900, and has absolutely refused to do so.

5. By reason of the matters above complained of [*here state the damage sustained by the plaintiff, as for instance*] the plaintiff has lost the benefit of the said agreement, and has been deprived of the said remainder of the said purchase-money, together with interest thereon from the said —— day of —— 18—, and has lost the expense, amounting to £——, to which he was put in deducing the said title and in preparing to perform the said agreement on his part, and in endeavouring to procure the performance thereof by the defendant.

Claim by Vendor against Purchaser on a Sale by Auction for not completing the Purchase.

1. The plaintiff, on the —— day of ——, 18—, caused to be put up for sale by public auction a messuage and land called —— House, situate in the parish of ——, in the county of ——, upon and subject to the following among other conditions of sale.

334; 44 L. J. C. P. 177); and in an action for the breach of such covenants he is, generally speaking, entitled, if evicted, to recover the whole value of the estate, besides any special damage sustained by him in consequence of the breach. Thus, in an action for a breach of the covenant for quiet enjoyment in a lease the value of the term is recoverable. (*Williams* v. *Burrell*, 1 C. B. 402; and see *Lock* v. *Furze*, 19 C. B. N. S. 96; 34 L. J. C. P. 201; L. R. 1 C. P. 441; 35 L. J. C. P. 141.) For mode of stating claims for breaches of covenant, see "*Landlord and Tenant*," *ante*, p. 243; "*Agreements*," *ante*, p. 51.

2. The said conditions of sale were as follows : [*State the conditions material to the cause of action, as for instance*] that the highest bidder should be the purchaser, and that the purchaser should pay the vendor a deposit of £—— per cent. in part of the purchase-money immediately after the sale, and the remainder of the purchase-money on the —— day of ——, 18—, on which day the purchase should be completed, and that the vendor should within 10 days from the date of the said sale deliver to the purchaser's solicitor an abstract of the vendor's title to the said premises [commencing with, &c., *according to the fact*], and that on payment of the remainder of the said purchase-money as aforesaid, the vendor should execute a conveyance of the said premises to the purchaser, and that such conveyance should be prepared by, and at the expense of the purchaser, and that if the purchaser should fail to comply with the said conditions, his said deposit should thereupon be forfeited, and the vendor should be at liberty to resell the said premises by public auction or private contract, as he should think fit, and the deficiency, if any, in price and all expenses attending such resale should be paid by the purchaser to the vendor.

3. Upon such putting up to sale of the said premises the defendant was the highest bidder for the same, and purchased the said premises from the plaintiff, and the plaintiff sold the same to the defendant for £——, upon and subject to the said conditions of sale [and the defendant signed an agreement of that date, whereby he agreed with the plaintiff to purchase the said premises at the said price, and upon and subject to the said conditions].

4. The defendant then paid the plaintiff such deposit as aforesaid, and the plaintiff within 10 days from the date of the said sale [*or* within due time in that behalf] duly delivered to the defendant's solicitor, Mr. —— ——, such abstract of the plaintiff's title to the said premises as specified in and by the said conditions as aforesaid, and duly verified the same [by producing to the defendant and his said solicitor the deeds and documents constituting the said title], and was always [*or* at all times material to this action] ready and willing to perform the said conditions in all respects on his part, and to execute to the defendant such conveyance of the said premises as aforesaid, and to complete the said sale of the said premises.

5. The defendant always [*or*, at all times material to this action] had notice of such readiness and willingness as above mentioned on the part of the plaintiff, and a reasonable time elapsed for the defendant to prepare, and tender for execution to the plaintiff such conveyance as aforesaid, and to entitle the plaintiff to have the said purchase completed, and the remainder of the said purchase-money paid by the defendant.

6. The defendant did not prepare or tender any such conveyance as aforesaid, and did not on the said —— day of ——, 18—, or at any time, pay the plaintiff the remainder of the said purchase-money, or complete the said purchase on his part.

7. By reason of the matters hereinbefore complained of, the plaintiff has been deprived of the said remainder of the said purchase-money, and of interest thereon, from the said —— day of ——, 18—, and has lost the expenses incurred by him, to the amount of £——, in making out and delivering the said abstract of his title, and in verifying the same, and in endeavouring to procure the completion of the said purchase on the part of the defendant.

8. After the defendant had failed as aforesaid to comply with the said conditions of sale, the plaintiff, in accordance with the said conditions, resold the said premises by public auction on the —— day of ——, 18—, for a less sum than the price aforesaid, viz., for £——, and there was a deficiency in price on such resale of £ ——, and the expenses attending such resale amounted to £——, of all which the defendant had notice, but did not pay the last-mentioned sums or either of them to the plaintiff.

Claim by Purchaser against Vendor on a Sale by Private Contract for not Completing.

1. By an agreement bearing date the —— day of ——, 18—, it was agreed by and between the plaintiff and the defendant that the defendant should sell to the plaintiff, and the plaintiff should purchase from the defendant [for an estate in fee simple] a messuage and land, situate &c. (*see the above precedents*), at the price of £——, upon the terms and conditions following, viz. [*state the conditions material to the cause of action, as follows*] that the plaintiff should pay the defendant a deposit of £—— in

part of the said purchase-money, on the signing of the said agreement, and the remainder on the —— day of —— 18—, on which day the said purchase should be completed, and that the defendant should on the —— day of ——, 18—, execute to the plaintiff a proper conveyance of the said premises, to be prepared at the plaintiff's expense.

2. The plaintiff paid the said deposit of £——, on the signing of the said agreement, and prepared such conveyance as aforesaid at his own expense, and tendered the same to the defendant on the said —— day of ——, 18—- [*or* within due time in that behalf, viz. on the —— day of ——, 18—], for execution, and was always [*or* at all times material to this action] ready and willing to pay to the defendant the said remainder of the said purchase-money, and to carry out the said agreement on his part.

3. The defendant always had notice of the facts above mentioned, and a reasonable time elapsed after such tender for the execution of the said conveyance and completion of the said sale by the defendant.

4. The defendant did not execute to the plaintiff such conveyance of the said premises, nor complete the said sale on his part [and wholly refused to do so].

5. By reason of the matters above complained of, the plaintiff has been deprived of the advantages and profits which he would have derived from the completion of the said purchase, and the performance of the said agreement, and has lost the money paid by him as such deposit as aforesaid, and the use of, and interest upon the money so paid [and other monies amounting to £——, provided and kept by him on and from the —— day of ——, 18—, for the completion of the said purchase], and has lost the amount of the expenses, amounting to £——, incurred by him in entering into, and preparing the said agreement, and in preparing the said conveyance, and in investigating the title of the defendant, and in preparing to perform the said agreement on his part, and in endeavouring to procure the performance thereof by the defendant.

6. The plaintiff also says that the consideration for the said sum of £——, paid by the plaintiff to the defendant as such deposit, as in the above 2nd paragraph mentioned, has, under the circumstances above mentioned wholly failed, and the said sum became due from, and

payable by the defendant to the plaintiff before the commencement of this action, yet the defendant has not paid the said sum, or any part thereof to the plaintiff.

Claim by Purchaser against Vendor on a Sale by Auction for not Delivering a proper Abstract of Title, and for not Making a Good Title.

1. The defendant, on the —— day of ——, 18—, caused to be put up for sale by public auction a messuage and land, situate, &c. [*describe the premises shortly, as in the above precedents*], upon, and subject to the following among other conditions of sale, viz. [*state the conditions material to the cause of action, as for instance*], that the highest bidder should be the purchaser, and that the purchaser should pay the vendor a deposit of £—— per cent. upon the amount of the purchase-money immediately after the sale, and the remainder of the purchase-money on the —— day of —— , 18—, on which day the purchase should be completed, and that the vendor should within 10 days from the date of the said sale deliver to the purchaser or his solicitor an abstract of the vendor's title to the said premises, commencing with an indenture, dated the —— day of ——, 18—, and that the title to be deduced and made by the vendor should commence with that indenture, and that the purchaser should not require the production of, or make any requisitions in respect of prior title, and that the expense of verifying the abstract with the deeds and documents should be borne by the purchaser, and that on payment of the remainder of the purchase-money as aforesaid, the vendor should execute a conveyance of the said premises to the purchaser at the purchaser's expense.

2. Upon such putting up for sale of the said premises, the plaintiff was the highest bidder for the same, and purchased the said premises from the defendant, and the defendant sold the same to the plaintiff for £——, upon and subject to the said conditions of sale.

3. The plaintiff paid the defendant the said deposit of £—— per cent. upon the amount of the said purchase-money, amounting to £——, immediately after the said sale, and was always [*or* at all times material to this action] ready and willing to pay the defendant the remainder of the said purchase money, in accordance with the said conditions of sale, and to do all things which

by the said conditions were required to be done and performed upon the part of the plaintiff, and to complete the said purchase, whereof the defendant always had notice.

4. The defendant has never delivered to the plaintiff, or to any solicitor of the plaintiff, any abstract [*or* any proper and sufficient abstract] of the defendant's title to the said premises, in accordance with the said conditions, although the time allowed for the delivery thereof as above stated by the conditions of sale expired before this action was commenced. [*If any abstract of title has been delivered, some particulars of the objections thereto should ordinarily be stated, as for instance,* and although the defendant on the —— day of ——, 18—, delivered to the plaintiff's solicitor a document purporting to be an abstract of the defendant's title to the said premises, the same was not a proper or sufficient abstract of such title within the meaning of the said conditions, and was defective in this, that &c., (*here state the defects complained of*)], and the defendant has never deduced, or made, or shown to the plaintiff, or to any solicitor of the plaintiff a good title, or any title of the defendant to the said premises, in accordance with the said conditions [and has wholly refused to carry out and complete the said sale on his part].

5. By reason of the matters above complained of, &c. [*here state the damage sustained by the plaintiff in consequence of the breaches of the contract by the defendant; see the last precedent, and see note* p. 312].

6. [*A claim may be added for the amount of the deposit as a debt; see paragraph* 6 *of the last precedent.*]

See a Form of Statement of Claim by a Purchaser against a Vendor claiming Specific Performance with an Additional or Alternative Claim of Damages. Hussey v. *Horne-Payne,* 8 Ch. D. 670; L. J. Ch. 519, 751; 4 App. Cas. 311; 48 L. J. Ch. 846.

SCHOOLMASTER.

Statement of Claim by a Schoolmaster for Tuition, Board, &c.

1. The plaintiff is the proprietor of a preparatory school at —— for the sons of gentlemen.

2. The plaintiff on the —— day of ——, 18—, at the request of the defendant received the defendant's son, G. H., at the said school upon the terms [contained in letters bearing date, *or as the case may be*] that the plaintiff should provide the said G. H. with education, board, and lodging, whilst he should continue at such school, and that the defendant should pay the plaintiff therefor £—— per term, on the —— of ——, the —— of ——, and the —— of —— in each year.

3. The said G. H. continued at the said school until the —— of ——, 18—, and was, whilst he so continued at the said school, provided by the plaintiff with education, board, and lodging on the terms aforesaid.

4. The defendant has not paid to the plaintiff the sum of £——, which on the —— of ——, 18—, became due from and payable by the defendant to the plaintiff in respect of the said education, board, and lodging of the said G. H.

By a Schoolmaster for removing a Pupil without a Term's Notice.

1. [*The same as in paragraph* 1 *of last preceding form.*]

2. [*The same as in paragraph* 2 *of last preceding form, and continue as follows:*] and that the defendant should continue the said G. H. at the said school to be educated, boarded, and lodged as aforesaid until the expiration of a term's notice to be given to the plaintiff by the defendant of his intention to take the said G. H. away from the said school, or in the absence of such notice should pay the plaintiff for one term at the rate aforesaid in addition to the terms during which the said G. H. had continued at the said school.

3. [*The same as in paragraph* 3 *of last preceding form, and continue as follows:*] and the plaintiff was always ready and willing to continue providing the said G. H. with education, board, and lodging upon the terms aforesaid, whereof the defendant had notice.

4. On the —— of ——, 18—, the defendant wrongfully took away the said G. H. from the said school without giving the plaintiff any such notice as agreed as aforesaid, and without making the plaintiff any such payment as aforesaid.

A like Form, Simeon v. *Watson,* 46 L. J. C. P. 679.

SHARES (*a*).

Statement of Claim for the price of Shares sold.

1. On the —— of ——, 18—, the plaintiff sold to the defendant, and the defendant purchased from the plaintiff —— shares in an undertaking called the —— Company, at the price of £—— per share, to be paid to the plaintiff upon the transfer of the said shares [*or* upon the —— of ——, 18—.]

(*a*) Shares are not "goods, wares, or merchandises" within the meaning of s. 17 of the Statute of Frauds (*Humble* v. *Mitchell*, 11 A. & E. 205 ; *Tempest* v. *Kilner*, 3 C. B. 249 ; and see Leake on Contracts, 258) ; nor are they an "interest in land" within the meaning of s. 4 of that statute, except in some few cases where they are such as to give the shareholders an actual interest in real estate. (*Humble* v. *Mitchell*, *supra* ; *Powell* v. *Jessopp*, 18 C. B. 336 ; 25 L. J. C. P. 199 ; and see Leake on Contracts, 254.)

Contracts relating to the sale and purchase of shares are regulated by the usages of the stock exchange or market in which they are made. (*Grissell* v. *Bristowe*, L. R. 4 C. P. 36, 49 ; 38 L. J. C. P. 10 ; *Maxted* v. *Paine*, L. R. 6 Ex. 132 ; 40 L. J. Ex. 57 ; *Nickalls* v. *Merry*, L. R. 7 H. L. 530 ; 45 L. J. Ch. 285 ; and see further as to such usages "*Broker*," *ante*, and Roscoe's Nisi Prius, 14th ed., p. 519 *et seq.*)

There is an implied contract between the vendor and purchaser of shares that the vendor shall be indemnified against the payment of calls made subsequently to the time fixed for the transfer of the shares, and that the purchaser shall be indemnified against the payment of calls made previously to such time. (*Walker* v. *Bartlett*, 17 C. B. 446 ; 18 C. B. 845 ; 25 L. J. C. P. 156, 263 ; *Rudge* v. *Bowman*, 37 L. J. Q. B. 193.) See as to wagers as to the price of shares or stocks "*Broker*," *ante*. p. 118.

By the 30 & 31 Vict. c. 29, s. 1, it is enacted "that all contracts, agreements, and tokens of sale and purchase which shall, from and after the 1st day of July, 1867, be made or entered into for the sale or transfer, or purporting to be for the sale or transfer of any share or shares, or of any stock or other interest, in any joint stock banking company in the United Kingdom of Great Britain and Ireland constituted under or regulated by the provisions of any Act of Parliament, Royal Charter, or Letters Patent, issuing shares or stock transferable by any deed or written instrument, shall be null and void to all intents and purposes whatsoever, unless such contract, agreement, or other token shall set forth and designate in writing such shares, stock, or interest by the respective numbers by which the same are distinguished at the making of such contract, agreement, or token on the register or books of such banking company as aforesaid, or where there is no such register of shares or stock by distinguishing numbers, then, unless such contract, agreement, or other token shall set forth the person or persons in whose name or names such shares, stock, or interest shall at the time of making such contract stand as the registered proprietor thereof in the books of such banking company."

2. The said shares were on the —— of ——, 18—, duly transferred by the plaintiff to the defendant, and such transfer was accepted by the defendant, and the price of the said shares became due from and payable by the defendant to the plaintiff before this action.

3. The said price, which amounts to £——, is still due and unpaid.

By Vendor of Shares against Purchaser for not accepting, whereby the Vendor was obliged to pay calls, and incurred other special damage (*b*).

1. On the —— of ——, 18—, it was [in conversation, *or as the case may be,*] agreed by and between the plaintiff and the defendant that the plaintiff should sell to the defendant —— shares in the —— Company, at £—— per share, and should do all things necessary on his part to transfer the said shares to the defendant on the —— of —— then next, and that the defendant should at the time aforesaid accept the transfer of the said shares and pay the said price for the same upon the transfer thereof.

2. The plaintiff within due time in that behalf did all things necessary on his part to transfer the said shares to the defendant in accordance with the said agreement, and was, at all times material to this action, ready and

---

(*b*) In an action for not accepting shares under a contract of sale, the measure of damages is the difference between the contract price and the price at the time appointed for acceptance, or upon a re-sale if re-sold by the vendor within a reasonable time after the breach. (*Stewart* v. *Cauty*, 8 M. & W. 160; *Pott* v. *Flather*, 11 Jur. 735; 16 L. J. Q. B. 366.) |As to the averment of conditions precedent, see "*Conditions Precedent*," *ante*, p. 158.

The measure of damages for the breach of a contract of sale of shares in not delivering or transferring the shares sold is the difference between the contract price and the market price when the contract was broken, allowing the purchaser a reasonable time for the purchase of like shares. (*Shaw* v. *Holland*, 15 M. & W. 136; *Tempest* v. *Kilner*, 3 C. B. 253; and see *Cockerell* v. *Van Diemen's Land Co.*, 18 C. B. 454.)

On a contract to replace on a given day stock or shares which have been lent by the plaintiff to the defendant, the measure of damages is the price at the time appointed by the contract for replacing the stock or shares, or the price at the day of the trial, at the option of the plaintiff. (*Shepherd* v *Johnson*, 2 East, 211; *M'Arthur* v. *Lord Seaforth*, 2 Taunt. 257; *Owen* v. *Routh*, 14 C. B. 327; and see *Gainsford* v. *Carroll*, 2 B. & C. 625; *Shaw* v. *Holland*, 15 M. & W. 136, 145; *Cockerell* v. *Van Diemen's Land Co.*, 18 C. B. 454.)

willing to perform the said agreement on his part in all respects, whereof the defendant always had notice, and before this action all times elapsed necessary to entitle the plaintiff to have the transfer of the said shares accepted by the defendant in accordance with the said agreement, and to be paid the said price for the same.

3. The defendant did not nor would on the said —— of ——, 18—, or at any other time, accept a transfer of the said shares, and did not nor would pay the said price for the same.

4. By reason of the said breach by the defendant of the said agreement, the plaintiff, as the legal owner of the said shares, became liable to pay, and paid calls to the extent of £—— made upon the said shares subsequently to the said breach, and lost the sum of £—— which was the difference between the market price of the said shares at the date of the said breach, and the said agreed price.

For Form of Statement of Claim by a Company registered under the Companies Act, 1862, *against a Shareholder, for Money payable by him as such Shareholder upon an Allotment of Shares, see* "*Company,*" *ante,* p. 151.

The like by a Company upon an Agreement with the Company to pay Money on Allotment of Shares, see "*Company,*" *ante,* p. 151.

For other Forms, see "*Broker,*" *ante,* p. 117.

SHIPPING (*a*).

(*a*) Common carriers of goods by water, in the absence of any express contract, are, in general, subject to the same duties as common carriers by land. See *ante,* "*Carriers,*" p. 120.

Owners or masters of general vessels, whether engaged in the coasting trade or on sea voyages, are common carriers (*Morse* v. *Slue,* 2 Lev. 69; *Benett* v. *P. & O. Steamboat Co.,* 6 C. B. 775; *Nugent* v. *Smith,* 1 C. P. D. 19; 45 L. J. C. P. 19; *reversed on another ground,* 1 C. P. D. 423; 45 L. J. C. P. 897); so are lightermen and bargemen. (*Maving* v. *Todd,* 1 Stark. 72; *Rich* v. *Kneeland,* Cro. Jac. 330; and see *Liver Alkali Co.* v. *Johnson,* L. R. 7 Ex. 267; L. R. 9 Ex. 338; 41 L. J. Ex. 110; 43 L. J. Ex. 216.) It has been doubted whether owners and masters of ships other than general ships are common carriers. (*Nugent* v. *Smith*, 1 C. P. D. 425 ; 45 L. J. C. P. 697, *per* Cockburn, C. J.) It is, however, usual for ship owners to make special contracts respecting the carriage of goods by charter-party, bill of lading, or otherwise ; and then their liability is regulated by the written document. Where the goods are sent under a special contract stating that the carrier accepts no liability, this does not exempt such carrier from liability for loss or damage arising wholly from his own or his agent's negligence. (*Martin* v. *Gt. Indian Peninsular Ry. Co.*, L. R. 3 Ex. 9 ; 37 L. J. Ex. 27 ; *Phillips* v. *Clark*, 2 C. B. N. S. 156 ; 26 L. J. C. P. 168 ; *Czech* v. *General Steam Nav. Co.*, L. R. 3 C. P. 14 ; 37 L. J. C. P. 3 ; *The Helene*, 35 L. J. C. P. 63.)

In the same way the ordinary exceptions of perils in a bill of lading do not exempt from liability for damage or loss through negligence of the owner or his servants. (*Grill* v. *Gen. Screw Colliery Co.*, L. R. 3 C. P. 476 ; *Hayn* v. *Culliford*, 4 C. P. D. 182 ; 48 L. J. C. P. 372 ; and cases cited *supra.*)

It is implied in contracts of affreightment, whether under a charter-party, bill of lading, or otherwise, that the ship shall at the commencement of the voyage be fit to carry the goods, or as it is usually termed "seaworthy." (*Lyon* v. *Mells*, 5 East, 428 ; *Richardson* v. *Stanton*, L. R. 7 C. P. 421 ; L. R. 9 C. P. 390 ; 43 L. J. C. P. 230 ; 45 L. J. C. P. 78 ; *Kopitoff* v. *Wilson*, 1 Q. B. D. 377 ; 45 L. J. Q. B. 436 ; *Cohn* v. *Davidson*, 2 Q. B. D. 455 ; 46 L. J. Q. B. 305 ; *Steel* v. *State Line Steam Ship Co.*, 3 App. Cas. 72 ; *Tully* v. *Howling*, 2 Q. B. D. 182 ; 46 L. J. Q. B. 388.)

A carrier of passengers by water does not, it would seem, impliedly warrant to his passengers that his ship is seaworthy, or warrant their safety any more than a carrier of passengers by land. See "*Carriers*," *ante*, p. 137 ; and *Readhead* v. *Mid. Ry. Co.*, L. R. 4 Q. B. 379, 390 ; 38 L. J. Q. B. 169.

In general, where the contract is not by deed, either the master or the owner may sue for freight. (*Shields* v. *Davis*, 6 Taunt. 65.)

Where the contract is in writing or by deed, the fact that it is by writing or deed should be stated in suing for freight due on such contract.

Freight paid in advance cannot be recovered back, although the vessel is lost on the voyage. (*Bryne* v. *Schiller*, L. R. 6 Ex. 20 ; *ib.* 319 ; 40 L. J. 40 ; *ib.* 177 ; *Allison* v. *Bristol Marine Ins. Co.*, 1 App. Cas. 209 ; 43 L. J. 311 ; and see "*Money Received*," *ante*, p. 287.)

Freight *pro ratâ itineris* may be recovered where the goods are delivered short of their destination, when the circumstances are such as to raise a fair inference that the owner of the goods, having an option in the matter, dispenses with their further carriage (*The Soblomsten*, L. R. 1 Ad. 293 ; 36 L. J. Ad. 5 ; *Vlierboom* v. *Chapman*, 13 M. & W. 238 ; *Hill* v. *Wilson*, 4 C. P. D. 329, 335 ; 48 L. J. C. P. 764 ; *Christy* v. *Row*, 1 Taunt. 300 ; and see also *Aca'os* v. *Burns*, 3 Ex. D. 282 ; 47 L. J. Ex. 566), but if the master justifiably sells part of the cargo at an intermediate port for the necessary repairs of the ship, freight *pro ratâ* cannot be charged. (*Hopper* v. *Burness*, 1 C. P. D. 137 ; 45 L. J. C. P. 377 ; *Metcalfe* v. *Britannia Iron Works Co.*, 1 Q. B. D. 613 ; 2 Q. B. D. 423 ; 45 L. J. Q. B. 837 ; 46 L. J. Q. B. 443.) As to claim for freight on delivery of incomplete cargo, see *Ritchie* v. *Atkinson*, 10 East, 295.

Claim against a Consignee for Freight Due under a Bill of Lading (b).

1. In January, 1880, A. B. caused to be shipped on board the ship *Vanilla*, at Bilbao, 2000 quarters of wheat,

---

(*b*) *Bill of Lading.*]—The bill of lading represents the goods shipped, and the indorsement and delivery of the bill of lading by the shipper or owner of the goods transfers the property to the indorsee. (*Lickbarrow* v. *Mason*, 2 T. R. 63 ; 6 East, 21 ; 1 Sm. L. C. 8th ed., p. 753 ; *Barber* v. *Meyerstein*, L. R. 4 H. L. 317 ; 39 L. J. C. P. 187.)

The indorsee for value of a bill of lading who takes it *bonâ fide* and without notice that the goods have not been paid for, and that the consignee is insolvent, has a right to the goods which is superior to the right of the unpaid vendor to stop in transit (*Lickbarrow* v. *Mason*, *supra ; Pease* v. *Gloahec*, L. R. 1 P. C. 219, 227 ; 35 L. J. P. C. 66 ; *Leask* v. *Scott*, 2 Q. B. D. 376 ; 46 L. J. Q. B. 576) ; and is liable, in the absence of notice, to those claims only on the goods which are specified or referred to in the bill of lading, provided his indorser had a right to indorse. See the cases *supra*, and *Foster* v. *Colby*, 3 H. & N. 705 ; 28 L. J. Ex. 81 ; *Shand* v. *Sanderson*, 4 H. & N. 381 ; 28 L. J. Ex. 278 ; *Gurney* v. *Behrend*, 3 E. & B. 622, 633.

At common law the indorsement of the bill of lading transferred only the property in the goods and not the contract ; and the indorsee could neither sue nor be sued upon it. (*Lickbarrow* v. *Mason*, *supra ; Thompson* v. *Dominy*, 14 M. & W. 403 ; *Howard* v. *Shepherd*, 9 C. B. 297.) But if the indorsee accepted the goods under it, this might be evidence of a new contract to pay freight, or even demurrage, according to the terms of it. (*Möller* v. *Young*, 5 E. & B. 755 ; 25 L. J. Q. B. 94 ; *Stindt* v. *Roberts*, 5 D. & L. 460 ; 17 L. J. Q. B. 166 ; *Smith* v. *Sievking*, 4 E. & B. 945 ; 5 E. & B. 589 ; *Chappel* v. *Comfort*, 10 C. B. N. S. 803 ; 31 L. J. C. P. 58 ; *Jesson* v. *Solly*, 4 Taunt. 52.) And if the freight was payable "as per charter-party," he might become liable according to the terms of that instrument. (*Sanders* v. *Vanzeller*, 4 Q. B. 260 ; *Wegener* v. *Smith*, 15 C. B. 285 ; *Fry* v. *Chartered Bank of India*, L. R. 1 C. P. 689 ; 35 L. J. C. P. 306 ; *Gray* v. *Carr*, L. R. 6 Q. B. 522 ; 40 L. J. Q. B. 257.)

By 18 & 19 Vict. c. 111, s. 1, "every consignee of goods named in a bill of lading, and every indorsee of a bill of lading, to whom the property in the goods therein mentioned shall pass upon or by reason of such consignment or indorsement, shall have transferred to and vested in him all rights of suit, and be subject to the same liabilities in respect of such goods as if the contract contained in the bill of lading had been made with himself."

By s. 2, "nothing herein contained shall prejudice or affect any right of stoppage *in transitu*, or any right to claim freight against the original shipper or owner, or any liability of the consignee or indorsee by reason or in consequence of his being such consignee or indorsee, or of his receipt of the goods by reason or in consequence of such consignment or indorsement."

By s. 3, "every bill of lading in the hands of a consignee or indorsee for valuable consideration representing goods to have been

and the master of the said ship then received the same to be carried to London, upon the terms contained in bills of lading then signed by the said master. The terms whereof, so far as is material, were as follows :—

"Shipped in good order and well conditioned by A. B. upon the good ship *Vanilla*, whereof is master for the present voyage H. P., 2000 quarters of wheat [in bulk], to be delivered in the like good order and well conditioned in the port of London to C. D., or his assignees" (certain risks and perils which are not ma-

---

shipped on board a vessel shall be conclusive evidence of such shipment as against the master or other person signing the same, notwithstanding that such goods or some part thereof may not have been so shipped, unless such holder of the bill of lading shall have had actual notice at the time of receiving the same that the goods had not been in fact laden on board." The owner is not bound by the signature of the master for goods not in fact shipped. (*Jessel* v. *Bath*, L. R. 2 Ex. 267 ; 36 L. J. Ex. 149 ; *Brown* v. *Powell Steam Coal Co.*, L. R. 10 C. P. 562 ; 44 L. J. C. P. 289.) The section only makes the bill of lading conclusive against the person by whom, or by whose authority it is signed ; in other cases it may be shown that the goods were not shipped. (*McLean* v. *Fleming*, L. R. 2 H. L. Sc. 128, and see *Meyer* v. *Dresser*, 16 C. B. N. S. 646 ; 33 L. J. C. P. 289.)

As to the effect of an innocent mistake in the statement of weight in a bill of lading, see *Blanchet* v. *Powell's Collieries Co.*, L. R. 9 Ex. 74 ; 43 L. J. Ex. 50. The above statute transfers the contract in the bill of lading to the indorsee, but the liability and right of the indorsee under the statute does not continue after he has indorsed it away, provided he does so before the arrival and delivery of the cargo. (*Smurthwaite* v. *Wilkins*, 11 C. B. N. S. 842 ; 31 L. J. C. P. 214 ; *The Felix*, L. R. 2 Ad. 273 ; 37 L. J. Ad. 48.) It seems that the indorsement of the bill of lading transfers to the indorsee the right of action for a breach of the contract previously accrued. (*Short* v. *Simpson*, L. R. 1 C. P. 248 ; 35 L. J. C. P. 147.) The indorsement of the bill of lading does not relieve the original shipper or owner of the goods from his liability for freight under it. (*Fox* v. *Nott*, 6 H. & N. 630 ; 30 L. J. Ex. 259 ; 18 & 19 Vict. c. 111, s. 2, *supra.*)

The bill of lading remains in force until the goods have been delivered thereunder to a person having a right to take such delivery. (*Meyerstein* v. *Barber*, L. R. 2 C. P. 661 ; L. R. 4 H. L. 317 ; 39 L. J. C. P. 187.) Bills of lading are usually drawn in sets of three, and the property in the goods passes to the first indorsee. (*Meyerstein* v. *Barber*, *supra.*)

Where an unpaid vendor shipping goods under a contract of sale takes a bill of lading making the goods deliverable to his own order, and retains such bill of lading in his own or his agent's hands for his own protection, he does not reserve the vendor's lien only in case of default in payment of the price, but reserves a right of disposing of the goods so long at least as the purchaser continues in default. (*Ogg* v. *Shuter*, 1 C. P. D. 47 ; 45 L. J. C. P. 44.)

terial in this action being excepted), "he or they paying freight for the same at the rate of £—— per quarter of 480lbs. delivered."

2. The said bills of lading were signed by the said master, as agent for, and with the authority of the plaintiffs, the owners of the said ship.

3. The said wheat was afterwards in accordance with the terms of the said bills of lading delivered in good order and well conditioned in the port of London to the said C. D., the defendant, who duly presented the first of the said bills of lading.

4. The said C. D., the defendant, has not paid the said freight, and there is now due from and payable by the defendant to the plaintiffs the sum of £—— in respect thereof.

Upon a Bill of Lading for not Delivering Goods Shipped in Good Order and Condition, in the like Good Order and Condition (*b*).

See Form No. 8 *in App.* (*C*) *to Jud. Act*, 1875.

1. In the month of February, 1873, Messrs. L. & Co., of Alexandria, caused to be shipped 6,110 ardebs of cotton seed on board the *Ida*, then lying in Port Said (Egypt), and the then master of the said vessel received the same, to be carried from Port Said to Hull, upon the terms of three bills of lading, signed by the master, on behalf of himself and the defendants, the owners of the said vessel, and delivered to Messrs. L. & Co.

2. The three bills of lading, being in form exactly similar to one another, were and are, so far as is material to the present case, in the words, letters, and figures following, that is to say:—

"Shipped in good order and well conditioned, by L. & Co., Alexandria (Egypt), in and upon the good ship called the *Ida*, whereof is master for the present voyage Ambrozio Chiapella, and now riding at anchor in the port of Port Said (Egypt), and bound for Hull, 6,110 ardebs of cotton seed, being marked and numbered as in the margin, and are to be delivered in the like good order and well conditioned at the aforesaid port of Hull (the act of God, the Queen's enemies, fire, and all and every other dangers and accidents of the seas, rivers, and navigation of whatever nature and kind soever, save risk of boats, so far as ships are liable thereto, excepted), unto order or to assigns paying freight for the said goods at the rate of (19*s.*), say 19*s.* sterling in full per ton of 20 cwt. delivered with £10 gratuity. Other conditions as per charter-party, dated London, 4th October, 1872, with primage and average accustomed. In witness whereof the master or purser of the said ship hath affirmed to three bills of lading, all of this tenor and date, the one of which three bills being accomplished the other two to stand void. Dated in Port Said (Egypt), 6th February, 1873. 100 dunnage mats. Fifteen working days remain for discharging."

3. The persons constituting the firm of Messrs. L. & Co. are identical with the members of the plaintiff's firm.

4. The vessel sailed on her voyage to Hull, and duly arrived there on or about the 7th day of May, 1873.

5. The cotton seed was delivered to the plaintiffs, but not in as good order and condition as it was in when shipped at Port Said; but was delivered to the plaintiffs greatly damaged.

6. The deterioration of the cotton seed was not occasioned by any of the perils or causes in the bills of lading excepted.

7. By reason of the premises the plaintiffs lost a great part of the value of the said cotton seed, and were put to great expense in and about keeping, warehousing, and improving the condition of the said cotton seed, and in and about having the same surveyed.

The plaintiffs claim the following relief:—

1. £—— for damages.
2. Such further relief as the nature of the case requires.

Against the Indorsee of the Bill of Lading for Freight and Demurrage where "Freight and all other Conditions" are expressed by the Bill of Lading to be "as per Charter-party" (*b*) (*c*).

1. The plaintiffs were and are owners of the steamship *Varna*.

(*c*) *Charter Party.*]—As to what are conditions precedent to the liability of the charterer to load, see Leake on Contracts, 658—660, and as to what are conditions precedent to the liability for freight, *ib.* 660, 661; and see generally as to the mutual rights and liabilities of freighter and shipowner, *Nelson* v. *Dahl*, 12 Ch. D. 568, 580;

2. On the —— day of ——, 18—, the master of the *Varna* entered into a charter-party on behalf of himself and the owners of the said ship with A. B., for the conveyance of a cargo of grain in the said ship, which, so far as is material, was as follows:—

"That the said ship being tight, staunch, and strong, and in every way fitted for the voyage, shall with all convenient speed load a full and convenient cargo of

---

6 App. Cas. 38, *Postlethwaite* v. *Freeland*, 5 App. Cas. 599; 49 L. J. Ex. 630.

Neglect or delay in the performance of the contract, in the absence of express stipulation, is only ground for a claim for damages; unless it be such as to frustrate the object of the charter-party, in which case the charterer would be discharged. (*Freeman* v. *Taylor*, 8 Bing. 124; *Jackson* v. *Union Marine Insurance Co.*, L. R. 8 C. P. 572; L. R. 10 C. P. 125; 42 L. J. C. P. 284; 44 L. J. C. P. 27; *MacAndrew* v. *Chapple*, L. R. 1 C. P. 643, 648; 35 L. J. C. P. 281.) A stipulation that the ship shall sail for the port of loading, or be ready to load on or before a particular day is, in general, a condition precedent to the liability of the charterer to load. (*Glaholm* v. *Hays*, L. M. & G. 257; *Segur* v. *Duthie*, 8 C. B. N. S. 45; 29 L. J. C. P. 253; *Tully* v. *Howling*, 2 Q. B. 182; 46 L. J. Q. B 383.)

Where the contract is silent as to time the law implies that the act shall be done within a reasonable time. See as to this *Nelson* v. *Dahl*, *supra*; "*Carriers*," *ante*, p. 123; *Ellis* v. *Thompson*, 3 M. & W. 445; *Postlethwaite* v. *Freeland*, *supra*.

Where the act to be done is one in which both parties to the contract are to concur, and both bind themselves to the performance of it, there is no principle on which, in the absence of a stipulation to that effect, the damage arising from an unforeseen impediment is to be cast by law on the one party more than on the other; what is implied by law in such a case is, not that either party contracts that it shall be done within either a fixed or a reasonable time, but that each contracts that he shall use reasonable diligence in performing his part. (*Ford* v. *Cotesworth*, L. R. 4 Q. B. 127; 5 *ib.* 544; 39 L. J. Q. B. 188; *Nelson* v. *Dahl*, 12 Ch. D. 568; 6 App. Cas. 38.)

If by the terms of the charter party the charterer binds himself to discharge the ship within a fixed period of time, that is an absolute and unconditional engagement for the non-performance of which he is answerable, but if there is no fixed time the discharge must be within a reasonable time having regard to the usage of the port and to the circumstances of the case. (*Postlethwaite* v. *Freeland*, *Ford* v. *Cotesworth*, *supra*.) A charter party in which there are stipulations as to loading or discharging cargo in a port is to be construed as made with reference to the custom of that port. (*Postlethwaite* v. *Freeland*, 5 App. Cas. 599; 49 L. J. Ex. 630, *per* Lord Blackburn.)

In charter parties it is usual to allow a certain number of days, termed *lay* days, for loading and unloading, with liberty, on payment of a specified sum, to detain the ship for a further specified number of days. Such further detention during the specified days is termed demurrage, as is the detention beyond the lay days when no further days are specified; but all detention beyond the specified demurrage

grain in bags, not exceeding what she can reasonably stow and carry over and above her tackle, apparel, provisions, and furniture, and being so loaded, shall therewith proceed to Hull, or so near thereto as she can safely get, and there make right and true delivery of the said cargo to the assigns of the freighter" (subject to certain conditions which are not material in this action), "on being paid freight 2*s.* 9*d.* per delivered quarter of wheat of 504 lbs. weight, other grain in proportion, according to the London Baltic printed rates of freight. The freight to be paid on unloading and right delivery of the cargo in cash without deduction. The cargo to be shipped at Copenhagen and discharged at Hull afloat."

"The loading and discharging is stipulated in four

---

days, where demurrage days are specified, is detention to be compensated by damage, and not demurrage. (*Sanguinetti* v. *The Pacific Steam Nav. Co.*, 2 Q. B. D. 238, 251; 46 L. J. Q. B. 105.)

The word "*demurrage*" properly signifies the agreed additional payment for an allowed detention beyond a period specified in the instrument; but it has also a popular or more general meaning of compensation for undue detention. (*Lockhart* v. *Falk*, L. R. 10 Ex. 135; 44 L. J. Ex. 108.)

In reckoning demurrage, in the absence of stipulation to the contrary, a fraction of a day is reckoned as a day. (*The Commercial Steam Ship Co.* v. *Boulton*, L. R. 10 Q. B. 346; 44 L. J. Q. B. 219.)

Whenever, in the charter party, it is agreed that a specified number of days shall be allowed for loading, or unloading, as the case may be, and that it shall be lawful for the freighter to detain the vessel for that purpose a further specified time, on payment of a daily sum, this constitutes a stipulation on the part of the freighter that he will not detain the ship for loading, or unloading, as the case may be, beyond those two specified periods. (*Ford* v. *Cotesworth*, *supra*; *Nelson* v. *Dahl*, 12 Ch. D. 568, 583, 584.) If in such a case it is detained beyond the specified lay days, the charterer must pay demurrage, or damages for detention in the nature of demurrage, though the delay arose from causes wholly beyond the charterer's control. (*Nelson* v. *Dahl*, *supra*.)

The right of the shipowner as to unloading is that the liability of the charterer as to his part of the joint act of unloading should accrue as soon as the ship is in the place named as that at which the carrying voyage is to end, and the ship is ready, so far as she is concerned, to unload; and when the ship is at the named place, or, where there is a stipulation to that effect, so near thereto as she may safely get, and is ready to discharge, the liability of the charterer as to unloading commences. (*Nelson* v. *Dahl*, *supra*.) See further, *Thiis* v. *Byers*, 1 Q. B. D. 244; 45 L. J. Q. B. 511; *Fowler* v. *Knoop*, 4 Q. B. D. 299; *Davies* v. *McVeagh*, 4 Ex. D. 265; *Jones* v. *Adamson*, 1 Ex. D. 60; 45 L. J. Ex. 64; *Straker* v. *Kidd*, 3 Q. B. D. 223; *Porteus* v. *Watney*, 3 Q. B. D. 223; *ib.* 534; *Norden Steamship Co.* v. *Dempsey*, 1 C. P. D. 654; 45 L. J. C. P. 764.

running working days, such days to be reckoned from the day the said ship shall be ready to load and unload, and for demurrage over and above the said lay days £15 to be paid per day."

3. The said ship was then duly loaded at Copenhagen with a cargo of barley, part of which was shipped under a duly signed bill of lading, which was, so far as is material, as follows:—

"Shipped in good order and well conditioned, by C. D., 1,960 bags of barley, to be delivered in the like good order and condition at Hull" (subject to certain exceptions which are not material) "unto E. F., or assigns, he or they paying freight for the said goods and all other conditions as per charter-party with primage and average accustomed."

4. The said bill of lading was duly indorsed by the said E. F. to the defendant, to whom upon and by reason of such indorsement the property in the goods therein mentioned passed.

5. The defendant accordingly duly presented the said bill of lading and took delivery of the said goods therein mentioned.

6. The defendant did not pay nor has he paid the freight for the said goods therein mentioned as per charter-party, or at all, and the amount thereof is still due and payable by the defendant to the plaintiff.

7. The amount of such freight is £——.

8. The defendant further kept the said ship on demurrage at Hull three days [namely from the —— to the —— of ——] over and above the said lay days, and the sum of £45 became by virtue of the said bill of lading due and payable by the defendant to the plaintiff in respect thereof.

9. The defendant has not paid the said £45 or any part thereof.

Upon a Charter-party to Recover a Balance due thereunder for the Hire of a Ship (*c*).

Form No. 10 *in App.* (*C*) *to Jud. Act*, 1875.

1. The plaintiffs were, on the 1st August, 1874, the owners of the steamship *British Queen*.

2. On the 1st August, 1874, the ship being then in

Calcutta, a charter-party was there entered into between John Smith, the master, on behalf of himself and the owners of the said ship, of the one part, and the defendants of the other part.

3. By the said charter-party it was agreed, amongst other things, that the defendants should be entitled to the whole carrying power of the said steamship for the period of four months certain, commencing from the said 1st August, 1874, upon a voyage or voyages between Calcutta and Mauritius and back; that the defendants should pay for such use of the said steamship to the plaintiffs' agents at Calcutta, monthly, the sum of £1000; that the charter should terminate at Calcutta; and that if at the expiration of the said period of four months the said steamship should be upon a voyage, then the defendants should pay *pro ratâ* for the hire of the ship up to her arrival at Calcutta, and the complete discharge of her cargo there.

4. The *British Queen* made several voyages in pursuance of the said charter-party, and the first three monthly sums of £1000 each were duly paid.

5. The period of four months expired on the 1st December, 1874, and at that time the steamship was on a voyage from Mauritius to Calcutta. She arrived at Calcutta on the 13th December, and the discharge of her cargo there was completed on the 16th December, 1874.

6. The plaintiffs' agents at Calcutta called upon the defendants to pay to them the fourth monthly sum of £1000, and a sum of £500 for the hire of the steamship from the 1st to the 16th December, 1874, but the defendants have not paid any part of the said sums.

The plaintiffs claim :—

The sum of £1,500 and interest upon £1000, part thereof, from the 1st December, 1874, until judgment.

By Shipowner against Charterer for not Loading a Cargo. Cunningham v. *Dunn,* 38 L. T. 631.

By a Co-owner of a Ship for an Account and for a Sale of the Ship, The Horlock, 36 L. T. 622; 2 P. D. 243.

By Shipowner for Demurrage upon a Charter-party, see Sanguinetti v. *The Pacific Steam Nav. Co.*, 2 Q. B. D. 238; 35 L. T. 658; *Swansea Shipping Co.* v. *Duncan*, 1 Q. B. D. 644.

By Shipowner against Charterer for refusal to take Delivery of Cargo as per Charter Party and for Lighterage Expenses incurred in Discharging; Hayton v. *Irwin*, 5 C. P. D. 130; 41 L. T. 666.

See for Form of Claim in an Action for Limitation of Liability The Andalusian, 3 P. D. 182; 47 L. J. Ad. 65 (*d*).

(*d*) *Limitation of Liability.*]—By "The Merchant Shipping Act, 1854," s. 503 (17 & 18 Vict. c. 104), "No owner of any sea-going ship or share therein shall be liable to make good any loss or damage that may happen without his actual fault or privity of or to any of the following things; (that is to say)

"(1.) Of or to any goods, merchandise, or other things whatsoever taken in or put on board any such ship, by reason of any fire happening on board such ship;

"(2.) Of or to any gold, silver, diamonds, watches, jewels, or precious stones taken in or put on board any such ship by reason of any robbery, embezzlement, making away with or secreting thereof, unless the owner or shipper thereof has, at the time of shipping the same, inserted in his bills of lading or otherwise declared in writing to the master or owner of such ship the true nature and value of such articles.

"To any extent whatever." This has been held to apply only to British ships. (*Cope* v. *Doherty*, 2 De Gex & J. 614; 29 L. J. Ch. 600.)

By "The Merchant Shipping Act Amendment Act, 1862" (25 & 26 Vict. c. 63, s. 54), "The owners of any ship, whether British or foreign, shall not in cases where all or any of the following events occur without their actual fault or privity, that is to say:

"(1.) Where any loss of life or personal injury is caused to any person being carried in such ship;

"(2.) Where any damage or loss is caused to any goods, merchandise, or other things whatsoever on board any such ship;

"(3.) Where any loss of life or personal injury is by reason of the improper navigation of such ship as aforesaid caused to any person carried in any other ship or boat;

"(4.) Where any loss or damage is by reason of the improper navigation of such ship as aforesaid caused to any other ship or boat, or to any goods, merchandise, or other things whatsoever on board any other ship or boat.

be answerable in damages in respect of loss of life or personal injury, either alone or together with loss or damage to ships, boats, goods, merchandise, or other things, to an aggregate amount exceeding fifteen pounds for each ton of their ship's tonnage; nor in respect of loss or damage to ships, goods, merchandise, or other things, whether there be in addition loss of life or personal injury or not, to an aggregate amount exceeding eight pounds for each ton of the ship's tonnage."

As to the mode of ascertaining tonnage, see the above statute, and *The Franconia*, 3 P. D. 164.

By s. 514 of the first-mentioned statute (17 & 18 Vict. c. 104), subject to the right given by the statute to the Board of Trade of recovering damages in respect of loss of life or personal injury, it is enacted that in cases where any liability has been, or is alleged to have been, incurred by any owner in respect of loss of life, personal injury, or loss of or damage to ships, boats, or goods, and several claims are made or apprehended in respect of such liability, it shall be lawful in England or Ireland, for the High Court of Chancery to entertain proceedings at the suit of any owner for the purpose of determining the amount of such liability, and for the distribution of such amount rateably amongst the several claimants, with power for such Court to stop all actions and suits pending in any other Court in relation to the same subject matter.

By "The Admiralty Court Act, 1861," s. 13 (24 Vict. c. 10), "Whenever any ship or vessel, or the proceeds thereof, are under arrest of the High Court of Admiralty, the said Court shall have the same powers as are conferred upon the High Court of Chancery in England by the ninth part of 'The Merchant Shipping Act, 1854,'" that is, amongst other powers, the powers conferred by the last cited section.

By "The Common Law Procedure Act, 1860," s. 35 (23 & 24 Vict. c. 126), "the Superior Courts, or any judge thereof, may upon summary application by rule or order, exercise such and the like jurisdiction as may be exercised by the Court of Chancery under the provisions of the ninth part of 'The Merchant Shipping Act, 1854.'"

For an example of such motion in a Common Law Division, see *Smith* v. *Kirby*, 1 Q. B. D. 131.

By "The Jud. Act, 1873," s. 16, subject as therein mentioned, the jurisdiction vested in the High Court of Chancery, the Superior Courts, and the High Court of Admiralty, is transferred to the High Court of Justice.

By s. 23, the jurisdiction so transferred is to be exercised, where no special provision is contained in the Act or in any rules or orders of Court with reference thereto, as nearly as may be in the same manner as it might have been exercised by the respective Courts from which such jurisdiction is transferred.

By s. 24 (5), no cause or proceeding in the High Court of Justice is to be restrained by prohibition or injunction, but the Court in which such cause or proceeding is pending may on motion in a summary way stay such cause or proceeding.

So that the proceedings in other Divisions are not now stayed, it would seem, by the Chancery and Admiralty Divisions under "The Merchant Shipping Act, 1854," and "The Admiralty Court Act, 1861," but application is made to the Division in which such proceeding is pending. (*Garbutt* v. *Fawcus*, 1 Ch. D. 155; 45 L. J. Ch. 130, 133; *In re People's Garden Co.*, 1 Ch. D. 44; 45 L. J. Ch. 129; *Walker* v. *Banagher's Dist. Co.*, 1 Q. B. D. 129; 45 L. J. Q. B. 134.)

By s. 34 all causes and matters commenced after the commencement of the Act, under any Act of Parliament, by which exclusive jurisdiction in respect to such causes or matters has been given to the Court of Chancery, or to any judges or judge thereof respectively, except appeals from County Courts, are assigned (subject as stated in the Act), to the Chancery Division.

By the same section all causes and matters which would have been within the exclusive cognizance of the High Court of Admiralty if the Act had not passed are assigned (subject as aforesaid) to the Probate, Divorce, and Admiralty Division.

By s. 36 a power of transfer from one Division to another is given, as also power to retain any cause or matter in the Division in which the same was commenced, although such may not be the proper Division to which the same cause or matter ought in the first instance to have been assigned.

Where reliance is placed upon the above sections as limiting liability the facts must be set out on the pleadings showing the right to have the liability thus limited. (*Wahlberg* v. *Young*, 45 L. J. C. P. 783.)

See further, *Chapman* v. *Royal Netherlands Steam Nav. Co.*, 4 P. D. 157.

See further, as to form of action for limitation of liability, *The Rajah*, L. R. 3 A. & E. 539 ; *The Clutha*, 3 Asp. Mar. Law Cas. 225 ; 35 L. T. 36 ; 45 L. J. Ad. 108 ; and see Seton on Decrees, 4th ed., p. 279—281.

The above sections do not, it would seem, apply to delay. (*L. & S. W. Ry. Co.* v. *James*, L. R. 8 Ch. Ap. 241.)

Before the Jud. Acts it was necessary to proceed by motion under the C. L. P. Act, 1860, s. 35, or to institute a separate suit for limitation of liability in the Admiralty Court, or the Court of Chancery, under the above enactments, but now it would appear that a defendant may, in the High Court of Justice, by counter-claim claim to have relief by having his liability limited (see *The Clutha*, 3 Asp. Mar. Law Cas. 225 ; 35 L. T. 36 ; 45 L. J. Ad. 108), or claim such relief by motion under "The Common Law Proc. Act, 1860," cited *supra*. (See Jud. Act, 1873, ss. 23, 24 ; Jud. Act, 1875, s. 11 ; O. XIX. r. 3 ; Jud. Act, 1875, s. 21.)

Sea Traffic of Railway Companies.]—"The Railway and Canal Traffic Act, 1854" (17 & 18 Vict. c. 31), is extended, so far as its provisions are applicable, to the sea traffic carried by Railway Companies in steam vessels by 31 & 32 Vict. c. 119, s. 16, and 34 & 35 Vict. c. 78, s. 12. (*Doolan* v. *Mid. Ry. Co.*, 2 App. Cas. 792 ; *Cohen* v. *S. E. Ry. Co.*, 2 Ex. D. 253 ; 46 L. J. Ex. 417.) As to the effect of "The Railway and Canal Traffic Act, 1854," see "Defences," "*Carriers*," and "*Carriers*," *ante* (*d*), p. 124.

By "The Regulation of Railways Act, 1868" (31 & 32 Vict. c. 119), s. 14, it is enacted that "Where a company by through booking contracts to carry any animals, luggage, or goods, from place to place, partly by railway and partly by sea, or partly by canal and partly by sea, a condition exempting the company from liability for any loss or damage which may arise during the carriage of such animals, luggage, or goods by sea from the act of God, the king's enemies, fire, accidents from machinery and boilers, and steam and all and every other dangers, and accidents of the seas, rivers, and navigation of whatever nature and kind soever, shall, if published in a conspicuous manner in the office where such through booking is effected, and if printed in a

Solicitor (*a*).

Statement of Claim for Work done as a Solicitor (*a*).

(See "*Agent,*" *ante*, p. 37.)

---

legible manner on the receipt or freight-note which the company gives for such animals, luggage, or goods, be valid as part of the contract between the consignor of such animals, luggage, or goods, and the company, in the same manner as if the company had signed and delivered to the consignor a bill of lading containing such condition."

As to equality of charges, see "*Carriers,*" *ante*, p. 132, and s. 16 of the above enactment.

Damages.]—See generally, "*Carriers by Land,*" "*Damages,*" *note, ante*, p. 128. In the case of carriage of goods by ship, damages for loss of market are not in general recoverable, even though the delay be due to defects in the ship. (*The Parana*, 2 P. D. 118.)

The measure of damages for not loading a cargo is, in general, the freight which would have been earned had the cargo been carried less the expenses of carrying it and any profit which the ship has made by being otherwise employed. (*Smith* v. *Maguire*, 3 H. & N. 554; 27 L. J. Ex. 465; *Morris* v. *Levison*, 1 C. P. D. 155, 158; 45 L. J. C. P. 409.)

As to limitation of liability by statute, see *ante*, p. 336.

(*a*) By "The Attorneys and Solicitors Act, 1874" (37 & 38 Vict. c. 68), s. 12, "No costs, fee, reward, or disbursement on account of, or in relation to, any act or proceeding done or taken by any person who acts as an attorney or solicitor, without being duly qualified so to act, shall be recoverable in any action, suit, or matter by any person or persons whomsoever."

A client who employs an uncertificated solicitor to conduct litigation cannot recover costs which he would otherwise be entitled to from the defeated party. (*Fowler* v. *Mon. Ry. and Canal Co.*, 4 Q. B. D. 334; 48 L. J. Q. B. 457.) See further as to unqualified persons practising, Archbold's Practice, 13th ed., p. 76, *et seq.*, and as to taxation of costs, *ib.*, p. 120.

Where an action is brought to recover solicitor's fees, charges, or disbursements, it is necessary that a signed bill of such fees, charges, and disbursements should at least one calendar month before such action have been delivered to the party to be charged therewith, or sent by the post to or left for him at his counting-house, office of business, dwelling-house, or last known place of abode, except in cases where a judge's order is obtained specially authorising the action, although one month has not expired from the delivery of the bill (6 & 7 Vict. c. 73, s. 37; 38 & 39 Vict. c. 79, s. 2; see "Defences," and further, Cordery on Solicitors, pp. 172—177, 204—209).

As to what written agreements a solicitor may make with his client as to costs, and as to the modes of enforcing them, see 33 & 34 Vict. c. 28; *Re Lewis*, 1 Q. B. D. 724; 45 L. J. Q. B. 816, and 44 & 45 Vict. c. 44.

The want of a signed bill, as required by the above enactment, must be specially pleaded as a defence, if relied on, and it would not

Against a Solicitor for Negligence in conducting an Action at the suit of the Plaintiff (*b*).

1. The defendant is a solicitor carrying on business at ——.

2. The plaintiff in the month of ——, 18—, retained the defendant as his solicitor to conduct an action [in the High Court of Justice, Queen's Bench Division] at the suit of the plaintiff against G. H. upon the terms amongst others that the defendant should for reward conduct the said action with due and proper care, skill, and diligence, and the defendant then accepted the said retainer upon the said terms.

3. The defendant did not conduct the said action with due and proper care, skill, or diligence [but wholly neglected to instruct or brief counsel to appear upon the trial of the said action on behalf of the plaintiff, and to procure the attendance of witnesses thereon for the plaintiff].

4. The plaintiff in consequence failed to obtain judgment in his favour in the said action, and lost the costs

---

seem necessary for the plaintiff in his statement of claim to aver in the first instance compliance with the requirements of the enactment. *Under the former system, see Lane* v. *Glenny*, 7 A. & E. 83.

There is in general no privity of contract between the client and the town agent of the solicitor employed by such client, and consequently no right of action by the client against such town agent for any breach of his contract or duty as solicitor, or by the town agent against such client for his charges. (*Robbins* v. *Fennell*, 11 Q. B. 248 ; 17 L. J. Q. B. 77 ; *Cobb* v. *Becke*, 6 Q. B. 930 ; *Scrace* v. *Whittington*, 2 B. & C. 11 ; *Collins* v. *Griffin*, 1 Barnes, 37.)

(*b*) Actions against solicitors by their clients for negligence might under the former system of pleading be framed, in general, either upon the contract, charging the injury as a breach of contract, or upon the duty imposed by law, charging the injury as a breach of duty, or wrong. See notes to "*Carriers*," *ante*, p. 120.

A solicitor impliedly contracts to use reasonable skill and diligence in the performance of his duty, but he is not liable for a mere error of judgment upon a point of law open to reasonable doubt. (*Purves* v. *Landell*, 12 Cl. & F. 91 ; *Hunter* v. *Caldwell*, 10 Q. B. 69, 83 ; 16 L. J. Q. B. 274 ; *Kemp* v. *Burt*, 4 B. & Ad. 424 ; *Hart* v. *Frame*, 6 Cl. & F. 193 ; *Godefroy* v. *Dalton*, 6 Bing. 460 ; *Godefroy* v. *Jay*, 7 Bing. 413 ; *Whiteman* v. *Hawkins*, 4 C. P. D. 13 ; and see Cordery on Solicitors, p. 71, *et seq.*)

A solicitor is liable to his client in an action for damages for compromising an action against the express directions of the client. (*Butler* v. *Knight*, L. R. 2 Ex. 109 ; 36 L. J. Ex. 66 ; *Fray* v. *Voules*, 1 E. & E. 839 ; 28 L. J. Q. B. 232.) As to "Agency," see *note* (*a*), *supra*.

amounting to £——, incurred by him in prosecuting the said action, and was obliged [*or* became liable] to pay the costs amounting to £——, incurred by the said G. H. in defending the same, and the plaintiff has been delayed in recovering [*or* has lost] the sum of £—— claimed by him in the said action from the said G. H.

Against a Solicitor for investing the Plaintiff's Money upon insufficient Security (*b*).

1. [*As in form next above.*]

2. The plaintiff in the month of —— 18—, retained and employed the defendant for reward to the defendant to invest certain money of the plaintiff [namely £——] upon good and sufficient security, and the defendant then accepted the said retainer and employment.

3. The defendant invested the said money upon bad and insufficient security.

4. By reason of the premises the plaintiff has lost the said money.

TRADE (*a*).

By the Vendor of the Goodwill of a Trade to recover the Price.

1. The plaintiff was possessed of a shop, situate at No. ——, High Street, ——, wherein he carried on the business of a ——, and also of certain stock-in-trade and plant used by him in carrying on such business.

2. On or about the —— of ——, 18—, it was agreed [by a memorandum of agreement, bearing date, &c., *or as the case may be*] by and between the plaintiff and the defendant that the plaintiff should yield up the possession of the said shop to the defendant, and assign over and deliver to the defendant the said stock-in-trade and plant, and should retire from the said business and

---

(*a*) A trader who sells his business and the "goodwill" thereof to another, in the absence of express agreement, impliedly contracts to abstain from soliciting orders from the old customers of the business. (*Leggott* v. *Barrett*, 15 Ch. D. 306; *Labouchere* v. *Dawson*, L. R. 13 Eq. 322; 41 L. J. Ch. 427.) See further Leake on Contracts, 734—741, 1132, 1133; "*Liquidated Damages*," *ante*, p. 262.

permit the defendant to carry on the said business in the plaintiff's stead, and that the defendant should pay to the plaintiff the sum of £—— upon receiving the possession of the said shop, and upon delivery to him by the plaintiff of the said stock-in-trade and plant.

3. The plaintiff did in accordance with the said agreement yield up possession of the shop to the defendant, who received the possession thereof, and assign over and deliver to the defendant the said stock-in-trade and plant, and retire from the said business and permit the defendant to carry it on in his stead.

4. The defendant has not paid to the plaintiff the said sum of £—— or any part thereof.

For a Claim by the Purchaser of the Goodwill of a Trade for Damages for Breach of Warranty of Amount of Earnings or Takings, see "Warranty," post, p. 350.

By the Purchaser of a Professional Practice on a Covenant by the Vendor in the Deed of Sale to Pay Liquidated Damages in the Event of his Practising within a Certain Distance, see "Liquidated Damages," ante, p. 262.

By an Employer against a late Servant for Carrying on Business in Breach of an Agreement to Abstain from so doing, Davey v. *Shannon,* 4 Ex. D. 80; 48 L. J. Ex. 459.

WARRANTY.

Upon an express Warranty on a Sale of Goods that the Vendor had Title to sell them (*a*).

1. The defendant on the —— of ——, 18—, by warranting that he then had lawful right and title to sell

---

(*a*) On a sale of a specific chattel there is, in general, no implied warranty of title; but such a warranty may be inferred from the usage or nature of a particular trade, or from the circumstances of the sale. (*Morley* v. *Attenborough*, 3 Ex. 500; *Sims* v. *Marryat*, 17 Q. B.

certain furniture, sold the same to the plaintiff for the sum of £—— [which sum the plaintiff then paid the defendant as the price thereof].

2. The defendant had not then lawful right and title to sell or dispose of the said furniture or any of it.

3. The plaintiff was in consequence afterwards obliged to deliver up the said furniture to G. H., who had the lawful right and title thereto, and lost the said furniture [and the said sum which he had paid as the price thereof].

For Breach of Warranty of a Horse (*b*).

1. The defendant on the —— of ——, 18—, by warranting [in writing] a horse to be then sound, sold the

---

281; 20 L. J. Q. B. 458; *Hall* v. *Conder*, 2 C. B. N S. 22, 40; *Bagueley* v. *Hawley*, L. R. 2 C. P. 625; 36 L. J. C. P. 328.) If a man sells goods affirming them to be his own, that amounts to an express warranty of title. (*Cross* v. *Garnet* or *Gardner*, 3 Mod. 261; 1 Show. 68; *Medina* v. *Stoughton*, 1 Salk. 210; 1 Ld. Raym. 593.) So upon a sale of goods in a shop the shopkeeper is considered as warranting that the goods are his to sell, and if the purchaser is deprived of the goods by reason of a defect of title he may recover back the price. (*Eicholz* v. *Bannister*, 17 C. B. N. S. 708; 34 L. J. C. P. 105.) A pawnbroker who had sold an article as a forfeited pledge was held to warrant only that it had been pledged with him and was irredeemable, and that he knew of no defect of title, and was not liable for breach of an implied warranty of title upon the article being claimed by the true owner. (*Morley* v. *Attenborough*, *supra.*)

A sale of goods taken in execution imports no warranty of title. (See *Chapman* v. *Speller*, 14 Q. B. 621; 19 L. J. Q. B. 239; and *Bagueley* v. *Hawley*, *supra.*)

A concealment by the vendor of defects in his title which are known to him, amounts to fraud, and is actionable. (*Ib.*; *Early* v. *Garrett*, 9 B. & C. 932.) An executory contract of sale of an unascertained chattel may import a warranty of title. (See *per* Parke, B., in *Morley* v. *Attenborough*, *supra.*)

In order to create a warranty it is not requisite that the word "warrant" should be used; any affirmance or representation made at the time of the sale is a warranty, if it appear to have been so intended and understood by the parties. (*Per* Buller, J., in *Pasley* v. *Freeman*, 3 T. R. 57; 2 Sm. L. C., 8th ed. p. 66; and see *Chandelor* v. *Lopus*, notes, 1 Sm. L. C. 184, and cases there cited; and see Benjamin on Sales, p. 455; Leake on Contracts, 403, 404.)

(*b*) Upon a sale or exchange of a specific chattel, or specific goods *in esse*, the actual condition of which may be ascertained, there is in general no implied warranty of soundness or quality. (*Parkinson* v. *Lee*, 2 East. 314; *Dickson* v. *Zizinia*, 10 C. B. 610; *Jones* v. *Just*, L. R. 3 Q. B. 197, 202; 37 L. J. Q. B. 89; *La Neuville* v. *Nourse*, 3 Camp. 351.) A breach of warranty of a specific chattel sold does not

said horse to the plaintiff for £—— [which the plaintiff then paid the defendant as the price thereof.]

2. The said horse was not then sound. [It was lame in both forelegs and blind.]

---

entitle the purchaser to rescind the contract and return the chattel and sue for the price, but only entitles him to an action for damages upon the warranty, or to counterclaim for such damages, when sued for the price, or to set up in reduction of the price the amount by which the value of the chattel itself is diminished by reason of the breach. (*Weston* v. *Downes*, 1 Doug. 23; *Street* v. *Blay*, 2 B. & Ad. 456; *Kennedy* v. *Panama, &c., Mail Co.*, L. R. 2 Q. B. 587; 36 L. J. Q. B. 263; *Gompertz* v. *Denton*, 1 C. & M. 207; *Allen* v. *Cameron*, 1 C. & M. 832, 840; *Poulton* v. *Lattimore*, 9 B. & C. 259.) If consequential or special damage is sought in an action or by a counterclaim upon the warranty, it must be specifically set forth and claimed in the pleadings. (O. XIX. rr. 4, 8; and see *Mondel* v. *Steel*, 8 M. & W. 858; *Rigge* v. *Burbidge*, 15 M. & W. 598.)

If in an action for the price, the purchaser reduces the amount of the claim by proving the breach of warranty, he is precluded from afterwards recovering damages for the mere breach of warranty in a cross action. (*Mondel* v. *Steel*, 8 M. & W. 858.)

The contract may, however, be made conditional upon the warranty being true (*Bannerman* v. *White*, 31 L. J. C. P. 28; 10 C. B. N. S. 844; and see *Dawson* v. *Collis*, 10 C. B. 523); or it may expressly provide for the return of the goods if they should turn out to be not according to the warranty, as in *Adam* v. *Richards*, 2 H. Bl. 573; and *Head* v. *Tattersall*, L. R. 7 Ex. 7; 41 L. J. Ex. 4, and *Hinchcliffe* v. *Barwick*, 5 Ex. D. 177; 49 L. J. Ex. 495. In such cases the purchaser may, upon a return of the goods, recover back the price. The purchaser would also be entitled to recover back the price where the vendor had agreed to rescind the contract and had accepted a return of the goods.

If at the time of the sale of a horse the horse warranted to be then sound has any disease, or congenital defect, or malformation which diminishes his usefulness so as to make him less fit for work, or which will in the ordinary course diminish his usefulness, or if he has, either from disease or accident, undergone any alteration in structure that actually does, or in its ordinary effect will, so diminish his usefulness, such horse is unsound. (*Kiddell* v. *Burnard*, 9 M. & W. 669; *Holliday* v. *Morgan*, 1 E. & E. 1; 28 L. J. Q. B. 9; Leake on Contracts, 403.)

A warranty may, however, be given so as to be a warranty only of soundness for particular purposes, or otherwise limited in its effect. It is in general to be implied that defects apparent at the time of the bargain are not included in a warranty however general; a party therefore, who should buy a horse knowing it to be blind in both eyes could not sue on a general warranty of soundness. (*Per* Tindal, C. J., in *Margetson* v. *Wright*, 7 Bing. 603; and see *Holliday* v. *Morgan*, 1 E. & E. 1; 28 L. J. Q. B. 9.)

An agent who gives a warranty in selling on his master's behalf binds his master by such warranty where it is within the limits of his authority to warrant, or where he acts in warranting within the apparent limits of his authority and position as employed by his

3. In consequence of the said unsoundness the said horse was of much less value than it would have been had it been sound [*or* was of no use to the plaintiff].

4. [By reason of the premises the plaintiff incurred

---

master, so that the person dealing with him has a right to, and does, believe that he has the authority to warrant which he assumes to have. Thus, the servant of a horse dealer, or livery stable keeper who deals in horses employed in the ordinary conduct of the business, may, if in the course of such business it is usual to warrant, bind his principal by a sale of a horse with a warranty, though he may on the particular occasion, unknown to the buyer, have express instructions not to warrant, such warranty being within the scope of his apparent authority. (*Howard* v. *Sheward*, L. R. 2 C. P. 148; 36 L. J. C. P. 42; *Brady* v. *Todd*, 9 C. B. N. S. 592; 30 L. J. C. P. 223; *Coleman* v. *Riches*, 16 C. B. 104; 24 L. J. C. P. 128.) So a servant employed to sell a horse at a public market or fair, where it is usual for the person selling to exercise all the powers of an owner, may there bind his principal by a sale with a warranty (*per cur.* in *Brady* v. *Todd*, *supra*). But the servant of a person not carrying on the business of a horse dealer employed on a particular occasion to sell a horse would have no implied authority to warrant the horse, and the master would not be bound by a warranty given by the servant, if, in fact, he had no authority to warrant. (*Brady* v. *Todd*, *supra*.) The owner in such case could either repudiate the sale, or affirm it, but if he affirm it, he must affirm it *in toto*, and adopt the warranty (*per cur.* in *Brady* v. *Todd*, *supra*).

In an action for a breach of the warranty of a specific chattel sold, as a particular horse, the measure of damages is, in general, the price paid for the horse, if it be returned, whilst if it be kept, it is the diminution in value by reason of it not being as warranted. (*Caswell* v. *Coare*, 1 Taunt. 566; *Clare* v. *Maynard*, 6 A. & E. 519.) If in consequence of the breach the purchaser resells, the price realised on such resale is evidence of its value, so that in general the difference between the contract price and the price so realised would be given by a jury. (*Clare* v. *Maynard*, *supra*.)

If the purchaser has been compelled to keep a horse sold to him with a warranty which was broken or untrue, for a time before he could, acting reasonably, resell it, he may claim and recover, the cost of so keeping it, as special damage. (*Caswell* v. *Coare*, 1 Taunt. 566; *Chesterman* v. *Lamb*, 2 A. & E. 132.) In such case, perhaps, the purchaser should, to entitle him to recover such special damage, in general, have given the vendor the option of taking back the horse. See cases *supra*.

The loss of profit on a resale at an advanced price cannot, in general, be recovered (*Clare* v. *Maynard*, *supra*); but in cases where it is known to both parties at the time of the bargain that the purchase is made to fulfil a contract for resale at an advanced price the loss on such contract may be recovered. (*Randall* v. *Raper*, E. B. & E. 84; 27 L. J. Q. B. 266.) The loss of profit on a resale at an advanced price may be evidence of what the value would have been had the chattel or horse been as warranted. See *Clare* v. *Maynard*, *supra*.

The cost of defending an action upon a similar warranty given

trouble, and also incurred expense to the amount of £—— in keeping and selling the said horse and endeavouring to induce the defendant to receive it back, and resold the said horse for £—— less than the sum paid as above stated to the defendant.]

The like, Hinchcliffe v. *Barwick,* 5 Ex. D. 177.

For a Breach of Warranty of the Quality of Goods sold by description (c).

1. By an agreement in writing bearing date the —— of ——, 18—, the defendant bargained and sold to the

---

upon a resale has been held recoverable as damages after notice of the action to the original seller who returned no answer to such notice. (*Lewis* v. *Peake*, 7 Taunt. 153.) A liability to pay such costs may be sufficient without actual payment. (*Randall* v. *Raper, supra.*) But if such action is defended by the purchaser at his own risk, when he might have discovered the breach of the warranty, and not at the request of his vendor, he cannot charge the costs as damages. (*Wrightup* v. *Chamberlain*, 7 Scott, 598, and Leake on Contracts, 1077.)

Where a person sold a cow which would in the ordinary course be placed by the purchaser with other cattle, with a warranty that it was sound, and the purchaser relying upon such warranty placed the cow with other cattle, to which it communicated an infectious disease from which it was suffering at the time of the sale, it was held that the purchaser could recover as special damage in an action upon the warranty the loss caused to him by such communication of disease. (*Smith* v. *Green*, 1 C. P. D. 92; 45 L. J. C. P. 29.)

(*c*) In general on a sale of goods by a particular description it is an implied term of the contract that they shall answer that description (*Wieler* v. *Schilizzi*, 17 C. B. 619; 25 L. J. C. P. 89; *Jones* v. *Just*, L. R. 3 Q. B. 197, 204, 205); and where the buyer has had no opportunity of inspecting the goods it is further an implied term of the contract that they shall be merchantable under that description. (*Jones* v. *Just, supra; Josling* v. *Kingsford*, 13 C. B. N. S. 447; 32 L. J. C. P. 94.)

As to sales by sample, see note (*d*), *post*, p. 347.

If goods sold by description or sample do not answer the description or sample, the vendee may refuse to accept or take delivery of them, or he may keep them a reasonable time for the purpose of efficient examination of them, and do whatever is reasonably necessary for that purpose, and then, if he find them not to answer such description or sample, reject them. (*Heilbutt* v. *Hickson*, L. R. 7 C. P. 438; 41 L. J. C. P. 228; *Lucy* v. *Mouflet*, 5 H. & N. 233; 29 L. J. Ex. 110.)

plaintiff and the plaintiff bought from the defendant —— tons of linseed, to be delivered *ex* ship *Argos* at Hull, at the price of £—— per ton, and by the said agreement the defendant warranted to the plaintiff the said linseed to be Calcutta linseed.

2. The —— tons of linseed were accordingly under the said agreement delivered to the plaintiff, *ex* ship *Argos*, at Hull, and he then received the same.

3. The linseed so delivered was not Calcutta linseed, but was linseed of quality and value inferior to Calcutta linseed.

4. The plaintiff in consequence lost £——, the difference between the value of the said linseed and the value of Calcutta linseed.

For a like Form, see Cowdy v. *Thomas*, 36 L. T. 22.

On an implied Warranty that Goods sold by Sample were equal to Sample (d).

1. On the —— of —— 18—, the defendant offered to sell to the defendant —— pockets of hops at the price of

---

If the goods so sold fail to answer to the sample or description and are rejected by the buyer, it is not, in general, incumbent on the buyer to incur the expense or trouble of returning them; it is enough if he gives clear notice of his rejection of the goods to the vendor, intimating that they are at his risk. (*Grimoldby* v. *Wells*, L. R. 10 C. P. 391; 44 L. J. C. P. 203; *Heilbutt* v. *Hickson*, L. R. 7 C. P. 438; 41 L. J. C. P. 228.) If goods so sold are retained, the purchaser may sue for damages for the loss caused by diminution of value owing to such goods not being as described, or according to sample. (See *per cur.* in *Heilbutt* v. *Hickson*, *supra*; and in *Behn* v. *Burness*, 3 B. & S. 755; 32 L. J. Q. B. 206.) See further as to sales by description, Benjamin on Sales, 2nd ed. p. 487; Leake on Contracts, 177, 406.

Under "The Merchandise Marks Act, 1862" (25 & 26 Vict. c. 88), ss. 19, 20, upon a sale of goods bearing a trade-mark or description, the sale is deemed to have been made with a warranty of such trade-mark or description, unless the contrary is expressed in writing. See "*Trade Marks*," post, p. 525.

See notes to "*Sale of Goods*," *ante*.

(*d*) In a sale by sample of goods not specifically ascertained, the goods may, in general, be rejected by the buyer if they do not correspond with the sample (see note (*c*), *ante*, p. 346). There is no implied warranty in a sale by sample that the article sold is merchantable so far as regards those qualities which can fairly be judged

£——, and then produced for the inspection of the plaintiff that which he alleged to be a fair sample of the said hops.

2. The plaintiff then after inspecting the said sample agreed to purchase the said —— pockets of hops at the said price, upon the terms that the said —— pockets of hops should be equal in quality and description to the said sample.

3. The plaintiff paid the said agreed price to the defendant and received the said hops.

4. The said —— pockets of hops were not equal in quality or description to the said sample but were inferior thereto, whereby the plaintiff lost £——, the difference between what the value of the said hops would have been had they been equal to sample and the value of the hops actually received by the plaintiff.

By a Purchaser of Machinery for a special purpose for Breach of Contract to supply Machinery reasonably fit for that purpose (*e*).

1. The plaintiff was and is a worsted spinner and manufacturer and the owner and occupier of the —— mill at ——.

---

of from the sample, but such implied warranty is not thereby excluded as to such matters as cannot be judged of by the sample. (*Mody* v. *Gregson*, L. R. 4 Ex. 49; 38 L. J. Ex. 12; *Heilbutt* v. *Hickson*, L. R. 7 C. P. 454; 41 L. J. C. P. 228.) See note (*c*), *ante*, p. 346.

(*e*) Where a manufacturer or dealer contracts to supply an article which he manufactures or produces, or in which he deals, for, or to be applied to, a particular purpose, so that the buyer necessarily trusts to the judgment or skill of the manufacturer or dealer, there is an implied term or warranty that it shall be reasonably fit for such purpose (*per cur.* in *Jones* v. *Just*, L. R. 3 Q. B. 197, 203; *Randall* v. *Newson*, 2 Q. B. D. 102; 46 L. J. Q. B. 259; *Gray* v. *Cox*, 4 B. & C. 108; *Brown* v. *Edgington*, 2 M. & G. 279; *Jones* v. *Bright*, 5 Bing. 533), and there is no exception as to latent defects (*Randall* v. *Newson*, 2 Q. B. D. 102; 46 L. J. Q. B. 259.)

Where a manufacturer undertakes to supply goods, manufactured by himself, or in which he deals, but which the vendee has not had the opportunity of inspecting, it is an implied term in the contract that he shall supply a merchantable article (*per cur.* in *Jones* v. *Just*, *supra*; *Laing* v. *Fidgeon*, 4 Camp. 169; 6 Taunt. 108; *Shepherd* v. *Pybus*, 3 M. & G. 868).

Where a known, described, and defined article is ordered of a manufacturer, although it is stated to be required for a particular

2. The defendants are and were a firm carrying on business at —— as engineers, millwrights and iron-founders, and were fully acquainted with the plaintiff's said mill, and the mode in which it was used and occupied.

3. In ——, 18—, some bevil wheels having broken in the plaintiff's said mill, the plaintiff consulted the defendants as to the best method of transmitting the steam power with an even motion from the engine to the machinery used by the plaintiff in his said mill at the place where the said wheels had broken, and in accordance with the advice which the defendants then gave him the plaintiff ordered the defendants to make and fit up for him for the above purpose at the said place a large strap pulley, and a leathern belt, for reward to be paid by him to the defendants.

4. The defendants accepted the said order, and made and fitted up a large strap pulley and leathern belt for the plaintiff at the said place, but the said pulley was negligently and carelessly made and fitted up, and was not properly balanced. It was half a hundredweight heavier and much thicker on one side than on the other, instead of being, as it should have been, of the same weight and thickness on both sides.

5. The said pulley was in consequence not reasonably fit for the purpose for which, as stated, it was ordered and supplied.

6. By reason of the above defects the said pulley did not transmit the steam power with an even motion from the engine to the machinery used by the plaintiff in his said mill at the said place, and it broke and twisted the shafting, and damaged the said machinery, and altogether failed to accomplish the said purpose for which it was ordered.

7. The plaintiff's work at the said mill was in consequence stopped for —— weeks, and his said mill and machinery rendered useless, and the plaintiff was put to an expense of £—— in repairing the said shafting and

---

purpose, still if the known, described, and defined thing be supplied, there is no warranty that it shall answer the particular purpose intended by the buyer (*per cur.* in *Jones* v. *Just, supra; Chanter* v. *Hopkins*, 4 M. & W. 399; *Ollivant* v. *Bayley*, 5 Q. B. 288).

As to articles of food, see *Burnby* v. *Bollett*, 16 M. & W. 644; *Emmerton* v. *Matthews*, 7 H. & N. 586; 31 L. J. Ex. 139; *Smith* v. *Baker*, 40 L. T. 261.

machinery, and lost £—— which he had paid to the defendants as the price of the said pulley.

8. The defendants, when they entered into the said contract with the plaintiff, were fully aware of the consequences which might and which did, in fact, ensue from their breaches of contract above stated.

On a Warranty that Goods supplied for a Particular Purpose were fit for that Purpose.

1. The defendant, by warranting that certain copper was then reasonably fit and proper to be used for the purpose of sheathing a ship of the plaintiff, sold the same to the plaintiff for the purpose of being so used.

2. The said copper was not then reasonably fit or proper to be used for the purpose of sheathing the said ship.

3. In consequence of the said copper not being then reasonably fit or proper to be used for the said purpose the plaintiff, after having sheathed his said ship with the said copper, incurred expense [to the amount of £——] in having the said copper removed, and in having his said ship sheathed with other copper.

For a like Form, see Randall v. *Newson*, 2 Q. B. D. 102.

For the Breach of a Warranty of the Takings of a Business.

1. At the date of the hereinafter-mentioned sale the defendant was possessed of the lease of a public-house at ——, called the ——, for an unexpired term of years, and of certain fixtures, goods, and stock-in-trade in the said house, and of the goodwill of the business carried on therein.

2. On the —— of ——, 18—, the defendant by warranting that the takings of the said business had been and were £—— per month, all retail over the counter, sold the said lease, fixtures, goods, stock-in-trade, and goodwill to the plaintiff for the price of £——, which the plaintiff then paid to the defendant for the same.

3. The takings of the said business had not been, and

were not at the time of the said sale, £—— per month, all retail over the counter. Such retail takings had been and were at the said time about £—— only per month.

4. By reason of the premises the said lease, fixtures, goods, stock-in-trade and goodwill are of much less value to the plaintiff than they would otherwise have been.

For a Claim against an Agent upon an Implied Warranty that he had Authority to Contract, see "Agent," ante, p. 44.

WORK.

Statement of Claim for Work done and Materials provided (*a*).

1. The plaintiff is a housefitter and decorator carrying on business at ——.

(*a*) Under the general term "work" any species of labour may be given in evidence (*Clark* v. *Mumford*, 3 Camp. 37), whether mental or physical, or both (*Grafton* v. *Armitage*, 2 C. B. 336; *Clay* v. *Yates*, 1 H. & N. 73; 25 L. J. Ex. 237); but it is usual and proper to describe the kind of work or the character in which the work has been done, as, work done by the plaintiff as a solicitor, an auctioneer, a broker, &c. If there is a claim for materials provided it must be stated (*Heath* v. *Freeland*, 1 M. & W. 543).

Where the work has been done by the plaintiff upon his own materials in making an article to be delivered to the defendant under a contract of sale, the work is done by the plaintiff for himself, and not for the purchaser, and the subject of the contract should be treated as goods sold, and not as work and labour. (*Atkinson* v. *Bell*, 8 B. & C. 277; *Lee* v. *Griffin*, 1 B. & S. 272; 30 L. J. Q. B. 252.) Contracts which fall under the description of work and labour, although they result in the delivery of completed goods are not within the 17th section of the Statute of Frauds. (*Clay* v. *Yates*, 1 H. & N. 73; 25 L. J. Ex. 237; *Lucas* v. *Godwin*, 3 Bing. N. C. 737; *Grafton* v. *Armitage*, 2 C. B. 336.)

Where work is done by one party under a special contract, but not according to its terms, the other may refuse to accept it (*Ellis* v. *Hamlen*, 3 Taunt. 52); but if he does accept it and takes the benefit of it, he may be sued for the value of it (*Burn* v. *Miller*, 4 Taunt. 745).

If the work is of such a nature that it cannot be rejected, so that the party has no option in accepting it, he is not necessarily liable for the value; as work done in building upon the defendant's land, but not according to contract. (*Ellis* v. *Hamlen*, *supra*; *Milner* v. *Field*, 5 Ex. 829; *Burn* v. *Miller*, *supra*; *Munro* v. *Butt*, 8 E. & B.

2. In the month of ——, 18—, the plaintiff was employed as such housefitter and decorator by the defendant to execute certain repairs at the defendant's house at ——, and to provide certain materials for the same for reward to the plaintiff.

3. The plaintiff duly executed the said repairs and provided the said materials for the said repairs.

4. The sum which the plaintiff was to receive for executing the said repairs and providing the said materials was not fixed by any express agreement. The fair and reasonable prices for the said repairs and materials amount altogether to the sum of £——.

5. [Full particulars of the said repairs and materials and of the said prices thereof have been delivered by the plaintiff to the defendant, *or* are as follows, *setting out the same.*]

6. The said sum of £—— was due from and payable by the defendant to the plaintiff before the commencement of this action, and is still due and unpaid.

738.) So where work is performed, notwithstanding the express dissent of the defendant, the defendant is not liable though he derive some benefit therefrom. (*Stokes* v. *Lewis*, 1 T. R. 20.)

Where the terms of the contract are such as to make the remuneration contingent upon the completion of the services, a partial performance will not alone give any claim against the employer (*Hulle* v. *Heightman*, 2 East, 145; *Cutter* v. *Powell*, 2 Sm. L. C. 8th ed., p. 1; 6 T. R. 320; *Appleby* v. *Dods*, 8 East, 300; *Jesse* v. *Ray*, 1 C. M. & R. 316; *Moffatt* v. *Laurie*, 24 L. J. C. P. 56; *Sinclair* v. *Bowles*, 9 B. & C. 92; *Green* v. *Mules*, 30 L. J. C. P. 343); so if the completion is prevented by some accident or event that may excuse the further performance, yet if there be no default in the employer, he is not liable for the value of the part performed where by the contract payment is contingent on completion (*Appleby* v. *Myers*, L. R. 2 C. P. 651; 36 L. J. C. P. 331; *Adlard* v. *Booth*, 7 C. & P. 108; *Gillett* v. *Mawman*, 1 Taunt. 140; *Metcalfe* v. *Britannia Ironworks Co.*, 1 Q. B. D. 613; 45 L. J. Q. B. 837; *Hopper* v. *Burness*, 1 C. P. D. 137; 45 L. J. C. P. 377).

But where the contract is to do work or render services to be paid for on completion, and the employer revokes the retainer before the work is completed, or prevents the completion of it, he must nevertheless reimburse the party employed, for his labour expended in pursuance of the employment, unless the contract is such as to admit the power of revocation in the employer without any compensation for the services rendered. See "*Agent*," *ante*, p. 42, *and cases cited there; and De Bernardy* v. *Harding*, 3 Ex. 822; 22 L. J. Ex. 340; *Pontifex* v. *Wilkinson*, 1 C. B. 75.

For Work done.

1. The plaintiffs are the owners of the Bute Docks at Cardiff, and the defendants are coal merchants carrying on business at Cardiff.

2. In the months of April and June, 18—, the plaintiffs did work for and rendered services to the defendants in and about weighing, tipping, loading, and transferring coal for the defendants at their request.

3. The rate at which the plaintiffs were to be paid for such work and services was not fixed by any express agreement, but at the usual fair and reasonable rate paid in Cardiff for such work and services; there is now due and payable from the defendants to the plaintiffs in respect of and as the price of such work and services the sum of £—— [*or if the rate was fixed, show what it was, and how fixed*].

Against a Workman for using Bad Materials and for Bad Workmanship (*b*).

1. The plaintiff in March, 18—, employed the defendant to roof for him a house at ——, upon the terms that he should use materials of the best description and quality, and complete the work in a good and workmanlike manner for the sum of £——.

2. The defendant accepted the said employment upon the said terms, but he did not use materials of the best description or quality, nor did he complete the said work in a good or workmanlike manner.

3. [The defendant used inferior slates and laid them on unskilfully and in an unworkmanlike manner.]

4. [In consequence of the premises the plaintiff had to incur an expense of £—— in putting the said roof into proper condition, and lost the said sum of £—— which he had paid to the defendant under the said agreement.]

(*b*) A person who carries on a particular trade requiring skill impliedly contracts that he will use reasonable skill in the exercise of such trade when employed in such trade. (*Harmer* v. *Cornelius*, 5 C. B. N. S. 236; 28 L. J. C. P. 85; *Jenkins* v. *Betham*, 15 C. B. 189.) If the work is useless owing to the workman's improper execution of the work he contracted to do with reasonable skill and care, such workman can recover nothing in respect of it. (*Farnsworth* v. *Garrard*, 1 Camp. 38; *Montriou* v. *Jefferys*, R. & M. 317; *Denew* v. *Daverell*, 3 Camp. 451; *Huntley* v. *Bulwer*, 6 N. C. 111; *Kannen* v. *McMullen*, Peake, 59.)

By a Builder to Recover Payment for his Work upon Production of the Architect's Certificate as required by the Contract (c).

1. [By an agreement in writing bearing date the —— of —— 18—] it was agreed by and between the plaintiff and the defendant that the plaintiff should build for the defendant a house at ——, upon the terms and subject to the conditions contained in a certain written specification and should be paid therefor by the defendant the sum of £—— upon production of the written certificate of A. B., the architect of the defendant, that the said house was completed to the satisfaction of the said A. B.

2. Afterwards and before this action the said house was duly completed by the plaintiff in accordance with the said specification, and the said A. B., the architect of the defendant, gave to the plaintiff his written certificate that the said house was completed to the satisfaction of him, the said A. B.

3. The plaintiff thereupon produced the said written certificate to the defendant, and required payment of the said sum of £——.

4. The defendant has not paid the plaintiff the said sum of £——, or any part thereof, and the same is due and payable by the defendant to the plaintiff.

For further Forms, see " Solicitor," "Agent," &c.

(c) It is common in building contracts and the like to make it a condition precedent to the payment of the price that the architect or engineer give his certificate of approval; and then there can be no claim for payment under the contract until it is given (*Morgan* v. *Birnie*, 9 Bing. 672; *Milner* v. *Field*, 5 Ex. 829), and that even where the certificate is wrongly or unreasonably withheld (*Clarke* v. *Watson*, 18 C. B. N. S. 278; 34 L. J. C. P. 148; *Scott* v. *Corporation of Liverpool*, 3 D. & J. 334; 28 L. J. Ch. 230; *De Worms* v. *Mellier*, L. R. 16 Eq. 554).

There may, however, be a claim or right of action on the ground of fraud where the certificate is withheld by the procurement of the employer in collusion with the architect. (*Batterbury* v. *Vyse*, 2 H. & C. 42; 32 L. J. Ex. 77; *M'Intosh* v. *G. W. R. Co.*, 2 Mac. & G. 74.) See as to form of pleading, *Stevenson* v. *Watson*, 4 C. P. D. 148; 48 L. J. C. P. 318. See further, Leake on Contracts, 640, 641, 955.

Where a contract stipulates that no extra work shall be paid for unless ordered in writing, the price of extra work done without such order cannot be recovered. (*Russel* v. *Viscount Sa da Bandiera*, 13 C. B. N. S. 149; 32 L. J. C. P. 68; *Kirk* v. *Bromley Union*, 2 Phill. 640.)

See further, "*Conditions Precedent*," *ante*, p. 158.

By a Builder against his Employer for Collusively Procuring his Architect to withhold his Certificate, such Certificate being a Condition precedent to the Right of the Builder to Payment for the Work done (c).

1. The plaintiff is a builder and contractor, carrying on business at ——.

2. On the —— of ——, 18—, by an agreement in writing made between the plaintiff and the defendant, it was agreed that the plaintiff should erect for the defendant a house at —— in accordance with certain plans and specifications for the sum of £——.

3. The said agreement was made upon, and subject to, the terms and conditions, amongst others, that the work in and about the erection of the said house should be executed by the plaintiff in the best and most workmanlike manner, with the best quality of materials, under the superintendence and to the satisfaction of the defendant's architect, and that if in the course of the said work any additions to or omissions from the said work should be required by the defendant or his architect, such additions or omissions should not in any way vitiate the said agreement, but the value of such additions or omissions should be estimated by the said architect, and added to or deducted from the said agreed sum, as the case might be, and that the decision of the said architect should be final and conclusive in all matters affecting the proposed works, and that the amount of the said agreement should be paid by monthly instalments equal to £—— per cent. of the value of the work executed, and the balance within one month after the final completion of the said house to the said architect's satisfaction, but that no payment should be considered due unless upon production of the said architect's certificate for payment.

4. Under and in pursuance of the said agreement the plaintiff erected the said house in accordance with the said plans and specifications, with the exception of certain omissions, which said omissions were duly required by the defendant and his architect, and executed the said work in and about the erection of the said house in the best and most workmanlike manner, and with the best quality of materials, and under the superintendence of the said architect.

5. In the course of the said work additions to the said work were required by the said architect and duly executed by the plaintiff.

6. The fair and reasonable prices for the said additions executed by the plaintiff as aforesaid amount to the sum of £——, and after deducting therefrom the sum of £——, the fair and reasonable prices of the said omissions, there remains a balance of £——, which with £——, the unpaid balance of the said agreed price, amounts to the sum of £——.

7. The said house was on the —— of —— 18—, duly completed by the plaintiff to the satisfaction of the said architect.

8. Although more than one month has elapsed since the said completion of the said house, the defendant has paid to the plaintiff only £——, and the said sum of £—— in the above 6th paragraph mentioned is still wholly unpaid.

9. All [conditions have been performed and all things have happened and all] times have elapsed necessary to entitle the plaintiff to have the value of the said omissions and additions estimated by the said architect, and to receive the said architect's certificate for payment for the same.

10. The said architect has wholly neglected and refused to estimate the value of the said omissions and additions and to give any certificate for any payment beyond the amount already paid as above stated, and he has so neglected in fraudulent collusion with and by procurement of the defendant.

CHAPTER III.

STATEMENTS OF CLAIM IN ACTIONS FOR WRONGS(*a*).

(*a*) Before the C. L. P. Act, 1852, causes of action were classed under the two divisions of actions of contract and actions of tort; the former comprising the actions of Assumpsit, Debt, and Covenant; and the latter the actions of Trespass, Case, Trover, Detinue (except in some points of view; *see Bryant* v. *Herbert*, 3 C. P. D. 389; 47 L. J. C. P. 670), and Replevin. But for certain technical reasons, and particularly in order to avoid the then rule, which prohibited the joinder of counts in contract with counts in tort, the declaration was framed in tort in many cases in which the cause of action was the breach of a duty essentially founded on contract, as in actions against carriers and other bailees. (*See* "*Carriers,*" *ante*, p. 120.)

Under the present system the facts are in all cases to be stated, and the question of whether an action is founded upon contract or in tort is immaterial, except for the purpose of convenience in classification, or for the purpose of determining the right to costs in certain cases under the County Courts Act, 1867 (30 & 31 Vict. c. 142), s. 5, or for the purpose of determining whether the action can be sent to the County Court for trial, from the High Court of Justice under the County Courts Act, 1856 (19 & 20 Vict. c. 108), s. 26, or remitted to the County Court under the County Courts Act, 1867 (30 & 31 Vict. c. 142), ss. 7, 10.

It is, however, convenient to retain the division of actions into *actions of contract*, and *for wrongs*, not excluding from the latter division those actions which are for breaches of duty arising out of contract, as, for example, for negligence of carriers, which partake of the character both of breaches of contract and wrongs. (*See* "*Carriers,*" *ante*, p. 120.)

It is never necessary to aver, as was the practice before the C. L. P. Act, 1852, the duty or legal liability charged for that duty is a mere inference of law from the facts stated, and is useless if the facts do not show a legal liability. (*Brown* v. *Mallett*, 5 C. B. 599; *Seymour* v. *Maddox*, 16 Q. B. 326; *Roberts* v. *Great Western Ry. Co.*, 4 C. B. N. S. 506; *Gautret* v. *Egerton*, L. R. 2 C. P. 371, 374; 36 L. J. C. P. 191; *Collis* v. *Selden*, L. R. 3 C. P. 495; 37 L. J. C. P. 233; *Dutton* v. *Powles*, 2 B. & S. 174; 30 L. J. Q. B. 169; *Benett* v. *P. & O. Steamboat Co.*, 6 C. B. 785.)

As to what are actions founded on contract, and what on tort within the meaning of sect. 5 of the County Courts Act, 1867 (30 & 31 Vict. c. 142), which is, by sect. 67 of the Jud. Act, 1873, applicable to all actions in the High Court of Justice in which relief is sought which can be given in a County Court, *see* "*Carriers,*" *ante*, p. 121.

ADMINISTRATORS. *See "Executors," post*, p. 416.

AGENT (*a*).

[*For forms see "Agent," ante*, p. 36.]

ARREST. *See post, "Malicious Prosecution;" "Sheriff;" "Trespass to the Person."*

ASSAULT. *See post, "Trespass to the Person."*

BAILMENTS.

See ante, "Bailments," p. 70; *and post, "Conversion,"* p. 372.

Against a Bailee for Reward.

1. The plaintiff, on the —— of ——, 18—, delivered to the defendant thirteen cases of eggs, to be safely kept and taken care of by the defendant for the plaintiff, for reward to the defendant, and the defendant received and had the said thirteen cases of eggs in his care and keeping for the purpose and on the terms aforesaid.

2. The defendant kept the said goods in a negligent manner, and took no care thereof.

3. In consequence of the said negligence and want of care of the defendant, the said cases were broken and the said eggs spoilt and rendered valueless.

(*a*) Actions against Agents for neglect or misconduct may in general be brought either as for a breach of contract, or as for a wrong. (*See "Carriers," ante*, p. 120; and *see* p. 357, *supra*.)

By a gratuitous Bailee of a Horse for Injuries caused him (*b*).

1. The defendant, on the —— of ——, 18—, lent the plaintiff a horse to ride.

2. The said horse was, as the defendant then knew, a vicious horse, and one that was in consequence dangerous to ride.

3. The plaintiff was ignorant of the fact that the said horse was vicious, and of the fact that it was dangerous to ride.

4. The defendant, though aware that the plaintiff was ignorant as aforesaid, did not inform the plaintiff that the said horse was vicious, or that it was dangerous to ride,

---

(*b*) Upon the gratuitous bailment of a chattel, lent for use, the liabilities and duties of the borrower and the lender have been laid down as follows :—The borrower is not responsible for reasonable wear and tear ; but he is for negligence, for misuse, for gross want of skill in the use, above all for anything that may be qualified as legal fraud. So, the lender must be responsible for defects in the chattel with reference to the use for which he knows the loan is accepted, of which he is aware, and owing to which directly the borrower is injured. By the necessarily implied purpose of the loan a duty is contracted towards the borrower not to conceal from him those defects which may make the loan perilous, or unprofitable, to him. (*Blakemore, or Blackmore*, v. *Bristol and Exeter Ry. Co.*, 8 E. & B. *per* Coleridge, J., 1057 ; 27 L. J. Q. B. 167 ; *Moffatt* v. *Bateman*, L. R. 3 P. C. 115.) Accordingly, it was held that a gratuitous lender of a scaffold was not liable for an injury sustained by the borrower, which was caused by the defective construction of the scaffold of which the lender was not aware ; although the jury found that he had been guilty of negligence in the construction, and that the injury was caused by that negligence. (*M'Carthy* v. *Young*, 6 H. & N. 329 ; 30 L. J. Ex. 227.)

So in the case of a gratuitous deposit for safe custody the bailee is only bound to take ordinary care of the thing deposited, and is only liable if his negligence is such that an ordinarily prudent man would not be guilty of with regard to his own property. (*Gibbin* v. *McMullen*, L. R. 2 P. C. 317; 38 L. J. P. C. 25.)

Bankers are not gratuitous bailees of documents or securities deposited with them by their customers in the ordinary course of their business as bankers, under circumstances which would create a lien on them for the customers' general banking accounts. (*In re United Service Co.*, L. R. 6 Ch. App. 212 ; 39 L. J. Ch. App. 730.)

The duty of a person who lets out carriages for hire appears to be to supply a carriage as fit for the purpose for which it is hired as care and skill can render it. He is bound to take the same care as railway companies or carriers who provide carriages for the public to travel in. (*Hyman* v. *Nye*, 6 Q. B. D. 685 ; see "*Carriers*," *ante*, p. 138.)

nor did he give him any warning of the said qualities of the said horse.

5. Whilst the said horse was so lent to the plaintiff as aforesaid, the plaintiff, in ignorance that the said horse was vicious, and in ignorance that it was dangerous to ride, rode it, and was by reason of its said viciousness thrown from it, and was thereby injured in his knee and his arm, and much bruised.

Against a Hotel Keeper for the Loss of a Horse intrusted to him as such Hotel Keeper.

1. The defendant is the landlord of the "Red Lion Hotel" at ——.

2. On the —— of ——, 18—, the plaintiff, who is a farmer residing at ——, and who was possessed of a mare called "Polly," delivered the said mare to the defendant at the said hotel to be kept and taken care of by the defendant for the plaintiff, for reward to the defendant, and re-delivered by the defendant to the plaintiff on demand.

3. The defendant, though he received the said mare upon the terms aforesaid, did not keep and take due care of the said mare, and did not re-deliver the said mare to the plaintiff, although required by the plaintiff so to do, and negligently and without the authority of the plaintiff delivered the said mare to, or allowed the said mare to be taken away from the said hotel by persons other than the plaintiff, whereby the said mare was lost to the plaintiff.

For further Forms see "Bailments," ante, p. 70.

Bankruptcy (*a*).

For Commencements of Statements of Claim by Trustees in Bankruptcy, see "Bankruptcy," ante, p. 78.

(*a*) Wrongs which are personal to the debtor do not vest in, or pass to, his trustees in bankruptcy. *See "Bankruptcy," ante,* p. 80.

It has been held (Martin, B., doubting) that under the Bankruptcy Act, 1869 (32 & 33 Vict. c. 71), an action will lie for maliciously, and without reasonable or probable cause, making a man bankrupt. (*Johnson* v. *Emerson*, L. R. 6 Ex. 329, 368; 40 L. J. Ex. 201, 222.)

CARRIERS.

CARRIERS BY LAND (*a*).

Against a Common Carrier for Refusing to Carry Goods.

1. The defendant is and was a common carrier of goods for hire from —— to ——.

2. The plaintiff on the —— of ——, 18—, at a reasonable and proper time in that behalf, tendered to the defendant at —— aforesaid, at his place of business for the receipt of goods to be carried by him as such carrier, certain goods of the plaintiff [namely, 13 bales of cotton], and requested the defendant as such carrier to receive the same and carry them from —— to —— aforesaid, and at the last mentioned place to deliver the same for the plaintiff, for hire to the defendant.

(*a*) As to the duties and liabilities of carriers of goods by land, and as to other forms, see "*Carriers,*" *ante*, p. 120.

A common carrier is not liable as an insurer after the carriage of the goods to their destination, though they are not accepted by their consignee; after completion of the carriage the carrier remains liable only for negligence. (*Garside* v. *Trent Nav.*, 4 T. R. 581; and see *Bourne* v. *Gatliffe*, 3 M. & G. 643; 11 Cl. & F. 45; *Crouch* v. *Great Western Ry. Co.*, 2 H. & N. 491; 27 L. J. Ex. 345; *Mitchell* v. *L. & Y. Ry. Co.*, L. R. 10 Q. B. 256; 44 L. J. Q. B. 107; *Shepherd* v. *Bristol and Exeter Ry. Co.*, L. R. 3 Ex. 189; 37 L. J. Ex. 113; *Great Northern Ry. Co.* v. *Swaffield*, L. R. 9 Ex. 132; 43 L. J. Ex. 89.)

Where the consignee makes default in receiving the goods, the carrier can recover from him the expenses reasonably incurred in taking care of the goods. (*Great Northern Ry. Co.* v. *Swaffield, supra*; *Cargo ex Argos*, L. R. 5 P. C. 134; 42 L. J. Ad. 47.)

A misdelivery of goods by the carrier to the wrong person amounts to a conversion (*Stephenson* v. *Hart*, 4 Bing. 483; *Youl* v. *Harbottle*, Peake, 49; *Wyld* v. *Pickford*, 8 M. & W. 443; *Devereux* v. *Barclay*, 2 B. & Ald. 704). It is the duty of a carrier to keep goods which are to be fetched away a reasonable time for the consignee to come and fetch them (*Bourne* v. *Gatliffe*, 3 M. & G. 643; 7 M. & G. 850; *Patscheider* v. *Great Western Ry. Co.*, 3 Ex. D. 153). But if the consignee is *in mord* by delaying to take the goods away within a reasonable time, the obligation of the carrier becomes that of an ordinary bailee, and is confined to taking proper care of the goods as a warehouseman (*Chapman* v. *Great Western Ry. Co.*, 5 Q. B. D. 278; 49 L. J. Q. B. 420); and this is so even if the goods are consigned "to be left till called for" (*Chapman* v. *Great Western Ry. Co., supra*).

3. The plaintiff was then ready and willing, and offered to pay to the defendant his reasonable hire in that behalf, whereof the defendant then had notice.

4. The defendant had then sufficient time, means, and convenience to receive and carry and deliver the said goods as aforesaid, and could and ought to have done so.

5. The defendant, nevertheless, did not and would not receive and carry the said goods for the plaintiff.

Against a Carrier for Losing Goods.

1. The defendant was a carrier of goods for hire from —— to ——.

2. The plaintiff, on the —— of ——, 18—, delivered to the defendant, and the defendant received as such carrier, certain goods of the plaintiff [namely, 20 quarters of wheat], to be by the defendant taken care of and safely and securely carried from —— to —— aforesaid, and there delivered to [*or* for] the plaintiff within a reasonable time in that behalf, for reward to the defendant.

3. A reasonable time for carrying and delivering the said goods as aforesaid has elapsed.

4. The defendant has not taken care of or safely or securely carried the said goods from —— to —— aforesaid, or there delivered the same to [*or* for] the plaintiff as aforesaid, whereby the said goods have been lost to the plaintiff.

The like, Fleming v. *Manchester, Sheffield, & Lincolnshire Ry. Co.*, 4 Q. B. D. 81.

For Claims against a Carrier for Damage to Goods, see Forms, ante, "Carriers," p. 127, and *Lewis* v. *Great Western Ry. Co.*, 3 Q. B. D. 195.

Against a Carrier for Misdelivery of Goods.

1. 2. 3. [*As in form above for losing goods.*]

4. The defendant has not delivered the said goods at —— aforesaid to the plaintiff as aforesaid, but has wrongfully and without the consent of the plaintiff delivered

them to a person or to persons other than the plaintiff, whereby the plaintiff has been and is deprived of the use and possession of the said goods, and the same have thereby been lost to the plaintiff.

The like, Pontifex v. *Midland Ry. Co.*, 3 Q. B. D. 23; 47 L. J. Q. B. 28; 37 L. T. 403.

CARRIERS OF PASSENGERS. *See "Carriers of Passengers," ante*, p. 137; *and see "Negligence," post*, p. 477.

CARRIERS BY WATER. *See "Shipping;" post*, p. 518, *and ante*, p. 326.

COMMON (*a*).

Claim for a Disturbance of the Plaintiff's Right of Common of Pasture by Digging up the Turf and Soil and Enclosing.

1. At the times hereinafter mentioned the plaintiff was possessed of [a messuage and] land, called —— ——, in the parish of ——, in the county of ——.

(*a*) *Commons.*]—By the Prescription Act, 2 & 3 Will. IV., c. 71, s. 1, it is enacted, "That no claim which may be lawfully made at the common law, by custom, prescription, or grant, to any right of common or other profit or benefit to be taken and enjoyed from or upon any land" of any "person or body corporate, except such matters and things as are herein specially provided for, and except tithes, rent, and services, shall, where such right, profit, or benefit shall have been actually taken and enjoyed by any person claiming right thereto, without interruption for the full period of thirty years, be defeated or destroyed by showing only that such right, profit, or benefit was first taken or enjoyed at any time prior to such period of thirty years, but nevertheless, such claim may be defeated in any other way by which the same is now liable to be defeated; and when such right, profit, or benefit shall have been so taken and enjoyed as aforesaid, for the full period of sixty years, the right thereto shall be deemed absolute and indefeasible, unless it shall appear that the same was taken and enjoyed by some consent or agreement expressly made or given for that purpose by deed or writing."

Section 2 provides in similar terms for rights of way or other easements, but assigning corresponding terms of twenty years and

2. By reason of his possession of his said [messuage and] land the plaintiff at the said times was entitled to have common of pasture for all the commonable cattle levant and couchant in and upon his said [messuage

---

forty years for the periods of prescription instead of thirty years and sixty years.

Section 4 enacts, "That each of the respective periods of years hereinbefore mentioned shall be deemed and taken to be the period next before some suit or action wherein the claim or matter to which such period may relate shall have been or shall be brought into question, and that no act or other matter shall be deemed to be an interruption, within the meaning of this statute, unless the same shall have been or shall be submitted to or acquiesced in for one year after the party interrupted shall have had or shall have notice thereof, and of the person making or authorizing the same to be made."

Section 6 enacts, "That in the several cases mentioned in and provided for by this Act, no presumption shall be allowed or made in favour or support of any claim, upon proof of the exercise or enjoyment of the right or matter claimed for any less period of time or number of years than for such period or number mentioned in this Act, as may be applicable to the case and to the nature of the claim."

Section 7 provides, "That the time during which any person otherwise capable of resisting any claim to any of the matters before mentioned shall have been or shall be an infant, idiot, *non compos mentis*, *feme covert*, or tenant for life, or during which any action or suit shall have been pending, and which shall have been diligently prosecuted until abated by the death of any party or parties thereto, shall be excluded in the computation of the periods hereinbefore mentioned, except only in cases where the right or claim is hereby declared to be absolute and indefeasible."

"Provided always," by s. 8, "that when any land or water upon, over, or from which any such way or other convenient (*sic*) water-course or use of water shall have been or shall be enjoyed or derived, hath been or shall be held under or by virtue of any term of life or any term of years exceeding three years from the granting thereof, the time of the enjoyment of any such way or other matter as herein last before mentioned during the continuance of such term, shall be excluded in the computation of the said period of forty years, in case the claim shall within three years next after the end or sooner determination of such term be resisted by any person entitled to any reversion expectant on the determination thereof." (The words "other convenient" in this section are supposed to be a misprint for "other easement or." See "Williams on Commons," p. 311.)

The interruption under ss. 1, 4, must be an obstruction by some adverse claimant, and not a mere cessation of user by the claimant himself. (*Carr* v. *Foster*, 3 Q. B. 581.)

An action or legal proceeding is not essential to show non-acquiescence in such interruption, which is a mere question of fact. (*Bennison* v. *Cartwright*, 5 B. & S. 1; 33 L. J. Q. B. 137.)

The periods prescribed by the Act are required to be next before some suit or action wherein the claim shall be brought in question (see s. 4); consequently until such suit or action the period is not

and] land in and over a waste or common called ——, situate in the said parish [*or as the case may be*], at all times of the year, as to the said [messuage and] land appertaining.

---

complete, and the right is not established (*Ward* v. *Robins*, 15 M. & W. 237); but the establishment of the right in any such suit or action is conclusive in any subsequent suit or action between the same parties without further proof of enjoyment for the period next before the pending suit or action. (*Cooper* v. *Hubbuck*, 12 C. B. N. S. 456; 31 L. J. C. P. 323.) As to the establishment of a right under the Prescription Act, see *Earl de la Warr* v. *Miles*, 17 Ch. D. 535.

A right of common of pasture for cattle levant and couchant cannot be prescribed for in respect of a messuage only without land. (*Scholes* v. *Hargreaves*, 5 T. R. 46; *Benson* v. *Chester*, 8 T. R. 396.)

'Cattle levant and couchant' imports such number of cattle as the land to which the right of common is appurtenant is capable of maintaining; but it does not necessarily import that the cattle using the common are actually maintained on the land. (*Carr* v. *Lambert*, 3 H. & C. 499; L. R. 1 Ex. 168; 34 L. J. Ex. 66; 35 *ib.* 121.)

With respect to the mode of pleading rights of common or other prescriptive rights, it was always the rule under the former practice that it was sufficient for a plaintiff suing in respect of such rights to state his title generally in a form somewhat similar to that given in the above precedents, although where such rights were set up by a *defendant* as a defence to actions of trespass, &c., a greater amount of particularity in the statement of his title to the rights alleged was required. (See 1 Wms. Saund. 1871 ed. p. 623; and see "Defences," "*Common.*")

And it was enacted by s. 5 of the Prescription Act "That in all actions upon the case and other pleadings, wherein the party claiming may now by law allege his right generally, without averring the existence of such right from time immemorial, such general allegation shall still be deemed sufficient, and if the same shall be denied, all and every the matters in this Act mentioned and provided, which shall be applicable to the case, shall be admissible in evidence to sustain or rebut such allegation; and that in all pleadings to actions of trespass, and in all other pleadings wherein before the passing of this Act it would have been necessary to allege the right to have existed from time immemorial, it shall be sufficient to allege the enjoyment thereof as of right by the occupiers of the tenement in respect whereof the same is claimed for and during such of the periods mentioned in this Act as may be applicable to the case, and without claiming in the name or right of the owner of the fee, as is now usually done; and if the other party shall intend to rely on any proviso, exception, incapacity, disability, contract, agreement, or other matter hereinbefore mentioned, or on any cause or matter of fact or of law, not inconsistent with the simple fact of enjoyment, the same shall be specially alleged and set forth in answer to the allegation of the party claiming, and shall not be received in evidence on any general traverse or denial of such allegation."

It would seem that the last cited section is repealed by the Judicature Acts and the Orders thereunder (see, as to similar repeals, the

3. The defendant between the month of ——, 18—, and the commencement of this action, disturbed the plaintiff in the use and enjoyment of his said common of pasture by wrongfully digging up and subverting the soil

---

notes to "*Conditions Precedent*," *ante*, p. 158, and O. XIX. rr. 1, 4, Jud. Act, 1875, ss. 21, 24, 33 (2)), and that in strictness either a plaintiff or a defendant should at least state in what manner the alleged right is claimed to have arisen. (See *Baylis* v. *Tyssen-Amhurst*, 6 Ch. D. 500; 46 L. J. Ch. 718; *Robinson* v. *Duleep Singh*, 11 Ch. D. 798; *Philipps* v. *Philipps*, 4 Q. B. D. 127; 48 L. J. Q. B. 135; *Turquand* v. *Fearon*, 48 L. J. Q. B. 703; 40 L. T. 543.)

To do so, however, would in most cases considerably lengthen the pleadings, and it has hitherto been the usual and convenient practice for plaintiffs in their statements of claim to state their title in a general form similar to that given in the above precedents. In some cases this mode of pleading might embarrass or otherwise prejudice the defendant, and in such case he would be entitled to have the statement of claim amended on that ground under O. XXVII. r. 1. See further "*Pleading in General*," *ante*, p. 7. The right should be described accurately in respect to its extent, with all the restrictions and qualifications, if any, to which it is subject. It is immaterial, however, that a right is alleged more narrowly than it really exists, provided the allegation is wide enough to cover the disturbance complained of. (See *Duncan* v. *Louch*, 6 Q. B. 904; *Tebbutt* v. *Selby*, 6 A. & E. 786.)

A right of common was held to be well laid as "for sheep at all times of the year," though it was proved to be subject to folding the sheep at night on a certain farm; the expression being held to mean all usual times. (*Brook* v. *Willet*, 2 H. Bl. 224.)

Where a declaration alleged a right of common for all commonable cattle, it was held to be some evidence in support of it that the plaintiff was shown to have turned on all the cattle which he kept, although he had never kept any sheep. (*Manifold* v. *Pennington*, 4 B. & C. 161.)

Where the declaration alleged a right of common by reason of the possession of a messuage and land, proof of a right of common in respect of land only without any messuage was held sufficient. (*Ricketts* v. *Salwey*, 2 B. & Ald. 360.)

If the allegation of the right is divisible, it seems that the plaintiff is entitled to a limited verdict for a divisible part of the right alleged, though he fails to prove the residue. See *Giles* v. *Groves*, 12 Q. B. 721; 1 Chit. Pl., 7th ed., 400.

Any division of the High Court of Justice has jurisdiction to grant an injunction against a wrongful inclosure or other interference with rights of common, and such injunction may be claimed accordingly in addition to claims of damages or other relief. (See "*Injunction*," *post*, p. 439, and see the cases below cited.)

One freehold tenant of a manor can maintain an action on behalf of himself and all other freehold tenants, or freehold and copyhold tenants of the manor (if numerous and having the same interest), to obtain a declaration of the title of such tenants to rights of common, and an injunction restraining the lord of the manor from interfering with those rights. See O. XVI. r. 9; *Warrick* v. *Queen's College*,

and carrying away the turf of the said waste, and by wrongfully enclosing and separating a part, that is to say [about —— acres of the said waste on the —— side thereof] from the rest of the said waste, and by wrongfully causing and permitting the said part to remain so enclosed and separated as aforesaid.

4. By reason of the wrongful acts respectively hereinbefore complained of the plaintiff was prevented from having the use and enjoyment of his said common of pasture in so ample and beneficial a manner as he otherwise might and would have done.

5. [*If an injunction is claimed, add any facts material for that purpose, as for instance:* The defendant made and continued the said enclosure and committed the other acts hereinbefore complained of under a claim of right

---

Oxford, L. R. 10 Eq. 105; *ib.* 6 Ch. Ap. 716; 39 L. J. Ch. 636; 40 *ib.* 780; *Betts* v. *Thompson*, L. R. 6 Ch. Ap. 733; 19 W. R. 1098; *Hall* v. *Byron*, 4 Ch. D. 667; 46 L. J. Ch. 297; and see *Commissioners of Sewers* v. *Glasse*, L. R. 19 Eq. 134; *ib.* 7 Ch. Ap. 456; 41 L. J. Ch. 409; *ib.* 415.

In cases where the plaintiff sues in such representative capacity, the writ must be indorsed accordingly. (O. XVI. r. 9; O. III. r. 4.)

But a right of common cannot be claimed on behalf of an indeterminate and fluctuating body of persons, such as the inhabitants of a parish, unless by virtue of a grant from the Crown or of an Act of Parliament. (*Gateward's Case*, 6 Co. 59b.; *Lord Rivers* v. *Adams*, 3 Ex. D. 361; 48 L. J. Ex. D. 47; *Chilton* v. *Corporation of London*, 7 Ch. D. 735; 47 L. J. Ch. 433.)

With respect to the inclosure of commons generally, see "The Inclosure Acts, 1845 to 1878."

The following instances of declarations under the former practice may be useful for purposes of reference, viz.:—A declaration for injury to a right of common of pasture to which the plaintiff claimed to be entitled as freeman of a borough. (*Beadsworth* v. *Torkington*, 1 Q. B. 782.)

The like by an owner of land in a common field claiming a right of common over the whole field. (*Cheesman* v. *Hardham*, 1 B. & Ald. 706.)

The like claiming a right of common for a certain number of cattle of different kinds. (*Nichols* v. *Chapman*, 5 H. & N. 643; 29 L. J. Ex. 461.)

A declaration for disturbing a right of common by surcharging. (*Bowen* v. *Jenkin*, 6 A. & E. 911.)

A declaration for disturbing a right of common by removing the manure of the cattle and so impoverishing the common. (*Pindar* v. *Wadsworth*, 2 East, 154.)

Declarations for disturbing the plaintiff's right of common of pasture by digging up the soil and inclosing. (*Carr* v. *Foster*, 3 Q. B. 581; *Ricketts* v. *Salwey*, 2 B. & Ald. 360.)

and title in that behalf, and has continued the said enclosure and separation of the said part of the said waste up to the present time, and threatens and intends to continue the same unless he is restrained by an injunction of this court from so doing.]

The plaintiff claims :—

1. £—— damages for the wrongs hereinbefore complained of.
2. [An injunction restraining the defendant [his servants, agents, and workmen] from enclosing or permitting to remain enclosed any part of the said waste, and from repeating or continuing any of the wrongful acts hereinbefore complained of, and from interfering in any manner with the plaintiff's use and enjoyment of the said right of common of pasture.]
3. Such further or other relief as the nature of the case may require.

Claim for Obstructing the Plaintiff's Right of Common by putting on Cattle.

1 and 2. [*The same as paragraphs* 1 *and* 2 *in the last precedent.*]

3. The defendant during the months of —— and ——, 18—, disturbed the plaintiff in the use and enjoyment of his said common of pasture, by wrongfully putting divers horses, cows, and sheep [*state the numbers, if known*] in and upon the said waste, and keeping and depasturing the same there a long time [*state the time or times respectively, if known*].

4. [*The same as paragraph* 4 *of the last precedent.*]

Statement of Claim by a Freehold Tenant of a Manor against the Lord for Wrongfully Enclosing and Disturbing a Fold-course or Right of Pasture for Sheep, claiming a Declaration of the Plaintiff's Right and an Injunction. Robinson v. *Duleep Singh,* 11 Ch. D. 798.

COMPANY.

Claim against a Joint-Stock Company for refusing to register the Plaintiff as a Shareholder, with a Claim for a Mandamus (*a*).

1. The defendants are a joint-stock company, registered and incorporated under the Companies Act, 1862 [*or*,

(*a*) With respect to companies registered in England under the Companies Act, 1862, 25 & 26 Vict. c. 89, if the name of any person is, without sufficient cause, entered in or omitted from the register of members of any such company, or if default is made or unnecessary delay takes place in entering on the register the fact of any person having ceased to be a member of the company, the person or member aggrieved, or any member of the company, or the company itself, may, under the provisions of s. 35 of that Act, by motion in the High Court of Justice, or by application to a judge sitting in chambers, or to the vice-warden of the Stannaries in the case of companies subject to his jurisdiction, or in such other manner as the Court may direct, apply for an order of the Court that the register may be rectified; and the Court may either refuse such application with or without costs, to be paid by the applicant, or it may, if satisfied of the justice of the case, make an order for the rectification of the register, and may direct the company to pay all the costs of such motion, application, or petition, and any damages the party aggrieved may have sustained: and the Court may in any proceeding under this section decide on any question relating to the title of any person who is a party to such proceeding to have his name entered in or omitted from the register, whether such question arises between two or more members or alleged members, or between any members or alleged members and the company; and generally the Court may in any such proceeding decide any question that it may be necessary or expedient to decide for the rectification of the register. (See the Companies Act, 1862, s. 35.)

It is a matter of discretion whether the Court or judge will exercise the summary jurisdiction conferred by the above section, and it has been held that in a complicated or doubtful case that jurisdiction ought not to be exercised, but when the legal title in the applicant is clear, and there is no question of fact in dispute, the order ought to be made on an application under the section. (*Ex parte Shaw*, 2 Q. B. D. 463; 46 L. J. Ex. 65; *Ex parte Parker*, L. R. 2 Ch. Ap. 685; 15 W. R. 1217; *Simpson's Case*, L. R. 9 Eq. 91; 39 L. J. Ch. 41.)

The party may also proceed against the company by action or by mandamus. (See "*Mandamus*," *post*, 459.)

By s. 37 of the Act it is provided that the register of members shall be *primâ facie* evidence of any matters by the Act directed or authorised to be inserted therein (as to which see s. 25).

With respect to companies which are constituted by private Acts or Royal Charter, and are thereby subjected to an obligation to register the names of shareholders in the company, an action for damages will lie at the suit of a person aggrieved by the neglect of

under the Companies Acts, 1862 and 1867; *or*, under the Companies Acts, 1862 to 1880 (see "*Company*," *ante*, p. 145)].

2. Before and at the time of the transfer hereinafter mentioned, one A. B. was the registered holder and proprietor of —— shares in the said company, numbered ——, and by a deed of transfer dated the —— of ——,

---

this duty on the part of the company or their officers (*Daly* v. *Thompson*, 10 M. & W. 309; *Norris* v. *Irish Land Co.*, 8 E. & B. 512; 27 L. J. Q. B. 115; *Copeland* v. *North Eastern Ry. Co.*, 6 E. & B. 277; *Catchpole* v. *Ambergate Ry. Co.*, 1 E. & B. 111; 22 L. J. Q. B. 35); and in such cases a mandamus may also be obtained under ordinary circumstances. (*Norris* v. *Irish Land Co.*, and *Copeland* v. *North Eastern Ry. Co.*, *supra*; *Ward* v. *South-Eastern Ry. Co.*, 2 E. & E. 812; 29 L. J. Q. B. 177; and see "*Mandamus*," *post*, p. 459.)

Similarly a mandamus or injunction may be obtained to compel the company to remove a name improperly inserted in the register (*Eustace* v. *Dublin Trunk Ry. Co.*, L. R. 6 Eq. 182; 37 L. J. Ch. 716; *Taylor* v. *Hughes*, 2 Jo. & Lat. 24; *Shortridge* v. *Bosanquet*, 16 Beav. 84; and see Lindley on Partnership, 3rd ed. p. 147.)

An action will also lie against a company for wrongfully declaring the plaintiff's shares forfeited and selling them. (*Catchpole* v. *Ambergate Ry. Co.*, *supra*.)

With respect to actions by and against companies for wrongs generally, see *post*, "*Corporation*," p. 387.

Where a person has been, by the fraudulent misrepresentations of directors, or by their fraudulent concealment of facts which it was their duty to disclose, drawn into a contract to purchase shares in a company, such contract is voidable and may be rescinded by him upon, or within a reasonable time after the discovery by him of such fraud (*Oakes* v. *Turquand*, L. R. 2 H. L. 325; 36 L. J. Ch. 949); unless innocent third parties have, in reliance upon such voidable contract, acquired rights which would be defeated by its rescission. (*Tennent* v. *City of Glasgow Bank*, *per* Cairns, L. C., 4 App. Cas. 615, 620; 40 L. T. 694.)

Such person is too late to exercise his option to rescind if he delay until the company is being wound up, as thereby creditors of the company would be prejudiced. (*Stone* v. *City and County Bank*, 3 C. P. D. 282; 47 L. J. C. P. 681; *Tennent* v. *City of Glasgow Bank*, *supra*; *Houldsworth* v. *City of Glasgow Bank*, *infra*.)

A person induced by the fraud of the agents of a joint-stock company to become a shareholder in the company can bring no action for damages against the company whilst remaining a shareholder or partner in the company. The contract must be rescinded; and if that becomes impossible, by the winding up of the company, or by other means, he cannot maintain such action. (*Houldsworth* v. *City of Glasgow Bank and Liquidators*, 5 App. Cas. 317; 42 L. T. 194; *Tennent* v. *City of Glasgow Bank*, 4 App. Cas. 615; 40 L. T. 694; *Oakes* v. *Turquand*, L. R. 2 H. L. 325; 36 L. J. Ch. 949; *Stone* v. *City and County Bank*, 3 C. P. D. 282; 47 L. J. C. P. 681; *Addie* v. *The Western Bank*, L. R. 1 H. L. Sc. 145.)

18—, and executed by the said A. B. and by the plaintiff, the said shares were, in consideration of £—— then paid by the plaintiff to the said A. B., transferred by the said A. B. to the plaintiff in accordance with the regulations of the said company, and were duly accepted by the plaintiff, who thereupon became the owner and proprietor of the said shares.

3. All things were done and happened necessary to entitle the plaintiff to have the defendants enter in the said register the name of the plaintiff as such member and shareholder as aforesaid in respect of the said shares, according to the provisions of the said Act [*or* Acts] in that behalf, and he was and is entitled to have his name so entered accordingly; and while so entitled as aforesaid and in due time in that behalf, he duly requested the defendants to make such entry in the said register, and a reasonable time for making such entry elapsed after the said request and before the commencement of this action.

4. The defendants neglected and refused to enter and wholly made default in entering in the said register the name of the plaintiff as a member and shareholder of the said company in respect of the said shares.

5. By reason of the premises [*here state the damage sustained by the plaintiff, as for instance*], the plaintiff has been deprived of the evidence of his title to the said shares, and has been prevented from selling and transferring the same, and has lost the profits, amounting to £——, which he would otherwise have made from the sale and transfer thereof, and has been prevented from receiving the dividends due upon the said shares, viz., a dividend of £—— per share, which was declared on the —— of ——, 18—.

6. [*If a mandamus is also sought, add this and the following paragraph.*] The plaintiff further says, that under the circumstances hereinbefore mentioned it became and was the duty of the defendants to enter in the said register the name of the plaintiff as a member and shareholder of the said company in respect of the said shares in accordance with the provisions of the said Act [*or* Acts], and that the plaintiff was and is personally interested in having his name entered by the defendants in the said register as aforesaid, and sustains and will sustain damage from the non-performance of the said duty by the defendants, and that all things were done

and happened and all times elapsed necessary to entitle the plaintiff to claim and have such mandamus or order as hereinafter mentioned and to maintain this action.

7. The defendants wrongfully and contrary to the provisions of the said Act [*or* Acts] have hitherto neglected and refused, and still neglect and refuse, to perform the said duty, and the said shares are still standing in the said register in the name of the said A. B.

And the plaintiff claims—

1. £—— damages for the wrongs above complained of.
2. [A mandamus or order of this Court commanding the defendants to enter in the said register the name of the plaintiff as a member and shareholder of the said company in respect of the said shares.]
3. Such further or other relief as the nature of the case may require.

CONVERSION (*a*).

Statement of Claim for a Conversion.

1. The defendant on the —— of ——, 18—, converted to his own use and wrongfully deprived the plaintiff of

---

(*a*) *Conversion of Goods.*]—This form of action was called *trover* from the original form of the declaration, when it was applicable only to the case of goods lost and found, and converted by the finder to his own use. When this form of action was extended to all conversions of goods, whether ensuing upon a loss and finding or not, the averment of the loss and finding inserted in the count became fictitious. (1 Chit. Pl. 7th ed. 163.) Since this fictitious averment was abolished by the C. L. P. Act, 1852 (15 & 16 Vict., c. 76), s. 49, the cause of action may perhaps be more correctly designated as a *conversion* of goods, which is the term adopted in the schedule to that Act.

In the forms of indorsements of writs given in App. (A), part ii. sect. 4, to the Judicature Act, 1875, the form for conversion is "for wrongfully *depriving* the plaintiff of goods, household furniture, &c." The law is unaltered by the Judicature Acts, as to what constitutes a conversion, although there has been a change in the mode of stating the cause of action for the wrong. (*Per* Bramwell, L. J., in *Hiort* v. *London and North-Western Ry. Co.*, 4 Ex. D. 188, 194; 48 L. J. Ex. 545, 546.)

A conversion is a wrongful interference with goods, as by taking,

the use and possession of the plaintiff's [goods, household furniture, &c., *give, where practicable, a sufficient description to avoid the necessity of having to give particulars of the property converted.*]

---

using, or destroying them, inconsistent with the owner's right of possession. (*Fouldes* v. *Willoughby*, 8 M. & W. 540; *Thorogood* v. *Robinson*, 6 Q. B. 769; *Jones* v. *Brown*, 25 L. J. Ex. 345; *Simmons* v. *Lillystone*, 8 Ex. 431; *Hiort* v. *London and North-Western Ry. Co.*, *supra*; *Hollins* v. *Fowler*, L. R. 7 H. L. 757; 44 L. J. Q. B. 169; *Cooper* v. *Chitty*, 1 Burr. 20; 1 Sm. L. C. 8th ed. p. 477; *Alexander* v. *Southey*, 5 B. & Ald. 247; *Heald* v. *Carey*, 11 C. B. 977; 21 L. J. C. P. 97; *Burroughes* v. *Bayne*, 5 H. & N 296; 29 L. J. Ex. 185; *Pillott* v. *Wilkinson*, 2 H. & C. 72; 3 *ib.*, 345; 32 L. J. Ex. 201; 34 *ib.*, 22; *Hiort* v. *Bott*, L. R. 9 Ex. 86; 43 L. J. Ex. 81; *Mulliner* v. *Florence*, 3 Q. B. D. 484; 47 L. J. Q. B. 700.)

To constitute this injury there must be some act of the defendant repudiating the owner's right, or some exercise of dominion inconsistent with it. (*Ib.*; *Jones* v. *Hough*, 5 Ex. D. 115; 49 L. J. Ex. 211.)

Any person who, however innocently, obtains possession of goods the property of another who has been fraudulently deprived of the possession of them, and disposes of them, whether for his own benefit or that of any other person, is guilty of a conversion. (*Per* Lord Chelmsford in *Hollins* v. *Fowler*, L. R. 7 H. L. 788, 795; 44 L. J. Q. B. 169, 190; *Hiort* v. *Bott*, L. R. 9 Ex. 86; 43 L. J. Ex. 81; *Cochrane* v. *Rymill*, 40 L. T. 744; *Hardman* v. *Booth*, 1 H. & C. 803; 32 L. J. Ex. 105; *Stephens* v. *Elwall*, 4 M. & S. 259.)

A mere contract of sale of goods, not in market overt, without delivery or change of possession, or transfer of the documents of title by which possession may be obtained, as it does not affect the property in the goods, is not a conversion by the seller. (*Lancashire Waggon Co.* v. *Fitzhugh*, 6 H. & N. 502; 30 L. J. Ex. 231; and see *Johnson* v. *Stear*, 15 C. B. N. S. 330; 33 L. J. C. P. 130; *as to which on other points see infra.*)

Where the plaintiffs sent the defendant an invoice of barley, and a delivery order which made it deliverable to the order of the consignor or consignee, the defendant having in fact ordered no barley, and one G. fraudulently procured the defendant to indorse the delivery order to him, and so procured and disposed of the barley, it was held that the defendant by so indorsing exercised dominion over the barley without authority, and was guilty of a conversion thereof. (*Hiort* v. *Bott*, L. R. 9 Ex. 86; 43 L. J. Ex. 81; *per* Cotton, L. J., and Thesiger, L. J., in *Jones* v. *Hough*, *supra.*)

The purchase of goods which the seller had no right to sell, accompanied by taking possession, is a conversion by the purchaser against the true owner, although the purchaser did not know the sale was wrongful; so where a principal ratifies the unauthorised purchase on his behalf by his agent of a chattel which the vendor had no right to sell, he is guilty of a conversion. (*Hilbery* v. *Hatton*, 2 H. & C. 822; 33 L. J. Ex. 190.)

Where the plaintiff placed his goods on board the defendant's ship to be carried, the refusal of the defendant to give the plaintiff bills of lading in his own name, and the denial of his title as owner, and the taking of the goods to a person not intended by the owner to have them, was held to amount to a conversion. (*Falk* v. *Fletcher*, 18 C. B. N. S. 403; 34 L. J. C. P. 146; and see *Jones* v. *Hough*, *supra*; *Peek* v. *Larsen*, L. R. 12 Eq. 378; 40 L. J. Ch. 763.) But a mere refusal to sign bills of lading containing a certain clause to which the owner was entitled, and the sailing with the cargo on board without any bills of lading being signed, but without any denial of the owner's title or demand by the owner of re-delivery, was held to be a breach of contract, but no conversion. (*Jones* v. *Hough*, *supra*.)

Where the conversion cannot be proved by any positive act, it may be inferred from proof of a demand of the goods by the plaintiff, and a refusal to deliver them by the defendant, he having the control over them at the time. (*Philpott* v. *Kelley*, 3 A. & E. 106; *Verrall* v. *Robinson*, 2 C. M. & R. 495; *Catterall* v. *Kenyon*, 3 Q. B. 310; *M'Kewen* v. *Cotching*, 27 L. J. Ex. 41; *Walker* v. *Clyde*, 10 C. B. N. S. 381; *France* v. *Gaudet*, L. R. 6 Q. B. 199; 40 L. J. Q. B. 121.)

A demand and refusal is always *evidence* of a conversion. If the refusal is in disregard of the plaintiff's title, and for the purpose of claiming the goods either for the defendant or a third person, it is a conversion. (*Per* Blackburn, J., in *Hollins* v. *Fowler*, L. R. 7 H. L. 757, 766; 44 L. J. Q. B. 169, 174.)

If the refusal is by a person who does not know the plaintiff's title, and having a *bonâ fide* doubt as to the title to the goods detains them for a reasonable time, for clearing up that doubt, it is not a conversion. (*Ib.*; *Isaac* v. *Clarke*, 2 Buls. 306, 312; *Vaughan* v. *Watt*, 6 M. & W. 492; 9 L. J. Ex. 272.)

So a finder, or an involuntary bailee of goods is justified in taking steps for their protection and safe custody until he finds the owner, and it is no conversion to remove them *bonâ fide* to a place of security. See *per* Blackburn, J., *Hollins* v. *Fowler*, L. R. 7 H. L. 757, 766; 44 L. J. Q. B. 169, 174. (*See to the same effect*, *Kirk* v. *Gregory*, 1 Ex. D. 55; 45 L. J. Ex. 186, *a case of trespass.*)

A warehouseman with whom goods have been deposited is not guilty of conversion by merely keeping, or restoring them to the depositor, though that person turns out to have had no authority from the true owner (*per* Blackburn, J., *Hollins* v. *Fowler*, *supra*; *Heald* v. *Carey*, 11 C. B. 977; 21 L. J. C. P. 97; *Alexander* v. *Southey*, 5 B. & Ald. 247; *Glyn* v. *East & West India Dock Co.*, 6 Q. B. D. 475 491); but he becomes guilty of a conversion if, after demand by the true owner, he nevertheless persists in restoring them to such depositor, the assumption and exercise of dominion over a chattel inconsistent with the title of the true owner being a conversion. (See *per* Brett, J., in *Hollins* v. *Fowler*, *supra*; *Hiort* v. *Bott*, L. R. 9 Ex. 86; 43 L. J. Ex. 81.)

The same principle would seem applicable to carriers and the like (*ib.*; *Greenway* v. *Fisher*, 1 C. & P. 190, *as to which see per* Blackburn, J., in *Hollins* v. *Fowler*, L. R. 7 H. L. 768; 44 L. J. Q. B. 175).

If a man steals a chattel and takes it to a carrier to be carried to A., and there delivered to X., and the carrier takes, carries, and delivers the chattel accordingly, it is clear and settled law that he would not be guilty of a conversion, *per* Bramwell, L. J., *Glyn* v. *East and West India Dock Co.*, *supra.*

As to the effect of a qualified demand or refusal, see *Alexander* v.

Southey, 5 B. & Ald. 247; *Cranch* v. *White*, 1 Bing. N. C. 414; *Rushworth* v. *Taylor*, 3 Q. B. 699; *Davies* v. *Vernon*, 6 Q. B. 443; *Lee* v. *Bayes*, 18 C. B. 599; *Clark* v. *Chamberlain*, 2 M. & W. 78; *Burroughes* v. *Bayne*, 5 H. & N. 296; 29 L. J. Ex. 185.

If some time is necessarily taken by the defendant to obtain actual possession of the goods, and deliver them up, and he does not make any unnecessary delay in doing so, he is not on that account guilty of a conversion. (*Towne* v. *Lewis*, 7 C. B. 608.)

An act of conversion differs from a mere trespass, inasmuch as the former must amount to a deprivation of the possession to such an extent as to be inconsistent with the right of the owner, and evidence an intention to deprive him of that right; whereas the latter includes every direct forcible injury or act disturbing the possession without the consent of the owner, however slight or temporary the act may be. (*Fouldes* v. *Willoughby*, 8 M. & W. 540; and see *per* Parke, J., *Smith* v. *Goodwin*, 4 B. & Ad. 420; and see *Burroughes* v. *Bayne*, *suprà*.)

Where a person is left in possession of his goods he cannot sue for a conversion thereof, unless his dominion over the property has been interfered with in such a way that he has been actually deprived of the use of his goods. A limited interference with the plaintiff's goods where all along the plaintiff is himself in possession, does not constitute conversion. (*England* v. *Cowley*, L. R. 8 Ex. 126; 42 L. J. Ex. 80.)

If a pawnbroker, with whom goods are wrongfully, and without the assent of the owner pledged, refuses on demand by the owner to restore them to him, this is a conversion by such pawnbroker, the indemnity, given by sect. 25 of the Pawnbrokers' Act, 1872 (35 & 36 Vict. c. 93), to the pawnbroker who delivers a pledge to the person producing the pawn ticket, applying only as between the pawnbroker and the pawnor or owner who has authorised the pledge. (*Singer Co.* v. *Clark*, 5 Ex. D. 37; 49 L. J. Ex. 224.)

If a bailee of chattels deals with the chattels in a manner inconsistent with the purpose for which they are held, he may be guilty of a conversion, as where a carrier delivers goods to the wrong person (*Devereux* v. *Barclay*, 2 B. & Ald. 702; *Stephenson* v. *Hart*, 4 Bing. 476, 483; *Wyld* v. *Pickford*, 8 M. & W. 443; *Hiort* v. *London and North Western Ry. Co.*, 4 Ex. D. 188, 194; 48 L. J. Ex. 545, 546); or where an innkeeper having a lien upon, but no power to sell, goods of his guest, sells them. (*Mulliner* v. *Florence*, 3 Q. B. D. 484; 47 L. J. Q. B. 700.) Now, by 41 & 42 Vict. c. 38 (Innkeepers Act, 1878), innkeepers may, under certain conditions, realise their lien by a sale by auction (see "Defences," "*Innkeeper*").

A mere omission or negligence of a bailee, or person entrusted with the possession for a special purpose, in the course of his employment, is not a conversion; thus, the loss of goods by a carrier is not a conversion (2 Wms. Saund. 1871 ed. 103; *Ross* v. *Johnson*, 5 Burr. 2825; *Williams* v. *Gesse*, 3 Bing. N. C. 849; *Kirkman* v. *Hargreaves*, 1 Selw. N. P., 13th ed., 364); nor is delivery of the goods in the ordinary course of business at the place directed, although they are delivered to some one not intended by the sender. (*M'Kean* v. *M'Ivor*, L. R. 6 Ex. 36; 40 L. J. Ex. 30.)

An active wrongful disposal by a bailee of property bailed in a manner inconsistent with the bailment is a conversion, and puts an end to the bailment. (*Mulliner* v. *Florence*, 3 Q. B. D. 484; 47 L. J. Q. B. 700.)

There is a distinction between a pledge, and a bailment giving a lien without power of sale. In the latter case an unauthorised sale or pledging of the property bailed terminates the bailment, and is a conversion, whilst in the former case a sub-pledge is not so inconsistent with the original contract or pledge as to terminate the pledge or amount to a conversion. (*Mulliner* v. *Florence*, 3 Q. B. D. 484, 492; 47 L. J. Q. B. 700, 703; *Halliday* v. *Holgate*, L. R. 3 Ex. 299; 37 L. J. Ex. 174; *Donald* v. *Suckling*, L. R. 1 Q. B. 585; 35 L. J. Q. B. 232; and see further, *Johnson* v. *Stear*, 15 C. B. N. S. 330; 33 L. J. C. P. 130; and observations upon that case in the cases cited, *suprà*.)

A right of lien, properly so called, is a mere personal right of detention, and an unauthorised transfer of the thing does not transfer that personal right. (*Per* Blackburn, J., in *Donald* v. *Suckling*, *suprà*; and see also, *Mulliner* v. *Florence*, *suprà*.)

In order to maintain an action for conversion the plaintiff must have the right to the immediate possession of the goods, and not merely a property in reversion, or future property. (*Bradley* v. *Copley*, 1 C. B. 685.) As to suing for injuries to reversionary interests in goods, see *post*, "*Reversion*."

The owner of goods let to another for a term still continuing cannot maintain this action (*Gordon* v. *Harper*, 7 T. R. 9); nor can the owner of goods in the possession of another who is entitled to a lien on them (*Milgate* v. *Kebble*, 3 M. & G. 100); but any special or temporary ownership with immediate possession, as under a lien or bailment, is sufficient to maintain the action (*Legg* v. *Evans*, 6 M. & W. 36; *Roberts* v. *Wyatt*, 2 Taunt. 268; *Brierly* v. *Kendall*, 17 Q. B. 937). Where goods are bailed to another for hire, the bailee is the proper person to sue for a conversion by a third party; but where the bailee terminates the bailment by any act inconsistent with it, as where the bailee of goods for hire, or a bailee having a mere personal lien without power of sale, sells them to a third party, the bailor may at once sue the purchaser or the bailee for a conversion. (*Cooper* v. *Willomatt*, 1 C. B. 672; *Fenn* v. *Bittleston*, 7 Ex. 152; *Bryant* v *Wardell*, 2 Ex. 479; *Mulliner* v. *Florence*, *suprà*.)

Upon any bailment of goods which does not exclude the absolute owner's right to the immediate possession, either the bailor or the bailee may maintain an action for conversion by a third party. (*Nicolls* v. *Bastard*, 2 C. M. & R. 659; *Rooth* v. *Wilson*, 1 B. & Ald. 59.)

The purchaser of goods which remain in the vendor's possession subject to the vendor's lien for the price, cannot maintain this action against a wrong-doer. (*Lord* v. *Price*, L. R. 9 Ex. 54.)

A joint owner of goods cannot maintain this action against his co-owner in respect of any act of the latter consistent with his ownership; but if the latter is guilty of an act inconsistent with joint ownership, as a complete destruction of the goods or a sale of them in market overt, it amounts to a conversion for which the joint owner can sue. (2 Wms. Saund. 116; *Higgins* v. *Thomas*, 8 Q. B. 908; *Jones* v. *Brown*, 25 L. J. Ex. 345; *Mayhew* v. *Herrick*, 7 C. B. 229.)

Where goods were pledged by four joint owners, a refusal to re-deliver upon a tender of the amount due, made by three of such joint owners acting on their own behalf, was held not to be a conversion. (*Harper* v. *Godsell*, L. R. 5 Q. B. 422; 39 L. J. Q. B. 185.)

As possession in fact is evidence of the right of possession, it is sufficient to maintain the action against the wrongdoer who cannot show a better title in himself, or authority under a better title. (*Elliott* v. *Kemp*, 7 M. & W. 312; *Northam* v. *Bowden*, 11 Ex. 70; *Armory* v. *Delamirie*, 1 Smith's L. C. 8th ed. 374; *Bourne* v. *Fosbrooke*, 18 C. B. N. S. 515; 34 L. J. C. P. 164.) But if a plaintiff was not in possession at the time of the conversion, and has to rely upon his right only, he must then be able to prove a good title in order to maintain the action, the defendant being in such case at liberty to rebut the plaintiff's title by showing a *jus tertii* (*Gadsden* v. *Barrow*, 9 Ex. 514; *Leake* v. *Loveday*, 4 M. & G. 972). A defendant cannot set up a *jus tertii* where he has disturbed the actual possession of the plaintiff, unless he can justify under the authority of the third party. (*Jeffries* v. *Great Western Ry. Co.*, 5 E. & B. 802; 25 L. J. Q. B. 107; *White* v. *Mullett*, 6 Ex. 713; and see *Thorne* v. *Tilbury*, 3 H. & N. 534; 27 L. J. Ex. 407; *Biddle* v. *Bond*, 6 B. & S. 225; 34 L. J. Q. B. 137.) Where the plaintiff had obtained possession of some tallow, part of the salvage from a fire, and his possessory right had been lawfully divested, he was held not entitled to maintain trover against a person who subsequently purchased it. (*Buckley* v. *Gross*, 3 B. & S. 566; 32 L. J. Q. B. 129.) An uncertificated bankrupt having been again adjudicated bankrupt, it was held that the second assignees might maintain trover for goods acquired by the bankrupt after his first bankruptcy against all persons except the first assignees. (*Morgan* v. *Knight*, 15 C. B. N. S. 669; 33 L. J. C. P. 168.)

Where a vendee has obtained goods by fraud or false pretences from a vendor who has delivered possession to him with the intention of passing the property to him, the property vests in the vendee, notwithstanding the vendor was induced to part with the goods by such fraud or false pretences, until the vendor has done some act to disaffirm the transaction. (*Kingsford* v. *Merry*, 11 Ex. 577, 579; 25 L. J. Ex. 166, 168; *The Marie Joseph*, L. R. 1 P. C. 219, 229.) If the vendor does not treat the sale as void before the vendee has resold the goods to an innocent purchaser, the property passes to such purchaser, and he cannot be sued in conversion, or otherwise made liable to the original vendor. (*White* v. *Garden*, 10 C. B. 919; 20 L. J. C. P. 166; *Kingsford* v. *Merry*, *suprà*; *Higgins* v. *Burton*, 26 L. J. Ex. 342; and see further *per* Lord Cairns in *Cundy* v. *Lindsay*, 3 App. Cas. 463, 461; 47 L. J. H. L. 481; *Clough* v. *L. & N. W. Ry. Co.*, L. R. 7 Ex. 26; 41 L. J. Ex. 17; *Moyce* v. *Newington*, 4 Q. B. D. 32; 48 L. J. Q. B. 125; *Stevenson* v. *Newnham*, 13 C. B. 285; Benjamin on Sales, 2nd ed. p. 342.)

Where certain goods were pledged with the plaintiffs as security for an advance, and the pledgors by fraudulently representing that they had sold them to the defendants and would hand over to the plaintiffs the money received in payment, obtained possession of the goods, and then pledged them to the defendants for an advance giving them a power of sale, it was held that, as the plaintiffs had parted with their special property to the pledgors, they could not recover against the defendants, who had obtained the goods *bonâ fide* and for good consideration. (*Babcock* v. *Lawson*, 4 Q. B. D. 394; 5 Q. B. D. 284; 48 L. J. Q. B. 524; 49 *ib.* 408.)

By 24 & 25 Vict. c. 96, s. 100: if any person guilty of any felony or misdemeanour mentioned in that Act, in stealing, taking, obtaining, extorting, embezzling, converting, or disposing of, or in knowingly receiving any chattel, money, valuable security, or other property whatsoever, shall be indicted for such offence, by or on the behalf of the owner of the property, or his executor or administrator, and convicted thereof, in such case the property shall be restored to the owner or his representative, and power to order such restitution is vested in the Court which tries the offender, provided that if it shall appear before any order made that any valuable security shall have been *bonâ fide* paid or discharged by some person or body corporate liable to the payment thereof, or being a negotiable instrument shall have been *bonâ fide* taken or received by transfer or delivery, by some person or body corporate, for a just and valuable consideration, without any notice or without any reasonable cause to suspect that the same had by any felony or misdemeanour been stolen, taken, obtained, extorted, embezzled, converted, or disposed of, in such case the Court shall not award or order the restitution of such security. It is also further provided that nothing in section 100 should apply to the case of any prosecution of any trustee, banker, merchant, attorney, factor, broker, or other agent intrusted with the possession of goods or documents of title to goods for any misdemeanour against that act.

The effect of such a conviction of the offender would appear to be, that as against any person other than innocent third parties who by purchase or otherwise acquire for good consideration an interest in the goods before the date of the conviction, the property in the goods is on the conviction revested in the original owners as from the time of such conviction. (*Lindsay* v. *Cundy*, 1 Q. B. D. 348, 357; 45 L. J. Q. B. 381; *afterwards reversed on other points*, see *infra*; *Moyce* v. *Newington*, 4 Q. B. D. 32, 36; 48 L. J. Q. B. 125; *Horwood* v. *Smith*, 2 T. R. 750.)

Accordingly where a person purchased and obtained delivery of sheep from the defendant by false pretences, and afterwards sold the sheep to the plaintiff, who had no knowledge of the fraud, it was held that the defendant by retaking the sheep after the conviction of such person out of the plaintiff's possession was guilty of a conversion, the sale from such person to the plaintiff having been prior to the conviction. (*Moyce* v. *Newington*, 4 Q. B. D. 32; 48 L. J. Q. B. 125.)

But where a vendor has sold goods to A., or has been led to believe that he has sold them to A., and the person who induced him so to sell, or led him into that belief receives and carries off the goods and disposes of them to another, there is no contract between the vendor and such person, and consequently he cannot, unless by a sale in market overt, confer a good title on any one else, the property never having vested in him. (*Hardman* v. *Booth*, 1 H. & C. 803; 32 L. J. Ex. 105; *Lindsay* v. *Cundy*, 2 Q. B. D. 96, 100; 3 App. Cas. 459; 45 L. J. Q. B. 381; 46 *ib.* 233; 47 *ib.* 481; *Hollins* v. *Fowler*, L. R. 7 H. L. 757; 44 L. J. Q. B. 169; *Higgins* v. *Burton*, 26 L. J. Ex. 342.)

The action for conversion lies only in respect of specific personal property; it will not lie for money, though certain in amount, unless it be identified in specie. (*Orton* v. *Butler*, 5 B. & Ald. 652; *Hall* v. *Wood*, Dyer, 22, Cro. Eliz. 841; *Harris' case*, Noy, 128; and see *Foster* v. *Green*, 31 L. J. Ex. 158.) It does not lie for fixtures, *eo nomine*, as they form part of the land, and therefore cannot be converted. (*Davis* v. *Jones*, 2 B. & Ald. 165; *Minshall* v. *Lloyd*, 2 M.

& W. 450; *Weeton* v. *Woodcock,* 5 M. & W. 587; *Mackintosh* v. *Trotter,* 3 M. & W. 184; *Wilde* v. *Waters,* 16 C. B. 637; 24 L. J. C. P. 193.) Though an action lies for wrongfully preventing the plaintiff from exercising his right to remove them. (*Lond. & Westminster Loan Co.* v. *Drake,* 6 C. B. N. S. 798; 28 L. J. C. P. 297.) If they have been reduced to the state of moveable goods by severance they become capable of being converted, though they should not then, strictly speaking, be described as fixtures. (See *Sheen* v. *Rickie,* 5 M. & W. 175; 7 Dowl. 335; and see *Niblet* v. *Smith,* 4 T. R. 504; *Dalton* v. *Whittem,* 3 Q. B. 961; *Wiltshear* v. *Cottrell,* 1 E. & B. 674.) So conversion lies for soil taken up from the land and *removed* (*Higgon* v. *Mortimer,* 6 C. & P. 616); and for coals or minerals wrongfully dug from the plaintiff's land (*Martin* v. *Porter,* 5 M. & W. 351; *Morgan* v. *Powell,* 3 Q. B. 278; *Powell* v. *Rees,* 7 A. & E. 426.) So too, it lies for a bank note, a cheque, or the like. (*Burn* v. *Morris,* 2 Cr. & M. 579; *Matthiessen* v. *London & County Bank,* 5 C. P. D. 7; 48 L. J. C. P. 529.) The goods should be described in the statement of claim with sufficient certainty to inform the defendant as to the goods taken, and particulars will be ordered as to the specific goods taken where the description is only general.

Though the measure of damages for a conversion is *primâ facie* the value of the goods converted, it is not necessarily so, the damages being compensation for the loss actually sustained by the wrongful act. (*Johnson* v. *Lanc. & York. Ry. Co.,* 3 C. P. D. 499; *Hiort* v. *L. & N. W. Ry. Co.,* 4 Ex. D. 188; 48 L. J. Ex. 545; *Brierly* v. *Kendall,* 17 Q. B. 937; *Chinery* v. *Viall,* 5 H. & N. 288; 29 L. J. Ex. 180; *Mulliner* v. *Florence,* 3 Q. B. D. 484; 47 L. J. Q. B. 700.) The value, where that is the proper measure of damages is, in general, the value to the owner, or price for which he could purchase similar goods to those converted. (*Livingstone* v. *Rawyards Coal Co.,* 5 App. Cas. 25, 32, 40; *France* v. *Gaudet,* L. R. 6 Q. B. 199; 40 L. J. Q. B. 121.) If the goods converted have been returned to the plaintiff he recovers the damages sustained by the wrongful act, and not their full value. (*Hiort* v. *L. & N. W. Ry. Co., supra.*)

The plaintiff claiming goods is assumed, if he recover the full value, to be in a position to convey or transfer to the defendant the dominion over and property in the goods, so far as regards any act of his own (*per* Thesiger, L. J. in *Hiort* v. *L. & N. W. Ry. Co., supra.*)

The true doctrine is, that whenever the plaintiff could have resumed the property, if he could lay hands on it, and could have rightfully held it when recovered as the full and absolute owner, he is entitled to the value as damages in conversion (*per* Williams, J., in *Johnson* v. *Stear,* 15 C. B. N. S. 330; 33 L. J. C. P. 130, approved in *Johnson* v. *Lanc. & York. Ry. Co., supra,* and in *Mulliner* v. *Florence, supra.*)

Thus, where a vendee sued a vendor for a conversion of the goods sold, the goods not having been delivered and the price not having been paid, and not being recoverable by reason of the conversion, the measure of damages was held to be the difference between the value of the goods and the contract price. (*Chinery* v. *Viall, supra; Martindale* v. *Smith,* 1 Q. B. 389; *Page* v. *Eduljee,* L. R. 1 P. C. 127.) A person having a special property in the goods, with immediate possession, can only recover against the absolute owner for a conversion by him damages in respect of such limited interest (*Roberts* v. *Wyatt,* 2 Taunt. 268; *Brierly* v. *Kendall,* 17 Q. B. 937); but in an

Against an Auctioneer for Selling the Plaintiff's Goods Wrongfully and without the Plaintiff's Authority (*b*).

1. The plaintiff was the owner of a piano-forte, which, by an agreement in writing between himself and one

---

action against a stranger who is guilty of a conversion he is entitled to recover the full value of the goods. (*Turner* v. *Hardcastle*, 11 C. B. N. S. 683; 31 L. J. C. P. 193.) Where the defendant, having obtained a judgment against the plaintiff, wrongfully refused to give up certain goods of the plaintiff then in his possession, and afterwards sold them under his judgment, the plaintiff was held entitled to recover the full value of the goods (*Edmondson* v. *Nuttall*, 17 C. B. N. S. 280; 34 L. J. C. P. 102); so where the defendant having obtained a judgment against the plaintiff, seized his goods under process, but in a place where the process did not run, the plaintiff was held entitled to recover the full value of the goods. (*Sowell* v. *Champion*, 6 A. & E. 407.)

Special damage sustained may be recovered, if stated and claimed. (*Moon* v. *Raphael*, 2 Bing. N. C. 310; *Bodley* v. *Reynolds*, 8 Q. B. 779; *France* v. *Gaudet*, L. R. 6 Q. B. 199; 40 L. J. Q. B. 121.)

Thus, where the plaintiff purchased champagne lying at the defendant's wharf which he resold at a profit, but which the defendants wrongfully refused to deliver, it was held, there being no market in which the plaintiff could purchase similar champagne, that the plaintiff was entitled to recover as damages the price at which he had so resold the wine, although the defendant had no knowledge of such resale. (*France* v. *Gaudet*, *suprà*.) By 3 & 4 Wm. IV. c. 42, s. 29, in all actions for conversion the jury may, if they shall think fit, give damages in the nature of interest over and above the value of the goods.

The recovery of judgment in conversion or detinue, if unsatisfied, does not change the property in the goods the subject matter of the action. (*Brinsmead* v. *Harrison*, L. R. 6 C. P. 584; L. R. 7 C. P. 547; 40 L. J. C. P. 281; 41 *ib.* 190; *Ex parte Drake*, 5 Ch. D. 866.) But where in an action for conversion the full value of the goods converted has been assessed and recovered as damages, the satisfaction of the judgment has the effect of vesting the property in the defendant. (*Brinsmead* v. *Harrison*, *suprà*; *Ex parte Drake*, *suprà*; *Morris* v. *Robinson*, 3 B. & C. 196, 206; *Marston* v. *Phillips*, 9 L. T. 289; *Hiort* v. *London and North Western Ry. Co.*, 4 Ex. D. 188, 199; 48 L. J. Ex. 545.)

In this action the Court will sometimes exercise a summary jurisdiction to stay proceedings upon a return of the goods and payment of nominal damages and costs, and on such other terms as the Court thinks proper to impose; but the general practice as to such applications would appear to be, that if the plaintiff will not consent to accept a return of the goods on the terms considered by the Court proper, he will be allowed to proceed with his action, but if he fail to get substantial damages, and so justify his refusal, he may be made to pay the costs of the action subsequent to the application. (See 2 Chit. Pr., 13th ed., p. 1103; O. LV.; *Moon* v. *Raphael*, 2 Bing. N. C. 310, 314; *Hiort* v. *London and North Western Ry. Co.*, 4 Ex. D. 188, 195; 48 L. J. Ex. 545.)

(*b*) An auctioneer, or other person, selling goods under the instruc-

A. B., bearing date the —— of ——, 18—, he let on hire for a term of three months from the said —— of ——, 18—, to the said A. B.

2. In pursuance of the said agreement, possession of the said piano-forte was given on the —— of ——, 18—, to the said A. B. by the plaintiff.

3. The said A. B., in violation of the said agreement, delivered the said piano-forte to the defendant, and instructed him to sell the same by auction on his behalf.

4. The defendant thereupon, on the —— of ——, 18—, sold the said piano-forte by auction and received the price thereof, and delivered the said piano-forte to the purchaser thereof at the said auction, whereby the plaintiff has been, and is deprived of his said piano-forte.

Against Wharfingers for a Conversion, by Refusing upon the Demand of the True Owner to Deliver to him his Goods.

1. The plaintiffs are merchants, carrying on business at ——, in Spain. The defendants are wharfingers, carrying on business in London.

2. The plaintiffs were and are the owners of 63 bales of wool marked C. H., which were shipped by them in June, 18—, from Lisbon to London, by the steamer "Achille."

3. On the arrival of the said steamer in London a person by falsely pretending that he was X. Y., to whom the said wool was consigned, wrongfully obtained possession of the said wool.

4. Afterwards the said wool was lodged with the defendants as wharfingers by such person, or by some person claiming the said wool through such person.

5. Thereupon, in December, 18—, the plaintiffs demanded of the defendants the return of the said wool, and informed the defendants that they, the plaintiffs, were the owners thereof.

6. The defendants denied the plaintiff's title to the

---

tions, or orders of, or in pursuance of a contract made by himself with a person having no right to dispose of such goods, and delivering possession to the purchaser, is guilty of a conversion. (*Cochrane* v *Rymill*, 40 L. T. 744 ; *Hollins* v. *Fowler*, L. R. 7 H. L. 757 ; 44 L. J. Q. B. 169 ; *Davis* v. *Artingstall*, 49 L. J. Ch. 609 ; 42 L. T. 507 ; *Ganly* v. *Ledwidge*, 10 Ir. C. L. 33.)

said wool, and refused to return, and have not returned the said wool to the plaintiffs [and have since sold and delivered the same to persons other than the plaintiffs, and received the price thereof, *or as the case may be*].

For a Form against a Carrier for a Conversion by a mis-delivery, see "Carriers," ante, p. 362.

Against Bankers, for Conversion of a Cheque, and to Recover the Proceeds, Matthiessen v. *London and County Bank*, 5 C. P. D. 7; 48 L. J. C. P. 529.

Against an Innkeeper, for Conversion of Goods of his Guest, Mulliner v. *Florence*, 38 L. T. 167 (*c*).

For Refusing after Demand by the Owner to Deliver to him his Goods, which the Defendants held to his Order, Johnson v. *Lanc. and York. Ry. Co.*, 3 C. P. D. 499.

By the Holders of a Bill of Sale, for Conversion by the Defendant of Property comprised in the Bill of Sale, National Merc. Bank v. *Hampson*, 5 Q. B. D. 177 (*d*).

Against Carriers, for Mis-delivery of Goods, Pontifex v. *Mid. Ry. Co.*, 3 Q. B. D. 23; 47 L. J. Q. B. 28; 37 L. T. 403.

(*c*) By The Innkeepers Act, 1878 (41 & 42 Vict. c. 38) an innkeeper may now in some cases realise his lien by sale. See "Defences," "*Innkeeper*."

(*d*) A bill of sale of stock in trade, when the trade is to be carried on, is subject to an implied condition that the grantor shall have liberty to deal with the goods in the ordinary way of his trade, and any *bonâ fide* purchaser buying from him in such way obtains a good title. (*National Merc. Bank* v. *Hampson*, 5 Q. B. D. 177; 49 L. J. Q. B. 480; *Walker* v. *Clay*, 49 L. J. C. P. 560; 42 L. T. 369.) But if the disposition of the goods is not *bonâ fide*, and in the ordinary course of business, the grantee under the bill of sale may demand such goods from such purchaser, and upon his refusal to give them up maintain an action against him for their conversion. (*Taylor* v. *M'Keand*, 5 C. P. D. 358; 49 L. J. C. P. 563; *Payne* v. *Fern*, 6 Q. B. D. 620.)

Against a Solicitor, to Recover Cheques received by him on behalf of the Plaintiffs, The General Share Trust Co. v. *Chapman*, 1 C. P. D. 771.

For Conversion by Refusing to Deliver to the Owner, after Demand, his Goods, or the Dock Warrants therefor, then held by the Defendants, Johnson v. *Crédit Lyonnais*, 2 C. P. D. 224 (*e*).

For Conversion of Goods, shipped under a Bill of Lading, by the Wrongful Sale and Delivery thereof at an Intermediate Port, Acatos v. *Burns*, 3 Ex. D. 282.

Copyright (*a*).

Statement of Claim for Infringing the Copyright in a Book by Printing Copies, and for an Injunction.

1. The plaintiff was and is the proprietor of a subsisting copyright in a book entitled ——, which was first

---

(*e*) In consequence of the decision in the above case (which see on appeal, 3 C. P. D. 32, 36 ; 47 L. J. C. P. 241, 245) further protection was given by statute 40 & 41 Vict. c. 39, to innocent parties purchasing from, or making advances to factors or agents. See "Defences," "*Agents.*"

(*a*) Copyright in works of literature after publication exists only by statute. (See *Jefferys* v. *Boosey*, 4 H. L. C. 876 ; 24 L. J. Ex. 81 ; *Reade* v. *Conquest*, 9 C. B. N. S. 755 ; 30 L. J. C. P. 209.)

Copyright is regulated by the following statutes :—

By 5 & 6 Vict. c. 45, as to books, which includes "every volume, part or division of a volume, pamphlet, sheet of letter-press, sheet of music, map, chart, or plan separately published" (s. 2). Secs. 3 & 4 of the Act define the endurance of the term of the copyright, and an action for infringement is given by s. 15. Sec. 23 provides that all copies of the book unlawfully printed or imported shall be deemed the property of the proprietor of the copyright, and he may, after demand in writing, sue for and recover the same, or damages for the detention, or damages for the conversion thereof. Sec. 24 makes registration of the copyright, in general, a condition precedent to an action on the part of the proprietor, see *Wood* v. *Boosey*, L. R. 2 Q. B. 340 ; 36 L. J. Q. B. 103 ; and *per* Malins, V.-C., in *Weldon* v. *Dicks*, 10 Ch. D. 252, 259 ; 48 L. J. Ch. 201, 202 ; and *Stannard* v. *Lee*, L. R. 6 Ch. Ap. 346 ; 40 L. J. Ch. 489 ; but it is doubtful whether the word "proprietor" in the above section applies to the assignee

published after the passing of the Act of Parliament passed in the 6th year of the reign of Queen Victoria to amend the law of copyright.

2. Before the commencement of this action [*or* on

---

of the copyright. (See *Wood* v. *Boosey*, *supra.*) No copyright is acquired by mere registration before publication. (*Maxwell* v. *Hogg*, L. R. 2 Ch. Ap. 307; 36 L. J. Ch. 433; *Henderson* v. *Maxwell*, 5 Ch. D. 892; 46 L. J. Ch. 891.)

By ss. 18 & 19 of the above statute registration of the first number of a periodical is sufficient to give copyright in any subsequent number. (*Henderson* v. *Maxwell*, 4 Ch. D. 163; 46 L. J. Ch. 59.) The assignment of a copyright must be in writing (*Leyland* v. *Stewart*, 4 Ch. D. 419; 46 L. J. Ch. 103), and should be so described in the pleadings. (See *Turquand* v. *Fearon*, 49 L. J. Q. B. 703; and see *ante*, p. 50.)

By s. 26, all actions for any offence against this Act must be brought within twelve months after the committing of the offence. See further *Hogg* v. *Scott*, L. R. 18 Eq. 444; 43 L. J. Ch. 705.

There is no copyright in immoral or illegal publications. (See *Southey* v. *Sherwood*, 2 Mer. 435, 439; *Stockdale* v. *Onwhyn*, 5 B. & C. 173.) As to infringing the copyright in a dictionary, see *Spiers* v. *Brown*, 6 W. R. 352; in a directory, *Kelly* v. *Morris*, L. R. 1 Eq. 697; 35 L. J. Ch. 423; *Morris* v. *Ashbee*, L. R. 7 Eq. 34; *Morris* v. *Wright*, L. R. 5 Ch. Ap. 279; *Kelly* v. *Byles*, 13 Ch. D. 682; 49 L. J. Ch. 181; in statistical returns, *Scott* v. *Stanford*, L. R. 3 Eq. 718; 36 L. J. Ch. 729; in a descriptive catalogue and books of designs, *Hotten* v. *Arthur*, 1 H. & M. 603; 32 L. J. Ch. 771; *Grace* v. *Newman*, L. R. 19 Eq. 623; 44 L. J. Ch. 298; *Cobbett* v. *Woodward*, L. R. 14 Eq. 407; 41 L. J. Ch. 656; in articles published in periodicals, *Smith* v. *Johnson*, 4 Giff. 632; 33 L. J. Ch. 137. As to copyright in newspapers, see *Kelly* v. *Hutton*, L. R. 3 Ch. Ap. 703; 37 L. J. Ch. 917; *Platt* v. *Walter*, 17 L. T. 157; and *Walter* v. *Howe*, 50 L. J. Ch. 621.

In order to constitute an infringement of a copyright there must be an appropriation of a substantial part of a protected publication. (*Bradbury* v. *Hotten*, L. R. 8 Ex. 1; 42 L. J. Ex. 28.)

Copyright is regulated as to oral lectures, by 5 & 6 Will. IV. c. 65, and to dramatic pieces and musical performances, by 3 & 4 Will. IV. c. 15, and the above statute, 5 & 6 Vict. c. 45, ss. 20, 21.

By s. 3 of 3 & 4 Will. IV. c. 15, actions must be commenced for any offence under the Act within twelve calendar months after such offence shall have been committed.

Dramatizing and representing a novel on the stage is not an infringement of the literary copyright in the novel. (*Reade* v. *Conquest*, 9 C. B. N. S. 755; 30 L. J. C. P. 209; *Toole* v. *Young*, L. R. 9 Q. B. 523; 43 L. J. Q. B. 170.) But printing and selling a drama in which the scenes and language of a novel are copied, is an infringement of the copyright in the latter. (*Tinsley* v. *Lacey*, 1 H. & M. 747; 32 L. J. Ch. 535.) And where the plaintiff wrote a drama and then turned it into a novel, and the defendant dramatized and represented the novel, without knowing of the plaintiff's drama, it was held an infringement of the dramatic copyright of the plaintiff. (*Reade* v. *Lacey*, 1 J. & H. 524; 30 L. J. Ch. 655; *Reade* v.

the —— of ——, 18—, *shewing the date to be before the issue of the writ in the action*] the plaintiff caused an entry to be made in the book of registry of the Stationers' Company, of such book, pursuant to the abovementioned Act.

Conquest, 11 C. B. N. S. 479; 31 L. J. C. P. 153; *Boosey* v. *Fairlie*, 7 Ch. D. 301; 4 App. Cas. 711; 46 L. J. Ch. 726; 47 L. J. Ch. 186.) The assignment of the copyright in a dramatic or musical piece does not convey the right of performing it, unless an entry to that effect is registered (5 & 6 Vict. c. 45, s. 22); before that enactment it was held otherwise. (*Cumberland* v. *Planché*, 1 A. & E. 580.)

The arrangement of the score of an opera for the pianoforte is an original composition for the purposes of the Act, so that the arranger, and not the composer of the opera, must be registered as the author. (*Wood* v. *Boosey*, L. R. 2 Q. B. 340; L. R. 3 Q. B. 223; 36 L. J. Q. B. 103; 37 L. J. Q. B. 84; as to which case see further *Fairlie* v. *Boosey*, 4 App. Cas. 711, 728; 47 L. J. Ch. 186.) In order to constitute an infringement under s. 2 of 3 & 4 Will. IV. c. 15, by a representation of any part of any production of which another has the sole right of performance, the part represented must be a material and substantial part. (*Chatterton* v. *Cave*, 3 App. Cas. 483; 47 L. J. H. L. 545.)

Copyright is regulated as to engravings, prints, and lithographs, by 8 Geo. II. c. 13; 7 Geo. III. c. 38; 17 Geo. III. c. 57; and 15 & 16 Vict. c. 12, s. 14. Copies made by photography are within these statutes. (*Gambart* v. *Ball*, 14 C. B. N. S. 306; 32 L. J. C. P. 166; *Graves* v. *Ashford*, L. R. 2 C. P. 410; 36 L. J. C. P. 139.)

Copyright is regulated as to sculptures, models, copies and casts, and designs for ornamenting articles of manufacture, by 54 Geo. III. c. 56; 5 & 6 Vict. c. 100; 6 & 7 Vict. c. 65; 13 & 14 Vict. c. 104; 21 & 22 Vict. c. 70; 24 & 25 Vict. c. 73; and see also 33 & 34 Vict. c. 27, s. 3, and 38 & 39 Vict. c. 93.

The portrait of a well-known public character, copied from a photograph and applied as a design upon earthenware, is not a new and original design within the meaning of the Copyright of Designs Act, 5 & 6 Vict. c. 100. (*Adams* v. *Clementson*, 12 Ch. D. 714.) As to the copyright in designs on rugs and carpets, see *Woodward* v. *London and North Western Ry. Co.*, 3 Ex. D., *per* Hawkins, J., at p. 125; 47 L. J. Ex. 265.

Copyright in works of the fine arts is protected by 25 & 26 Vict. c. 68. A photograph taken from a picture is an original photograph within the meaning of the Act. (*Graves's Case*, L. R. 4 Q. B. 715; 39 L. J. Q. B. 31.)

International copyright is regulated by 7 & 8 Vict. c. 12; 15 & 16 Vict. c. 12; and 38 & 39 Vict. c. 12.

As to copyright in the colonies, see 10 & 11 Vict. c. 95.

The protection of copyright in a work given by 5 & 6 Vict. c. 45, extends over the whole of the British dominions and is afforded to every author, whether an alien or not, who being at the time of first publication a resident within any portion of the British dominions, first publishes such work in the United Kingdom. (*Routledge* v. *Low*, L. R. 3 H. L. 100; 37 L. J. Ch. 454; and *per* Lord Cairns,

3. The defendant, without the consent in writing of the plaintiff, who then was such proprietor as aforesaid, did, contrary to the said Act, print and cause to be printed for sale [and exportation] a large number of copies of the said book.

4. The plaintiff has thereby been prevented from selling a large number of copies of the said book, and his profits from the said copyright have been thereby diminished.

5. [The defendant has in his possession or under his control a large number of copies of the said book so printed or caused to be printed by him as aforesaid.

6. The plaintiff before this action demanded the said copies from the defendant. The defendant refuses to deliver them to the plaintiff and threatens to sell the same unless prevented therefrom by injunction.]

The plaintiff claims as follows :—

1. £—— damages.
2. An injunction to restrain the defendant from a continuance and repetition of the said injury and the committal of any injury of a like kind relating to the said copyright, and an order for cancelling all plates used by the defendant in and about printing the said book [and for the delivery up of all copies of the said book printed by the defendant which are in the defendant's possession or under his control].

For Infringing the Copyright in a Book by Selling Copies unlawfully Printed.

1 and 2. [*As in the form next above.*]

3. In or about the year 18— one G. H., without the consent of the plaintiff in writing, and contrary to the

---

L. C., and Lord Westbury, the protection of the statute is given to every author who first publishes in the United Kingdom wherever he may then be resident. *Ib.*)

A first publication abroad deprives the author, whether British or a foreigner, of any copyright save such as he may acquire under the International Copyright Act. (*Jefferys* v. *Boosey*, 4 H. L. 815; 24 L. J. Ex. 81; *Boucicault* v. *Delafield*, 1 H. & M. 597; 33 L. J. Ch. 38; *Boucicault* v. *Chatterton*, 5 Ch. D. 267; 46 L. J. Ch. 305.)

See further as to copyright, Roscoe's N. P. Evd., 14th ed., p. 748 *et seq.*

said Act, printed or caused to be printed and published for sale [or exportation] a large number of copies of the said book.

4. The defendant, well knowing the premises, afterwards, without the consent in writing of the plaintiff, and contrary to the said Act, sold [and published and exposed for sale and hire] divers copies of the said book so printed or caused to be printed by the said G. H. as aforesaid.

5. [*As in paragraph 4 of the form next above.*]

6. [*Add, if necessary, paragraphs to the same effect as paragraphs 5 and 6 in the form next above.*]

Statement of Claim for Infringing the Copyright in the Title of a Book: Weldon v. *Dicks*, 10 Ch. D. 247.

For an Injunction to Restrain the use of the Title of a Book: Kelly v. *Byles*, 40 L. T. 623.

CORPORATION (*a*).

Statement of Claim against a Life Assurance Company to Recover Money obtained by the Fraud of their Agent, with a Claim for the Cancellation of a Policy: Blake v. *Albion Life Assurance Society*, 4 C. P. D. 94.

(*a*) An action will lie against a corporation for a wrong which they cause to be committed, as a nuisance, a trespass to the person, or to land, or goods, or a conversion or detention of goods; and the authority of their agent may be sufficiently proved against a corporation without showing an appointment under seal. (*Yarborough* v. *Bank of England*, 16 East, 6; *Smith* v. *Birmingham Gas Co.*, 1 A. & E. 526; *Maund* v. *The Monmouthshire and Staffordshire Canal Co.*, 2 Dowl. N. S. 113; *Eastern Counties Ry. Co.* v. *Broom*, 6 Ex. 314; *Goff* v. *Great Northern Ry. Co.*, 3 E. & E. 672; 30 L. J. Q. B. 148; *Met. Asylum Dist.* v. *Hill*, 6 App. Cas. 193; 50 L. J. H. L. 353; and see *Mill* v. *Hawker*, L. R. 9 Ex. 309; L. R. 10 Ex. 92; 43 L. J. Ex. 129; 44 ib. 49.)

Such authority may be inferred from the nature of the employment of the agent or servant, and generally speaking a corporation is liable for the acts of an agent or servant acting within the scope of his employment (*Limpus* v. *London General Omnibus Co.*, 1 H. & C. 526; 32 L. J. Ex. 34; *Barwick* v. *English Joint Stock Bank*, L. R. 2 Ex.

Against a Municipal Corporation for pulling down Buildings erected by the Plaintiff: Baker v. *Mayor, &c., of Portsmouth,* 3 Ex. D. 4.

259; 36 L. J. Ex. 147; *Weir* v. *Bell*, L. R. 3 Ex. D. 238; 47 L. J. Ex. 702; *Mackay* v. *Commercial Bank of New Brunswick*, L. R. 5 P. C. 394; *Betts* v. *De Vitre*, L. R. 3 Ch. Ap. 441; 37 L. J. Ch. 325; *Swift* v. *Winterbotham*, L. R. 8 Q. B. 244; *reversed on another point*, see *Swift* v. *Jewsbury*, L. R. 9 Q. B. 301; *Bank of New South Wales* v. *Owston*, 4 App. Cas. 270; 48 L. J. C. P. 301; *Bayley* v. *M. S. and L. Ry. Co.*, L. R. 7 C. P. 415; ib. 8 C. P. 148; 42 L. J. C. P. 78); though where the act complained of is one which the corporation is not under any circumstances authorised to do, no such authority to the agent will be implied. (*Poulton* v. *London and South Western Ry. Co.*, L. R. 2 Q. B. 534; 36 L. J. Q. B. 294; see *Moore* v. *Metropolitan Ry. Co.*, L. R. 8 Q. B. 36; 42 L. J. Q. B. 23.) But, generally speaking, there is an implied authority to the agent or servant to do all those things that are necessary for the protection of the property entrusted to him, or for the fulfilment of the duty that he has to perform. (See *Allen* v. *London and South Western Ry. Co.*, L. R. 6 Q. B. 65, 69; 40 L. J. Q. B. 55, 57; *Bank of New South Wales* v. *Owston, supra.*)

An action for a wrong will lie against a corporation where the matter complained of is a thing done within the scope of their incorporation, and is one which would constitute an actionable wrong if done by an individual; as an action against a company conducting an electric telegraph for publishing a libellous message (*Whitfield* v. *South Eastern Ry. Co.*, 1 E. B. & E. 115; 27 L. J. Q. B. 229); an action against a company engaged in running omnibuses for driving them in such a manner as to obstruct the plaintiff in the use of the highway (*Green* v. *London General Omnibus Co.*, 7 C. B. N. S. 290; 29 L. J. C. P. 13; *Limpus* v. *London General Omnibus Co., supra*); an action against a railway company for arresting a passenger upon a false charge of travelling without having paid his fare (*Goff* v. *Great Northern Ry. Co.*, 3 E. & E. 672; 30 L. J. Ex. 148; *Moore* v. *Metropolitan Ry. Co., supra*); an action for infringing a patent (*Betts* v. *De Vitre, supra*), an action for knowingly keeping a mischievous animal (*Stiles* v. *Cardiff Steam Navigation Co.*, 33 L. J. Q. B. 310); an action for deceit by the fraud of their agent (*Blake* v. *The Albion Life Assurance Co.*, 4 C. P. D. 94; 48 L. J. C. P. 169; *Barwick* v. *English Joint Stock Bank, supra;* and *Mackay* v. *Commercial Bank of New Brunswick, supra*); an action against a Local Board, in whom sewers were vested, for injuries caused by negligence in not properly repairing or constructing such sewers. (*White* v. *Hindley Local Board*, L. R. 10 Q. B. 219; 44 L. J. Q. B. 114; *Borough of Bathurst* v. *Macpherson*, 4 App. Cas. 256; 48 L. J. P. C. 61.)

An action lies against a corporation for damages for injuries caused by their negligence in the performance or non-performance of their duties. (*Henly* v. *Mayor of Lyme*, 5 Bing. 91; and see *Geddis* v. *Proprietors of the Bann Reservoir*, 3 App. Cas. 430; *Winch* v. *Thames Conservators*, L. R. 7 C. P. 458; 41 L. J. C. P. 458.)

It was formerly thought that an action would not lie against a corporation for a malicious prosecution (*Stevens* v. *Midland Ry. Co.*, 10 Ex. 252; and see *Henderson* v. *Midland Ry. Co.*, 24 L. T.

By a Municipal Corporation for disturbance of Market and refusal to pay Tolls: Mayor of Penryn v. *Best,* 3 Ex. D. 292.

For further Forms see "*Company,*" *ante,* p. 369.

COUNTY COURTS (*a*).

---

881), but it is now clear that such an action is maintainable. (*Edwards* v. *Midland Ry. Co.*, 6 Q. B. D. 287; 50 L. J. Q. B. 281; *Bank of New South Wales* v. *Owston*, 4 App. Cas. 270; 48 L. J. P. C. 25; *Kelly* v. *Midland Ry. Co.*, I. R. 7 C. L. 8; see *Whitfield* v. *South Eastern Ry. Co., supra*; *Barwick* v. *English Joint Stock Bank, supra; Mackay* v. *Commercial Bank of New Brunswick, supra*; and see *Walker* v. *South Eastern Ry. Co.*, L. R. 5 C. P. 640.)

An action will lie at the suit of a corporation for a libel. (*Metropolitan Saloon Omnibus Co.* v. *Hawkins,* 4 H. & N. 87; 28 L. J. Ex 201.)

A corporation is liable for the negligence of its servants upon the same principle on which an individual is liable; and it makes no difference in the liability that the corporation is appointed to perform duties of a public nature or receives no profits for its own benefit (*Mersey Docks Trustees* v. *Gibbs*, L. R. 1 H. L. 93; *Coe* v. *Wise*, L. R. 1 Q. B. 711; and see "*Master and Servant*," *post*, p. 464; "*Negligence*," p. 477); and the property of the corporation is liable to executions against them. (*Worall Waterworks Co.* v. *Lloyd*, L. R. 1 C. P. 719.)

(*a*) By the "County Courts Act, 1846," (9 & 10 Vict. c. 95), s. 138, it is enacted (*inter alia*) that all actions to be commenced against any person for anything done in pursuance of that Act shall be commenced within three calendar months after the fact committed, and not afterwards or otherwise, and that notice in writing of such action and of the cause thereof shall be given to the defendant one calendar month at least before the commencement of the action; and that no plaintiff shall recover in any such action if tender of sufficient amends shall have been made before such action brought, or if after such action brought a sufficient sum of money shall have been paid into court, with costs, by or on behalf of the defendant. (See *Burton* v. *Le Gros*, 34 L. J. Q. B. 91; and see "*Notice of Action*," "Defences.")

The section also contained a provision with respect to the venue of such actions, which, so far as relates to actions in the High Court of Justice, has been impliedly repealed by O. XXXVI. r. 1, abolishing local venues.

With respect to actions against any high bailiff or bailiff of a county court, or against any person acting by the order and in aid of such high bailiff, for anything done in obedience to any warrant under the hand of the clerk or clerks of the county court and the

Defamation (*a*).

Statement of Claim for a Libel.

1. The defendant, on or about the —— of ——, 18—, falsely and maliciously printed and published of the plaintiff [in a newspaper called "——,"] the words following, that is to say, "He is a regular prover under bank-

---

seal of such court, see the provisions contained in s. 19 of "The County Courts Act, 1850" (13 & 14 Vict. c. 61). The special provision in this act as to pleading the general issue is repealed by the Stat. Law Rev. Act, 1875.

By "The County Courts Act, 1852" (15 & 16 Vict. c. 54), s. 6, it is enacted (*inter alia*) that "if any action or suit shall be brought against any person for anything done in pursuance of this Act, or any other Act relating to county courts, such person may plead the general issue, and give the special matter in evidence; and the warrant under the seal of the county court, being produced in any such action or suit, shall be deemed sufficient proof of the authority of the said county court previous to the issuing of such warrant."

The above provisions with respect to pleading the general issue of "*not guilty*," and giving the special matter in evidence thereunder, are not affected by the Judicature Acts, but it is now provided that if a defendant so plead, he shall not plead any other defence without the leave of the court or a judge. (O. XIX. r. 16, and see "Defences.")

The high bailiff of a county court is liable for the acts of persons employed by him to execute process to the same extent as the sheriff of a county, and such high-bailiff was accordingly held liable for the acts of a person employed by his under-bailiff in wrongfully selling goods seized in execution, contrary to the 9 & 10 Vict. c. 95, s. 106. (*Burton* v. *Le Gros*, 34 L. J. Q. B. 91; and see "*Sheriff*," *post*, p. 514.)

(*a*) *Libel and Slander.*]—*Libel* consists in the publication by the defendant, by means of printing, writing, pictures, or the like signs, of matter defamatory to the plaintiff (3 Bl. Com. 125).

Slander consists in the publication by the defendant, by means of words spoken, of matter defamatory to the plaintiff (3 Bl. Com. 123).

The nature of the defamatory matter which is actionable in a written publication or libel, and that which is actionable when spoken, with the distinction between them, may be seen from the following descriptions.

Matter imputing criminal offences. This is actionable equally in the form of libel and of slander.

Matter imputing misconduct in the discharge of a public office. This is also actionable both as libel and as slander.

Matter imputing misconduct, or want of care or of qualification or of skill in a lawful profession, trade, or business. This is also actionable both as libel and as slander.

Matter imputing to a person that he is suffering from a contagious disease such as leprosy or the pox. This is also actionable both as

ruptcies," the defendant meaning thereby that the plaintiff had proved and was in the habit of proving fictitious debts against the estates of bankrupts, with the knowledge that such debts were fictitious.

---

libel and slander. No proof of special damage is required to render such matter actionable as slander because it causes the person as a natural consequence to be shunned by society.

Matter imputing conduct or qualities tending to degrade or disparage the plaintiff, or exposing him to public hatred, contempt, or ridicule, is actionable as libel when published in print, writing, or other permanent form, but not as slander when merely spoken. (See *I'Anson* v. *Stuart*, 1 T. R. 748; 2 Smith's L. C. 6th ed. 57; *Thorley* v. *Kerry*, 4 Taunt. 364; *Clement* v. *Chivis*, 9 B. & C. 175; *Parmiter* v. *Coupland*, 6 M. & W. 105, 108; *Fray* v. *Fray*, 17 C. B. N. S. 603; 34 L. J. C. P. 45; *Cox* v. *Lee*, L. R. 4 Ex. 284; 38 L. J. Ex. 219.)

Defamatory words merely spoken, and not actionable under any of the above descriptions, but which cause special damage to the plaintiff, are actionable as slander. (See *Kelly* v. *Partington*, 5 B. & Ad. 645.)

Whether matter, written or spoken, is defamatory, within the above descriptions, is a question for the jury. It is for the judge to direct the jury what constitutes defamation in law, and for the jury to say whether according to such direction, the matter in question is defamatory. (*Parmiter* v. *Coupland*, 6 M. & W. 105; *Baylis* v. *Lawrence*, 11 A. & E. 920; *per* Williams, J., *Paris* v. *Levy*, 9 C. B. N. S., 342, 352, and see *per* Brett, L.J. in *Capital & Counties Bank* v. *Henty*, 5 C. P. D. 539; 49 L. J. C. P. 830.) The judge may state his opinion to the jury whether the matter is defamatory (*ib.*). If the words sued on are reasonably susceptible of a libellous or slanderous construction, it is for the jury to decide whether they bear that meaning. (*Hart* v. *Wall*, 2 C. P. D. 146; 46 L. J. C. P. 227; *Jenner* v. *A'Beckett*, L. R. 7 Q. B. 11; 41 L. J. Q. B. 14; *Botterill* v. *Whytehead*, 41 L. T. 588; *Simmonds* v. *Mitchell*, 6 App. Cas. 156.) But if they are incapable of such construction, the statement of claim may be demurred to, or the case may be withdrawn from the jury, and judgment entered for the defendant. (*Hearne* v. *Stowell*, 12 A. & E. 719; *Miller* v. *David*, L. R. 9 C. P. 118; 43 L. J. C. P. 84; *Capital & Counties Bank* v. *Henty*, *supra*; *Mulligan* v. *Cole*, L. R. 10 Q. B. 549; 44 L. J. Q. B. 153.)

The profession, trade, or occupation must be a lawful one in order to entitle the plaintiff to recover damages for defamation in respect of it. (*Morris* v. *Langdale*, 2 B. & P. 284; *Hunt* v. *Bell*, 1 Bing. 1.) But the business need not necessarily be one of which the Court will take judicial notice. (*Foulger* v. *Newcomb*, L. R. 2 Ex. 327; 36 L. J. Ex. 169.)

Words spoken imputing general immorality are not a sufficiently specific injury to a person's trade or profession to be actionable without special damage (*Lumby* v. *Allday*, 1 Cr. & J. 301; *Ayre* v. *Craven*, 2 A. & E. 2; *Gallwey* v. *Marshall*, 9 Ex. 294); though such imputations might be actionable if written, or printed, and published, as imputing conduct tending to degrade or bring into contempt the person so charged.

For sending a Libellous Letter to, and publishing it in, a Newspaper.

1. The plaintiff is and was the Chief Constable of the Borough of ——.

2. On the —— of ——, 18—, the defendant falsely and maliciously wrote and published of and concerning

---

It has been held that a shopkeeper whose wife assisted him in his shop, can maintain an action for defamatory words spoken and published of his wife, imputing to her adultery committed at such shop, followed, as a natural consequence, by a falling off in his business, occasioned by such words. (*Riding* v. *Smith*, 1 Ex. D. 91 ; 45 L. J. Ex. 21.)

The ordinary rule is that from the publishing of the defamatory matter, whether written or spoken, malice is inferred, though where the occasion is privileged, this *primâ facie* inference is rebutted, and malice must be proved in order to maintain the action. (*Wright* v. *Woodgate*, 1 C. M. & R. 577 ; *Laughton* v. *Bishop of Sodor & Man*, L. R. 4 P. C. 495, 505 ; 42 L. J. P. C. 11 ; *Davies* v. *Snead*, L. R. 5 Q. B. 608 ; 39 L. J. Q. B. 202 ; *Webb* v. *East*, 5 Ex. D. 108 ; 49 L. J. Ex. 250.) See the following note.

Privileged Communications.]—On certain occasions a person is privileged to write or to speak honestly according to the best of his belief, and he is not liable to an action for matter written or spoken on such privileged occasions, although it be false, unless he has written or spoken maliciously, in fact, has not made a *bonâ fide* use of the occasion. (*Stevens* v. *Sampson*, 5 Ex. D. 53 ; 49 L. J. Q. B. 120 ; *Clark* v. *Molyneux*, 3 Q. B. D. 237, 246, 249 ; 47 L. J. Q. B. 230.) A communication made *bonâ fide* upon any subject-matter in which the party communicating has an interest, or in reference to which he has a duty, is privileged, if made to a person having a corresponding interest or duty, the duty not being confined merely to legal duties, but including moral and social duties of imperfect obligation. (*Harrison* v. *Bush*, 5 E. & B. 344 ; 25 L. J. Q. B. 25 ; *Henwood* v. *Harrison*, L. R. 7 C. P. 606, 622, 623 ; 41 L. J. C. P. 206, 215 ; *Davies* v. *Snead*, L. R. 5 Q. B. 608, 611 ; 39 L. J. Q. B. 202 ; *Waller* v. *Lock*, 45 L. T. 242 ; *Coxhead* v. *Richards*, 2 C. B. 569 ; *Blackham* v. *Pugh*, 2 C. B. 611 ; *Laughton* v. *Bishop of Sodor and Man*, L. R. 4. P. C. 495 ; 42 L. J. P. C. 11 ; *Hamon* v. *Falle*, 4 App. Cas. 247.)

A common instance of a privileged occasion is that of a master answering inquiries about a servant. (*Per* Blackburn, J., in *Davies* v. *Snead*, *supra*.) On such occasions of privilege malice is not inferred from the mere falsehood of the defamatory statement, but must be proved to exist in fact. (*Taylor* v. *Hawkins*, 16 Q. B. 308 ; *Hemmings* v. *Gasson*, E. B. & E. 346 ; 27 L. J. Q. B. 252 ; *Webb* v. *East*, 5 Ex. D. 108 ; 49 L. J. Ex. 250.) The wording of the libel itself may, however, be such as to afford evidence of malice, from the language being unnecessarily exaggerated or violent. (*Gilpin* v. *Fowler*, 9 Ex. 615 ; 23 L. J. Ex. 152 ; *Wright* v. *Woodgate*, 2 C. M. & R. 573 ; *Spill* v. *Maule*, L. R. 4 Ex. 232, 236 ; 38 L. J. Ex. 138.) So may the mode in which the communication is made, as for instance where it is unnecessarily made by telegraph or post card instead of by sealed letter. (*Williamson* v. *Freer* L. R. 9 C. P. 393;

the plaintiff, in the form of a letter addressed to the editor of a newspaper called "——," the words [and figures] following, that is to say [*here set out libel verbatim*].

---

43 L. J. C. P. 161.) Whether the occasion is privileged is a question for the judge; the existence of express malice, if there is any evidence of it, is one for the jury. (*Cooke* v. *Wildes*, 5 E. & B. 328; 24 L. J. Q. B. 367; *Huntley* v. *Ward*, 6 C. B. N. S. 514; *Cowles* v. *Potts*, 34 L. J. Q. B. 247; *Gilpin* v. *Fowler*, *supra*; *Spill* v. *Maule*, L. R. 4 Ex. 232, 237; 38 L. J. Ex. 138; *Stace* v. *Griffith*, L. R. 2 P. C. 420.)

Proof that the defendant when he spoke or wrote the defamatory matter complained of knew it, or a portion of it, to be false, affords evidence of malice. (*Fountain* v. *Boodle*, 3 Q. B. 5.) If the defendant, at the time of making the privileged communication complained of, honestly believed it to be true, it is immaterial that he had no reasonable grounds for so believing. (*Clark* v. *Molyneux*, 3 Q. B. D. 237; 47 L. J. Q. B. 230.) As to newspaper reports of public meetings see "The Newspaper Libel and Registration Act, 1881," (44 & 45 Vict., c. 60) s. 2, and see further "*Defamation*," "Defences."

There are some occasions which, on grounds of public policy, are absolutely privileged, and in which no inquiry is permitted as to the intent of the party making use of such occasion. Thus, the statements made by a witness in examination, or by deposition, or affidavit, in the course of a trial or inquiry before a judicial, parliamentary or military tribunal or court, with reference to such trial or inquiry, are privileged, and cannot be made the subject of an action. (*Dawkins* v. *Lord Rokeby*, L. R. 7 H. L. 744; 45 L. J. H. L. 8; *Seaman* v. *Netherclift*, 1 C. P. D. 540; 2 C. P. D. 53; 45 L. J. C. P. 798; 46 ib. 128; *Goffin* v. *Donnelly*, 6 Q. B. D. 307; 50 L. J. Q. B. 303; *Revis* v. *Smith*, 18 C. B. 126; 25 L. J. C. P. 195; *Henderson* v. *Broomhead*, 4 H. & N. 569; 28 L. J. Ex. 360.) So, also, are the speeches or observations of an advocate, whether a barrister or solicitor, in the course of such a trial or inquiry, having reference to such trial or inquiry (*Wood* v. *Gunston*, Styles, 462; *R.* v. *Skinner*, Lofft. 55, 56; *Dawkins* v. *Rokeby*, *supra*; *Hodgson* v. *Scarlett*, 1 B. & A. 232; *Mackay* v. *Ford*, 5 H. & N. 792; 29 L. J. Ex. 404); as also are the judgments or observations of the judge or presiding officer on such trial or inquiry. (*Scott* v. *Stansfield*, L. R. 3 Ex. 220; 37 L. J. Ex. 155; *Thomas* v. *Chirton*, 2 B. & S. 475; 31 L. J. Q. B. 139; *Jekyll* v. *Moore*, 2 N. R. 341.) So, too, words spoken by a member of Parliament in his place in Parliament are absolutely privileged (*R.* v. *Lord Abingdon*, 1 Esp. 228; *Davison* v. *Duncan*, 7 E. & B. 229, 233; 26 L. J. Q. B. 104, 107); as are statements made in a petition to Parliament. (*Lake* v. *King*, 1 Wms. Saund. 1871 ed., p. 137.) The defence of privilege is one that must, in general, be pleaded, though where the facts which give rise to the privilege appear upon the statement of claim, it may be raised by demurrer.

The Form of the Statement of Claim.]—The defamatory matter must be *false*, and must be so charged in the statement of claim; it is then, unless it appears that the occasion was a privileged one, presumed to have been published maliciously. (*Bromage* v. *Prosser*, 4 B. & C. 247, 255; *Haire* v. *Wilson*, 9 B. & C. 643; *Huntley* v. *Ward*, 6 C. B.

3. The defendant falsely and maliciously printed and published, or caused and procured to be printed and published the said letter in all the copies of the said newspaper printed and published on the —— of ——, 18—.

N. S. 514; *Davies* v. *Snead*, L. R. 5 Q. B. 608, 611; 39 L. J. Q. B. 202; *Toogood* v. *Spyring*, 1 C. M. & R. 193; *Hamon* v. *Falle*, 4 App. Cas. 247, 251.)

It is usually alleged that the words were printed, or written, or spoken *maliciously*, but this is not strictly necessary, unless it appear that the occasion was a privileged one, as the malice is sufficiently implied from the falseness of the defamatory words. (*Bromage* v. *Prosser*, 4 B. & C. at p. 255; Styles, 392; *Mercer* v. *Sparks*, Owen, 51; Noy, 35; *Clark* v. *Molyneux*, 3 Q. B. D. 237, 247; 47 L. J. Q. B. 230.) Where it appears that the occasion is a privileged one it is sufficient to allege *malice* as a fact without setting out the circumstances from which it is to be inferred. (O. XIX. rr. 4, 25.) Subsequent libels or slanders published by the defendant of the plaintiff are admissible in evidence to prove malice. Evidence of actual malice may in all cases be given to increase the damages. See further "*The body of the statement of claim*," *ante*, p. 11.

It must appear upon the statement of claim that the defamatory matter was written, printed, or spoken, "of the plaintiff," either by express averment to that effect or by necessary implication. (*Clement* v. *Fisher*, 7 B. & C. 459; *O'Brien* v. *Clement*, 4 D. & L. 583.) It is necessary to set out the words spoken or published exactly; it is not enough to set out their effect, the words being the "material facts" (*Harris* v. *Warre*, 4 C. P. D. 125; 48 L. J. C. P. 310; *Gutsole* v. *Mathers*, 1 M. & W. 495; *Solomon* v. *Lawson*, 8 Q. B. 823; *R.* v. *Berry*, 4 T. R. 217; and see *M'Pherson* v. *Daniels*, 10 B. & C. 274; *Wood* v. *Adams*, 6 Bing. 431; *Wright* v. *Clements*, 3 B. & Ald. 503); nor is it enough to set out the "substance" or "purport" of the words. (*Wright* v. *Clements*, *supra*; *Wood* v. *Brown*, 6 Taunt. 169; *Cook* v. *Cox*, 3 M. & S. 110; *Harris* v. *Warre*, *supra*.)

The libel or slander, if in a foreign language, should be set out in the original (*Zenobio* v. *Axtell*, 6 T. R. 162; *Jenkins* v. *Phillips*, 9 C. & P. 766), and should be translated with allegations of its actionable meaning; and the statement of claim should aver that the persons in whose presence it was spoken, or to whom it was published, understood the foreign language. (*Amann* v. *Damm*, 8 C. B. N. S. 597; 29 L. J. C. P. 313.) Where the ground of action is that the words impute misconduct, or want of qualification, or skill, in a lawful profession or business, it must appear upon the statement of claim by express averment or by necessary implication that the words were spoken of the plaintiff in relation to such profession or business. (*Miller* v. *David*, L. R. 9 C. P. 118; 43 L. J. C. P. 84.)

Innuendo.]—Expressions which are actionable in their plain and ordinary meaning, as calling a man a "thief," saying that he has committed "perjury," &c., might always be alleged simply without any explanation. (*Harvey* v. *French*, 1 C. & M. 11; *Day* v. *Robinson*, 1 A. & E. 558; *Homer* v. *Taunton*, 5 H. & N. 661; 29 L. J. Ex. 318.) But where the words are innocent or uncertain in their natural meaning, and are actionable only in consequence of the peculiar

[A very large number of such copies were circulated in —— and the North of England.]

4. In consequence of the premises the plaintiff has been and is greatly injured in his credit and reputation. [*Add special damage, if any.*]

---

meaning conveyed by them on the particular occasion, as calling a man a "lame duck," a "black sheep," or saying that he is "forsworn," or where the words are used ironically, it is necessary to add an *innuendo*, or statement of the meaning intended by the words, whereby they are rendered actionable. (*Sweetapple* v. *Jesse*, 5 B. & Ad. 27; *Jackson* v. *Adams*, 2 Bing. N. C. 402; *Cox* v. *Cooper*, 12 W. R. 75.)

Whether the words are capable of the meaning alleged, and whether such meaning is actionable are questions for the Court; whether they in fact were used with that meaning is a question for the jury. (*Blagg* v. *Sturt*, 10 Q. B. 899; *Broome* v. *Gosden*, 1 C. B. 728; *Hemmings* v. *Gasson*, E. B. & E. 346; 27 L. J. Q. B. 252; *Burnett* v. *Allen*, 3 H. & N. 376; *Cox* v. *Cooper*, 12 W. R. 75; *Hart* v. *Wall*, 2 C. P. D. 146; 46 L. J. C. P. 227; *Jenner* v. *A'Beckett*, L. R. 7 Q. B. 11; 41 L. J. Q. B. 14; *Botterill* v. *Whytehead*, 41 L. T. 588; *Mulligan* v. *Cole*, L. R. 10 Q. B. 549; 44 L. J. Q. B. 153; *Shepheard* v. *Whitaker*, L. R. 10 C. P. 502; *Ruel* v. *Tatnell*, 43 L. T. 507; *Capital & Counties Bank* v. *Henty*, 5 C. P. D. 514; 49 L. J. C. P. 830.)

The Damage.]—Where the defamatory words are actionable in themselves it is not necessary to state any special damage, unless it is intended to claim it in addition to the general damages resulting from the injury. Where the defamatory words are actionable only by reason of the damage caused by them, the special damage must be alleged in the statement of claim.

The special damage must be the natural and proximate consequence of the defamation. Illness of body caused by defamatory words not actionable in themselves cannot be relied on as special damage, because not a consequence which generally happens under the same circumstances. (*Allsop* v. *Allsop*, 5 H. & N. 534; 29 L. J. Ex. 315.) The loss of the hospitality of friends consequent upon slander may be charged as special damage. (*Moore* v. *Meagher*, 1 Taunt. 39; *Davies* v. *Solomon*, L. R. 7 Q. B. 112.) Exclusion from membership of a congregation of Protestant dissenters, as not involving temporal or pecuniary loss, is not sufficient special damage. (*Roberts* v. *Roberts*, 5 B. & S. 384; 33 L. J. Q. B. 249.)

A wife cannot maintain an action for words imputing unchaste conduct to her without proof of special damage occasioned thereby (*Lynch* v. *Knight*, 9 H. L. C. 577), and the loss of the consortium of her husband, if due to her own repetition of the charge against her to her husband, is not such special damage. (*Lynch* v. *Knight*, *supra*; *Parkins* v. *Scott*, 1 H. & C. 153; 31 L. J. Ex. 331.) Whether the loss of the consortium of her husband alone without other damage of a pecuniary or material nature is sufficient special damage to enable her to maintain an action for defamatory words spoken of her which are not actionable without special damage is doubtful. (*Lynch* v. *Knight*, *supra*; *Davies* v. *Solomon*, *supra*.) Damage caused by an unauthorised repetition of defamatory words spoken by the defendant

For a Libel imputing Felony to the Plaintiff.

1. The defendant falsely and maliciously wrote and published of the plaintiff [in the form of a letter addressed and sent by the defendant to A. B., bearing date the —— of ——, 18—,] the words following, that is to say, "He

---

cannot, in general, be charged as special damage. (*Ward* v. *Weeks* 7 Bing. 211; *Dixon* v. *Smith*, 5 H. & N. 450; 29 L. J. Ex. 125; *Bateman* v. *Lyall*, 7 C. B. N. S. 638.) But where there is a duty or moral obligation to repeat such words, then it would seem such a repetition may be a natural consequence of the original wrong, and charged as special damage against the original utterer. (*Derry* v. *Handley*, 16 L. T. 263.)

The wrongful acts of third parties cannot be charged as special damage, unless such damage is the immediate and natural consequence of the defamatory words. (*Vicars* v. *Wilcocks*, 8 East, 1; but see *Green* v. *Button*, 2 C. M. & R. 713; *Lynch* v. *Knight*, *supra*.)

When a third party acts upon the defamatory words to the prejudice of the plaintiff, although he did not believe them, the consequence may be charged as special damage. (*Knight* v. *Gibbs*, 1 A. & E. 43.)

The special damage must be alleged in the statement of claim with sufficient particularity to inform the defendant of what the plaintiff intends to prove.

Where it is intended to prove that particular customers have, in consequence of the defamation complained of, ceased to deal with the plaintiff, the names of such customers should be stated in the statement of claim. Damages may, however, be recovered for a general loss of trade, if such general loss be alleged, without stating or proving the ceasing of any particular customer to deal with the plaintiff. (*Evans* v. *Harries*, 1 H. & N. 251; 26 L. J. Ex. 31; *Riding* v. *Smith*, 1 Ex. D. 91; 45 L. J. Ex. 281.)

In actions for defamation express malice may be proved in aggravation of damages; and for this purpose subsequent libels published by the defendant of the plaintiff are admissible in evidence, and cannot be excluded on the ground that they may disclose distinct causes of action; but, if they disclose distinct causes of action, the jury cannot give damages in respect of them. (*Chalmers* v. *Payne*, 2 C. M. & R. 156, 157; *Pearson* v. *Lemaitre*, 5 M. & G. 700; and see *Hemmings* v. *Gasson*, E. B. & E. 346; 27 L. J. Q. B. 252.)

The defendant may give evidence in answer to the evidence of special damage adduced by the plaintiff, or in mitigation of the damage proved. He may prove in mitigation of damages that the plaintiff published libels of him, provided they relate to the same matter (*Watts* v. *Fraser*, 7 A. & E. 223; *May* v. *Brown*, 3 B. & C. 113; *Tarpley* v. *Blabey*, 2 Bing. N. C. 437); he may also give evidence of the general bad reputation of the plaintiff at the time of the defamation (*Richards* v. *Richards*, 2 M. & Rob. 557; and see *Thompson* v. *Nye*, 16 Q. B. 175); and he may rely upon the plaintiff's conduct in the matter as provoking the libels and as reducing his claim to damages. (*Kelly* v. *Sherlock*, L. R. 1 Q. B. 686.) But he cannot give in evidence in mitigation of damages, matter which if pleaded would be a defence to the action. (*Watson* v. *Christie*, 2 B.

is the person who took my horse," the defendant meaning thereby that the plaintiff feloniously stole a horse of the defendant.

2. By reason of the premises the plaintiff was injured in his character and reputation, [and in his business of a ——.]

For a Libel in a Foreign Language.

1. The defendant falsely and maliciously wrote and published [in a placard affixed to, &c., *or as the case may be*] of the plaintiff in the Welsh language the words following, that is to say [*here set out the libel verbatim in Welsh*], which said words, being translated into the English language, have, and were understood by the persons to whom they were so published to have the meaning and effect following, that is to say [*here set out a literal translation of the libel in English, and add any innuendo which may be necessary, as in the ordinary form*].

For Slander.

1. On the —— day of ——, 18—, the defendant [in a conversation which he then had with one A. B., *or as the case may be*] falsely and maliciously spoke and published of the plaintiff the words following, that is to say, "He is a thief."

2. [*If there be any special damage, here state it with such reasonable particularity as to give notice to the defendant of the particular injury complained of; as, for instance,* Thereby the plaintiff lost his situation as gamekeeper in the employ of ——].

For a Slander of the Plaintiff in his Trade, with Statement of Special Damage.

1. The plaintiff carried on and still carries on the business of a —— at ——, and the defendant on the

---

& P. 224; *Underwood* v. *Parks*, 2 Str. 1200.) Evidence that an apology was offered before the commencement of the action may be given in mitigation of damages, after notice in writing of the defendant's intention to do so, under 6 & 7 Vict. c. 96, s. 1.

The County Court has no jurisdiction in this action (9 & 10 Vict. c. 95, s. 58); except by consent (19 & 20 Vict. c. 108, s. 23); or in cases remitted for trial before a County Court under the 30 & 31 Vict. c. 142, s. 10.

—— of ——, 18—, falsely and maliciously spoke and published of the plaintiff in relation to his said business and the carrying on and conducting thereof by him, the words following, that is to say [*state the slander verbatim, with innuendoes, if necessary; as, for instance,* meaning thereby that the plaintiff cheated and was guilty of fraudulent conduct in his said business, *or as the case may be*].

2. The plaintiff in consequence was injured in his credit and reputation as a —— and in his said business, [and G. H. and K. L., who had dealt with him before in his said business, ceased to so deal with him, and he thereby lost profits which he otherwise would have made in his said business.]

For a Slander in respect of Words not actionable in themselves, but only in respect of the Special Damage caused thereby.

1. The plaintiff is a milliner carrying on business at ——.

2. The defendant falsely and maliciously spoke and published to A. B. of the plaintiff the words following, that is to say, "She," meaning the plaintiff, "is a disgrace to the town; she is a most immoral and abandoned woman," meaning thereby that the plaintiff had been guilty of acts of incontinence and immorality.

3. By reason of the premises the said A. B., who had previously employed the plaintiff as such milliner, ceased so to employ her, and the plaintiff thereby lost profits which she otherwise would have made.

Against a Bank Manager for Disclosing to a Third Party an Anonymous Letter containing Statements Defamatory of the Plaintiff: Robshaw v. *Smith*, 38 L. T. 423.

Against the Printers and Publishers of a Newspaper for Publishing therein Defamatory Comments upon the Conduct of the Plaintiff, the Medical Officer of a Union Workhouse: Purcell v. *Sowler*, 1 C. P. D. 781; 46 L. J. C. P. 308; 36 L. T. 416.

Against the Proprietors, Printers, and Publishers of a Newspaper for Publishing a Libel upon the Plaintiff therein: Leyman v. *Latimer,* 3 Ex. D. 15 (*affirmed ib.* 352); 46 L. J. Ex. 765 (*affirmed* 47 L. J. Ex. 470).

For a Libel contained in a Letter commenting on an Advertisement which had been put forth by the Plaintiffs, with a Claim for Special Damage: Hart v. *Wall,* 2 C. P. D. 146; 46 L. J. C. P. 227.

By an Architect, for Libels contained in Letters and in a Petition or Memorial imputing to him Want of Skill and Experience in the Class of Work upon which he was Employed: Botterill v. *Whytehead,* 41 L. T. 588.

By a Patentee, for a Libel imputing that he had Dishonestly Pirated an Invention of another Person, with a Claim for an Injunction to Restrain the Defendants from Publishing further Libels of a like nature: Saxby v. *Easterbrook,* 3 C. P. D. 339 (*b*).

By a Banking Co. upon a Letter the meaning of which is by an innuendo alleged to be Defamatory, Capital and Counties Bank v. *Henty,* 5 C. P. D. 514.

For Wantonly Publishing a False and Defamatory Statement as to the Goods the Plaintiff deals in, and as to his Conduct as a Tradesman, whereby he lost Custom in his Trade (*c*).

1. The plaintiff is a butcher carrying on business at ——.

(*b*) The Court has power, it would seem, to issue an injunction to restrain a defendant from publishing of the plaintiff, to the injury of his trade, matter which has been decided to be libellous. (*Saxby* v. *Easterbrook*, 3 C. P. D. 339; *Thorley's Cattle Food Co.* v. *Massam*, 6 Ch. D. 582; 46 L. J. Ch. 713; *Ib.* 14 Ch. D. 763; *Thomas* v. *Williams*, 14 Ch. D. 864.)

(*c*) An action lies for wantonly, without lawful occasion, publishing, either by words spoken or in writing or print, a false and

2. The defendant on the —— of ——, 18—, falsely and maliciously printed and published of the plaintiff as such butcher, and in relation to his said business and the carrying on thereof by him, [in the form of a handbill,] the words following, that is to say, "He," meaning the plaintiff, "kills old cows and sells them as prime beef, and buys rotten and diseased sheep and passes them off upon the public as the primest of mutton, underselling all respectable butchers," meaning thereby that the plaintiff was not a respectable butcher, and was in the habit of selling bad meat and deceiving his customers.

3. By reason of the premises the plaintiff has sustained great loss in his said business, and lost customers he otherwise would have had in his said business.

Detention of Goods, or Detinue (a).

Statement of Claim for the Detention of a Horse.

1. The plaintiff is the owner of a race-horse called ——.

2. The defendant has wrongfully detained, and still wrongfully detains, the said horse from the plaintiff.

---

defamatory statement disparaging the goods wherein a man deals, and thereby causing him special damage. (*Western Counties Manure Co.* v. *Lawes' Chemical Manure Co.*, L. R. 9 Ex. 218; *distinguishing Young* v. *Macrae*, 3 B. & S. 264; 32 L. J. Q. B. 6.) As to granting an injunction to restrain such statements, see preceding *note*, and see *Saxby* v. *Easterbrook*, 3 C. P. D. 339 for form of pleading.

This action is analogous to that for slander of title. (See *post*, "*Slander of Title.*")

(*a*) *Detention of Goods.*]—An action lies for the specific recovery of personal chattels wrongfully detained from the person entitled to the possession of them, and also for damages occasioned by the wrongful detainer. (3 Bl. Com. 151.) The form of action adapted for suing for the wrongful detention of personal property is called *detinue*. The declaration in detinue formerly commenced with a statement either that the plaintiff had lost the goods and that they had come to the possession of the defendant by finding, or that the plaintiff had delivered them to the defendant to be re-delivered to him on request; and the count was spoken of as *detinue sur trover* or *detinue sur bailment*, according to the form adopted; but these allegations, which were generally fictitious, were immaterial and not traversable, and were abolished by the C. L. P. Act, 1852, s. 49. See as to them, *Gledstane* v. *Hewitt*, 1 C. & J. 565.

The gist of the action is the wrongful detention of goods, and it is therefore, in general, an action for a wrong independent of contract, and is "founded on tort" within the meaning of sec. 5 of 30 &

For the Detention of a Lease, whereby the Plaintiff was Prevented from Selling the Premises.

1. The defendant detained [and still detains] from the plaintiff a deed of the plaintiff, that is to say, a lease

---

31 Vict. c. 142, as to costs. (*Gledstane* v. *Hewitt*, *suprà*; *Broadbent* v. *Ledward*, 11 A. & E. 209; *Clements* v. *Flight*, 16 M. & W. 42; *Bryant* v. *Herbert*, 3 C. P. D. 389; 47 L. J. C. P. 670.)

To support this action, the plaintiff must have the right to the immediate possession of the goods at the time of commencing the action, arising out of an absolute or a special property; an interest in reversion is not sufficient. See "*Conversion*," *ante*, p. 372, and "*Trespass to Goods*," *post*, p. 532.

In this action the goods must be sufficiently ascertained and distinguishable to be capable of being recovered. Thus, the action cannot be brought for a sum of money or a quantity of corn, unless they be specifically distinguished from other property of the same kind, as by being in a bag or a sack. (3 Bl. Com. 152.)

This action may be brought for the title-deeds of a real estate; and the proper party to sue in such case is the person entitled to the legal interest in the estate. See *Atkinson* v. *Baker*, 4 T. R. 229; *Philips* v. *Robinson*, 4 Bing. 106; *Plant* v. *Cotterill*, 5 H. & N. 430; 29 L. J. Ex. 198. Thus, the legal tenant for life may maintain an action of detinue to recover the title-deeds against the remainderman. (*Lord Buckhurst's case*, 1 Co. Rep. 2 *a*; *Allwood* v. *Heywood*, 1 H. & C. 745; 32 L. J. Ex. 153; *Leathes* v. *Leathes*, 5 Ch. D. 221; 46 L. J. Ch. 562.) On the death of the tenant for life the reversioner may recover the deeds from the assignee of the tenant for life to whom they have been assigned as security for an advance. (*Easton* v. *London*, 33 L. J. Ex. 34.) The lessor is not entitled to the possession of a lease for an expired term as against the lessee. (*Hall* v. *Ball*, 3 M. & G. 242; *Elworthy* v. *Sandford*, 34 L. J. Ex. 42.)

The injurious act being the wrongful detention of the goods, and not the original taking or obtaining of the possession, it is immaterial whether they were obtained by the defendant by lawful means, as by a bailment or finding, or by a wrongful act, as by a trespass or conversion. (1 Chit. Pl. 7th ed. 137.) The usual evidence of the detention is, that the defendant, having the possession or control over the goods, does not deliver them to the plaintiff when demanded. The defendant cannot excuse himself from such delivery by reason of his having lost the possession by his own wrongful act, as where the defendant, having had the possession of the plaintiff's goods, has wrongfully sold them (*Jones* v. *Dowle*, 9 M. & W. 19); or carelessly lost them. (*Reeve* v. *Palmer*, 5 C. B. N. S. 84; 27 L. J. C. P. 327; 28 *ib.* 168.)

The goods must be described with sufficient certainty and accuracy for the purpose of identification, because the judgment and execution are for the recovery of the specific goods. (2 Wms. Saund. 74 *b.*)

The judgment for the plaintiff in this action is, that he recover against the defendant the goods, or the sum assessed by the jury for the value of them if the plaintiff cannot have his goods again, and also his damages and costs assessed by the jury beyond the value of the goods, and also the costs of increase. (Chit. Forms, 11th ed.

bearing date the —— day of ——, 18—, and made between G. H. of the one part, and the plaintiff of the other part, whereby the said G. H. demised to the plaintiff a house and premises at —— for an unexpired term of years.

353.) Before the C. L. P. Act, 1854, the defendant, under the judgment in this action, had the option to deliver the goods, or to retain them and pay the value assessed by the jury. (*Phillips* v. *Jones*, 15 Q. B. 859.) By sect. 78 of that Act, "the Court or a judge shall have power, if they or he see fit so to do, upon the application of the plaintiff in any action for the detention of any chattel, to order that execution shall issue for the return of the chattel detained, without giving the defendant the option of retaining such chattel upon paying the value assessed; and that if the said chattel cannot be found, and unless the Court or judge should otherwise order, the sheriff shall distrain the defendant by all his lands and chattels in the said sheriff's bailiwick, till the defendant renders such chattel, or, at the option of the plaintiff, that he cause to be made of the defendant's goods the assessed value of such chattel; provided that the plaintiff shall, either by the same or a separate writ of execution, be entitled to have made of the defendant's goods the damages, costs, and interest in such action." This section does not apply where the jury have not assessed the value. (*Chilton* v. *Carrington*, 15 C. B. 730.) The writ of delivery is retained by O. XLII. r. 4 & O. XLIX. Where the defendant improperly detained photographs belonging to the plaintiff, and had taken and sold copies of them, the plaintiff was held entitled to recover the photographs or their value in detinue, and also to have an injunction to prevent the defendant from taking or selling any more copies. (*Mayall* v. *Higbey*, 1 H. & C. 148; 31 L. J. Ex. 329; see "*Injunction*," *post*, p. 439.)

If there are distinct goods or parcels of goods claimed, the jury should assess the value of each separately. (*Sandford* v. *Alcock*, 10 M. & W. 689.) Where the goods have been redelivered, the jury may confine their assessment to the damages for the detention. (*Williams* v. *Archer*, 5 C. B. 318; *Crossfield* v. *Such*, 8 Ex. 159.) Special damage may be recovered if properly claimed. (*Ib.*) Where the goods have been redelivered after the commencement of the action, the defendant should plead the redelivery as a defence arising after action. Thus pleaded it affords a bar to the further maintenance of the action for the redelivery of the goods, but leaves unanswered any claim there may be for damages for the previous detention. (*Leader* v. *Rhys*, 10 C. B. N. S. 369; 30 L. J. C. P. 345; O. XX.) See further "Defences," "*Detention*."

In this action the Court will sometimes exercise a summary jurisdiction to stay proceedings upon delivery up of the deeds or goods sought to be recovered, and upon payment of nominal damages and costs, and upon such other terms as the Court thinks proper to impose. (2 Chit. Pr. 13th ed. p. 1103.)

The County Courts have jurisdiction in actions of detinue where the value of the goods does not exceed £50. (*Taylor* v. *Addyman*, 13 C. B. 309.)

The right to costs subject to the powers over costs of the judge

2. In consequence of such detention the plaintiff was prevented from selling the said lease and his term and interest in the said house and premises to J. K., and lost the sum of £ ——, the price he would have received for the same, and incurred an expense of £—— in maintaining and repairing the said house.

Dilapidations (*a*).

---

or Court under the Jud. Acts, depends on the value of the goods. (*Leader* v. *Rhys*, 10 C. B. N. S. 369; 30 L. J. C. P. 345.)

Metropolitan police magistrates have a summary jurisdiction to order the delivery up of goods detained, and to adjudicate upon liens upon them, where the value of the goods is not greater than £15. (2 & 3 Vict. c. 71, s. 40.) A refusal by such magistrate to make an order for the delivery up of certain goods below £15 in value, is not a bar to a subsequent action for them. (*Dover* v. *Child*, 1 Ex. D. 172; 45 L. J. Ex. 462.)

Judgment for the plaintiff in an action of detinue does not, without satisfaction of the value of the chattel detained as found by the judgment, change the property in the detained chattel. (*Ex parte Drake*, 5 Ch. D. 866; and see "*Conversion*," *ante*, p. 380.)

(*a*) The incumbent of a benefice is bound to keep the buildings and fences belonging to his benefice in good and substantial repair, and also to restore and rebuild such buildings when necessary; though he is not bound to maintain or supply matters of ornament or luxury. (*Wise* v. *Metcalfe*, 10 B. & C. 299; see *Bird* v. *Relph*, 4 B. & A. 826; 2 A. & E. 773; and *Ross* v. *Adcock*, L. R. 3 C. P. 655; 37 L. J. C. P. 290.)

By the common law of England (which was extended to Wales by the 27 Hen. VIII. c. 26), the non-fulfilment of this obligation subjected the incumbent, if living, and if he was not living, his executors or administrators (having assets), to an action at the suit of his successor, or of the representatives of the successor, to recover the value of the dilapidations (whenever they may have happened) as damages. (*Ib.*; and see *Radcliffe* v. *D'Oyly*, 2 T. R. 630; *Mason* v. *Lambert*, 12 Q. B. 795; *Bunbury* v. *Hewson*, 3 Ex. 558; *Bryan* v. *Clay*, 1 E. & B. 38; *Gleaves* v. *Parfitt*, 7 C. B. N. S. 838; 29 L. J. C. P. 216.) But this common-law remedy by action for damages has been in the great majority of cases taken away by "The Ecclesiastical Dilapidations Act, 1871" (34 & 35 Vict. c. 43), which by s. 34 empowers the bishop of the diocese, after an inspection of the buildings and fences of a vacated benefice and a report by a surveyor, to make an order stating the repairs and their cost for which the late incumbent, his executors or administrators, is or are liable, and by s. 36 enacts that the sum stated in the order as the cost of the repairs shall be a debt due from the late incumbent, his executors or administrators, to the new incumbent, and shall be recoverable as such, while by s. 53 it is enacted that "no sum shall be recoverable for dilapidations in respect of any benefice becoming vacant after the commencement of this Act, and to which

DISTRESS (*a*).

this Act shall be applicable, unless the claim for such sum be founded on an order made under the provisions of this Act." Hence in nearly all cases an action for debt is now substituted for the former action for damages as the remedy in respect of dilapidations of the buildings or fences of the benefice. See *Wright* v. *Davies*, 1 C. P. D. 638; *ib.* 649, 651; 46 L. J. C. P. 41.

The provision of s. 29 of the Act with reference to the time within which the bishop is to direct the surveyor to inspect and report upon the buildings of a benefice after its avoidance, is directory only and not imperative, and the fact that such direction was not given by the bishop within the time mentioned by the Act, is no defence to an action brought to recover the amount of the costs of repairs specified in an order subsequently made by the bishop under s. 34. (*Caldow* v. *Pixell*, 2 C. P. D. 562; 46 L. J. C. P. 541; *Gleaves* v. *Marriner*, 1 Ex. D. 107.)

Where a benefice was under sequestration at the death of the incumbent, and the buildings were afterwards inspected by the surveyor, and an order made by the bishop stating the cost of the repairs, and declaring the executors or administrators of the incumbent liable for the amount, it was held that the sequestrator was not liable for the cost of the repairs. (*Jones* v. *Dangerfield*, 1 Ch. D. 438; 45 L. J. Ch. 161.)

An agreement between two incumbents, with the consent of the patrons of their livings and of the respective diocesans, to exchange the livings in their then state and condition, and without any payment being made for dilapidation on either side, was held a good defence to an action by one of such incumbents against the other for the amount of an order made by the bishop for the cost of repairs under the above Act, such agreement not being necessarily simoniacal or contrary to the policy of the Act. (*Wright* v. *Davies*, *supra*; and see also *Goldham* v. *Edwards*, 16 C. B. 437; 17 *ib.* 141; 24 L. J. C. P. 189; 25 *ib.* 223; *Downes* v. *Craig*, 9 M. & W. 166.)

(*a*) *Wrongful Distress.*]—In actions for *illegal* distresses, as for a distress where no rent is due, or after tender of the rent due, or for distraining things privileged from distress, the particular facts may be alleged in the statement of claim, showing that there was a distress, and setting forth the circumstances under which it was levied, and which made it *illegal*, or the wrongful acts merely which are complained of may be set forth. (*as in the forms given under the titles*, "*Trespass*," *post*; "*Conversion*," *ante*), or for the taking of the goods the plaintiff may proceed by replevin. (See "*Replevin*," *post*.)

In an action for an illegal distress, where the defendant is a trespasser *ab initio* as to the whole, the full value of the goods taken is recoverable as damages. (*Attack* v. *Bramwell*, 3 B. & S. 520; 32 L. J. Q. B. 146.) So in an action for taking things not distrainable. (*Keen* v. *Priest*, 4 H. & N. 236; 28 L. J. Ex. 157.) If it is desired to set off the amount of rent in arrear this can only be done by counterclaim. But if a portion only of the goods distrained are privileged, the landlord is a trespasser *ab initio* only as to such portion, and in such a case where the tenant paid the rent and costs, and the distress was withdrawn,

For Distraining and Selling where no Rent was due, for double value of the Goods sold, under 2 W. & M. sess. 1, c. 5, s. 5 (b).

1. The plaintiff was tenant to the defendant of a messuage at —— at a certain rent payable by the plaintiff to the defendant, and the defendant on the —— of ——, 18—, wrongfully distrained in the said messuage divers goods of the plaintiff as a distress for pretended

---

it was held that only the actual damage sustained by taking the particular goods privileged could be recovered, and not the whole amount paid. (*Harvey* v. *Pocock*, 11 M. & W. 740.)

An action for an *excessive* distress lies under the Statute of Marlbridge, and the plaintiff cannot maintain trespass or conversion.

Actions for *irregular* distresses lie only in respect of the special damage occasioned by irregularities in conducting distresses; and the statement of claim must be framed upon the particular description of irregularity complained of. See *post*, p. 412.

In order to create a distress it is not necessary that there should be an actual seizure; it is enough if the landlord or his agent takes effectual means to prevent the removal of the article from the premises, on the ground of rent being in arrear, as by declaring that it shall not be removed until the rent is paid, and prohibiting removal. (*Cramer* v. *Mott*, L. R. 5. Q. B. 357; 39 L. J. Q. B. 172.)

The metropolitan police magistrates have a summary jurisdiction in cases of unlawful, irregular, and excessive distresses, where the tenancy is by the week or month, or the rent does not exceed £15 a year, to order a return of the distress on payment of the rent, or, if it has been sold, a payment of the value, deducting the rent (2 & 3 Vict. c. 71, s. 39).

Justices have a summary jurisdiction to order a restoration of goods of lodgers distrained contrary to the Lodgers' Goods Protection Act, 1871 (34 & 35 Vict. c. 79, s. 2). (See *post*, p. 409.)

(*b*) The statute 2 W. & M. sess. 1, c. 5, which enables, though it does not compel the sale of goods distrained for rent (*Hudd* v. *Ravenor*, 2 B. & B. 662; 5 Moore, 542; *Philpott* v. *Lehain*, 35 L. T. 855), by sec. 5, enacts, "that in case any such distress and sale as aforesaid shall be made by virtue or colour of this present Act for rent pretended to be arrear or due, where in truth no rent is arrear or due to the person or persons distraining, or to him or them in whose name or names, or right, such distress shall be taken as aforesaid, that then the owner of such goods or chattels distrained and sold as aforesaid, his executors or administrators, shall and may, by action of trespass, or upon the case, to be brought against the person or persons so distraining, any or either of them, his or their executors or administrators, recover double of the value of the goods or chattels so distrained and sold, together with full costs of suit."

Upon the trial of an action brought upon this section the jury ought to be directed, if they find for the plaintiff, to give damages to double the amount of the value of the goods. (*Masters* v. *Fariss*, 1 C. B. 715.)

The costs are now regulated by Jud. Act, 1875, O. LV.

arrears of the said rent, and on the —— of ——, 18—, wrongfully sold the said goods as such distress.

2. At the time of the making of the said distress and of the said sale as aforesaid, no rent was due or in arrear for or in respect of the said messuage.

3. The value of the goods so distrained is £——.

4. By reason of the premises the plaintiff is entitled to recover from the defendant, by virtue of the statute in such case made and provided, double of the value of the said goods so distrained and sold as aforesaid.

For Distraining twice for the same Rent (*c*).

1. The plaintiff was tenant to the defendant of a house No. 5, —— Street, ——, at a yearly rent of £—— payable half-yearly by equal payments by the plaintiff to the defendant on the 24th of June and the 25th of December in each year.

2. The defendant, on the —— of ——, 18—, distrained divers goods of the plaintiff in the said house as a distress for [one half year's] arrears of the said rent.

3. At the time of making the said distress there were in the said house goods of the plaintiff liable to the said distress of more than sufficient value to have satisfied the said arrears and the charges of a distress for the

---

(*c*) Trespass or conversion will lie for the wrongful taking or conversion under the second distress. (*Dawson* v. *Cropp*, 1 C. B. 961; and see *Bagge* v. *Mawby*, 8 Ex. 641; 22 L. J. Ex. 236.)

If there has been some mistake as to the value of the goods, and the landlord fairly supposed the distress to be of the proper value at the time of levying the first distress, and he afterwards finds it to be insufficient, he may then distrain for the remainder; or if the tenant has done anything equivalent to saying "forbear to distrain now and postpone your distress to some other time," the landlord may distrain a second time. But, if there is fair opportunity, and there is no legal cause why he should not work out the payment of the rent by the first distress, his duty is to work it out by the first distress, and he cannot distrain again. (*Bagge* v. *Mawby*, *supra*.) So where by misconduct the tenant prevents the first distress being realised, a second may lawfully be made. (*Lee* v. *Cooke*, 2 H. & N. 584; 3 H. & N. 203; 27 L. J. Ex. 337.)

After a distress, and before the sale of the goods distrained, no action can, whether the distress is sufficient or not, be maintained for any rent distrained for (*Lehain* v. *Philpott*, L. R. 10 Ex. 242; 44 L. J. Ex. 225), though after the sale an action will lie for any balance remaining due after such sale, giving credit for the proceeds of such sale. (*Philpott* v. *Lehain*, 35 L. T. 855.)

same and of the appraisement and sale thereof, and which the defendant could then have distrained to satisfy the same, of which the defendant then had notice.

4. The defendant afterwards, on the —— of ——, 18—, wrongfully made a second distress on certain goods of the plaintiff in the said house for the same arrears of rent for which the first mentioned distress was made as above stated, and for the charges of such second distress.

For Distraining Beasts of the Plough, under 51 Hen. III. c. 4 (d).

1. The plaintiff was tenant to the defendant of land at —— at a certain rent payable by the plaintiff to the defendant.

(*d*) The statute 51 Hen. III., st. 4, enacts that no man shall be distrained by his beasts that gain his land, nor by his sheep, so long as the distrainer can find other chattels sufficient for the demand. (2 Inst. 132.) As to what are such beasts, see *Keen* v. *Priest*, 4 H. & N. 236; 28 L. J. Ex. 157.

The plaintiff may also in this case sue as for a trespass or conversion, or replevy the goods unlawfully taken. (*Nargett* v. *Nias*, 1 E. & E. 439; 28 L. J. Q. B. 143; *Davies* v. *Aston*, 1 C. B. 746.) Similar to this is the action for distraining implements of trade and other things privileged from distress, whether absolutely or conditionally. (*Ib.*; *Harvey* v. *Pocock*, 11 M. & W. 740.)

Fixtures are absolutely privileged from distress, and the removal of fixtures under a distress amounts to a conversion. (*Dalton* v. *Whittem*, 3 Q. B. 961; *Darby* v. *Harris*, 1 Q. B. 895; *Turner* v. *Cameron*, L. R. 5 Q. B. 306; 39 L. J. Q. B. 125.)

A distrainer is not liable for claiming to take fixtures unless he actually removes them. (*Beck* v. *Denbigh*, 29 L. J. Ch. 273.)

As to what things are privileged as fixtures, see *Duck* v. *Braddyll*, 13 Price, 455; *Hellawell* v. *Eastwood*, 6 Ex. 295; and see *Holland* v. *Hodgson*, L. R. 7 C. P. 328, 337; 41 L. J. C. P. 146.

Growing crops are distrainable by statute 11 Geo. II., c. 19, s. 8, and may be cut when ripe, and appraised and sold. See *Peacock* v. *Purvis*, 2 B. & B. 362; *Owen* v. *Legh*, 3 B. & Ald. 470.

Trees and shrubs growing in a nursery ground are not distrainable. (*Clark* v. *Gaskarth*, 8 Taunt. 431; 2 B. Mowe, 491.)

The provisions of 11 Geo. II., c. 19, s. 8, apply only to distresses made by the lessor or landlord. (*Miller* v. *Green*, 2 C. & J. 142.)

Commodities of a perishable nature, and which cannot be restored in the same state as that in which they were taken, as meat, milk, fruit, &c., cannot be distrained. (*Morley* v. *Pincombe*, 2 Ex. 101.) Formerly corn and hay were thus privileged, but they have been made distrainable by 2 W. & M. c. 5, s. 3.

Implements of trade or husbandry are privileged from distress for rent conditionally, that is to say, if other sufficient distress can be

2. The defendant, on the —— of ——, 18—, wrongfully distrained for £—— arrears of the said rent upon the said land the beasts of the plough of the plaintiff wherewith the plaintiff tilled the said land, namely, upon three horses.

---

found. (*Gorton* v. *Falkner*, 4 T. R. 565; *Simpson* v. *Hartopp*, Willes, 512; 1 Sm. L. C. notes to 7th ed., 439, 445; *Nargett* v. *Nias*, *supra.*)

Goods necessarily delivered to a person exercising a trade for the purpose of having them dealt with in the way of his trade are absolutely privileged whilst on the premises where such trade is carried on. (Co. Lit. 47 *a*; *Simpson* v. *Hartopp*, *supra*; *Wood* v. *Clarke*, 1 C. & J. 484; *Lyons* v. *Elliott*, 1 Q. B. D. 210; 45 L. J. Q. B. 159.) As in the following cases:—Goods sent to an auctioneer, factor or commission agent, to his premises to be sold (*Adams* v. *Grane*, 1 C. & M. 380; *Findon* v. *M'Laren*, 6 Q. B. 891; *Thompson* v. *Mashiter*, 1 Bing. 283; *Lyons* v. *Elliott*, *supra*); materials delivered to a manufacturer to be worked up (*Gibson* v. *Ireson*, 3 Q. B. 39; *Read* v. *Buxley*, Cro. Eliz. 596; *Lyons* v. *Elliott*, *supra*); an animal sent to a butcher to be slaughtered (*Brown* v. *Shevill*, 2 A. & E. 138); goods pledged with a pawnbroker (*Swire* v. *Leach*, 18 C. B. N. S. 479; 34 L. J. C. P. 150); goods of guests at a common inn, and goods in a market or fair (see *per* Parke, B., *Muspratt* v. *Gregory*, 1 M. & W. 633, 654; *Lyons* v. *Elliott*, *supra*); goods stored at a furniture depository to be taken care of (*Miles* v. *Furber*, L. R. 8 Q. B. 77; 42 L. J. Q. B. 41); goods in the hands of a carrier, or being taken to market,[1] are privileged absolutely, even when not on the premises of the carrier or person taking them to market. (*Lyons* v. *Elliott*, *supra*; Co. Litt. 47 *a*; *Gisbourne* v. *Hurst*, 1 Salk. 249.)

Where a horse was sent to an inn, and the innkeeper put it into a stable which had been temporarily lent to him, at a distance from the inn, it was held that the horse was not privileged from distress by the landlord of the stable, on the ground that the privilege did not extend beyond the privileged premises. (*Crosier* v. *Tomkinson*, Barnes, 472; 2 Ld. Ken. 439; *Lyons* v. *Elliott*, *supra.*)

The goods are not privileged in such cases as the following:—A boat sent by the buyers of goods to the manufacturers' to carry away the goods bought (*Muspratt* v. *Gregory*, 1 M. & W. 633; 3 *ib.* 677); brewers' casks sent to a public-house and left until the beer is consumed (*Joule* v. *Jackson*, 7 M. & W. 450); goods sent to an auctioneer to be sold at a sale held, not on the auctioneer's premises, but at a private house, whilst at such private house. (*Lyons* v. *Elliott*, 1 Q. B. D. 210; 45 L. J. Q. B. 159.)

It has been held that horses and carriages standing at livery are not privileged. (*Parsons* v. *Gingell*, 4 C. B. 545; see as to this, *Swire* v. *Leach*, *supra.*)

Things in actual use of a person are privileged whilst they are being used, as a horse on which a person is riding (*Storey* v. *Robinson*, 6 T. R. 138); a loom with which a person is weaving. (*Simpson* v. *Hartopp*, Willes, 512; 1 Sm. L. C. 7th ed., p. 439.)

See further as to what things are privileged from distress, Co. Lit. 47 a; notes to *Simpson* v. *Hartopp*, *supra*; Bullen on Distress, 89—104; Roscoe's N. P. Ev., 14th ed. p. 835.

3. There were then upon the said land other goods of the plaintiff, not being beasts of the plough or sheep, liable to the said distress, and sufficient to satisfy the said arrears and the charges of a distress for the same, and of the appraisement and sale thereof, and which the defendant might then have distrained for the said arrears and charges, whereof the defendant then had notice, and the said distress was contrary to the statute in such case made and provided.

By section 1 of 34 & 35 Vict. c. 79, if a superior landlord distrains on the goods of a lodger for arrears of rent due to him by his immediate tenant, such lodger may serve the superior landlord, or the person employed by him to distrain, with a declaration in writing setting forth that such immediate tenant has no interest in the goods distrained, or threatened to be distrained upon, and that they are the property, or in the lawful possession of such lodger; and also setting forth whether any and what rent is due, and for what period, from such lodger to his immediate landlord, and to such declaration a correct inventory subscribed by the lodger is to be annexed of the goods referred to in the declaration, and such lodger may pay the superior landlord, or the person employed by him to distrain, the rent, if any, so due as aforesaid, or so much thereof as shall be sufficient to discharge the superior landlord's claim.

Section 2 provides that if, after service of such declaration and inventory, and after payment or tender by the lodger to the superior landlord, or person employed to distrain, of the said rent, if any, which by the preceding section such lodger is authorised to pay, the superior landlord or bailiff, or other person employed by him, shall levy, or proceed with a distress, on the lodger's goods, he shall be deemed guilty of an illegal distress and liable to an action at the suit of the lodger, or the lodger may apply to a justice of the peace for an order for the restoration of the goods distrained.

As to who is a lodger under this Act, see *Phillips* v. *Henson*, 3 C. P. D. 26; 47 L. J. C. P. 273.

By "The Railway Rolling Stock Protection Act, 1872," sec. 3 (35 & 36 Vict. c. 50), railway rolling stock being in "a work" is not liable to distress for rent payable by a tenant of the work, if such rolling stock is not the property of the tenant, and has upon it a distinguishing metal plate affixed to a conspicuous part thereof, or a distinguishing brand or other mark conspicuously impressed or made thereon, sufficiently indicating the actual owner thereof.

By section 5, the protection from distress is not to extend to the interest which such tenant may have in the rolling stock.

By section 4, where rolling stock is distrained contrary to the Act, power is given to justices to make a summary order for restoration of the rolling stock or payment of its value.

The word "work" in the above Act, by section 2 thereof, includes any colliery, quarry, mine, manufactory, warehouse, wharf, pier or jetty, in or on which is any railway siding.

This statute protects railway companies from the risk to which their wagons would be otherwise exposed of distress upon sidings in private works.

For Refusing to Restore Goods Distrained on Tender of the Rent and Charges before Impounding (*e*).

1. The plaintiff was tenant to the defendant of a house [*or* land] situate at ——, at a rent of £—— a year, payable upon the usual quarter days, by equal quarterly instalments [*or as the case may be*] by the plaintiff to the defendant.

2. The defendant on the —— of ——, 18—, distrained divers goods of the plaintiff in the said house (*or* on the said land) as a distress for £——, being —— quarters' arrears of the said rent.

3. Afterwards, on the —— of ——, 18—, whilst the defendant was in possession of the said goods under such distress, and before the same were impounded, the plaintiff tendered to the defendant in satisfaction and discharge of the said arrears and of the charges of the said distress the sum of £——, and requested the defendant to redeliver to the plaintiff his said goods.

(*e*) Tender before the distress makes the distress wrongful; tender after the distress and before impounding makes the detainer and not the taking wrongful; tender after the impounding makes neither the taking nor the detainer wrongful, for then it comes too late. (*Per* Lord Coke in *Six Carpenters' case*, 8 Co. Rep. 147 *a*; cited by Tindal, C. J. in *Gulliver* v. *Cosens*, 1 C. B. 788, 795; *West* v. *Nibbs*, 4 C. B. 172; *Singleton* v. *Williamson*, 7 H. & N. 747; 31 L. J. Ex. 287.) Tender may be made at any time before the impounding is complete (see *Thomas* v. *Harries*, 1 M. & G. 695), which may be without removal of the goods (*Ib.*), as by mere agreement with the party distrained upon to consider the goods as impounded. (*Washborn* v. *Black*, 11 East, 405 n. *a*; *Tennant* v. *Field*, 8 E. & B. 336.) Tender may be made to a bailiff authorized to make a distress, but not to a man put in by the bailiff to keep possession. (*Boulton* v. *Reynolds*, 29 L. J. Q. B. 11.) Tender before actual distress need not include the costs incurred, although the warrant to distrain has been delivered for execution. (*Bennett* v. *Bayes*, 5 H. & N. 391; 29 L. J. Ex. 224.)

Trespass, detinue, trover, or replevin will lie for a wrongful distress made after tender. See *Branscomb* v. *Bridges*, 1 B. & C. 145; *Holland* v. *Bird*, 10 Bing. 15. Detinue or replevin will lie for a wrongful detainer after tender made before impounding (*Gulliver* v. *Cosens*, 1 C. B. 788; *Evans* v. *Elliott*, 5 A. & E. 142); and trespass or trover also, if the goods have been afterwards removed by the distrainer. (*Vertue* v. *Beasley*, 1 M. & Rob. 21.) Trover or detinue will lie, if the landlord refuses to deliver the goods after tender and acceptance of the rent in arrear and the expenses of the distress after impounding. (*West* v. *Nibbs*, 4 C. B. 172.)

An action may be maintained for selling after a tender of the rent made within the five days allowed by the statute 2 W. & M. sess. 1, c. 5, s. 2, although the tender is made after impounding. (*Johnson* v. *Upham*, 28 L. J. Q. B. 252.)

4. The said sum of £—— was equal to the amount of the said arrears and charges, and sufficient to satisfy and discharge the same.

5. The defendant refused to accept and did not accept the said sum so tendered as aforesaid, and refused to redeliver and did not redeliver to the plaintiff his said goods, and wrongfully impounded [and afterwards sold] the said goods.

For Taking an Excessive Distress under the Statute of Marlbridge, 52 Hen. III. c. 4 (f).

1 and 2. [*As in form next above.*]

3. The said goods of the plaintiff so distrained were of much greater value than the amount of the said arrears

---

(*f*) *Excessive distress.*]—This action lies upon the Statute of Marlbridge, 52 Hen. III. c. 4, which enacts that "distresses shall be reasonable, and not too great." (See 2 Inst. 107.) If any rent be due, no action will lie for a distress merely because it is made under a claim of more than is due, unless it be followed by some special damage. (*Leyland* v. *Tancred,* 16 Q. B. 669; *Lucas* v. *Tarleton,* 3 H. & N. 116; 27 L. J. Ex. 246; *Stevenson* v. *Newnham,* 13 C. B. 285; *Glynn* v. *Thomas,* 11 Ex. 870; 25 L. J. Ex. 125; *French* v. *Phillips,* 1 H & N. 564; 26 L. J. Ex. 82.) But if more goods are taken than are reasonably sufficient to cover the arrears of rent and expenses, an action will lie for an excessive distress. In this case trespass or trover will not lie. (*Lynn* v. *Moody,* 2 Str. 851; *Hutchins* v. *Chambers,* 1 Burr. 590; *Whitworth* v. *Smith,* 5 C. & P. 250.)

If a larger sum than is due for arrears is paid under a distress, the excess cannot be recovered back in an action for money received. (*Knibbs* v. *Hall,* 1 Esp. 84; *Glynn* v. *Thomas,* 11 Ex. 870; 25 L. J. Ex. 125; and see "*Money Received,*" *ante,* p. 280.)

The mere distraining of the goods to an excessive value above the rent due, without sale or removal, is sufficient to support this action. (*Sells* v. *Hoare,* 1 Bing. 401; *Swann* v. *Earl of Falmouth,* 8 B. & C. 456; and see *Bayliss* v. *Fisher,* 7 Bing. 153; *Chandler* v. *Doulton,* 3 H. & C. 553; 34 L. J. Ex. 89.) The action lies for the excessive taking of things distrainable by statute, as growing crops, as well as things distrainable at common law. (*Piggott* v. *Birtles,* 1 M. & W. 441, 449.) The excess of the value of the goods distrained above the arrears of rent due must be unreasonably great. The landlord is not bound to calculate very nicely the value of property seized; but he must take care that some proportion is kept between that and the sum for which he is entitled to take it. (*Per* Bailey, J., *Willoughby* v. *Backhouse,* 2 B. & C. 821, 823; *Roden* v. *Eyton,* 6 C. B. 427.) The landlord is not bound by the amount of rent claimed at the time of distraining; but the plaintiff must show an excess above the amount really due. See *Tancred* v. *Leyland,* 16 Q. B. 669; *Phillips* v. *Whitsed,* 29 L. J. Q. B. 164.

The test of value of the goods seized is what they would have sold

and of the charges of the said distress and of the appraisement and sale thereof.

4. Part of the said goods was then of sufficient value to have satisfied the said arrears and charges, and might then have been distrained by the defendant for the same.

5. The defendant, in distraining as above stated, made an excessive and unreasonable distress for the said arrears, contrary to the statute in such case made and provided.

For Selling without Five Days' Notice of the Distress, under 2 W. & M. sess. 1, c. 5, s. 2 (g).

1 and 2. [*As in form next but one above.*]

3. The defendant on the —— of ——, 18—, sold the said goods towards satisfaction of the said arrears and

---

for at a broker's sale. (*Wells* v. *Moody*, 7 C. & P. 59.) An actual sale made under the distress, though not proved to be unfair, is not a conclusive test of value; and an action may be maintained for an excessive distress, if the excess be proved, though at the sale the goods did not in fact realize the rent due. (*Smith* v. *Ashforth*, 29 L. J. Ex. 259.) Where the goods have been appraised by brokers under the statute 2 W. & M. c. 5, s. 2, the amount of the appraisement is *primâ facie* evidence of their value. (*Walter* v. *Rumbal*, 1 Ld. Raym. 53.)

The measure of damages in this action, if the goods are removed and impounded off the land, is the loss of the use and enjoyment of the surplus of the goods, and if the goods are not restored before action, the plaintiff may claim the full value of the surplus. (*Piggott* v. *Birtles*, 1 M. & W. 441, 448.) The plaintiff may recover substantial damages, although the goods are not removed or sold, and the plaintiff retains the use of them while under the distress (*Bayliss* v. *Fisher*, 7 Bing. 153); and the plaintiff upon proof of an excessive distress is entitled to nominal damages, though he cannot prove substantial damages. (*Chandler* v. *Doulton*, 3 H. & C. 553; 34 L. J. Ex. 89.) Upon an excessive distress of growing crops, the measure of damages was held to be the compensation for the additional expense of the distress, and for the loss of ownership and power of disposition, or, if the tenant replevied, for the additional expense and inconvenience of replevying to a larger amount. (*Piggott* v. *Birtles*, 1 M. & W. 441.)

(*g*) *Irregular distresses.*]—By the common law goods distrained for rent could not be sold, but could only be detained as a pledge for enforcing payment of the rent. A power of selling the goods was given by the statute 2 W. & M. sess. 1, c. 5, subject to certain restrictions and formalities which, so far as they are still in force, must be strictly complied with. tels s2 of that statute it was enacted "that where any goods or chatleasehall be distrained for any rent reserved and due upon any demise, lease, or contract whatsoever, and the tenant or owner of the goods so distrained shall not within five days next after such distress taken, and notice thereof (with the cause of such taking) left at

of the charges of such distress and of the appraisement and sale of the said goods, without notice of the said distress, and of the cause of taking the same having been given to the plaintiff or left on the said premises five

---

the chief mansion, house, or other most notorious place on the premises charged with the rent distrained for, replevy the same, *with sufficient security to be given to the sheriff according to law*, that then in such case, after such distress and notice as aforesaid, and expiration of the said five days, the person distraining shall and may, *with the sheriff or under-sheriff of the county, or with the constable of the hundred, parish, or place where such distress shall be taken (who are hereby required to be aiding and assisting therein)*, cause the goods and chattels so distrained to be appraised by two *sworn* appraisers (*whom such sheriff, under-sheriff, or constable are hereby empowered to swear*), to appraise the same truly, according to the best of their understandings; and after such appraisement shall and may lawfully sell the goods and chattels so distrained for the best price can be gotten for the same, towards satisfaction of the rent for which the said goods and chattels shall be distrained, and of the charges of such distress, appraisement and sale, *leaving the overplus (if any) in the hands of the said sheriff, under-sheriff, or constable, for the owner's use*."

By sec. 13 of 35 & 36 Vict. c. 92, so much of the above Act as requires any sheriff or under-sheriff, or constable, to be aiding or assisting at any distress for rent, or to swear any appraiser thereof, is repealed, and no oath, it is enacted, shall be required from appraisers. This statute does not, in express words, repeal the provision as to leaving the overplus in the hands of the sheriff, but it would seem to do so by necessary implication, the sheriff not being required to aid or assist at such distresses. And by sec. 63 of 19 & 20 Vict. c. 108, the powers and responsibilities of the sheriff with respect to replevin bonds and replevins are put an end to, and the registrar of the County Court of the District in which the distress is taken is empowered to approve of replevin bonds, &c., see "*Replevin*," *post*, p. 510.

Various causes of action frequently arise from irregularities committed by persons availing themselves of the 2 W. & M. sess. 1, c. 5. In suing upon such causes of action the facts must be stated, as in the examples of pleadings above given.

At common law an irregularity in the conduct or treatment of a distress made the party distraining a trespasser *ab initio*, and liable to be sued as such. (*Six Carpenters' Case*, 8 Co. 146, *a*; 1 Smith, L. C. 8th ed. 143.) This doctrine occasioned great hardship in cases of distress for rent, particularly after the above statute of W. & M. had allowed the sale of the distress subject to the formalities mentioned above; and consequently the rule was altered in these cases by the 11 Geo. II. c. 19, s. 19, which enacted, that where any distress shall be made for any kind of rent justly due, and any irregularity or unlawful act shall be afterwards done by the party distraining or his agent, the distress itself shall not be deemed to be unlawful nor the party making it be therefore deemed a trespasser *ab initio*; but the party aggrieved by such unlawful act or irregularity shall or may recover full satisfaction for the special damages sustained thereby

days before sale of the said goods, contrary to the statute in such case made and provided.

4. The plaintiff, in consequence of the matters above complained of, [*state special damage*].

For Selling the Distress without Appraisement, under 2 W. & M. sess. 1, c. 5, s. 2 (g).

1 and 2. [*As in preceding forms.*]

3. The defendant afterwards sold the said goods to-

---

and no more. In respect of distresses other than for rent, the common law doctrine still prevails.

An action for any irregularity in dealing with a distress cannot be maintained without proof of actual damage, on failure of which the plaintiff is not entitled to a verdict for even nominal damages, but the defendant is entitled to the verdict (*Proudlove* v. *Twemlow*, 1 C. & M. 326; *Rogers* v. *Parker*, 18 C. B. 112; 25 L. J. C. P. 220; *Lucas* v. *Tarleton*, 3 H. & N. 116; 27 L. J. Ex. 246); therefore it would seem advisable to set forth in the statement of claim the damage sustained. The landlord is liable for the irregularities committed by his broker in conducting the distress; but he is not, in general, liable for acts wholly unlawful committed by the broker, as where the latter distrains on the wrong premises, or on goods privileged from distress, as fixtures, unless he expressly sanctioned such acts by prior authority or subsequent assent after notice. (*Lewis* v. *Reed*, 13 M. & W. 834; *Gauntlett* v. *King*, 3 C. B. N. S. 59; *Haseler* v. *Lemoyne*, 5 C. B. N. S. 530; 28 L. J. C. P. 103.) The person who authorises the broker is liable, although he is only an agent of the landlord. (*Bennett* v. *Bayes*, 5 H. & N. 391; 29 L. J. Ex. 224.)

The notice required by the statute must be in writing. (*Wilson* v. *Nightingale*, 8 Q. B. 1034.) The damages for selling without appraisement are the real value of the goods sold *minus* the rent. (*Knight* v. *Egerton*, 7 Ex. 407, 408.)

Where the distrainer abuses a distress, as by working it, it is considered as no longer impounded or in the custody of the law, and the owner may interfere to prevent the working of the distress without being guilty of a pound-breach or rescue. (*Smith* v. *Wright*, 6 H. & N. 821; 30 L. J. Ex. 313; and see for forms under the former system of declarations upon this cause of action, *Wilder* v. *Speer*, 8 A. & E. 547; *Bignell* v. *Clark*, 5 H. & N. 485; 29 L. J. Ex. 257.)

It would seem that an action against the landlord for the overplus is a proper mode of disputing the propriety of the charges made. See *Lyon* v. *Tomkies*, 1 M. & W. 603; Roscoe's N. P. Ev. 14th ed. p. 831, and see 35 & 36 Vict. c. 92, above cited.

Where goods have been redeemed, and excessive charges have been paid to the broker in order to redeem them, the excess may be recovered back from him under a count for money received to the plaintiff's use. (*Hills* v. *Street*, 5 Bing. 37.) Where the rent distrained for does not exceed £20, the charges are limited by 57 Geo. III. c. 93; where the rent exceeds that sum the charges must be reasonable. (*Lyon* v. *Tomkies*, 1 M. & W. 603.)

wards satisfaction of the said arrears and of the charges of such distress and of the sale of the said goods, without causing the same to be appraised by two appraisers, contrary to the statute in such case made and provided.

4. The plaintiff in consequence [*state special damage*].

For not Selling for the Best Price, under 2 *W. & M. sess.* 1, *c.* 5, *s.* 2 (*h*).

1 and 2. [*As in preceding forms.*]

3. The defendant afterwards sold the said goods towards satisfaction of the said arrears and of the charges of such distress and of the appraisement and sale of the said goods.

4. The defendant did not sell the said goods for the best price that could be gotten for the said goods, contrary to the statute in such case made and provided.

5. The plaintiff in consequence [*state special damage, as for instance,* lost a large sum of money he would have otherwise received as the balance after satisfaction of the said arrears and charges].

See for a like Form, Hawkins v. *Walrond,* 35 L. T. 210; 1 C. P. D. 280.

For Pound-breach, Claiming Treble Damages, under 2 *W. & M. sess.* 1, *c.* 5, *s.* 4 (*i*).

1 and 2. [*As in preceding forms.*]

3. Afterwards, on the —— of ——, 18—, the plaintiff

(*h*) A sale to the landlord himself at the appraised price is not a sale within the statute, and if made without the consent of the owner it does not change the property in the goods. (*King* v. *England,* 4 B. & S. 782; 33 L. J. Q. B. 145.)

Where a landlord sells hay or other goods of his tenant under a distress for rent, he cannot lawfully impose upon the purchaser a stipulation that it, or they, are to be consumed or used only on the land demised, even if the tenant is bound to him by covenant so to consume or use such hay or other goods, the statute requiring the best price to be gotten. (*Hawkins* v. *Walrond,* 1 C. P. D. 280; 45 L. J. C. P. 772.)

(*i*) By 11 Geo. II. c. 19, s. 10, any distress for any rent may now be impounded or otherwise secured in such place or on such part of the

impounded and secured the said goods so distrained, as above stated, on the part of the said premises chargeable with the said rent which was most fit and convenient for the impounding and securing such distress.

4. The defendant on the —— of ——, 18—, whilst the said goods were so impounded and secured, as above stated, broke the said pound, and seized and carried away the said goods so distrained for rent as aforesaid, contrary to the statute in such case made and provided.

5. The plaintiff, in consequence, has been delayed in recovering the said arrears of rent, and deprived of the means of obtaining satisfaction of the said rent, and of the costs and charges of the said distress, and is likely to lose the same.

6. The plaintiff has thereby sustained damages to the amount of £——.

The plaintiff claims:—

(1). £——, treble the amount of the said damages.

(2). Such further or other relief, &c.

Executors (*a*).

---

premises chargeable with the rent, as shall be most fit and convenient for such impounding and securing. Goods when impounded are not regarded as in the possession of the landlord, but are treated as in *custodia legis*. (See *R.* v. *Cotton*, Parker, 121; *Cotsworth* v. *Bettison*, 1 Salk. 247; 1 Ld. Raym. 105.) The proper remedy for the landlord to pursue in case of any wrongful interference with the goods impounded is not conversion or trespass, but action for pound-breach or rescue founded upon the statute 2 W. & M. sess. 1, c. 5, in which action treble damages are recoverable by s. 4 of that statute. (*Moneux* v. *Goreham*, 2 Sel. N. P. 10th ed. 1351; *Turner* v. *Ford*, 15 M. & W. 212. See further Bullen on Distress.)

For forms of declarations under the former system of pleading, see *Parrett Navigation Co.* v. *Stower*, 6 M. & W. 564; *Smith* v. *Wright*, 6 H. & N. 821; 30 L. J. Ex. 313.

(*a*) *Actions by and against executors and administrators.*]—With respect to actions for wrongs independent of contract done either to or by a deceased person in his lifetime, the rule of the common law was, *actio personalis moritur cum personâ*; and the executor could neither sue nor be sued.

This rule still remains in force with respect to injuries to the person; as, assault, battery, false imprisonment, libel, and slander: but by 9 and 10 Vict. c. 93 (Lord Campbell's Act), with respect to injuries to the person from the wrongful act or default of another resulting in death, an action is given to the executor or administrator of the deceased for the benefit of the relatives of the deceased. See *post*, p. 418.

For injuries to the personal estate of the testator an action was given to the executor by the statute 4 Edw. III. c. 7, which was afterwards extended to executors of executors by 25 Edw. III. c. 5, and to administrators upon their institution under 31 Edw. III. c. 11. Upon the construction of this statute an executor now has the same action for any injury done to the personal estate of the testator in his lifetime, whereby it has become less beneficial to the executor, as the testator himself might have had (*Twycross* v. *Grant*, 4 C. P. D. 40 ; 48 L. J. C. P. 1.)

For injuries to the real estate of the deceased in his lifetime an action is given to the executor by the statute 3 & 4 Will. IV. c. 42. By s. 2, after reciting that no remedy is provided by law for injuries to the real estate of any person deceased committed in his lifetime, it is enacted that an action may be maintained by the executors or administrators of any person deceased, for any injury to the real estate of such person, committed in his lifetime, for which an action might have been maintained by such person, so as such injury shall have been committed within six calendar months before the death of such deceased person, and provided such action shall be brought within one year after the death of such person, and the damages, when recovered, shall be part of the personal estate of such person.

And with respect to injuries done by a person deceased in his lifetime to another in respect of his property real or personal, the last mentioned statute, by s. 2, after reciting that no remedy is provided by law for such injuries, enacts that an action may be maintained against the executors or administrators of any person deceased, for any wrong committed by him in his lifetime to another, in respect of his property, real or personal, so as such injury shall have been committed within six calendar months before such person's death, and so as such action shall be brought within six calendar months after such executors or administrators shall have taken upon themselves the administration of the estate and effects of such person ; and the damages to be recovered in such action shall be payable in like order of administration as the simple contract debts of such person. See *Woodhouse* v. *Walker*, 5 Q. B. D. 404 ; 49 L. J. Q. B. 609.

In actions brought under these sections the statement of claim should show that the facts bring the case within these provisions. This may be done either incidentally in describing the plaintiff or defendant, and in stating the injury, or by a distinct allegation. Such allegation where the executor is suing may be as follows :— "The injury herein complained of was committed within six calendar months before the death of the said *C. D.*, and this action was brought within one year after his death." Where the action is brought against the executor the allegation may be thus :—"The injury herein complained of was committed within six calendar months before the death of the said *G. H.*, and this action was brought within six calendar months after the defendant took upon himself the administration of the estate and effects of the said *G. H.*" No such allegation is required in an action brought under the above statutes of Edw. III.

See further as to actions by and against executors for wrongs, Wms. Exs. 8th ed. pp. 796, 884, 1735.

Statement of Claim against Carriers by the Executor or Administrator of a Passenger killed by the Negligence of the Defendants, under 9 & 10 Vict. c. 93 (b).

1. The plaintiff is the executor of the last will and testament of C. D., deceased [*or* is the administrator of

---

(*b*) By the 9 & 10 Vict. c. 93 (Lord Campbell's Act), s. 1, it is enacted, "that whensoever the death of a person shall be caused by wrongful act, neglect, or default, and the act, neglect, or default is such as would (if death had not ensued) have entitled the party injured to maintain an action and recover damages in respect thereof, then and in every such case the person who would have been liable if death had not ensued shall be liable to an action for damages, notwithstanding the death of the person injured, and although the death shall have been caused under such circumstances as amount in law to felony." By s. 2, it is enacted, "that every such action shall be for the benefit of the wife, husband, parent, and child of the person whose death shall have been so caused, and shall be brought by and in the name of the executor or administrator of the person deceased; and in every such action the jury may give such damages as they may think proportioned to the injury resulting from such death to the parties respectively for whom and for whose benefit such action shall be brought; and the amount so recovered, after deducting the costs not recovered from the defendant, shall be divided amongst the before-mentioned parties in such shares as the jury by their verdict shall find and direct." By s. 3, it is provided "that not more than one action shall lie for and in respect of the same subject-matter of complaint; and that every such action shall be commenced within twelve calendar months after the death of such deceased person." By s. 5, the word "person" shall apply to bodies politic and corporate; and the word "parent" shall include father and mother, and grandfather and grandmother, and stepfather and stepmother; and the word "child" shall include son and daughter, and grandson and granddaughter, and stepson and stepdaughter.

The 27 & 28 Vict. c. 95, amending the above Act, enacts by s. 1, that "if, and so often as it shall happen at any time or times hereafter, in any of the cases intended and provided for by the said Act, that there shall be no executor or administrator of the person deceased, or that, there being such executor or administrator, no such action as in the said Act mentioned shall within six calendar months after the death of such deceased person as therein mentioned have been brought by and in the name of his or her executor or administrator, then and in every such case such action may be brought by and in the name or names of all or any of the persons (if more than one) for whose benefit such action would have been, if it had been brought by and in the name of such executor or administrator; and every action so to be brought shall be for the benefit of the same person or persons, and shall be subject to the same regulations and procedure as nearly as may be, as if it were brought by and in the name of such executor or administrator."

And by s. 2, after reciting the 2nd section of the former Act (*supra*), it is enacted and declared "that it shall be sufficient, if the defendant is advised to pay money into court, that he pay it as a compensation

the personal estate and effects which were of C. D., deceased, who died intestate], and as such executor [*or* administrator] as aforesaid sues for the benefit of and on behalf of I. D., the wife, and K. D. and L. D., the children of the said C. D.

---

in one sum to all persons entitled under the said Act for his wrongful act, neglect, or default, without specifying the shares into which it is to be divided by the jury; and if the said sum be not accepted, and an issue is taken by the plaintiff as to its sufficiency, and the jury shall think the same sufficient, the defendant shall be entitled to the verdict upon that issue."

By s. 3, the two Acts are to be read together as one Act.

The statement of claim should show clearly for whom, and on whose behalf, the action is brought, and the nature of the loss in respect of which damages are claimed. See "*Particulars and their effect on Pleading,*" *ante*, p. 29; *and sec.* 4 *of the above statute there cited.*

The defendant is liable for negligence under these statutes only where he would have been liable to an action for the same cause at the suit of the deceased had he survived. Thus, where a servant is killed in the employment of his master, the master is not liable for negligence for which the servant could not have sued him. (*Senior* v. *Ward*, 1 E. & E. 385; 28 L. J. Q. B. 139.)

Where a person is injured by the negligence of another, and within six months afterwards dies in consequence of such injury, the death does not create a new cause of action, as the negligence alone is the cause of action; and an accord and satisfaction made with the deceased in respect of such cause of action would be a good defence to any action brought by the representative under the above acts. (*Read* v. *The Gt. E. Ry. Co.*, L. R. 3 Q. B. 555.)

In such action the position of the executor or administrator suing, is as trustee of particular persons designated by the Act, of the action thereby given. See *Bradshaw* v. *L. and Y. Ry. Co.*, *infra.* Where a person is killed by the negligence of another it has been held that the executor of the deceased may maintain an action for the loss which thereby resulted to the personal estate of the deceased during his lifetime in respect of medical expenses, &c., incurred by him in consequence of the negligence of the defendant (*Bradshaw* v. *L. and Y. Ry. Co.*, L. R. 10 C. P. 189; 44 L. J. C. P. 148; *Potter* v. *Met. District Ry. Co.* 30 L. T. 765; 32 L. T. 36); and such action may be brought, although damages under Lord Campbell's Act (the above statute) have been recovered in a previous action by the representative of the deceased. (*Leggott* v. *G. N. Ry. Co.*, 1 Q. B. D. 599; 45 L. J. Q. B. 557.)

Where the action is in the names of the persons beneficially entitled under the statute (see 27 & 28 Vict. c. 95, s. 1, *supra*), if any of such persons are under a disability they should, it would seem, sue as such persons do in other cases; for example, if infants, they should sue by a next friend. (O. XVI. r. 8.)

The measure of damages is the pecuniary loss occasioned to the relatives by the death; and in estimating the damages the reasonable expectation of pecuniary advantage which the relatives had

2. The defendants were and are carriers of passengers on a railway between —— and ——.

3. On the —— of ——, 18—, the said C. D. was received by the defendants at —— aforesaid as a passenger,

---

from the deceased, and the probable pecuniary loss sustained by his death, are to be taken into account. Funeral and mourning expenses are not to be included. (*Dalton* v. *South-Eastern Ry. Co.*, 4 C. B. N. S. 296 ; 27 L. J. C. P. 227 ; *Franklin* v. *South-Eastern Ry. Co.*, 3 H. & N. 211 ; *Pym* v. *Great Northern Ry. Co.*, 4 B. & S. 396 ; 31 L. J. Q. B. 249 ; 32 *ib.* 377.) The pecuniary loss is the only damage recoverable. (*Blake* v. *Midland Ry. Co.*, 18 Q. B. 93 ; see also *Condon* v. *Gt. S. and W. Ry. Co.*, 16 Ir. C. L. R. 418.) The expectation of life of the deceased is an element to be considered. (*Rowley* v. *L. and N. W. Ry. Co.*, L. R. 8 Ex. 221.) Pecuniary loss arising from a contract merely with the deceased cannot be taken into consideration in assessing damages under the above statute. (*Sykes* v. *N. E. Ry. Co.*, 44 L. J. C. P. 191.) The plaintiff is not entitled to a verdict with nominal damages on proof merely of the death by negligence, without further proof of damage. (*Duckworth* v. *Johnson*, 4 H. & N. 653 ; 29 L. J. Ex. 25.)

The statement of claim need not negative the existence of any relations entitled to compensation other than those named therein. (See *Barnes* v. *Ward*, 9 C. B. 392.) The word "child" in the Act means legitimate child only. (*Dickinson* v. *North-Eastern Ry. Co.*, 2 H. & C. 735 ; 33 L. J. Ex. 91.) It includes a child *in ventre sa mère.* (*The George and Richard*, L. R. 3 Adm. 466.)

The Act applies to loss of life arising from collisions at sea, but subject to the limitations of liability contained in the Merchant Shipping Amendment Act, 1862, 25 & 26 Vict. c. 63, s. 54. See *Glaholm* v. *Barker*, L. R. 1 Ch. Ap. 223 ; 35 L. J. Ch. 259.

It was enacted by s. 7 of "The Admiralty Court Act, 1861" (24 Vict. c. 10), that the High Court of Admiralty should have jurisdiction over any claim for *damage* done by any ship, and it has been held that under this enactment the Probate, Divorce, and Admiralty Division has jurisdiction to entertain actions *in rem* against vessels in respect of claims under Lord Campbell's Act. (*The Franconia*, 2 P. D. 163 ; 46 L. J. P. 71. See, however, the judgments of Bramwell and Brett, L.JJ. in that case, and *Smith* v. *Brown*, L. R. 6 Q. B. 729 ; 40 L. J. Q. B. 219.)

As to the limitation of the liability of shipowners in cases of loss of life without their actual fault or privity, see "*Shipping*," *ante*, p. 336.

By the Regulation of Railways Act, 1868 (31 & 32 Vict. c. 119), s. 25, "Where a person has been injured or killed by an accident on a railway, the Board of Trade, upon application in writing made jointly by the company from whom compensation is claimed, and the person if he is injured, or his representatives if he is killed, may, if they think fit, appoint an arbitrator, who shall determine the compensation (if any) to be paid by the company."

As to actions by the legal personal representatives of a deceased wor man whose death resulted from an injury within "The Employers Liability Act, 1880" (43 & 44 Vict. c. 42), see "*Master and Servant*," *post*, p. 466.

to be carefully carried by them upon the said railway on a journey from —— to —— aforesaid, for reward to the defendants.

4. The train in which the said C. D. was being carried as such passenger upon the said journey came into collision with certain goods waggons then standing or being upon the said railway.

5. The said collision was caused by the negligence of the servants of the defendants, in not stopping the said train before it came into collision with the said goods waggons [*or as the case may be*].

6. The said C. D. had his spine injured in and by the said collision, and in consequence of such injury died on the —— of ——, 18—.

7. The said C. D., before and at the time of his death, carried on the business of a ——, and out of the profits of such business entirely supported his said wife and children, and paid for the education of his said children, and would, but for his said death, have continued to do so.

8. In consequence of the death of the said C. D., his said wife and children have been deprived of the said support, and his said children have been deprived of the said education.

For Statement of Claim by an Administratrix for Expenses and Costs incurred by the Estate of the Deceased in consequence of his being Injured by the Negligence of the Defendants, see *Leggott* v. *Gt. N. Ry. Co.*, 1 Q. B. D. 599; 35 L. T. 334.

FENCES (*a*).

Claim for not Repairing the Fences between adjacent Closes of Land.

1. At the times hereinafter mentioned the plaintiff was possessed and in the occupation of a close of land in the

---

(*a*) The general rule of law is that the owner of cattle is bound to take care that they do not trespass on the land of others. But the owner of land may be bound by prescription or otherwise to maintain and repair a fence for the benefit of the owner of the adjoining land who may have a corresponding right to have the fence so main-

parish of ——, in the county of —— and the defendant was possessed and in the occupation of another close of land next adjoining the said close of the plaintiff, and divided therefrom by a fence.

---

tained and repaired. (1 Wms. Saund. 559; *Churchill* v. *Evans*, 1 Taunt. 529; *Dovaston* v. *Payne*, 2 H. Bl. 527; *Boyle* v. *Tamlyn*, 6 B. & C. 329; and see *Ricketts* v. *East and West India Docks Ry. Co.*, 12 C. B. 160; *Erskine* v. *Adeane*, L. R. 8 Ch. Ap. 756; 42 L. J. Ch. 835; *Lawrence* v. *Jenkins*, L. R. 8 Q. B. 274; 42 L. J. Q. B. 147.)

As to fences between common land and ancient enclosure, see *Barber* v. *Whiteley*, 34 L. J. Q. B. 212. A person having the right to dig shafts for minerals is impliedly bound to fence the shafts for the protection of the owner of the surface. (*Groucott* v. *Williams*, 32 L. J. Q. B. 237; 4 B. & S. 149; and see *Sybray* v. *White*, 1 M. & W. 435.)

Where cattle trespass on the plaintiff's land through a defect in the fence which the defendant is bound to repair, the plaintiff may maintain an action in the above form in respect of the damage done, or he may maintain an action of trespass against the owner of the cattle (see *post* "*Trespass*," and *Ellis* v. *Loftus Iron Co.*, L. R. 10 C. P. 10; 44 L. J. C. P. 24), or he may distrain the cattle *damage feasant*; and the defendant is liable for mischief done by his cattle so straying, without proof that he knew they were of a mischievous disposition. (*Lee* v. *Riley*, 18 C. B. N. S. 722; 34 L. J. C. P. 212; see "*Mischievous Animals*," *post*, p. 475.)

Where cattle escape from the plaintiff's land through a defect in the fence which the defendant is bound to repair, the plaintiff may maintain an action for not repairing the fence in respect of any damage thereby occasioned to his cattle, or even to cattle not his own, but kept by him on his land for another person to whom he was liable. (*Rooth* v. *Wilson*, 1 B. & Ald. 59; and see *Carruthers* v. *Hollis*, 8 A. & E. 113; *Singleton* v. *Williamson*, 7 H. & N. 410; 31 L. J. Ex. 17; *Dawson* v. *Midland Ry. Co.*, L. R. 8 Ex. 8; 42 L. J. Ex. 49.)

Where the evidence showed a prescriptive obligation on the defendant to maintain a sufficient fence at all times, the act of God or *vis major* only excepted, the fact that the defendant had no knowledge or notice of the fence being out of repair did not relieve him from liability, and it was held that damage occasioned by the death of the plaintiff's cows, which, having escaped through the defective fence, were poisoned by eating the leaves of a yew-tree felled on the defendant's land, was not too remote. (*Lawrence* v. *Jenkins*, *sup.*; and see *Ellis* v. *Loftus Iron Co.*, *sup.*; *Powell* v. *Salisbury*, 2 Y. & J. 391.)

A plaintiff whose cattle trespassed on the land adjoining the defendant's cannot maintain an action against him for damage occasioned to them by the defect in the fence, although the defendant is bound to repair it as against the owner of the adjoining land. (*Ricketts* v. *East and West India Docks Ry. Co.* 12 C. B. 160.) So, where the defendant was bound to repair the fence between his land and the highway, it was held that the plaintiff, in order to maintain this action, must show that his cattle were lawfully using the highway. (*Dovaston* v. *Payne*, 2 H. Bl. 527; see *Fawcett* v. *York and North Midland Ry. Co.*, 16 Q. B. 610.)

The action must be brought against the person bound to repair

2. The defendant, by reason of the possession of his said close, then of right ought to have maintained and repaired, and kept maintained and repaired the said fence, so as to prevent cattle lawfully feeding or being in the said respective closes from escaping from and out of the one into the other of the said closes through defects of the said fence (*b*).

---

who is, in general, the occupier, and not the owner. (*Cheetham* v. *Hampson*, 4 T. R. 318.)

With respect to the statutory obligation of railway companies to maintain fences between the railway and the adjoining land under the Railways Clauses Consolidation Act, 1845 (8 & 9 Vict. c. 20), s. 68, see *Ricketts* v. *East and West India Docks Ry. Co.*, 12 C. B. 160; *Bessant* v. *Great Western Ry. Co.*, 8 C. B. N. S. 368; *Marfell* v. *South Wales Ry. Co.*, 8 C. B. N. S. 525; *Roberts* v. *Great Western Ry. Co.*, 4 C. B. N. S. 506; 27 L. J. C. P. 266; *Sharrod* v. *London and North Western Ry. Co.*, 4 Ex. 580; *Dawson* v. *Midland Ry. Co.*, L. R. 8 Ex. 8; 42 L. J. Ex. 49; *Child* v. *Hearn*, L. R. 9 Ex. 176; 43 L. J. Ex. 100; *Wiseman* v. *Booker*, 3 C. P. D. 184; 38 L. T. 292; *Corry* v. *G. W. Ry. Co.*, 6 Q. B. D. 237; 7 *ib.* 322; 50 L. J. C. P. 313; ib. 386.

The obligation created by that section exists solely between a railway company and adjoining owners and occupiers, and does not impose on the company any duty towards their passengers to keep up the fences, so that as to passengers the company are merely bound by their common law duty of taking reasonable care to prevent cattle straying on to the line. (*Buxton* v. *The North Eastern Ry. Co.*, L. R. 3 Q. B. 549; 37 L. J. Q. B. 258.)

With respect to actions against railway companies for not maintaining sufficient gates or stiles on a level crossing, under the Railways Clauses Consolidation Act, 1845 (8 & 9 Vict. c. 20), ss. 47, 61, see *Ellis* v. *London and South Western Ry. Co.*, 2 H. & N. 424; 26 L. J. Ex. 349; *Williams* v. *Great Western Ry. Co.*, L. R. 9 Ex. 157; 43 L. J. Ex. 105; and see *Fawcett* v. *York and North Midland Ry. Co.*, 16 Q. B. 610; and "*Negligence*," *post*, p. 479.

With respect to the statutory duty of fencing certain machinery in factories, see the Factory and Workshop Act, 1878 (41 Vict. c. 16), ss. 5–8; and see *Caswell* v. *Worth*, 5 E. & B. 849; 25 L. J. Q. B. 121; *Doel* v. *Sheppard*, 5 E. & B. 856; 25 L. J. Q. B. 124; *Holmes* v. *Clarke*, 6 H. & N. 349; 7 Ib. 397; 30 L. J. Ex. 135; 31 Ib. 356; *Britton* v. *Great Western Cotton Co.*, L. R. 7 Ex. 130; *Watling* v. *Oastler*, L. R. 6 Ex. 73; 40 L. J. Ex. 43.

(*b*) The mode of stating a prescriptive obligation to fence which is adopted in the above precedent, is the same as that which was in ordinary use before the Judicature Acts, and was then held to be sufficient. See *Rider* v. *Smith*, 3 T. R. 766. Strictly speaking, it would seem that since the Judicature Acts (see O. XIX.) the mode in which the obligation arose should be stated more explicitly; but for the sake of conciseness it is thought that the above mode of pleading may still be adopted, subject to the exercise of the power of amendment in cases where a general averment of this nature would embarrass the defendant. See "*Common*," *ante*, p. 365, and "*Pleading in General*," *ante* p. 7.

3. The defendant, throughout the period from January, 18—, to October, 18—, wrongfully suffered the said fence to be and continue defective and out of repair.

4. In consequence of the said fence being defective and out of repair as aforesaid, certain cattle, viz. two cows, of the plaintiff lawfully being, on or about the —— of ——, 18—, in the said close of the plaintiff, then escaped through the said fence out of the said close of the plaintiff into the said close of the defendant, and were lost to the plaintiff, and certain other cattle, as well of the defendant as of other persons, at various times during the said period [*state the times and the number of cattle more particularly, if known*], then being in the said close of the defendant, escaped through the said fence out of the said close of the defendant into the said close of the plaintiff, and trod down, consumed, and spoiled the grass and herbage of the last mentioned close.

Ferry (*a*)

Claim for Disturbing the Plaintiff's Ferry.

1. The plaintiff, at the times hereinafter mentioned, was possessed of an ancient ferry, called —— ferry, in

(*a*) Strictly speaking the mode in which the right to the ferry arises, should be more explicitly stated in the statement of claim (see O. XIX.); but it is thought that the above mode of pleading may still be adopted under ordinary circumstances, and subject to the power of amendment. See "*Common,*" *ante*, p. 365, and "*Pleading in General,*" *ante*, p. 7. Where the right alleged is for a ferry both ways across a river, and the right proved is for a ferry one way only, the allegation is divisible. See *Giles* v. *Groves*, 12 Q. B. 721.

In cases of substantial and continued disturbance of a ferry, an injunction may ordinarily be obtained, when properly claimed by the plaintiff. See "*Injunction,*" *post*, p. 439, and *Attorney-General* v. *Richards*, 2 Anstr. at p. 608; *Huzzey* v. *Field*, 2 C. M. & R. 432; *Letton* v. *Gooden*, L. R. 2 Eq. 123; 35 L. J. Ch. 427.

It is doubtful whether the exclusive right of the owner of a ferry extends beyond the carriage of passengers by boat, and whether the building of a *bridge* even in the line of a ferry would be actionable as a disturbance. (*Hopkins* v. *Great Northern Ry. Co.*, 2 Q. B. D. 224; 46 L. J.Q. B. 265.) And it would appear that the owner of a ferry cannot maintain an action for loss of traffic caused by a new highway by bridge or ferry built or established near to the old ferry in order to provide for a new kind of traffic different from that which was accommodated by the old ferry. (Ib.; *Newton* v. *Cubitt*, 12 C. B. N. S. 32; 31 L. J. C. P. 246.) For other instances of actions for disturbance of ferry, see *Peter* v. *Kendal*, 6 B. & C. 703; *Pim* v. *Curell*, 6 M. & W. 234; *Blacketer* v *Gillett*, 9 C. B. 26.

the parish of ——, in the county of ——, for the carriage [of foot passengers and their goods] across the river —— from —— to —— in the said parish, taking for the carriage of such [passengers and goods] across such ferry certain reasonable freights and ferryages.

2. From the month of ——, 18—, up to the commencement of this action, the defendant wrongfully disturbed the plaintiff in the enjoyment of his said ferry by carrying in boats kept by or by the authority of the defendant divers [foot passengers and their goods] for hire across the said river where the plaintiff had the said ferry, and over and in the line of the said ferry [*or* near to the said ferry of the plaintiff, viz., (*state shortly the termini between which the defendant's boats plied and their distance from the termini of the plaintiff's ferry*)].

3. By reason of the matters above complained of, the plaintiff was disturbed in the enjoyment of his said ferry, and lost the profits which he would otherwise have received from his said ferry between the said month of ——, 18—, and the commencement of this action, amounting in the whole to £——.

Fishery (*a*).

Claim for Trespass to the Plaintiff's Fishery.

The defendant, at various times between ——, 18—, and ——, 18—, broke and entered the several fishery of

---

(*a*) Strictly speaking the statement of claim should be somewhat more precise and circumstantial in its allegations, but the above form may suffice under ordinary circumstances, and subject to the power of amendment. See "*Common,*" *ante*, p. 365, and "*Pleading in General,*" *ante*, p. 7.

It seems that an action is maintainable for trespass, where the defendant has broken and entered a several fishery even *in alieno solo*. (*Holford* v. *Bailey*, 8 Q. B. 1000; 13 Ib. 426; *Mayor of Carlisle* v. *Graham*, L. R. 4 Ex. 363; 38 L. J. Ex. 226; *Foster* v. *Wright*, 4 C. P. D. 438.)

A "sole and exclusive fishery" is not a sufficient description of a several fishery. (*Holford* v. *Bailey*, *sup.*)

Where the plaintiff had an exclusive right of fishery over a river under a crown grant, the facts that the river by a gradual change of its course had encroached on part of the defendant's land, and that the defendant had fished only over the land which was so submerged, were held to be no defence. (*Foster* v. *Wright*, *supra.*) But it is otherwise where the change in the course of the river is not gradual,

the plaintiff in the river ——, and fished in the said fishery for fish, and chased and disturbed the fish therein, and caught, took, and carried away and converted to his own use large quantities of the plaintiff's fish therein.

A like Claim: Foster v. *Wright*, 4 C. P. D. 438.

Fixtures (*a*).

Fraud (*aa*).

Statement of Claim for Fraud in Selling a Picture by a False Representation that it was painted by a certain Master.

1. The defendant on the —— of ——, 18—, by fraudulently representing to the plaintiff that a certain

---

or where the grant is so expressed as to restrict the right to the original channel. (Ib., and see *Mayor of Carlisle* v. *Graham*, *supra*.) The crown has no *de jure* right to the soil or fisheries of an inland non-tidal lake, and therefore a crown grant of a several fishery therein is not of itself sufficient to establish the title thereto. (*Bristow* v. *Cormican*, 3 App. Cas. 641.) As to the effect of a re-grant of a fishery which had been resumed by the Crown, see *Northumberland* v. *Houghton*, L. R. 5 Ex. 127; 39 L. J. Ex. 66; and *Foster* v. *Wright*, *supra*.

For instances of actions for trespass to fisheries besides the cases above cited, see *Smith* v. *Kemp*, 2 Salk. 637; *Mannall* v. *Fisher*, 5 C. B. N. S. 856; *Marshall* v. *Ulleswater Steam Navigation Co.*, 3 B. & S. 732; 32 L. J. Q. B. 139; *Ford* v. *Lacey*, 7 H. & N. 151; 30 L. J. Ex. 351.

(*a*) Fixtures while unremoved remain part of the realty, but if they have been removed and carried away, the plaintiff may sue for a wrongful conversion of them. (*London and Westminster Loan, &c., Co.* v. *Drake*, 6 C. B. N. S. 798; 28 L. J. C. P. 297; *Saint* v. *Pilley*, L. R. 10 Ex. 137; 44 L. J. Ex. 33; and see *Ex parte Brook*, 10 Ch. D. 100; 48 L. J. B. 22.)

A reversioner may maintain an action for an injury to the reversion by removing fixtures. See "*Reversion*," *post*, p. 512.

(*aa*) An action to recover damages arising from fraud will lie where the defendant has stated or represented as a matter of fact what is untrue, knowing it to be untrue, with intent to induce the plaintiff to act upon it, and has thereby induced the plaintiff to act upon it,

picture was painted by ——, induced the plaintiff to buy the said picture from the defendant for £——, which sum the plaintiff then paid to the defendant.

2. The said picture was not painted by ——.

---

to his loss. (*Pasley* v. *Freeman*, 3 T. R. 51 ; 2 Smith's L. C. 8th ed. 66 ; *Langridge* v. *Levy*, 2 M. & W. 519 ; *Eastwood* v. *Bain*, 3 H. & N. 738 ; 28 L. J. Ex. 74 ; *Behn* v. *Kemble*, 7 C. B. N. S. 260 ; *Bedford* v. *Bagshaw*, 4 H. & N. 538 ; 29 L. J. Ex. 59.) Such action will not lie upon a statement made by the defendant without an intention of inducing the plaintiff to act upon it. (*Way* v. *Hearn*, 13 C. B. N. S. 292 ; 32 L. J. C. P. 34 ; *Rawlings* v. *Bell*, 1 C. B. 951 ; *Barley* v. *Walford*, 9 Q. B. 197 ; and see *Freeman* v. *Cooke*, 2 Ex. 654.)

An action will also lie where the defendant fraudulently, in order to induce the plaintiff to act upon his representation, represents as true a matter of fact of which he knows nothing, and which is, in reality, untrue. (*Evans* v. *Edmonds*, 13 C. B. 777 ; 22 L. J. C. P. 211, *per* Maule, J. ; *Behn* v. *Burness*, 3 B. & S. 751 ; 32 L. J. Q. B. 204.)

If persons recklessly or dishonestly take upon themselves to make positive assertions as to which they are ignorant whether they are true or not, they are as responsible in civil proceedings as if they had asserted that which they knew to be untrue. (*Reese River Silver Mining Co.* v. *Smith*, L. R. 4 H. L. 64, 79 ; 39 L. J. Ch. 849, *per* Lord Cairns ; *Taylor* v. *Ashton*, 11 M. & W. 401, 415 ; *Evans* v. *Edmonds*, *supra ; Hart* v. *Swaine*, 7 Ch. D. 42, 46 ; 47 L. J. Ch. 5 ; *Behn* v. *Burness*, *supra ; Slim* v. *Croucher*, 2 Giff. 37 ; 37 L. J. Ch. 273.) As to fraudulent concealment, see *Smith* v. *Hughes*, L. R. 6 Q. B. 597 ; 40 L. J. Q. B. 221 ; *Hill* v. *Gray*, 1 Stark. 434 ; *Peek* v. *Gurney*, L. R. 6 H. L. 377 ; 43 L. J. Ch. 19 ; Leake on Contracts, 358 *et seq.*, and cases cited *infra*.

The active concealment of a material fact may operate as a misrepresentation (*Schneider* v. *Heath*, 3 Camp. 506 ; *Baglehole* v. *Walters*, *ib.* 154 ; *Udell* v. *Atherton*, 7 H. & N. 172 ; 30 L. J. Ex. 337 ; *Hill* v. *Gray*, *supra ; Peek* v. *Gurney*, *supra*) ; thus, where a vessel, sold "with all faults," was, previously to the sale, placed by the vendor so as to prevent examination of her bottom, which was known to be unsound, it was held that this was a fraud entitling the buyer to avoid the contract. (*Schneider* v. *Heath*, *supra.*)

Mere non-disclosure of facts, where there is no duty to disclose them, will not give a cause of action. (*Fletcher* v. *Krell*, 42 L. J. Q. B. 55 ; *Smith* v. *Hughes*, *supra* ; *Beechey* v. *Brown*, E., B. & E. 976 ; 29 L. J. Q. B. 105 ; *Ward* v. *Hobbs*, 3 Q. B. D. 150 ; 47 L. J. Q. B. 90 ; 4 App. Cas. 13 ; 48 L. J. H. L. 281.)

Upon an express warranty given on a sale, or where the contract of sale implies a warranty, the statement of claim may be framed either upon the contract or upon the wrong. (See *forms*, "*Warranty*," *ante*, p. 342.) Where no warranty exists in the contract, but the contract is induced by false representations, known by the seller to be false, the action is grounded on the fraud, and should be so framed. (*Ormrod* v. *Huth*, 14 M. & W. 651 ; *Meyer* v. *Everth*, 4 Camp. 22.)

Where fraud is intended to be charged there should be a clear and distinct allegation of fraud upon the pleadings, and though it is not necessary that the word *fraud* should be used, the facts must

3. The defendant, at the time of making the said representation, knew that the said picture was not painted by ——.

4. The plaintiff, by reason of the premises, lost the said £ ——.

---

be so stated as to show distinctly that fraud is charged. (*Davy* v. *Garrett*, 7 Ch. D. 473, 489; 47 L. J. Ch. 218, *per* Thesiger, L.J.)

It may in some cases be useful to join with a claim upon a warranty an alternative claim upon the ground of fraud. Where it is intended to rely upon alternative cases the facts ought to be distinctly stated, so as to show on what facts each alternative of the relief sought is founded; the facts ought not to be mixed up, leaving the defendant to pick out the facts applicable to each case. (*Davy* v. *Garrett*, *supra*, *per* Thesiger, L.J.)

It has been held that where the title to relief is rested in the pleadings entirely upon a charge of fraud, it is not open to the plaintiff, if he fails in establishing the charge of fraud, to pick out facts, which might, if not put forward as material facts in support of the charge of fraud, have entitled him to relief apart from fraud. (*Hickson* v. *Lombard*, L. R. 1 H. L. 324; *London Chartered Bank of Australia* v. *Lempriere*, L. R. 4 P. C. 572; *Noad* v. *Murrow*, 40 L. T. 100.) The rule under the former system of pleading at common law was, that if a declaration disclosed a state of facts upon which an action might be maintained without fraud, the plaintiff might recover upon the facts disclosed, though fraud was alleged and disproved. (*Swinfen* v. *Lord Chelmsford*, 5 H. & N. 890, 921; *Thom* v. *Bigland*, 8 Ex. 725, *per* Parke, B.)

But where charges of fraud are made which are not sustained, the Judge has power to order the party making such charges to pay the costs occasioned thereby. (O. LV.; see *Parker* v. *McKenna*, L. R. 10 Ch. Ap. 96; 44 L. J. Ch. 425; *London Chartered Bank of Australia* v. *Lempriere*, *supra*.)

A principal is, in general, responsible civilly for the fraud of his authorised agent acting within the scope of his authority. (*Barwick* v. *English Joint Stock Bank*, L. R. 2 Ex. 259; 36 L. J. Ex. 174; *Houldsworth* v. *City of Glasgow Bank*, 5 App. Cas. 317, 326, 339; *Mackay* v. *Com. Bank of New Brunswick*, L. R. 5 P. C. 394; 43 L. J. P. C. 31; *Swire* v. *Francis*, 3 App. Cas. 106; 47 L. J. P. C. 18.)

The agent actually committing the fraud is also personally responsible. (*Weir* v. *Bell*, 3 Ex. D. 238, 248; 48 L. J. Ex. 704; *Eaglesfield* v. *Marquis of Londonderry*, 4 Ch. D. 693, 708.) See further, "*Agent*," "*Company*," "*Corporation*," *ante*, and "*Husband and Wife*," *post*.

The damages recoverable are such as are the direct and natural consequence to the plaintiff of acting upon the faith of the fraudulent representations made to him by the defendant. (*Mullett* v. *Mason*, L. R. 1 C.P. 559; 35 L. J. C. P. 299; see also *Smith* v. *Green*, 1 C. P. D. 92; 45 L. J. C. P. 29; *Twycross* v. *Grant*, 2 C. P. D. 469; 46 L. J. C. P. 636; *Waddell* v. *Blockey*, 4 Q. B. D. 678; 48 L. J. Q. B. 517.) Thus, where a cattle dealer sold the plaintiff a cow by fraudulently representing that it was free from infectious disease, and the plaintiff, in reliance upon this misrepresentation,

For Fraud in Selling an Unsound Horse by a False Representation that it was sound.

1. The defendant was possessed of a brown horse, which was, as the defendant well knew, unsound.

2. The defendant, on the —— of ——, 18——, in order to induce the plaintiff to buy the said horse, falsely and fraudulently represented to the plaintiff that the said horse was then sound.

3. By the above stated false and fraudulent representation the defendant induced the plaintiff to buy the said horse, and to pay the defendant in respect thereof the sum of £——.

4. The said horse was, by reason of its unsoundness, useless to the plaintiff, and the plaintiff thereby lost the said £——.

For Fraud in Selling Lambs by a false Representation that they were the Property of a certain Farmer, and were sound.

1. On the —— of ——, 18—, the plaintiff met the defendant at —— Fair, when the defendant called the attention of the plaintiff to—— lambs, which the defendant there had for sale.

2. The defendant, for the purpose of inducing the plaintiff to buy the said lambs, then stated to the plaintiff that he was the salesman of the said lambs, that they were not his own property, but were sent to him for sale by a farmer at ——, and, further, that he believed the said lambs to be sound.

3. The defendant in answer to questions by the plaintiff then also further stated to the plaintiff for the purpose aforesaid that he knew the farmer who had sent him the said lambs for sale, and that such farmer had never had a rotten sheep on his farm, and that he,

---

which was false, placed it with other cattle which caught the disease from it and died, it was held that the plaintiff could recover, as damages, the value of such other cattle. (*Mullett* v. *Mason*, *supra*.)

A misrepresentation of matter of law, that is as to the legal consequences of true facts, does not, at any rate in the absence of actual fraud, give a right to relief. (*Beattie* v. *Lord Ebury*, L. R. 7 Ch. Ap. 777, 800; 41 L. J. Ch. 804; *Rashdall* v. *Ford*, L. R. 2 Eq. 750; 35 L. J. Ch. 769; *Eaglesfield* v. *Marquis of Londonderry*, *supra*; and see *Hirschfeld* v. *L. B. and S. C. Ry. Co.*, 2 Q. B. D. 1; 46 L. J. Q B. 94.)

the defendant, believed the said lambs to be all right and sound.

4. The plaintiff was induced by the above statements of the defendant to buy the said —— lambs for the sum of —— each, and to pay the said price of them to the defendant.

5. The said lambs were not in fact the property of a farmer at ——, or of any farmer, nor were they then either sound or all right.

6. The said lambs were then the property of a dealer at ——, who had lost certain other sheep and lambs from rot and unsoundness, and who had sent the said lambs to the defendant to be sold by him.

7. The defendant was fully aware of the above facts, and did not believe the said lambs to be either sound or all right at the time when he made the above statements, and he made the said statements fraudulently and with a full knowledge of their falseness.

8. The said lambs were, when the plaintiff so bought them, rotten and unsound, and in consequence of such rotteness and unsoundness —— of them died soon afterwards.

9. By reason of the premises the plaintiff lost the said price of the said lambs, and the expenses incurred by him in keeping and attending to them, and the profits which he would otherwise have made by the sale of the said lambs.

Statement of Claim for Damages for Fraud upon the Sale of a Business. Form No. 15 in App. (C) to Jud. Act, 1875.

1. In or about —— March, 1875, the defendant caused to be inserted in the *Daily Telegraph* newspaper an advertisement, in which he offered for sale the lease, fixtures, fittings, goodwill, and stock-in-trade of a baker's shop and business, and described the same as an increasing business, and doing 12 sacks a week. The advertisement directed application for particulars to be made to X. Y.

2. The plaintiff having seen the advertisement applied to X. Y., who placed him in communication with the defendant, and negotiations ensued between the plaintiff and the defendant for the sale to the plaintiff of the

defendant's bakery, at ——, with the lease, fixtures, fittings, stock-in-trade, and goodwill.

3. In the course of these negotiations the defendant repeatedly stated to the plaintiff that the business was a steadily increasing business, and that it was a business of more than 12 sacks a week.

4. On the 5th of April, 1875, the plaintiff, believing the said statements of the defendant to be true, agreed to purchase the said premises from the defendant for £500, and paid to him a deposit of £200 in respect of the purchase.

5. On the 15th April the purchase was completed, an assignment of the lease executed, and the balance of the purchase money paid. On the same day the plaintiff entered into possession.

6. The plaintiff soon afterwards discovered that at the time of the negotiations for the said purchase by him and of the said agreement, and of the completion thereof, the said business was and had long been a declining business; and at each of those times, and for a long time before, it had never been a business of more than 8 sacks a week. And the said premises were not of the value of £500, or any saleable value whatever.

7. The defendant made the false representations hereinbefore mentioned well knowing them to be false, and fraudulently, with the intention of inducing the plaintiff to make the said purchase on the faith of them.

For Damages against Directors of a Joint-Stock Company for inducing a person to take Shares by false and fraudulent Statements contained in a Prospectus (*b*).

1. The defendants were the directors of the —— Company Limited, a company incorporated for the purpose of &c., and duly registered.

(*b*) If the officers of a company knowingly and fraudulently concoct false and deceitful reports to induce persons to invest in the shares or securities of the company, and investments are made by such persons on the faith of such reports, whereby a loss is sustained by them, the officers so acting are responsible in damages. (*Cullen* v. *Thompson*, 4 Macq. 441; *Clarke* v. *Dickson*, 6 C. B. N. S. 453; 28 L. J. C. P. 225; *Eaglesfield* v. *Marquis of Londonderry*, 4 Ch. D. 693.) But an officer of a company is not liable for a fraud (such as the issue

2. On or about the —— of ——, 18—, the defendants fraudulently issued to the plaintiff, with the intent to induce him to take shares in the said company, a prospectus signed by the defendants, stating, amongst other things, that the land and buildings of the said company had been valued by Mr. —— at £ ——, and were fully worth that amount.

---

of a fraudulent prospectus of the company) committed by his fellow officers, if he has neither expressly authorised nor tacitly permitted its commission. (*Weir* v. *Barnett*, 3 Ex. D. 32 ; *Weir* v. *Bell*, 3 Ex. D. 238 ; 47 L. J. Ex. 704 ; *Cargill* v. *Bower*, 10 Ch. D. 502 ; 47 L. J. Ch. 649 ; and see *Peek* v. *Gurney*, L. R. 6 H. L. 377 ; 43 L. J. Ch. 19.)

Where the act of the plaintiff, whereby the injury was sustained by him, was not directly induced by the representation of the defendant, no action will lie (*Peek* v. *Gurney*, *supra*) ; though a person is responsible to a third party for the consequences of a fraudulent misrepresentation made to another with the direct intent that it should be acted on as true by such third party in the manner that directly occasioned the injury. (*Peek* v. *Gurney*, L. R. 6 H. L. 377, 412, 413, *per* Ld. Cairns ; 43 L. J. Ch. 19 ; *Barry* v. *Croskey*, 2 J. & H. 1, 23.)

So where the prospectus of a company containing false and fraudulent representations was issued to persons about to apply for shares to be allotted to them, and the shares were applied for and allotted, it was held that a plaintiff who afterwards was shown by third parties the prospectus, and bought shares in reliance upon it in the market, could not sue on the representations contained in the prospectus, the representations not having been made by the defendant to him. (*Peek* v. *Gurney*, *supra*.) But where the directors of a bank issued a report, known by them to be false, intended for the information of any person desiring to deal in the shares of the bank, and the plaintiff, through a broker, obtained a copy, and was thereby induced to purchase shares, it was held that he could sue on the misrepresentations therein contained. (*Scott* v. *Dixon*, 29 L. J. Ex. 62, n.)

The statute 30 & 31 Vict. c. 131, s. 38, enacts that every prospectus of a company, and every notice inviting persons to subscribe for shares in any joint-stock company, shall specify the dates and the names of the parties to any contract entered into by the company, or the promoters, directors, or trustees thereof, before the issue of such prospectus or notice, whether subject to adoption by the directors or the company, or otherwise ; and any prospectus or notice not specifying the same shall be deemed fraudulent on the part of the promoters, directors, and officers of the company knowingly issuing the same, as regards any person taking shares in the company on the faith of such prospectus, unless he shall have had notice of such contract.

This statute gives to shareholders a remedy against the person making the omission. (*Cornell* v. *Hay*, L. R. 8 C. P. 328 ; 42 L. J. C. P. 136 ; *Gover's case*, 1 Ch. D. 182 ; 45 L. J. Ch. 83.)

As to what contracts are required to be stated, see *Twycross* v. *Grant*, 2 C. P. D. 469 ; 46 L. J. C. P. 636 ; 2 C. P. D. 491 ; 46 L. J. C. P. 645 ; *Gover's case*, *supra* ; *Cornell* v. *Hay*, *supra* ; *Charlton* v. *Hay*, 31 L. T. 437 ; *Sullivan* v. *Mitcalfe*, 5 C. P. D. 455 ; 49 L. J. C. P. 815 ; *Arkwright* v. *Newbold*, 17 Ch. D. 301 ; 49 L. J. Ch. 684.

3. The said land and buildings had been valued by Mr. ——, but they had been valued by him at £——, and no more. They were not worth £——, but were only worth a much smaller sum.

4. The defendants were well aware of the above mentioned facts when they so issued the prospectus.

5. The plaintiff was by the above mentioned false and fraudulent representations induced to take and pay for —— shares in the said company at a price of £—— per share.

6. By reason of the premises the plaintiff lost the said price so paid for the said shares, and became and is liable to pay £—— to the said company as calls upon the said shares.

For fraudulently representing that a third person might be trusted with Goods on Credit (*c*).

1. The defendant, by a letter bearing date the —— of ——, 18—, signed by the defendant, fraudulently repre-

(*c*) By the 9 Geo. IV. c. 14 (Lord Tenterden's Act), s. 6, "no action shall be brought whereby to charge any person upon or by reason of any representation or assurance made or given concerning or relating to the character, conduct, credit, ability, trade or dealings of any other person, to the intent or purpose that such other person may obtain credit, money, or goods upon (*sic*), unless such representation or assurance be made in writing, signed by the party to be charged therewith." A representation partly written and partly verbal is sufficient, if the written part forms a material part of the representation. (*Tatton* v. *Wade*, 18 C. B. 371; 25 L. J. C. P. 240; and see *Clarke* v. *Dickson*, 6 C. B. N. S. 453; 28 L. J. C. P. 225.)

The representation must be signed by the party, a signature by his agent will not suffice. (*Swift* v. *Jewsbury*, L. R. 9 Q. B. 301; 43 L. J. Q. B. 56; *Hosegood* v. *Bull*, 36 L. T. 617.) The word "person" applies to a corporation. (*Boyd* v. *Croydon Rail. Co.*, 4 Bing. N. C. 669.) One partner of a firm signing such a representation in the name of the firm, with the authority of the firm, will thereby make himself only, and not his partners, liable on such representation. (*Mason* v. *Williams*, 28 L. T. 232.)

It was formerly unnecessary to aver in a declaration that the representation was in writing, or that it was signed by the defendant, that being merely matter of evidence; but it would now seem advisable for the plaintiff to aver in the statement of claim that the representation was in writing. If the statement of claim does not contain such an averment, the defendant should, if he relies on the absence of such writing, expressly plead the want of it in his defence.

As to form of pleading, see the statement of claim in *Hosegood* v. *Bull*, 36 L. T. 617, and the grounds upon which it was held bad.

sented to the plaintiff that G. H. then held a responsible situation, and was then in good circumstances, and might safely be trusted with goods on credit.

2. The said G. H. did not then hold a responsible situation, and was not then in good circumstances, and could not then be safely trusted with goods on credit, as the defendant then well knew.

3. The defendant, as he intended, did, by so representing, induce the plaintiff to sell and deliver to the said G. H. goods [namely, 5 tons of hay] on credit.

4. In consequence of the premises the plaintiff lost the price of the said goods, amounting to £ ——, and incurred expense amounting to £ —— in endeavouring to recover the same.

Highways (*a*).

See "*Nuisance*," "*Ways*," "*Negligence*," *post*.

(*a*) *Highways*.—The highways in England are regulated by 5 & 6 Will. IV., c. 50; 25 & 26 Vict. c. 61; 27 & 28 Vict. c. 101, [which Acts are to be construed together as one Act, and called, collectively, "The Highway Acts," and, severally, "The Highway Act, 1835," "The Highway Act, 1862," and "The Highway Act, 1864" (see 27 & 28 Vict. c. 101, ss. 1, 2),] by 41 & 42 Vict. c. 77, which amends the above, and, in the case of highways within urban sanitary districts, also by 38 & 39 Vict. c. 55 (The Public Health Act, 1875.)

The statute 5 & 6 Will. IV., c. 50, s. 109, requires notice of action to be given before suing any person for "anything done in pursuance of or under the authority of" that Act, and further enacts that such action shall not be brought "after sufficient satisfaction, or tender of satisfaction, has been made to the party aggrieved, nor after three calendar months next after the fact committed" in respect of which the action is brought.

The notice of action required must be given one calendar month at least before the action is commenced. (5 & 6 Vict. c. 97, s. 4; see "Defences," "*Notice of Action*.")

"The Public Health Act, 1875" (38 & 39 Vict. c. 55), by s. 144, enacts that "every urban authority shall within their district, exclusively of any other person, execute the office of and be surveyor of highways, and have, exercise, and be subject to, all the powers, authorities, duties, and liabilities of surveyors of highways, under the law for the time being in force, save so far as such powers, authorities, or duties, are or may be inconsistent with the provisions of this Act; every urban authority shall also have, exercise, and be subject to, all the powers, authorities, duties, and liabilities which, by 'The Highway Act, 1835,' or any Act amending the same, are vested in and given to the inhabitants in vestry assembled of any parish within their district."

By s. 149 of the same Act, "all streets being, or which at any time become, highways repairable by the inhabitants at large within any urban district, and the pavements, stones, and other materials thereof, and all buildings, implements, and other things provided for the purposes thereof, shall vest in and be under the control of the urban authority."

This section vests in the urban authority a right of property in such "streets," and the materials composing them. (*Coverdale* v. *Charlton*, 3 Q. B. D. 376; 4 Q. B. D. 104; 47 L. J. Q. B. 446; 48 L. J. Q. B. 128.) No such right is so vested in the mines or minerals below the roadway. (See *Coverdale* v. *Charlton*, *supra*, and 41 & 42 Vict. c. 77, s. 27.) "*Street*" is, by s. 4 of the Act 38 & 39 Vict. c. 55, to include "any highway (not being a turnpike road), and any public bridge (not being a county bridge), and any road, lane, footway, square, court, alley, or passage, whether a thoroughfare or not." (See further, *Coverdale* v. *Charlton*, *supra*; *Nutter* v. *Accrington Local Board*, 4 Q. B. D. 375; 48 L. J. Q. B. 487; *R.* v. *Fullford*, 33 L. J. M. C. 122; *Taylor* v. *Corporation of Oldham*, 4 Ch. D. 395; 46 L. J. Ch. 105; *Rolls* v. *Vestry of St. George's, Southwark*, 14 Ch. D. 785; 49 L. J. Ch. 691.)

By s. 264 of the same Act, notice of action must be given one month at least before a writ or process is sued out against, or served on, any local authority, or any member thereof, or any officer of a local authority, or person acting in his aid for anything done or intended to be done or omitted to be done under the provisions of the Act. And every such action must be commenced within six months next after the accruing of the cause of action. And further, any person to whom such notice of action is given may tender amends at any time within a month after service of notice of action, and may, in case the same be not accepted, plead the tender in bar.

By s. 15 of the above Act, every local authority is bound to keep in repair all sewers belonging to it (as to which see s. 13), and is consequently liable to persons lawfully using a highway in which such sewers are placed for injuries caused to such persons by the sewers being negligently allowed to remain in a defective and dangerous state. (*White* v. *Hindley Local Board*, L. R. 10 Q. B. 219; 44 L. J. Q. B. 114; *Smith* v. *West Derby Local Board*, 3 C. P. D. 423; 47 L. J. C. P. 607; *Borough of Bathurst* v. *Macpherson*, 4 App. Cas. 256, 265 *et seq.*)

A surveyor of highways is not, nor are corporate bodies executing that office, liable, as such, for damages caused to individuals by non-repair of a highway within the district for which they hold office. (*Young* v. *Davis*, 7 H. & N. 760; 31 L. J. Ex. 250; *Parsons* v. *St Matthew, Bethnal Green*, L. R. 3 C. P. 56; 37 L. J. C. P. 62; *Gibson* v. *Mayor of Preston*, L. R. 5 Q. B. 218; 39 L. J. Q. B. 121; *Harris* v. *Baker*, 4 M. & S. 27; *White* v. *Hindley Local Board*, *supra*.) But a person is not, by reason of his holding the office of surveyor, exempted from liability for the consequences of his own personal negligence. (*Pendlebury* v. *Greenhalgh*, 1 Q. B. D. 36; 45 L. J. Q. B. 3.) Nor are corporate bodies executing that office free from liability for injuries caused by their negligence, or that of their servants acting within the scope of their employment, whether in discharging obligations imposed on them by statute or otherwise. (*Borough of Bathurst* v. *Macpherson*, 4 App. Cas. 256; *Hartnall* v. *Ryde Commissioners*, 4 B. & S. 361; 33 L. J. Q. B. 39. (Thus where the servants of a corporate body, executing the office of surveyor of highways, negli-

HUNDREDORS (*a*).

HUSBAND AND WIFE.

By Husband and Wife for Damages for Injury to the Wife by Negligent Driving, coupled with a Claim by the Husband for Loss to Himself consequent thereon (*aa*).

Between A. B. and C. (*Christian name of wife*), his wife . . } Plaintiffs.

and

D. E. . . . . . Defendant.

1. The plaintiff C. is, and was on the —— of ——,

---

gently left a heap of stones by the side of one of the highways within the district, without a light or guard at night, whereby the plaintiff drove against it and was injured, it was held that such corporate body was liable to the plaintiff in damages. (*Foreman* v. *Mayor of Canterbury*, L. R. 6 Q. B. 214; 40 L. J. Q. B. 138.)

The use of locomotives on highways is regulated by 24 & 25 Vict. c. 70; 28 & 29 Vict. c. 83; 41 & 42 Vict. c. 77. Those statutes do not protect the owner of a locomotive engine from his common law liability to make compensation for damage done to property by the escape of sparks from such locomotive while passing along the highway. (*Powell* v. *Fall*, 5 Q. B. D. 597; 49 L. J. Q. B. 428.)

As to obstructions to highways, see *post*, "*Nuisance*," "*Ways*." See also "*Negligence*," *post*.

(*a*) See note to "*Corporations*," *ante*, p. 167, and see also 2 Chit. Pr., 13th ed., p. 987, and the notes to *Pinkney* v. *Inhabitants de Rotel*, 2 Wm. Saund., 1871 ed., p. 758.

(*aa*) With respect to injuries to the person of the wife during coverture, the husband and wife must join in suing. The husband cannot sue alone for damages in respect of the injury to the wife; but may sue alone for the damages occasioned thereby to himself solely. If the wife sues for damages alone, it was formerly matter for a plea in abatement; it is now ground for a summons to stay until joinder of the husband. (O. XIX. r. 13; O. XVI. rr. 13, 14; and see "*Abatement*," "Defences."

Claims by or against husband and wife may be joined with claims by or against either of them separately (O. XVII. r. 4), subject to the power of the court or judge to order separate actions. (O. XVII. rr. 8, 9.) If two actions are unnecessarily brought, the costs of the second action may, if the judge think fit, be disallowed. (O. LV.)

With respect to torts with regard to separate property of the wife, see "*Husband and Wife*," *ante*, p. 203, the "Married Women's Property Act, 1870" (33 & 34 Vict. c. 93), and the "Married Women's Property Act (1870) Amendment Act, 1874," 37 & 38 Vict. c. 50), there cited.

18— (*the date of the cause of action*), the wife of the plaintiff A. B.

2. On the —— of ——, 18—, a van of the defendant's was, about 4 P.M., being driven in a public street called ——Street, ——, by one of the servants of the defendant in the course of his employment as such servant.

3. It was then so negligently [*the circumstances should be stated where practicable*] driven and managed by the said servant of the defendant, that it was driven with great force against the plaintiff C. who was then crossing the said street.

4. The right leg of the plaintiff C. was thereby broken, and she was in consequence obliged to remain in her bedroom for —— weeks, and suffered much pain.

5. By reason of the premises, the plaintiff A. B. lost the benefit and comfort of the plaintiff C.'s society, and her assistance in the management of his house for —— weeks, and was put to an expense of £ —— for medical attendance, and was compelled to employ for —— weeks an additional servant at a cost of £ —— [*or as the case may be*].

A wife cannot sue in respect of any injuries to personal property, other than separate estate, committed during the coverture, as all such property vests in the husband exclusively. The husband alone can sue for such injuries. (*Chambers* v. *Donaldson*, 9 East, 471; *Boggett* v. *Frier*, 11 East, 301; see *Shingler* v. *Holt*, 7 H. & N. 65; 30 L. J. Ex. 322.)

With respect to injuries done during coverture to the real property of which the husband and wife are seised, or to which they are entitled in right of the wife, the husband may sue alone, or the husband and wife may join in suing. (*Bidgood* v. *Way*, 2 Bl. 1236; 1 Ch. Pl. 7th ed. 84; *Wallis* v. *Harrison*, 5 M. & W. 142.)

Upon the bankruptcy of the husband the trustees must join with the wife in suing upon causes of action in right of the wife which if vested in the husband would pass to the trustees, as for a conversion of the wife's goods before marriage; and the husband cannot join in the action. See under former practice, *Richbell* v. *Alexander*, 10 C. B. N. S. 324; 30 L. J. C. P. 268; *Sherrington* v. *Yates*, 12 M. & W. 855.

The rule with respect to injuries to the person, or to the personal or real estate of the wife committed before the marriage is, that the husband and wife must join in suing. If the wife sued alone the mode of objecting was by plea in abatement, and is now by summons. (O. XIX. r. 13; O. XVI. rr. 13, 14; and see "*Abatement*," "Defences.")

As to the effect of Divorce, Judicial Separation, and Protection Orders, see "*Husband and Wife*," *ante*, p. 199.

Against a Husband and Wife for Damages for a Wrong committed by the Wife during Coverture (*b*).

1. The defendant C. (*Christian name of the wife*) is the wife of the defendant E. F. and was his wife on the —— of ——, 18— [*date of the cause of action*].

2. On the said —— of ——, 18—, the said C. wrongfully seized and took possession of a diamond ring belonging to the plaintiff, of which said ring she still retains possession.

(*b*) With regard to torts committed by the wife before marriage, the husband and wife must be sued jointly, and the same rule applies to torts committed by the wife during coverture; but by s. 2 of the "Married Women's Property Act (1870) Amendment Act, 1874" (37 & 38 Vict. c. 50), the husband, if married after 30th July, 1874, in any action brought for damages sustained by reason of any tort committed by the wife before marriage, is liable only to the extent of the assets thereinafter specified (as to which see, "*Husband and Wife*," *ante*, p. 207), but unless the husband by his pleading shows the contrary he is taken to admit sufficient assets.

If the wife is wrongly sued alone she may apply to have the action stayed until joinder of her husband. Formerly she could have pleaded in abatement, see "*Abatement*," "Defences."

A married woman is liable for all torts committed by her, including frauds; but when the fraud is directly connected with a contract with her, and is the means of effecting it and part of the same transaction, she is exempt from liability; thus, an action will not lie against husband and wife for a fraudulent representation by the wife that she was unmarried, whereby the plaintiffs were induced to take her promissory note. (*Liverpool Adelphi Loan Ass.* v. *Fairhurst*, 9 Ex. 422.) Where the wife fraudulently represented that a bill was accepted by her husband, whereby the plaintiff was induced to discount it, the Court was equally divided as to the right to maintain the action. (*Wright* v. *Leonard*, 11 C. B. N. S. 258; 30 L. J. C. P. 365.)

The separation of husband and wife, except under a judicial separation, makes no difference with respect to the joinder of husband and wife as parties to actions. (*Head* v. *Briscoe*, 5 C. & P. 484.) Upon a divorce *a vinculo matrimonii*, the disability of the wife to sue or be sued alone ceases, and the husband ceases to be liable for wrongs previously committed by her. (*Capel* v. *Powell*, 17 C. B. N. S. 743; 34 L. J. C. P. 168.)

The property of a married woman settled to her separate use may be charged by her fraudulent acts relating to the property, but not by wrongful acts of a general kind (Leake on Contracts, 559; *Wainford* v. *Heyl*, L. R. 20 Eq. 321; 44 L. J. Ch. 567), but property settled without power of anticipation cannot be thus reached, so as to effect an anticipation. (*Stanley* v. *Stanley*, 7 Ch. D. 589; 47 L. J. Ch. 256.) See "*Husband and Wife*," *ante*, p. 204.

As to marriage pending action, see O. L.

By a Husband for Enticing Away and Harbouring his Wife (c).

1. A. B. is and was the wife of the plaintiff C. B.

2. The defendant wrongfully and without the consent of the plaintiff enticed away from the plaintiff his said wife, and procured her to absent herself from the plaintiff unlawfully and without his consent from the —— of ——, 18—, to the time of the commencement of this action [*or as the case may be*].

3. The defendant was always aware that the said A. B. was the wife of the plaintiff.

4. By reason of the said absence of his said wife the plaintiff lost the society and services of his said wife.

Imprisonment.

See "*Trespass to the Person,*" *post*, p. 529.

Infant.

See "*Infant,*" *ante*, p. 213, and "Defences," "*Infant.*'

Injunction (*a*).

For Form of Injunction to Restrain Working of Mines so as to Cause Subsidence of Plaintiff's Land, see Siddons v. *Short*, 2 C. P. D. 572; 46 L. J. C. P. 795; 37 L. T. 230; *Mayor of Birmingham* v. *Allen*, 46 L. J. Ch. 673; 37 L. T. 207.

(*c*) By the 20 & 21 Vict. c. 85, s. 59, "no action shall be maintainable in England for criminal conversation." The above claim for enticing away and harbouring a wife discloses entirely distinct causes of action from the old action for criminal conversation, and is not affected by the above provision. Where the defendant harbours the wife from motives of humanity, the action will not lie. (*Philp* v. *Squire*, Peake, 115; *Berthon* v. *Cartwright*, 2 Esp. 480.)

(*a*) Where an action is brought to obtain an injunction, it should be distinctly claimed in the statement of claim, and the material facts

The like, to Restrain the Managers of a Hospital from so managing it as to cause a Nuisance, see Hill v. Managers of Metrop. Asylum District, 4 Q. B. D. 433, 446; 40 L. T. 491; 48 L. J. Q. B. 562, 569.

---

should be stated which are relied upon as entitling to such injunction. (O. XIX. rr. 1 & 4. See Jud. Act, 1875, App. (C.), Form, No. 27, and "*Relief other than Damages or Payment of Debts,*" *ante*, p. 23.) The statement of claim should distinctly show against what description of acts the injunction sought is required. (*Ib.*)

It is enacted by section 25 (8) of the Jud. Act, 1873, that "a mandamus or an injunction may be granted, or a receiver appointed, by an interlocutory order of the Court in all cases in which it shall appear to the Court to be just or convenient that such order should be made; and any such order may be made either unconditionally or upon such terms and conditions as the Court shall think just; and if an injunction is asked either before, or at, or after the hearing of any cause or matter to prevent any threatened or apprehended waste or trespass, such injunction may be granted, if the Court shall think fit, whether the person against whom such injunction is sought is or is not in possession under any claim of title or otherwise, or (if out of possession) does or does not claim a right to do the act sought to be restrained under any colour of title; and whether the estates claimed by both or by either of the parties are legal or equitable."

This section has not altered the principles on which injunctions are granted or refused, though it has somewhat enlarged the powers of the Courts as to injunctions. (*Gaskin* v. *Balls*, 13 Ch. D. 324; *Shaw* v. *Earl of Jersey*, 4 C. P. D. 120; *ib.* 359; 48 L. J. C. P. 308; *Beddow* v. *Beddow*, 9 Ch. D. 89; 47 L. J. Ch. 588; *Day* v. *Brownrigg*, 10 Ch. D. 294, 307; 48 L. J. Ch. 173; *Aslatt* v. *Corporation of Southampton*, 16 Ch. D. 143, 148; 50 L. J. Ch. 31; and see "*Defamation,*" *ante*, p. 399.)

An injunction is no longer granted by writ, but by judgment or order. (O. LII. r. 32, of April, 1880.)

As to the principles upon which injunctions are granted, see cases cited *supra et infra*, and see *Doherty* v. *Allman*, 3 App. Cas. 709; *Krehl* v. *Burrell*, 7 Ch. D. 551; 11 Ch. D. 146; 47 L. J. Ch. 353; 48 L. J. Ch. 252.

As to interlocutory injunctions, see *Aynsley* v. *Glover*, L. R. 18 Eq. 544; 44 L. J. Ch. 523; *Shaw* v. *Earl of Jersey*, *supra*; and *Elwes* v. *Payne*, 12 Ch. D. 468; 48 L. J. Ch. 831; *Ecclesiastical Commissioners* v. *Kino*, 14 Ch. D. 213; 49 L. J. Ch. 529.

The Court has jurisdiction by injunction to protect property from an act threatened which, if completed, would give a right of action, and this jurisdiction is especially exercised in cases in which damages given for the injury done by such completed act would afford no adequate remedy. (*Emperor of Austria* v. *Day*, 3 D. F. & J. 217, 240; 30 L. J. Ch. 706; *Pattison* v. *Gilford*, L. R. 18 Eq. 259, 263; 43 L. J. Ch. 524; *Hext* v. *Gill*, L. R. 7 Ch. Ap. 699; 41 L. J. Ch. 761; *Lord Cowley* v. *Byas*, 5 Ch. D. 944; *Siddons* v. *Short*, 2 C. P. D. 572; 46 L. J. C. P. 795.)

The Court has power to grant a mandatory injunction requiring the removal of a building already erected. (*Durell* v. *Pritchard*,

The like, to Restrain Pollution of a Stream, see Atty.-Gen. v. Colney Hatch Asylum, L. R. 4 Ch. Ap. 146, 161; 38 L. J. Ch. 265, 271; *Pennington* v. *Brinsop Hall Coal Co.,* 5 Ch. D. 769, 774; 46 L. J. Ch. 773, 775; *Lingwood* v. *Stowmarket Co.,* L. R. 1 Eq. 77, 336.

L. R. 1 Ch. Ap. 244; 35 L. J. Ch. 223; *Kelk* v. *Pearson,* L. R. 6 Ch. Ap. 809; 24 L. T. 890; *City of London Brewery Co.* v. *Tennant,* L. R. 9 Ch. Ap. 212; 43 L. J. Ch. 457; *Krehl* v. *Burrell, supra; Gaskin* v. *Balls, supra; Smith* v. *Day,* 13 Ch. D. 651; *Smith* v. *Smith,* L. R. 20 Eq. 500; 44 L. J. Ch. 630.) But the Court will rarely interfere to pull down a building erected without complaint or objection. See *Gaskin* v. *Balls, supra, per* Thesiger, L.J. There is not the same objection to order the pulling down of a building erected after action, and after notice that an action will be brought. (*Smith* v. *Day,* 13 Ch. D. 651.)

An injunction may be claimed by a defendant as part of the relief sought by a counterclaim. See *Duke of Norfolk* v. *Arbuthnot,* 4 C. P. D. 291; 48 L. J. C. P. 737.

Where a party to a contract agrees not to do a particular act, the fact that the contract stipulates for the payment of a sum of money by way of penalty for a breach of this agreement does not prevent the granting of an injunction against acts constituting such breach. (*Howard* v. *Hopkyns,* 2 Atk. 371; *Bird* v. *Lake,* 1 H. & M. 111; *Howard* v. *Woodward,* 34 L. J. Ch. 47; *Jones* v. *Heavens,* 4 Ch. D. 636.) But where a fixed sum is stipulated to be paid as *liquidated damages* for a breach of such agreement, and it appears to be the real meaning of the contract that the defendant, if he chooses, is to have the right of doing the act on payment of the fixed sum as an equivalent, an injunction will not be granted. (*French* v. *Macabe,* 2 Dr. & War. 276; *Sainte* v. *Ferguson,* 1 Mac. & G. 286; *Coles* v. *Sims,* 5 De G., M. & G. 1; *Young* v. *Chalkley,* 16 L. T. 286; *Carnes* v. *Nisbett,* 7 H. & N. 158, 778; 30 L. J. Ex. 348.)

An injunction will not be granted to restrain an obstruction to a right of light unless the damage is of a substantial nature (*Kino* v. *Rudkin,* 6 Ch. D. 160; 46 L. J. Ch. 807; *Dent* v. *Auction Mart Co.,* L. R. 2 Eq. 238; 35 L. J. Ch. 555; *Kelk* v. *Pearson, supra*); nor will an injunction be granted to restrain waste where the damages are trivial. (*Doherty* v. *Allman,* 3 App. Cas. 709, 733.) An injunction will be granted to restrain an injury, such as the pollution of a stream, even in cases where the actual damage is but trifling, that, rather than damages, being the appropriate remedy. (*Pennington* v. *Brinsop Hall Coal Co.,* 5 Ch. D. 769; 46 L. J. Ch. 773; *Clowes* v. *Staff. Potteries Waterworks Co.,* L. R. 8 Ch. Ap. 125; 42 L. J. Ch. 107.)

Mere lapse of time alone will not prevent the Courts from granting an injunction in aid of a legal right, which has been established, and which is not itself barred by lapse of time. (*Fullwood* v. *Fullwood,* 9 Ch. D. 176; 47 L. J. Ch. 459; and see *Atty.-Gen.* v. *Colney Hatch Asylum,* L. R. 4 Ch. Ap. 146, 160; 38 L. J. Ch. 265.) As to what amounts to such delay or acquiescence as to bar the right to an injunction, see *Hogg* v. *Scott,* L. R. 18 Eq. 444; 43 L. J. Ch. 705; *Stanley* v. *Earl of Shrewsbury,* L. R. 19 Eq. 616; 44 L. J. Ch. 389; *Allen* v. *Seckham,* 11 Ch. D. 790; 48 L. J. Ch. 611; *Gaunt* v. *Fynney,* L. R.

The like, to Restrain Defendant from Causing or Continuing a Nuisance, see Sturges v. *Bridgman*, 11 Ch. D. 852; 48 L. J. Ch. 785; *Broder* v. *Saillard*, 2 Ch. D. 692, 703; 45 L. J. Ch. 414, 417; *Ball* v. *Ray*, L. R. 8 Ch. Ap. 467, 472.

The like, to Restrain Obstruction of Right of Way, see Cannon v. *Villars*, 8 Ch. D. 415, 423; 47 L. J. Ch. 597, 600; *Original Hartlepool Collieries Co.* v. *Gibb*, 5 Ch. D. 713; 46 L. J. Ch. 311, 316.

The like, to Restrain Acts of Trespass, see Duke of Norfolk v. *Arbuthnot*, 4 C. P. D. 290; 48 L. J. C. P. 737; *Newcomen* v. *Coulson*, 5 Ch. D. 133; *London & N. W. Ry. Co.* v. *L. & Y. Ry. Co.*, L. R. 4 Eq. 174; *and see Form No.* 27, *App.* (*C*) *to Jud. Act*, 1875.

---

8 Ch. Ap. 8; 42 L. J. Ch. 122. The provisions as to notice of action contained in various statutes for the protection of various public officers and bodies do not apply to proceedings for an injunction. (*Atty.-Gen.* v. *Hackney Local Board*, L. R. 20 Eq. 626; 44 L. J. Ch. 545; *Flower* v. *Local Board of Leyton*, 5 Ch. D. 347; 46 L. J. Ch. 321.)

By 21 & 22 Vict. c. 27, s. 2 (*Lord Cairns' Act*), it was enacted as follows:—"In all cases in which the Court of Chancery has jurisdiction to entertain an application for an injunction against a breach of any covenant, contract, or agreement, or against the commission or continuance of any wrongful act, or for the specific performance of any covenant, contract, or agreement, it shall be lawful for the same Court, if it shall think fit, to award damages to the party injured, either in addition to or in substitution for such injunction or specific performance, and such damages may be assessed in such manner as the Court shall direct."

The damages which may be given under this section are not limited to such as may have accrued at the date of the writ. (*Fritz* v. *Hobson*, 14 Ch. D. 542; 49 L. J. Ch. 321; *Beddall* v. *Maitland*, 17 Ch. D. 174, 178; 50 L. J. Ch. 401; *National Provincial Assurance Co.* v. *Prudential Insurance Co.*, 6 Ch. D. 757, 769; 46 L. J. Ch. 871.) The above statute is not repealed by the Jud. Acts, but the powers thereby conferred upon the Court of Chancery may now be exercised by any Division of the High Court of Justice. (Jud. Act. 1873, ss. 16, 24, 76; *Fritz* v. *Hobson*, *supra*; *Krehl* v. *Burrell*, *supra*; *Bowen* v. *Hall*, 6 Q. B. D. 333, 341; 50 L. J. Q. B. 305; *Matthews* v. *Jeffrey*, 6 Q. B. D. 290, 294; *White* v. *Boby*, 26 W. R. 133.)

The like, to Restrain Obstruction to Light, see Ecclesiastical Commissioners v. *Kino,* 14 Ch. D. 212, 229; *Allen* v. *Seckham,* 11 Ch. D. 790; 47 L. J. Ch. 742; *Kino* v. *Rudkin,* 6 Ch. D. 160; 46 L. J. Ch. 807; *Dent* v. *Auction Mart Co.,* L. R. 2 Eq. 238, 255; 35 L. J. Ch. 555, 557.

The like, to Restrain the Publication of Defamatory Matter Injurious to the Plaintiff's Trade, see Saxby v. *Easterbrook,* 3 C. P. D. 339; *Thomas* v. *Williams,* 14 Ch. D. 864, 875; 43 L. T. 91.

For other Forms, see "Common," "Copyright," "Light," &c., and Daniel's Ch. Forms and Precedents, and Seton on Decrees.

INNKEEPER (*a*).

By a Guest against an Innkeeper for the Loss of Goods.

1. The defendant is an innkeeper, and keeps a common inn, called the ——, at ——, for the accommodation of travellers.

(*a*) By the custom of the realm an innkeeper who professes to entertain and lodge all travellers is bound to receive a traveller at any hour of the day or night, provided the traveller offers himself in proper condition to be received into the inn, and is ready to pay for his accommodation, and there is room to accommodate him (*Fell* v. *Knight,* 8 M. & W. 269; *R.* v. *Ivens,* 7 C. & P. 213; *Hawthorn* v. *Hammond,* 1 C. & K. 404; *Spice* v. *Bacon,* 36 L. T. 896; *R.* v. *Rymer,* 2 Q. B. D. 136); but he is not bound to receive a guest who is not a traveller. (*R.* v. *Luellin,* 12 Mod. 445; *R.* v. *Rymer,* 2 Q. B. D. 136.) As to what constitutes an innkeeper, see *Thompson* v. *Lacy,* 3 B. & Ald. 283. Where goods were lost at a hotel, of which a company were proprietors, and an action was brought to recover their value against the paid manager in whose name the justices' licence had been granted, it was held that the company were the real "innkeepers," and, therefore, that the action was not maintainable. (*Dixon* v. *Birch,* L. R. 8 Ex. 135.)

An innkeeper at common law is not an insurer of the goods of his guests, but is liable only for negligence or default in keeping the goods by himself or his servants. (*Calye's Case,* 8 Co. Rep. 32; 1 Smith's L. C. 6th ed. 105; *Dawson* v. *Chamney,* 5 Q. B. 164; *Spice* v. *Bacon,* 36 L. T. 896.) The loss of the goods is presumptive

2. On the —— of ——, 18—, the plaintiff as and being a traveller, was received into the said inn by the defendant, with his goods, consisting of a portmanteau containing his wearing apparel.

---

evidence of such negligence, which it lies upon the innkeeper to rebut. He may do this by showing that the loss happened by the negligence of the guest, or by the act of God or the Queen's enemies. (*Richmond* v. *Smith*, 8 B. & C. 9; *Armistead* v. *Wilde*, 17 Q. B. 261; *Morgan* v. *Ravey*, 6 H. & N. 265; 30 L. J. Ex. 131.) In order to exonerate the innkeeper, the negligence of the guest must have occasioned the loss in such a way as that the loss would not have happened if the guest had used the ordinary care that a prudent man might reasonably be expected to take under the circumstances. (*Cashill* v. *Wright*, 6 E. & B. 891, 900; *Oppenheim* v. *White Lion Hotel Co.*, L. R. 6 C. P. 515; 25 L. T. 93.) Whether such care has been used is a question for the jury, and in deciding upon such question the circumstances of the case, such as the value of the goods and the means of securing them, should be taken into consideration. (*Spice* v. *Bacon, supra.*) The law implies a promise on the part of the innkeeper to take care of the goods of his guest according to his common-law duty, and a claim against him for loss of the goods may be framed either in tort, or upon such promise. (*Morgan* v. *Ravey*, 6 H. & N. 265; 30 L. J. Ex. 131.)

By the 26 & 27 Vict. c. 41, s. 1, it is enacted that "no innkeeper shall, after the passing of this Act, be liable to make good to any guest of such innkeeper any loss of or injury to goods or property brought to his inn, not being a horse or other live animal, or any gear appertaining thereto, or any carriage, to a greater amount than the sum of £30, except in the following cases (that is to say):—

(1.) Where such goods or property shall have been stolen, lost, or injured, through the wilful act, default, or neglect of such innkeeper, or any servant in his employ:

(2.) Where such goods or property shall have been deposited expressly for safe custody with such innkeeper:

Provided always, that in the case of such deposit it shall be lawful for such innkeeper, if he think fit, to require, as a condition of his liability, that such goods or property shall be deposited in a box or other receptacle, fastened and sealed by the person depositing the same."

By s. 2, "if any innkeeper shall refuse to receive for safe custody, as before mentioned, any goods or property of his guest, or if any such guest shall, through any default of such innkeeper, be unable to deposit such goods or property as aforesaid, such innkeeper shall not be entitled to the benefit of this Act in respect of such goods or property."

By s. 3, "every innkeeper shall cause at least one copy of the first section of this Act, printed in plain type, to be exhibited in a conspicuous part of the hall or entrance to his inn, and he shall be entitled to the benefit of this Act in respect of such goods or property only as shall be brought to his inn while such copy shall be so exhibited."

The word "wilful" in s. 1 applies only to the word "act." (*Squire* v. *Wheeler*, 16 L. T. 93, *per* Byles, J.)

3. The defendant did not, whilst the plaintiff was staying at his said inn as such traveller as aforesaid, keep the said portmanteau and its said contents safely and without diminution or loss, and the said portmanteau and its said contents were then wrongfully taken and carried away from the said inn by some person to the plaintiff unknown, and were thereby lost to the plaintiff.

4. The said portmanteau and its said contents were so taken and carried away owing to the neglect and default of the defendant and his servants.

5. The value of the said portmanteau and of its said contents was £ ——.

A like Form against an Innkeeper, where the Plaintiff's Watch and Purse were Stolen at an Inn: Spice v. *Bacon*, 2 Ex. D. 463.

JUDGE (*a*).

As to what is a sufficient "copy" under s. 3, see *Spice* v. *Bacon*, 2 Ex. D. 463; 46 L. J. Ex. 713; 36 L. T. 896.

As to the lien of an innkeeper upon the goods brought into his inn and his right to dispose of them, see "*Conversion*," *ante*, p. 375, and "Defences," "*Innkeeper*," and "The Innkeepers' Act, 1878" (41 &42 Vict. c. 38), there cited.

(*a*) No action will lie against a judge for an act within his jurisdiction, although it may be irregular or founded on an erroneous judgment. (*Calder* v. *Halket*, 3 Moore, P. C. 28; *Dicas* v. *Lord Brougham*, 6 C. & P. 249; *Kemp* v. *Neville*, 10 C. B. N. S. 523; 31 L. J. C. P. 158; and see the cases there cited, and *Scott* v. *Stansfield*, L. R. 3 Ex. 220.) But a judge of a court of limited jurisdiction is liable to an action of trespass for an act done by his authority for which he had no jurisdiction (*Houlden* v. *Smith*, 14 Q. B. 841; *Carratt* v. *Morley*, 1 Q. B. 18; *Beaurain* v. *Scott*, 3 Camp. 388; *per* Parke, B., 3 Moore, P. C. 28, 77); and such judge is responsible for mistakes of law respecting his jurisdiction; but is justified in determining his jurisdiction upon the facts as they appear before him, although they may subsequently be found to be false. (*Lowther* v. *Earl Radnor*, 8 East, 113; *Houlden* v. *Smith*, 14 Q. B. 841, 852; and see *Pease* v. *Chaytor*, 1 B. & S. 658; 31 L. J. M. C. 1; 32 *Ib.* 121.)

The judge of a court is not answerable for the wrongful acts or defaults of the ministerial officers of the Court in executing the commands of the Court. (*Holroyd* v. *Breare*, 2 B. & Ald. 473; *Tunno* v. *Morris*, 2 C. M. & R. 298.)

As to the liability of a judge for defamatory words, see "*Defamation*," *ante*, p. 393.

As to actions against justices of the peace, see *infra*.

Justice of the Peace (*a*).

(*a*) Actions against justices of the peace are regulated by 11 & 12 Vict. c. 44.

Magistrates are not liable for acting erroneously in point of law in matters within their jurisdiction, unless they act maliciously and without reasonable and probable cause; and the statement of claim must show that they so acted. See s. 1 of the above Act, and *Sommerville* v. *Mirehouse*, 1 B. & S. 652. They are liable for acts done without jurisdiction, although not done maliciously and without reasonable and probable cause. See s. 2 of the above Act, and *Pease* v. *Chaytor*, 1 B. & S. 658; 31 L. J. M. 1; 32 *Ib.* 121. They are not liable for a wrong decision as to jurisdiction, unless they have proceeded without reasonable and probable cause. (*Pease* v. *Chaytor*, *supra.*)

By s. 2 of the above Act it is further provided that no action shall be brought against a justice of the peace for anything done under a conviction or order, until the conviction has been quashed, either upon appeal or upon application to the High Court of Justice; and that no such action shall be brought for anything done under a warrant issued by such justice to procure the appearance of a party and which has been followed by a conviction or order in the same matter, until after such conviction or order has been quashed, or for anything done under a warrant to compel appearance if a summons has been previously served and not obeyed.

By s. 8 of the above Act, "no action shall be brought against any justice of the peace for anything done by him in the execution of his office, unless the same be commenced within six calendar months next after the act complained of had been committed." See "Defences," "*Limitations*," and see as to the time in which an action should be brought against a magistrate of the police courts of the metropolis, "Defences," "*Police.*"

By s. 9, "no action shall be commenced against any such justice of the peace until one calendar month at least after a notice in writing of such intended action shall have been delivered to him, or left for him at his usual place of abode, by the party intending to commence such action, or by his attorney or agent, in which said notice the cause of action, and the court in which the same is intended to be brought, shall be clearly and explicitly stated; and upon the back thereof shall be indorsed the name and place of abode of the party so intending to sue, and also the name and place of abode or of business of the said attorney or agent, if such notice have been served by such attorney or agent." See "Defences," "*Notice of Action.*"

By s. 11, he may tender amends. See "Defences," "*Tender of Amends.*"

See further as to actions against justices, 2 Arch. Pr. 13th ed. 1050; Addison on Torts, 5th ed. 617 *et seq.*

Light (*a*).

For Obstructing the Access of Light to a House, where the Right is Acquired under the Prescription Act, 2 & 3 W. IV., c. 71, ss. 3, 4.

1. The plaintiff was and is possessed of a dwelling-house, No. ——, —— Street, ——.

(*a*) By the Prescription Act, 2 & 3 Will. IV., c. 71, s. 3, it is enacted, "That when the access and use of light to and for any dwelling-house, workshop, or other building shall have been actually enjoyed therewith for the full period of twenty years without interruption, the right thereto shall be deemed absolute and indefeasible, any local usage or custom to the contrary notwithstanding, unless it shall appear that the same was enjoyed by some consent or agreement expressly made or given for that purpose by deed or writing."

As to the period here prescribed, and as to what constitutes an interruption, see s. 4 of the same Act, cited "*Common*," *ante*, p. 364, and *Flight* v. *Thomas*, 11 A. & E. 688; 8 Cl. & F. 231.

The access of light to a house may be "actually enjoyed" within the above section, although the house is unoccupied and not completed internally nor fit for habitation, if windows have been opened in it, through which the light in fact enters. (*Courtauld* v. *Legh*, L. R. 4 Ex. 126; 38 L. J. Ex. 45.)

The custom of the City of London, authorising the building on ancient foundations so as to obstruct a neighbour's ancient lights, is abolished by the above enactment in cases where there has been an enjoyment of the access and use of light for the statutory period without interruption. (*Salters Co.* v. *Jay*, 3 Q. B. 109; *Truscott* v. *Merchant Taylors' Co.*, 11 Ex. 855; 25 L. J. Ex. 173.)

In stating a claim of such right by actual enjoyment under the statute, it is not necessary to allege such enjoyment to have been "as of right," and this observation applies also to defences on the ground of such statutory right. (See *Truscott* v. *Merchant Taylors' Co.*, *supra*; *Frewen* v. *Phillips*, 11 C. B. N. S. 449; 30 L. J. C. P. 356; Gale on Easements, 5th ed., p. 177.)

A right to air is quite distinct from a right to light. A claim to have free access for all the winds of heaven to the sails of a windmill has been held too large and indefinite in its nature to be acquired by use, and not to be within the statute. (*Webb* v. *Bird*, 10 C. B. N. S. 268; 13 *Ib.* 841; 30 L. J. C. P. 384; 31 *Ib.* 335; *Dalton* v. *Angus*, 44 L. T. 844); and a grant of such a right cannot be presumed from mere enjoyment. (*Ib.*; and see *Angus* v. *Dalton*, 3 Q. B. D. 85; 4 *Ib.* 162; 47 L. J. Q. B. 163; 48 *Ib.* 225; 14 L. T. 844; *Allen* v. *Seckham*, 11 Ch. D. 797; 47 L. J. Ch. 742.) But there is a right at common law to the passage of a proper quantity of wholesome air to a house or land, and its stoppage is actionable as a nuisance (*Webb* v. *Bird*, *supra*); and in some rare cases, as where there is danger to health, may be restrained by injunction. (*Gale* v. *Abbott*, 10 W. R. 748; 8 Jur. N. S. 987; *City of London Brewery Co.* v. *Tennant*, L. R. 9 Ch. Ap. 212; 43 L. J. Ch. 457; see *Baxter* v. *Bower*, 44 L. J. Ch. 625.) It has been held that a right to have access of wind or air to a chimney, in order to create a sufficient

2. Upon the west side of the said house there were and are five windows.

3. The access and use of light through the said windows to and for the said house has been actually enjoyed therewith

---

draft, cannot be claimed, either as a natural right, or by immemorial prescription, or by the fiction of a lost grant, or under the statute. (*Bryant* v. *Lefever*, 4 C. P. D. 172; 48 L. J. C. P. 380.)

The right to light may be acquired by one tenant as against another tenant of land under the same landlord. (*Frewen* v. *Phillips*, 11 C. B. N. S. 449; 30 L. J. C. P. 356; see *Daniel* v. *Anderson*, 31 L. J. Ch. 610.) But the acquiring of a right to light under the statute is suspended during the continuance of a unity of possession of the two tenements. (*Ladyman* v. *Grave*, L. R. 6 Ch. Ap. 763; 24 L. T. 55; see *Ecclesiastical Commissioners* v. *Kino*, 14 Ch. D. 213; 49 L. J. Ch. 529.)

The Metropolitan Building Act enabling the owner to rebuild a party-wall, on making good all damage, does not authorize him in so doing to obstruct the ancient lights of the adjoining owner. (*Crofts* v. *Haldane*, L. R. 2 Q. B. 194; 36 L. J. Q. B. 85; see *Wells* v. *Ody*, 1 M. & W. 452; *Weston* v. *Arnold*, L. R. 8 Ch. Ap. 1084; 43 L. J. Ch. 123.)

It was formerly held that if the plaintiff altered or enlarged his lights, or added new ones, the defendant might obstruct them wholly, and the plaintiff had no remedy until he had reduced his lights to the original form and number. (*Renshaw* v. *Bean*, 18 Q. B. 112; *Hutchinson* v. *Copestake*, 8 C. B. N. S. 102; 9 C. B. N. S. 863; 31 L. J. C. P. 19; *Cooper* v. *Hubbuck*, 30 Beav. 160; 31 L. J. Ch. 123.) But this doctrine is overruled; and it is now held that if a person opens new lights or alters and enlarges old ones, the adjoining proprietor is entitled to obstruct the new lights or alterations only, and in so doing he is not entitled to obstruct the original lights, though he cannot otherwise obstruct the new ones. (*Tapling* v. *Jones*, 11 H. L. C. 290; 34 L. J. C. P. 342; *Aynsley* v. *Glover*, L. R. 18 Eq. 544; L. R. 10 Ch. Ap. 283; 43 L. J. Ch. 777; 44 *Ib.* 523; and see *National, &c., Insurance Co.* v. *Prudential Assurance Co.*, 6 Ch. D. 757; 46 L. J. Ch. 871; *Barnes* v. *Loach*, 4 Q. B. D. 494; 48 L. J. Q. B. 756.)

In such cases an injunction may be granted against any obstruction of the ancient lights, without putting the plaintiff on the terms of restoring the windows to their former state. (*Aynsley* v. *Glover*, *supra*; *Staight* v. *Burn*, L. R. 5 Ch. Ap. 163; 39 L. J. Ch. 289.) Such injunction may be granted even where the buildings in respect of which the right is claimed have been pulled down, provided that they were pulled down with the intention that they should be re-built, or that similar buildings should be substituted for them, by the owner or his vendees. (*Ecclesiastical Commissioners* v. *Kino*, 14 Ch. D. 213; 49 L. J. Ch. 529.)

The right to ancient lights is abandoned, or extinguished by closing them up with the intention of abandoning them. (*Moore* v. *Rawson*, 3 B. & C. 332; and see *Jones* v. *Tapling*, 11 C. B. N. S. 289; 31 L. J. C. P. 110; *Stokoe* v. *Singers*, 8 E. & B. 31; and as to abandonment of rights, see *Crossley* v. *Lightowler*, L. R. 3 Eq. 279; 2 Ch. Ap. 478; 36 L. J. Ch. 584; *Cook* v. *Mayor of Bath*, L. R. 6 Eq. 177; 18 L. T. 123; *Ecclesiastical Commissioners* v. *Kino*, *supra*.)

as an easement for the full period of 20 years next before the commencement of this action [*or*, next before a certain suit or action (*describing the same*), wherein the claim to the said access and use of light to and for

---

Where a man grants a house in which there are windows, neither he nor anyone claiming under him can stop up the windows or destroy the light (*Palmer* v. *Fletcher*, 1 Lev. 122; 1 Sid. 167, 227; *Allen* v. *Taylor*, 16 Ch. D. 355; 50 L. J. Ch. 178); but if having a house and land he grants the land, reserving the house, the grantee of the land can block up the windows of the house (*Ib.*). If, however, the owner of a house and land sells the house "with all lights, &c.," and as part of the same transaction sells to another person the land, the purchaser of the land cannot take away the lights from the house. (*Swansborough* v. *Coventry*, 9 Bing. 305; *Allen* v. *Taylor*, *supra*).

The grant of part of a tenement ordinarily implies a grant of all those continuous and apparent easements (such as access of light) over the other part of the tenement retained by the grantor which are necessary to the enjoyment of the part granted, and have been hitherto used therewith; and the fact that the part retained by the grantor is at the time of the grant in the possession of a lessee does not prevent the presumption of such implied grant of a right to the access of light. (*Barnes* v. *Loach*, 4 Q. B. D. 494; 48 L. J. Q. B. 756; and see *Leech* v. *Schweder*, L. R. 9 Ch. Ap. 463; 43 L. J. Ch. 487.) But, except in the case of ways of necessity and in some few similar cases, there is no corresponding implication of a reservation in favour of the grantor of part of a tenement in respect of the part retained by him, and if he desires to retain a right of access of light to that part over the part granted, he should expressly reserve such right, as no reservation of it will ordinarily be implied. (*Wheeldon* v. *Burrows*, 12 Ch. D. 31; 48 L. J. Ch. 853; *Allen* v. *Taylor*, *supra*.)

As to conveyances after 1881, see 44 & 45 Vict. c. 41, s. 6.

The plaintiff, whether tenant or reversioner, may maintain repeated actions for damages so long as the obstruction continues. (*Shadwell* v. *Hutchinson*, 2 B. & Ad. 97; *Battishill* v. *Reed*, 18 C. B. 696; 25 L. J. C. P. 290; *Spurr* v. *Hall*, 2 Q. B. D. 615.) In order to give a right of action for damages there must be a substantial deprivation of light sufficient to render the occupation of the house uncomfortable, or to prevent the plaintiff from carrying on business on the premises as beneficially as he formerly could. (*Back* v. *Stacey*, 2 C. & P. 465; *Dent* v. *Auction Mart Co.*, L. R. 2 Eq. 238, 245; 35 L. J. Ch. 555; *Ecclesiastical Commissioners* v. *Kino*, 14 Ch. D. 213, 224; 49 L. J. Ch. 529; *Moore* v. *Hall*, 3 Q. B. D. 178; 47 L. J. Q. B. 334.)

In a proper case an injunction may be claimed, either alone, or coupled with a claim for damages, either as an alternative or additional relief. An injunction will be granted where the obstruction materially interferes with the use and enjoyment of premises, and causes, or is likely to cause, material and substantial damage. (*Robson* v. *Whittingham*, L. R. 1 Ch. Ap. 442; 35 L. J. Ch. 227; *Dent* v. *Auction Mart Co.*, L. R. 2 Eq. 238; 35 L. J. Ch. 555; *Martin* v. *Headon*, L. R. 2 Eq. 425; 35 L. J. Ch. 602; *Durell* v. *Pritchard*, L. R. 1 Ch. Ap. 244; 35 L. J. Ch. 223; *Staight* v. *Burn*, *supra*; *Aynsley* v. *Glover*, *supra*; *Kino* v. *Rudkin*, 6 Ch. D. 160; *Kelk* v. *Pearson*, L. R. 6 Ch

the said house through the said windows was brought into question] without interruption, within the meaning of the statute 2 & 3 W. IV. c. 71, ss. 3 & 4 [such enjoyment not being by any consent or agreement expressly made or given for that purpose by deed or writing (*b*)].

4. The defendant has interfered with such enjoyment by erecting, and keeping so erected, a high wall near to the said windows, and thereby preventing the light from

---

Ap. 809; 24 L. T. 890.) As to interlocutory injunctions in such cases, see *Aynsley* v. *Glover, supra;* see further, "*Injunction,*" *ante*, p. 440.

It was formerly said that the Court would not in an ordinary case restrain the erection of a building the height of which above an ancient light is not greater than the distance from the light (*Beadel* v. *Perry*, L. R. 3 Eq. 465; 15 L. T. 345; *Hackett* v. *Baiss*, L. R. 20 Eq. 494; 45 L. J. Ch. 13); but there is no rule of law to that effect, and, although proof of that fact will, ordinarily, be *primâ facie* evidence that there is no obstruction of the light, such proof may be rebutted by evidence that an obstruction and diminution of light in fact exist. See *City of London Brewery Co.* v. *Tennant*, L. R. 9 Ch. Ap. 212; 43 L. J. Ch. 457; *Theed* v. *Debenham*, 2 Ch. D. 165; *Ecclesiastical Commissioners* v. *Kino, supra*.

The right to light is not restricted to the quantity made use of for present purposes where a right to a greater quantity has been previously acquired; and the possibility that the premises may subsequently be used for a different purpose ought to be taken into account. (*Yates* v. *Jack*, L. R. 1 Ch. Ap. 295; 35 L. J. Ch. 539; *Dent* v. *Auction Mart Co., supra; Aynsley* v. *Glover, supra; Moore* v. *Hall, supra.*)

An injunction will not be granted against an obstruction merely on the ground that it obscures the view of a shop from the outside. (*Smith* v. *Owen*, 35 L. J. Ch. 317; *Butt* v. *Imperial Gas Co.*, L. R. 2 Ch. Ap. 158; and see *Rickett* v. *Metropolitan Ry. Co.*, L. R. 2 H. L. 175; 36 L. J. Q. B. 205.)

An injunction may be granted in an action by a reversioner where material injury to the reversion is proved. See *Kino* v. *Rudkin, supra; Aynsley* v. *Glover, supra;* and *Jackson* v. *Duke of Newcastle*, 3 De G. J. & S. 275; 33 L. J. Ch. 698.

The right to light may sometimes be established on the ground of prescription from time immemorial, where, by reason of interruption or other causes, a prescription under the Prescription Act cannot be made out. See *Aynsley* v. *Glover, supra.* But ordinarily a claim of such right by immemorial prescription is liable to be negatived by the known date of the buildings; and in such cases, where proof cannot be given of a prescriptive right under the statute, the right to light may sometimes be supported on the ground of the presumption of a lost grant from the owner of the servient tenement. See *Leech* v. *Schweder, supra; Angus* v. *Dalton, supra; Allen* v. *Seckham, supra;* and see "Defences," "*Light.*") As to stating the mode in which the right claimed arises, see further, note (*c*), *post*, p. 451.

(*b*) See "Defences," "*Lights.*"

entering through the said windows, as it formerly did, as above stated, into the said house.

5. The said house has in consequence been rendered dark and unwholesome [*state special damage, if any*].

For a Form of Claim for Obstruction to Light, see *Spurr* v. *Hall,* 2 Q. B. D. 615; 37 L. T. 313.

Claim by a Reversioner for an Obstruction to Light (*c*).

1. At the times hereinafter mentioned a dwelling-house, situate, &c. (*describe the house shortly, as in the last Precedent*), was in the possession of A. B. as tenant thereof to the plaintiff, under an indenture of lease, dated the —— of ——, 18—, for a term of —— years from that day, the reversion thereof at the times of the grievances hereinafter mentioned [and still] belonging to the plaintiff.

2. In the said house there of right were at the times aforesaid, and still ought to be, on the —— side of the said house, three windows, through which at the times aforesaid the light [and air] of right ought to have entered, and still ought to enter into the said house.

3. In ——, 18—, the defendant wrongfully erected and built a wall [—— feet high] on the —— side of the said house, near to the said windows [and within a distance of —— feet therefrom], and has kept and continued the said wall so erected up to the present time [*or if the wall has been removed, state the time during which the defendant allowed it to remain standing*].

(*c*) See note (*a*), *supra*, p. 447. It is probably more correct to state the facts, showing how the right arises, whether under the statute, as in the form first given, or by immemorial prescription, or lost grant, or in the alternative in any or all of the above modes, but unless the defendant is embarrassed in his defence by the above mode of pleading, the above form is sufficient; though it is conceived that if the defendant is so embarrassed, he may obtain an order that it should be amended, so as to show the mode in which the right is claimed, or may obtain particulars. (O. XXVII. r. 1; and see "*Pleading in General*," *ante*, p. 7.)

The above form would generally, it is thought, be sufficient. (See *Spurr* v. *Hall*, 2 Q. B. D. 615; *Duke of Norfolk* v. *Arbuthnot*, 4 C. P. D. 291; 48 L. J. C. P. 737; and see "*Common*," *ante*, p. 365.)

4. By so erecting and continuing the said wall as aforesaid, the defendant prevented and obstructed and hindered the light [and air] from entering through the said windows into the said house, and the said house has been thereby rendered dark [unwholesome] and of less value, and the plaintiff has been injured in his reversionary estate therein, and has been put to an expense of £ —— in constructing and opening other windows to obtain light [and air] in the said house.

5. [*If an injunction is claimed, state any facts which may be material for the granting thereof, as for instance:* The plaintiff, as soon as he became aware of the intended erection of the said wall by the defendant, and at the time of the commencement of the building thereof [by letters bearing date ——], warned the defendant that the erection thereof would occasion such obstruction of light [and air] as aforesaid, and requested the defendant to desist from the erection of the said wall.

6. The defendant nevertheless erected and continued the said wall as aforesaid, and threatens and intends to continue the same, and to raise it to a greater height, unless he is restrained by the order and judgment of this Court from so doing.]

The plaintiff claims:—

1. £ —— damages for the wrongs above complained of.
2. [That the defendant may be restrained by the order and judgment of this Court from continuing or allowing the said wall to remain erected, and from further raising the same, and from erecting or permitting to remain any wall or other building or erection which shall in any way obstruct or hinder the access of light [and air] to the said windows.]
3. Such further or other relief as the nature of the case may require.

For a Form of Counterclaim for Obstruction of Light, with a Claim for an Injunction, see *Duke of Norfolk* v. *Arbuthnot*, 4 C. P. D. 291; 48 L. J. C. P. 737.

Malicious Prosecution (*a*).

For a Malicious Prosecution before a Justice of the Peace.

1. The plaintiff was in the service of the defendant as his cook [and had been in his service in that capacity for

---

(*a*) This cause of action consists in the prosecution by the defendant of legal proceedings, of a civil or criminal nature, against the plaintiff, maliciously, and without any reasonable or probable cause; whereby the plaintiff is injured, as by being arrested and imprisoned or put to expense. (*Johnstone* v. *Sutton*, 1 T. R. 493, 544.)

The statement of claim must show the legal proceedings instituted by the defendant against the plaintiff, and the termination of them in his favour, where the proceedings are capable of such a termination (*Basébé* v. *Matthews*, L. R. 2 C. P. 684; 36 L. J. M. C. 93); the absence of reasonable or probable cause for instituting the proceedings, and the malice of the defendant in so doing, and also the arrest or other loss or injury suffered by the plaintiff. (*Johnson* v. *Emerson*, L. R. 6 Ex. 329, 344, 372; 40 L. J. Ex. 201; *Saxon* v. *Castle*, 6 A. & E. 652; *De Medina* v. *Grove*, 10 Q. B. 168; *Dimmock* v. *Bowley*, 2 C. B. N. S. 542; *Harris* v. *Warre*, 4 C. P. D. 125; 48 L. J. C. P. 310.)

The malice may be alleged as a fact, without setting out the circumstances from which it is to be inferred (O. XIX. r. 25).

All the circumstances under which the wrong was committed may be stated and proved in order to aggravate and enhance the damages. (*Millington* v. *Loring*, 6 Q. B. D. 190; 50 L. J. Q. B. 214, and see "*Damages*," *ante*, p. 19.) Where the proceedings were *ex parte*, and the plaintiff had no opportunity of preventing an unfavourable termination, as where the defendant maliciously exhibited articles of the peace against him, it was held that notwithstanding such termination the plaintiff might recover. (*Steward* v. *Gromett*, 7 C. B. N. S. 191; 29 L. J. C. P. 170.) The exhibition of articles of the peace is always an *ex parte* proceeding. (*Lort* v. *Hutton*, 45 L. J. M. C. 95; 33 L. T. 730.)

In an action for maliciously arresting the plaintiff on a *ca. sa.* for a larger sum than was really due under the judgment, it was held not necessary that the plaintiff should have obtained his discharge by an order of the Court before action, because the illegality of the arrest did not depend upon the result of any legal proceedings, but only on the amount for which execution might issue. (*Gilding* v. *Eyre*, 10 C. B. N. S. 592; 31 L. J. C. P. 174.)

The absence of reasonable and probable cause is a question of law for the judge to determine, the facts and inferences of fact are for the jury. (*Venafra* v. *Johnson*, 10 Bing. 301; *Panton* v. *Williams*, 2 Q. B. 169; *James* v. *Phelps*, 11 A. & E. 483; *Douglas* v. *Corbett*, 6 E. & B. 511; *Lister* v. *Perryman*, L. R. 4 H. L. 521; 39 L. J. Ex. 177.)

The *onus* of showing that there was not reasonable and probable cause rests in the first instance upon the plaintiff. (*Lister* v. *Perryman*, *supra*; *Walker* v. *South Eastern Ry. Co.*, L. R. 5 C. P. 640, 644; 39 L. J. C. P. 346.)

"In order to justify a defendant there must be a reasonable cause—such as would operate on the mind of a discreet man; there must

five years] at the time of the grievances hereinafter mentioned.

2. On the —— of ——, 18—, the defendant, missing a five-pound note which belonged to him, charged the

---

also be a probable cause—such as would operate on the mind of a reasonable man; at all events such as would operate on the mind of the party making the charge; otherwise there is no probable cause for him." (*Per* Tindal, C. J. in *Broad* v. *Ham*, 5 Bing. N. C. 725; *Lister* v. *Perryman*, L. R. 4 H. L. 521, 532, 540; 39 L. J. Ex. 177; *Shrosbery* v. *Osmaston*, 37 L. T. 792.)

As to what constitutes reasonable and probable cause, see *James* v. *Phelps*, 11 A. & E. 483; *Haddrick* v. *Heslop*, 12 Q. B. 267; *Heslop* v. *Chapman*, 23 L. J. Q. B. 49; *Hinton* v. *Heather*, 14 M. & W. 131; *Busst* v. *Gibbons*, 30 L. J. Ex. 75; *Turner* v. *Ambler*, 10 Q. B. 252; *Lister* v. *Perryman*, *supra*; *Johnson* v. *Emerson*, *supra*.

The malice necessary to support this action consists in the defendant being actuated by indirect and improper motives. Malice is a question of fact for the jury, and may generally be inferred by them from the fact of the defendant having acted without reasonable and probable cause (*Mitchell* v. *Jenkins*, 5 B. & Ad. 588; and see *Moore* v. *Guardner*, 16 M. & W 595; *Weston* v. *Beeman*, 27 L. J. Ex. 57); but a prosecution instituted with malicious motives is not a ground of action, unless also without reasonable and probable cause. See *Musgrove* v. *Newell*, 1 M. & W. 582.

No action will lie for malicious and unfounded prosecution of civil proceedings where special damage is not proved to have resulted therefrom, such as, for example, an arrest of the plaintiff, where such arrest was part of the proceedings (*Cotterell* v. *Jones*, 11 C. B. 713; *Johnson* v. *Emerson*, *supra*, *per* Martin B.; *notes to Skinner* v. *Gunton*, 1 Wms. Saund. p. 269; and *see Wren* v. *Weild*, L. R. 4 Q. B. 730; 38 L. J. Q. B. 327.) The extra costs incurred in successfully defending a civil action, beyond the amount awarded by the Court, are not damage sufficient to maintain this action. (*Cotterell* v. *Jones*, *supra*.)

As to the distinction between malicious prosecution and false imprisonment, see *Austin* v. *Dowling*, L. R. 5 C. P. 534; 39 L. J. C. P. 260.

The arrest and prosecution of offenders or supposed offenders not being within the scope of employment of servants in general, a master, in the absence of proof of authority to the servant to arrest or prosecute on his behalf, or of ratification by the master of the arrest or prosecution by the servant on his behalf, is not responsible for an arrest or prosecution by an ordinary servant or employé. A servant in charge of property has, in general, an implied authority to do all that is necessary for the protection of such property, but no implied authority to punish for an infringement of the law. See *Allen* v. *L. & S. W. Ry. Co.*, L. R. 6 Q. B. 65, 69; 40 L. J. Q. B. 55; *Edwards* v. *L. & N. W. Ry. Co.*, L. R. 5 C. P. 445; 39 L. J. C. P. 241; *Bank of New South Wales* v. *Owston*, 4 App. Cas. 270; 48 L. J. P. C. 25. Thus it has been held that neither the arrest, nor the prosecution, of offenders is within the ordinary scope of a bank manager's authority, and that unless there is express evidence of such authority, or evidence thereof to be implied from the exigency of the particular occasion, his

plaintiff with having stolen it. The plaintiff at once denied the said charge.

3. Thereupon the defendant falsely and maliciously, and without any reasonable or probable cause, appeared before a justice of the peace and charged the plaintiff with having feloniously stolen the said note, and upon such charge procured the said justice to grant his warrant for apprehending the plaintiff, and bringing her before the said justice, to be dealt with according to law, and under and by virtue of the said warrant caused the plaintiff to be arrested and to be imprisoned [for —— hours], and then brought in custody before the said justice on the —— of ——, 18—.

4. [On the said —— of ——, 18—, the defendant procured the said justice to remand the plaintiff to prison, and caused the plaintiff to be imprisoned until the —— of ——, 18—, and then again brought in custody before the said justice.]

5. Upon the said —— of ——, 18—, the said justice having heard the said charge dismissed the same, and

---

principals are not responsible for his action in arresting or prosecuting persons for stealing the bank property (*Bank of New South Wales* v. *Owston, supra*); so a foreman porter in the service of a railway company, who is left in charge of a station, has no implied authority to give in charge a person whom he suspects to be stealing the company's property; and if he gives an innocent person in charge on such suspicion, the company are not liable. (*Edwards* v. *L. & N. W. Ry. Co., supra.*)

The scope of employment of a servant may in some particular cases be such as to include authority to arrest or prosecute offenders on behalf of his master. Such authority may be implied where the employment is such that its duties could not be efficiently performed for the benefit of the employer without such authority (*Bank of New South Wales* v. *Owston, supra*; *Moore* v. *Met. Ry. Co.*, L. R. 8 Q. B. 36; 42 L. J. Q. B. 23; *Edwards* v. *Mid. Ry. Co.*, 6 Q. B. D. 287; 50 L. J. Q B. 281; *Allen* v. *L. & S. W. Ry. Co., supra*).

As to arrest, see further "*Trespass*," *post*, p. 530.

As to actions for a malicious prosecution against a corporation, see "*Corporation*," *ante*, p. 388.

It was held (*Martin, B. dissenting*) in the case of *Johnson* v. *Emerson, supra*, that an action would lie for wrongfully and maliciously and without reasonable or probable cause procuring a person to be adjudicated a bankrupt under the Bankruptcy Act, 1869 (32 & 33 Vict. c. 71). Under former Bankruptcy Acts such action was maintainable. See *Farley* v. *Danks*, 4 E. & B. 493; 24 L. J. Q. B. 244; *Cotton* v. *James*, 1 B. & Ad. 128; *Whitworth* v. *Hall*, 2 B. & Ad. 695; *Hay* v. *Weakley*, 5 C. & P. 361; *Atkinson* v. *Raleigh*, 3 Q. B. 79.

discharged the plaintiff out of custody, whereby the said prosecution was determined.

6. The plaintiff has, by reason of the above conduct of the defendant, been injured in her character and put to an expense of £—— in obtaining her release from the said imprisonment.

For a Malicious Prosecution by Indictment (b).

1. The plaintiff has for many years carried on and still carries on business as a wine and spirit merchant at ——; the defendant is a wholesale wine and spirit merchant carrying on business at ——.

2. On the —— of ——, 18—, the plaintiff gave the defendant an order for 50 quarter casks of brandy and 25 quarter casks of sherry, to be put on board the ship "Victoria Nyanza" by the defendant for the plaintiff.

3. The defendant accepted the said order, and put the said brandy and sherry ordered on board the said ship for the plaintiff.

4. The mate's receipt for the said goods was, in the usual course of business, handed by the defendant to the plaintiff.

5. Afterwards, on the —— of——, 18—, the plaintiff was adjudicated a bankrupt.

6. The defendant thereupon falsely and maliciously, and without reasonable or probable cause, presented to the grand jury at the assizes holden in and for the county

(b) The defendant is liable for maliciously and without reasonable or probable cause procuring the prosecution of a criminal charge against the plaintiff, notwithstanding he has also procured himself to be bound over by recognizance to prosecute. (*Dubois* v. *Keats*, 11 A. & E. 329.) Where the defendant gave false evidence as a witness in a previous action, whereupon the presiding judge, at his own instance, ordered the prosecution for perjury of the plaintiff who was another witness in that action, and bound over the defendant to prosecute, and the defendant appeared to prosecute, and repeated his false evidence before the grand jury, it was held that he was liable in an action for maliciously, and without reasonable or probable cause, causing the plaintiff to be prosecuted for perjury. (So held by a majority of one in the Exchequer Chamber in *Fitzjohn* v. *Mackinder*, 9 C. B. N. S. 505; reversing the judgment of a majority of one in the Court below; 8 C. B. N. S. 78; 30 L. J. C. P. 257). A remand is the act of the magistrate, and may be sued for in an action for malicious prosecution. It cannot, even in an action for false imprisonment, be charged as the act of the defendant. See *Lock* v. *Ashton*, 12 Q. B. 871.

of ——, on the —— of ——, 18—, a Bill of Indictment against the plaintiff.

7. The said Bill of Indictment charged the plaintiff with having unlawfully obtained from the defendant, by false and fraudulent pretences knowingly made by the plaintiff to the defendant, a certain valuable security, to wit, the said mate's receipt.

8. The defendant further falsely and maliciously, and without reasonable and probable cause, prosecuted and caused and procured the plaintiff to be tried upon the said false charge at the said assizes.

9. Upon such trial the plaintiff was acquitted of the said charge, whereby the said prosecution was determined.

10. By reason of the premises the plaintiff was injured in his character, reputation, and business, and put to an expense of £—— in defending himself upon the said trial.

For a Malicious Arrest under 32 *&* 33 *Vict. c.* 62, *s.* 6 (*c*).

1. The plaintiff resides, and has for some time resided, at ——. The defendant also resides at ——.

(*c*) By the Debtors' Act, 1869 (32 & 33 Vict. c. 62), s. 6 : "Where the plaintiff, in any action in any of her Majesty's superior courts of law at Westminster, in which, if brought before the commencement of this Act, the defendant would have been liable to arrest, proves at any time before final judgment, by evidence on oath, to the satisfaction of a judge of one of those courts, that the plaintiff has good cause of action against the defendant to the amount of £50, or upwards, and that there is probable cause for believing that the defendant is about to quit England, unless he be apprehended, and that the absence of the defendant from England will materially prejudice the plaintiff in the prosecution of his action, such judge may, in the prescribed manner, order such defendant to be arrested and imprisoned for a period not exceeding six months, unless and until he has sooner given the prescribed security, not exceeding the amount claimed in the action, that he will not go out of England without the leave of the court. Where the action is for a penalty or sum in the nature of a penalty, other than a penalty in respect of any contract, it shall not be necessary to prove that the absence of the defendant from England will materially prejudice the plaintiff in the prosecution of his action, and the security given, instead of being that the defendant will not go out of England, shall be to the effect that any sum recovered against the defendant in the action shall be paid, or that the defendant shall be rendered to prison." The plaintiff can only, it would seem, be "materially prejudiced" by the absence of the defendant "in the

2. On the —— of ——, 18—, the plaintiff accepted a bill of exchange drawn upon him by the defendant for £——, payable three months after date.

3. This bill of exchange was dishonoured at maturity, and an action was brought by the now defendant against the now plaintiff to recover the amount thereof.

4. After the said action was commenced, the defendant maliciously, and without reasonable or probable cause procured and caused the plaintiff to be arrested on the —— day of ——, 18—, under an order of the Hon. Mr. Justice ——, dated the —— of ——, 18— [in the presence of numerous persons acquainted with the plaintiff in —— Street, ——], and under and by virtue of the said order to be imprisoned and kept in custody [for —— days.]

5. On the —— day of ——, 18—, the plaintiff was discharged from the said custody under and by virtue of an order of the Hon. Mr. Justice ——.

6. The first mentioned order of the Hon. Mr. Justice —— was caused and procured by the defendant maliciously, and without reasonable or probable cause, producing to the said Hon. Mr. Justice —— an affidavit wherein he deposed, amongst other things, that the now plaintiff was a necessary and material witness for him, the defendant, in the said action upon the said bill of exchange, and that without the evidence of the now plaintiff he could not prove in the said action that the now plaintiff was the acceptor of the said bill of ex-

---

prosecution" of the action, if the presence of the defendant is required for the purpose of obtaining discovery from him, or taking his evidence as a witness. (*Yorkshire Engine Co.* v. *Wright*, 21 W. R. 15; *Hume* v. *Druyff*, L. R. 8 Ex. 214; 42 L. J. Ex. 145.) An action is maintainable for falsely or fraudulently and maliciously, and without reasonable or probable cause, making or procuring an affidavit under the above section, and thereby obtaining an order for the plaintiff's arrest. See *Daniels* v. *Fielding*, 16 M. & W. 200; and *Grainger* v. *Hill*, 4 Bing. N. C. 212; Roscoe's N. P. Ev. 14th ed. 822.

A person privileged from arrest on the ground that he is attending a court of justice as a witness, or on any similar ground, if arrested, cannot maintain an action, although the arrest was made maliciously and with knowledge of the privilege: for the privilege is that of the Court granting it, and not that of the person, and it is discretionary in the Court to allow the privilege even if claimed by the plaintiff. (*Magnay* v. *Burt*, 5 Q. B. 381; *Yearsley* v. *Heane*, 14 M. & W. 322; *Philips* v. *Naylor*, 3 H. & N. 14; 4 *Ib.* 565; 27 L. J. Ex. 222; 28 *Ib.* 225.)

change, and that the absence of the now plaintiff from England would materially prejudice the now defendant in the prosecution of the said action.

7. The said statements contained in the said affidavit were false to the knowledge of the defendant. The defendant then knew the handwriting of the now plaintiff perfectly well, and could have himself proved in the said action that the now plaintiff was the acceptor of the said bill. Further, the defendant then well knew that numerous persons at —— were acquainted with the handwriting of the now plaintiff, and that he could obtain their evidence, and so prove in the said action that the plaintiff was the acceptor of the said bill. The defendant further, as he then well knew, could have proved that the plaintiff had actually admitted that he accepted the said bill. The now defendant then knew perfectly well that the absence of the now plaintiff could not prejudice him, the now defendant, in the prosecution of the said action, and that the now plaintiff was not a necessary witness in the said action.

8. [*State damage.*]

MANDAMUS (*a*).

For Claim against a Joint-Stock Company for a Mandamus requiring them to Register the Plaintiff as a Shareholder, see "Company," ante, p. 369.

(*a*) By the C. L. P. Act, 1854, ss. 68–73, the Superior Courts of Common Law at Westminster were empowered to grant to the plaintiff in any action (except replevin and ejectment), in pursuance of a claim to be made in the action as therein mentioned, and as part of the judgment in such action, a peremptory writ of mandamus commanding the defendant to fulfil any [public or *quasi*-public] duty in the fulfilment of which the plaintiff was personally interested. The jurisdiction given by the above-cited enactments of granting a writ of mandamus as part of the judgment in an action has, by the Judicature Acts, been transferred to, and vested in, the High Court of Justice and the Court of Appeal respectively, subject to the modifications introduced by the Judicature Acts and Rules. See Jud. Act, 1873, ss. 16 and 19; *Glossop* v. *Heston Local Board*, 12 Ch. D. 102; 49 L. J. Ch. 89.

It is also provided, by s. 25 (8) of the Jud. Act, 1873, that a writ of mandamus may be granted by an interlocutory order of the Court in all cases in which it shall appear to the Court to be just or con-

For Claim against a Railway Company for a Mandamus requiring them to issue a Warrant for a Jury to Assess Compensation for Land taken by the Company, see "Company," ante, p. 154.

---

venient that such order should be made. See the section, *ante*, p. 440; and see O. LII., rule 4; *Glossop* v. *Heston Local Board*, 12 Ch. D. 102; 49 L. J. Ch. 89; *In re Paris Skating Rink Co.*, 6 Ch. D. 731; 46 L. J. Ch. 831.

Where the plaintiff seeks to obtain a mandamus, the writ of summons should be indorsed with a claim of such mandamus accordingly. (O. II., r. 1; and see s. 68 of the C. L. P. Act, 1854, and "*Injunction*," *ante*, p. 439.) As to the form of such indorsement, see O. III. r. 3, and Part II. of App. (A.) to Jud. Act, 1875, sect. 4, Form 74; and *Ward* v. *South Eastern Ry. Co.*, 2 E. & E. 812; 29 L. J. Q. B. 77; *Morgan* v. *Metropolitan Ry. Co.*, L. R. 3 C. P. 553; 4 *Ib.* 97; 37 L. J. C. P. 275; 38 *Ib.* 87.

The statement of claim in an action for a mandamus should distinctly claim the mandamus, and should sufficiently show what is the duty of which performance is sought to be enforced, and should state the material facts relied upon in support of the claim, and set forth that the plaintiff is personally interested in the fulfilment of such duty, and that he sustains or may sustain damage by the non-performance thereof, and that performance thereof has been demanded by him, and refused or neglected. (O. XIX., rr. 2 and 4; and see ss. 69 and 70 of the C. L. P. Act, 1854.)

A writ of mandamus may be claimed either together with claims for damages or other relief, or separately.

The duty for the performance of which a mandamus is obtainable as part of the judgment in an action must be one of a public, or *quasi*-public, nature, as well as one in the performance of which the plaintiff is personally interested. See *Benson* v. *Paul*, 6 E. & B. 273; 25 L. J. Q. B. 274; *Norris* v. *Irish Land Co.*, 8 E. & B. 512; 27 L. J. Q. B. 115; *Fotherby* v. *Metropolitan Ry. Co.*, *supra*; Day's C. L. P. Acts, 4th ed., p. 320. Hence a claim for a writ of mandamus will not lie for the specific performance of a mere personal contract, as to accept a lease under an agreement. (*Benson* v. *Paul*, *supra*.)

Nor will an action for a writ of mandamus lie where there is any other equally effectual remedy, as for a personal debt for which an action may be brought in the ordinary manner. (*Bush* v. *Beavan*, 1 H. & C. 500; 32 L. J. Ex. 54.)

The following are instances of actions in which a claim for a mandamus has been held to lie, viz.; an action against a public company for a mandamus requiring them to register the plaintiff as a shareholder in respect of his shares (*Norris* v. *Irish Land Co.*, 8 E. & B. 512; 27 L. J. Q. B. 115; and see *Copeland* v. *North-Eastern Ry. Co.*, 6 E. & B. 277); a like action for a mandamus requiring the company to replace on the register the name of the plaintiff which had been wrongfully removed (*Swan* v. *North British Australasian Co.*, 7 H. & N. 603; 31 L. J. Ex. 425; 2 H. & C. 175; 32 L. J. Ex. 273); an action against a railway company for a mandamus requiring them to issue a warrant for a jury to assess compensation for land which they had given notice to take for the purposes of their undertaking

MARKET (*a*).

For Form of Statement of Claim for Disturbance of Market and Refusal to Pay Tolls: Mayor of Penryn v. *Best*, 3 Ex. D. 292; 48 L. J. Ex. 103 (*b*).

(*Fotherby* v. *Metropolitan Ry. Co.*, L. R. 2 C. P. 188; 36 L. J. C. P. 88; and see *Morgan* v. *Metropolitan Ry. Co.*, L. R. 3 C. P. 553; 4 *Ib.* 97; 37 L. J. C. P. 265; 38 *Ib.* 87; *Tyson* v. *Mayor, &c., of London*, L. R. 7 C. P. 18; 41 L. J. C. P. 6); an action against a railway company for a mandamus requiring them to enter a transfer of stock, to register the plaintiff as proprietor thereof, and to deliver a certificate of his being such proprietor (*Ward* v. *South-Eastern Ry. Co.*, 2 E. & E. 812; 29 L. J. Q. B. 177); an action against Improvement Commissioners for a mandamus requiring them to levy a rate for the payment of a debt due to the plaintiff (*Ward* v. *Lowndes*, 1 E. & E. 940, 956; 28 L. J. Q. B. 265; 29 *Ib.* 40; *Worthington* v. *Hulton*, L. R. 1 Q. B. 63); an action against Improvement Commissioners to compel them to apply their funds in payment of certain bonds in compliance with their duty (*Webb* v. *Herne Bay Commissioners*, L. R. 5 Q. B. 642; 39 L. J. Q. B. 221).

(*a*) The mere grant of a market does not of itself confer the right to prevent persons from selling on market days in their private houses, though within the town or manor where the market may be held (*Mayor of Macclesfield* v. *Chapman*, 12 M. & W. 18; *Mayor of Penryn* v. *Best*, 3 Ex. D. 292; 48 L. J. Ex. 103), but such right may be acquired by immemorial enjoyment or prescription. (*Mosley* v. *Walker*, 7 B. & C. 40; *Mayor of Macclesfield* v. *Pedley*, 4 B. & Ad. 397; *Mayor of Penryn* v. *Best, supra.*)

Market owners are bound to provide a reasonably safe place for the receipt and storage of cattle brought into the market at their invitation, and for their profit, and where any injury arises from neglect of this obligation the sufferer therefrom, will, in the absence of contributory negligence or acceptance of the risk which caused such injury, be entitled to sue the owners for the loss sustained by him. (*Lax* v. *Corporation of Darlington*, 5 Ex. D. 28; 49 L. J. Ex. 105.)

See the Markets and Fairs Clauses Act, 1847 (10 Vict. c. 14), as to markets authorized by statutes incorporating that Act.

(*b*) As to what acts constitute a disturbance of a market, see *Mosley* v. *Chadwick*, 7 B. & C. p. 47, n. (*a*); *Mosley* v. *Walker*, 7 B. & C. 40; *Bridgland* v. *Shapter*, 5 M. & W. 375; *Yard* v. *Ford*, 2 Wms. Saund. 1871 ed. p. 500; *Mayor of London* v. *Low*, 49 L. J. Q. B. 144; 42 L. T. 16.

For forms under old practice see: *For disturbing the plaintiff's market by selling goods near the market: Bridgland* v. *Shapter*, 5 M. & W. 375; *Mayor of Brecon* v. *Edwards*, 1 H. & C. 51; 31 L. J. Ex. 368; *for disturbing the plaintiff's market by selling goods in private shops on market days: Mayor of Devizes* v. *Clark*, 3 A. & E. 506; *Mosley* v. *Walker*, 7 B. & C. 40; *Mayor of Macclesfield* v. *Chapman*, 12 M. & W. 18; *for disturbing the plaintiff's right of holding a stall in a market adjoining his house by removing the market: Ellis* v. *Mayor of Bridgnorth*, 15 C. B. N. S. 52; 32 L. J. C. P. 273.

Master and Servant.

Statement of Claim for Enticing Away the Plaintiff's Servant (a).

1. The plaintiff carries on the business of a —— at ——.

2. G. H. was [and is] the servant of the plaintiff [in his said business].

3. In the month of ——, 18—, whilst the said G. H. was such servant of the plaintiff as above stated, the defendant wrongfully enticed and procured the said G. H., unlawfully and without the consent and against the will of the plaintiff, to depart from the said service of the plaintiff.

4. The defendant then well knew that the said G. H. was then such servant of the plaintiff as above stated.

5. In consequence of the above wrongful acts of the defendant, the plaintiff was deprived of the services of the said G. H. [in his said business] and suffered great loss and inconvenience.

For Form of Declaration under the Old Practice for Maliciously Enticing and Procuring a Singer Engaged to Perform at the Plaintiff's Theatre to Break her Engagement, see Lumley v. *Gye,* 2 E. & B. 216; 22 L. J. Q. B. 463.

(a) In order to maintain this action there must be a valid contract of service, or an actual subsisting service in fact (*Sykes* v. *Dixon*, 9 A. & E. 693; *Hartley* v. *Cummings*, 5 C. B. 247; *Bowen* v. *Hall*, 6 Q. B. D. 333; 50 L. J. Q. B. 305), to the knowledge of the defendant (*Fores* v. *Wilson*, Peake, 55), and an actual loss of service by the act of the defendant. See *Eager* v. *Grimwood*, 1 Ex. 61. An action will not lie for enticing away an apprentice if the indentures of apprenticeship are void. (*Cox* v. *Muncey*, 6 C. B. N. S. 375.) The services of a daughter residing at home are sufficient to entitle the father to maintain an action for enticing her away. (*Evans* v. *Walton*, L. R. 2 C. P. 615; 36 L. J. C. P. 307.) Where the defendant has enticed away the plaintiff's apprentice, or has kept him after notice, the plaintiff may waive the tort and sue as upon a contract for the value of his services. (*Lightly* v. *Clouston*, 1 Taunt. 112; *Foster* v. *Stewart*, 3 M. & S. 191.)

For Loss of Services caused by the Seduction of the Plaintiff's Servant (*b*).

1. The plaintiff carries on the business of a —— at ——, and the defendant is a —— residing at ——.

2. G. H. is the daughter of the plaintiff, and at the times hereinafter mentioned assisted him in the conduct of his said business and in the management of his household affairs.

3. In or about the month of ——, 18—, the defendant seduced the said G. H., whereby she became pregnant with child, and was delivered thereof on the —— of ——, 18—.

4. In consequence of the said seduction, the plaintiff was deprived of the services of the said G. H. for a long time [*or state the period*], and incurred £—— expense in nursing and taking care of her and about the delivery of the said child.

Statement of Claim by a Master for Injury to his Servant. Berringer v. *Gt. Eastern Ry. Co.*, 4 C. P. D. 163; 48 L. J. C. P. 400 ; 27 W. R. 681 (*c*).

(*b*) In order to maintain an action for seduction, the relation of master and servant must subsist at the time of the seduction (*Davies* v. *Williams*, 10 Q. B. 725, *and see preceding note*). Where the relation is contracted after the seduction the action is not maintainable. (*Ib.*)

A father can maintain an action for the seduction of his daughter only in respect of his loss of his daughter's services occasioned by the seduction, and not in respect of his being compelled to maintain her by reason of the seduction. (*Grinnell* v. *Wells*, 7 M. & G. 1033.) The loss of service must be alleged in the statement of claim, and proved.

As to the kind of service required to support the action see *Thompson* v. *Ross*, 5 H. & N. 16 ; 29 L. J. Ex. 1 ; *Manley* v. *Field*, 7 C. B. N. S. 96 ; 29 L. J. C. P. 79 ; *Rist* v. *Faux*, 4 B. & S. 409 ; 32 L. J. Q. B. 386 ; *Evans* v. *Walton*, *supra* ; *Terry* v. *Hutchinson*, L. R. 3 Q. B. 599 ; 37 L. J. Q. B. 257 ; *Hedges* v. *Tagg*, L. R. 7 Ex. 283 ; 41 L. J. Ex. 169 ; and see Addison on Torts, 5th ed. 534.

The loss of service must be occasioned by the act of the defendant ; where the jury found that the defendant seduced the plaintiff's daughter, but was not the father of the child whose birth occasioned the loss of service, he was held entitled to a verdict. (*Eager* v. *Grimwood*, 1 Ex. 61.)

(*c*) A master may, in general, sue for loss of services caused by an injury to his servant inflicted by the defendant. See the cases cited above and *Hodsoll* v. *Stallebrass*, 11 A. & E. 301. And he may maintain the action although the injury done to the servant was not direct, but consequential, and for which the servant could not have

Against a Master for Injuries occasioned by the Negligent Driving of his Servant (d).

Form No. 20, App. (C.) to Jud. Act, 1875.

1. The plaintiff is a shoemaker, carrying on business at ——. The defendant is a soap and candle manufacturer, of ——.

---

maintained an action of trespass (*Martinez* v. *Gerber*, 3 M. & G. 88); but where the injury to the servant is actionable only by reason of a contract between the servant and the defendant, to which the plaintiff is not a party, the plaintiff cannot maintain the action; as where the servant became a passenger on the defendant's railway, and was injured in the carriage by the defendant's neglect of duty, it was held that the plaintiff could not recover for the loss of services. (*Alton* v. *Midland Ry. Co.*, 19 C. B. N. S. 213; 34 L. J. C. P. 292).

The loss of service is the gist of the action, as in the action for seduction, *ante*, p. 463.

A master cannot maintain an action for loss of services caused by an injury which resulted in the immediate death of his servant (*per* Kelly, C. B. and Pigott, B., Bramwell, B. *dissenting*, *Osborn* v. *Gillett*, L. R. 8 Ex. 88; 42 L. J. Ex. 53).

An action may be maintained by a parent for the loss of service of his child, if the child is living with the parent, and capable of performing acts of service; but where the child was incapable of performing any service by reason of his tender age, the action was held not maintainable. (*Hall* v. *Hollander*, 4 B. & C. 660.)

(*d*) The master is, in general, liable for the negligence of his servant in the course of his employment, and he is also liable for wrongful acts done by the servant wilfully and intentionally, if done in the course of the employment and for the purposes of the master. (*Limpus* v. *Lond. Gen. Omnibus Co.*, 32 L. J. Ex. 34; *Huzzey* v. *Field*, 2 C. M. & R. 432; *Croft* v. *Alison*, 4 B. & Ald. 590; *Greenwood* v. *Seymour*, 7 H. & N. 355; 30 L. J. Ex. 327; *Patten* v. *Rea*, 2 C. B. N. S. 606; 26 L. J. C. P. 235; *Whatman* v. *Pearson*, L. R. 3 C. P. 422; 37 L. J. C. P. 156; *Betts* v. *De Vitre*, L. R. 3 Ch. Ap. 429; 37 L. J. Ch. 325; *Bayley* v. *M. S. & L. Ry. Co.*, L. R. 8 C. P. 148; 42 L. J. C. P. 78.) He is liable for every such wrong of his servant or agent as is committed in the course of his service, and for the master's benefit, though no express command or privity of the master be proved, because, although the master may not have authorized the particular act, he has put the agent in his place to do that class of acts, and he must be answerable for the manner in which that agent has conducted himself in doing the business which it was the act of his master to place him in. (*Barwick* v. *English Joint Stock Bank*, L. R. 2 Ex. 259; 36 L. J. Ex. 147, *per* Willes, J.; *Mackay* v. *Commercial Bank of New Brunswick*, L. R. 5 P. C. 394; 43 L. J. P. C. 31; *Swire* v. *Francis*, 3 App. Cas. 106; 47 L. J. P. C. 18; *Houldsworth* v. *City of Glasgow Bank*, 5 App. Cas. 317.) The master, however, is not liable for the negligence of his general servant whilst acting under the orders and control of another person (*Swainson* v. *N. E. Ry. Co.*, 3 Ex. D. 341; 47 L. J. Ex. 372; *Rourke* v. *White Moss Col. Co.*, 2 C. P. D. 205; 46 L. J. C. P. 283); nor is he liable for acts

2. On the 23rd May, 1875, the plaintiff was walking eastward along the south side of Fleet Street, in the city of London, at about three o'clock in the afternoon. He was obliged to cross —— Street, which is a street

---

done by the servant beyond the scope of his employment, or for acts done for his own purposes. (*Lyons* v. *Martin*, 8 A. & E. 512; *Williams* v. *Jones*, 3 H. & C. 256; 33 L. J. Ex. 297; *Mitchell* v. *Crassweller*, 13 C. B. 237; 22 L. J. C. P. 100; *McKenzie* v. *McLeod*, 10 Bing. 385; 3 L. J. C. P. 75; *Storey* v. *Ashton*, L. R. 4 Q. B. 476; 38 L. J. Q. B. 223; *Rayner* v. *Mitchell*, 2 C. P. D. 357; *Stevens* v. *Woodward*, 6 Q. B. D. 318; 50 L. J. C. P. 231.)

The master is not in general liable for the negligence of persons employed by the servant to do his work, between whom and the master the relation of master and servant does not exist. (*Milligan* v. *Wedge*, 12 A. & E. 737; *Rapson* v. *Cubitt*, 9 M. & W. 710; *Murray* v. *Currie*, L. R. 6 C. P. 24; 40 L. J. C. P. 26.)

The hirer of a carriage and horses to be driven by the servant of the owner, is not liable for the negligent driving of the servant. (*Laugher* v. *Pointer*, 5 B. & C. 547; *Quarman* v. *Burnett*, 6 M. & W. 499; and see *McLaughlin* v. *Pryor*, 4 M. & G. 48.)

A cab proprietor under the statutes relating to Hackney Carriages is liable for the negligence of his driver. (*Powles* v. *Hider*, 6 E. & B. 207; *Venables* v. *Smith*, 2. Q. B. D. 279; 46 L. J. Q. B. 470.)

Where a person employs a contractor to do certain work, the work being proper to be done and the contractor a proper person to do it, the employer is not in general liable for injuries caused by the negligence of the contractor or of the servants employed by the contractor in the performance of the work (*Reedie* v. *London and North Western Ry. Co.*, 4 Ex. 244; *Overton* v. *Freeman*, 11 C. B. 867; *Peachey* v. *Rowland*, 13 C. B. 182; *Steel* v. *South Eastern Ry. Co.*, 16 C. B. 550; *Allen* v. *Hayward*, 7 Q. B. 960; *Butler* v. *Hunter*, 7 H. & N. 826; 31 L. J. Ex. 214; *Pearson* v. *Cox*, 2 C. P. D. 369; *Murray* v. *Currie*, *supra*; *Murphy* v. *Caralli*, 3 H. & C. 462; 34 L. J. Ex. 14; *questioning Randelson* v. *Murray*, 8 A. & E. 109); but he is liable where the work contracted for is wrongful, and causes the injury. (*Ellis* v. *Sheffield Gas Co.*, 2 E. & B. 767; *Hole* v. *Sittingbourne Ry. Co.*, 6 H. & N. 488; 30 L. J. Ex. 81; *Blake* v. *Thirst*, 2 H. & C. 20; 32 L. J. Ex. 188.) And he may be liable where he retains a control over the contractor, or personally interferes with the work. (*Burgess* v. *Gray*, 1 C. B. 578.) And where a duty is incumbent upon a person, he is not excused the omission or imperfect performance of the duty by reason of his having engaged a contractor to do it, who neglected it. (*Pickard* v. *Smith*, 10 C. B. N. S. 470; *Hole* v. *Sittingbourne Ry. Co.*, *supra*; *Gray* v. *Pullen*, 5 B. & S. 970; 32 L. J. Q. B. 169; 34 Ib. 265; *Tarry* v. *Ashton*, 1 Q. B. D. 314; 45 L. J. Q. B. 260; *Bower* v. *Peate*, 1 Q. B. D. 321; 45 L. J. Q. B. 446; *Angus* v. *Dalton*, 4 Q. B. D. 162; 48 L. J. Q. B. 225; 44 L. T. 844.)

As to when a master is liable for the acts of his servants in prosecuting or arresting another, see "*Malicious Prosecution*," *ante*, p. 454.

See further as to the liability of a master for the acts of his servant,

running into Fleet Street at right angles on the south side. While he was crossing this street, and just before he could reach the foot pavement on the further side thereof, a two-horse van of the defendant's, under the charge and control of the defendant's servants, was negligently, suddenly, and without any warning, turned at a rapid and dangerous pace out of Fleet Street into —— Street. The pole of the van struck the plaintiff and knocked him down, and he was much trampled by the horses.

3. By the blow and fall and trampling the plaintiff's left arm was broken, and he was bruised and injured on the side and back, as well as internally; and in consequence thereof the plaintiff was for four months ill and in suffering, and unable to attend to his business, and incurred heavy medical and other expenses, and sustained great loss of business and profits.

The plaintiff claims £—— damages.

For Forms against Corporations for the Wrongful Acts of their Servants see "Corporation," ante, p. 387.

Statement of Claim in an Action removed by Certiorari from a County Court, by a Workman for a Personal Injury caused by the Negligence of a Fellow-Servant. (43 & 44 *Vict. c.* 42, *ss.* 1, 6) (*e*).

1. On the —— of ——, 18—, the plaintiff entered a plaint and issued a summons in the County Court

---

"*Corporation,*" *ante*, p. 387; "*Highways,*" *ante*, p. 435; "*Negligence,*" *post*, p. 477; and "*Nuisance,*" *post*, p. 487.

Where the act of the servant complained of was specifically ordered by the master, or necessarily followed upon or was comprised in his specific order, it may be charged in the statement of claim as the immediate act of the master. Where it was an independent act of the servant not specifically ordered, although one for which the master may be liable, it should not be charged as the immediate act of the master. In the latter case the liability of the master will depend upon whether the act of the servant was done in the course of his employment or not, as explained above.

(*e*) Before the passing of the Employers' Liability Act, 1880 (43 & 44 Vict. c. 42), a master was not in general liable to an action at the

of ——, holden at ——, against the defendants in respect of the cause of action hereinafter set forth, and by a writ of certiorari duly issued on the —— of ——, 18—, out of the Queen's Bench Division of Her

---

suit of a servant for an injury arising from the negligence of a fellow-servant in the course of their common employment (*Priestley* v. *Fowler*, 3 M. & W. 1; *Hutchinson* v. *York, Newcastle & Berwick Ry. Co.*, 5 Ex. 343; *Wigmore* v. *Jay*, 5 Ex. 354; 46 L. J. C. P. 283; *Degg* v. *Midland Ry. Co.*, 1 H. & N. 773; 26 L. J. Ex. 171; *Vose* v. *Lanc. & York Ry. Co.*, 2 H. & N. 728; 27 L. J. Ex. 249; *Griffiths* v. *Gidlow*, 3 H. & N. 648; 27 L. J. Ex. 404; *Searle* v. *Lindsay*, 11 C. B. N. S. 429; 31 L. J. C. P. 106; *Morgan* v. *Vale of Neath Ry.*, L. R. 1 Q. B. 149; 35 L. J. Q. B. 23; *Lovell* v. *Howell*, 1 C. P. D. 161; 45 L. J. C. P. 387; *Rourke* v. *White Moss Col. Co.*, 2 C. P. D. 205; 46 L. J. C. P. 283; *Allen* v. *The New Gas Co.*, 1 Ex. D. 251; 45 L. J. Ex. 668; *Charles* v. *Taylor*, 3 C. P. D. 492), and this is still the law with regard to actions begun in the High Court of Justice, but by the above Act (43 & 44 Vict. c. 42) a special action, to be brought in a County Court, is given after the commencement of the Act (1st Jan. 1881) in respect of personal injury caused to a workman under the circumstances therein set forth. As such action may, by s. 6 of the above Act, upon the application of either plaintiff or defendant, be removed into a superior court in like manner and upon the same conditions as an action commenced in a County Court may by law be removed, it will be convenient to set out the more important sections.

By s. 8. for the purposes of this Act, unless the context otherwise requires,—

The expression "person who has superintendence entrusted to him" means a person whose sole or principal duty is that of superintendence, and who is not ordinarily engaged in manual labour:

The expression "employer" includes a body of persons corporate or unincorporate:

The expression "workman" means a railway servant and any person to whom the Employers and Workmen Act, 1875, applies.

By s. 1. where after the commencement of this Act personal injury is caused to a workman

(1.) By reason of any defect in the condition of the ways, works, machinery, or plant connected with or used in the business of the employer; or

(2.) By reason of the negligence of any *person* in the service of the employer *who has any superintendence entrusted to him* whilst in the exercise of such superintendence; or

(3.) By reason of the negligence of any person in the service of the employer to whose orders or directions the workman at the time of the injury was bound to conform, and did conform, where such injury resulted from his having so conformed; or

(4.) By reason of the act or omission of any person in the service of the employer done or made in obedience to the rules or byelaws of the employer, or in obedience to particular

Majesty's High Court of Justice, and directed to the Judge of the said Court, the said plaint, with all things touching the same, were sent into the said Queen's Bench Division of the said High Court of Justice.

---

instructions given by any person delegated with the authority of the employer in that behalf; or

(5.) By reason of the negligence of any person in the service of the employer who has the charge or control of any signal, points, locomotive engine, or train upon a railway,

the workman, or in case the injury results in death, the legal personal representatives of the workman, and any persons entitled in case of death, shall have the same right of compensation and remedies against the employer as if the workman had not been a workman of nor in the service of the employer, nor engaged in his work.

By s. 2. a workman shall not be entitled under this Act to any right of compensation or remedy against the employer in any of the following cases; that is to say,

(1.) Under sub-section one of section one, unless the defect therein mentioned arose from, or had not been discovered or remedied owing to the negligence of the employer, or of some person in the service of the employer, and entrusted by him with the duty of seeing that the ways, works, machinery, or plant were in proper condition.

(2.) Under sub-section four of section one, unless the injury resulted from some impropriety or defect in the rules, byelaws, or instructions therein mentioned; provided that where a rule or byelaw has been approved or has been accepted as a proper rule or byelaw by one of Her Majesty's Principal Secretaries of State, or by the Board of Trade or any other department of the Government, under or by virtue of any Act of Parliament, it shall not be deemed for the purposes of this Act to be an improper or defective rule or byelaw.

(3.) In any case where the workman knew of the defect or negligence which caused his injury, and failed within a reasonable time to give, or cause to be given, information thereof to the employer or some person superior to himself in the service of the employer, unless he was aware that the employer or such superior already knew of the said defect or negligence.

By s. 3. the amount of compensation recoverable under this Act shall not exceed such sum as may be found to be equivalent to the estimated earnings, during the three years preceding the injury, of a person in the same grade employed during those years in the like employment and in the district in which the workman is employed at the time of the injury.

By s. 4. an action for the recovery under this Act of compensation for an injury shall not be maintainable unless notice that injury has been sustained is given within six weeks, and the action is commenced within six months from the occurrence of the accident causing the injury, or, in case of death, within twelve months from the time of death: Provided always, that in case of death the want of such notice shall be no bar to the maintenance of such action if

2. The defendants are the —— Railway Company.

3. Previously to, and at the times hereinafter mentioned, the plaintiff was an engine-driver in the service of the defendants, upon the defendants' said railway, and one

---

the judge shall be of opinion that there was reasonable excuse for such want of notice.

By s. 5. there shall be deducted from any compensation awarded to any workman, or representatives of a workman, or persons claiming by, under, or through a workman in respect of any cause of action arising under this Act, any penalty or part of a penalty which may have been paid in pursuance of any other Act of Parliament to such workman, representatives, or persons in respect of the same cause of action; and where an action has been brought under this Act by any workman, or the representatives of any workman, or any persons claiming by, under, or through such workman, for compensation in respect of any cause of action arising under this Act, and payment has not previously been made of any penalty or part of a penalty under any other Act of Parliament in respect of the same cause of action, such workman, representatives, or person shall not be entitled thereafter to receive any penalty or part of a penalty under any other Act of Parliament in respect of the same cause of action.

By s. 7. notice in respect of an injury under this Act shall give the name and address of the person injured, and shall state in ordinary language the cause of the injury and the date at which it was sustained, and shall be served on the employer, or, if there is more than one employer, upon one of such employers.

The notice may be served by delivering the same to or at the residence or place of business of the person on whom it is to be served.

The notice may also be served by post by a registered letter addressed to the person on whom it is to be served at his last known place of residence or place of business; and, if served by post, shall be deemed to have been served at the time when a letter containing the same would be delivered in the ordinary course of post; and, in proving the service of such notice, it shall be sufficient to prove that the notice was properly addressed and registered.

Where the employer is a body of persons corporate or unincorporate, the notice shall be served by delivering the same at or by sending it by post in a registered letter addressed to the office, or, if there be more than one office, any one of the offices of such body.

A notice under this section shall not be deemed invalid by reason of any defect or inaccuracy therein, unless the judge who tries the action arising from the injury mentioned in the notice shall be of opinion that the defendant in the action is prejudiced in his defence by such defect or inaccuracy, and that the defect or inaccuracy was or the purpose of misleading.

By s. 10. this Act may be cited as the Employers' Liability Act, 1880, and shall continue in force till the thirty-first day of December one thousand eight hundred and eighty-seven, and to the end of the then next Session of Parliament, and no longer, unless Parliament shall otherwise determine, and all actions commenced

——, who was employed by the defendants as a signalman upon their said railway, had the charge and control of certain signals for regulating the movements of trains at —— Junction upon the said railway.

---

under this Act before that period shall be continued as if the said Act had not expired.

If the plaintiff proceeds with an action after it has been removed into the superior court, he must, after appearance has been entered, begin by delivering a statement of claim, at whatever stage the action may have been when removed, unless the defendant under O. XIX. r. 2. dispenses with the delivery thereof. Such statement of claim must of course be drawn in compliance with the rules of pleading under the Judicature Acts, and should commence in a form similar to that given above. The date of the plaint and summons should be stated as it might be material in the event of the Statute of Limitations being pleaded, or in case of a demurrer.

As to the removal of causes from inferior courts, and proceedings after removal, see Arch. Pr. 13th ed. p. 1404 *et seq.*

See further as to the jurisdiction of County Courts in disputes between employers and workmen "The Employers and Workmen Act, 1875." (38 & 39 Vict. c. 90.)

In order to exempt the master from liability in an action not within "the Employers' Liability Act, 1880" (43 & 44 Vict. c. 42), there must be a common employment and a common master; it is not necessary that there should be a common service for a definite time or at fixed wages (*per* Brett, L. J. in *Swainson* v. *N. E. Ry. Co.*, 3 Ex. D. 341, 349; 47 L. J. Ex. 372, 376). Where two servants are servants of the same master, and where the service of each will bring them so far to work in the same place and at the same time that the negligence of one in what he is doing, as part of the work which he is bound to do, may injure the other whilst he is doing the work which he is bound to do, the master is not liable to the one servant for the negligence of the other (*per* Brett, L. J. in *Charles* v. *Taylor*, 3 C. P. D. at p. 496).

Workmen do not cease to be fellow-workmen, because they are not all equal in point of station or authority. (*Wilson* v. *Merry*, L. R. 1 H. L. Sc. 326.)

A person who volunteers to assist a servant in his work is in the same position as a servant in respect of the right of action for personal injury against the master. (*Degg* v. *Midland Ry. Co.*, 1 H. & N. 773; 26 L. J. Ex. 171; *Potter* v. *Faulkner*, 1 B. & S. 800; 31 L. J. Q. B. 30; *and see Abraham* v. *Reynolds*, 5 H. & N. 143.) But where, while a person is on the defendants' premises with their consent for the purpose of assisting in the delivery of his own goods, an accident happens to him through the negligence of the defendants' servants, the defendants are liable to him for the consequences of their negligence. (*Wright* v. *The Lond. & N. W. Ry. Co.*, L. R. 10 Q. B. 298; 1 Q. B. D. 252; 45 L. J. Q. B. 570; and see *Holmes* v. *N. E. Ry. Co.*, L. R. 4 Ex. 254; L. R. 6 Ex. 123; 38 L. J. Ex. 151.) Where a railway station was used by two companies, it was held that the respective servants of the two companies, in the course of their ordinary duties, were not on that account engaged in a common employment. (*Warburton*

4. On the —— of ——, 18—, the plaintiff was driving the —— A.M. up —— express train towards the said junction, and had arrived within about —— yards of the signal-box at the said junction in which the said —— was then on duty in the course of his said employment, when the said —— negligently and improperly signalled to him that the line was clear, and that he might drive the said train through the said junction with safety.

5. The said line was, at the time when the said —— so signalled as aforesaid, obstructed at the said junction by a goods train, which was in the course of being shunted into an adjoining siding.

6. In consequence of the said negligent and improper conduct of the said ——, the plaintiff, in attempting to drive his said train through the said junction, brought it into violent collision with the rear of the said goods train.

7. The plaintiff was, by reason of the said collision, greatly cut about the head, and bruised and wounded, and was scalded by the steam and water from the boiler of the said engine, and was for a long time confined to his bed and incurred £—— expense for surgical and medical attendance.

---

v. *Gt. W. Ry. Co.*, L. R. 2 Ex. 30; 36 L. J. Ex. 9.) In an ordinary contract of service, there is no implied promise on the part of the master not to expose the servant to extraordinary risk in the course of the employment. (*Riley* v. *Baxendale*, 6 H. & N. 445; 30 L. J. Ex. 87.) Where the plaintiff, a workman in the employ of a contractor engaged by the defendants, had to work in a dark tunnel rendered dangerous by the passing of trains, and after he had been working a fortnight was injured by a passing train, it was held, by the majority of the Court of Appeal, that the plaintiff, having continued in his employment with full knowledge of the circumstances, could not make the defendants liable for an injury arising from danger to which he voluntarily exposed himself. (*Woodley* v. *The Met. Dis. Ry. Co.*, 2 Ex. D. 384; 46 L. J. Ex. 521.) A master is not liable to an action at the suit of a servant for an injury incurred in the service, consequent upon the insufficient number of servants employed. (*Skipp* v. *Eastern Counties Ry. Co.*, 9 Ex. 223.)

See further, as to what constitutes common employment, the cases cited *supra*, and *Lovegrove* v. *Lond. and Brighton Ry. Co.*, 16 C. B. N. S. 669; 33 L. J. C. P. 329; *Waller* v. *S. E. Ry. Co.*, 2 H. & C. 102; 32 L. J. Ex. 205; *Gallagher* v. *Piper*, 16 C. B. N. S. 669; 33 L. J. C. P. 329; *Hall* v. *Johnson*, 3 H. & C. 589; 34 L. J. Ex. 222; *Tunney* v. *Midland Ry. Co.*, L. R. 1 C. P. 291; *Feltham* v. *England*, L. R. 2 Q. B. 33; 36 L. J. Q. B. 14; *Wilson* v. *Merry*, L. R. 1 H. L. Sc. 326.

8. £—— are the estimated earnings, during the 3 years preceding the said injuries, of a person in the same grade employed during the said 3 years in the like employment, and in the district in which the plaintiff was employed at the time of the said injuries.

By a Servant against his Master, for Employing him to Work upon an Unsafe Scaffolding (f).

1. The plaintiff is a bricklayer, and the defendant is a builder and contractor.

2. In the month of ——, 18—, the plaintiff was employed by the defendant as such bricklayer, to work for the defendant in and about the erection of a house at ——.

3. In the course of his said employment the plaintiff had to work upon a certain scaffolding, constructed by the defendant for that purpose in front of the said house.

4. The said scaffolding was, by the negligence and default of the defendant, constructed unsafely and with defective and improper materials, and was in an unsafe condition and unfit for the purpose aforesaid.

(*f*) An action will lie at the suit of a servant against his master for knowingly providing bad materials or instruments for the work, whereby injury is caused to the servant, unless the servant undertook the work with the knowledge of the state of the materials or instruments. It is the master's duty to be careful that his servant is not induced to work under a notion that tackle or machinery is staunch and secure, when in fact the master knows, or ought to know, that it is not so; and if from any negligence in this respect damage arises to the servant the master is responsible. (*Per* Ld. Cranworth, C., *Paterson* v. *Wallace*, 1 Macq. H. L. C. 748; *Bartonshill Coal Co.* v. *Reid*, 3 Macq. H. L. C. 266, 288; *Roberts* v. *Smith*, 2 H. & N. 213; 26 L. J. Ex. 319; *Ashworth* v. *Stanwix*, 30 L. J. Q. B. 183; *Mellors* v. *Shaw*, 1 B. & S. 437; 30 L. J. Q. B. 333; *Watling* v. *Oastler*, L. R. 6 Ex. 73; *Wilson* v. *Merry*, L. R. 1 H. L. Sc. 326; *Murphy* v. *Phillips*, 35 L. T. 477.)

So also an action will lie at the suit of a servant against the master for negligently employing an incompetent fellow-servant, through whose incompetency the plaintiff is injured, although there is no generally implied warranty by the master of the competency of his workmen. (*Tarrant* v. *Webb*, 18 C. B. 797; 25 L. J. C. P. 261; *Wilson* v. *Merry*, *supra*; *Allen* v. *The New Gas Co.*, 1 Ex. D. 251.)

See, further, as to masters' liability with regard to unfenced machinery, *Holmes* v. *Clarke*, 6 H. & N. 349; 7 *Ib.* 937; 30 L. J. Ex. 135; 31 *Ib.* 356; *Britton* v. *Gt. Western Cotton Co.*, L. R. 7 Ex. 130, and "*Fences*," *ante*, p. 423.

5. The defendant well knew that the said scaffolding was constructed unsafely and with defective and improper materials, and was in an unsafe condition and unfit for the purpose aforesaid, but the plaintiff had no reasonable means of knowing the above facts, and was ignorant thereof.

6. By reason of the premises, whilst the plaintiff was so employed as such bricklayer as aforesaid, doing the said work upon the said scaffolding, the said scaffolding broke and gave way, and thereby the plaintiff fell to the ground.

7. The plaintiff's leg and ribs were broken by the said fall, and he was permanently injured and rendered unfit for work, and incurred £—— expense for surgical and medical attendance.

Medical Men.

Statement of Claim against a Medical Man for Negligence and Unskilfulness in the Treatment of a Patient.

1. Previously to, and at the time of the happening of the grievances hereinafter mentioned, the plaintiff carried on the business of an architect at ——, and the defendant was a surgeon in practice at ——.

2. In the month of ——, 18—, the plaintiff, who was then suffering from a slight inflammation of his eyes, retained the services of the defendant as such surgeon as aforesaid, for reward in that behalf, for the purpose of being properly treated by him for the said inflammation.

3. The defendant negligently, improperly, and unskilfully treated the plaintiff for the said inflammation.

4. In consequence of such last-mentioned treatment the said inflammation became much worse, and the plaintiff was rendered permanently blind. [*Add further special damage, if any.*]

Mesne Profits.

See "*Landlord and Tenant,*" *ante*, p. 256, *and* "*Trespass to Land,*" *post*, p. 534.

METROPOLIS MANAGEMENT ACTS (*a*).

(*a*) By "The Metropolis Management Amendment Act, 1862," (25 & 26 Vict. c. 102) s. 106, it is enacted that "No writ or process shall be sued out against or served upon, and no proceeding shall be instituted against the Metropolitan Board of Works, or any vestry or district board, or their clerk, or any clerks, surveyor, contractor, officer or person whomsoever, acting under their or any of their directions, for anything done or intended to be done under the powers of such board or vestry under the said Acts ('The Metropolis Management Act, 1855,' 18 & 19 Vict. c. 120; 'The Metropolis Management Amendment Act, 1856,' 19 & 20 Vict. c. 112; 'The Metropolis Management Amendment Act, 1858,' 21 & 22 Vict. c. 104), or this Act, until the expiration of one calendar month next after notice in writing shall have been served upon such board or vestry, or, where the action or proceeding shall be against such officer or other person acting under their or any of their directions, shall have been delivered to him or left at his office or place of abode, stating the cause of action or grounds of the proceeding or demand, and the name and place of abode of the intended plaintiff or claimant, and of his attorney or agent in the cause or proceeding; and upon the trial of any action the plaintiff shall not be permitted to go into evidence of any cause of action except such as is stated in the notice so served or delivered, and unless such notice be proved the jury shall find for the defendant; and every such action and proceeding shall be brought or commenced within six months next after the accrual of the cause of action or ground of claim or demand and not afterward; * * * and the defendant shall in any such action be at liberty to plead the general issue and give the said recited Acts, and this Act and all special matter in evidence thereunder; and it shall be lawful for the board or vestry, or any person to whom such notice is given as aforesaid, to tender amends to the plaintiff, his attorney or agent, at any time within one calendar month after service of such notice, and in case the same be not accepted, to plead such tender in bar and (by leave of the Court) with the general issue or other plea or pleas; and if upon issue joined upon any plea pleaded to the whole action the jury find generally for the defendant, or if the plaintiff be nonsuited or discontinue, or if judgment be given for the defendant, then the defendant shall be entitled to full costs of suit and have judgment accordingly; and in case amends have not been tendered as aforesaid, or in case the amends tendered be insufficient, it shall be lawful for the defendant, by leave of the Court at any time before trial to pay into Court under plea such sum of money as he may think proper, and (by the like leave) to plead the general issue or other plea or pleas, any rule of Court or practice to the contrary notwithstanding."

This section does not apply to a claim for injuriously affecting property in the exercise by the Board of the powers conferred upon them, nor to an action on an award in respect of such a claim, but only to illegal acts done by them or their contractors in respect of which compensation may be tendered. (*Delany* v. *Metropolitan Board of Works*, L. R. 2 C. P. 532; L. R. 3 C. P. 111; 37 L. J. C. P. 59.)

By s. 5 of "The Metropolis Management and Building Acts

Mines (*a*).

Statement of Claim for a Trespass in Breaking and Entering the Plaintiff's Coal Mine and Taking his Coals. *See " Trespass to Land," post,* p. 534.

For Working a Mine under or near to the Plaintiff's Land, whereby it lost its Natural or Acquired Right to Support, and sank : *see " Support," post,* p. 521.

Mischievous Animals (*aa*).

Statement of Claim for Knowingly Keeping a Fierce Dog, which Injured the Plaintiff.

1. The plaintiff is a milkman carrying on business at ——.

Amendment Act, 1878" (41 & 42 Vict. c. 32), Part I. of that Act, and "The Metropolis Management Act, 1855," and the Acts amending the same, are to be construed together as one Act, subject to the proviso mentioned in such section.

(*a*) See notes to "*Trespass,*" *post*, p. 534 ; "*Support,*" *post*, p. 520 ; and "*Conversion,*" *ante*, p. 379.

The law relating to the regulation and inspection of coal mines and certain other mines is consolidated and amended by "The Coal Mines Regulation Act, 1872" (35 & 36 Vict. c. 76), and the law as to the regulation and inspection of mines not included in the last-mentioned Act is amended by "The Metalliferous Mines Regulation Acts, 1872 and 1875" (35 & 36 Vict. c. 77, and 38 & 39 Vict. c. 39).

(*aa*) An action lies against one who keeps a mischievous animal knowing it to be mischievous, in respect of any damage done by the animal to the plaintiff. (4 Co. 18, b ; *Thomas* v. *Morgan*, 2 C. M. & R. 496 ; *Card* v. *Case*, 5 C. B. 622.) The wrongful act consists in insecurely keeping the dangerous animal after knowledge of its propensities. (*May* v. *Burdett*. 9 Q. B. 101.) The averment that the animal was of a fierce and mischievous nature and accustomed to bite, may be supported by evidence that it was of a fierce disposition and attempted to bite, to the knowledge of the defendant, without proof that it had ever bitten any one before (*Worth* v. *Gilling*, L. R. 2 C. P. 1) ; but it is not sufficient to show merely that the dog was of a fierce disposition and usually tied up by the defendant. (*Beck* v. *Dyson*, 4 Camp. 198.) If the owner of a dog appoints a servant to keep it, the servant's knowledge of the dog's ferocity is the knowledge of the master. (*Baldwin* v. *Casella*, L. R. 7 Ex. 325 ; 41 L. J. Ex. 167.) A complaint made to defendant's wife on the premises, for the purpose of being communicated to the defendant was held to be evidence of defendant's knowledge. (*Gladman* v. *Johnson*, 36 L. J.

2. The defendant is a gentleman residing at ——.

3. On and before the —— of ——, 18—, the defendant kept at his said residence a large mastiff, which was of a fierce and mischievous nature, and accustomed to attack mankind.

4. The defendant at the said times was fully acquainted with the nature and propensity of the said mastiff.

5. On the said —— of ——, 18—, the plaintiff, whilst delivering milk at the defendant's said residence in accordance with the defendant's orders, was attacked and severely bitten about the throat and hands by the said mastiff.

6. [*State special damage, if any.*]

MISREPRESENTATION.

See notes to "*Fraud*," *ante*, p. 426.

C. P. 153.) So also was a complaint made to defendant's barmaids on the premises. (*Applebee* v. *Percy*, L. R. 9 C. P. 647 ; 43 L. J. C. P. 365 ; *per* Coleridge, C. J., and Keating, J. ; Brett, J., *dissenting*.)

As to trespasses by animals of the defendant, see "*Trespass*," *post*, p. 534.

With respect to injuries done to sheep and cattle by dogs, it is enacted, by 28 & 29 Vict. c. 60, s. 1, that "the owner of every dog shall be liable in damages for injury done to any cattle or sheep by his dog ; and it shall not be necessary for the party seeking such damages to show a previous mischievous propensity in such dog, or the owner's knowledge of such previous propensity, or that the injury was attributable to neglect on the part of such owner. Such damages shall be recoverable in any court of competent jurisdiction by the owner of such cattle or sheep killed or injured. Where the amount of the damages claimed shall not exceed five pounds, the same shall be recoverable in a summary way before any justice or justices sitting in petty sessions under the provisions of the Act Eleven and Twelve Victoria Chapter Forty-three."

By s. 2 it is provided that "the occupier of any house or premises where any dog was kept or permitted to live or remain at the time of such injury shall be deemed to be the owner of such dog, and shall be liable as such, unless the said occupier can prove that he was not the owner of such dog at the time the injury complained of was committed, and that such dog was kept or permitted to live or remain in the said house or premises without his sanction or knowledge : provided always, that where there are more occupiers than one in any house or premises let in separate apartments, or lodgings, or otherwise, the occupier of that particular part of the premises in which such dog shall have been kept or permitted to live or remain at the time of such injury shall be deemed to be the owner of such dog."

Negligence (*a*).

For Injuries done by the Negligent Driving of the Defendant.

1. The plaintiff is a ——, residing at ——, and the defendant is a jobmaster.

(*a*) *Negligence.*—An action lies for the omission or negligent performance of any duty of the defendant whereby the plaintiff has sustained damage. The negligence in respect of the duty which is ctionable has been described as being the omission to do something which a reasonable man would do, or the doing of something which a reasonable man would not do. (*Per* Alderson, B., *Blyth* v. *Birmingham Waterworks Co.*, 11 Ex. 781, 784 ; 25 L. J. Ex. 212.) If such negligence causes damage to another, an action will lie in respect of the damage so caused.

The mere happening of an accident is not in general *primâ facie* evidence of negligence, but the plaintiff must show affirmative evidence of negligence on the part of the defendant. (*Cotton* v. *Wood*, 8 C. B. N. S. 568 ; 29 L. J. C. P. 333 ; *Hammack* v. *White*, 11 C. B. N. S. 588 ; 31 L. J. C. P. 129 ; *Welfare* v. *London, Brighton & South Coast Ry. Co.*, L. R. 4 Q. B. 693 ; 38 L. J. Q. B. 241 ; *Holmes* v. *Mather*, L. R. 10 Ex. 261 ; 44 L. J. Ex. 176 ; *Abbot* v. *Freeman*, 35 L. T. 783 ; *Allen* v. *New Gas Co.*, 1 Ex. D. 251 ; 45 L. J. Ex. 668 ; *Manzoni* v. *Douglas*, 6 Q. B. D. 145 ; 50 L. J. C. P. 289.) Thus, the mere fact of the defendant's omnibus running over the plaintiff while crossing the road, is not evidence of negligence against the defendant. (*Cotton* v. *Wood*, *supra* ; and see *Singleton* v. *Eastern Counties Ry. Co.*, 7 C. B. N. S. 287.) And where the defendant rode a horse in the public street which he had just bought, and of which he had no experience, and which became unmanageable and knocked down the plaintiff, it was held that these facts afforded no evidence of negligence. (*Hammack* v. *White*, *supra* ; and see *Holmes* v. *Mather*, *supra*.) So where a horse drawing a brougham in a public street, suddenly and without any explainable cause bolted, and, notwithstanding the utmost efforts of the defendant's servant who was driving to control him, swerved on to the footway and injured the plaintiff, it was held that there was no evidence of negligence for a jury. (*Manzoni* v. *Douglas*, *supra*.)

But in some cases the circumstances of the accident alone raise a sufficient presumption of negligence ; thus, a barrel falling from the defendant's warehouse on to the plaintiff below was held to afford *primâ facie* proof of negligence against the defendant. (*Byrne* v. *Boadle*, 2 H. & C. 722 ; 33 L. J. Ex. 13 ; and see *Pearson* v. *Cox*, 2 C. P. D. 369 ; 36 L. T. 495.) So, a packing-case of the defendant on his premises falling down against the plaintiff (*Briggs* v. *Oliver*, 4 H. & C. 403 ; 35 L. J. Ex. 163, Martin, B., dissentiente) ; so where goods fell upon the plaintiff from a crane fixed over a doorway upon the defendant's premises under which the plaintiff was passing, no explanation being given of the cause, it was held that there was sufficient evidence of negligence. (*Scott* v. *London Dock Co.*, 34 L. J. Ex. 17, *ib.* 220 ; 3 H. & C. 596.) In the latter case it was laid down by the

2. The defendant, on the —— day of ——, 18—, so negligently drove a brougham in a public highway called —— Street, ——, that he drove it against the plaintiff, and knocked him down and injured him in his arm and shoulder.

Court that "when a thing is solely under the management of the defendant or his servants, and the accident is such as in the ordinary course of things does not happen to those who have the management of machinery, and use proper care, it affords reasonable evidence, in the absence of explanation by the defendant, that the accident arose from want of care." So, where a brick from a railway bridge fell upon the plaintiff while passing on the road underneath, this circumstance was in itself held to furnish sufficient evidence of negligence. (*Kearney* v. *London, Brighton & South Coast Ry. Co.*, L. R. 5 Q. B. 411 ; 39 L. J. Q. B. 200 ; L. R. 6 Q. B. 759 ; 40 L. J. Q. B. 285.) On the point generally as to what is evidence of negligence see also *Cockle* v. *South Eastern Ry. Co.*, L. R. 5 C. P. 457, 39 L. J. C. P. 226 ; L. R. 7 C. P. 321 ; 41 L. J. C. P. 140 ; *Metropolitan Ry. Co.* v. *Jackson*, 3 App. Cas. 193 ; 47 L. J. C. P. 303 ; *Dublin, &c. Ry. Co.* v. *Slattery*, 3 App. Cas. 1155. Whether there is reasonable evidence of negligence to be left to the jury is a question for the judge to decide, whilst it is for the jury to say whether, and how far, the evidence is to be believed ; in other words, it is for the Court to say whether on the facts negligence can legitimately be inferred, and for the jury to say whether negligence ought to be inferred. (*Bridges* v. *North London Ry. Co.*, L. R. 7 H. L. 213 ; 43 L. J. Q. B. 151 ; explained in *Metropolitan Ry. Co.* v. *Jackson, supra.*) The plaintiff cannot recover unless the negligence of the defendant connects itself, or is connected by the evidence, with the accident ; the negligence must be *incuria dans locum injuriae.* (*Per* Lord Cairns, *Metropolitan Ry. Co.* v. *Jackson, supra.*)

The omission to guard against extraordinary accidents is not negligence ; thus, a water company whose pipes were constructed with reasonable care with reference to ordinary frost was held not to be liable for the breaking of the pipes by an extraordinary frost. (*Blyth* v. *Birmingham Waterworks Co.*, 11 Ex. 781 ; 25 L. J. Ex. 212 ; and see *Nichols* v. *Marsland*, 2 Ex. D. 1 ; 46 L. J. Ex. 174 ; *Thomas* v. *Birmingham Canal Co.*, 49 L. J. Q. B. 851 ; 43 L. T. 435.) Nor is the omission of a merely voluntary precaution actionable. (*Skelton* v. *London & North Western Ry. Co.*, L. R. 2 C. P. 631 ; 36 L. J. C. P. 249.)

The following cases have been decided as to accidents on railways :—Railway Companies are not liable for accidental fires occasioned by their engines, if they have taken all possible precautions, and are not guilty of some negligence in fact (*Vaughan* v. *Taff Vale Ry. Co.*, 5 H & N. 679 ; 29 L. J. Ex. 247 ; *Hammersmith Ry. Co.* v. *Brand*, L. R. 4 H. L. 171 ; 38 L. J. H. L. 265) ; provided the use of such engines is authorized by their Act (*Jones* v. *Festiniog Ry. Co.*, L. R. 3 Q. B. 733 ; 37 L. J. Q. B. 214; and see *Fremantle* v. *London & North Western Ry. Co.*, 10 C. B. N. S. 89 ; 31 L. J. C. P. 12 ; *Smith* v. *London & South Western Ry. Co.*, L. R. 5 C. P. 98 ; 39 L. J. C. P. 68 ; L. R. 6 C. P. 14 ; 40 L. J. C. P. 21 ; see also *Powell* v. *Fall*, 5 Q. B. D. 597 ; 49 L. J. Q. B. 428). Where two trains

3. **The plaintiff was thereby put to great pain, and was put to expense in procuring medical and other attendance, and was prevented from carrying on his business of a —— as aforesaid.** [*Give particulars where practicable.*]

---

both belonging to the same company came into collision upon their railway, it was held that this alone showed a *primâ facie* case of negligence (*Skinner* v. *London, Brighton & South Coast Ry. Co.*, 5 Ex. 787); and so it has been held where an accident occurred to a train on a railway while the train and the railway were under the exclusive management of the defendants. (*Carpue* v. *London, Brighton & South Coast Ry. Co.*, 5 Q. B. 747; and see *Ayles* v. *South Eastern Ry. Co.*, L. R. 3 Ex. 146; 37 L. J. Ex. 104.) But if the accident is not inconsistent with due care having been taken, *primâ facie* evidence of negligence can at most be inferred: thus, where a train ran off the line in an unexplained manner, this was held not to be conclusive proof of negligence. (*Bird* v. *Great Northern Ry. Co.*, 28 L. J. Ex. 3.) So the fact of a train running over a child without evidence how the child got upon the railway is not evidence of negligence against the company. (*Singleton* v. *Eastern Counties Ry. Co.*, 7 C. B. N. S. 287.) As to negligence in respect of precautions necessary where dangerous works are being constructed on the line, see *Daniel* v. *Metropolitan Ry. Co.*, L. R. 5 H. L. 45; 40 L. J. C. P. 121. The mere fact of a carriage, forming part of a train, being pulled up either short of, or beyond the platform at a station is not in itself evidence of negligence (*Siner* v. *Great Western Ry. Co.*, L. R. 3 Ex. 150; 37 L. J. Ex. 98; *Ib.* 4 Ex. 117; 40 L. J. Ex. 67; *Cockle* v. *South Eastern Ry. Co.*, L. R. 5 C. P. 457; 39 L. J. C. P. 226; *Ib.* 7 C. P. 321; 41 L. J. C. P. 140; *Praeger* v. *Bristol & Exeter Ry. Co.*, 24 L. T. 105; *Bridges* v. *North London Ry. Co.*, L. R. 6 Q. B. 377; 40 L. J. Q. B. 188; L. R. 7 H. L. 213; *Lewis* v. *London, Chatham & Dover Ry. Co.*, L. R. 9 Q. B. 66; 43 L. J. Q. B. 8; *Weller* v. *London, Brighton & South Coast Ry. Co.*, L. R. 9 C. P. 126; 43 L. J. C. P. 127; *Robson* v. *North Eastern Ry. Co.*, L. R. 10 Q. B. 271; 44 L. J. Q. B. 112; 2 Q. B. D. 85; 46 L. J. Q. B. 50; *Rose* v. *North Eastern Ry. Co.*, 2 Ex. D. 248; 46 L. J. Ex. 374); but railway companies are bound to find reasonable means for their passengers to alight (*per* Mellish, L. J., *Robson* v. *North Eastern Ry. Co.*, *supra*); and the bringing up of a train to a final standstill at a station amounts to an invitation to them to alight, at all events after such a time has elapsed that they may reasonably infer that it is intended that they should alight. (*Per* Cockburn, C. J., *Cockle* v. *South Eastern Ry. Co.*, L. R. 7 C. P. at p. 326.) When railway companies are bound by statute to place gates, fences, or other protections at level crossings on their lines, and to keep such gates closed upon the approach of the trains, the omission to take either of such precautions amounts to negligence, and if an accident ensue in consequence of such omission the company may be liable. (*Stapley* v. *London, Brighton & South Coast Ry. Co.*, L. R. 1 Ex. 21; 35 L. J. Ex. 7; *Williams* v. *Great Western Ry. Co.*, L. R. 9 Ex. 157; 43 L. J. Ex. 105; *Wanless* v. *North Eastern Ry. Co.*, L. R. 6 Q. B. 481; L. R. 7 H. L. 12.) See also as to liability for accidents at level crossings:—*Stubley* v. *London & North Western Ry. Co.*, L. R. 1 Ex. 13; 35 L. J. Ex. 3; *Bilbee* v. *London, Brighton & South Coast Ry. Co.* 18

For other Forms, see Form No. 20, App. (C.) *to the Judicature Act,* 1875, *cited ante, "Master and Servant,"* p. 464; *and Horwell* v. *London Gen. Omnibus Co.,* 2 Ex. D. 365.

C. B. N. S. 584; 34 L. J. C. P. 182; explained in *Cliff* v. *Midland Ry. Co.*, L. R. 5 Q. B. 258; *Ellis* v. *Great Western Ry. Co.*, L. R. 9 C. P. 551; 43 L. J. C. P. 304; *Clarke* v. *Mid. Ry. Co.*, 43 L. T. 381; *Dublin, &c. Ry. Co.* v. *Slattery*, 3 App. Cas. 1155; and "*Fences*," *ante*, p. 423. As to liability for leaving a level crossing in an improper or defective state, see *Oliver* v. *North Eastern Ry. Co.*, L. R. 9 Q. B. 409; 43 L. J. Q. B. 198.

The plaintiff in an action for negligence cannot succeed if it is found by the jury that he has himself been guilty of any negligence or want of care which contributed to cause the injury: unless the defendant could, by the exercise of ordinary care and diligence, have avoided the mischief which happened; in other words, the plaintiff, notwithstanding his own negligence, may still recover, if such negligence was not the proximate cause of the injury he has sustained. (*Butterfield* v. *Forrester*, 11 East, 60; *Davies* v. *Mann*, 10 M. & W. 546; *Tuff* v. *Warman*, 5 C. B. N. S. 573; 27 L. J. C. P. 322; *Radley* v. *London & North Western Ry. Co.*, 1 App. Cas. 754; 46 L. J. Ex. 573.) The contributory negligence of a plaintiff disentitling him to succeed is relative to his condition, age, knowledge, &c.; thus an act which would be contributory negligence in a grown person might not amount to such in a child of tender years. (*Lynch* v. *Nurdin*, 1 Q. B. 29; but see *Hughes* v. *Macfie*, 2 H. & C. 744; 33 L. J. Ex. 177; *Mangan* v. *Atterton*, L. R. 1 Ex. 239; 35 L. J. Ex. 161; commented on in *Clark* v. *Chambers*, 3 Q. B. D. 327; 47 L. J. Q. B. 427.) But if a child is injured by causes, one of which is the direct contributory negligence of a person to whose care it has been intrusted, the child is held to be so far identified with that person as to be disentitled to recover. (*Waite* v. *North Eastern Ry. Co.*, E. B. & E. 719, 728.) And this principle of identification extends to all cases where one person having for certain purposes in hand surrendered his will to another, sustains injury from causes one of which is the direct contributory negligence of that other person; for instance, a passenger in a public vehicle is in this respect held to be "identified" with his driver or other person in charge. (*Thorogood* v. *Bryan*, 8 C. B. 115; *Armstrong* v. *Lancashire & Yorkshire Ry. Co.*, L. R. 10 Ex. 47; 44 L. J. Ex. 89.)

A statement of claim merely alleging that the defendant acted "negligently," and that damage ensued to the plaintiff, does not alone show a cause of action, unless it is also shown, or can be inferred from the facts alleged, that the negligence amounted to a breach of duty or wrong. (*Dutton* v. *Powles*, 2 B. & S. 174; 31 L. J. Q. B. 191, 192; *Gautret* v. *Egerton*, L. R. 2 C. P. 371; 36 L. J. C. P. 191; *Jones* v. *Egerton*, *Ib.*; *Metcalfe* v. *Hetherington*, 11 Ex. 257; *Collis* v. *Selden*, L. R. 3 C. P. 495; 37 L. J. C. P. 233.) Where the cause of action is founded on contract, or arises out of a relationship created by bailment or retainer, it is necessary to show expressly the creation of the duty alleged to have been broken; and where it arises independently of contract, the statement of the facts must show that the defendant was bound to do or not to do what he is alleged to have negligently

The like, where the Injuries were sustained in a Collision.

1. The plaintiff is a milkman, carrying on business at ——. The defendant is a butcher.

2. On the —— of ——, 18—, whilst the plaintiff was driving his milk-cart in a public highway called —— Street, ——, the defendant so negligently drove a horse and gig of the defendant's, that the same was driven with great violence against the said milk-cart of the plaintiff.

3. The plaintiff was in consequence thrown out of his said cart, and had his right arm broken, and his said cart was damaged to such an extent that he was obliged to incur an expense of £—— in repairing it.

4. [*State further special damage, if any.*]

For Injuries caused to a Railway Passenger by the Company's Servants' Negligence in Starting a Train.

1. The plaintiff is a ——, residing at ——, and the defendants are the —— Railway Company.

2. The plaintiff, on the —— of ——, 18—, became

---

omitted or committed, or that he was bound, as regarded the plaintiff, not to do negligently what he did. An express allegation of duty on the part of the defendant is a mere inference of law. If the facts stated do not raise the duty, the express allegation will not supply the defect; and if the facts sufficiently show the duty, the express allegation is unnecessary, and therefore ought not to be introduced. (*Cane* v. *Chapman*, 5 A. & E. 647; *Seymour* v. *Maddox*, 16 Q. B. 326; and see *per* Cotton, L. J., *Hurdman* v. *North Eastern Ry. Co.*, 3 C. P. D. 168; 47 L. J. C. P. 368; 38 L. T. 339.) See also *ante*, "*Pleading in General*," p. 7.

As regards damages, although the defendant is responsible for all the consequences which he could reasonably foresee as the result of his negligent act (*Scott* v. *Shepherd*, 2 W. Bl. 892; *Hill* v. *New River Co.*, 9 B. & S. 303; *Collins* v. *Middle Level Commissioners*, L. R. 4 C. P. 279; 38 L. J. C. P. 236; *Sneesby* v. *Lancashire & Yorkshire Ry. Co.*, L. R. 9 Q. B. 263; 43 L. J. Q. B. 69; 1 Q. B. D. 42; 45 L. J. Q. B. 1; *Clark* v. *Chambers*, 3 Q. B. D. 327; 47 L. J. Q. B. 427; *Harris* v. *Mobbs*, 3 Ex. D. 268), he is not responsible for occurrences which are not the necessary and reasonable consequences of such act. (*Sharp* v. *Powell*, L. R. 7 C. P. 253; 41 L. J. C. P. 95; and see *per* Pollock, C. B., *Greenland* v. *Chaplin*, 5 Ex. 243.) See "*Damages*," *ante*, p. 19.

As to claims under Lord Campbell's Act, (9 & 10 Vict. c. 93, amended by 27 & 28 Vict. c. 95) see "*Executors*," *ante*, p. 418.

See also "*Shipping*," "*Corporation*," "*Nuisance*," "*Carriers of Passengers*," "*Solicitor*," &c. And see further "*Shearman & Redfield on Negligence*"; "*Addison on Torts*"; "*Smith on Negligence*."

a passenger to be carried on the defendants' railway from A. to B. for reward paid to the defendants.

3. Upon the arrival at B. of the train in which the plaintiff was being carried, the guard of the said train, being the servant of the said company who had charge of the said train, negligently and carelessly started the said train before the plaintiff had time to get clear and out of the way thereof, whereby the plaintiff was thrown and fell between the platform and the said train.

4. By the said fall, and the movement of the said train, the plaintiff was cut and bruised and was crushed between the platform and the said train, and was seriously injured, and in consequence thereof the plaintiff was for six months ill and in suffering, and was unable to attend to his said business for twelve months, and incurred medical and other expenses amounting to £——.

For other Forms of Pleadings in Actions against Railway Companies for Negligence, see "Carriers of Passengers," ante, p. 137, *and "Executors," ante, p.* 418.

The like, where the Injuries arose from the Negligence of the Defendants' Servants in leaving an Obstruction upon the Platform, which the Plaintiff fell over.

1. The plaintiff is a ——, residing at ——, and the defendants are a company possessed of a railway and passenger station thereon at ——, in the county of ——.

2. On the evening of the —— of ——, 18—, the plaintiff came to the defendants' said station for the purpose of travelling on the defendants' said railway.

3. The plaintiff had taken a ticket to travel upon the said railway, and was obliged to pass through the defendants' booking-office in order to get to the platform, from which the train by which the plaintiff was to travel started.

4. There was a crowd of people in the said booking-office, which, together with the said platform, owing to the negligence of the defendants, was insufficiently lighted at the time, and a luggage barrow was negligently allowed by the defendants to remain in the said booking-office close to the door of the said booking-office, leading to the said platform.

5. In consequence of the negligence of the defendants

as aforesaid, the plaintiff fell over the said barrow and severely injured his leg, and broke his thumb, and suffered internal and other injuries.

6. [*State special damage, if any.*]

The like, where the Injuries arose from a Neglect to provide Proper Accommodation at a Platform: Foulkes v. *Metr. Distr. Ry. Co.*, 4 C. P. D. 267.

For Injuries sustained by the Negligence of the Defendant's Servants in allowing a Heavy Substance to fall from a Window upon the Plaintiff passing underneath: Pearson v. *Cox*, 36 L. T. 496.

Against a Defendant for negligently Building a Wall and placing Soil upon his Land, so that the Rain-water percolated through the wall, and Injured the Plaintiff's House: Hurdman v. *N. Eastern Ry. Co.*, 3 C. P. D. 168; 47 L. J. C. P. 368; 38 L. T. 339.

Against a Railway Company for Negligence by which the Plaintiff, a Passenger, was Injured: Hirschfeld v. *L. B. & S. C. Ry. Co.*, 2 Q. B. D. 1.

Against a Railway Company for Negligence by which the Plaintiff's Servant was Injured: Berringer v. *Great Eastern Ry. Co.*, 4 C. P. D. 163.

Statement of Claim against a Telegraph Company for the Negligence of their Servants in Misdelivering a Telegram: Dickson v. *Reuter's Telegraph Co.*, 2 C. P. D. 62.

Against a Landlord by his Tenant for Negligence in the Construction of a Cistern, &c., Anderson v. *Oppenheimer*, 5 Q. B. D. 602.

For Negligently pulling down a House, whereby the Plaintiff's House adjoining was Injured (*b*).

1. The plaintiff was possessed of a house, No. ——, —— Street, ——, and the defendant was possessed of a house adjoining the plaintiff's said house.

2. The defendant so negligently and unskilfully pulled down his said house that the walls of the plaintiff's said house were cracked and injured, and the plaintiff was put to an expense of £—— in repairing the injury thereby caused to his said house.

Against the Trustees of a Hospital for Injuries caused by the Negligence of their Servants in Repairing their Property (*c*).

1. The defendants were and are the trustees of the —— County Hospital.

(*b*) When the plaintiff is not entitled to a right to support for his house from the adjoining house, an action will not lie for pulling down the adjoining house without shoring up the plaintiff's. (*Peyton* v. *Mayor of London*, 9 B. & C. 725; see "*Support*," *post*, p. 523.) But an action may be maintained for any damage caused to the plaintiff's house by pulling down the adjacent house in a negligent and improper manner, as distinct from the damage done by the removal of the support to which the plaintiff was entitled. (*Dodd* v. *Holme*, 1 A. & E. 493; *Langford* v. *Woods*, 7 M. & G. 625; *Bradbee* v. *Christ's Hospital*, 4 M. & G. 714; *Trower* v. *Chadwick*, 3 Bing. N. C. 334; 6 *Ib.* 1.) There is no obligation towards a neighbour cast by law on the owner of a house, merely as owner, to keep it repaired; the only duty is to keep it in such a state, that his neighbour may not be injured by its fall. (*Chauntler* v. *Robinson*, 4 Ex. 163.)

(*c*) Corporate bodies, trustees, and commissioners, carrying on public works or performing public duties, are liable for negligence upon the same principles as those upon which individuals are liable, notwithstanding they undertake such duties gratuitously or derive no profit from them. (*Mersey Docks Trustees* v. *Gibbs*, L. R. 1 H. L. 93; *Coe* v. *Wise*, L. R. 1 Q. B. 711; *Winch* v. *Conservators of the Thames*, L. R. 7 C. P. 458; *Ib.* 9 C. P. 378.) And they are liable for the acts of their servants in the same manner as an individual is liable. (*Ib.*; see "*Corporation*," *ante*, p. 387; "*Master and Servant*," *ante*, p. 464.)

Officers of government performing public duties are not responsible for the negligence or misconduct of inferior officers in their several departments, although they appoint and may dismiss them, as the postmaster-general, commissioners of customs, military and naval officers. (*Whitfield* v. *Lord Le Despencer*, 2 Cowp. 754; *Lane* v. *Cotton*, 1 Ld. Raym. 646; *Nicholson* v. *Mouncey*, 15 East, 384; and see *Tobin* v. *The Queen*, 14 C. B. N. S. 505; 16 *Ib.* 310; 32 L. J. C. P. 216; 33 *Ib.* 199.)

2. The defendants by their servants were repairing the front of the said hospital on the —— of ——, 18—.

3. The said servants of the defendants, whilst so repairing the said hospital on the said —— of ——, 18—, so negligently conducted themselves that they caused a plank to fall from the said hospital upon the plaintiff whilst lawfully using the highway in front of the said hospital.

4. The plaintiff was thereby bruised and injured [*state special damage, if any.*]

For a Form of Claim by Husband and Wife for Damages for Injury to the Wife by Negligent Driving, coupled with a Claim by the Husband for Loss to Himself consequent thereon, see "Husband and Wife," ante, p. 436.

NUISANCE (*a*).

For Placing on a Highway an Obstruction which the Plaintiff fell over.

1. The defendant on the —— of ——, 18—, wrongfully heaped up earth and stones in a public highway,

---

(*a*) Nuisances are either *public* nuisances, as obstructions to highways, noxious trades, &c., which are indictable offences, or private nuisances, which are injuries to private property, as obstructing lights or rights of way, diverting watercourses, &c. (3 Bl. Com. 216.) The latter are for the most part injuries to easements, and will be found arranged under the titles "*Ways,*" "*Water,*" "*Light,*" &c. Some, however, may be conveniently collected under the present title, as, polluting the air, nuisances by noise, smoke, &c.

No action will lie for a public nuisance at the suit of a private person, unless he has thereby sustained particular damage over and above what is common to others (3 Bl. Com. 220); thus, no action will lie merely for placing an obstruction on a public highway, but if a person suffers damage by driving or falling against such obstruction, he may maintain an action for such damage; so if an obstruction of the highway prevents access to a person's abode and hinders his business, he may maintain an action for the damage thereby done to his trade. (*Iveson* v. *Moore,* 1 Ld. Raym. 486; 12 Mod. 262; *Wilkes* v. *Hungerford Market Co.,* 2 Bing. N. C. 281; *Rose* v. *Groves,* 5 M. & G. 613; *Simmons* v. *Lillystone,* 8 Ex. 431; *Benjamin* v. *Storr,* L. R. 9 C. P. 400; 43 L. J. C. P. 162; *M'Carthy* v. *Metropolitan Board of Works,* L. R.

in the parish of —— [*describe locality*], so as to obstruct the said highway.

2. The plaintiff in consequence, whilst lawfully passing

---

7 C. P. 508; *Ib.* 8 C. P. 191; *Ib.* 7 H. L. 243; *Fritz* v. *Hobson*, 14 Ch. D. 542; 49 L. J. Ch. 321; *Lyon* v. *Fishmongers' Co.*, 1 App. Cas. 662; 46 L. J. Ch. 68.)

But mere delay caused by the obstruction, or the trouble and expense of removing it, being common to all, is not sufficient damage to enable an individual to maintain an action. (*Winterbottom* v. *Lord Derby*, L. R. 2 Ex. 316; 36 L. J. Ex. 194.) That the plaintiff and his servants were compelled to go by a longer route, and their work was thereby increased, and the plaintiff was prevented from employing his servants otherwise, is sufficient peculiar damage. (*Blagrave* v. *Bristol Waterworks Co.*, 1 H. & N. 369.)

A highway may be dedicated to the public subject to an obstruction or to the exercise of some private right upon it, which is then not actionable. (*Fisher* v. *Prowse*, *Cooper* v. *Walker*, 2 B. & S. 770; 31 L. J. Q. B. 212; *Morant* v. *Chamberlain*, 6 H. & N. 541; 30 L. J. Ex. 299; *Mercer* v. *Woodgate*, L. R. 5 Q. B. 26; 39 L. J. M. C. 21; *Arnold* v. *Blaker*, L. R. 6 Q. B. 433; 40 L. J. Q. B. 185; *Robbins* v. *Jones*, 15 C. B. N. S. 221; 33 L. J. C. P. 1; *St. Mary Newington* v. *Jacobs*, L. R. 7 Q. B. 47; 41 L. J. M. C. 72.)

If the defendant persists in continuing a nuisance after a verdict against him for nominal damages, the jury in a second action may give vindictive damages to compel him to abate the nuisance. (*Shadwell* v. *Hutchinson*, 2 B. & Ad. 97; *Battishill* v. *Reed*, 18 C. B. 696; 25 L. J. C. P. 290.)

In actions for nuisances, when the circumstances make it advisable, the plaintiff may claim an injunction. (See "*Injunction*," *ante*, p. 439, and "*Light*," *ante*, p. 449.)

An action for a nuisance may be maintained by the reversioner where there is damage done to his reversion; this may be, either by the damage being of a permanent nature, or by its being such as to be an injury to his title to the premises, as by establishing, or furnishing evidence of some right adverse to his title thereto. (*Kidgill* v. *Moor*, 9 C. B. 364; 19 L. J. C. P. 177; *Jesser* v. *Gifford*, 4 Burr. 2141; *Dobson* v. *Blackmore*, 9 Q. B. 991; *Mott* v. *Shoolbred*, L. R. 20 Eq. 22; 44 L. J. Ch. 380; and see "*Lights*," *ante*, p. 451.)

See further, "*Reversion*," *post*, p. 512.

Where by statute a thing is directed to be done, the doing of which, if not so directed, would amount to a nuisance or entitle persons injured thereby to an action, no action is maintainable in respect of such thing, but the persons thereby injured can recover only such compensation, if any, as the statute directing the thing to be done, or the statutes incorporated therewith have provided. (*Hammersmith Ry. Co.* v. *Brand*, L. R. 4 H. L. 171, 215; 38 L. J. H. L. 265; *Met. Asylum District* v. *Hill*, 6 App. Cas. 193, 203; 50 L. J. Q. B. 353; *Dixon* v. *Met. Board of Works*, 7 Q. B. D. 418.) But if the thing directed to be done would not amount to a nuisance or cause damage, unless done negligently, the statute does not, in general, afford any answer to an action brought by a person injured by reason of such negligence. (*Geddis* v. *Proprietors of Bann Reservoir*, 3 App. Cas. 430 456; *Brine* v. *Gt. W. Ry. Co.*, 31 L. J. Q. B. 101.)

along the said highway on the —— of ——, 18—, fell over the said earth and stones so heaped up, and broke his arm.

3. [*State special damage, if any.*]

For Keeping a Dangerous Cellar Open adjoining a Public Highway (*b*).

1. The defendant was, on the —— of ——, 18—, the occupier of a house, No. ——, —— Street, ——, and of a vault or cellar belonging thereto under the footway of the said street.

Where, however, by statute a thing is permitted, not directed, to be done, it is not, in general, to be inferred that the right of action is taken away for a nuisance caused by the doing of such thing, even if such nuisance is not due to any negligence in the manner of the doing, at all events where there is no provision for compensation of persons injured. (*Met. Asylum District* v. *Hill*, *supra; Powell* v. *Fall*, 5 Q. B. D. 597; 49 L. J. 428; *Vernon* v. *Vestry of St. James*, 16 Ch. D. 449; 50 L. J. Ch. 81.)

As to asylums for the care and cure of sick poor under the Metropolitan Poor Act, 1867, (30 Vict. c. 6) see *Met. Asylum District* v. *Hill*, *supra*.

As to locomotives on highways, see *Powell* v. *Fall*, *supra*, and "*Highways*," *ante*, p. 436.

As to locomotives on railways, see "*Negligence*," *ante*, p. 478.

(*b*) Making an excavation, cellar, or area adjoining a public way, or keeping such an excavation, cellar, or area insecurely fenced and guarded, so as to render the way unsafe to those who use it with ordinary care, is a nuisance, for which an action will lie at the suit of the person who is injured by falling into it or otherwise while using the public way. (*Barnes* v. *Ward*, 9 C. B. 392; *Hadley* v. *Taylor*, L. R. 1 C. P. 53.)

The occupier of land is liable for allowing the continuance on his premises of any artificial work which causes a nuisance to a neighbour, even though it has been put there before he took possession. (*Broder* v. *Saillard*, 2 Ch. D. 692; 45 L. J. Ch. 414; *Coupland* v. *Hardingham*, 3 Camp. 397; *White* v. *Jameson*, L. R. 18 Eq. 303.)

The occupier is liable for any nuisance which is the natural result of operations which he has licensed another to carry on upon the land;—thus, where the occupier gave to another a licence to burn bricks upon the land, he was held liable for the nuisance thereby naturally caused. (*White* v. *Jameson*, *supra; Harris* v. *James*, 45 L. J. Q. B. 545; 35 L. T. 240.)

A man who procures work to be done upon his land likely to cause danger to his neighbour, as for instance pulling down and re-erecting a house adjoining that of a neighbour entitled to support, is bound to see that proper precautions to avoid such injury are taken, and is not relieved from such duty and liability by employing a competent contractor. (*Bower* v. *Peate*, 1 Q. B. D. 321; 45 L. J. Q. B. 446; *Angus*

2. On the said —— of ——, the defendant wrongfully suffered the said vault or cellar to be open to the said street and unguarded, so as to be dangerous to persons lawfully passing along the said footway.

---

v. *Dalton*, 4 Q. B. D. 162; 48 L. J. Q. B. 225; 44 L. T. 844, and see *Pearson* v. *Cox*, 2 C. P. D. 369.)

An occupier who maintains a lamp projecting over a highway, is bound to keep it in repair so as not to be dangerous to passers-by, and is liable for injury occasioned by its falling through want of repair upon a passer-by, notwithstanding he may have employed a competent contractor to repair it. (*Tarry* v. *Ashton*, 1 Q. B. D. 314; 45 L. J. Q. B. 260.)

A landlord is liable for an injury to a stranger by the defective repair of demised premises only when he has contracted with the tenants to repair, or when he has been guilty of misfeasance, as, for instance, in letting the premises in a ruinous condition. (*Nelson* v. *Liverpool Brewery Co.*, 2 C. P. D. 311; 46 L. J. C. P. 675; *Payne* v. *Rogers*, 2 H. Bl. 349; *Todd* v. *Flight*, 9 C. B. N. S. 377; 30 L. J. C. P. 21; *Pretty* v. *Bickmore*, L. R. 8 C. P. 401; *Russell* v. *Shenton*, 3 Q. B. 449; *Gwinnell* v. *Eamer*, L. R. 10 C. P. 658.)

Thus, where the landlord lets land with a standing and continuing nuisance upon it, and suffers it to continue, as with a wall which obstructed the plaintiff's light (*Rosewell* v. *Prior*, 2 Salk. 460; 1 Ld. Raym. 713), with a noxious privy (see *R.* v. *Pedly*, 1 A. & E. 822, explained in *Rich* v. *Basterfield*, 4 C. B. 783, 804), with a dangerous stack of chimneys (*Todd* v. *Flight*, 9 C. B. N. S. 377), the landlord is liable. He is not liable for nuisances occasioned by the use of the premises by the occupiers, and not by the premises alone, as for a nuisance of smoke from a chimney let with the premises (*Rich* v. *Basterfield*, 4 C. B. 783); unless, it would seem, the premises are let for the express purpose of using them in the precise way which causes the nuisance. (*Harris* v. *James*, *supra.*)

Where the servant of the defendant causes the nuisance in the course of his employment the defendant may be liable, even though he is not the occupier, as where the servant of a coal merchant in delivering coals at a customer's house removed the cover of the hole in the footway through which the coals were shot into the customer's cellar, but neglected to guard the hole, or to give any warning to the plaintiff who was using the footway, in consequence of which neglect the plaintiff fell into the hole and was injured, it was held that the coal-merchant was liable. (*Whiteley* v. *Pepper*, 2 Q. B. D. 276; 46 L. J. Q. B. 436.)

A person voluntarily using private premises as a mere licensee for purposes of his own unconnected with the premises or the business there carried on, and not for the purpose of carrying out a contract with the occupier, or in pursuance of a contract with the occupier for such use of the premises, cannot maintain an action to recover damages for an injury occasioned to him by the dangerous state of the premises, unless such danger was one which was hidden, or unusual, so as to be in the nature of a trap. (*Gautret* v. *Egerton*, L. R. 2 C. P. 371; 36 L. J. C. P. 191; *Corby* v. *Hill*, 4 C. B. N. S. 556; 27 L. J. C. P. 318; *Bolch* v. *Smith*, 7 H. & N. 736; 31 L. J. Ex. 201;

3. The said street, with the said footway thereof, was a public highway.

4. The plaintiff [about —— P.M. of the said —— of ——, when it was getting dusk, *or as the case may be, giving details where practicable*] in consequence of the above stated dangerous condition of the said vault or cellar, whilst lawfully passing along the said footway, fell into the said vault or cellar.

5. [*State damage, as for instance*, The effect of the said fall upon the plaintiff was, that his right leg was broken, and he was much shaken and bruised.]

6. The plaintiff was thereby prevented from attending to his business of a tailor for —— months, and lost £——, profits which he would otherwise have made on his said business during the said —— months, and was put to an

---

Smith v. *London and St. Katherine Docks Co.*, L. R. 3 C. P. 326; 37 L. J. C. P. 257; *White* v. *France*, 2 C. P. D. 308; 46 L. J. C. P. 823.) But the occupier is bound to use reasonable care to protect persons coming to his premises by invitation, or upon business, from unusual dangers, which he knows, or ought to know, to be there. (*Indermaur* v. *Dames*, L. R. 1 C. P. 274; 2 *Ib.* 311; 36 L. J. C. P. 181; *Holmes* v. *North Eastern Ry. Co.*, L. R. 4 Ex. 254; *Ib.* 6 Ex. 123; 38 L. J. Ex. 161; 40 *Ib.* 121; *Wright* v. *London and North Western Ry. Co.*, L. R. 10 Q. B. 298; 1 Q. B. D. 252; 45 L. J. Q. B. 570; *Smith* v. *London and St. Katherine Docks Co.*, *supra*.) Where a person is upon the premises, by the invitation or permission of the occupier, on lawful business in which both he and the occupier have an interest, there is a duty towards such person cast upon the occupier to keep the premises in a reasonably secure condition. (*Holmes* v. *North Eastern Ry. Co.*, *supra*; *Wright* v. *London and North Western Ry. Co.*, *supra*; and see *Woodley* v. *Met. Dist. Ry. Co.*, 2 Ex. D. 384.) Where the plaintiff was lawfully using a road on private premises, and was injured by driving against an unguarded obstruction placed thereon by the defendant, he was held entitled to recover. (*Corby* v. *Hill*, *supra*; see *Gautret* v. *Egerton*, *supra*.) Where the defendant left a trap-door open in the entrance of his shop, he was held liable for an injury to a customer falling into it. (*Chapman* v. *Rothwell*, E. B. & E. 168; 27 L. J. Q. B. 315.) Where the defendant left a shoot in his sugar refinery unprotected, and the plaintiff being lawfully there on business fell down the shoot, the defendant was held liable. (*Indermaur* v. *Dames*, *supra*.) Where the plaintiff was permitted to go along a flagged path of the defendants to unload coals carried for him by the defendants, and was injured owing to the flag he stepped on being so worn as to give way, it was held that the defendants had a duty to the plaintiff to keep the way in a reasonably safe condition. (*Holmes* v. *North Eastern Ry. Co.*, *supra*.)

As to the liability to trespassers, see *Bird* v. *Holbrook*, 4 Bing. 628; *Ilott* v. *Wilkes*, 3 B. & Ald. 304; and see *Lynch* v. *Nurdin*, 1 Q. B. 29, 37; *Jordin* v. *Crump*, 8 M. & W. 782; *Clark* v. *Chambers*, 3 Q. B. D. 327; 47 L. J. Q. B. 427.

expense of £—— for medical and surgical attendance, and for nursing; and further, his business as a tailor was thereby permanently injured, and he was himself put to much pain, and rendered, for a long time, less able to carry on his said business than formerly.]

For a Statement of Claim, alleging that the Surface of the Defendants' Land had been Artificially Raised by Earth placed thereon by the Defendants, and that in consequence Rain-water falling on the Defendants' Land made its way through the Defendants' Wall into the adjoining House of the Plaintiff, and caused substantial Damage, see Hurdman v. *North Eastern Ry. Co.*, 3 C. P. D. 168; 47 L. J. C. P. 368 (*c*).

(*c*) Where the owner of land, without negligence, innocently uses his land in the ordinary manner of its use, though mischief is thereby occasioned to his neighbour, he is not liable in damages (*Rylands* v. *Fletcher*, L. R. 3 H. L. 330; L. R. 1 Ex. 265; 37 L. J. Ex. 171; *Smith* v. *Kenrick*, 7 C. B. 515; *Wilson* v. *Waddell*, 2 App. Cas. 95; *Hurdman* v. *North Eastern Ry. Co.*, 3 C. P. D. 168; 47 L. J. C. P. 368); but if he brings upon the land for his own purposes anything which is in itself dangerous, and liable to do mischief if it escapes, he must keep it in, at his peril; and if he fails to do so, he is *primâ facie* answerable for all damage which is the natural consequence of its escape. (*Rylands* v. *Fletcher*, *supra*; *Tenant* v. *Goldwin*, 2 Ld. Raym. 1089; Salk. 360; *Crowhurst* v. *Amersham Burial Board*, 4 Ex. D. 5; 48 L. J. Ex. 109; *Smith* v. *Fletcher*, L. R. 9 Ex. 64; *Ib.* 7 Ex. 305; 41 L. J. Ex. 193.)

He can excuse himself by showing that the escape was owing to the plaintiff's default, or that it was due to *vis major*, or the act of God, and occurred in spite of all reasonable care on his part. (*Rylands* v. *Fletcher*, *supra*; *Nichols* v. *Marsland*, L. R. 10 Ex. 255; 2 Ex. D. 1; 44 L. J. Ex. 134; 46 L. J. Ex. 174; *Nitro-Phosphate Co.* v. *London and St. Katherine Docks Co.*, 9 Ch. D. 503; *Carstairs* v. *Taylor*, L. R. 6 Ex. 217; 40 L. J. Ex. 29; *Box* v. *Jubb*, 4 Ex. D. 76; 48 L. J. Ex. 417; *Thomas* v. *Birmingham Canal Co.*, 49 L. J. Q. B. 851; 43 L. T. 435.)

An occupier of land is, in the absence of any right of easement or contract to the contrary, bound to keep all filth, sewage, and the like, arising on his land, from escaping on to the land of his neighbour. (*Tenant* v. *Goldwin*, *supra*; *Rylands* v. *Fletcher*, *supra*; *Alston* v. *Grant*, 3 E. & B. 128.)

So if any one by artificial erections or works upon his own land causes rain water, water brought artificially upon his land, or liquid filth, to pass into his neighbour's land, so as to interfere substantially with his enjoyment thereof, it is, in general, an actionable wrong. (*Broder* v. *Saillard*, 2 Ch. D. 692, 700; 45 L. J. Ch. 414; *Tenant* v. *Goldwin*, *supra*; *Humphries* v. *Cousins*, 2 C. P. D. 239; 46 L. J. C. P.

For a Form of Injunction to restrain the Defendant from so using his Stable as to be a Nuisance to the Occupier of an adjoining House, see Ball v. *Ray*, L. R. 8 Ch. Ap. 472; *and Broder* v. *Saillard*, 2 Ch. D. 692; 45 L. J. Ch. 417.

For a Statement of Claim for Negligently allowing Sewage to Escape into a Neighbour's Premises, see Humphries v. *Cousins*, 2 C. P. D. 239; 46 L. J. C. P. 488.

For a Nuisance in carrying on a Noxious Manufacture (d).

1. The plaintiff is the owner and occupier of a house called Cliffe House, ——, and of the gardens, plantations,

---

438; *Hurdman* v. *North Eastern Ry. Co.*, 3 C. P. D. 168, 173; 47 L. J. C. P. 368.) But it is held that a mine owner is exempt from liability for water which, in consequence of his works, flows by gravitation into an adjoining mine, if his works are carried on with skill and in the usual manner, so excavating and raising minerals being regarded as the natural use of mineral land. (*Hurdman* v. *North Eastern Ry. Co.*, *supra*; *Wilson* v. *Waddell*, 2 App. Cas. 95; *Rylands* v. *Fletcher*, L. R. 3 H. L. 330; 37 L. J. Ex. 171; *West Cumberland Iron and Steel Co.* v. *Kenyon*, 11 Ch. D. 782; 48 L. J. Ch. 793; *Fletcher* v. *Smith*, 2 App. Cas. 781; 47 L. J. Ex. 4.)

Upon the above principle in a suit by the owner and occupier of a house against the occupier of an adjoining house, complaining of noise from the defendant's stable and of damp from an artificial mound on which it stood, an injunction was granted to prevent the defendant from keeping horses in his stable so as to be a nuisance; and it was also held that the defendant was liable for not preventing the damp from going through the plaintiff's wall. (*Broder* v. *Saillard*, *supra*; and see also *Ball* v. *Ray*, L. R. 8 Ch. Ap. 472.)

But where the dangerous matter is brought upon the land for the joint purposes of the defendant and the plaintiff, with the consent of the plaintiff, there is no such absolute obligation to keep it in as exists where it is brought by the defendant upon his land for his own purposes, the defendant in the former case not being liable for injury caused by its escape in the absence of negligence on his part. (*Carstairs* v. *Taylor*, L. R. 6 Ex. 217; 40 L. J. Ex. 29; *Anderson* v. *Oppenheimer*, 5 Q. B. D. 602; 49 L. J. Q. B. 708; and see *Ross* v. *Fedden*, L. R. 7 Q. B. 661; 41 L. J. Q. B. 270.)

One who takes a part of a house, takes it subject to the ordinary risks arising from the ordinary use of the rest of the house, and therefore cannot, in the absence of negligence, recover against an occupier of the other part of the house for damage done by an escape of water from the pipes in the possession of such occupier. (*Ross* v. *Fedden* *supra*; *Anderson* v. *Oppenheimer*, *supra*.)

(*d*) Smoke, noise, and smells may severally constitute a nuisance

and fields thereto adjoining. The defendant is a manufacturer of chemical products, carrying on his business at his works called "The Phœnix Works," near the plaintiff's said premises.

2. On the —— of ——, 18—, and the —— following days [*or as the case may be*] the defendant wrongfully caused to issue and proceed from his said works large quantities of offensive, poisonous and unwholesome smoke, vapours, gases, and noxious matter.

3. The above-mentioned smoke, vapours, gases, and noxious matter, spread themselves over the plaintiff's said premises and damaged the grass growing in the plaintiff's said fields, and the trees in his said plantations, and the plants and flowers in his said gardens, and rendered his said house unwholesome and uncomfortable to live in. [*Give details where practicable.*]

See as to Claims for Injunction, "Injunction," ante, and "Light," ante.

---

and be ground for an action for damages or for an injunction. (*Crump* v. *Lambert*, L. R. 3 Eq. 409, *and cases there cited; Walter* v. *Selfe*, 4 De G. & Sm. 315; 20 L. J. Ch. 433; *Sturges* v. *Bridgman*, 11 Ch. D. 852; 48 L. J. Ch. 785; *St. Helen's Smelting Co.* v. *Tipping*, 11 H. L. C. 642; 35 L. J. Q. B. 66; *Walker* v. *Brewster*, L. R. 5 Eq. 25; 37 L. J. Ch. 33; *Soltau* v. *De Held*, 2 Sim. N. S. 133; 31 L. J. Ch. 159; *Inchbald* v. *Robinson*, L. R. 4 Ch. Ap. 388; *Broder* v. *Saillard*, 2 Ch. D. 692; 45 L. J. Ch. 414; *Ball* v. *Ray*, L. R. 8 Ch. Ap. 467.)

In order to constitute a nuisance it must appear that physical injury is inflicted on the plaintiff's property, or that the ordinary comfort or healthfulness of human existence in the plaintiff's premises is materially interfered with. (*Crump* v. *Lambert, supra*; *St. Helen's Smelting Co.* v. *Tipping, supra*; *Cavey* v. *Lidbetter*, 12 C. B. N. S. 470; 32 L. J. C. P. 104; *Inchbald* v. *Robinson, supra.*)

A material addition to previously existing nuisances is separately actionable. (*Crump* v. *Lambert, supra*; *Baxendale* v. *M'Murray*, L. R. 2 Ch. Ap. 790.) The acts of several persons together may constitute a nuisance which the Court will restrain, though the damage done by the acts of each one, if taken alone, would be inappreciable. (*Thorpe* v. *Brumfitt*, L. R. 8 Ch. Ap. 650.)

Whether anything is a nuisance is to be determined, not merely by an abstract consideration of the thing itself, but with reference to the locality, and all the circumstances. (*Sturges* v. *Bridgman*, 11 Ch. D. 852, 865; 48 L. J. Ch. 785; *Bamford* v. *Turnley*, 3 B. & S. 62; 31 L. J. Q. B. 286; *Cavey* v. *Lidbetter, supra*; *St. Helen's Smelting Co.* v. *Tipping, supra.*) A nuisance caused by a noxious or noisy trade or manufacture is not, however, justifiable merely on the ground that the trade is carried on in a convenient and proper place. (*Ib.*)

For a Form of Injunction to Restrain Pollution of a Stream, see Lingwood v. *Stowmarket Co.*, L. R. 1 Eq. 77, 336 (*e*).

Officers (*a*).

(*e*) The pollution of a stream with refuse or filth to the injury of riparian proprietors, or others having a right to the beneficial use of the water in its normal or ordinary state, is a nuisance, for which damages may be obtained. (*Murgatroyd* v. *Robinson*, 7 E. & B. 391; 26 L. J. Q. B. 233.)

Where there is continuing damage, or a threatened continuance of damage, an injunction may be claimed, either in addition to damages, or as the sole remedy. (See "*Injunction*," *ante*; *Pennington* v. *Brinsop Hall Coal Co.*, 5 Ch. D. 769; 46 L. J. Ch. 773; *Attorney-General* v. *Colney Hatch Lunatic Asylum*, L. R. 4 Ch. Ap. 146; 38 L. J. Ch. 265.)

The fact that a stream is fouled by others as well as by the defendant is no answer to an action to restrain the fouling by him. (*Crossley* v. *Lightowler*, L. R. 3 Eq. 279; *Ib.*, 2 Ch. Ap. 478; 36 L. J. Ch. 584; *Attorney-General* v. *Leeds Corporation*, L. R. 5 Ch. Ap. 583; 39 L. J. Ch. 711.)

If a Local Board under the *Public Health Act*, 1875 (38 & 39 Vict. c. 55), do no act themselves to cause a nuisance, but merely neglect their duty of providing a proper and satisfactory system of drainage, such neglect of duty is no ground of action by an individual injured for damages or injunction, the remedy is by prerogative writ of mandamus. (*Glossop* v. *Heston Local Board*, 12 Ch. D. 102; 48 L. J. Ch. 736; and see "*Mandamus*," *ante*, p. 459.)

See further "*Injunction*," *ante*, p. 439, and "*Water*," *post*, p. 541.

(*a*) With respect to actions against officers of the army, navy, marines, coastguard, customs, excise, police, or other persons, acting for or under the direction of the Commissioners of Customs, or duly employed in the prevention of smuggling, for anything done in the execution of or by reason of their office, see the 39 & 40 Vict. c. 36, ss. 268—272, and the 40 & 41 Vict. c. 13, s. 4. These enactments provide that a month's notice in writing shall be given before action, that tender of amends may be made within a month from service of the notice, and, if not accepted, may be pleaded in bar of the action; that if there is no tender or no sufficient tender of amends before action, money may by leave of the Court be paid into Court by way of amends; and that every such action must be commenced within two months after the cause of action shall have arisen (with an extension of time in certain cases therein mentioned), and that the defendant may plead "Not guilty," and give the special matter in evidence on the trial. See also the 7 & 8 Geo. IV. c. 53, ss. 114—118, as to actions against officers of Excise or other persons for anything done in pursuance of that Act. As to actions against any person for any act done in pursuance or execution or intended execution of the Army Act, 1881 (44 & 45 Vict. c. 58), or in respect of any neglect or default in the execution thereof, see s. 170 of that Act.

As to similar provisions in other cases, see "Defences," "*Limitations of Actions*," and "*Notice of Action*."

PARTNERS (*a*).

PATENTS (*aa*).

(*a*) If several persons are jointly entitled to property injured, they should ordinarily join in suing in respect of such injury, although in some exceptional cases one or more of the joint-owners may properly sue without joining the others as co-plaintiffs. See "*Number of the parties,*" *ante*, p. 4, where see as to the effect of non-joinder.

If one of the joint-owners sues alone and solely on his own behalf, and no objection is taken on the ground of non-joinder, he can recover damages proportionate to his own interest, and the other joint-owners may afterwards sue for and recover damages for the injury done to their share or interest in the property. See *Sedgworth* v. *Overend*, 7 T. R. 279; *Bloxam* v. *Hubbard*, 5 East, 407; *Broadbent* v. *Ledward*, 11 A. & E. 209. As to actions by persons jointly interested in a patent or in a trade-mark, see "*Patents,*" *post*, p. 500; "*Trade-marks,*" *post*, p. 525.

Partners in trade may join in suing for a slander concerning their trade (*Le Fanu* v. *Malcolmson*, 1 H. L. C. 637; *Cook* v. *Batchellor*, 3 B. & P. 150; *Maitland* v. *Goldney*, 2 East, 426; *Booth* v. *Briscoe*, 2 Q. B. D. 496); so partners in a bank may join in suing for a libel respecting the business of the bank. (*Forster* v. *Lawson*, 3 Bing. 452.)

See further as to parties suing jointly or separately in actions for wrongs, Jud. Act, 1875, O. XVI.; "*Number of the Parties,*" *ante*, p. 4; "*Partners,*" *ante*, p. 290; and *Booth* v. *Briscoe*, 2 Q. B. D. 496.

A partner is liable for a tort committed by his co-partner in the course of the partnership business. Thus the proprietors of a stage coach were held liable for an injury caused by one of them in negligently driving the coach (*Moreton* v. *Hardern*, 4 B. & C. 223); and the proprietors of a mine were held liable for an injury to a workman caused by the negligence of one of the proprietors while engaged in the work of the mine. (*Ashworth* v. *Stanwix*, 30 L. J. Q. B. 183; *Mellors* v. *Shaw*, 1 B. & S. 437; 30 L. J. Q. B. 333.)

By s. 5 of the Carriers Act (11 Geo. IV. & 1 Will. IV. c. 68) any one or more of several persons carrying on business jointly as mail contractors, stage coach proprietors, or common carriers by land for hire shall be liable to be sued by his, her, or their name or names only, and no action for loss or injury to any parcel, package, or person, abates for want of joining any co-proprietor or co-partner.

(*aa*) Patent rights, though emanating from the royal prerogative, are regulated by statute law. The principal statutes relating to patents are the Statute of Monopolies, 21 Jac. I. c. 3; 5 & 6 Will. IV. c. 83; 2 & 3 Vict. c. 67; 7 & 8 Vict. c. 69, ss. 2-5; 15 & 16 Vict. c. 83 (the Patent Law Amendment Act, 1852); 16 & 17 Vict. c. 5; and 16 & 17 Vict. c. 115.

Under the provisions of the Judicature Acts, the whole jurisdiction of the former courts of common law and of equity in relation to patents (with the exception of the jurisdiction vested in the Lord Chancellor in relation to grants of letters-patent) has been transferred to the High Court of Justice and the Court of Appeal respectively. See especially ss. 16, 17 (4), 18, 24 (1) (2) and (7), of the Judicature Act, 1873.

The enactments of s. 42 of the Patent Law Amendment Act, 1852, whereby, in any action for the infringement of a patent, power was given to make an order for an injunction, inspection, or account, are now virtually superseded by the wider provisions of the Judicature Acts.

As to injunction, see "*Injunction*" *ante*, p. 439, and see *Frearson* v. *Loe*, 9 Ch. D. 48; 27 W. R. 183; *Bovill* v. *Goodier*, L. R. 2 Eq. 195; 35 L. J. Ch. 132; *Plimpton* v. *Spiller*, 4 Ch. D. 286; 35 L. T. 656.

As to inspection, &c., see O. LII., r. 3.

As to orders for an account, see *Walton* v *Lavater*, 8 C. B. N. S. 162; 29 L. J. C. P. 275; *Ellwood* v. *Christy*, 18 C. B. N. S. 494; 34 L. J. C. P. 130.

It was held prior to the Judicature Acts that the plaintiff in a suit in equity for the infringement of a patent was not entitled to have both an account of profits and an enquiry into damages under Sir H. Cairns' Act (21 & 22 Vict. c. 27, ss. 2, 5), and that he must elect which of those two forms of relief he would adopt (*De Vitre* v. *Betts*, L. R. 6 H. L. 319; 42 L. J. Ch. 841; *Neilson* v. *Betts*, L. R. 5 H. L. 1; 40 L. J. Ch. 317); and similarly it was held at law that if the plaintiff in an action for infringement obtained an order for an account of profits, he was not entitled to recover more than a nominal amount as damages. See *Vidi* v. *Smith*, 3 E. & B. 969; *Holland* v. *Fox*, ib. 977; *Walton* v. *Lavater*, 8 C. B. N. S. 162; 29 L. J. C. P. 275. The rule is the same under the Judicature Acts.

As to the ordinary measure of damages in actions for infringement of patent-right, see *Penn* v. *Jack*, L. R. 5 Eq. 81; 37 L. J. Ch. 136.

As to what amounts to infringement, where a patent is granted for a combination of instruments, see *Dudgeon* v. *Thomson*, 3 App. Cas. 34.

In an action by a patentee of an exclusive right to "vend," it was held not to be sufficient to charge that the defendant "exposed to sale," as this allegation did not show an infringement. (*Minter* v. *Williams*, 4 A. & E. 251.)

But the sale in this country of articles which have been manufactured, either here or abroad, by the unauthorised use of a patent process, is itself an infringement of the patent right, although the defendant did not know them to be so manufactured. (*Walton* v. *Lavater*, 8 C. B. N. S. 162; 29 L. J. C. P. 275; *Wright* v. *Hitchcock*, L. R. 5 Ex. 37; 39 L. J. Ex. 97; *Elmslie* v. *Boursier*, L. R. 9 Eq. 217; 39 L. J. Ch. 328; *Von Heyden* v. *Neustadt*, 14 Ch. D. 230; and see *Neilson* v. *Betts*, L. R. 5 H. L. 1; 40 L. J. Ch. 317.)

Letters-patent in the ordinary form do not bind the Crown or its agents or servants, but contractors who manufacture for the Crown according to a patent process and sell the completed article to the Crown without the patentee's licence are not mere agents or servants of the Crown, and are therefore liable to an action for infringing the patent. (*Dixon* v. *The London Small Arms Co.*, 1 App. Cas. 632; 46 L. J. Q. B. 617; and see *Vavasseur* v. *Krupp*, 9 Ch. D. 351; 39 L. T. 437.)

S. 7 of the 5 & 6 Will. IV. c. 83 imposes a penalty for the un-

Claim for the Infringement of a Patent (*b*).

1. The plaintiff was the first and true inventor of a certain new manufacture, that is to say, of [*state the title*

---

authorised use of the name of a patentee or imitation of the stamp or mark or other device of a patentee. See, for an instance of an action brought for a penalty under this section, *Myers* v. *Baker*, 3 H. & N. 802; 28 L. J. Ex. 90.

(*b*) Where a complete specification is filed in the first instance, the letters-patent, in lieu of the condition mentioned in the above precedent, are conditioned to become void if such complete specification is not sufficient (see s. 9 of the Patent Law Amendment Act, 1852), and the statement of claim must be framed accordingly.

By the Patent Law Amendment Act, 1852, s. 41, it was enacted that "in any action for the infringement of letters-patent, the plaintiff shall deliver with his declaration particulars of the breaches complained of in the said action, and the defendant, on pleading thereto, shall deliver with his pleas particulars of any objections on which he means to rely at the trial in support of the pleas in the said action; and at the trial of such action no evidence shall be allowed to be given in support of any alleged infringement or of any objection impeaching the validity of such letters-patent which shall not be contained in the particulars delivered as aforesaid; provided always that the place or places at or in which and in what manner the invention is alleged to have been used or published prior to the date of the letters-patent shall be stated in such particulars." And a similar enactment with respect to the delivery by a defendant in an action for infringing any letters-patent (or by a plaintiff in any *scire facias* to repeal such letters-patent), of a notice of any objections on which he intended to rely, as impeaching the validity of such letters-patent, was contained in the previous statute, 5 & 6 Will. IV. c. 83, s. 5.

This practice as regards particulars of breaches was adopted by the Court of Chancery before the passing of the Judicature Acts (see *Finnegan* v. *James*, L. R. 19 Eq. 73; *Flower* v. *Lloyd*, 6 Ch. D. 297; 45 L. J. Ch. 746.) It seems the better opinion, however, that these enactments with respect to the delivery of particulars of breaches by the plaintiff, and of particulars of objections by the defendant in actions for the infringement of patent right, have been virtually overruled and repealed by the provisions of the Judicature Acts and the orders thereunder, and that in strictness it is now the proper course to give such particulars in the pleadings themselves, instead of delivering particulars separately. See *ante*, p. 31. But in practice it is a convenient and usual course to deliver such particulars separately. See *Finnegan* v. *James*, *sup.*; *Sykes* v. *Howarth*, 12 Ch. D. 826; 48 L. J. Ch. 769; *Edison Telephone Co.* v. *India Rubber Co.*, 17 Ch. D. 137.

With respect to such particulars of breaches, see further *Talbot* v. *La Roche*, 15 C. B. 310; *Walton* v. *Lavater*, *sup.*; *Sykes* v. *Howarth*, 12 Ch. D. 826; 48 L. J. Ch. 769; *Needham* v. *Oxley*, 1 H. & M. 248; *Curtis* v. *Platt*, 8 L. T. 657; *Batley* v. *Kynock*, L. R. 19 Eq. 229; 44 L. J. Ch. 565; *Edison Telephone Co.* v. *India Rubber Co.*, *supra*.

or description of the patent, as for instance, certain improvements in the manufacture of sulphuric acid].

2. Her Majesty Queen Victoria thereupon, by letters patent under the Great Seal of the United Kingdom, bearing date the —— day of ——, 18—, granted to the plaintiff the sole privilege to make, use, exercise, and vend the said invention within the United Kingdom of Great Britain and Ireland, the Channel Islands, and the Isle of Man [*or as the case may be*], for the term of 14 years from the said —— day of ——, 18—, subject to a condition that the plaintiff should, within six calendar months next after the date of the said letters patent, cause to be filed in the Great Seal Patent Office [*or as the case may be*] an instrument in writing under his hand and seal particularly describing and ascertaining the nature of the said invention, and in what manner the same was to be and might be performed.

3. The plaintiff did, within six calendar months from the date of the said letters patent, cause to be filed in the Great Seal Patent Office [*or as the case may be, see* 43 & 44 Vict. c. 10, s. 5] such instrument in writing under his hand and seal as was prescribed by the said letters patent as aforesaid.

4. During the said term the defendant, between the —— day of ——, 18—, and the commencement of this action, infringed the said patent right, by using and putting in practice the said invention in the manufacture of [sulphuric acid] at his manufactory at ——, in the county of ——, and by there manufacturing large quantities [amounting in the whole to —— tons] of [sulphuric acid], in accordance with, and by means of the said invention, and by the process described in the specification of the said letters patent, and by selling to A. B. and C. D. [*or* to divers persons] the [sulphuric acid] so manufactured. Particulars of the said infringements are as follows, viz. [*or* are delivered herewith].

5. By reason of the premises [*here state any special damage sustained by the plaintiff, as for instance,* the plaintiff has lost the profits which he would otherwise have gained from manufacturing and selling the above-mentioned quantities of [sulphuric acid]].

6. [*If an injunction or an account of future profits is claimed, state any material circumstances in support of such claim, as for instance,* The defendant, though well knowing the premises, still continues to infringe the said

patent right in manner aforesaid, and to use the said invention and process in the manufacture of [sulphuric acid] without the licence or permission, and against the consent of the plaintiff, and claims the right of so doing, and intends and threatens to continue to do so, unless he is restrained by injunction from so doing.]

The plaintiff claims—

1. £—— damages for the wrongs hereinbefore complained of.
2. [That an account may be taken of the profits which have been, or during the pendency of this action may be, made or obtained by the defendant by means of the infringement of the said patent, and by the use of the said invention in the manufacture of [sulphuric acid], and that the defendant may be ordered to pay the amount of such profits, when ascertained, to the plaintiff.]
3. [That the defendant may be restrained by injunction from continuing or repeating the said injuries, and from hereafter using or putting in practice the said invention in the manufacture of [sulphuric acid], and from selling the [sulphuric acid] so manufactured.]
4. Such further or other relief as the nature of the case may require.

A like Claim, stating a Disclaimer or Alteration of part of the Title of the Invention or of part of the Specification. (See 5 & 6 *Will.* IV. *c.* 83, *s.* 1; 7 & 8 *Vict. c.* 69, *s.* 5; 15 & 16 *Vict. c.* 83, *s.* 39) (*c*).

1, 2, and 3. [*Same as paragraphs* 1, 2, *and* 3 *of the preceding form.*]

4. Afterwards the plaintiff, on the —— day of ——, 18—, pursuant to the statutes in such case made and

---

(*c*) As to the disclaimer and alteration of patents and specifications, see 5 & 6 Will. IV. c. 83, s. 1, 7 & 8 Vict. c. 69, s. 5 (partially repealed by the Statute Law Revision Act, 1874 (No. 2)), and 15 & 16 Vict. c. 83, s. 39. The latter section provides that no action shall be brought upon any letters-patent in which or on the specification of which any disclaimer or memorandum of alteration shall have been filed in respect of any infringement committed prior

provided, and by and with the leave of her Majesty's Attorney- [*or* Solicitor-] General first duly had and obtained for that purpose certified by his fiat and signature in that behalf, duly filed a disclaimer [*or* memorandum of alteration] of part of the title of the said invention and of the said specification, stating the reason for such disclaimer, such disclaimer [*or* alteration] not being such as extended the exclusive right granted by the said letters-patent; and the title of the said invention as altered by the said disclaimer [*or* memorandum of alteration] was and is [*state the title*], and the said disclaimer [*or* memorandum of alteration] was duly filed with the said specification to which the same related pursuant to the statutes in that case made and provided.

5. During the said term and after the said disclaimer [*or* memorandum of alteration] was filed as aforesaid, the defendant between the —— day of ——, 18—, and the commencement of this action infringed, &c. [*continue as in paragraph* 4 *of the preceding form*].

6 and 7. [*Same as paragraphs* 5 *and* 6 *of the preceding form, which see also as to the claims of damages and other relief.*]

Claim by the Assignee of a Patent for Infringement (*d*).

1, 2, and 3. A. B. was the first and true inventor, &c. [*Same as paragraphs* 1, 2, *and* 3 *of the first of the above precedents, except that the inventor must be mentioned by*

---

to the filing of such disclaimer or memorandum of alteration, unless the law-officer shall certify in his fiat that any such action may be brought notwithstanding the entry or filing of such disclaimer or memorandum of alteration.

As to the operation of a disclaimer see *Seed* v. *Higgins*, 8 E. & B. 755, 771; 8 H. L. C. 550; *Ralston* v. *Smith*, 11 C. B. N. S. 471; 11 H. L. C. 223; *Thomas* v. *Welsh*, L. R. 1 C. P. 192; 35 L. J. C. P. 200; *Dudgeon* v. *Thomson*, 3 App. Cas. 34. And for examples of former declarations after a disclaimer or alteration see *Seed* v. *Higgins*, *supra; Stocker* v. *Warner*, 1 C. B. 148; *Talbot* v. *La Roche*, 15 C. B. 310; *Platt* v. *Else*, 8 Ex. 364; *Titley* v. *Easton*, 2 C. B. N. S. 706; 26 L. J. C. P. 269.

With respect to the extension of the term of a patent, see the statutes 5 & 6 Will. IV. c. 83, s. 4; 2 & 3 Vict. c. 67; 7 & 8 Vict. c. 69, ss. 1–4; 15 & 16 Vict. c. 83, s. 40; 16 & 17 Vict. c. 115, s. 7, and see *Russell* v. *Ledsam*, 14 M. & W. 574.

(*d*) Where the action is brought by an assignee of a patent-right, the statement of claim must be framed accordingly, and must state the fact of the assignment.

his name, and that the letters patent must be stated to have been granted to him and his assigns, instead of to him simply].

4. Afterwards the said A. B. by deed bearing date the —— day of ——, 18—, granted and assigned to the plaintiff the said sole privilege to make, use, exercise and vend the said invention as aforesaid for the term aforesaid, together with the said letters patent, and all the liberties and privileges by the said letters patent granted to the said A. B. as aforesaid. [*State the assignment according to the fact.*]

5. The said assignment was duly entered in the Register of Proprietors, in pursuance of the Patent Law Amendment Act, 1852.

6, &c. Afterwards, and during the said term, the defendant, between the —— day of ——, 18—, and the —— day of ——, 18—, infringed, &c. [*continue as in the first of the above precedents down to the end*].

Penal Statutes.

(See *ante*, p. 296.)

Police.

See "Defences," "*Police*," "*Notice of Action*," "*Not Guilty by Statute*."

By the Patent Law Amendment Act, 1852, s. 35, assignments of letters-patent, or of any share or interest therein, and licences under letters-patent; are to be entered in the Register of Proprietors; and such entry is made essential to the title of the assignees and licensees. (*Chollet* v. *Hoffman*, 7 E. & B. 686; 26 L. J. Q. B. 249.) But it appears that such entry relates back to the date of the assignment, so as to entitle the assignee to maintain a suit to restrain infringement instituted between the dates of the assignment and the registration. (*Hassall* v. *Wright*, L. R. 10 Eq. 509; 40 L. J. Ch. 145; and see *Ellwood* v. *Christy*, 18 C. B. N. S. 494; 34 L. J. C. P. 130.)

As to *partial* assignments of patents, see *Cornish* v. *Keene*, 3 Bing. N. C. 570; *Dunnicliff* v. *Mallett*, 7 C. B. N. S. 209; 29 L. J. C. P. 70; *Walton* v. *Lavater*, 8 C. B. N. S. 162; 29 L. J. C. P. 275.

Each of several co-owners of a patent may maintain an action for its infringement (*Dunnicliff* v. *Mallet*, *supra*; *Walton* v. *Lavater*, *supra*; *Mathers* v. *Green*, L. R. 5 Ch. Ap. 29; 35 L. J. Ch. 1; *Sheehan* v. *Gt. E. Ry. Co.*, 17 Ch. D. 59; 50 L. J. Ch. 68), and so also a person who has an *exclusive* licence to use a patent. (*Renard* v. *Levinstein*, 2 H. & M. 628.)

Pound.

See "*Distress*," *ante*, p. 415.

Prison (*a*).

Public Health (*aa*).

Railway.

See "*Carriers*," *ante*, p. 361, "*Company*," *ante*, p. 369, "*Fences*," *ante*, p. 423, "*Negligence*," *ante*, p. 478.

(*a*) By the "Prison Act, 1865," 28 & 29 Vict. c. 126, s. 49, it is enacted that if any action is prosecuted against any person for anything done in pursuance of that Act, such person may plead the general issue, and give that Act and the special matter in evidence See "Defences," "*Not Guilty by Statute*." And by s. 50 all actions and prosecutions commenced against any person for anything done in pursuance of that Act shall be commenced within six calendar months after the committal of the act complained of.

As to prisons generally, see further the "Prison Act, 1877," (40 & 41 Vict. c. 21).

(*aa*) See the "Public Health Act, 1875," (38 & 39 Vict. c. 55); "*Corporati*..." *ante*, p. 387; *Highways*, *ante*, p. 434.

As to the requisites of a notice of action under the above statute, see *Smith* v. *West Derby Local Board*, 3 C. P. D. 423; 47 L. J. C. P. 607 (which was a decision with respect to a notice under s. 139 of the Public Health Act, 1848), and see "Defences," "*Notice of Action*."

Where the real and principal object of the action is to obtain an injunction to prevent the continuance of a nuisance, and the case is one in which the former Court of Chancery would have granted such injunction, no notice of action is necessary, even though the plaintiff also claims damages by way of subsidiary relief. (*Flower* v. *Local Board of Low Leyton*, 5 Ch. D. 347; 46 L. J. Ch. 621.)

By s. 265 of the above Act, "No matter or thing done, and no contract entered into by any local authority or joint board or port sanitary authority, and no matter or thing done by any member of such authority or by any officer of such authority or other person whomsoever acting under the direction of such authority, shall, if the matter or thing were done or the contract were entered into bonâ fide for the purpose of executing this Act, subject them or any of them personally to any action, liability, claim or demand whatsoever."

See as to this section *Mill* v. *Hawker*, L. R. 9 Ex. 309; L. R. 10 Ex. 92; 44 L. J. Ex. 49; *Bailey* v. *Cuckson*, 32 L. T. 124.

By s. 1 of the Public Health (Water) Act, 1878 (41 & 42 Vict. c. 25) that Act is to be construed as one with the Public Health Act, 1875.

RECOVERY OF LAND (*a*).

(*a*) Formerly in actions of ejectment there were no pleadings as in ordinary actions; but now the action for the recovery of land is placed substantially on the same footing as other actions, though the right of a landlord, when such action is brought against his tenant in possession of the land, to intervene and defend the action is preserved, and no defendant in such action who is in possession by himself or his tenant need plead his title except in certain specified cases. See "Defences," "*Recovery of Land*"; *Danford* v. *McAnulty*, 6 Q. B. D. 645; 50 L. J. Q. B. 294. The plaintiff in an action for the recovery of land is also restricted in joining therewith other causes of action. See Jud. Act, O. XVII. r. 2, and "*Joinder of Causes of Action*," *ante*, p. 17.

All persons in whom title to possession is alleged to exist should be joined as plaintiffs in the action. The plaintiff in such action must upon the statement of claim show that he is entitled, by stating such facts as, if true, show that he has an interest entitling him to possession of the premises sought to be recovered, or show that the defendant is estopped from disputing his title. (See "*Landlord and Tenant*," *ante*, pp. 255, 256; *O'Connor* v. *O'Hara*, 8 L. R. Ir. 249.) Where the defendant is not so estopped, the title of the plaintiff should be stated in such a way as to afford notice to the defendant of the case he has to meet. (*Philipps* v. *Philipps*, 4 Q. B. D. 127; 48 L. J. Q. B. 135.) Thus where the plaintiff has never been in possession, but claims as heir of some ancestor formerly in possession, the statement of claim should show how he is heir, tracing the title, and stating upon what deeds and documents he relies in deducing his title; and it is not enough that there is a general allegation that the plaintiff is so entitled heir by virtue of certain deeds and documents in the possession of the defendant. (*Philipps* v. *Philipps*, *supra*; and see *Heirs and Devisees*," *ante*, p. 194.) Where the facts in a pedigree are facts to be relied upon to establish the right or title, they must be set out. (*Philipps* v. *Philipps*, *supra*, *per* Brett, L. J.) It is not in general necessary to state negative facts, as that a person made no will, or did not bar an entail. The statement of claim need not show how the defendant came into possession, or deal with the title he alleges. (*Hodgins* v. *Hickson*, 39 L. T. 644 (Ir.).) It must show that there was a right of entry at the date of the writ; and for the purpose of recovery of *mesne profits* from an earlier date, it must be shown that the right of entry accrued at such earlier date. Prior possession, however short, is a sufficient *primâ facie* title against a wrong doer. (*Doe* d. *Hughes* v. *Dyeball*, M. & M. 346; 3 C. & P. 610; *Asher* v. *Whitlock*, L. R. 1 Q. B. 1.) It may sometimes be inexpedient to claim more than the mere recovery of the premises, and in such a case judgment and execution in the original action is no bar to a subsequent action for *mesne profits*. (See C. L. P. A., 1852, ss. 214, 218.) In such subsequent action, the judgment in the original action, even though it may have been by default, is conclusive evidence of the plaintiff's title at the date of the writ in such original action, if pleaded, as against the same defendant and persons claiming under him (*Wilkinson* v. *Kirby*, 15 C. B. 430; 23 L. J. C. P. 224; *Harris* v. *Mulkern*, 1 Ex. D. 31, 36; 45 L. J. Ex. 244); and *primâ facie*

Statement of Claim by Mortgagee against Mortgagor for Recovery of Land (*b*).

1. At the time of the making of the indenture hereinafter mentioned, the defendant was seised in fee of a certain farm, buildings, and premises, called the —— Farm, at ——, in the county of ——.

---

evidence of the defendant's possession at the same date. (*Pearse* v. *Coaker*, L. R. 4 Ex. 92, 99; 38 L. J. Ex. 82.) If the defendant should set up a title prior to that which the plaintiff has set out, the plaintiff may amend his statement of claim and set out his earlier title. (See further "*Landlord and Tenant*," *ante*, p. 256.)

By 37 & 38 Vict. c. 57, s. 1, "no person shall make an entry or distress or bring an action or suit to recover any land or rent but within 12 years next after the time at which the right to make such entry or distress, or to bring such action or suit, shall have first accrued to some person through whom he claims; or if such right shall not have accrued to any person through whom he claims, then within 12 years next after the time at which the right to make such entry or distress, or to bring such action or suit, shall have first accrued to the person making or bringing the same."

In the case of any of the following disabilities, viz., infancy, coverture, idiotcy, lunacy, and unsoundness of mind, six years is allowed from the termination of the disability (s. 3); but no time is allowed for absence beyond seas (s. 4); and 30 years is the utmost limit allowed, notwithstanding a person may have remained under disability or successive disabilities during the whole of the 30 years (s. 5).

By s. 7, a mortgagor is barred at the end of 12 years from the time when the mortgagee took possession or from the last written acknowledgment; and by s. 2, provision is made as to estates and interests in reversion or remainder, and as to other future estates or interests; and by s. 6, for defective assurances by tenants in tail. The said 12 years bar under the above act to a redemption suit is absolute, and not to be extended by reason of any disability of the mortgagor. (*Forster* v. *Patterson*, 17 Ch. D. 132; 50 L. J. Ch. 603; *Kinsman* v. *Rouse*, 17 Ch. D. 104; 50 L. J. Ch. 486.)

The effect of 3 & 4 Will. IV. c. 27 (which so far as the same is unrepealed is to be construed with 37 & 38 Vict. c. 57), is not merely to bar the remedy, but the title itself is extinguished, and the right of action wholly disappears. (*Dawkins* v. *Lord Penrhyn*, *per* Jessel, M. R., 6 Ch. D. 318; 4 App. Cas. 51; 48 L. J. Ch. 304; and see *Scott* v. *Nixon*, 3 Dr. & War. 388.)

If the statement of claim shows upon the face of it that the plaintiff and the persons through whom he claims have been out of possession more than 12 years, it must show also the facts which entitle the plaintiff to a longer period, otherwise the statement of claim may be demurred to. (*Dawkins* v. *Lord Penrhyn*, *supra*; *Noyes* v. *Crawley*, 10 Ch. D. 31, 36; 48 L. J. Ch. 112.) See further as to the Statutes of Limitation, "Defences," "*Limitation, Statutes of.*"

(*b*) Where the mortgage deed contains no proviso or stipulation amounting in law to a redemise and the mortgagor remains in possession after the execution of the deed, the mortgagee may bring an

2. On the —— of ——, 18--, the defendant, by an indenture of that date, made between himself and the plaintiff, granted the said —— Farm unto and to the use of the plaintiff and his heirs by way of mortgage.

3. The defendant has never given up possession of the said —— Farm to the plaintiff, and is still in possession thereof.

The plaintiff claims :—

To have possession of the said farm, buildings and premises.

Statement of Claim by Mortgagee against Tenant of Mortgagor under a Lease made after Mortgage (c).

1. By deed, dated the —— of ——, 18—, and made between A. B. and the plaintiff, the said A. B.,

---

action against the mortgagor for possession of the premises, unless a tenancy, other than one of sufferance, has been created between them. (*Doe* d. *Roylance* v. *Lightfoot*, 8 M. & W. 553; *Doe* d. *Parsley* v. *Day*, 2 Q. B. 147.) Where no tenancy other than a tenancy by sufferance has been created it is unnecessary for the mortgagee before bringing such action to give any notice to quit or to make any demand of possession. (*Doe* d. *Roby* v. *Maisey*, 8 B. & C. 767; *Doe* d. *Fisher* v. *Giles*, 5 Bing. 421.)

If the deed contains any proviso or stipulation that the mortgagor may remain in possession until a certain day or until default in payment of a certain sum at a particular time, and it is executed by the mortgagee, it in general amounts in law to a redemise; and no action for the recovery of the premises can be maintained until after such day, or default. (*Wilkinson* v. *Hall*, 3 Bing. N. C. 504; *Doe* d. *Lister* v. *Goldwin*, 2 Q. B. 141.) In some cases, however, the proviso or stipulation may amount only to a covenant. See Shep. Touch. 272; *Doe* d. *Parsley* v. *Day*, *supra*; Cole on Ejectment, p. 464 *et seq.*

Where the mortgage deed stipulates for payment of a certain sum on a particular day, and the mortgagor makes default in payment and remains in possession of the premises after such default, an action may, in the absence of any new tenancy, be brought against him by the mortgagee for recovery of the premises without any previous notice to quit, or demand of possession. (*Doe* d. *Fisher* v. *Giles*, *supra*; *Doe* d. *Roby* v. *Maisey*, *supra*.) See further, Cole on Ejectment, p. 462 *et seq.*

(*c*) Where the mortgagor has no title to possession, the mortgagee may, without giving notice to quit, recover possesion of the mortgaged premises against a tenant who claims under a lease from the mortgagor granted after the mortgage without the privity or consent of the mortgagee, unless such tenant has become tenant to the mortgagee, or unless the lease is one made under 44 & 45 Vict. c. 41, s. 18. (*Keech* v. *Hall*, 1 Doug. 21; 1 Smith, L. C. 8th ed. p. 574; *Lows* v. *Telford*, 1 App. Cas. 414, 425.) A mere notice by the mortgagee to the tenant to pay rent to him, not assented to by the tenant,

being seised in fee of the mansion house and lands at ——, in the county of ——, known as the M. estate, granted the said house and lands unto and to the use of the plaintiff and his heirs by way of mortgage.

2. The said A. B. subsequently to the making of the said deed let the said house and lands to the defendant without being entitled so to do, and without the privity or consent of the plaintiff.

3. The plaintiff has never in any way accepted or recognised the defendant as tenant of the said house and lands.

4. The defendant is in possession of the said house and lands as tenant thereof to the said A. B. under the said letting.

For a Form of Statement of Claim for Foreclosure, see Jud. Act, 1875, *App. C. Form No.* 14 (*d*).

Statement of Claim by Heir-at-law of the last Purchaser against a Tenant and a Person who has been admitted to appear and defend as Landlord under O. XII. r. 18 (*e*).

Between John F. . . Plaintiff.
and
A. B. and C. D., Defendants.

---

will not create a new tenancy; but a notice assented to by payment of rent, or otherwise, is evidence from which a jury may infer a new contract of tenancy from year to year as between the mortgagee and the tenant in possession. (*Brown* v. *Storey*, 1 M. & G. 117; *Rogers* v. *Humphreys*, 4 A. & E. 299, 313; *Doe* d. *Higginbotham* v. *Barton*, 11 A. & E. 307.)

In the case of a tenancy created before the mortgage, the tenant will be entitled to possession until the tenancy has been determined by notice to quit, or otherwise.

Where a person was in possession before the mortgage adversely to the mortgagor, the plaintiff must rely upon the title conferred upon him by the mortgage deed, and must proceed against him as in ordinary cases between strangers. See further Cole on Ejectment, pp. 473, 475 *et seq.*

(*d*) Actions of Foreclosure and Redemption are assigned to the Chancery Division of the High Court of Justice. (Jud. Act, 1873, s. 34 (3).) An action for foreclosure is not an action for the recovery of land within the meaning of O. XVII. r. 2. (*Tawell* v. *Slate Co.*, 3 Ch. D. 629.)

(*e*) In the case of a person who died before January 1st, 1834, descent is traced from the person last *seised* of the land. For Canons of descent under the old law see 2 Black. Com. c. 14; Stephens' Com. 8th ed. p. 388 n.; Williams on Seisin, p. 52.

1. George F. was, at the time of his decease hereinafter mentioned, seised in fee and in possession of the messuage known as No. 9, High Street, ——, which said messuage had been granted and conveyed by L. M.

In the case of persons who died on or since the above date the descent is traced from the last purchaser. (3 & 4 Will. IV. c. 106, s. 2.) By s. 1 of the last-mentioned Act the *purchaser* "shall mean the person who last acquired the land otherwise than by descent, or than by any escheat, partition, or enclosure, by the effect of which the land shall have become part of or descendible in the same manner as other land acquired by descent; and the word '*descent*' shall mean the title to inherit the land by reason of consanguinity, as well where the heir shall be an ancestor or collateral relation as where he shall be a child or other issue." By s. 2 it is further enacted that "to the intent that the pedigree may never be carried further back than the circumstances of the case and the nature of the title shall require, the *person last entitled to the land* shall, for the purposes of this Act, be considered to have been the *purchaser* thereof, unless it shall be proved that he inherited the same, in which case the person from whom he inherited the same shall be considered to have been the *purchaser*, unless it shall be proved that he inherited the same; and in like manner the last person from whom the land shall be proved to have been inherited shall in every case be considered to have been the purchaser, unless it shall be proved that he inherited the same." By s. 1 "The expression '*the person last entitled*' to land shall extend to the last person who had a right thereto, whether he did or did not obtain the possession or the receipt of the rents and profits thereof."

By s. 3, an heir who is also devisee will take in the latter capacity.

By s. 4, where heirs take by purchase under limitations to the heirs of their ancestor the land shall descend as if the ancestor had been the purchaser.

By s. 5 "No brother or sister shall be considered to inherit immediately from his or her brother or sister, but every descent from a brother or sister shall be traced through the parent."

By ss. 6, 7, and 8 provisions are made for the tracing of descent through the male line in preference to the female line and for tracing descent in cases of half-blood.

For a table of descents under the above Act see Stephens' Com. 8th ed. p. 388.

See further, "Defences," "*Recovery of Land*," and Cole on Ejectment, p. 483, and Roscoe's N. P. p. 958 *et seq.*

By O. XII. r. 18, "Any person not named as a defendant in a writ of summons for the recovery of land may by leave of the Court or judge appear and defend, on filing an affidavit showing that he is in possession of the land either by himself or his tenant." The application under this rule is an *ex parte* one, and should be in general made at chambers. Where the person making such application is in possession by his tenant, he should state in his appearance that he appears as landlord (O. XII. r. 19), and any person making such application who has obtained leave to appear and defend must after entering an appearance in the action "forthwith give notice of such appearance to the plaintiff's solicitor, or to the plaintiff if he sues in

unto and to the use of the said George F. by a deed bearing date the —— of ——, 18—.

2. The said George F. died on the 8th of April, 1869, leaving Henry F., his eldest son, and the plaintiff, John F., his second son, him surviving.

3. The said Henry F. died on the 15th of November, 1878, seised in fee of the said messuage which he had inherited from his father.

4. The said Henry F. was never married.

5. The writ in this action was issued against the defendant A. B., who then was and still is wrongfully in possession of the said messuage.

6. Since the issuing of the said writ the defendant C. D., who claims that he is in possession of the said messuage by the defendant A. B., his tenant, has been, pursuant to the order of Master ——, dated the —— of ——, 18—, admitted to appear to this action, and to defend for the whole of the property claimed therein, and he has accordingly entered an appearance in the said action as landlord of the defendant A. B.

Statement of Claim by Devisees of Freehold (f).

(Form No. 25 in App. (C) to Jud. Act, 1875.)

1. K. L., late of Sevenoaks, in the county of Kent, duly executed his last will, dated the 4th day of April,

---

person, and shall in all subsequent proceedings be named as a party defendant to the action. (O. XII. r. 20.)

By O. XII. r. 21 "Any person appearing to a writ of summons for the recovery of land shall be at liberty to limit his defence to a part only of the property mentioned in the writ, describing that part with reasonable certainty in his memorandum of appearance, or in a notice intituled in the cause and signed by him or his solicitor; such notice to be served within four days after appearance; and an appearance where the defence is not so limited shall be deemed an appearance to defend for the whole."

(*f*) All property may now be disposed of by will (1 Vict. c. 26, s. 3), and it is therefore only necessary for the devisee of a freehold suing for recovery of the land devised to show that the testator was at the time of his death seised in fee of or was entitled to the land, that he died after having by his last will devised it to the plaintiff, that the title of the plaintiff is not extinguished by the Statute of Limitations, and that the defendant is in possession. If any estates are limited by the will prior to the devise to the plaintiff, or if the testator had demised the property, the determination of such estates, or of such tenancy, must also be shown. Where land has been devised

1870, and thereby devised his lands at or near Sevenoaks, and all other his lands in the county of Kent, unto and to the use of the plaintiffs and their heirs, upon the trusts therein mentioned for the benefit of his daughters Margaret and Martha, and appointed the plaintiffs executors thereof.

2. K. L. died on the 3rd day of January, 1875, and his said will was proved by the plaintiffs in the Court of Probate on or about the 4th day of February, 1875.

3. K. L. was at the time of his death seised in fee of a house at Sevenoaks, and two farms near there called respectively ——, the Home Farm containing 276 acres, and the Longton Farm containing 700 acres, both in the county of Kent.

4. The defendant, soon after the death of K. L., entered into possession of the house and two farms, and has refused to give them up to the plaintiffs.

The plaintiffs claim :—

1. Possession of the house and two farms.
2. £ —— for mesne profits of the premises from the death of K. L. till such possession shall be given.

By Legatee of Leasehold (*g*).

1. C. D., being seised in fee of a messuage and land situate at ——, let the same by deed bearing date the 25th of March, 1865, to E. F., to hold for 99 years from the said 25th of March, 1865.

2. The said E. F. thereupon, under and in pursuance of the said lease, entered into possession of the said messuage and land, and remained thenceforth in possession thereof, and entitled thereto, until his death, which occurred on the 29th of June, 1880.

3. The said E. F., by his last will, dated the 4th of January, 1880, bequeathed all his estate and interest in

---

to the heir of the testator, he takes it as devisee and should be sued in that character. (3 & 4 Will. IV. c. 106, s. 3.) See further Cole on Ejectment, 492 *et seq.*

(*g*) The statement of claim must show that the testator had only a chattel interest, as otherwise if he died in possession the presumption would be that he was seised in fee. It must also show the assent of the executors to the bequest, for until such assent the term vests in the executors (1 Wms. Exors. 7th ed. 303), where see as to what is sufficient to constitute assent.)

the said messuage and land to the plaintiff, and appointed G. H. his executor.

4. The said will was duly proved by the said G. H. in the Probate Division of the High Court of Justice on the 17th of July, 1880.

5. The said G. H. afterwards, on or about the 30th of July, 1880, expressly assented to the said bequest of the said messuage and land to the plaintiff, and authorized the plaintiff to take possession of the said messuage and land.

6. The plaintiff, upon going to take possession of the said messuage and land, in pursuance of the said authority, found the defendant in prior possession thereof, and the defendant refused, and still refuses to give up the possession thereof to the plaintiff.

By Devisee of Copyhold (*h*).

1. A. B. was, previously to and at the time of his death, seised in his demesne as of fee at the will of the Lord of the Manor of ——, according to the custom of the said manor, of certain land situate at ——, known as —— [*describe the land sufficiently for the purpose of identification*], and which said land is part and parcel of the said manor.

2. The said A. B. died on the —— of ——, 18—.

3. By his last will, which was dated the —— of ——, 18—, and was duly executed on the —— of ——, 18—, the said A. B. devised the said land to the plaintiff his heirs and assigns according to the custom of the said manor.

4. The plaintiff was on the —— of ——, 18—, duly admitted, according to the custom of the said manor, as devisee of the said land.

5. The defendant, after the death of the said A. B., took possession of the said land and refused, and still refuses to give up the possession thereof to the plaintiff.

For Forms by Landlord against Tenant, see "Landlord and Tenant," ante, p. 255.

(*h*) By 1 Vict. c. 26, s. 3, copyhold estates may be devised by will, and the effect of that Act is to enable a copyholder to devise his estate in every case, dispensing with a surrender to the use of the will, but leaving the estate in the customary heir till the admittance of the devisee. (*Garland* v. *Mead*, L. R. 6 Q. B. 441.) The devisee must show that he has been admitted.

For Statement of Claim by Trustees and Mortgagees in Possession against Defendant, who entered by False Representations, pending Negotiations for a Lease (*i*), *see Hillman* v. *Mayhew*, 1 Ex. D. 132.

See also for a Form of Statement of Claim for Recovery of Land, Hodgins v. *Hickson*, 39 L. T. 644.

Replevin (*a*).

(*i*) Where a person is let into possession of land under a contract for the purchase of it, which afterwards goes off, he is a tenant at will, and a demand of possession is necessary before an action can be maintained against him for recovery of the land. (*Doe* d. *Newby* v. *Jackson*, 1 B. & C. 448; *Right* d. *Lewis* v. *Beard*, 13 East, 210.)

(*a*) *Replevin.*]—The action of replevin, it is said, lies wherever goods have been unlawfully taken out of the possession of the owner. (Com. Dig. "Pleader," 3 K. 1, and "Replevin" (A.); *Galloway* v. *Bird*, 4 Bing. 299; *Mellor* v. *Leather*, 1 E. & B. 619; *George* v. *Chambers*, 11 M. & W. 149; *Allen* v. *Sharp*, 2 Ex. 352; *Gay* v. *Mathews*, 4 B. & S. 425; 32 L. J. M. 58.) But it is not usual to have recourse to this remedy, except in cases of goods unlawfully distrained; and it has been questioned whether it was ever applicable in any other case. (*Mennie* v. *Blake*, 6 E. & B. 842; 25 L. J. Q. B. 399.)

Replevin consists in the re-delivery of the goods taken to the owner. This was formerly made by the sheriff, who took the goods from the distrainor, and re-delivered them to the owner upon the execution of a replevin bond by the owner and two sureties, conditioned to prosecute his suit with effect and without delay against the distrainor, and to return the goods if a return should be awarded. Stat. Marlbridge, 52 Hen. III. c. 21; Stat. Westm. 2nd, 13 Edw. I. c. 2; 11 Geo. II. c. 19, s. 23. By the Act 19 & 20 Vict. c. 108 (to amend the Acts relating to the county courts), ss. 63–66, the powers and responsibilities of the sheriff with respect to replevin bonds and replevins were taken away; and the same or similar powers were transferred to the registrar of the county court, who now grants replevin upon security being given for prosecuting the suit, under ss. 64, 65, and 66 of the above Act. See *post*, "*Sheriff,*" p. 515.

Formerly the action of replevin could not be commenced in the superior courts. It was commenced in the old county court, from which it might be removed by either party into a superior court. Upon the establishment of the new county courts, by the statute 9 & 10 Vict. c. 95, s. 119, all actions of replevin in cases of distress for rent in arrear and damage feasant were transferred to those courts subject to a power of removing the action into the superior courts.

But now, by the above statute, 19 & 20 Vict. c. 108, ss. 65, 66, an action of replevin may be commenced in any superior court, or in the county court at the option of the plaintiff, upon his giving the security required by the Act (see *infra*). And by s. 67 the action may be removed into any superior court by writ of certiorari, upon application by the defendant to the Court or a judge for such writ, and upon his giving the security required by that section. By s. 70 the security required to be given for the above purposes is to be in the form of a bond, with sureties to the other party in the action or proceeding. If the defendant does not remove the action by certiorari into the superior court, the County Court has full jurisdiction, though title come in question, notwithstanding 9 & 10 Vict. c. 95, s. 58. (*Fordham* v. *Akers*, 4 B. & S. 578; 33 L. J. Q. B. 67.)

By the C. L. P. Act, 1860, s. 22, the provisions of the above Act, 19 & 20 Vict. c. 108, which relate to replevin shall be deemed and taken to apply to all cases of replevin in like manner as to the replevin of goods distrained for rent or damage feasant. It was held that in the declaration in this action the place where the goods were taken, and also the goods taken, must be described with sufficient particularity to inform the defendant. (1 Wms. Saund. 636; *Banks* v. *Angell*, 7 A. & E. 843, 855.)

By 19 & 20 Vict. c. 108, s. 65, "an action of replevin may be commenced in any Superior Court in the form applicable to personal actions therein, and such Court shall have power to hear and determine the same; and if the replevisor shall wish to commence proceedings in any superior court, he shall, at the time of replevying, give security, to be approved of by the registrar, for such an amount as such registrar shall deem sufficient to cover the alleged rent or damage in respect of which the distress shall have been made, and the probable costs of the cause in a superior court, conditioned to commence an action of replevin against the distrainor in such superior court as shall be named in the security, within one week from the date thereof, and to prosecute such action with effect, and without delay; and unless judgment thereon be obtained by default, to prove before such superior court that he had good ground for believing either that the title to some corporeal or incorporeal hereditament, or to some toll, market, fair, or franchise, was in question, or that such rent or damage exceeded twenty pounds, and to make return of the goods, if a return thereof shall be adjudged."

"With effect" means in the above section "with success." (*Morgan* v. *Griffith*, 7 Mod. 380; *Tumman* v. *Ogle*, 6 E. & B. 571; 25 L. J. Q. B. 403; Woodfall's Land. & Ten. 11th ed. pp. 455, 469.)

A judgment in replevin is a bar to a subsequent action of trespass for the same wrongful taking of the goods seized, and for any special damage arising therefrom. (*Gibbs* v. *Cruikshank*, L. R. 8 C. P. 454; 42 L. J. C. P. 273.) But it is not a bar to a claim for trespass to the land. (*Ib.*)

The declaration used to be, "That the defendant, in a certain dwelling-house called ——, took the goods of the plaintiff, that is to say, *household furniture*, and unjustly detained the same against sureties and pledges until, &c., whereby the plaintiff has sustained damage." Now, however, it would seem by Ord. XIX. the facts should be plainly narrated. See further, Woodfall's Land. & Ten. 11th ed. pp. 454, *et seq.*; "*Distress*," *ante*, p. 404; and, *as to certiorari*, see *a form*, "*Master and Servant*," *ante*, p. 466.

Reversion.

Statement of Claim for an Injury to the Plaintiff's Reversion in Land (a).

1. A farm at ——, known as the —— Farm, was [and is] in the possession of G. H. as tenant thereof to the

---

(*a*) The claim must either state something which is necessarily an injury to the reversion, as the cutting down timber trees or the like; or, if it state something which may or may not be an injury to the reversion, it must go on to aver that the reversionary interest of the plaintiff is thereby injured. Where that which is stated cannot be injurious to the reversion, the allegation that the reversion is thereby injured will not help the plaintiff; where it must be an injury to the reversion, that concluding allegation is unnecessary. (*Per* Willes, J., *Metropolitan Ass.* v. *Petch*, 5 C. B. N. S. 504, 513; *Jackson* v. *Pesked*, 1 M. & S. 234; *Kidgill* v. *Moor*, 9 C. B. 364.) The allegation may be supported by proof of any act injurious to the land of a permanent character, although the damage might be remedied before the reversion came into possession; thus, opening a new door in a house (*Young* v. *Spencer*, 10 B. & C. 145), obstructing a right of way (*Kidgill* v. *Moor*, 9 C. B. 364; *Bell* v. *Midland Ry. Co.*, 10 C. B. N. S. 287), obstructing ancient lights (*Jesser* v. *Gifford*, 4 Burr. 2141; *Metropolitan Ass.* v. *Petch*, 5 C. B. N. S. 504; 27 L. J. C. P. 330; see "*Light*," *ante*), building a roof with eaves which discharge the rain-water on the land (*Tucker* v. *Newman*, 11 A. & E. 40), may be injurious to the reversion, and will warrant the jury in so finding.

The action will not lie for an act which is necessarily of a temporary character, as for a nuisance of mere noise, although less rent is paid by the tenant in consequence of the noise (*Mumford* v. *Oxford W. & W. Ry. Co.*, 1 H. & N. 36; 25 L. J. Ex. 265; *Jones* v. *Chappell*, L. R. 20 Eq. 539; 44 L. J. Ch. 658); or for a nuisance of smoke (*Simpson* v. *Savage*, 1 C. B. N. S. 347; 26 L. J. C. P. 50; see further, "*Nuisance*," *ante*). The action will not lie for an act which is not in fact injurious to the reversion, merely in respect of its being done with the intent to establish an easement in and upon the land by prescription, as the exercise of a right of way (*Baxter* v. *Taylor*, 4 B. & Ad. 72; but see *Dobson* v. *Blackmore*, 9 Q. B. 991, 1004; and *Tucker* v. *Newman*, 11 A. & E. 40); such act would not be evidence against the reversioner where the right is claimed by reason of forty years' user under the Prescription Act, 2 & 3 Will. IV. c. 71, which by s. 8 reserved to the reversioner three years for resisting any such claim after his estate has come into possession, although the full period of prescription has previously elapsed. See *Bright* v. *Walker*, 1 C. M. & R. 220; *Palk* v. *Skinner*, 18 Q. B. 568.

The action by the reversioner is independent of the remedy which the tenant may have for the same act in respect of the damage to his possession; and the reversioner also may bring repeated actions for a continuing injury. (*Battishill* v. *Reed*, 18 C. B. 696; 25 L. J. C. P. 290; *Shadwell* v. *Hutchinson*, 2 B. & Ad. 97; *Spurr* v. *Hall*, 2 Q. B. D. 615; 46 L. J. Q. B. 693.) If the defendant persists in continuing the nuisance after a verdict against him for nominal damages, the jury in a second action may give vindictive damages to compel him to abate the nuisance. (*Ib.*)

plaintiff, the reversion thereof then [and still] belonging to the plaintiff.

2. The defendant, on the —— of ——, 18—, and the —— of ——, 18—, wrongfully cut down 12 trees growing on the said farm [*or as the case may be*].

3. The plaintiff's said reversion in the said farm was thereby injured.

For a like Claim see *Lamb* v. *Walker*, 3 Q. B. D. 389, 391; 47 L. J. Q. B. 461; 38 L. T. 643.

For a Claim by a Reversioner for Obstruction to Light, see "*Light*," *ante*, p. 451.

For a Claim by a Reversioner for an Injury to Reversionary Property in Goods (*b*).

1. The plaintiff was the owner of certain drawing-room furniture let to hire for 3 months to G. H.

2. On the —— of ——, 18—, G. H. had possession of the said drawing-room furniture under the said letting to hire, the reversionary property and interest therein belonging to the plaintiff.

3. The defendant, on the said —— of ——, broke and damaged the said furniture, whereby the plaintiff's said reversionary property and interest therein was injured.

SEDUCTION.

See "*Master and Servant*," *ante*, p. 463.

As to damages, see "*Damages*," *ante*, p. 19; *Spurr* v. *Hall*, *supra*; *Lamb* v. *Walker*, 3 Q. B. D. 389; 47 L. J. Q. B. 451. The reversioner may in a proper case claim an injunction; as to this, see "*Injunction*," *ante*, p. 439.

(*b*) The owner of a future or reversionary interest in goods can sue in respect of injury done to his reversionary interest therein, though he cannot in general sue as for a *conversion* of them or for *trespass* to them. See "*Conversion*," *ante*, p. 376.

In order to support the action it must appear upon the face of the pleading and be proved that actual damage to the reversion has been sustained. (*Tancred* v. *Allgood*, 4 H. & N. 438; 28 L. J. Ex. 362; *Lancashire Waggon Co.* v. *Fitzhugh*, 6 H. & N. 502; 30 L. J. Ex. 231; *Mears* v. *London and South-Western Ry. Co.*, 11 C. B. N. S. 850; 31 L. J. C. P. 220.) A mere sale of the goods, not in market overt, and without a delivery of them to the purchaser and taking or user of them by him, is not an injury to the reversionary property in the goods. *Ib.*)

Sheriff (*a*).

Statement of Claim against a Sheriff for not Levying under a Writ of Fi. Fa.

1. During all the material times herein referred to the defendant was the sheriff of ——.

(*a*) Actions for default of duty in the office of sheriff must be brought against the high-sheriff, though the default is occasioned by the under-sheriff or bailiff. (*Cameron* v. *Reynolds*, Cowp. 403.)

The sheriff is liable for every irregularity or default committed under colour of process (*Gregory* v. *Cotterell*, 5 E. & B. 571; 25 L. J. Q. B. 33), whether by his bailiffs or their agents (*Ib.*); as for arresting the debtor under a writ of *fi. fa.* (*Smart* v. *Hutton*, 8 A. & E. 568 n.; and see *Raphael* v. *Goodman*, 8 A. & E. 565); but not for what is done irrespectively of the process, unless it is subsequently adopted by the sheriff (*Underhill* v. *Wilson*, 6 Bing. 697; *Crowder* v. *Long*, 8 B. & C. 598); nor for what is done after the bailiff's authority is terminated by a *supersedeas* (*Brown* v. *Copley*, 7 M. & G. 558); nor is he liable at the suit of the execution creditor for what is done by the bailiff with the execution creditor's authority (*Crowder* v. *Long*, 8 B. & C. 598); nor for what is done by a bailiff specially appointed by the execution creditor (*Alderson* v. *Davenport*, 13 M. & W. 42; *Ford* v. *Leche*, 6 A. & E. 699); nor is he liable at the suit of the execution debtor for what is done with the consent and authority of the latter. See *Wright* v. *Child*, L. R. 1 Ex. 358; 35 L. J. Ex. 209.

Actions against the sheriff for breach of duty can in general only be maintained in respect of actual damage, as an actual delay of the plaintiff's suit. (*Wylie* v. *Birch*, 4 Q. B. 566, 577; *Williams* v. *Mostyn*, 4 M. & W. 145; *Randell* v. *Wheble*, 10 A. & E. 719; *Stimson* v. *Farnham*, L. R. 7 Q. B. 175; 41 L. J. Q. B. 52; and as to the measure of damages, see *Moore* v. *Moore*, 25 Beav. 8; 27 L. J. C. 385; *Hobson* v. *Thelluson*, L. R. 2 Q. B. 642; 36 L. J. Q. B. 302; *Dennis* v. *Whetham*, L. R. 9 Q. B. 345; 43 L. J. Q. B. 129.)

An exception occurs in actions for an escape out of the custody of the sheriff when the custody is on final process, or for default in arresting on final process, in which actions the plaintiff is entitled to nominal damages, although no actual damage be proved. (*Clifton* v. *Hooper*, 6 Q. B. 468; *Hobson* v. *Thelluson*, *sup.*)

An action will not lie against the sheriff for arresting a person privileged from arrest by reason of his attending a court of justice, or other similar ground. (*Magnay* v. *Burt*, 5 Q. B. 381; and see *Watson* v. *Carroll*, 4 M. & W. 592; *Philips* v. *Naylor*, 3 H. & N. 14; 4 *Ib.* 565; 27 L. J. Ex. 222; 28 *Ib.* 225; and "*Malicious Prosecution*," *ante*.)

If the sheriff seizes under a writ of *fi. fa.* and the amount of the writ is paid, either directly, by virtue of the seizure, or indirectly by means of a compromise which is the consequence of the seizure, the sheriff is entitled to poundage, just as in the case where there is a sale under the writ (*Mortimore* v. *Cragg*, 3 C. P. D. 216; 47 L. J. C. P. 348; *Bissicks* v. *The Bath Colliery Co.*, 2 Ex. D. 459; 3 Ex. D. 174; 46 L. J. Ex. 611; 47 L. J. Ex. 408); but there must be a seizure to

2. On the —— day of ——, 18—, the plaintiff, by the judgment of this Court in this division, recovered against A. B. £——.

3. On or about the —— day of ——, 18—, the plaintiff caused a writ of *fieri facias*, upon the said judgment, directed to the sheriff of ——, to be issued out of this Court in this division, whereby her Majesty the Queen commanded the said sheriff that of the goods and chattels of the said A. B. in the said sheriff's bailiwick, he should cause to be made the amount of the said judgment with interest thereon at £4 per centum per annum from the said —— day of ——, 18—, and should have the said money and interest before her said Majesty in her said Court immediately after the execution of the said writ, to be paid to the said A. B. in pursuance of the said judgment, and in what manner he should have executed the writ the said sheriff should make appear to her said Majesty in her said Court immediately after the execution thereof.

4. On or about the said —— day of ——, 18—, the plaintiff delivered the said writ to the defendant, as and being sheriff of ——, to be executed, indorsed with a direction to levy £—— and interest thereon from the —— day of ——, 18—, and with such other matters as are required by the rules of the Supreme Court.

5. At the time of the delivery of the said writ by the plaintiff to the defendant, and during a reasonable time afterwards, goods and chattels of the said A. B. were

---

entitle the sheriff to poundage. (*Bissicks* v. *The Bath Colliery Co.*, *supra*.) As to what is a seizure, see *Bissicks* v. *The Bath Colliery Co.*, *supra*; *Gladstone* v. *Padwick*, L. R. 6 Ex. 203; 40 L. J. Ex. 154; *Cole* v. *Davies*, 1 Ld. Raym. 724.

When the sheriff had jurisdiction to grant replevins, he was liable to an action for refusing to grant replevin of goods at the suit of the person whose goods were taken. (*Sabourin* v. *Marshall*, 3 B. & Ad. 440.) He was also liable to an action at the suit of the person who had taken the goods for granting replevin without taking a replevin bond (*R.* v. *Lewis*, 2 T. R. 617); and for taking a replevin bond with insufficient sureties. (*Tesseyman* v. *Gildart*, 1 B. & P. N. R. 292.) But by the Act 19 & 20 Vict. c. 108 (to amend the Acts relating to the County Courts), ss. 63, 64, the powers and responsibilities of the sheriff with respect to replevin bonds and replevins are taken away, and the registrar of the County Court is empowered, according to the Act, to approve of replevin bonds and to grant replevins. (See "*Replevin*," *ante*, p. 510.) The high bailiff of a County Court incurs a liability similar to that which the sheriff was subject to before. (*Burton* v. *Le Gros*, 34 L. J. Q. B. 91.)

within the said bailiwick of the defendant, of which the defendant then had notice, and out of which the defendant could and ought to have levied the money and interest indorsed on the said writ as aforesaid.

6. The defendant, being such sheriff as aforesaid, did not and would not levy the said money and interest, or any part thereof, and made default in the execution of the said writ.

7. By reason of the premises the plaintiff has been unable to obtain the said money and interest, and is likely to lose the same.

Against a Sheriff for a False Return of Nulla Bona to a Writ of Fi. Fa. after Levying.

1.—5. (*As in preceding form.*)

6. The defendant, thereupon, as being such sheriff as aforesaid, by virtue of the said writ duly levied of the goods and chattels of the said A. B. in his bailiwick the money and interest so indorsed on the said writ.

7. The defendant had not the said money and interest so levied as aforesaid before her said Majesty in her said Court immediately after the execution of the said writ as required by the said writ, or at all, nor has the defendant paid the said money and interest or any part thereof to the plaintiff.

8. The defendant, as being such sheriff as aforesaid, falsely returned to the said Court upon the said writ that the said A. B. had not any goods or chattels in his bailiwick whereof he could cause to be made the money and interest so indorsed on the said writ as aforesaid, or any part thereof.

9. The plaintiff has in consequence been unable to obtain the said money and interest, and the same is still wholly unpaid.

Against a Sheriff for Trespass.

1. The plaintiff is and was a draper, residing and carrying on business at ——, and the defendant is the sheriff of ——.

2. On the —— day of ——, 18—, the defendant, by his agents and servants or officers, broke and entered the plaintiff's house and shop at —— aforesaid, and stayed

therein a long time, and interfered with and hindered the plaintiff in the carrying on of his said business of a draper in his said shop and seized and carried away £—— of the monies of the plaintiff from his said shop.

3. The defendant's said agents and servants or officers committed the acts above mentioned in pretended or intended execution of a writ of *fieri facias* directed to him as sheriff of ——, commanding him as such sheriff to cause to be made the said sum of £—— [*or as the case may be,*] of the goods and chattels of some person other than the plaintiff.

4. [The plaintiff, at the time when the defendant's said agents and servants or officers committed the acts above mentioned, pointed out to them that the said writ was not against him or his goods and chattels, but they nevertheless persisted and hindered the plaintiff as above stated, and seized and carried away the said sum of £—— of the monies of the plaintiff.]

5. The plaintiff has by reason of the premises been injured in his credit and reputation and in his said business of a draper.

By a Landlord against a Sheriff for the Removal of Goods taken in Execution against the Tenant, without Payment of Rent due (8 Anne, c. 14, s. 1) (*b*).

1. G. H. was tenant to the plaintiff from year to year [*or as the case may be*] of a messuage situate at ——, at

---

(*b*) As to this action, see Woodfall's Land. & Ten. 11th ed. pp. 445–453; Addison on Torts, 5th ed. 639; *Cocker* v. *Musgrove*, 9 Q. B. 223. The statute (8 Anne, c. 14, s. 1,) only applies to subsisting tenancies. (*Cox* v. *Leigh*, L. R. 9 Q. B. 333; 43 L. J. Q. B. 123.) In order to make the sheriff liable as a wrongdoer for the removal, it must appear that he had notice, or knew, of the claim for rent in arrear. (*Arnitt* v. *Garnett*, 3 B. & A. 441; *Smith* v. *Russell*, 3 Taunt. 400; *Riseley* v. *Ryde*, 11 M. & W. 20; *Andrews* v. *Dixon*, 3 B. & A. 645.) See further 7 & 8 Vict. c. 96, s. 67 (by which in case of a tenancy at a weekly rent the landlord's claim is limited, when there is an execution, to four weeks' arrears; and where the tenement is let for any other term less than a year, to arrears accruing during four such terms or times of payment). By 19 & 20 Vict. c. 108, s. 75, the 8 Anne, c. 14, s. 1, does not apply to goods taken in execution under the warrant of a County Court. The course of proceeding in such case is regulated by that section. As to the course of proceeding where a claim in respect of rent or otherwise is made to goods taken in execution under process of the Court of Admiralty, see the Admiralty Court Act, 1861 (24 Vict. c. 10), s. 16.

the yearly rent of £——, payable quarterly [*or as the case may be*].

2. Whilst the said G. H. was such tenant to the plaintiff as aforesaid, on the —— of ——, 18—, the defendant, as and being the sheriff of ——, under a writ of *fieri facias* against the goods and chattels of the said G. H., sued out of the High Court of Justice, Queen's Bench Division, at the suit of I. K., and directed to the sheriff of ——, seized and took the goods and chattels of the said G. H., being in the said messuage.

3. Afterwards, and before the removal of the said goods and chattels, the plaintiff gave notice to the defendant, as and being such sheriff as aforesaid, that there was, as was the fact, due and payable to him, the plaintiff, from the said G. H., as such tenant as aforesaid, £——, being the rent of the said messuage for one year, and requested the defendant not to remove the said goods and chattels from the said messuage unless the said arrears of rent should be first paid.

4. The defendant, notwithstanding the said notice and request, removed the said goods and chattels from the said messuage without the said arrears of rent being first paid or satisfied, contrary to the statute in such case made and provided.

5. The said arrears of rent are still unpaid.

6. [The said goods and chattels so removed were of greater value than the said arrears of rent, *or* were of the value of £——.]

SHIPPING (*a*).

(*a*) By sec. 25 (9) of the Judicature Act, 1873, "In any cause or proceeding for damages arising out of a collision between two ships, if both ships shall be found to have been in fault, the rules hitherto in force in the Court of Admiralty, so far as they have been at variance with the rules in force in the Courts of Common Law, shall prevail." This section modifies the common law rule as to contributory negligence furnishing in general a defence (*per* James, L. J., *The City of Manchester*, 5 P. D. 221, 222; 48 L. J. P. D. & A. 70).

By the "Merchant Shipping Act, 1854" (17 & 18 Vict. c. 104), sec. 298, if in any case of collision it appears to the court before which the case is tried that such collision was occasioned by the non-observance of any rule for the exhibition of lights or the use of fog-signals issued in pursuance of the powers thereinbefore contained, or of the rules therein as to the passing of steam and sailing ships, or as to a steam

Slander of Title (*a*).

See for a Form of Statement of Claim, Halsey v. *Brotherhood,* 15 Ch. D. 514; 49 L. J. Ch. 786.

---

ship keeping to that side of a narrow channel which lies on the starboard side, the owner of the ship by which such rule has been infringed shall not be entitled to recover any recompence whatever for any damage sustained by such ship in such collision, unless it is shown to the satisfaction of the court that the circumstances of the case made a departure from the rule necessary; and by the "Merchant Shipping Act, 1873" (36 & 37 Vict. c. 85), s. 17, it is enacted that if, in any case of collision, it is proved to the court before which the case is tried that any of the regulations for preventing collision contained in or made under the Merchant Shipping Acts, 1854 to 1873, has been infringed, the ship by which such regulation has been infringed shall be deemed to be in fault, unless it is shown to the satisfaction of the court that the circumstances of the case made departure from the regulation necessary. The rule of the Court of Admiralty, subject to the above enactments, is that if both vessels are to blame for a collision the damage as between the owners of the vessels is divided. As to the construction of the above enactments, see *Stoomvaart Maatschappy Nederland* v. *P. & O. Steam Navigation Co.*, 5 App. Cas. 876; *The Tirzah,* 4 P. D. 33; 48 L. J. P. D. & A. 15.

See for forms of claims in the Admiralty Division, App. (C.) to Judicature Act 1875, No. 11; and *The City of Brooklyn,* 34 L. T. 932; *The Transit,* 34 L. T. 934; *The Tirzah,* 4 P. D. 33; *The Mary Hounsell,* 4 P. D. 204; *The Parlement Belge,* 4 P. D. 129 (*reversed on* app. 5 P. D. 197); *The Princeton,* 3 P. D. 90; *The Andalusian,* 2 P. D. 231; and see further "*Shipping,*" *ante,* p. 326, and Addison on Torts, 5th ed. 573 et seq.

(*a*) *Slander of title.*]—This action lies to recover compensation for special damage sustained by reason of the speaking or writing and publishing slander of the plaintiff's title to property. No action lies unless special damage has been sustained. (*Malachy* v. *Soper,* 3 Bing. N. C. 371.)

The statement constituting the slander must be false; it must have been spoken or published maliciously, and must have occasioned the damage. A statement made *bonâ fide* and under a reasonable belief of its truth, by a person having an interest in the matter, is not actionable. (*Rawe* v. *Roach,* 1 M. & S. 304; *Pitt* v. *Donovan,* 1 M. & S. 639; *Smith* v. *Spooner,* 3 Taunt. 246; *Pater* v. *Baker,* 3 C. B. 831, 868; *Brook* v. *Rawl,* 4 Ex. 521; *Wren* v. *Weild,* L. R. 4 Q. B. 730; 38 L. J. Q. B. 327; *Steward* v. *Young,* L. R. 5 C. P. 122; 39 L. J. C. P. 85; *Halsey* v. *Brotherhood,* 15 Ch. D. 514; 49 L. J. Ch. 786; *Dicks* v. *Brooks,* 15 Ch. D. 22, 39; 49 L. J. Ch. 812.) But a person is responsible in law for mistakes in law in making false assertions respecting title in which he is not concerned. (*Mildmay's case,* 1 Co. Rep. 175.)

The words complained of must be set out in the Statement of Claim as in ordinary actions of slander. (*See Gutsole* v. *Mathers,* 1 M. & W. 495; and *ante* "*Defamation.*")

SUPPORT OF LAND (*a*).

As this action is in respect of special damage only, it is immaterial whether the words are written or spoken. (*Malachy* v. *Soper*, *supra.*)

A statement wantonly, without lawful occasion depreciating the quality of goods offered for sale by a person, although not conveying any imputation of fraud or misrepresentation against him, is likewise actionable in respect of special damage occasioned thereby, but not otherwise. (*Thorley's Cattle Food Co.* v. *Massam*, 14 Ch. D. 763; *Thomas* v. *Williams*, 14 Ch. D. 864; 49 L. J. Ch. 605; *Evans* v. *Harlow*, 5 Q. B. 624; *Western Counties Manure Co.* v. *Lawe's Chemical Manure Co.*, L. R. 9 Ex. 218; 43 L. J. Ex. 171; and see *Jenner* v. *A'Beckett*, L. R. 7 Q. B. 11; 41 L. J. Q. B. 14.) See further, "*Defamation*," *ante*, p. 399.

(*a*) Where the surface of land belongs to one person and the subjacent soil and minerals to another, the owner of the surface is entitled, *primâ facie*, to a natural right of support by the subjacent strata. (*Humphries* v. *Brogden*, 12 Q. B. 739; *Smart* v. *Morton*, 5 E. & B. 30; 24 L. J. Q. B. 260; *Rowbotham* v. *Wilson*, 8 E. & B. 123; *Angus* v. *Dalton*, 4 Q. B. D. 162, 167, 184, 192; 48 L. J. Q. B. 225; 44 L. T. H. L. 844. The owner of land is also entitled to a right of support for his land by the adjacent land as a natural incident to his property, independently of grant or prescription. (*Micklin* v. *Williams*, 10 Ex. 259; 23 L. J. Ex. 335; *Bonomi* v. *Backhouse*, E. B. & E. 622; 27 L. J. Q. B. 378; 28 *ib.* 378; 9 H. L. C. 503; *Lamb* v. *Walker*, 3 Q. B. D. 389; 47 L. J. Q. B. 451; *Angus* v. *Dalton*, *supra.*) These rights, however, may be qualified or altogether abandoned by statute, express reservation, grant, or covenant, or by prescription. (*Rowbotham* v. *Wilson*, 6 E. & B. 593; 8 *ib.* 123; 8 H. L. C. 348; 30 L. J. Q. B. 49; *Murchie* v. *Black*, 19 C. B. N. S. 190; 34 L. J. C. P. 337; *Gill* v. *Dickinson*, 5 Q. B. D. 159; 49 L. J. Q. B. 262; *Eadon* v. *Jeffcock*, L. R. 7 Ex. 379; 42 L. J. Ex. 36; *Smith* v. *Darby*, L. R. 7 Q. B. 716; 42 L. J. Q. B. 140; *Aspden* v. *Seddon*, L. R. 10 Ch. Ap. 394; 44 L. J. Ch. 359; *Aspden* v. *Seddon*, 1 Ex. D. 496; 46 L. J. Ex. 353.)

Appreciable damage is necessary to support an action for damages for a disturbance of these rights (*Smith* v. *Thackerah*, L. R. 1 C. P. 564; 35 L. J. C. P. 276; *Lamb* v. *Walker*, *supra*), and the cause of action arises, and the statute of limitation begins to run, upon the happening of such damage. (*Backhouse* v. *Bonomi*, 9 H. L. C. 503.) All such prospective damage as may fairly be anticipated as likely to accrue from the wrongful removal of support appears to be recoverable in such action. (*Lamb* v. *Walker*, *supra.*) An injunction may be obtained in a proper case to prevent threatened damage. (*Siddons* v. *Short*, 2 C. P. D. 572; 46 L. J. C. P. 795.) And see "*Injunction*," *ante*, p. 439.

The support to which an owner of land is entitled from the adjacent land is confined to such an extent of adjacent land as in its natural undisturbed state was sufficient to afford the requisite support. (*Corporation of Birmingham* v. *Allen*, 6 Ch. D. 284; 46 L. J. Ch. 673.)

The natural right of the owner of land to support from the adjacent land only extends to the land in its natural unincumbered

Statement of Claim for Damages for taking away the Support of the Plaintiff's Land by Mining (*b*).

1. The plaintiff was possessed of a field, situate at ——, in the county of ——.

2. The defendant in the year 18— wrongfully excavated and worked certain coal-mines under the said field, and dug out and removed the coal under the said field, without leaving proper or sufficient support for the said field of the plaintiff.

3. In consequence of the above-mentioned acts of the defendant the said field of the plaintiff sank and gave way.

---

state, and not with the additional weight of buildings erected thereon. (*Dodd* v. *Holme*, 1 A. & E. 493 ; *Humphries* v. *Brogden*, 12 Q. B. 743 ; *Wyatt* v. *Harrison*, 3 B. & Ad. 871 ; *Smith* v. *Thackerah*, *supra*.) But a right to support from adjacent or subjacent land for the additional weight of buildings on land may be acquired as an easement, by twenty years' uninterrupted enjoyment or otherwise. (*Ib.*; *Angus* v. *Dalton*, *supra*; *Rogers* v. *Taylor*, 2 H. & N. 828; 27 L. J. Ex. 173 ; *Partridge* v. *Scott*, 3 M. & W. 220 ; *Brown* v. *Robins*, 4 H. & N. 186 ; 28 L. J. Ex. 250 ; *Hunt* v. *Peake*, 1 Johns. 705 ; 29 L. J. Ch. 785 ; *N. E. Ry. Co.* v. *Elliot*, 20 L. J. Ch. 808.) It would appear that such a right is within sec. 2 of the Prescription Act (2 & 3 W. 4, c. 71). *Angus* v. *Dalton*, 44 L. T. H. L. 844. Mere possession is sufficient to support an action against a stranger who interferes with the support of a building by the adjacent land. (*Bibby* v. *Carter*, 4 H. & N. 153 ; 28 L. J. Ex. 182 ; *Jeffries* v. *Williams*, 5 Ex. 792.) But although the owner of land may be entitled to a right of support for the natural surface, without any right of support for additional buildings, he cannot acquire a prescriptive right to support for buildings independently of a right of support for the surface. (*Rowbotham* v. *Wilson*, 6 E. & B. 593 ; 8 *Ib.* 123 ; 8 H. L. C. 348 ; 25 L. J. Q. B. 362 ; 27 *Ib.* 61 ; 30 *Ib.* 49.) The owner of the land may maintain an action for a disturbance of the natural right to support for the surface, notwithstanding buildings have been erected thereon, provided the weight of the buildings did not cause the injury. (*Brown* v. *Robins*, 4 H. & N. 186 ; 28 L. J. Ex. 250; *Stroyan* v. *Knowles*, *Hamer* v. *Knowles*, 6 H. & N. 454 ; 30 L. J. Ex. 102.)

An owner of land has no natural right to the support of subterranean water. (*Chasemore* v. *Richards*, 7 H. L. C. 349 ; *Hurdman* v. *N. E. Ry. Co.*, 3 C. P. D. 168, 175 ; 47 L. J. C. P. 368.) There is nothing, apart from contract, to prevent an adjoining landowner from draining his land to render it more capable of being utilised for building or other purposes. (*Popplewell* v. *Hodkinson*, L. R. 4 Ex. 248 ; 38 L. J. Ex. 126.)

(*b*) In this form it is not necessary to state expressly the right to support, because it is naturally incident to the right to the surface, see *note* (*a*) *supra*. An acquired right to support for buildings must be expressly stated, see *note* (*c*) *infra*, and *Jeffries* v. *Williams*, 5 Ex. 792 ; *Peyton* v. *Mayor*, *&c. of London*, 9 B. & C. 725.

For a Like Form see *Gill* v. *Dickinson*, 5 Q. B. D. 159; 42 L. T. 510; 49 L. J. Q. B. 262.

For Forms of Statement of Claim for Injury to Land and Buildings by Wrongful Removal of Adjacent and Subjacent Support to which they were entitled, see *Lamb* v. *Walker*, 3 Q. B. D. 389, 391; 38 L. T. 643; and *Angus* v. *Dalton*, 3 Q. B. D. 85 (*c*).

The Like where the Working of the Defendant was under a Lease giving him a Right to Work, subject to leaving sufficient Support for Houses built upon the Plaintiff's Land, and such Support was not left (*d*).

1. At the date next hereinafter mentioned A. was seised in fee of certain land, and of the mines and minerals thereunder, situate at ——, in the county of ——.

2. The said A., by an indenture bearing date the ——

(*c*) The right to have buildings supported not being a natural right, it is necessary in general to show that the plaintiff is entitled in the particular case to such support. It would seem to be sufficient, in general, to state that the plaintiff is so entitled, as in the form for loss of the support of an adjoining house, *post*, p. 523, and in *Lamb* v. *Walker*, and *Angus* v. *Dalton*, *supra*; though it may be more correct to state the facts from which the right arises, see further "*Light*," and "*Common*," *ante*.

(*d*) Where minerals are conveyed apart from the surface, or reserved when the surface is conveyed, it must *primâ facie* be presumed that the minerals are to be enjoyed, and therefore that a power to get them must also be granted or reserved as a necessary incident. A similar presumption, *primâ facie*, arises that the owner of mines is not to injure the owner of the soil above by getting them, if such injury can be avoided (*per* Lord Wensleydale in *Rowbotham* v. *Wilson*, 8 H. L. C. 348,* 360; 30 L. J. Q. B. 49; *Smith* v. *Darby*, L. R. 7 Q. B. 716, 722; 42 L. J. Q. B. 140.) Such presumptions, however, may be rebutted by the terms of the deed conveying or reserving the minerals; the rights of the parties in such cases depending upon the terms of the deed and the true construction of the contract into which they have thereby entered. (*Rowbotham* v. *Wilson*, *supra*; *Davis* v. *Treharne*, 6 App. Cas. 460; *Aspden* v. *Seddon*, L. R. 10 Ch. Ap. 394, 396 *n.*, 401; 44 L. J. Ch. 359; *Eadon* v. *Jeffcock*, L. R. 7 Ex. 379, 388; 42 L. J. Ex. 36; *Smith* v. *Darby*, *supra*.) If an owner of both the surface and the minerals beneath grants the minerals to A. with liberty to let down the surface, making compensation to the owner thereof for the damage done, and afterwards grants the surface to B., the latter may recover such compensation for damage done to the surface by A. (*Aspden* v. *Seddon*,

of ——, 18—, granted and conveyed the said land to the plaintiff in fee, reserving to himself the mines and minerals thereunder, with liberty to him, his assigns, his and their agents and workmen, to search for, dig, work, win, get, and carry away the same, leaving always sufficient and proper support for the houses then being, or which thereafter should be, or be erected, on the said land.

3. Afterwards, by an indenture bearing date the —— of ——, 18—, the said A. leased to the defendant for a term of years still unexpired, the said mines and minerals so reserved as aforesaid, with liberty to the defendants, his assigns, agents, and workmen, to search for, dig, work, win, get, and carry away the said mines and minerals, leaving always sufficient and proper support for the houses then being, or which should thereafter be, or be erected, on the said land.

4. The defendant afterwards entered upon and worked the said mines and minerals under the said land.

5. The defendant carried away the whole of the coal under the said land, and did not leave sufficient or proper support for a house which, at the dates of the said indentures, was and still is upon the said land, nor did the defendant leave sufficient or proper support for a certain other house erected after the date of the said indenture of the —— of ——, 18—, and still existing on the said land.

6. In consequence of such sufficient and proper support for the said two houses not having been left by the defendant, the said two houses sank and the walls thereof were cracked and injured.

For Taking away from the Plaintiff's House the Support to which it was Entitled from the Adjoining House (*e*).

1. The plaintiff was possessed of a house, No. ——, —— Street, ——, adjoining a certain other house known

---

supra.) As of common right the surface owner is entitled to the support of the subjacent strata, the burden of showing that such right of support has been taken away by virtue of some lease, reservation, or contract, lies on the party alleging that it has been so taken away. (*Davis* v. *Treharne, supra; Hext* v. *Gill*, L. R. 7 Ch. App. 699, 713.)

(*e*) As between adjoining houses, there is no obligation towards a neighbour cast by law on the owner of a house, merely as such, to

as No. ——, —— Street, ——, belonging to the defendant.

2. The plaintiff was entitled to have his said house supported by the said house of the defendant.

3. The defendant in or about the month of ——, 18—, wrongfully deprived the plaintiff of the support to his said house of the said adjoining house by pulling down his said adjoining house without propping up or in any way supporting or securing the plaintiff's said house.

4. The walls of the plaintiff's said house were thereby cracked, damaged, and injured.

For a Statement of Claim for an Injunction by Purchasers of Building Land to Restrain their Vendors from Working Mines adjacent to the Land Purchased, in such a Manner as to Cause Subsidence of the Land Purchased and of the Buildings thereon, see *Siddons* v. *Short*, 2 C. P. D. 572; 37 L. T. 230; 46 L. J. C. P. 795 (*f*).

---

keep it standing and in repair; his only duty being to prevent it from being a nuisance, and from falling on to his neighbour's property. (*Chauntler* v. *Robinson*, 4 Ex. 163.) Where houses are built by the same owner adjoining one another, and depending upon one another for support, and are afterwards conveyed to different owners, there exists by a presumed grant and reservation a right of support to each house from the adjoining ones. (*Richards* v. *Rose*, 9 Ex. 218.) As to the acquisition of a similar right where adjoining houses are built by the separate owners of adjacent lands by twenty years' user, see *Angus* v. *Dalton*, *supra*; *Hide* v. *Thornborough*, 2 C. & K. 250; and see *Solomon* v. *Vintners' Co.*, 4 H. & N. 585; 28 L. J. Ex. 370. No such right can be thus acquired by the owner of a house against the owners of the houses beyond the adjoining one. (*Solomon* v. *Vintners' Co.*, *supra*.)

(*f*) Where land is conveyed for building purposes, the vendor excepting and reserving to himself the mines and minerals beneath the land, there is *primâ facie* the grant of a right to have, not only the surface in its natural state, but also the buildings to be erected supported by the subjacent and adjacent minerals of the vendor. (*Caledonian Ry. Co.* v. *Sprott*, 2 Macq. 449; *Aspden* v. *Seddon*, L. R. 10 Ch. Ap. 394, 401; 44 L. J. Ch. 359; *Siddons* v. *Short*, 2 C. P. D. 572; 46 L. J. C. P. 795. See further "*Injunction*," *ante* p. 439.)

TRADE MARKS (*a*).

Claim by a Manufacturer against the Defendant for Manufacturing and Selling Goods Marked with the Plaintiff's Registered Trade Mark.

1. The plaintiff is, and was before and at the times hereinafter mentioned, a [cutlery manufacturer], carrying on business at ——.

(*a*) By the "Trade Marks Registration Acts, 1875–77" (38 & 39 Vict. c. 91, 39 & 40 Vict. c. 33, and 40 & 41 Vict. c. 37), it is enacted that a person shall not be entitled to institute any proceeding to prevent, or to recover damages for, the infringement of any trade mark as defined by the Trade Marks Registration Act, 1875, unless such trade mark is registered in pursuance of that Act, or unless, with respect to any device, mark, name, combination of words, or other matter or thing in use as a trade mark before the passing of the last mentioned Act, registration thereof as a trade mark under that Act shall have been applied for and refused. (38 & 39 Vict. c. 91, ss. 1 and 7; 39 & 40 Vict. c. 33, ss. 1 and 2; 40 & 41 Vict. c. 37, s. 1.)

By s. 2 of the Act of 1875, "a trade mark must be registered as belonging to particular goods or classes of goods; and when registered shall be assigned and transmitted only in connection with the goodwill of the business concerned in such particular goods or classes of goods, and shall be determinable with such goodwill, but, subject as aforesaid, registration of a trade-mark shall be deemed equivalent to public use of such mark."

By s. 3, "The registration of a person as first proprietor of a trade-mark shall be *primâ facie* evidence of his right to the exclusive use of such trade-mark, and shall, after the expiration of five years from the date of such registration, be conclusive evidence of his right to the exclusive use of such trade-mark, subject to the provisions of this Act as to its connection with the goodwill of a business." And by s. 4, "Every proprietor registered in respect to a trade-mark subsequently to the first registered proprietor shall, as respects his title to that trade-mark, stand in the same position as if his title were a continuation of the title of the first registered proprietor."

With respect to what is a trade-mark within the meaning of the above-mentioned Acts, see the 38 & 39 Vict. c. 91, s. 10; *Ex parte Stephens*, 3 Ch. D. 659; 46 L. J. Ch. 46; *In re Barrow's Trade-marks*, 5 Ch. D. 353; 46 L. J. Ch. 450; *In re Mitchell's Trade-mark*, 7 Ch. D. 36; 46 L J. Ch. 876; *Orr-Ewing* v. *Registrar of Trade-marks*, 4 App. Cas. 479; 48 L. J. Ch. 707.

"The Merchandise Marks Act, 1862" (25 & 26 Vict. c. 88), enacts, by s. 19, that in every case in which any person shall sell, or contract to sell (whether by writing or not), any article with any trade-mark thereon, or upon any cask, bottle, stopper, vessel, case, cover, wrapper, band, reel, ticket, label, or other thing, together with which such article shall be sold, or contracted to be sold, the sale or contract shall be

2. The plaintiff before and at the times aforesaid manufactured at —— aforesaid and sold for profit large quantities of [penknives], which he was accustomed to mark with a certain trade-mark of the plaintiff, that is, with

---

deemed to have been made with a warranty or contract that every such trade-mark was genuine and true, and not forged or counterfeit, and not wrongfully used, unless the contrary shall be expressed in some writing signed by or on behalf of the vendor, and delivered to and accepted by the vendee.

By s. 20, in every case in which any person shall sell, or contract to sell (whether by writing or not), any article upon which, or upon any cask, etc., there shall be any description, statement, or other indication of or respecting the number, quantity, measure, or weight of such article, or the place or country in which it was made, manufactured, or produced, the sale or contract shall be deemed to have been made with a warranty or contract that no such description, etc., was in any material respect false or untrue, unless the contrary shall be expressed in some writing signed by or on behalf of the vendor, and delivered to and accepted by the vendee.

By s. 21, in any suit for forging or counterfeiting, etc., any trade-marks, etc., or for preventing such acts, when the plaintiff obtains a judgment, the Court may direct any counterfeit articles to be destroyed or otherwise disposed of.

By s. 22, in every case in which any person shall do, or cause to be done, any of the wrongful acts following; (that is to say) shall forge or counterfeit any trade-mark, or for the purpose of sale, or for the purpose of any manufacture or trade shall apply any forged or counterfeit trade-mark to any article or to any cask, bottle, stopper, vessel, case, cover, wrapper, band, reel, ticket, label, or thing in or with which any article shall be intended to be sold, or shall be sold or uttered, or exposed for sale, or for any purpose of trade or manufacture; or shall enclose or place any article in, upon, under, or with any cask, etc., to which any trade-mark shall have been falsely applied, or to which any forged or counterfeit trade-mark shall have been applied; or shall apply or attach to any article any case, cover, reel, wrapper, band, ticket, label, or other thing to which any trade-mark shall have been falsely applied, or to which any forged or counterfeit trade-mark shall have been applied; or shall enclose, place, or attach any article in, upon, under, with, or to any cask, etc., having thereon any trade-mark of any other person; every person aggrieved by any such wrongful act shall be entitled to maintain an action or suit for damages in respect thereof against the person who shall be guilty of having done such act, or causing or procuring the same to be done, and for preventing the repetition or continuance of the wrongful act, and the committal of any similar act.

The common law action to recover damages for the infringement of a trade-mark was based on the ground of fraud and intention to deceive. See per Mellish, L.J., in *The Singer Co.* v. *Wilson*, 2 Ch. D. 434, 454; 45 L. J. Ch. 490, 498; *Rodgers* v. *Nowill*, 5 C. B. 109; *Crawshay* v. *Thompson*, 4 M. & G. 357; but proof of knowledge or fraudulent intent on the defendant's part was not necessary in equity, and an injunction was obtainable in a court of equity to restrain

the words " —— —— " impressed in a bracket upon the blades thereof [*or, with a device of ——, describe the trade-mark used by the plaintiff according to the fact*], in order to denote that they were manufactured by him, and

---

even an innocent infringement of a trade-mark. (*Millington* v. *Fox*, 3 M. & Cr. 338; *Dixon* v. *Fawcus*, 3 E. & E. 537; 30 L. J. Q. B. 137; *Burgess* v. *Hills*, 26 Beav. 244; 28 L. J. Ch. 356.)

The right to use a trade-mark is a right of property, and the jurisdiction to restrain the infringement is founded upon the invasion of such property, and not upon the ground of the fraud committed upon the public. (*Leather Cloth Co.* v. *American Leather Cloth Co.*, 11 H. L. C. 523; 32 L. J. Ch. 199; 35 *Ib.* 53; *Hall* v. *Barrows*, 4 De G. J. & S. 150; 33 L. J. Ch. 204; *The Singer Co.* v. *Wilson*, 2 Ch. D. 434; 3 App. Cas. 376; 45 L. J. Ch. 490; 47 *Ib.* 481.)

The Trade Marks Registration Acts clearly recognize this right of property in the case of trade-marks registered under the Acts. (See the 38 & 39 Vict. c. 91, ss. 3–5.)

It appears, therefore, that damages for the infringement of a trade-mark would now be recoverable in an action in any Division of the High Court of Justice, without proof of any fraudulent intent on the part of the defendant, at any rate in cases where the plaintiff would be entitled to an injunction.

Where a trade-mark has been infringed, the plaintiff in an action for the infringement may ordinarily claim an injunction (see "*Injunction*," *ante*, p. 439), and may also claim a declaration of his right to the exclusive use of the trade-mark, and an account of the profits made by the defendant from wrongful sales of goods improperly marked with the trade-mark. As to when an account of profits will be granted, see *Moet* v. *Couston*, 33 Beav. 578; 10 L. T. 395; *Edelsten* v. *Edelsten*, 1 De G. J. & G. 185; 10 L. T. 780; *Neilson* v. *Betts*, L. R. 5 H. L. 1; 40 L. J. Ch. 317; and see "*Patents*," *ante*, p. 494.

An action for infringing a trade-mark is maintainable without any allegation or proof of special damage. (*Rodgers* v. *Nowill*, 5 C. B. 109; *Blofeld* v. *Payne*, 4 B. & Ad. 410; and see *The Singer Co.* v. *Wilson*, *supra*; *Braham* v. *Beachim*, 7 Ch. D. 848; 38 L. T. 640.)

Proof of the defendant having sold goods under the forged trade-mark does not of itself entitle the plaintiff to recover as damages the profits which he would have made by the sale of the same amount of goods, as it cannot be assumed that he would have sold them if the defendant had not. (*Leather Cloth Co.* v. *Hirschfield*, L. R. 1 Eq. 299; 13 L. T. 427.)

As to what constitutes an infringement of a trade-mark, and what degree of resemblance is allowable, see *Leather Cloth Co.* v. *American Leather Cloth Co.*, *supra*; *Blackwell* v. *Crabb*, 36 L. J. Ch. 504; *Seixo* v. *Provezende*, L. R. 1 Ch. Ap. 192; 14 L. T. 314; *Cope* v. *Evans*, L. R. 18 Eq. 138; 30 L. T. 292; *Braham* v. *Beachim*, *supra*; *Siegert* v. *Findlater*, 7 Ch. D. 801; 47 L. J. Ch. 233; *Orr-Ewing* v. *Johnston*, 13 Ch. D. 434; 42 L. T. 67; *Mitchell* v. *Henry*, 15 Ch. D. 181.

If a trade-mark contains any material misrepresentation, as by representing an article to be patented when in fact it is not, the person using such mark is not entitled to any protection in respect of it. (*Leather Cloth Co.* v. *American Leather Cloth Co.*, 11 H. L. C. 523; 35

to distinguish them from articles of the same kind manufactured by other persons, and the plaintiff enjoyed great reputation with the public on account of the good quality of the said [penknives], and made large profits by the sale of them.

3. The said trade-mark was duly registered in the Register of Trade Marks as a trade-mark for the [penknives] of the plaintiff, in pursuance of the Trade Marks Registration Acts, 1875–77 [and the plaintiff is, and was at the times hereinafter mentioned, the registered proprietor thereof].

4. The defendant, at various times between the —— day of ——, 18—, and the commencement of this action [*state the dates where practicable*], wrongfully and fraudulently, and without the consent of the plaintiff, manufactured at ——, in the county of ——, large quantities of [penknives], amounting in the whole to [the number of ——], and caused them to be marked with the words "—— ——," impressed in a bracket upon the blades thereof [*or*, with a device of ——, *describe the mark used by the defendant*], in imitation of the said trade-mark of the plaintiff, and in order to cause it to be believed

---

L. J. Ch. 53; *Morgan* v. *M'Adam*, 36 L. J. Ch. 228; *Ford* v. *Foster*, L. R. 7 Ch. Ap. 611; 27 L. T. 219; *Cheavin* v. *Walker*, 5 Ch. D. 850; 46 L. J. Ch. 486.)

As to the assignment and transmission of trade-marks see the 38 & 39 Vict. c. 91, ss. 2 and 4; and the rules under the Trade Marks Registration Acts, rr. 23–29, and see *Leather Cloth Co.* v. *American Leather Cloth Co.*, *supra*; *Hall* v *Barrows*, *supra*; *Bury* v. *Bedford*, 4 De G. J. & S. 352; 33 L. J. Ch. 465.

One of the two joint owners of a trade-mark may sue separately in respect of the injury to his separate interest by infringement. (*Dent* v. *Turpin*, 2 J. & H. 139; 30 L. J. Ch. 495; *Sheehan* v. *G. E. Ry. Co.*, 16 Ch. D. 59; 50 L. J. Ch. 68.)

As to registration in cases of joint-ownership or co-ownership of a trade-mark, see rules 28 and 29 of the above-mentioned Rules.

An action will lie for fraudulently procuring the plaintiff to manufacture goods with the trade-mark of another manufacturer, whereby the plaintiff was subjected to a suit for an injunction, which was compromised. (*Dixon* v. *Fawcus*, *supra*.)

As to the right to the name of a business, see *Lawson* v. *Bank of London*, 18 C. B. 84; 25 L. J. C. P. 188; *Colonial Life Assurance Co.* v. *Colonial Assurance Co.*, 33 Beav. 548; 33 L. J. Ch. 591; *Lee* v. *Haley*, L. R. 5 Ch. Ap. 155; 39 L. J. Ch. 284; and see *Ainsworth* v. *Walmsley*, L. R. 1 Eq. 518; 35 L. J. Ch. 352; *The Singer Co.* v. *Wilson*, *supra*; *Massam* v. *Thorley's Cattle Food Co.*, 14 Ch. D. 748.

See further as to trade-marks generally, Roscoe, N. P. Ev., 14th ed., p. 771 *et seq.*, and Sebastian on Trade-Marks.

that the last-mentioned [penknives] were manufactured by the plaintiff, and wrongfully and fraudulently sold the last-mentioned [penknives] as and for [penknives] manufactured by the plaintiff.

5. By reason of the premises the plaintiff was prevented from selling great quantities of the said [penknives] manufactured by him, and lost the profits [amounting to £——], which he would otherwise have gained by the sale thereof, and has been injured in his reputation in his said business by reason of the said [penknives] so manufactured and sold by the defendant being inferior in quality to those manufactured by the plaintiff.

6. [*If an injunction is also sought, state any material facts in support of the claim for an injunction, as for instance,* The defendant continues to manufacture large quantities of [penknives] at ——, as aforesaid, and to cause them to be marked in the manner mentioned in the above 4th paragraph, and to sell and offer for sale the same [penknives] so marked as last aforesaid, and in such a manner as to induce the belief that the same have been manufactured by the plaintiff, and threatens and intends to continue so to do.]

TRESPASS. I.—TO THE PERSON (*a*).

Claim for Assault and Battery.

1. The defendant on the —— of ——, 18—, at ——, assaulted and beat the plaintiff.

(*a*) *Trespass to the Person.*]—Trespass to the person consists in any direct injury to the person, as a battery, an assault, or an imprisonment.

A *battery* is the unlawful beating of another. The least touching of another's person hostilely or against his will is a battery. (*Rawlings* v. *Till*, 3 M. & W. 28; 3 Bl. Com. 120.) It includes the striking another with a missile. (*Pursell* v. *Horn*, 8 A. & E. 602.) The act may be a trespass although unintentional (*Covell* v. *Laming*, 1 Camp. 497); thus, for the result of misdirected force exercised by the defendant, in a place where the natural and probable result of misdirected force would be injury to others, the defendant may be responsible, though he did not intend to inflict injury. (*Leame* v. *Bray*, 3 East, 599; *Winsmore* v. *Greenbank*, Willes, 577; *Dickenson* v. *Watson*, 2 Jones, 205; *Weaver* v. *Ward*, Hob. 134; Addison on Torts, 5th ed., pp. 17, 18.) But if the damage be the result of pure accident, without fault on the part of the defendant, or of some agency

2. The plaintiff was thereby injured in his arm, and much bruised about his chest and face, and was thereby rendered unfit for —— days to attend to his business of a —— [*State further special damage, if any*].

---

over which the defendant had no control, so as not to be his act, it is not a trespass. (*Gibbons* v. *Pepper*, 1 L. Raym. 38; *Hall* v. *Fearnley*, 3 Q. B. 919; *Wakeman* v. *Robinson*, 1 Bing. 213; *Holmes* v. *Mather*, L. R. 10 Ex. 261; 44 L. J. Ex. 176.) Touching a person for the purpose of calling his attention is not a battery. (*Wiffin* v. *Kincard*, 2 B. & P. N. R. 471; *Coward* v. *Baddeley*, 4 H. & N. 478; 28 L. J. Ex. 260.)

An *assault* is an attempt at a battery; a menacing attitude, as holding up a hand or stick to strike a person who is within reach thereof at the time, constitutes an assault. (3 Bl. Com. 120; *Stephens* v. *Myers*, 4 C. & P. 349; *Read* v. *Coker*, 13 C. B. 850.) A mere verbal threat of bodily hurt, if followed by actual damage through fear thereof, as by the interruption of a man's business, will, it is said, support an action of trespass. (3 Bl. Com. 120.)

An *imprisonment* consists in the restraint of the liberty of a person, as by confining him in a prison or within walls, or by forcibly detaining him in an open place. (3 Bl. Com. 127.) It must amount to a total restraint of his liberty for some period, however short. A partial obstruction of his will, as the prevention of his going in one direction or in all directions but one, does not constitute an imprisonment. (*Bird* v. *Jones*, 7 Q. B. 742, Lord Denman, C.J., *dissentiente*.) A restraint by authority submitted to may be an imprisonment, although the person is not actually touched. (*Grainger* v. *Hill*, 4 Bing. N. C. 212; *per* Willes, J., *Warner* v. *Riddiford*, 4 C. B. N. S. 180, 204.) If a person order another, as a policeman, to take a third person, it is an imprisonment by the first as well as by the policeman, and is ground for an action of trespass against him. (*Wheeler* v. *Whiting*, 9 C. & P. 262; *Stonehouse* v. *Elliott*, 6 T. R. 315.) If he merely states the facts to a policeman (or other person), who takes the person on his own responsibility (*Gosden* v. *Elphick*, 4 Ex. 445; *Grinham* v. *Willey*, 4 H. & N. 496; 28 L. J. Ex. 242, where signing the charge sheet by direction of the police-constable was held not to amount to giving in charge); or if he procures a magistrate to issue a warrant for taking the person (*Brown* v. *Chapman*, 6 C. B. 365), it is no imprisonment or trespass by him. Where, however, a person puts the law in motion maliciously and without reasonable or probable cause, it is the ground of an action for malicious prosecution. (*Ib.*; *Barber* v. *Rollinson*, 1 C. & M. 330; see *ante*, p. 453.) As to the distinction between an action for a trespass and one for a malicious prosecution, see *Austin* v. *Dowling*, L. R. 5 C. P. 534; 39 L. J. C. P. 260; *Chivers* v. *Savage*, 5 E. & B. 697; 25 L. J. Q. B. 85; *Brandt* v. *Craddock*, 27 L. J. Ex. 314; *Guest* v. *Warren*, 9 Ex. 379; and see "*Malicious Prosecution*," *ante*, p. 453.

An action will lie for false imprisonment under colour of legal process where the process has been set aside for irregularity, etc. Both the party and his attorney are in general liable for the trespass committed in such cases. (*Bates* v. *Pilling*, 6 B. & C. 38; *Codrington* v. *Lloyd*, 8 A. & E. 449; *Jarmain* v. *Hooper*, 6 M. & G. 827; *Collett*

Claim for False Imprisonment.

1. The plaintiff was, on the —— of ——, 18—, the shopman of the defendant.

2. The defendant, on the said —— of ——, 18—, gave the plaintiff into the custody of a policeman upon a false charge, then made by the defendant, of stealing 10 yards of cloth, and caused the plaintiff to be imprisoned in a police-office for —— hours [until the plaintiff was brought in custody before a magistrate upon the said charge, and then procured the said magistrate to remand the plaintiff to prison upon the said charge until the —— of ——, 18—, when he was again brought in custody before the said magistrate upon the said charge, when the said charge was dismissed].

3. The plaintiff was in consequence put to an expense of £—— in defending himself upon the said charge. [*State further special damage, if any.*]

A Like Form, No. 13 in App. (C) to Jud. Act, 1875.

1. The plaintiff is a journeyman painter. The defendant is a builder, having his building-yard, and carrying on business at ——, and for six months before and up to the —— of ——, 18—, the plaintiff was in the defendant's employment as a journeyman painter.

2. On the said —— of ——, 18—, the plaintiff came to work as usual in the defendant's yard, at about six o'clock in the morning.

3. A few minutes after the plaintiff had so come to work the defendant's foreman, X. Y., who was then in the yard, called the plaintiff to him, and accused the

---

v. *Foster*, 2 H. & N. 356; 26 L. J. Ex. 412; and see *Sowell* v. *Champion*, 6 A. & E. 407; see such actions, *Ib.*; and *Blanchenay* v. *Burt*, 4 Q. B. 707; *Prentice* v. *Harrison*, 4 Q. B. 852.) So also an action will lie for a trespass committed under legal process where the judgment and execution have been set aside as against good faith. (*Brown* v. *Jones*, 15 M. & W. 191; and see *Cash* v. *Wells*, 1 B. & Ad. 375.)

An act done by the command of the Crown is not a trespass (*Buron* v. *Denman*, 2 Ex. 167); nor is the act of a judge acting judicially within his jurisdiction. (*Dicas* v. *Lord Brougham*, 6 C. & P. 249.)

A remand being the act of the magistrate cannot be charged as a substantive trespass, but may form the ground of a claim for malicious prosecution. (*Holtum* v. *Lotun*, 6 C. & P 726: *Lock* v. *Ashton*, 12 Q. B. 871.)

plaintiff of having on the previous day stolen a quantity of paint, the property of the defendant, from the yard. The plaintiff denied the charge, but X. Y. gave the plaintiff into the custody of a constable, whom he had previously sent for, upon a charge of stealing paint.

4. The defendant was present at the time when the plaintiff was given into custody, and authorised and assented to his being so given into custody; and in any case X. Y., in giving him into custody, was acting within the scope and in the course of his employment as the defendant's foreman, and for the purposes of the defendant's business.

5. The plaintiff upon being so given into custody, was taken by the said constable a considerable distance through various streets, on foot, to the —— police-station, and he was there detained in a cell till late in the same afternoon, when he was taken to the —— police-court, and the charge against him was heard before the magistrate then sitting there, and was dismissed.

6. In consequence of being so given into custody, the plaintiff suffered annoyance and disgrace, and loss of time and wages, and loss of credit and reputation, and was thereby unable to obtain any employment or earn any wages for three months.

TRESPASS. II.—TO GOODS (*b*).

Claim for Trespass to Goods.

1. The plaintiff is a farmer residing at —— Farm, at ——; the defendant is a grazier residing at ——.

(*b*) *Trespass to Goods.*]—The ground of this action is an actual taking of, or any direct and immediate injury to goods. (*Leame* v. *Bray*, 3 East, 593; *Fouldes* v. *Willoughby*, 8 M. & W. 540.) An indirect interference with the owner's possession, as preventing him from having access to his goods, or locking the door of the defendant's room in which they are, will not support the action. (*Hartley* v. *Moxham*, 3 Q. B. 701; and see *Thorogood* v. *Robinson*, 6 Q. B. 769.) In order to constitute a trespass, it is not necessary that the act should be intentional. (*Covell* v. *Laming*, 1 Camp. 497; *Colwill* v. *Reeves*, 2 Camp. 575, 576.) Trespass will lie for goods taken under an illegal distress, as where no rent is due, or where the goods were privileged, but not for irregularities in dealing with goods under a distress, see "*Distress*," *ante*, p. 404. Trespass will lie for beating the plaintiff's dog or horse. (*Dand* v. *Sexton*, 3 T. R. 37; and see *Slater*

2. On the —— of ——, 18—, the defendant at —— seized and took possession of a horse and gig, the property of the plaintiff, and carried away the same.

3. [The defendant has never returned the said horse and gig to the plaintiff, but still retains possession thereof, and the plaintiff has lost the use and possession thereof.]

4. The value of the said horse and gig is £——.

The Like.

1. The defendant, on the —— of ——, 18—, at ——, seized and took possession of a china dinner service of the plaintiff, and broke and injured the same.

---

v. *Swann*, 2 Str. 872.) If a bailee of goods for a special purpose destroys them, it is a trespass. (Co. Lit. 57 *a*; see *Countess of Salop* v. *Crompton*, Cro. Eliz. 777, 784; and see "*Conversion*," *ante*, p. 375.) One tenant in common of a chattel may maintain trespass against another for a destruction of it, see "*Conversion*," *ante*, p. 376.

The plaintiff in this action must at the time of the trespass have the present possession of the goods (*Ward* v. *Macauley*, 4 T. R. 489; *Young* v. *Hichens*, 6 Q. B. 606), either actual or constructive (*Smith* v. *Milles*, 1 T. R. 475, 480); or a legal right to the immediate possession, which is said in the case of personal property to draw to it the possession. (*Balme* v. *Hutton*, 9 Bing. 471, 477; 2 Wms. Saund. 47 *b*.) A trustee having the legal property may sue, though the beneficial interest and possession are in another. (*Wooderman* v. *Baldock*, 8 Taunt. 676.) A special or temporary right to the present possession, as that of a hirer of goods, or of a carrier, or bailee who has had actual possession, is sufficient to support an action of trespass. (*Colwill* v. *Reeves*, 2 Camp. 575; 2 Wms. Saund. 47 *e*.) And the person having such special property in the goods, may maintain an action of trespass even against the absolute owner for a wrongful taking of the goods by the latter, and recover damages in respect of his limited interest. (*Brierley* v. *Kendall*, 17 Q. B. 937; and see *Turner* v. *Hardcastle*, 11 C. B. N. S. 683; 31 L. J. C. P. 193.)

The fact of possession is *primâ facie* evidence of the right to possession, and therefore sufficient to maintain the action against a wrongdoer who cannot show a better right, or authority under a better title. (*Elliott* v. *Kemp*, 7 M. & W. 312.) Hence it is not open to a defendant in an action of trespass to set up a *jus tertii*, under which he cannot justify, to rebut the title of the plaintiff who was in actual possession at the time of the injury complained of. But where the plaintiff relies upon a mere right of property without actual possession in fact, the defendant may rebut his title by showing a *jus tertii*.

By 3 & 4 Wm. IV. c. 42, s. 29, in all actions of trespass *de bonis asportatis* the jury may, if they shall think fit, give damages in the nature of interest over and above the value of the goods at the time of seizure.

TRESPASS. III.—TO LAND (*c*).

Claim for Trespass to Land.

1. The plaintiff was, on the —— of ——, 18—, in possession of a field, called the Big Field, at ——, in the county of ——.

(*c*) *Trespass to Land.*]—A trespass to land is an entry upon or any direct and immediate act of interference with the possession of land; it is commonly described by the terms "breaking and entering." A trespass may be committed by driving a nail into the plaintiff's wall (*Lawrence* v. *Obee*, 1 Stark. 22); or by placing anything against his wall (*Gregory* v. *Piper*, 9 B. & C. 591); or by shooting into the plaintiff's land (*Pickering* v. *Rudd*, 1 Stark. 56, 58; where see also as to shooting over plaintiff's land, or placing anything above and overhanging the land). Where the plaintiff held apartments in the defendant's house as tenant of the defendant, and the defendant locked the outer door and refused the plaintiff access to the apartments, it was held that this was evidence of a breaking and entering of the apartments by the defendant. (*Lane* v. *Dixon*, 3 C. B. 776.)

The owner of animals, as horses, cattle, etc., in which property exists, is bound to keep them from straying into the land of another, and if they do so, it is actionable as a trespass, without any proof of negligence on the part of the owner; and he is liable to the person trespassed upon for the ordinary consequences of the trespass, and for any damage not too remote; but he is not liable for damage caused by a peculiar mischievous disposition of such animals, unless he had a previous knowledge of such disposition, or was guilty of negligence. See *Star* v. *Rookesby*, 1 Salk. 335; *Cox* v. *Burbidge*, 13 C. B. N. S. 430; 32 L. J. C. P. 89; *Lee* v. *Riley*, 18 C. B. N. S. 722; 34 L. J. C. P. 212; *Ellis* v. *Loftus Iron Co.*, L. R. 10 C. P. 10; 44 L. J. C. P. 24; except in the case of injuries to cattle or sheep by dogs, since the 28 & 29 Vict. c. 60, see "*Mischievous Animals*," *ante*, p. 475. As to trespasses by dogs, see *Read* v. *Edwards*, 17 C. B. N. S. 245; 34 L. J. C. P. 31.

So if the owner of land collects and keeps upon his land water or filth, or anything which escapes into or upon land of another, he is liable without proof of negligence. (*Rylands* v. *Fletcher*, L. R. 3 H. L 339; *Norton* v. *Scholefield*, 9 M. & W. 665; *Tennant* v. *Golding*, 1 Salk. 21; and see "*Nuisance*," *ante*, p. 490.)

An omission or nonfeasance by the defendant does not constitute a trespass, as an omission to take away his tithes from the plaintiff's land. (*Shapcott* v. *Mugford*, 1 L. Raym. 187; and see *Laurence* v. *Obee*, 1 Stark. 22.) The continuance of a trespass is a fresh trespass, and is actionable in the same manner as the original commission of it (*Holmes* v. *Wilson*, 10 A. & E. 503); and notwithstanding a recovery for the original act. (*Bowyer* v. *Cook*, 4 C. B. 236; and see *Battishill* v. *Reed*, 18 C. B. 696; 25 L. J. C. P. 290.)

A trespass is actionable though committed unintentionally or by mistake, as where the defendant mowed the plaintiff's grass by mistake for his own. (*Basely* v. *Clarkson*, 3 Lev. 37.) As to when the acts of a servant may be charged as the acts of his master, see *ante*,

2. The defendant [by his servants and agents], on the said —— of ——, and while the plaintiff was in possession as aforesaid, broke and entered the said field and depastured the same with cattle.

"*Master and Servant.*" And as to the liability of a principal for the acts of his agent, see *Wilson* v. *Tumman*, 6 M. & G. 236; *Woollen* v. *Wright*, 1 H. & C. 554; 31 L. J. Ex. 513; *Bird* v. *Brown*, 4 Ex. 786, 799.

The subject of the trespass must be real and corporeal property; as land or houses; or the vesture of land or herbage or pasture, to the exclusive possession of which the plaintiff is entitled, although he may have no other interest in the land (Co. Lit. 4 *b*; *Crosby* v. *Wadsworth*, 6 East, 602; *Burt* v. *Moore*, 5 T. R. 329; and see *Cox* v. *Glue*, 5 C. B. 533); an exclusive right of cutting turf (*Wilson* v. *Mackreth*, 3 Burr. 1824); or a several right of fishing or of free warren (*Smith* v. *Kemp*, Salk. 637; *Lord Dacre* v. *Tebb*, 2 W. Bl. 1151; *Holford* v. *Bailey*, 8 Q. B. 1000; 13 Q. B. 426). An incorporeal right is not the subject of a trespass; as a right of common of pasture, or of fishing, or of digging turf, or of a right of way, or a right to a pew or any easement annexed to land. (*Wilson* v. *Mackreth*, 3 Burr. 1824; *Mainwaring* v. *Giles*, 5 B. & Ald. 356, 361; *Bryan* v. *Whistler*, 8 B. & C. 288, 292.) The owner of the soil may maintain an action of trespass against a person entitled to rights over the surface for acts of trespass not justified by the exercise of such rights. (*Stammers* v. *Dixon*, 7 East, 200; *Earl Lonsdale* v. *Rigg*, 1 H. & N. 924; 26 L. J. Ex. 196.) Thus the owner of land subject to a highway over it may maintain an action of trespass for any act amounting to a trespass upon it other than a user of it as a highway. (*Lade* v. *Shepherd*, 2 Str. 1004; and see *Goodtitle* v. *Alker*, 1 Burr. 133.) So the owner of land subject to a public market held thereon. (*Mayor of Northampton* v. *Ward*, 1 Wils. 107.) And the owner of the subsoil of land of which the surface belongs to another, may maintain an action for a trespass to the subsoil. (*Stammers* v. *Dixon*, 7 East, 200; *Cox* v. *Glue*, 5 C. B. 533.) The term "close" is often used to describe the place trespassed upon, and is applicable equally either to surface or subsoil, or to an open or an enclosed parcel of land; if the plaintiff charging a trespass to his close proves a sufficient interest in the *locus in quo* to maintain an action of trespass, though he fails to prove exclusive possession of the soil for all purposes, he is entitled to recover. (*Cox* v. *Glue*, 5 C. B. 533, 551; and see *Smith* v. *Royston*, 8 M. & W. 381.)

In order to maintain an action for this wrong the plaintiff must have a present possessory title. The owner legally entitled cannot maintain an action of trespass before entry (*Litchfield* v. *Ready*, 5 Ex. 939; *Turner* v. *Cameron Coal Co.*, 5 Ex. 932); thus, the assignee of a term cannot maintain trespass before entry (*Ryan* v. *Clark*, 14 Q. B. 65; *Harrison* v. *Blackburn*, 17 C. B. N. S. 678; 34 L. J. C. P. 109); but an actual entry will relate back to the time of the legal right to enter, so as to support an action for a preceding trespass (*Barnett* v. *Guildford*, 11 Ex. 19; *Anderson* v. *Radcliffe*, E. B. & E. 806; 29 L. J. Q. B. 128); and upon entry the rightful owner may maintain an action against a party previously in possession. (*Butcher* v. *Butcher*, 7 B. & C. 399.) Actual possession as owner is presumptive proof of property, and is sufficient against a mere wrongdoer who cannot show

A Like Form, No. 27 *in App.* (*C*) *to Jud. Act*, 1875, *Claiming an Injunction.*

1. The plaintiff was on the 5th March, 1876, and still is, the owner and occupier of a farm called Highfield Farm, in the parish of ——, and county of ——.

2. A private road, known as Highfield Lane, runs

---

any better title or authority. (*Graham* v. *Peat*, 1 East, 244; *Purnell* v. *Young*, 3 M. & W. 288; *Pugh* v. *Roberts*, 3 M. & W. 458; *Matson* v. *Cook*, 4 Bing. N. C. 392; *Browne* v. *Dawson*, 12 A. & E. 624; and see *Asher* v. *Whitlock*, L. R. 1 Q. B. 1.) And it is not open to the defendant to set up a *jus tertii* to rebut the mere possessory title of the plaintiff, unless he acted under the authority of such right. The possession of a servant or agent is the possession of the owner (*Bertie* v. *Beaumont*, 16 East, 33); and seems not to be sufficient to entitle the servant to maintain trespass. (*Per* Byles, J., *White* v. *Bailey*, 10 C. B. N. S. 227, 235; 30 L. J. C. P. 253, 256.) A person who has contracted merely for board and lodging, and not for any interest in the premises, cannot maintain trespass. (See *Wright* v. *Stavert*, 2 E. & E. 721; 29 L. J. Q. B. 161.)

One joint tenant or tenant in common of land cannot maintain an action of trespass against another in respect of the exercise of any acts of ownership on the land by the latter, consistent with the right of the former (*Martyn* v. *Knowlys*, 8 T. R. 145; *Cubitt* v. *Porter*, 8 B. & C. 257; *Jacobs* v. *Seward*, L. R. 5 H. L. 464; 41 L. J. H. L. 221; and see Co. Lit. 200); but trespass lies by one tenant in common against another for an actual expulsion of the plaintiff from the land by the defendant (*Murray* v. *Hall*, 7 C. B. 441); or for digging up and carrying away the soil (*Wilkinson* v. *Haygarth*, 12 Q. B. 837); or for destroying buildings (*Cresswell* v. *Hedges*, 1 H. & C. 421; 31 L. J. Ex. 497); or for the occupation of a party-wall to the exclusion of the plaintiff (*Stedman* v. *Smith*, 8 E. & B. 1; 26 L. J. Q. B. 314); but not for pulling down a party-wall for the purpose of rebuilding it. (*Cubitt* v. *Porter*, 8 B. & C. 257.)

As soon as a person is entitled to possession, and enters in the assertion of that possession, the law vests in him the actual possession to the exclusion of a wrongdoer who, but for such entry, would be deemed in possession. (*Jones* v. *Chapman*, 2 Ex. 803, 821; *Lows* v. *Telford*, 1 App. Cas. 414, 426.)

An owner of land, having a right of entry thereon, who by force enters upon his land and evicts an occupier wrongfully in possession thereof is not liable in damages to such occupier for the eviction and forcible entry, even though he may have rendered himself liable to be indicted for a forcible entry under 5 Ric. 2, Stat. 1, c. 8. (*Newton* v. *Harland*, 1 M. & G. 644; 1 Sc. N. R. 474; *Burling* v. *Read*, 11 Q. B. 904; *Davison* v. *Wilson*, 11 Q. B. 890; 17 L. J. Q. B. 196; *Pollen* v. *Brewer*, 7 C. B. N. S. 373; *Beddall* v. *Maitland*, 17 Ch. D. 174; 44 L. T. 248; Addison on Torts, 5th ed., pp. 350, 351); though whenever in the course of such entry the owner of the land commits an independent wrong he is answerable in damages therefor. (*Pollen* v. *Brewer*, *Newton* v. *Harland*, *Beddall* v. *Maitland*, *supra*.)

See further, "*Nuisance*" and "*Injunction*," *ante*. As to the action of trespass for *mesne* profits, see "*Landlord and Tenant*," *ante*, p. 256.

through a portion of the plaintiff's farm. It is bounded upon both sides by fields of the plaintiff's, and is separated therefrom by a hedge and ditch.

3. For a long time prior to the said 5th March, 1876, the defendant had wrongfully claimed to use the said road for his horses and carriages, on the alleged ground that the same was a public highway, and the plaintiff had frequently warned him that the same was not a public highway, but the plaintiff's private road, and that the defendant must not so use it.

4. On the 5th March, 1876, the defendant came with a cart and horse, and a large number of servants and workmen, and forcibly used the road, and broke down and removed a gate which the plaintiff had caused to be placed across the same.

5. The defendant and his servants and workmen on the same occasion pulled down and damaged the plaintiff's hedge and ditch upon each side of the road, and went upon the plaintiff's field beyond the hedge and ditch, and injured the crops there growing, and dug up and injured the soil of the road, and in any case the acts mentioned in this paragraph were wholly unnecessary for the assertion of the defendant's alleged right to use, or the user of the said road as a highway.

The plaintiff claims:—

(1.) Damages for the wrongs complained of.
(2.) An injunction restraining the defendant from any repetition of any of the acts complained of.
(3.) Such further relief as the nature of the case may require.

Claim for Trespass to a House and Seizure of Furniture therein.

1. The plaintiff is, and was on the —— of ——, 18—, a chemist, residing at No. —, —— Street, ——. The defendants are money-lenders.

2. On the —— of ——, 18—, the defendants, by their servants and agents, broke and entered the plaintiff's said house, No. —, —— Street, and seized and carried away therefrom the household furniture, stock-in-trade, goods, and effects of the plaintiff, which were therein.

3. By reason of the premises the plaintiff has been, and is deprived of his said household furniture, stock-

in-trade, goods, and effects [and prevented from carrying on his said business as a chemist, and deprived of the profits thereof, amounting to £——, which he would otherwise have earned in his said business, *or as the case may be*].

Claim for Trespass to Coal (*d*).

1. The plaintiff is the owner and occupier of certain land situate at ——, and of the mines and minerals thereunder. The defendant is the occupier of a coal mine adjacent to the said land of the plaintiff.

2. The defendant broke and entered the said land of the plaintiff, and took and carried away large quantities of coal of the plaintiff [amounting in the whole to —— tons] from under the said land of the plaintiff.

For a Like Form see *Lamb* v. *Walker*, 38 L. T. 643; 3 Q. B. D. 389; 45 L. J. Q. B. 451.

For Forms of Trespass to Land, see *Duke of Norfolk* v. *Arbuthnot*, 4 C. P. D. 290; 41 L. T. 317; 48 L. J. C. P. 737; *Hurdman* v. *N. E. Ry. Co.*, 3 C. P. D. 168; 47 L. J. C. P. 368; 38 L. T. 339; *Cook* v. *Ward*, 2 C. P. D. 255; 46 L. J. C. P. 554; 36 L. T. 893; *Parrott* v. *Watts*, 37 L. T. 755; *Chapman* v. *Mid. Ry. Co.*, 5 Q. B. D. 167, 431.

(*d*) In the absence of fraud, negligence, or wilful trespass, the measure of damages for the wrongful working and abstracting of another's coal is the value of the coal to the person from whose property it was taken at the time of the taking. (*Jegon* v. *Vivian*, L. R. 6 Ch. Ap. 742; 40 L. J. Ch. 389; *Livingstone* v. *Rawyards Coal Co.*, 5 App. Cas. 25; *Wood* v. *Morewood*, 3 Q. B. *n.* 440.)

But if a man furtively and in bad faith robs his neighbour of his minerals, the party so offending may be charged with the whole value of the minerals taken, and allowed no deduction in respect of his labour and expenses in winning it. (*Martin* v. *Porter*, 5 M. & W. 351; *Jegon* v. *Vivian*, *supra*; *Livingstone* v. *Rawyards Coal Co.*, *supra*.)

Waste (*a*).

Statement of Claim for Permissive Waste in a Dwelling-house.

1. The defendant was tenant to the plaintiff of a house, No. —, —— Street, ——, for a term of —— years from the —— of ——, 18—.

(*a*) *Waste.*]—There are two kinds of waste: viz. voluntary or commissive waste, and permissive waste; the former consisting in acts, as pulling down a house; the latter in omissions, as suffering a house to fall into decay. As to what acts and omissions constitute waste, see Co. Lit. 53 *a*, *b*; Cruise's "Digest," tit. *Waste.* Where trees are excepted out of a lease and the tenant cuts them down, it is not waste, but a trespass. (*Goodright* v. *Vivian*, 8 East, 190.) As to the distinction between waste and trespass, see *Lowndes* v. *Bettle*, 33 L. J. Ch. 451.

A tenant at will is not liable for permissive waste (*Harnett* v. *Maitland*, 16 M. & W. 257); and a tenant for life or for years seems to be liable for such waste according to the terms and obligations of his particular tenancy. (1 Wms. Saund. 323 (*d*); *Yellowly* v. *Gower*, 11 Ex. 274, 294; *Jones* v. *Hill*, 7 Taunt. 392; *Harnett* v. *Maitland*, 16 M. & W. 257; *Woodhouse* v. *Walker*, 5 Q. B. D. 404; 49 L. J. Q. B. 609.) It is an implied term of the tenancy in the absence of express agreement, that the tenant shall use the premises in a tenant-like manner (*Standen* v. *Chrismas*, 10 Q. B. 135, and see "*Landlord and Tenant*," *ante*); and that a tenant of a farm shall use it in a husband-like manner (*Powley* v. *Walker*, 5 T. R. 373, and see *ante*, "*Landlord and Tenant*"); but the tenant is not impliedly liable for injury due to fair wear and tear. (*Torriano* v. *Young*, 6 C. & P. 8; and see *Martin* v. *Gilham*, 6 C. & P. 8, 11.) The terms of the lease or covenant may restrict the liability for acts which would otherwise be waste. (*Doe* v. *Jones*, 4 B. & Ad. 126; *Yellowly* v. *Gower*, *supra*.)

In order to maintain this action, the plaintiff must have a vested interest in the reversion at the time when the waste was committed; thus an heir cannot sue for waste done in the life of his ancestor. (2 Inst. 305; 2 Wms. Saund. 252; and see *Bacon* v. *Smith*, 1 Q. B. 345.) It may be brought by him in the reversion or remainder for life or years, as well as in fee or in tail. (2 Wms. Saund. 252 (*a*); *Woodhouse* v. *Walker*, *supra*.)

The action may lie at the suit of one tenant in common against another, where one does waste against the will of the other (see per Littledale, J., in *Cubitt* v *Porter*, 8 B. & C. 257, 268); but it does not lie where one cuts down trees fit to cut, reaps crops, or cuts grass for hay. (*Martyn* v. *Knowlys*, 8 T. R. 145; *Jacobs* v. *Seward*, L. R. 5 H. L. 464; 41 L. J. C. P. 221.) So where there are two tenants in common of a coal mine, one cannot sue the other for working the coal as for waste. (*Job* v. *Potton*, L. R. 20 Eq. 84; 44 L. J. Ch. 262.) By 4 Anne, c. 16, s. 27, joint tenants and tenants in common, and their executors and administrators, have a remedy given, in the form of an action for an account, see *Jacobs* v. *Seward*, *supra*.

2. During the said tenancy the defendant wrongfully permitted waste to the said house, by suffering the same to become and be ruinous and in decay in the doors, windows, and roof of the said house for want of needful and necessary repairing thereof. [*Where practicable, details should be stated.*]

For Voluntary Waste in Woods, Hedges, &c.

1. The defendant was tenant to the plaintiff of a farm, lands, and woods, situate at ——, in the county of ——, [for a term of —— years from the —— of ——, 18—, *or as the case may be*].

2. During the said tenancy the defendant wrongfully

An action will lie at the suit of the reversioner, for any act of commissive waste which is injurious to his reversion, whether committed by a stranger or by the tenant. See "*Reversion*," *ante*, p. 512.

There is a further branch of commissive waste termed *equitable* waste, formerly cognisable only in Courts of Equity, but which is now recognised in all Divisions of the High Court of Justice.

By s. 25 (3) of the Jud. Act, 1873, "An estate for life without impeachment of waste shall not confer, or be deemed to have conferred, upon the tenant for life any legal right to commit waste of the description known as equitable waste, unless an intention to confer such right shall expressly appear by the instrument creating such estate."

Equitable waste consists in doing acts of destructive injury to the property to the detriment of the persons entitled in remainder (Addison on Torts, 5th ed. p. 384, *Baker* v. *Sebright*, 13 Ch. D. 179; 49 L. J. Ch. 65.) It is equitable waste to cut down trees unfit for cutting, to the detriment of the property (*Chamberlayne* v. *Dummer*, 1 Bro. Ch. C. 160; 3 *ib.* 548), or trees required for the shelter or ornament of a mansion house (*Micklethwaite* v. *Micklethwaite*, 26 L. J. Ch. 721; *Wellesley* v. *Wellesley*, 6 Sim. 497; and see *Baker* v. *Sebright*, *supra*), or to commit any wanton or malicious act, destructive of the property. (*Aston* v. *Aston*, 1 Ves. sen. 265; *Duke of Leeds* v. *Lord Amherst*, 14 Sim. 357; *Bishop of London* v. *Web*, 1 P. Wms. 528.)

A tenant in fee simple subject to an executory devise over may not commit equitable waste (*Blake* v. *Peters*, 31 L. J. Ch. 889; *Turner* v. *Wright*, Johns. 740; 2 De G. F. & J. 234; 29 L. J. Ch. 470); nor may a lessee for years without impeachment of waste commit acts destroying and causing lasting injury to the inheritance. (*Bishop of London* v. *Web*, *supra.*)

An injunction to restrain waste may, in a proper case, be claimed, see *Doherty* v. *Allman*, 3 App. Cas. 709; "*Injunction*," *ante*, and see further Addison on Torts, 5th ed. pp. 384 *et seq.* Woodfall's Land. and Ten., 11th ed. p. 570, *et seq.*

committed waste to the said farm, lands, and woods, by felling, lopping, topping, and shrouding the trees of the plaintiff there growing and being, and by rooting up and destroying the hedges and fences of the plaintiff there also growing and being [*giving details as to time and acts where practicable*].

WATER AND WATERCOURSES (*a*) (*b*).

(*a*) *Watercourses.*]—The proprietor of land has a right to have the natural streams of water which run through or by his land run in their natural course and in their natural state. (*Wood* v. *Waud*, 3 Ex. 748, 775; *Orr Ewing* v. *Colquhoun*, 2 App. Cas. 839, 854.)

He has also a right to use the water as it passes. (*Ib.; Mason* v. *Hill*, 5 B. & Ad. 17; *Embrey* v. *Owen*, 6 Ex. 369.) These rights are not founded on a right of property in the water, nor on prescription, but they exist *ex jure naturæ* as incident to the property in the land. (*Ib.; Sampson* v. *Hoddinott*, 1 C. B. N. S. 590; 26 L. J. C. P. 148; *Chasemore* v. *Richards*, 7 H. L. C. 349; 29 L. J. Ex. 81; *Swindon Waterworks Co.* v. *Wilts, &c., Co.*, L. R. 9 Ch. Ap. 451; L. R. 7 H. L. 696; 43 L. J. Ch. 393; 45 L. J. Ch. 638.) All riparian proprietors have these rights, and the right of each is subject to the same rights in the others. (*Embrey* v. *Owen*, 6 Ex. 369.) As to the manner and extent of the use of running water to which the riparian proprietors are naturally entitled, see the cases of *Wood* v. *Waud*, *Embrey* v. *Owen*, *Sampson* v. *Hoddinott*, *Swindon Waterworks Co.* v. *Wilts, &c., Co, supra;* and *Nuttall* v. *Bracewell*, L. R. 2 Ex. 1; 36 L. J. Ex. 1.

The bed of a natural stream *primâ facie* belongs in severalty to the respective riparian proprietors *usque ad medium filum aquæ;* but such proprietors have not the right of using it in a manner to interfere with the natural flow of the stream. (*Bickett* v. *Morris*, L. R. 1 Sc. Ap. 47; and see *Crossley* v. *Lightowler*, L. R. 3 Eq. 279; *Ib.* 2 Ch. Ap. 478; 36 L. J. Ch. 584; *Orr Ewing* v. *Colquhoun*, *supra.*) The bed of a navigable tidal river belongs *primâ facie* to the crown, so far at least as the tide flows (*Williams* v. *Wilcox*, 8 A. & E. 314); but the above-mentioned rights of riparian proprietors exist also in navigable tidal rivers, subject to the public rights of navigation and to any authority conferred by statute. (*Lyon* v. *Fishmongers' Co.*, 1 App. Cas. 662; 46 L. J. Ch. 68.)

As to encroachments on the beds of such rivers, see *Att.-Gen.* v. *Lonsdale*, L. R. 7 Eq. 377; 38 L. J. Ch. 335; *Att.-Gen.* v. *Terry*, L. R. 9 Ch. Ap. 423; 29 L. T. 716.

Besides the rights to flowing water arising *ex jure naturæ* as above mentioned, other rights in excess of the natural rights of a riparian proprietor, and in derogation of the rights of the other riparian proprietors situated above or below the stream, may be acquired by grant or by prescription. (*Bealey* v. *Shaw*, 6 East, 207, 214; *Acton* v. *Blundell*, 12 M. & W. 324, 353; *Carlyon* v. *Lovering*, 1 H. & N. 784; 26 L. J. Ex. 251; *Sampson* v. *Hoddinott*, *supra.*) Such rights are within the Prescription Act, 2 & 3 Will. IV. c. 71, s. 2.

A riparian proprietor is entitled to an action for any injury to the above natural or acquired rights; as by diverting the stream, or by abstracting the water, or by fouling the water. And he is entitled to nominal damages in such an action, in order to prevent the injury, although no actual damage be in fact sustained. (*Wood* v. *Waud*, 3 Ex. 748; *Embrey* v. *Owen*, 6 Ex. 369; *Crossley* v. *Lightowler*, L. R. 2 Ch. Ap. 478; 36 L. J. Ch. 584; and see *Harrop* v. *Hirst*, L. R. 4 Ex. 43; 38 L. J. Ex. 1.) Similarly the injury to the plaintiff's right is sufficient ground for an injunction, without proof of any actual damage. (*Clowes* v. *Staffordshire, &c. Co.*, L. R. 8 Ch. Ap. 125; 42 L. J. Ch. 107; *Pennington* v. *Brinsop Hall Coal Co.*, 5 Ch. D. 769; 46 L. J. Ch. 773; and see *Swindon Waterworks Co.* v. *Wilts, &c. Co.*, *Att.-Gen.* v. *Lonsdale*, and *Att.-Gen.* v. *Terry*, *supra*.)

As to when injunctions will be granted to restrain such injuries, see *Ib.* and *Crossley* v. *Lightowler*, *supra*; *Grand Junction Canal Co.* v. *Shugar*, L. R. 6 Ch. Ap. 483; 24 L. T. 402; *Ivimey* v. *Stocker*, L. R. 1 Ch. Ap. 396; 35 L. J. Ch. 467; *Goldsmid* v. *Tunbridge Wells Commissioners*, L. R. 1 Eq. 161; L. R. 1 Ch. Ap. 349; 35 L. J. Ch. 88, 382; *Att.-Gen.* v. *Bradford Canal*, L. R. 2 Eq. 71; 35 L. J. Ch. 619; and see "*Injunction*," *ante*, p. 439.

The plaintiff in an action for such injuries may also claim a declaration of his title to the right claimed. (See forms of such declarations in *Seton on Decrees*, 4th ed., Vol. I., p. 213, and *Swindon Waterworks Co.* v. *Wilts, &c. Co.*, *supra*.)

Defined streams of water flowing underground are, it is said, subject to the same rules as streams on the surface. (*Chasemore* v. *Richards*, 2 H. & N. 168; 7 H. L. C. 349; 26 L. J. Ex. 393; 29 *Ib.* 81, 85; *Grand Junction Canal Co.* v. *Shugar*, *sup.*)

With respect to water, whether on the surface or underground, not running in defined streams, no similar rights subsist. Such water is the absolute property of the owner of the soil of which it forms part, and no action will lie for abstracting it, although such abstraction may diminish the water under neighbouring lands. (*Ib.*; *Acton* v. *Blundell*, 12 M. & W. 324; *Rawstron* v. *Taylor*, 11 Ex. 369; 25 L. J. Ex. 33; *Broadbent* v. *Ramsbotham*, 11 Ex. 602; 25 L. J. Ex. 115; *R.* v. *Metropolitan Board of Works*, 3 B. & S. 710; 32 L. J. Q. B. 105; *Brain* v. *Marfell*, 41 L. T. 455.)

But the owner of the soil is liable to an action for fouling the water under his land and allowing it to flow in a foul state on to his neighbour's land. (*Hodgkinson* v. *Ennor*, 4 B. & S. 229; 32 L. J. Q. B. 231.)

If the owner of a mine pumps up water so that it is thereby caused to flow into an adjacent mine, he is liable to an action (*Baird* v. *Williamson*, 15 C. B. N. S. 376; 33 L. J. C. P. 101); but where mineral workings have caused a subsidence of the surface, and a consequent flow of rainfall into an adjacent lower coalfield, the injuries, being entirely from gravitation and percolation, are not a valid ground for any claim for damages. (*Wilson* v. *Waddell*, 2 App. Cas. 95; 35 L. T. 639.) An owner of land has, in general, a right on his own land to do anything with regard to the diversion or storage of water he chooses, provided that he does not allow or cause that water to go upon his neighbour's land so as to affect that land in some other way than the way in which it has been affected before, and does not interfere with any easement his neighbour may have. (*West Cumberland, &c. Co.* v. *Kenyon*, 11 Ch. D. 782; 48 L. J. Ch. 793.)

So if a land owner by artificial means brings water on to his land for his own purposes which would not naturally come there, he is bound at his peril to keep it on his land, and if it escapes, he is liable, even without negligence, for any damage thereby occasioned to his neighbour's land, as by flooding his neighbour's mine. (*Rylands* v. *Fletcher*, L. R. 3 H. L. 330; 37 L. J. Ex. 171; and see *Fletcher* v. *Smith*, 2 App. Cas. 781; S. C. *Smith* v. *Musgrave*, 47 L. J. H. L. 4; *West Cumberland Co.* v. *Kenyon*, *sup.*; *Nield* v. *London & N. W. Railway. Co.*, L. R. 10 Ex. 4; 44 L. J. Ex. 15.) But this liability apart from negligence does not exist, where the escape of such water is proximately caused by the act of God or *vis major*, as by extraordinary floods which could not reasonably have been anticipated. (*Nichols* v. *Marsland*, 2 Ex. D. 1; 46 L. J. Ex. 174; *Thomas* v. *Birmingham Canal Co.*, 43 L. T. 435; 49 L. J. Q. B. 851, *affirmed on appeal.*)

See further "*Nuisance*," *ante*, p. 490.

An owner of land is not as such entitled to a right of support for his land from subterranean water. (*Popplewell* v. *Hodkinson*, L. R. 4 Ex. 248; 38 L. J. Ex. 126; see *Wilson* v. *Waddell*, *sup.*; and see "*Support*," *ante*, p. 521.)

A right to discharge an artificial stream of water into another person's land may be acquired by grant or prescription. A proprietor of land having acquired a right to discharge pure water into his neighbour's land, has no right to discharge water in a polluted state, and would be liable to an action for so doing. (*Wood* v. *Waud*, 3 Ex. 748; *Magor* v. *Chadwick*, 11 A. & E. 571.) Under this head may be included the right to discharge water and drainage through channels, gutters, and drains, on to the adjacent property, as in *Thomas* v. *Thomas*, 2 C. M. & R. 35; also the right to discharge the rain-water from the eaves of buildings, as in *Battishill* v. *Reed*, 18 C. B. 696; 25 L. J. C. P. 290. In the case of an artificial stream no right to compel the continuance of its flow is necessarily acquired by riparian proprietors against the person discharging it (*Arkwright* v. *Gell*, 5 M. & W. 203; *Greatrex* v. *Hayward*, 8 Ex. 291; 22 L. J. Ex. 137; *Gaved* v. *Martyn*, 19 C. B. N. S. 732; 34 L. J. C. P. 353); nor against the proprietors through whose land it flows. (*Wood* v. *Waud*, 3 Ex. 748.) But an artificial watercourse may have been made orignally under such circumstances, and may have been so used as to give all the rights that the riparian proprietors would have had if it had been a natural stream. (*Sutcliffe* v. *Booth*, 32 L. J. Q. B. 136; *Ivimey* v. *Stocker*, L. R. 1 Ch. Ap. 396; 35 L. J. Ch. 467.) The right to an artificial watercourse, as against the party creating it, must depend upon the character of the watercourse and the circumstances under which it was created. (*Rameshur, &c., Singh* v. *Pattuk*, 4 App. Cas. 121; *Greatrex* v. *Hayward*, 8 Ex. 293.)

A natural stream of water flowing in an ancient artificial channel is in general subject to the same rules of law as the natural stream in its natural channel. (*Beeston* v. *Weate*, 5 E. & B. 986; 25 L. J. Q. B. 115; *Nuttall* v. *Bracewell*, L. R. 2 Ex. 1; 36 L. J. Ex. 1; *Holker* v. *Porritt*, L. R. 8 Ex. 107; L. R. 10 Ex. 59; 42 L. J. Ex. 85; 44 L. J. Ex. 52.) As to what amounts to abandonment of water rights, see *Crossley* v. *Lightowler*, L. R. 2 Ch. Ap. 478; 36 L. J. Ch. 584.

A mere variation in the mode of enjoying riparian rights does not prevent an action for injury caused by their infringement. (*Holker* v. *Porritt*, *sup.*, *Pennington* v. *Brinsop, &c. Co.*, *sup.*; and see *Saunders*

v. *Newman*, 1 B. & Ald. 258; *Baxendale* v. *McMurray*, L. R. 2 Ch. Ap. 790.)

As to the effect of a grant of "watercourses," &c., see *Taylor* v. *Corporation of St. Helen's*, 6 Ch. D. 264; 46 L. J. Ch. 857; and see *Northam* v. *Hurley*, 1 E. & B. 665; 22 L. J. Q. B. 183. As to implied grants or reservations, see *Wheeldon* v. *Burrows*, 12 Ch. D. 31; 48 L. J. Ch. 853, and the authorities there cited. As to actions by reversioners in respect of injuries to water rights, see "*Reversion*," *ante*, p. 512; *Sampson* v. *Hoddinott*, *sup.*; *Wright* v. *Williams*, 1 M. & W. 77; *Tucker* v. *Newman*, 11 A. & E. 40; *Battishill* v. *Reed*, *sup.*

(*b*) It is usually sufficient in practice to allege the plaintiff's title to the right claimed in a general form, as in the above precedents. Strictly speaking, however, it is more correct to state the facts showing whether the right is claimed simply as a natural right, or as arising by grant, or by Act of Parliament, or by prescription from time immemorial, or during the statutory period, or in all or any of those modes (see "*Common*," *ante*, p. 365; "*Light*," *ante*, p. 451); and in cases where the above-mentioned general allegation of title on the part of the plaintiff embarrasses the defendant in his defence, the latter would be entitled to have the statement of claim amended, so as to show the mode in which the right is claimed, or to obtain particulars. See *Ib.* If, however, the title is set forth, it should be stated accurately. (*Fentiman* v. *Smith*, 4 East, 107; *Coryton* v. *Lithebye*, 2 Wms. Saund. 362; *Hewlins* v. *Shippam*, 5 B. & C. 221; *Whaley* v. *Laing*, 2 H. & N. 476; 27 L. J. Ex. 422.) A possessory title is in general sufficient evidence to support the right. (*Whaley* v. *Laing*, *supra*.) Where the right was claimed as an acquired right by reason of the possession of a mill, and the evidence showed only a natural right to the flow of the stream through the premises, the variance was held to be material, as it might affect the defence. (*Frankum* v. *Earl Falmouth*, 2 A. & E. 452.)

The right should be described accurately in respect of its extent, with all the restrictions and qualifications, if any, to which it is subject. It would be immaterial for the right to be stated more narrowly than it really exists, provided the statement is wide enough to cover the disturbance complained of. (*Duncan* v. *Louch*, 6 Q. B. 904; *Tebbutt* v. *Selby*, 6 A. & E. 786.) The right should not be stated too largely; but, where the allegation of the right is divisible, it would seem that the plaintiff may have a limited verdict for a divisible part of the right alleged, though he fails to prove the residue. See *Giles* v. *Groves*, 12 Q. B. 721; and see "*Common*," *ante*, p. 366. If a person having the right to send clean water through the drain of another chooses to send dirty water, every particle of the water may be stopped because it is dirty. (*Cawkwell* v. *Russell*, 26 L. J. Ex. 34.) A right for the passage of *water and soil* does not include the refuse from manufactures. (*Chadwick* v. *Marsden*, L. R. 2 Ex. 285; 36 L. J. Ex. 177.)

See further as to water rights generally, Roscoe, N. P. Ev. 14th ed., p. 742 *seq.* See also, "*Ferry*," *ante*, p. 424; "*Fishery*," *ante*, p. 425; "*Trespass*," *ante*, p. 534.

Statement of Claim for an Injury to the Plaintiff's Natural Right to the Flow of a Stream by Obstructing and Diverting the Water.

1. The plaintiff was at the times hereinafter mentioned [and still is] possessed of certain land, called ——, situate at ——.

2. The plaintiff then was [and still is] entitled to the flow of a stream, called ——, to and through the said land (*b*).

3. The defendant, in and during the month of ——, 18—, [and thenceforth until, &c., *state how long the acts complained of were continued*] obstructed the said stream, and diverted [large quantities of] the water thereof away from the said land of the plaintiff, by placing and keeping earth and stones in the bed of the said stream about —— yards higher up the said stream than the last-mentioned land, and by there making and maintaining a cutting in the bank of the said stream, and drawing off [large quantities of] the water of the said stream through the said cutting [into a reservoir constructed on certain adjacent land of the defendant].

4. The defendant thereby diminished the quantity of water which flowed down the said stream to and through the said land of the plaintiff, and deprived the plaintiff of the flow of water to which he was entitled as aforesaid.

5. By reason of the premises, &c. [*here state any special damage sustained by the plaintiff*].

6. [*If an injunction is also claimed, state any material facts in support of such claim, as for instance,* The defendant has continued such obstruction and diversion as aforesaid up to the present time, and although requested by the plaintiff to discontinue the same, has threatened and intends to continue such obstruction and diversion.]

The plaintiff claims :—

1. £—— damages for the wrongs above complained of.
2. [That the defendant [his agents, servants, and workmen] may be restrained by injunction from continuing or repeating any of the wrongful acts hereinbefore complained of, and from in any manner obstructing or diverting the water of the said stream, and from in any manner interfering with the plaintiff's said rights].
3. [Such further or other relief as the nature of the case may require].

For Diverting the Water from the Plaintiff's Mill, and Depriving the Plaintiff of the Use of the Water for the Irrigation of a Meadow.

1. The plaintiff was at the times hereinafter mentioned [and still is] possessed of certain land at ——, and of a water-mill erected thereon.

2. The plaintiff then was [and still is] entitled to have the benefit and advantage of the water of a stream [*or* watercourse], which flowed, and of right ought to have flowed, to and through the said land, and to use the said water for the purpose of working his said mill, and for the purpose of irrigating a meadow which formed part of the said land (*b*).

3. [*Same as paragraph* 3 *of the first precedent.*]

4. The defendant thereby hindered and prevented the plaintiff from having the benefit and advantage to which he was entitled as aforesaid, and from using the said water for the purposes hereinbefore mentioned.

5 and 6. [*Same as paragraphs* 5 *and* 6 *of the first precedent.*]

For Penning Back the Water of a Stream on to the Plaintiff's Land.

1. The plaintiff was at the times hereinafter mentioned [and still is] possessed of a meadow called ——, adjoining the river ——, at ——.

2. The plaintiff then was [and still is] entitled to have the said river flow by and away from the said meadow without obstruction or hindrance (*b*).

3. The defendant, in the month of ——, 18—, [and thenceforth until, &c., *state how long the obstruction continued*] obstructed the flow of the said river at a point about —— yards lower down the said river than the said meadow, by there erecting and continuing a wall or dam in the bed of the river, and thereby penned and forced back the water of the said river so that it was hindered and prevented from flowing by and away from the said meadow as it of right ought to have done, and otherwise would have done.

4. By reason of the premises, the water of the said river on the —— day of ——, 18—, overflowed and flooded the said meadow, and remained thereon for ——

weeks, and spoilt the herbage thereof, and the plaintiff was deprived of the use of the said meadow, and was put to an expense of £—— in removing the water therefrom, and the said meadow was, and is much diminished in value.

5. [*If an injunction is claimed, state any material facts in support of such claim.* See "*Injunction,*" *ante,* p. 439.]

For Polluting the Water of a Stream running through the Plaintiff's Land.

1. The plaintiff at the times hereafter mentioned was [and still is] possessed of certain pasture land at ——.

2. The plaintiff then was [and still is] entitled to have the use of the water of a stream [*or* watercourse] which flowed through his said land for his cattle to drink, and for other purposes, viz. [*state for what purposes*], without the same being polluted and disturbed as hereinafter mentioned (*b*).

3. The defendant, at various times between —— and ——, 18— [*state the dates, where practicable*], polluted and disturbed the water of the said stream [*or* watercourse] by throwing and causing to flow into the same noxious substances and fluids, that is to say ——, from a manufactory of the defendant at ——, so that the said water became foul, noxious, and unfit for the plaintiff's cattle to drink, and for the other purposes above mentioned.

4. By reason of the matters above complained of —— cows of the plaintiff which were watered in and from the said stream [*or* watercourse] became sick and disordered, and the plaintiff was compelled to drive his said cows to a pond, called ——, at a distance of —— hundred yards from his said land for water, and lost the use of the water of the said stream [*or* watercourse] for the said other purposes [*state any further items of damage sustained*], and his said land was and is lessened in value.

5. [*If an injunction is claimed, state any material facts in support of such claim.* See "*Injunction,*" *ante,* p. 439.]

See for further Forms, "Nuisance," ante, p. 493.

Ways (*a*).

Statement of Claim for Obstructing a Private Right of Way.

1. The plaintiff was possessed of a messuage at ——, in the county of —— [and the defendant was possessed of a field, called the Big Field, near the said messuage].

2. The plaintiff was entitled to a right of way from the said messuage over a field, called the Big Field, near thereto [*or* the said field], to a public highway, called the —— Road, and back again from the said highway over the said field to the said messuage, for himself, his servants, and workpeople on foot [and with horses, carriages, and cattle], at all times of the year.

3. The defendant, on or about the —— of ——, 18—, wrongfully obstructed the said way [by placing a fence in the said field, blocking up the said way].

4. [The defendant has thence hitherto kept the said way so obstructed by the said fence].

See Form, No. 27 App. (C) to Jud. Act, 1875, *ante*, p. 536; *and see Mayor, &c., of London* v. *Riggs*, 13 Ch. D. 798; 49 L. J. Ch. 297.

(*a*) Rights of way are *public* or *private*. As to public rights of way, see "*Highways*," *ante*, p. 434; "*Nuisance*," *ante*, p. 485.

The owner of a private right of way would be entitled to maintain an action and recover nominal damages for an obstruction, although no special or substantial damage was suffered thereby.

Qualified rights of way should be pleaded according to the facts. (See *Brunton* v. *Hall*, 1 Q. B. 792.)

A right of way to a piece of land is limited to the ordinary and reasonable use of such land, in the absence of evidence of any larger use, and every larger use is an excess. (*Williams* v. *James*, L. R. 2 C. P. 577; 36 L. J. C. P. 256; *Wimbledon, &c. Conservators* v. *Dixon*, 1 Ch. D. 362; 45 L. J. Ch. 353; *Bradburn* v. *Morris*, 3 Ch. D. 812; *Mayor, &c. of London* v. *Riggs*, 13 Ch. D. 798; 49 L. J. Ch. 297.)

Where there is an express grant the right must depend on the terms of the grant, and not upon the nature of the user. (*Finch* v. *G. W. Ry. Co.*, 5 Ex. D. 254.)

It is thought that the above mode of stating the right would be in general sufficient; see however as to this, "*Common*," *ante*, p. 365.

See further, "*Reversion*," "*Injunction*," "*Trespass*," "*Nuisance*."

Witness (*a*).

(*a*) An action for damages will lie against a witness for not attending to give evidence in a cause in pursuance of a *subpœna* duly served upon him, where a reasonable sum was paid or tendered to him as conduct-money, and where the evidence of such witness was material and necessary to the case of the party serving the *subpœna*, and such party has sustained actual damage by the non-attendance of the witness. See for instances of such actions, *Mullett* v. *Hunt*, 1 C. & M. 752; *Lamont* v. *Crook*, 6 M. & W. 615; *Needham* v. *Fraser*, 1 C. B. 815; 3 D. & L. 190; *Couling* v. *Coxe*, 6 C. B. 703; *Masterman* v. *Judson*, 8 Bing. 224; *Davis* v. *Lovell*, 4 M. & W. 678; *Amey* v. *Long*, 9 East, 473; and see also *Yeatman* v. *Dempsey*, 7 C. B. N. S. 628; 29 L. J. C. P. 177. An action for such non-attendance might also be brought against such witness under the 5 Eliz. c. 9, s. 12, to recover the penalty of £10, which is thereby made recoverable by the party grieved, together with a further sum to be awarded by the Court. (See *Pearson* v. *Iles*, 2 Doug. 556.) The witness may also be proceeded against by attachment for contempt of Court in disobeying the *subpœna*. See 1 Archb. Pr., 13th ed., p. 327.

See further, 1 Archb. Pr. 320 *et seq.*, and "*Defamation*," *ante*, p. 393.

Ex. G. A. A.

LONDON
BRADBURY, AGNEW, & CO., PRINTERS, WHITEFRIARS.

www.ingramcontent.com/pod-product-compliance
Ingram Content Group UK Ltd.
Pitfield, Milton Keynes, MK11 3LW, UK
UKHW021351120925
7876UKWH00023B/353

9 781015 447585